The Billboard Book of

GW00391048

NUMBER ONE

The
INSIDE STORY
behind
POP MUSIC'S

BLOCKBUSTER

RECORDS

CRAIG ROSEN

ALBUMS

BILLBOARD BOOKS • An imprint of Watson-Guptill Publications / New York

To my wife, Patti, son, Tyler,
and parents, Barbara and Harry.
Thanks for the love and support.
You're all Number One to me.

Edited by Paul Lukas
Cover and interior design by Bob Fillie, Graphiti Graphics
Graphic production by Hector Campbell

Copyright © 1996 by Craig Rosen

First published in 1996 in the United States by Billboard Books,
an imprint of Watson-Guptill Publications, a division of BPI
Communications, Inc., 1515 Broadway, New York, NY 10036

All rights reserved. No part of this publication may be reproduced,
stored in a retrieval system, or transmitted, in any form or by any means—
electronic, mechanical, photocopying, recording, or otherwise—without
prior written permission from the publisher.

A CIP data card for this publication is on file with the Library of Congress.

Manufactured in the United States of America.

First printing, 1996

1 2 3 4 5 6 7 8 9 / 00 99 98 97 96

CONTENTS

CONTENTS

CONTENTS

CONTENTS

ACKNOWLEDGMENTS

When I proposed this project more than three years ago, I had two goals in mind. One was obviously to complete the book and see it through to publication. The other was to enhance my knowledge about popular music. Hopefully, in writing about these 423 chart-toppers and interviewing hundreds of artists, producers, and executives, I learned a thing or two.

Thanks first and foremost to those who participated in the making of this book. It's refreshing to find that there are some artists gracious enough to talk about their past triumphs, rather than simply promoting their latest album.

I have to recognize Fred Bronson for paving the way with the *Billboard Book of Number One Hits*; Joel Whitburn, whose numerous chart-reference books made writing this book a lot easier; and Jerry Biederman for his inspiration and advice.

To Barbara Rosen, Chris Morris, and Steve Appleford, I'm grateful that you took the time to read along.

Special thanks to Paul Lukas, my editor, for enthusiastically embracing this project from our first conversation. Although he left Billboard Books while we were in the home stretch, he stayed on the project and saw the book through to the end. Thumbs up also to Bob Fillie for the fine layouts and design.

Thanks to all at *Billboard,* past and present, including Dave DiMartino, Ken Schlager, and Sean Ross, who hired me on back in 1989; and Timothy White, Howard Lander, Susan Nunziata, Marilyn Gillen, Melinda Newman, J.R. Reynolds, Paul Verna, Ken Terry, Thom Duffy, Doug Reece, Brett Atwood, Carrie Borzillo, Paul Grein, and Terri Horak.

Special thanks to Geoff Mayfield and Sylvio Pietroluongo in charts.

I'm grateful to the following for helping me with photos: Erik Himmelsbach, Dave DiMartino, Rebecca Edelson, Hillary Smoot, Larry Solters, Jessica Bumsted, Zona Hayhoe, Steve Karas, Geary Chansley, Laura Swanson, Gene Sculatti, Porter Hall, Dalet Brady, Stephanie McCormick, Christine Jardine-Bourdeau, Brett Kaufman, Kathy Acquaviva, Claudia Depkin, Bianca Moreno, Joanne Sloan, Chris Barsa, Sujata Murthy, Bob Kaus, and Dave Booth.

I'm also indebted to the following people, who assisted in setting up interviews, providing contacts, or offering some sort of support: Paul Wasserman, Brian O'Neal, David Horowitz, Julie Farman, Richard Chadwick, Bob Merlis, Linda Rowles, Liz Rosenberg, Christine Wolf, Joel Oberstein, Benjie Gordon, Rob Gordon, Todd Sullivan, Stevo Glendinning, Lisa Millman, Stacy Nick, Jolyn Matsumuro, Mitch Schneider, Dave Schulps, Jonathan Taylor, Robert Hilburn, Kip Cohen, Heidi Robinson, Suzan Crane, Margaret Sterlacci, Susan DuBow, Michelle Steinberg, Barbara Shelley, David Dorn, David McLees, Kate Blacklock, Howard Parr, Patti Matsui, Susan Rike, Sandy Brokaw, Jane Arginteanu, Denise McGeever, Linda Roles, Ramon Bain, Sheldon Roskin, Gene Hanson, Marsha Groff, Bob Fogerty, Laura Gold, Maria Kleinman, Amy Malsin, Mark Beavens, Clive Corcoran, Kerry Cooley, Cary Mansfield, Bob Bernstein, Andy McKaie, Ellen Bello, Dan Perloff, Tony D'Amato, Susan Silver, Bert Fink, Hanna Bolte, Susan Stewart, and all others who I may have inadvertingly forgotten.

INTRODUCTION

As shocking as it may seem, some of the greatest and most influential popular music acts in history never scored a Number One single on *Billboard*'s Hot 100 chart, but nonetheless recorded albums that appealed to the collective consciousness of the public in such a manner that their sales pushed them to the top of the *Billboard* album chart. Artists in this elite group include Jimi Hendrix, Cream, Bob Dylan, Creedence Clearwater Revival, Led Zeppelin, and contemporary superstars such as Garth Brooks, Bruce Springsteen, R.E.M., Nirvana, and Pearl Jam.

This book tells the stories behind the 423 albums that have topped the album chart during the rock era. As you will see, the list of artists and titles is incredibly diverse, ranging from the Singing Nun, Bob Newhart, and *The Sound of Music* to Snoop Doggy Dogg, Garth Brooks, Nirvana, and *The Lion King*. For the purposes of this book, the coverage starts on May 5, 1956, with *Elvis Presley*, the first rock 'n' roll album to top the album chart (rather than July 9, 1955, when Bill Haley's "Rock Around the Clock" became the first rock 'n' roll single to top the Hot 100). The book runs through the end of 1995, when, oddly enough, the Beatles returned to score their 16th chart-topper.

Some have said that the single is the ultimate form artistic expression in popular music. True, there's nothing like a great single for its immediacy and brevity, but even some marginal artists have somehow managed to record three minutes of magic.

I'd argue that an album is a greater barometer of artistic worth, as an album can contain several singles and gives an artist the opportunity to stretch out and record material that may not be commercially viable enough for release as a single, but further illustrates the artist's vision.

On the *Billboard* charts, topping the Hot 100 is one of the pinnacles of success most acts dream of, yet having an album top the album chart is even a greater accomplishment, for an album represents months or even years of work.

While the Hot 100 rankings are computed from a combination of radio airplay and sales, the album chart is based solely on sales, so the albums that top The Billboard 200 are the true favorites of the public, not of a select group of radio programmers. Although an occasional album will reach Number One on the strength of chart-topping single, usually it is the combination of several hits and an act's hard-earned reputation that push an album to the top. Therefore, the album chart has been more immune to "one-hit wonders" than the Hot 100.

This book doesn't offer a critical perspective or review of the 423 records that have topped the *Billboard* album chart. However, those who feel an artist's work alone is more important than commercial success will be happy to find that many of the greatest and most influential albums ever made—from *Elvis Presley*, the Beatles' *Sgt. Pepper's Lonely Hearts Club Band*, and the Rolling Stones' *Exile on Main St.* to Michael Jackson's *Thriller*, R.E.M.'s *Out of Time*, and Nirvana's *Nevermind*—have gone to Number One.

This book follows a format established with Fred Bronson's *Billboard Book of Number One Hits*. With a few exceptions, each entry contains quotes from among the hundreds of interviews I conducted with artists, producers, engineers, session players, and record executives. The point of this book is to pay tribute to the albums and the artists who have topped the *Billboard* album chart. The ultimate tribute, however, would be if readers of this book went and sought out an old chart-topper at a record store to experience a Number One album for the first time, or delved into their own personal collections to reacquaint themselves with an old favorite. After all, this book is only made up of words, and ultimately it's the music that matters.

Some practical concerns: *Billboard* introduced one of its most important features, a top 5 pop albums chart, in 1945. Since then, the chart has been through several name changes and incarnations. One significant change worth noting is the advent of the separate stereo and mono charts from May 25, 1959 through August 17, 1963. During that period, I've opted to include all the Number One albums, whether they topped the mono chart, stereo chart, or both. The entry for each album topping an album chart during this period lists the total weeks at Number One (if different from its stay at the stereo or mono chart) and the weeks it spent at Number One on the stereo and/or mono charts.

Also please note that all chart-related dates in this book, in keeping with long-established *Billboard* style, refer to the *week ending* on the date shown.

The label notations and stock numbers that appear at the beginning of each entry refer to the record labels and catalog numbers that appeared on the version of the album that went to Number One. Scores of albums in this book have been reissued on CD, often with a different catalog number, and occasionally on a different label; some of the others, sadly, are out-of-print as of this writing.

While *Billboard*'s charts have long been regarded as the most reputable source in the business, that's not to say they couldn't be even more accurate. The biggest breakthrough in this area came in 1991, when *Billboard* pacted with SoundScan, a firm that collects point-of-sale data from scanning machines that read an album's bar code. *Billboard* began using SoundScan data on May 25, 1991. As a result, a broader range of titles appeared on the album chart. Another effect of SoundScan was that albums began to debut at Number One more frequently. In fact, in the SoundScan era it seems that more albums debut at Number One than actually climb to Number One in subsequent weeks.

Thanks to SoundScan technology, The Billboard 200 is more exciting and accurate than ever. Every week millions of pop music lovers—whether they be record company executives, retail store clerks, or just dedicated fans—wait anxiously to hear the news about who is on top of the album chart. On a week-to-week basis, those die-hards will have to keep checking out *Billboard*, but for those who want to know about the past, they'll find it here in these pages.

CRAIG ROSEN
March 1996

RCA LPM 1254 **Elvis Presley**

ELVIS PRESLEY

1

Producer: None listed

Track listing: Blue Suede Shoes / I'm Counting on You / I Got a Woman / One-Sided Love Affair / I Love You Because / Just Because / Tutti Frutti / Tryin' to Get to You / I'm Gonna Sit Right Down and Cry / I'll Never Let You Go (Little Darlin') / Blue Moon / Money Honey

May 5, 1956
10 weeks

It's only appropriate that Elvis's debut album was the first rock 'n' roll LP to top *Billboard*'s Best Selling Popular Albums chart. After all, it was Elvis who brought rock 'n' roll to the masses.

Elvis Aron Presley was one of two twins born on January 8, 1935, in Tupelo, Mississippi. His twin brother, Jesse Garon, was stillborn. Throughout his youth, from church to grade school talent shows, music was a big influence on Elvis. One day in the summer of 1953, Elvis cut a record as a gift for his mother at the Memphis Recording Service, owned by Sun Records proprietor Sam Phillips, which allowed people to record a 10-inch disc for four dollars. When Elvis returned in January 1954 to cut another recording, he met Phillips.

Intrigued by his singing, Phillips signed Elvis to Sun Records and hooked him up with guitarist Scotty Moore and bassist Bill Black, from the country and western group the Starlight Ramblers. Between July 1954 and August 1955, Sun released five Presley singles. On November 22, 1955, RCA Records purchased Elvis's contract, including his singles and unreleased masters, from Phillips for $35,000.
By late 1955, Elvis was voted "most promising C&W artist" by *Billboard*, as "I Forgot to Remember to Forget" hit Number One on the country charts. The following year, Elvis would take over the pop charts as well.

In March of 1956, RCA issued *Elvis Presley*. "Heartbreak Hotel," Elvis's debut single for RCA, became his first pop Number One on April 21, 1956, but it wasn't included on the album, which instead featured five tracks (including the ballads "I Love You Because," "Blue Moon," and "I'll Never Let You Go (Little Darlin')," cut during the summer of 1954 and 1955, long before Elvis signed with RCA.

"We were just there to give Elvis a little accompaniment so Sam could hear what his voice sounded like in tape," Moore says of the Sun sessions. "After we did the first single, 'That's All Right,' we were trying to figure out what direction to go in. They were just auditions. We were just experimenting, but for some reason Sam kept those tapes."

There were also some new tracks, cut in January 1956 at RCA's studios in Nashville and New York, that made the album. "There wasn't any pressure," Moore says of the first RCA sessions. "They were just bigger studios with different equipment. We basically just went in and did the same thing we always did." The best known of the seven new recordings on *Elvis Presley* were covers of Carl Perkins's "Blue Suede Shoes" and Little Richard's "Tutti Frutti." Perkins's version of "Blue Suede Shoes," released on Sun Records, entered the singles chart on February 22 alongside "Heartbreak Hotel."

In the midst of the friendly chart battle, tragedy struck. In March 1956, Perkins was involved in a car accident that left him in the hospital for months and killed his brother and back-up singer, Jay. "We did 'Blue Suede Shoes' on a TV show as a tribute to Carl," Moore says. As a show of respect for Perkins, Elvis would not allow his version to be released as a single. "Blue Suede Shoes" was included on the *Elvis Presley* EP, a top 20 best seller, but no match for Perkins's single, which peaked at number three. Still the song remained an Elvis favorite—he would record it again as an album track [see 38—*G.I. Blues*].

THE TOP FIVE
Week of May 5, 1956

1. **Elvis Presley**
   Elvis Presley

2. **Belafonte**
   Harry Belafonte

3. **The Man with the Golden Arm**
   Soundtrack

4. **Carousel**
   Soundtrack

5. **Songs for Swingin' Lovers**
   Frank Sinatra

2 My Fair Lady COLUMBIA 5090
ORIGINAL CAST

Producer: Goddard Lieberson

Track listing: Overture [orchestra] / Why Can't the English? [Rex Harrison] / Wouldn't It Be Loverly [Julie Andrews, ensemble] / With a Little Bit of Luck [Stanley Holloway, Gordon Dilworth, Rod McLennan] / I'm an Ordinary Man [Harrison] / Just You Wait [Andrews] / The Rain in Spain [Harrison, Andrews, Robert Coote] / I Could Have Danced All Night [Andrews, Philippa Bevans] / Ascot Gavotte [ensemble] / On the Street Where You Live [Michael King] / You Did It [Harrison, Coote, Bevans] / Show Me [Andrews, King] / Get Me to the Church on Time [Holloway, Dilworth, McLennan] / A Hymn to Him [Harrison] / Without You [Andrews] / I've Grown Accustomed to Her Face [Harrison]

July 14, 1956
15 weeks (nonconsecutive)

Elvis and the arrival of rock 'n' roll couldn't stop the popularity of show tunes. That point was proven when Elvis's 10-week run at the summit was ended by the original cast album of *My Fair Lady*, which went on to become the most popular Broadway cast title in history.

My Fair Lady, a musical adaptation of George Bernard Shaw's *Pygmalion*, initially opened at the Shubert Theatre in New Haven, Connecticut, on February 4, 1956, before moving to the Erlander Theatre in Philadelphia on February 15, and finally to the Mark Hellinger Theater on Broadway on March 15, where it would run an amazing 2,717 performances.

The musical was produced by Herman Levin. Alan Jay Lerner wrote the book and music and his partner Frederick Loewe composed the music. The production was staged by Moss Hart.

The show starred Rex Harrison, making his musical comedy debut, and Julie Andrews. At the time Harrison was already a star, having appeared on the stage in such productions as *Bell, Book and Candle* and *Anne of the Thousand Days*, and in such films as *The King of Siam* and *Major Barbara*. Andrews had only recently made her debut in *The Boyfriend* and had appeared alongside Bing Crosby [see 11] in the television adaptation of *High Tor*.

Like most Broadway cast albums, *My Fair Lady* was recorded on a single day off, shortly after the play opened on Broadway. Given the show's grueling performance schedule, recording the album was not easy. "One had to be very careful of vocal fatigue," says Andrews, "as the show was very tough on all of us."

Andrews says she still has "fond memories of Moss, Alan, and Fritz. They really were the gentle giants of Broadway and they were kind and encouraging to one as green as myself."

On April 28, 1956, *My Fair Lady* first appeared on the charts. Nearly three months later, it hit Number One, becoming the first of nine original cast titles to top the *Billboard* album chart during the rock era. But its legacy wouldn't end there. During its first stay at Number One, the album held the top spot for eight weeks. It went on to return to the Number One position again for one week in 1957 and for another three weeks in 1958.

With the album's popularity still riding high, Columbia executives decided that a new version of *My Fair Lady* should be recorded to take advantage of the new stereo technology. The stereo version was recorded in London on February 1, 1959. For Andrews, the chance to record the album again was a thrill. "I was very glad to have the opportunity to re-record the album," she says. "From my point of view, I feel that the stereo recording is far superior to the original mono version."

The public was also happy to buy the album again, as the stereo version of the album (Columbia 34197) spent three weeks on top of the stereo album chart in 1959.

Together, the mono and stereo versions of *My Fair Lady* spent a remarkable 480 weeks on the album chart, more than any other cast album in the rock era. As Andrews says, "*My Fair Lady* was virtually the perfect musical in every way."

THE TOP FIVE
Week of July 14, 1956

1. **My Fair Lady**
   Original Cast

2. **Elvis Presley**
   Elvis Presley

3. **Calypso**
   Harry Belafonte

4. **Carousel**
   Soundtrack

5. **Songs for Swingin' Lovers**
   Frank Sinatra

RCA VICTOR 1248 ## Calypso

HARRY BELAFONTE

3

Producer: None listed

Track listing: Day O / I Do Adore Her / Jamaica Farewell / Will His Love Be Like His Rum? / Dolly Dawn / Star O / The Jack-Ass Song / Hosanna / Come Back Liza / Brown Skin Girl / Man Smart (Woman Smarter)

September 8, 1956
31 weeks (nonconsecutive)

Harry Belafonte had already scored two hit albums in 1956. His first album, *"Mark Twain" and Other Folk Favorites,* reached number three. A few months later, on March 24, the Harlem-born singer's *Belafonte* spent six weeks at Number One until it was knocked from the summit by *Elvis Presley* [see 1]. Despite his success with "straight pop" music, Belafonte decided to do something different on his third album.

"There were things that I had a big interest in that came from places that were not reflective of where popular American culture was headed at the time," says Belafonte. "I talked about doing this album of music that came from the Caribbean region with a cross-section of folk music coming from Jamaica, Trinidad, and other islands. There was significant resistance to that concept."

Executives at RCA urged the young Belafonte, who was just 28 at the time, to stick with the winning formula. Yet the singer had a vision influenced by his heritage. His mother was Jamaican and his father West Indian. "I took my appeal to George Merek, who then was the president of RCA. I told him about my desire to do this album. He felt my

request wasn't outside the purview of RCA's ability and game plan for me."

Once Belafonte got the green light, the album was recorded fairly quickly with accompaniment by Tony Scott and His Orchestra, guitarist Millard Thomas, and composer/conductor Norman Luboff. Most of the songs were well-rehearsed before Belafonte and company entered the studio. "The only kind of spontaneous thing that went on was the creation of a throwaway song to fill out the album called 'Day O,'" says Belafonte. A second version of the song, retitled "Star O," was featured on side two. Although *Calypso* climbed to Number One less than three months after it debuted on the chart, the album didn't develop its legs until "Day O," now retitled as "Banana Boat," was released as a single.

While RCA focused on "Jamaica Farewell" and Belafonte's Christmas single "Mary's Boy Child," a folk trio called the Tarriers, which featured the then-unknown actor Alan Arkin, scored a hit with a cover of "Day O." The single, which Glory Records titled "The Banana Boat Song," hit number four.

When RCA finally released Belafonte's original version of the song, it peaked at number five. That hit and Belafonte's growing legion of fans were enough to keep *Calypso* lodged firmly on top of the album chart.

With a total of 31 weeks at the summit, *Calypso* set the early standard as the Number One album with the most weeks at the top. Two years later, *South Pacific* [see 15] would tie that mark, and in 1962, *West Side Story* [see 52] broke the record with 54 weeks on top.

THE TOP FIVE
Week of September 8, 1956

1. **Calypso**
   Harry Belafonte

2. **The King and I**
   Soundtrack

3. **My Fair Lady**
   Original Cast

4. **Elvis Presley**
   Elvis Presley

5. **The Eddy Duchin Story**
   Soundtrack

4 The King and I CAPITOL 740
SOUNDTRACK

Supervisor and conductor: Alfred Newman

Track listing: Overture / I Whistle a Happy Tune / My Lord and Master / Hello, Young Lovers / The March of Siamese Children / A Puzzlement / Getting to Know You / We Kiss in a Shadow / I Have Dreamed / Shall I Tell You What I Think of You? / Something Wonderful / Song of the King / Shall We Dance? / Something Wonderful (Finale)

October 6, 1956
1 week

Rodgers and Hammerstein

Although the soundtrack to the film version of *South Pacific* wouldn't be released until 1958, the play and the original cast album had made composer Richard Rodgers and lyricist Oscar Hammerstein II stars. In fact, its success proved to be somewhat of an obstacle when the duo began working on a new musical called *The King and I.* "The trouble is that people aren't interested in whether it's a good show or a bad show; they want to know whether it's better than *South Pacific*," said Rodgers in Stanley Green's *The Rodgers and Hammerstein Story.*

The King and I proved to be a musical challenge for Rodgers and Hammerstein as well. It was the first production that the pair had penned with no American characters. In fact, the story, set in 19th-century Siam, featured mostly Siamese characters. The setting called for music with an Oriental flavor, but Rodgers had to walk a fine line in composing the material—it had to contain some Asian trademarks yet be accessible enough for American audiences.

THE TOP FIVE
Week of October 6, 1956

1. **The King and I**
   Soundtrack

2. **Calypso**
   Harry Belafonte

3. **The Eddy Duchin Story**
   Soundtrack

4. **My Fair Lady**
   Original Cast

5. **High Society**
   Soundtrack

To achieve that balance, Rodgers used an approach that he compared to the work of American artist Grant Wood. Much like Wood's paintings, Rodgers's music would capture the authentic flavor of Siam, but through the lens of a decidedly American perspective. Rodgers and Hammerstein accomplished this in a number of the selections, including "The March of the Siamese Children." The songs also served the essential purpose of giving the listener insight into the play's characters, whether it be the king in "A Puzzlement," or Anna in "Hello, Young Lovers" and the appropriately titled "Getting to Know You."

The King and I opened on March 29, 1951. More than 1,000 performances of the show were staged on Broadway, making it the third Rodgers and Hammerstein production to achieve such a feat.

Yul Brynner, who starred in the Broadway production, was also cast as the male lead in the big screen version of the musical. Others featured in the film and its accompanying soundtrack included Deborah Kerr, Rita Moreno, Terry Saunders, and Carlos Rivas.

Perhaps more important than the Number One status of the *The King and I* soundtrack was the fact that the musical proved that Rodgers and Hammerstein could successfully follow their own muse without pandering to the public. Just before the play opened on Broadway, Green reported that the duo wrote: "Writers who repeat themselves will eventually bore themselves. And this condition is a short and automatic step toward boring the public." The success of *The King and I* soundtrack was proof that the public was anything but bored with the music of Rodgers and Hammerstein.

DECCA 8289 # The Eddy Duchin Story

CARMEN CAVALLARO/SOUNDTRACK

5

Orchestra director: Morris Stoloff

Track listing: To Love Again (Main Title) / Manhattan / Shine on Harvest Moon / It Must be True / Whispering / Dizzy Fingers / You're My Everything / Chopsticks / On the Sunny Side of the Street / Brazil / La Vie En Rose / To Love Again (Finale)

October 13, 1956
1 week

Pianist-bandleader Eddy Duchin had an incredible life filled with triumphs and heartbreak. His story was so interesting that Columbia Pictures opted to make a film about his life five years after his 1951 death from leukemia. The film starred Tyrone Power— a close friend of Duchin's who visited him in the hospital shortly before his death—and Kim Novak. The movie featured a score performed by another famed pianist, Carmen Cavallaro.

The young Duchin was trained as a pharmacist and was expected to carry on the family business. His father owned several drug stores. Duchin, however, opted to pursue his dream of being a professional musician. Initially, in the late '20s, he played piano in Leo Reis-man's Orchestra before setting out on his own.

In 1935, with his career in full swing, Duchin married Marjorie Oelrichs, an artist and decorator; together they socialized with New York City's elite. Tragedy struck two years later, when Marjorie died shortly after giving birth to the couple's son, Peter.

Duchin carried on and became even more popular, appearing in such films as *Coronado* in 1935 and *The Hit Parade* in 1937. In 1941, he scored his biggest hit when "You Walk By," which featured Johnny Drake on vocals, reached number six. With the outbreak of World War II, Duchin enlisted in the Navy and eventually worked his way up to lieutenant-commander.

After the war, he resumed his career and remarried, but in March 1950, Duchin began to feel ill. He continued to perform an engagement at the Waldorf Hotel Wedgewood Room, but soon his condition deteriorated. He spent Christmas with his family before he died the following February.

Cavallaro was a natural choice to score the film, since he was a friend of Duchin's and had a similar style of piano playing. He also was contracted to Decca Records, which had secured the rights to the film's soundtrack. "We were one of the first labels to get into promoting soundtrack albums from movies," says Milt Gabler, Vice President of artists and repertoire for Decca.

Prior to his work on *The Eddy Duchin Story*, Cavallaro racked up a number of hits from films, including "I Can't Begin to Tell You." The song, which featured Bing Crosby's vocals and Cavallaro's piano, spent six weeks at Number One in late 1945. It was featured in the Betty Grable film *The Dolly Sisters*.

Cavallaro's greatest commercial triumph, however, had to be the *The Eddy Duchin Story*, since it was an LP release. "The picture was so great and Cavallaro's recording was so nice that the album sold incredibly well," says Gabler.

The film was so popular, in fact, that Columbia Records, Duchin's final record label, tried to cash in on the success of the film by releasing an album full of Duchin's original recordings. *The Eddy Duchin Story*, however, was the album that ended up topping the chart. It would be the first and only time an album that Duchin and Cavallaro were associated with reached Number One on the *Billboard* chart.

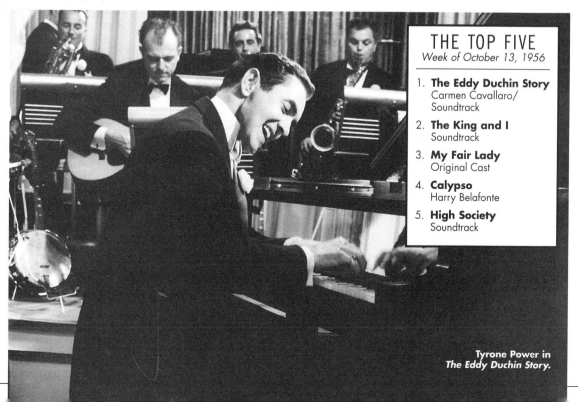

THE TOP FIVE
Week of October 13, 1956

1. **The Eddy Duchin Story**
   Carmen Cavallaro/
   Soundtrack

2. **The King and I**
   Soundtrack

3. **My Fair Lady**
   Original Cast

4. **Calypso**
   Harry Belafonte

5. **High Society**
   Soundtrack

Tyrone Power in
The Eddy Duchin Story.

6 Elvis RCA LPM 1382
ELVIS PRESLEY

Producer: None listed

Track listing: Rip It Up / Love Me / When My Blue Moon Turns to Gold Again / Long Tall Sally / First in Line / Paralyzed / So Glad You're Mine / Old Shep / Ready Teddy / Anyplace is Paradise / How's the World Treating You / How Do You Think I Feel

December 8, 1956
5 weeks

When *Elvis* was released in October 1956, the rising star had already racked up three Number One singles. A few weeks later, "Don't Be Cruel"/"Hound Dog" vacated the top spot, and Elvis scored yet another Number One with "Love Me Tender," the title track from his first film.

The songs from *Love Me Tender*, which were released on an EP in November 1956, were recorded at 20th Century Fox in Hollywood during August, September, and October of that year. For the first time in his professional career, Elvis recorded without his ace sidemen, who, much to his displeasure, were replaced by session players. Elvis was also reportedly unhappy about recording in a soundstage [see 9—*Loving You*].

While the *Love Me Tender* sessions were a bad experience, they proved to be a shot in the arm for Elvis and his regular backing band. When they reunited on September 1, 1956, at Radio Recorders in Hollywood, the sessions would result in the most productive recording dates of his young career. In a mere three days, Elvis and the boys laid down 13 tracks, 11 of which would be released on *Elvis*, making it a much more cohesive album than his debut

THE TOP FIVE
Week of December 8, 1956

1. **Elvis**
   Elvis Presley

2. **Calypso**
   Harry Belafonte

3. **My Fair Lady**
   Original Cast

4. **The Eddy Duchin Story**
   Soundtrack

5. **The King and I**
   Soundtrack

[see 1]. "We were serious when we were working on a tune, but the atmosphere was always loose," says guitarist Scotty Moore. "We were all friends, and there was not any one watching the clock." Moore was a key figure in Elvis's support cast, which also included bassist Bill Black, drummer D.J. Fontana, and the vocal group the Jordanaires. Gordan Stoker of the Jordanaires also played piano.

Elvis provided further evidence of the young performer's versatility with its diverse selection of material ranging from country and ballads to blues and barn-burning rock 'n' roll. Elvis turned to many familiar sources for this wide-ranging batch of material. "Love Me," which was released as a single and climbed to number two, was provided by Leiber & Stoller, the songwriting duo that penned Elvis's Number One hit "Hound Dog." "Paralyzed" was written by Otis Blackwell, whose "Don't Be Cruel" also became a Number One single for Elvis. For the more raucous material, Elvis once again turned to the catalog of his contemporary Little Richard, covering "Rip It Up," "Long Tall Sally," and "Ready Teddy."

The most personal number on *Elvis* was "Old Shep," a song about a boy

and his dog, which 10-year-old Elvis had performed at the Mississippi–Alabama Fair, winning second prize. Elvis played piano on that track, marking his recorded debut on the instrument.

There were no credits for a producer on most of Elvis's albums, but there were key individuals behind the scenes that helped shape his sound. Sam Phillips produced the Sun sessions. RCA executives Steve Sholes and Chet Atkins were listed as "producer" of several singles, but at the start of the *Elvis* sessions, Presley himself decided that he would take command of his future Hollywood recordings.

Elvis worked closely with house engineer Thorne Nogar. "The engineer knew the room and he placed us where he knew things would work," says Moore. "But we tried to work as close together as we could spacewise." With Elvis at the helm, the band got into more experimentation, often recording dozens of takes. "Once we decided we were going to do a certain number, we would try different tempos and different things, but nobody told you you had to play certain notes," Moore says. "Elvis was just looking for an overall feel." On *Elvis*, he found it, scoring his second Number One in seven months.

CAPITOL 824 # Love Is the Thing
NAT "KING" COLE

7

Arranger and conductor: Gordon Jenkins

Track listing: Stardust / It's All in the Game / When I Fall in Love / Ain't Misbehavin' / When Sunny Gets Blue / Love Is the Thing / At Last / Stay as Sweet as You Are / I Thought About Marie / Where Can I Go Without You

*May 27, 1957
8 weeks*

By the dawn of the rock era, Nat "King" Cole was already an established star, having scored several Number One singles, including "Nature Boy," "Mona Lisa," and "Too Young" in the late '40s and early '50s, first with the Nat "King" Cole Trio and later as a solo artist. Although Cole had nothing to do with rock 'n' roll, his popularity wasn't affected by the arrival of Elvis Presley.

In 1956, Cole's *Ballads of the Day* reached a respectable number 16. The following year, *After Midnight*, the first of four Cole albums released during 1957, peaked at number 13.

In December 1956, Cole entered the studio with an orchestra conducted by Gordon Jenkins to cut *Love Is the Thing*, a collection of a dozen popular ballads. Composer Hoagy Carmichael said that Cole's version of "Stardust," included on the album, was his favorite. The album also included "Ain't Misbehavin'," first popularized in the nightclub revue *Connie's Hot Chocolate* by Louis Armstrong [see 68], and "When Sunny Gets Blue," previously performed by Johnny Mathis [see 16].

Natalie Cole, the singer's daughter, recalls that he frequently socialized with his peers and listened to their recordings. "I met all these people through my dad—Sarah Vaughn, Count Basie, Ella Fitzgerald, Nancy Wilson, Rosemary Clooney, and Peggy Lee," she says. "I got turned on to that music at parties my parents had and by listening to the records my dad would bring home. Every afternoon my mother would sit in the library and turn on the music."

Three of the tracks on *Love Is the Thing*—the title track, "When I Fall in Love," and "Where Can I Go Without You?"—were composed by Victor Young, songwriter of the earlier Cole hit "Mona Lisa." The song "I Thought About Marie" was Jenkins's written contribution to the album.

Like other popular singers of the day, Cole attempted to branch out into television and film. He began hosting his own TV show for NBC in November 1956. Although the show was popular with viewers, the fact that it was hosted by a black performer scared away potential advertisers. Cole fared better on the big screen, appearing in such films as *Blue Gardenia* and *Small Town Girl* in 1953, *Istanbul* and *China Gate* in 1957, and *St. Louis Blues* in 1958.

Yet music remained Cole's forte. *Love Is the Thing* was the first and only chart-topping album in his lifetime. On February 15, 1965, he died of cancer. His music and legacy would live on, however, as his daughter Natalie would top the charts more than 25 years after his death with her version of songs made popular by her father [see 352].

THE TOP FIVE
Week of May 27, 1957

1. **Love Is the Thing**
   Nat "King" Cole

2. **Hymns**
   Tennessee Ernie Ford

3. **Calypso**
   Harry Belafonte

4. **An Evening with Harry Belafonte**
   Harry Belafonte

5. **My Fair Lady**
   Original Cast

8 Around the World in 80 Days DECCA 79046
SOUNDTRACK

Composer and conductor: Victor Young

Track listing: Around the World—Part I / Passepartout / Paris Arrival / Sky Symphony / (A) Invitation to a Bull Fight (B) Entrance of the Bull March / India Country Side / Around the World—Part II / The Pagoda of Pillagi / Temple of Dawn / Prairie Sail Car / Land Ho / Epilogue

July 22, 1957
10 weeks (nonconsecutive)

Victor Young didn't get to enjoy the success of his greatest work, *Around the World in 80 Days*. The composer died on November 11, 1956, five months before the soundtrack to Michael Todd's spectacular film was released in April of 1957. Prior to his death, however, Young had certainly made a name for himself composing and conducting music for such films as *Wells Fargo, Golden Boy, For Whom the Bell Tolls,* and *Rio Grande*.

Following Young's death, the album was released on Decca, which had already proven adept at marketing soundtracks with *The Eddy Duchin Story* [see 5]. However, Decca almost didn't get the album. "After Young's death, I had trouble getting the tracks from [the film's producer] Mike Todd, because he wanted the album to go to RCA-Victor," says Milt Gabler, who was the head of A&R for Decca at the time.

The controversy over which record company had the rights to the album resulted in a delay in its release. "It came out four to six weeks after it should have," says Gabler. Yet the delay didn't affect its sales, as the soundtrack, like the film that inspired it, turned out to be a blockbuster.

The film, which starred David Niven, the Mexican comedian Cantinflas, Robert Newton, and Shirley MacLaine, was shot, as its title suggests, around the world. More than 68,000 people in 13 countries were captured in the film. Todd's film crew traveled more than four million miles in the course of the shooting.

The story, based on the Jules Verne novel, traces the adventures of Phileas Fogg, played by Niven, who bets 20,000 pounds that he can circle the globe in 80 days.

Young's music not only suited the mood of the film perfectly, it also struck a nerve with his peers and the public. The title track was covered by some of the biggest names in popular music, including Bing Crosby, Frank Sinatra [see 13], and Mantovani. In fact, in 1957 alone, Young, Crosby, Mantovani, and the McGuire Sisters charted with versions of "Around the World." Mantovani's version, which reached number 12 on September 2, 1957, proved to be the highest-charting. Young's own instrumental rendition, which was released with Crosby's vocal interpretation on the flipside, reached number 13 on July 22, 1957. The same day, *Around the World in 80 Days* soared to the top of the album chart, giving Young a posthumous Number One. His effort also garnered him an Oscar for best score.

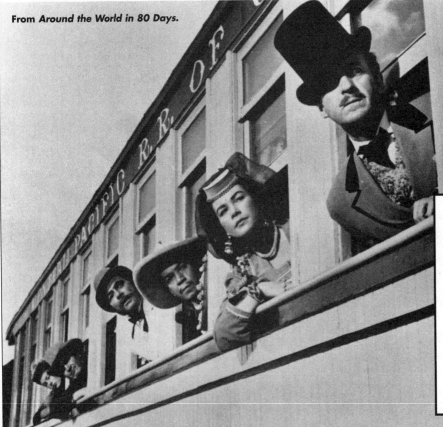

From *Around the World in 80 Days*.

THE TOP FIVE
Week of July 22, 1957

1. **Around the World in 80 Days**
   Soundtrack

2. **My Fair Lady**
   Original Cast

3. **Love Is the Thing**
   Nat King Cole

4. **Film Encores**
   Mantovani

5. **A Swingin' Affair**
   Frank Sinatra

RCA LPM 1515 **Loving You** **9**
ELVIS PRESLEY

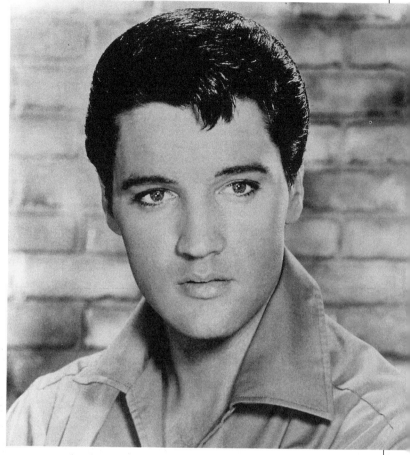

Producer: None listed

Track listing: Mean Woman Blues / Teddy Bear / Loving You / Got a Lot o' Livin' to Do / Lonesome Cowboy / Hot Dog / Party / Blueberry Hill / True Love / Don't Leave Me Now / Have I Told You Lately / I Need You So

July 29, 1957
10 weeks

The top of the Best Selling Pop Albums chart was a familiar place for Elvis Presley, as he spent 15 weeks of 1956 in the Number One position with *Elvis Presley* [see 1] and *Elvis* [see 6]. So no one was too surprised when *Loving You*, his third album, also hit the summit of the album chart, for Elvis had truly arrived.

Elvis was reportedly unhappy with the way the recording sessions for his first film, *Love Me Tender,* were handled. When it was time to record songs for his next film, he took command. "We started *Loving You* at a soundstage at Paramount Studios and it was huge," says guitarist Scotty Moore. "We just couldn't get a feel for it, it was just too big, so Elvis turned to the [film] producer [Hal Wallis] and told him we couldn't do it there, so we went back to Radio Recorders. From then on, just about everything we did in Hollywood was done at that studio."

Radio Recorders was the sight of Elvis's most fruitful recording session to date [see 6]. During January and February of 1957, Elvis and company holed up at the studio to work on several projects. On January 12 and 13, he recorded some gospel tunes, which

would initially comprise the *Peace in the Valley* EP and would later be included on *Elvis' Christmas Album* [see 10]. During those sessions, Elvis also laid down "Got a Lot o' Livin' to Do" and "Mean Woman Blues" for the *Loving You* album.

Elvis recorded several songs for the *Loving You* movie soundtrack on January 15–18, 21–22, and February 14, but only the takes of "Party," "Hot Dog," and "Lonesome Cowboy," the original title track of the picture, were used on the album. The album's first side featured music from the film; side two offered some surprises, including Elvis's rendition of the Cole Porter standard "True Love," a song made famous by Bing Crosby and Grace Kelly, and "Blueberry Hill," a hit for R&B belter Fats Domino.

The film's plot and music were customized for Elvis, allowing him to flaunt his teen-idol looks and his musical chops for his growing legion of fans. In fact, at least three of the performance scenes— "Teddy Bear," "Mean Woman Blues," and "Got a Lot o' Livin' to Do"—can stand alone apart from the film. Film producer Wallis attended the January sessions. He was so impressed with "Teddy Bear" that he insisted it be included in the movie. But another Elvis favorite from the same sessions didn't make the cut: a smoking take of Smiley Lewis's 1956 R&B hit "One Night of Sin," which was deemed too suggestive for the film and the album. A month later, Elvis recut the song, retitled "One Night," with less racy lyrics. But it didn't see the light of day until October 1958, when it was finally released as a single.

The single "(Let Me be Your) Teddy Bear" with "Loving You" on the flip side, was released in June. On July 8, it topped the Hot 100, becoming Elvis's fifth Number One single. The next day, the film opened. Seven weeks later, *Loving You* became Elvis's third consecutive Number One album.

10 Elvis' Christmas Album RCA VICTOR LOC 1035
ELVIS PRESLEY

Producer: None listed

Track listing: Santa Claus is Back in Town / White Christmas / Here Comes Santa Claus (Right Down Santa Claus Lane) / I'll be Home for Christmas / Blue Christmas / Santa Bring My Baby Back (to Me) / O Little Town of Bethlehem / Silent Night / (There'll be) Peace in the Valley (for Me) / I Believe /Take My Hand, Precious Lord / It is No Secret (What God Can Do)

December 16, 1957
4 weeks (nonconsecutive)

Following his 10-week reign atop the Best Selling Pop LP's chart with *Loving You* [see 9], Elvis Presley was temporarily displaced from the Number One position by the *Around the World in 80 Days* soundtrack. But that was only until Elvis gave his fans a present that would become the first Christmas album of the rock era to top the chart.

Eight of the 12 tracks on *Elvis' Christmas Album* were recorded at Radio Recorders in Hollywood, California, on September 5–7, 1957. Presley's guitar player Scotty Moore says those sessions weren't too different from any others. "We were just recording some more songs," he says. Also cut during those same sessions were the Number One single "Don't" and the B-sides "My Wish Came True" and "Treat Me Nice."

"It was fun to do," Moore says of the sessions. "But we were all laughing about playing Christmas songs in Los Angeles in September." To help set the mood, RCA A&R executive Steve Sholes had a fully decorated Christmas tree, complete with presents underneath, set up in the studio.

For material, Elvis turned to some proven classics, including "White Christmas," a song made famous by Bing Crosby [see 11], yet Elvis recorded the song using the Drifters' arrangement, backed by the Jordanaires and Millie Kirkham, who was flown in for the sessions (despite the fact she was six months pregnant). Also featured were a version of Ernest Tubb's "Blue Christmas" and "Santa Claus Is Back in Town," which Jerry Leiber and Mike Stoller reportedly penned in a matter of minutes in the studio at Elvis's request.

The other four tracks featured on the album were recorded at Radio Recorders in January and were initially released in April on Elvis's gospel EP, *Peace in the Valley*. The remaining cuts on *Elvis' Christmas Album* would also be divided up to fill two subsequent EPs— *Elvis Sings Christmas Songs*, which topped the Best Selling Pop EP's chart in December 1957, and *Christmas with Elvis*, which was released a year later. While the EPs offered a low-priced value for the casual fans, the initial pressing of *Elvis' Christmas Album* was aimed at the fanatic, as the deluxe edition contained 10 pages of color photos.

Despite the album's commercial success, many radio stations banned the songs from their playlists because some program directors believed a suggestive performer like Elvis had no business singing religious songs.

Nonetheless, Elvis celebrated his fourth Number One album in less than two years as two of the songs on the album—"I'll be Home for Christmas" and "White Christmas"—rang especially true: Elvis spent his first holiday at his new home, Graceland. And, as luck would have it, it snowed in Memphis that year.

THE TOP FIVE
Week of December 16, 1957

1. **Elvis' Christmas Album**
   Elvis Presley

2. **My Fair Lady**
   Original Cast

3. **Merry Christmas**
   Bing Crosby

4. **Around the World in 80 Days**
   Soundtrack

5. **Ricky**
   Ricky Nelson

DECCA 8128 **Merry Christmas**
BING CROSBY

11

Crosby and Carol Richards for the film *The Lemon Drop Kid*, reached number 78, while "How Lovely Is Christmas," featuring Crosby backed by the Arthur Norman Choir, stalled at number 97.

The latter track was not included on *Merry Christmas*, but the album did include "Jingle Bells," "Santa Claus Is Coming to Town," and "Mele Kalikimaka," which featured Crosby backed by the Andrews Sisters and the Vic Schoen Orchestra.

"It was a natural thing to put out a Bing Crosby Christmas album, because 'White Christmas' and 'Silent Night' were such gigantic sellers. We knew the public would accept an LP from him," says producer Milt Gabler, then vice president of artists and repertoire for Decca Records. With the popularity of the album, Crosby became "Mr. Christmas," Gabler says.

With his film career in full swing, Crosby allowed the executives at Decca to focus on his recording career. "He didn't have anything to say about what went on the album, but he didn't have to," says Gabler. "We ran his record career in those days. He was busy making movies, playing golf, going fishing, and hunting."

While Crosby was off enjoying the other aspects of his life, *Merry Christmas* hit Number One in its sixth week on the chart in 1957, knocking *Elvis' Christmas Album* from the summit. Elvis would return to the top the following week. However, that wasn't the last of *Merry Christmas* by any means. It returned to the album chart every Christmas from 1958 through 1962, and remains a perennial favorite on the Christmas charts.

Producer: None listed

Track listing: Silent Night / Adeste Fideles / White Christmas / God Rest Ye Merry, Gentlemen / Faith of Our Fathers / I'll Be Home for Christmas / Jingle Bells / Santa Claus is Coming to Town / Silver Bells / It's Beginning to Look Like Christmas / Christmas in Killarney / Mele Kalikimaka

December 30, 1957
1 week

On December 16, 1957, *Elvis' Christmas Album* [see 10] became the first holiday album to top the album chart in the rock era. But when the future king of rock 'n' roll was just an infant, another multimedia superstar was already scoring hits with seasonal favorites. Bing Crosby, known as "Der Bingle" to his fans, recorded "Silent Night, Holy Night," in November 13, 1935, just 10 months after Presley's birth on January 8, 1935.

It was Jack Kapp, the head of Decca Records, who convinced Crosby to record the holiday favorites that would become a staple of his catalog. Following the warm reception of "Silent Night," Crosby went on to record several other seasonal sides, including "Adeste Fiedelis (O Come, All Ye Faithful)" in June 1942, "I'll Be Home For

Christmas" in October 1943, and "Silver Bells" in September 1950, but the holiday standard that became Crosby's most popular seasonal song and signature tune was "White Christmas."

It was written by Irving Berlin, known for his work on Broadway. Crosby recorded the song, accompanied by John Scott Trotter & His Orchestra and the Ken Darby Singers, on May 29, 1942, for the film *Holiday Inn*. The single hit Number One in 1942, 1945, and 1946, and returned to the chart every year for two decades. Its popularity was such that the song ended up inspiring a movie of the same name in 1954, starring Crosby.

Decca first released a Crosby holiday album titled *Merry Christmas*, compiled from the singer's Christmas sides, in 1945. In 1956, a second Crosby Christmas set, *A Christmas Sing with Bing Around the World*, culled from a CBS Radio program, reached number 21. The following holiday season, a revised version of *Merry Christmas* was back on the charts competing with Elvis's holiday fare.

At the time, Crosby also had a huge presence on the singles chart. "White Christmas" was once again released as a single. It reached number 34, while a second version of "Silent Night," recorded in 1947, reached number 54. A third single, "Silver Bells," recorded by

THE TOP FIVE
Week of December 30, 1957

1. **Merry Christmas**
   Bing Crosby

2. **Elvis' Christmas Album**
   Elvis Presley

3. **My Fair Lady**
   Original Cast

4. **Hymns**
   Tennessee Ernie Ford

5. **Christmas Hymns and Carols**
   Robert Shaw

12 Ricky IMPERIAL 9048
RICKY NELSON

Producer: None listed

Track listing: Honeycomb / Boppin' the Blues / Be-Bop Baby / Have I Told You Lately That I Love You / Teenage Doll / If You Can't Rock Me / Whole Lotta Shakin' Goin' On / Baby I'm Sorry / Am I Blue / I'm Confessin' / Your True Love / True Love

January 20, 1958
2 weeks

Decades before the advent of MTV, a teenage would-be rock star named Ricky Nelson was able to expose his music to millions on television. Ricky, of course, was the real-life son of Ozzie and Harriet Nelson and began appearing on their *The Adventures of Ozzie & Harriet* TV show in 1952 at the age of 11. (He'd first appeared on the radio version of the series in 1948 when he was eight.) By the time he had hit his middle teens, Ricky Nelson's rock 'n' roll dreams were becoming a reality on TV and in real life.

In a 1956 episode of the ABC-TV situation comedy, Nelson formed a high school rock 'n' roll band. In real life, Nelson, inspired by his girlfriend's interest in Elvis Presley, decided that he too should became a pop star. Eventually, Nelson was featured playing his favorite song, Fats Domino's "I'm Walking," on the TV show. An audio tape of the performance was shopped to several record labels, but there were no takers until Ozzie Nelson set up a handshake deal with Verve Records. Within months, Nelson scored three top 20 hits: "A Teenager's Romance," "I'm Walking," and "You're My One and Only Love."

THE TOP FIVE
Week of January 20, 1958

1. **Ricky**
   Ricky Nelson

2. **My Fair Lady**
   Original Cast

3. **Around the World in 80 Days**
   Soundtrack

4. **Pat's Great Hits**
   Pat Boone

5. **The King and I**
   Soundtrack

Since Nelson had not actually signed a contract with Verve, Ozzie decided to move his son to a label more equipped to handle the sales of a pop superstar. While Verve dealt primarily with jazz, Imperial Records, headed by Lew Chudd, specialized in rock 'n' roll. In fact, Imperial was the label that had released Fats Domino's version of "I'm Walking."

When Chudd heard the news that Nelson was looking for a label, he went after the teen star with a vengeance. A&R executive Jimmie Haskell, who was later assigned to work with Nelson, still remembers Chudd's enthusiasm. "I could hear him yelling at the lawyers, 'I don't care how many points Ozzie wants. Give it to him. I want to put a record out now!'"

The first songs Nelson cut for Imperial were "Be-Bop Baby" and a cover of "Have I Told You Lately That I Love You," which was also recorded by Presley. "Rick chose that as his first [Imperial] backside, because he admired Elvis and loved that song," says Haskell, who oversaw the recording of *Ricky*. "He wanted to pay homage to him by recording one of his songs."

Guitarist Barney Kessel, who served as arranger of Nelson's Verve singles,

was also featured on the first Imperial single. The material featured on the album was chosen by Haskell, Ozzie, and Ricky. "I would sift through about 100 songs submitted to Imperial and narrow it down to about 50, which I would play for Rick at his bungalow on the set of *Ozzie and Harriet*," Haskell says. Sometimes, Ozzie Nelson rejected songs because the lyrical content was not consistent with the wholesome image projected on the TV show. "If Ricky liked a song and Ozzie didn't, they would have a discussion about it. And if Ricky still insisted, Ozzie would let him do it, but he would tell him to be aware of this or that," Haskell says.

Aside from Elvis, Nelson drew his song from other popular hitmakers of the day (Carl Perkins's "Boppin' the Blues" and "Your True Love," Jerry Lee Lewis's "Whole Lotta Shakin' Goin' On") and even recorded a standard (Cole Porter's "True Love"). With Nelson's performances of the songs on the album conveniently featured in the episodes of *Ozzie and Harriet*, *Ricky* reached the top of the Best Selling Pop LP's list in its 11th week. Yet as Haskell points out, "Ricky wasn't just a TV idol, he was a great singer." Millions of record-buyers agreed.

CAPITOL 920 # Come Fly with Me

FRANK SINATRA

13

Producer: Voyle Gilmore

Track listing: Come Fly with Me / Around the World / Isle of Capri / Moonlight in Vermont / Autumn in New York / On the Road to Mandalay / Let's Get Away from It All / April in Paris / London by Night / Brazil / Blue Hawaii / It's Nice to Go Trav'ling

February 10, 1958
5 weeks

Before Elvis Presley arrived on the music scene, Frank Sinatra was already an established superstar and one of the best-known vocalists in the world. From 1942 through 1954, he racked up 40 top 10 hits, including the Number One singles "Oh! What It Seemed to Be," "Five Minutes More," and "Mam'selle." Sinatra also had an impressive run on the album chart after 1955: In the Wee Small Hours, Songs for Swingin' Lovers!, A Swingin' Affair!, and Pal Joey all climbed to number two, but were unable to reach the summit. In fact, In the Wee Small Hours spent an amazing 18 weeks at number two, but did not reach the top spot.

With the release of Come Fly with Me in early 1958, Sinatra's fortunes would change. The album marked a reunion of sorts between the crooner and arranger-conductor Billy May. "I first worked for Frank in 1944, when Axel Stordahl was doing his conducting," says May. "I did some arranging for Axel."

When Sinatra joined Capitol Records in 1953 after a lengthy run on Columbia, Sinatra suggested that he work with May, but the bandleader was unavailable, since he was touring with his own band.

In the interim, the Sinatra–May pairing began to take on mythical proportions. Sinatra's 1953 single "South of the Border (Down Mexico Way)" was credited to "Frank Sinatra and Billy May with His Orchestra," but it was actually Sinatra's other well-known collaborator, Nelson Riddle, performing a May-like arrangement.

"I've always been a fan of Sinatra," says May. "I was very flattered that he wanted to work with me, because he had made a lot of successful records with Nelson, who was also working with Capitol at the time."

Finally, in the fall of 1957, the collaboration began to take shape. May had high hopes for the project from the get-go. "I went down to Frank's house in Palm Springs and Jimmy Van Heusen and Sammy Cahn were there," he recalls. "The material was so good, because Jimmy was such a good songwriter and Sammy was a good lyricist. The whole idea that they presented to me was so good, I figured we couldn't go far from wrong."

The Cahn–Van Heusen compositions "Come Fly with Me" and "It's Nice to Go Trav'ling," which open and close the album, set the tone for the album's traveling theme. Also included was Sinatra's interpretation of Victor Young's "Around the World" [see 8].

The sessions, held at Capitol Records' studios in Hollywood, went smoothly. "We did three sessions in October," says May. "They were all in the evening. We would start around eight or nine P.M. and end around midnight." The atmosphere was loose. "I was always relaxed around Frank and he was always relaxed around me," says May. "I know he gave a lot of people a lot of trouble, but I never had any difficulty with him."

Sinatra's involvement wasn't simply limited to his vocal contribution. He also had input on the arrangements. "When we did 'On the Road to Mandalay,' I had a big ending in mind," says May. "When it came to the part where it says, 'When the dawn comes up like thunder,' I had a big Chinese gong. Frank liked it so much that he considered that the end of the record." As a result, the remaining four to eight bars of the song were left off.

Come Fly with Me became Sinatra's first album-chart topper in its second

14 The Music Man CAPITOL 0990
ORIGINAL BROADWAY CAST

Musical director: Morton Da Costa

Track listing: Overture and Rock Island / Iowa Stubborn / Ya Got Trouble / Piano Lesson / Goodnight My Someone / Seventy-Six Trombones / Sincere / The Sadder-But-Wiser Girl / Pick-A-Little, Talk-A-Little, and Goodnight Ladies / Marian the Librarian / My White Night / Wells Fargo Wagon / It's You / Shipoopi / Lida Rose and Will I Ever Tell You / Gary, Indiana / Till There Was You / Finale

March 17, 1958
12 weeks, nonconsecutive

When *The Music Man* opened on December 17, 1957, at the Majestic Theatre, the play's writer, composer, and lyricist Meredith Willson already had a hefty list of credits. He played flute with John Philip Sousa's group and the New York Philharmonic Symphony under the direction of Toscanini. He conducted orchestras for radio, TV, and motion pictures. He composed popular songs, appeared on radio and TV, and had written a novel. Yet *The Music Man* marked Willson's debut on Broadway, and what a debut it was.

Based primarily on Willson's boyhood memories of growing up in Mason City, Iowa, *The Music Man* is a musical comedy about a salesman who peddles instruments and band uniforms to people in small towns with the promise of teaching the would-be musicians how to play. Yet since he himself cannot play a note, he skips town before fulfilling his promise. In River City, the protagonist's usual operation is thrown off track when he falls for a local librarian.

The original cast album was cut soon after the play opened on Broadway to enthusiastic audiences and rave reviews. Barbara Cook, who played the part of the librarian Marian Paroo, still remembers the all-day session in which the album was cut. Robert Preston was cast as the lead character, Harold Hill, after Gene Kelly, Danny Kaye, and Phil Harris passed on the part. "Robert was so nervous because he wasn't used to doing that type of thing," Cook says. "But he still did 'Ya Got Trouble' in one take, while we all cheered him on."

While Cook admits it was often hard to recreate the stage performance in the studio, conductor Herbert Greene was able to keep the energy flowing. "He really had a strong hand and kept everything in control," she says.

It was the unique material that made *The Music Man* stand out, Cook says. "The first time I heard the score, I was just bowled over," she says. "I'd really never heard that kind of rhythmic, talk-ing thing that Meredith had come up with. It was so unusual."

The Music Man was the third-longest-running Broadway musical of the 1950s, with a total of 1,375 performances. The album reached Number One in its fourth week on the chart and enjoyed an impressive 12-week run at the top. Yet its influence wouldn't end there. "Seventy-Six Trombones" went on to become an American standard, the soundtrack to the film version of the production reached number two in 1962, and even the Beatles took a cue from *The Music Man* when they covered "Till There Was You" on *Meet the Beatles!* [see 65].

THE TOP FIVE
Week of March 17, 1958

1. **The Music Man**
   Original Cast

2. **My Fair Lady**
   Original Cast

3. **Come Fly with Me**
   Frank Sinatra

4. **The Late, Late Show**
   Dakota Staton

5. **Pal Joey**
   Soundtrack

Scene from *The Music Man*.

Mitzi Gaynor and Rossano Brazzi in *South Pacific*.

Music supervisor and conductor:
Alfred Newman

Track listing: South Pacific Overture /
Dites-moi / A Cockeyed Optimist /
Twin Soliloquies / Some Enchanted
Evening / Bloody Mary / My Girl Back
Home / There is Nothin' Like a Dame /
Bali Ha'i / I'm Gonna Wash That Man
Right Outa My Hair / A Wonderful Guy
/ Younger Than Springtime / Happy
Talk / Honey Bun / Carefully Taught /
This Nearly Was Mine / Finale

May 19, 1958
31 weeks; 28 weeks stereo
(nonconsecutive)

When the soundtrack album for *South Pacific* made its debut on the Best Selling Pop LP's chart on March 31, 1958, the original cast album of *South Pacific* had already logged an incredible 208 weeks on the chart. The musical was adapted from James A. Michener's *Tales of the South Pacific*. The team of Richard Rodgers and Oscar Hammerstein II wrote the music and lyrics, respectively, for the production, which started Mary Martin and opera star Ezio Pinza. When the production opened on Broadway in 1949, it garnered the largest advance ticket sale in Broadway history.

When Rodgers and Hammerstein set out to cut the soundtrack album to the big-screen version of *South Pacific*, they

attempted to make an even more majestic production, while retaining the magic of the original cast album. For the film soundtrack, the pair even opted to include "My Girl Back Home." The song, composed for the original production, had been cut from the stage show to keep it down to a reasonable running time. However, Rodgers and Hammerstein had a second thought about the move and decided to restore the song to the score for the film.

Rising film star Mitzi Gaynor was cast as the female lead for the big-screen version of the film. "I was chosen to do it, because I sang in Mary Martin's keys and Rodgers and Hammerstein wanted to hear that particular sound," says Gaynor. For the actress, landing the role almost seemed like an act of fate. When Gaynor, a veteran of the stage, did her screen test for 20th Century-Fox Studios in 1950, she sang "A Wonderful Guy." Says Gaynor, "the Broadway show had just opened and I thought it was a wonderful song. That had a lot to do with me getting a contract with Fox, and then eight years later, ironically, I played the part of Nellie and sang the song on the screen."

While Gaynor starred in both the film and on the soundtrack album, the same could not be said of her co-stars. "Rossano Brazzi wanted to sing the Emile de Becque part, but he couldn't because he wasn't an opera singer and thats what the world wanted to hear,"

Gaynor says. Despite Brazzi's protests, the voice of opera star Giorgio Tozzi was dubbed in during the musical numbers and is featured on the soundtrack album.

South Pacific was recorded on the sound stages of 20th Century-Fox Studios in Hollywood with Alfred Newman conducting the orchestra. "Alfred Newman had known Rodgers and Hammerstein for centuries," Gaynor says. "They had been friends just about all of their lives." Prior to the sessions, Newman worked with vocal director Kenneth Darby to ensure that the cast was set to record its vocal performances. "We rehearsed for three weeks before we went into record, so we knew pretty much what we were going to do," says Gaynor. Hammerstein attended the sessions, but Rodgers, who was feeling ill at the time, did not.

The sessions ran approximately two weeks. "I was in particularly good voice," Gaynor says. "I didn't have a cold and Giorgio Tozzi naturally was in good voice." While the soundtrack album was being cut, a stage version of *South Pacific*, starring Martin and Tozzi, was playing locally in Los Angeles.

During the sessions, Gaynor was convinced that the soundtrack album, like the original cast recording that came before it, would be a smash. "The music was so thrilling, it knocked your socks off," she says. "The first time we heard 'Bali Ha'i,' it was a remarkably moving moment."

The soundtrack album of *South Pacific* hit the summit in its eighth week on the chart, leapfrogging over the original cast album, which had once again began climbing the chart due to the publicity from the film version.

THE TOP FIVE
Week of May 19, 1958

1. **South Pacific**
   Soundtrack

2. **South Pacific**
   Original Cast

3. **The Music Man**
   Original Cast

4. **Johnny's Greatest Hits**
   Johnny Mathis

5. **My Fair Lady**
   Original Cast

16 Johnny's Greatest Hits COLUMBIA 8634
JOHNNY MATHIS

Producer: Mitch Miller

Track listing: Chances Are / All the Time / The Twelfth of Never / When Sunny Gets Blue / When I Am with You / Wonderful! Wonderful! / It's Not for Me to Say / Come to Me / Wild Is the Wind / Warm and Tender / No Love / I Look at You

June 9, 1958
3 weeks, nonconsecutive

By the spring of 1958, young Johnny Mathis had already scored eight hit singles and three top 10 albums. *Wonderful Wonderful*, his debut album, climbed to number four in the fall of 1957. The follow-up, *Warm*, reached number two later that same year, while *Good Night, Dear Lord* stalled at number 10 in the spring of 1958. It would take a combination of Mathis's greatest recordings to put him on top.

The son of a vaudeville singer, Mathis was born in San Francisco on September 30, 1935. As a youth, he divided his time between singing in the church choir and competing in a number of track and field events and basketball. It was only after Columbia Records flew him to New York for an audition that Mathis decided to skip the 1956 Olympic trials and focus on singing.

After Mathis had scored a number of hits, Columbia A&R executive Mitch Miller [see 19] had plans to bring the singer's popularity to new heights. "I was in England at the time and I was supposed to go in the studio and record a new album," recalls Mathis. "Mitch Miller decided to release all the early singles that I had made as a compila-

tion. That was the beginning of all the greatest-hits stuff. It was just another marketing ploy, but no one had really started doing that until that album. I was glad, because it gave people an opportunity to have all of my most popular stuff on one album."

Many of Mathis's early sides, such as "When Sunny Gets Blue," "It's Not For Me to Say," and "Wonderful! Wonderful!" were recorded with Ray Conniff serving as arranger. "Columbia found Ray and paid $25 or $30 to do the singles. He was a genius. He did all of those songs with only eight to 10 musicians," says Mathis. The early tracks were recorded quickly at the Columbia Records 30th Street Studio, an old renovated church on 30th Street and Third Avenue in New York City. "Each song only took about 30 minutes or so," he adds. "It was get it or don't get it.

Whatever was on the record was what went out."

The singer shared a songwriting credit on "I Look at You" with J.M. Robinson, but Mathis downplays his role. "All I did was change the middle part and the bridge around and she gave me writing credit," he says. "But I did a very minimal amount of work on that. I don't know how to write music."

Johnny's Greatest Hits hit the top of the Best Selling Pop LP's chart in its ninth week on the chart and spent three weeks in the Number One position. In November 1959, Mathis would hit the summit again [see 28], but *Johnny's Greatest Hits* was his greatest chart accomplishment. It remained on the album chart for 490 weeks, a record that would remain in tact until it was eclipsed by Pink Floyd's *Dark Side of the Moon* 15 years later [see 157].

THE TOP FIVE
Week of June 9, 1958

1. **Johnny's Greatest Hits**
   Johnny Mathis

2. **South Pacific**
   Soundtrack

3. **The Music Man**
   Original Cast

4. **South Pacific**
   Original Cast

5. **Elvis' Golden Records**
   Elvis Presley

Producer: Jesse Kaye

Track listing: Overture / Thank Heaven for Little Girls / It's a Bore / The Parisians / Waltz at Maxim's (She is Not Thinking of Me) / The Night They Invented Champagne / I Remember It Well / Say a Prayer for Me Tonight / I'm Glad I'm Not Young Anymore / Gigi (Gaston's Soliloquy) / Finale: Thank Heaven for Little Girls

*July 21, 1958
10 weeks; 4 weeks mono (nonconsecutive)*

Lyricist Alan Jay Lerner and composer Frederick Loewe became stars with *My Fair Lady*. With *Gigi*, the pair achieved legendary status.

The story of *Gigi* dates back to 1942, when it was published in the form of a 60-page novella by the 70-year-old French writer Colette. The book inspired a 1950 French film that did not feature music, but four years later Anita Loos adapted the story for the stage with Audrey Hepburn cast in the lead role.

When the play opened in London in 1956, Leslie Caron was in the title role, which she would also hold in the big-screen version. It was producer Arthur Freed who bought the film rights to *Gigi*, which was shot on location in Paris.

Aside from Caron, the film starred Maurice Chevalier and Louis Jourdan. Andre Previn conducted the MGM Studio Orchestra for the soundtrack recording.

In his autobiography, *The Street Where I Live*, Lerner admitted that "Waltz at Maxim's (She's Not Thinking of Me)" was one of the most difficult lyrics for him to complete in his entire career. In fact, Freed was so intrigued by Lerner's agonizing over the song, he asked Previn to sneak into Lerner's room and steal his work in progress. Previn refused. After nine days, Lerner finally finished the lyric.

The film's most important song, the title song, was the last to be penned for the movie. In *The Street Where I Live*, Lerner wrote that the pair had attempted to write the song several times without any luck. When Loewe finally came up with the right tune, Lerner happened to be seated in the bathroom. "Fritz was at the piano in the living room, dressed in the Bryon-esque costume in which he

always works—his baggy underwear," Lerner wrote. "Suddenly an exquisite melody came wafting down the hall, causing me to drop my newspaper. 'My God!' I yelled. 'That's beautiful.' Leaping from my perch with my trousers still clinging to my ankles, I made my way to the living room like a man on tiny stilts."

While Caron starred in the film, her voice is not heard on the soundtrack. Lerner, Loewe, and Freed all agreed that her voice had to be dubbed by another singer for the soundtrack. Marni Nixon was the vocalist hired by Previn for the job. An awkward situation arose when Caron, unaware that her voice was inadequate, showed up at the sessions only to find Nixon singing her parts.

In the end, it all worked out for the best. *Gigi* was a huge hit at the box office and the music struck a chord with the public. "Gigi (Gaston's Soliloquy)," performed by Jourdan, won an Oscar for best song and the album won the first-ever Grammy for best original cast motion picture soundtrack.

In its fifth week on the chart, *Gigi* hit the top of the chart, making a big jump from number 14 to the summit.

Leslie Caron and Louis Jourdan in *Gigi*.

THE TOP FIVE
Week of July 21, 1958

1. **Gigi**
   Soundtrack

2. **South Pacific**
   Soundtrack

3. **The Music Man**
   Original Cast

4. **Sing Along with Mitch**
   Mitch Miller

5. **Johnny's Greatest Hits**
   Johnny Mathis

18 Tchaikovsky: Piano Concerto No. 1 RCA 2252
VAN CLIBURN

Conductor: Kiril Kondrashin

Track listing: Tchaikovsky: Piano Concerto No. 1 in B-Flat Minor, Op. 23—First movement: Allgro non troppo e molto meaestoso; Allegro con spirito / Second movement: Andante simplico; Prestissimo; Tempo I / Third movement: Allegro con fuoco

August 11, 1958
7 weeks (nonconsecutive)

On April 11, 1958, a tall, 23-year-old Texan by the name of Van Cliburn shocked the music world by winning the prestigious International Tchaikovsky Competition in Moscow.

On his return to the United States, the six-foot-four-inch pianist found that he had become a national hero. On May 19, he performed Tchaikovsky's First Concerto and Rachmaninoff's Third, the same program that wowed the Soviet audience, in front of an adoring crowd at Carnegie Hall. Despite his relatively young age, the music and the hall were not new to Cliburn. "I played in Carnegie Hall when I was 13 and I made my debut with the New York Philharmonic when I was 20 at Carnegie," Cliburn says. As for Tchaikovsky, Cliburn had been playing the program for more than a decade. "I made my debut with the Houston Symphony with the Tchaikovsky Concerto when I was 12, as the result of a Texas competition for young people," he recalls.

The day following his triumphant return to Carnegie Hall, Van Cliburn was treated to a ticker-tape parade. Three days later, he was interviewed by Edward R. Murrow. And the day after that, May 24, he recorded an album. After winning the Tchaikovsky competition, Cliburn had entered into a "gentlemen's agreement" with RCA to record his award-winning performance. The result was *Tchaikovsky: Piano Concerto No. 1*.

It was only fitting that Cliburn opted to record the album at Carnegie. But there was no audience, as the album was recorded in one overnight session running from midnight to 4:30 A.M. "We were going to record it at a studio on 42nd Street," says Cliburn, "but I didn't like the ambiance, so I had the idea to do it at Carnegie, but the only time we could do it was at night, which suited me just wonderfully, because I like performing at night."

Conducting the session was Kiril Kondrashin, who also served as conductor of the Moscow Radio Symphony, which had accompanied Cliburn during his award-winning performance in Moscow. "I got permission from Mr. Krushchev to bring him back with me," says Cliburn, referring to the then-head of the Soviet Union. "He was the first Soviet conductor to come to the U.S. There was a very good relationship between us."

The success of *Tchaikovsky: Piano Concerto No. 1* caught even *Billboard* by surprise. In the August 11, 1958, issue, another RCA album, Perry Como's *Como's Golden Records* was incorrectly placed in the Number One position. In the following issue, the error was corrected with an explanation, "Thru an error in tabulating, the sales of Van Cliburn's recording of *Tchaikovsky's Piano Concerto No. 1* were inadvertently credited to *Como's Golden Records*, both on RCA Victor."

The magazine also ran a front-page story on Cliburn's surprise success, sporting the headline, "Cliburn Album Sells Like Hot Single." The article noted that "at Victor these days they mention the names of Presley and Cliburn in one breath."

Although the perfectionist Cliburn only considered the recording of *Tchaikovsky: Piano Concerto No. 1* "passable," he has nothing put praise for the music. "It's a world-beloved treasure," he says. "When you examine the piece, you know why it is famous, because it has equal parts intelligence and emotion, and equal parts intelligence and emotion give you a masterpiece."

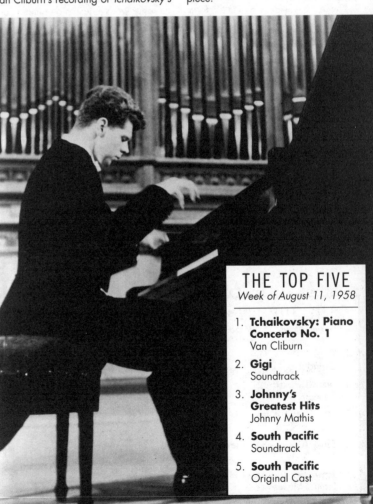

THE TOP FIVE
Week of August 11, 1958

1. **Tchaikovsky: Piano Concerto No. 1**
   Van Cliburn

2. **Gigi**
   Soundtrack

3. **Johnny's Greatest Hits**
   Johnny Mathis

4. **South Pacific**
   Soundtrack

5. **South Pacific**
   Original Cast

Producer: Mitch Miller

Track listing: That Old Gang of Mine / Down By the Old Mill Stream / By the Light of the Silvery Moon / You Are My Sunshine / Till We Meet Again / Let the Rest of the World Go By / Sweet Violets / I've Got Sixpence / I've Been Working on the Railroad / That's Where My Money Goes / She Wore a Yellow Ribbon / Don't Fence Me In / There Is a Tavern in the Town / Show Me the Way to Go Home / Bell Bottom Trousers; Be Kind to Your Web-Footed Friends

*October 6, 1958
8 weeks (nonconsecutive)*

Mitch Miller (left) and Guy Miller.

Columbia Records' head of artist and repertoire Mitch Miller first hit the top of the album chart as producer of *Johnny's Greatest Hits* [see 16]. Yet Miller was more than a producer/A&R man—he was a talent in his own right, having scored a Number One single in 1955 with "The Yellow Rose of Texas." However, with the arrival of Elvis Presley [see 1] and rock 'n' roll, Miller's brand of sophisticated and melodic pop music was in danger of extinction, at least until he developed the "sing-along" concept.

The concept took shape one night in Columbia's New York headquarters. "One of the sales guys came up to my office and said, 'Why don't you do an album of World War II songs, you can call it *Barracks Ballads*," Miller says. "I played devil's disciple and asked, 'Who's going to buy it?' Certainly the guys that came back from the service couldn't give a goddamn about it and

the people at home couldn't relate to it, but the idea of an album that people could sing along to just kept nagging me."

With that thought in the back of his head, Miller began conducting his own research. "I asked everyone I knew what were the songs that they sung at parties, at camp, at Lion's and Rotary Club meetings," he says. Miller kept tabs of the most popular songs and decided to include them on his first album, *Sing Along with Mitch*.

With the list of classic popular songs complete, Miller assembled a group of backing musicians and a chorus, collectively known as "the Gang," and entered the Columbia Records 30th Street Studio. "It was very simple," he says. "I had three pluckers I called my Guitar Mafia, an accordion player, a harmonica player, a bass player, a piano player, and a drummer." The chorus consisted of 25 men. "I used 25 guys for two reasons," says Miller. "I wanted that mass sound, and also the base salary per singer from AFTRA was less expensive if you used a large group."

Although all of the musicians and singers featured on the album were professionals, Miller wanted the album to sound informal, so that the amateur vocalists at home would feel free to sing along. "I wanted it to sound casual, yet that's the hardest thing in the world to do," he says. "When you try to make something sound casual, it usually ends up sounding like dreck."

Thanks to early exposure from WCCO Minneapolis DJ Howard Viken, who was also instrumental in the career of Bob Newhart [see 39], *Sing Along with Mitch* began to take off. At one point a department store in the Minneapolis area sent a telegram to Columbia requesting 50,000 copies.

In its 13th week on the chart, *Sing Along With Mitch* hit the summit, preventing Elvis Presley's *King Creole* from reaching Number One. (Presley was serving in the Army at the time and was unable to promote the album.) It was a victory for Miller, a staunch critic of rock 'n' roll, and it signaled that there was still plenty of interest in good old-fashioned music the whole family could sing along with.

THE TOP FIVE
Week of October 6, 1958

1. **Sing Along with Mitch**
   Mitch Miller and the Gang

2. **King Creole**
   Elvis Presley

3. **Only the Lonely**
   Frank Sinatra

4. **Gigi**
   Soundtrack

5. **Tchaikovsky: Piano Concerto No. 1**
   Van Cliburn

20 Frank Sinatra Sings for Only the Lonely CAPITOL 1053
FRANK SINATRA

Producer: Voyle Gilmore

Track listing: Only the Lonely / Angel Eyes / What's New / It's a Lonesome Old Town / Willow Weep for Me / Good-bye / Blues in the Night / Guess I'll Hang My Tears Out to Dry / Ebb Tide / Spring is Here / Gone with the Wind / One for My Baby

October 13, 1958
5 weeks

In 1965, Frank Sinatra had a hit with his version of "It Was a Very Good Year." If Sinatra had recorded the song in 1958, it would have been appropriate, as Ol' Blue Eyes had four top 20 albums that year. The run began with his first Number One, *Come Fly With Me* [see 13]. It continued with a greatest-hits compilation on Capitol, *This Is Sinatra, Volume Two*, which reached number eight. Another retrospective, *The Frank Sinatra Story*, released on his original label, Columbia, peaked at number 12. Then came *Frank Sinatra Sings for Only the Lonely*.

On the album, the carefree swing of Sinatra's travel-themed *Come Fly with Me* was replaced by blue moods, as Sinatra returned to work with arranger/conductor Nelson Riddle after a brief stint with Billy May.

For the album's opening number, "Only the Lonely," Sinatra once again called on the veteran songwriting team of lyricist Sammy Cahn and composer James Van Heusen, who also penned the title track for *Come Fly with Me*. Initially, the album was to be titled *For Losers Only*, but that moniker was scrapped in favor of *Only the Lonely*. The album was recorded at Capitol Records Studios in Hollywood in three days in late May and late June of 1958. On May 29, a particularly fruitful evening, Sinatra cut six of the album's tracks, "Only the Lonely," "Angel Eyes," "Willow Weep for Me," "Guess I'll Hang My Tears Out to Dry," "Ebb Tide," and "Spring Is Here." Nearly a month later, on June 24, Sinatra and company returned to the studio to record "What's New?," "Blues in the Night," and "Gone with the Wind." The recording sessions were completed the next day,

when "It's a Lonesome Old Town," "Good-Bye," and "One for My Baby (and One More for the Road)" were laid down.

As usual, Sinatra was in fine form, both in voice and in presence. "We always had such great respect for Frank," says bass trombone player George Roberts. "He was always the immaculate dresser and he always looked great." Sinatra's influence wore off on Roberts, who often showed up for Sinatra's recording sessions wearing a tie. "Nobody ever did that, but I had a lot of respect for Frank and wanted to be like him," Roberts says.

Also bent on pleasing the crooner was Riddle, Sinatra's longtime conductor/arranger. "Nelson told me whenever we did something with Frank that he wanted a first reading on everything we did," Roberts says. "He wanted the first things we did with Frank to be clean."

The singer's often unpredictable moods kept Riddle on his toes. "Nelson said that there is only one man in the world that I'm frightened of," Roberts says. "He was frightened of Frank, not physically, but because he could be in one mood and turn around and be in a completely different mood. That scared him, because when he arranged something, he wasn't sure if Frank was going to like it."

Yet Sinatra had to be pleased with *Only the Lonely*. In its third week on the chart, it became the crooner's second Number One album of 1958, the capper of what was indeed a very good year for Frank Sinatra.

THE TOP FIVE
Week of October 13, 1958

1. **Frank Sinatra Sings for Only the Lonely**
   Frank Sinatra

2. **The Music Man**
   Original Cast

3. **King Creole**
   Elvis Presley

4. **Tchaikovsky: Piano Concerto No. 1**
   Van Cliburn

5. **Sing Along with Mitch**
   Mitch Miller

The Kingston Trio
THE KINGSTON TRIO

21

The Kingston Trio was recorded in a mere two days during February 1958. "We started in the afternoon," recalls Reynolds. "One of the first songs we did was 'Tom Dooley.' " That song, about a convicted murderer named Tom Dula, became a Number One hit for the Trio on November 17, 1958, helping to push the group's self-titled debut album to the top of the chart.

"We learned 'Tom Dooley' at the Purple Onion from someone who was auditioning," Reynolds recalls. "Every Tuesday they had an audition afternoon and some guy played [the song]. We asked him if he would teach it to us. We sat around and had a beer and he showed it to us. We arranged it in the dressing room that night."

Following the album's release on June 1, 1958, two disc jockeys at KLUB in Salt Lake City started playing the song, although it had not been released as a single. "People started going crazy for that song," Reynolds recalls. Eventually, the Trio racked up five songs in the top 10 in Salt Lake City, and "Tom Dooley" spread to other cities, prompting Capitol to issue the single.

The Trio concentrated on obscure traditional material or songs written by such folk pioneers as Woody Guthrie, whose "Hard, Ain't It Hard" was covered on the album. Some songs, including "Scotch and Soda," were passed on to the Trio by friends. According to Reynolds, Guard learned "Scotch and Soda" from the Seavers, not the Weavers—Guard was dating the older sister of Tom Seaver, who would later go on to stardom as a major league baseball player. Seaver's parents taught him the tune during a visit the family's Fresno, California, home.

Producer: Voyle Gilmore

Track listing: Three Jolly Coachmen / Bay of Mexico / Banua / Tom Dooley / Fast Freight / Hard, Ain't It Hard / Saro Jane / (The Wreck of the) "John B" / Santy Anno / Scotch and Soda / Coplas / Little Maggie

November 24, 1958
1 week

"We had no idea we'd ever sell one album," says the Kingston Trio's Nick Reynolds, "and neither did Capitol. They said, 'You guys are a visual act. You're young, sort of semi-clean cut,' which is strictly a ruse, because we were not all that clean-cut. I had been around a lot."

Nonetheless, with their clean-cut image—accurate or not—and a safer brand of folk music than that of the political-leaning protest-singers, the Kingston Trio went on to top the Billboard album chart five times within the span of two years [see 27, 29, 34, and 36].

The Kingston Trio was formed by three college students in the San Francisco area in 1957. Bob Shane and Reynolds attended Menlo College, while Dave Guard studied at nearby Stanford University. At first, the Trio performed at the campus beer gardens, singing Hawaiian songs and covers of tunes by Harry Belafonte and the Weavers. Those gigs landed the group a spot at the Purple Onion, a renowned San Francisco night spot. "We packed the place every night, six nights a week for approximately eight months," Reynolds recalls.

Word of the Trio spread to the Capitol tower in Hollywood. The label promptly sent out a talent scout to catch the phenomenon and the group was more than happy to sign with the label. "We were thrilled," recalls Reynolds. "The thought of giving my mother an album with my picture on cover—what more can you do in life?"

THE TOP FIVE
Week of November 24, 1958

1. **The Kingston Trio**
   The Kingston Trio

2. **South Pacific**
   Soundtrack

3. **My Fair Lady**
   Original Cast

4. **Sing Along With Mitch**
   Mitch Miller

5. **Only the Lonely**
   Frank Sinatra

22 Christmas Sing-Along with Mitch COLUMBIA 1205
MITCH MILLER AND THE GANG

Producer: Mitch Miller

Track listing: Joy to the World / Hark! The Herald Angels Sing / What Child Is This / We Three Kings of Orient Are / It Came Upon the Midnight Clear / Silent Night, Holy Night / Deck the Halls with Boughs of Holly / God Rest Ye Merry, Gentlemen / O Come, All Ye Faithful / The First Noel / The Coventry Carol / Away in a Manger / O Little Town of Bethlehem

December 29, 1958
2 weeks

Not one to miss an opportunity, Mitch Miller jumped on the "sing-along" craze and attempted to milk it for everything it was worth. Following the success of Sing Along With Mitch [see 19], Columbia rush-released More Sing Along with Mitch. It debuted on the Best Selling LP's chart a mere five weeks after the first Sing Along album hit the summit. With Christmas on the horizon, Miller and Columbia knew they would have another winner with a seasonal sing-along album. After all, such chart-toppers as Elvis Presley [see 10] and Bing Crosby [see 11] had demonstrated the sales power of star appeal mixed with holiday fare only a year before. Thus, Christmas Sing-Along with Mitch was born.

Miller stuck to the classics, but he did mix up the sound a bit. "I figured with the Christmas album, we would add women's voices with the guys," he says. "I wanted to make an album for all the people to join in and sing with, or just enjoy listening to. But the songs had to be played at the right tempo and the right key, so people felt comfortable singing along with the record."

By December 1958, Mitch Miller mania was sweeping the country. More Sing Along with Mitch had peaked at number four and was still holding at number eight when Christmas Sing-Along hit the summit. "I remember I went to a department store in Cleveland where a radio station was broadcasting from, and I signed 8,000 albums in one day. I had blisters on my fingers," Miller says.

Miller wasn't the only one who gained notoriety from Christmas Sing-Along. The album cover photo featured Miller and his family—his son Mitchell Jr., daughter Margaret, and wife Fran—posing festively in front of candles and holiday decorations. "I wanted the feeling of warmth and family for my Christmas album," he recalls. "I thought, 'Why not put my own family on the cover?'" Miller got the idea from the family photo Christmas cards he and his wife sent out every year.

In only its second week on the chart, Christmas Sing-Along knocked Miller's first album, Sing Along With Mitch from the top of the album chart. Miller had scored his second Number One album in less than three months, giving him plenty to sing about.

Christmas Sing-Along with Mitch became something of an annual favorite for the next several years and made numerous return visits to the top 10, reaching number eight in 1959, number six in 1960, and number nine in 1961.

THE TOP FIVE
Week of December 29, 1958

1. **Christmas Sing-Along with Mitch**
   Mitch Miller and the Gang

2. **Sing Along with Mitch**
   Mitch Miller and the Gang

3. **Christmas Carols**
   Mantovani

4. **Johnny's Greatest Hits**
   Johnny Mathis

5. **Merry Christmas**
   Bing Crosby

Producer: Goddard Lieberson

Track listing: Overture / You Are Beautiful / A Hundred Miracles / I Enjoy Being a Girl / I Am Going to Like It Here / Like a God / Chop Suey / Don't Marry Me / Grant Avenue / Love Look Away / Fan Tan Fannie / Gliding Through My Memoree / The Other Generation / Sunday / The Other Generation (Reprise) / Finale

February 2, 1959
3 weeks

Scene from *Flower Drum Song.*

The original cast recording of *Flower Drum Song* is significant for a number of reasons. It was the first show album produced by legendary Columbia Records executive Goddard Lieberson to top the chart in the rock era. *Flower Drum Song* also marked the first time that Richard Rodgers and Oscar Hammerstein II collaborated with Joseph Field, another legend of the theater, who co-authored and co-produced the book with Hammerstein. Additionally, the show marked the Broadway directorial debut of the multi-talented Gene Kelly.

With such a strong cast of players involved, little wonder the musical about life in San Francisco's Chinatown became a hit on the stage and on the charts. The musical, based on the novel by C.Y. Lee, opened at the Shubert Theatre in Boston on October 27, 1958. Less than two months later, on December 1, 1958, it opened on Broadway at the St. James Theatre in New York City, the same theater that played host to such earlier Rodgers and Hammerstein

favorites as *Oklahoma!* and *The King and I.*

By the time the cast of *Flower Drum Song* entered the Columbia Records Studio in New York to record the album, Rodgers and Hammerstein were already a proven commodity on the album chart. The soundtrack from their initial pairing, *Oklahoma!,* hit Number One in January 1956. In October of that same year, the soundtrack of *The King and I* also hit the summit [see 4], as did *South Pacific* in 1958 [see 15].

Like many of Rodgers and Hammerstein's earlier efforts, *Flower Drum Song* proved to be a launching pad for young talents. Two performers who rose to the challenge were Miyoshi Umeki, a recording artist signed to Mercury Records, and Pat Suzuki, who was signed to RCA Victor.

For Suzuki, making her Broadway debut in the musical and working on the cast album was a thrill. "It was the most exciting and huge experience of a lifetime," she says. "Columbia did everything they could. It felt like we had 60 acres of strings." Leading the magical session was Lieberson, who Suzuki says "made probably the best musical recordings of all. He was a very classy guy and he was gorgeous."

Since Suzuki was an artist familiar with the studio, she had little trouble adapting to the recording sessions. "Studios are the most fun," she says. "Your imagination takes off and you don't have to worry about the audience."

The material also wasn't a problem for the young star. "I played this chickie-boo that was supposed to be a little delirious, but I didn't even stop to think if it was rational. I had to suspend belief and become part of this personality," she says. "Thirty years later, you can look at it and say, 'Nobody talks like that,' but as a performer, you make it come to life when you sing it."

Suzuki and the other cast members were convincing enough to help push *Flower Drum Song* to the top in its fourth week on the chart.

THE TOP FIVE
Week of February 2, 1959

1. **Flower Drum Song**
   Soundtrack

2. **Sing Along with Mitch**
   Mitch Miller

3. **Tchaikovsky: Piano Concerto No. 1**
   Van Cliburn

4. **The Music Man**
   Original Cast

5. **More Sing Along with Mitch**
   Mitch Miller

24 The Music from Peter Gunn RCA VICTOR 1956
HENRY MANCINI

Producer: Simon Rady

Track listing: Peter Gunn / Sorta Blue / The Brothers Go to Mother's / Dreamsville / Session at Pete's Pad / Soft Sounds / Fallout! / The Floater / Slow and Easy / A Profound Gass / Brief and Breezy / Not from Dixie

February 23, 1959
10 weeks

When *The Music from Peter Gunn* exploded onto the Best Selling LP's chart on February 9, 1959, at number three, it was a surprise to everyone, especially Henry Mancini and RCA Victor. "It all happened so fast," Mancini recalled. "The day after the first show went on NBC, the mail started coming in about the music."

Recorded in Hollywood on August 26 and 31 and September 4 and 29, 1958, *The Music from Peter Gunn* wasn't originally cut for an album, but for the NBC-TV show starring Craig Stevens as a detective named Peter Gunn. Mancini, working as a staff composer, had met aspiring director Blake Edwards at Universal Studios in Hollywood in the mid-'50s, and it was Edwards who had asked Mancini to compose the music for the pilot of his new show. With much of the show originating from a jazz club called Mother's, the primary sound of the series was jazz—except, that is, for the throbbing, rhythmic pulse of the famed theme song. "I just felt that when you said, 'Peter Gunn,' the name was very strong with a exclamation point," said Mancini. "I never even thought of the fact that it wasn't jazz."

THE TOP FIVE
Week of February 23, 1959

1. **The Music from Peter Gunn**
   Henry Mancini

2. **Flower Drum Song**
   Original Cast

3. **Sing Along with Mitch**
   Mitch Miller

4. **Come Dance with Me**
   Frank Sinatra

5. **Tchaikovsky: Piano Concerto No. 1**
   Van Cliburn

Although RCA Victor funded the album, the company wasn't completely behind it at first. "They didn't have much faith in it at all," Mancini recalled. "They didn't know me from Adam." In fact, RCA tried to get trumpeter/arranger Shorty Rogers, who was signed to the label, involved in the project. "I went to lunch with Shorty and he said, 'This is your music. I have no business coming in here to record this. Why don't you do it?' And that's what he told the RCA people, so I did it," said Mancini.

Reluctantly, RCA gave Mancini the go-ahead to record the album himself, but he didn't have enough material. "I had music that I had written for the show, but there wasn't enough. I had to write other stuff that we would use in later shows," he said. When the album was released, much to RCA's surprise, it became a hit, climbing to number two in its second week on the chart, and hitting the summit in its third week. "They were completely overwhelmed," said Mancini. "They had only printed 8,000 covers, so they ran out of covers and had to put some out in plain sleeves with no artwork."

The all-instrumental album included a ballad called "Dreamsville," which Mancini said paved the way for the big-band sound he would use later for much of his career. "It was the first time I had used the four horns and four trombones," he recalled.

Yet it was the title track that would become one of Mancini's signature tunes, alongside such greats as "Moon River" [see *Breakfast at Tiffany's*—51] and "The Pink Panther Theme." Ray Anthony scored a number eight hit with his version of "Peter Gunn" in 1959, while Duane Eddy had a top 30 hit with the song in 1960, and even covered it again in 1986 with the British pop band the Art of Noise. "The thing about that piece is, just about every garage band and bar band in the world plays it. It's so easy," Mancini said. "Anybody who plays that bass line feels like they have arrived and they can play something."

The Music from Peter Gunn was so successful that it spawned a sequel, *More Music from Peter Gunn*, which climbed to number seven in the summer of 1959.

LIBERTY 3034

Exotica

MARTIN DENNY

25

Producer: Sy Waronker

Track listing: Quiet Village / Return to Paradise / Hong Kong Blues / Busy Port / Lotus Land / Similau / Stone God / Jungle Flower / Ah Me Furi / Waipo / The Love Dance

June 22, 1959
5 weeks mono

"**H**awaii to me was a laboratory," says pianist/composer Martin Denny. "I was able to try out new things and if they worked, fine; if they didn't, I discarded them." It was in the tropical paradise of Hawaii that Denny invented his famed "exotic sounds."

The New York–born Denny first ventured to Honolulu, Hawaii, in 1954, when he landed a gig playing piano at Don The Beachcomber. By 1955, Denny had formed a trio. Shortly thereafter, he was hired away by industrialist Henry J.

Kaiser's Hawaiian Village complex to headline at the Shell Bar. During that engagement, Denny's group expanded to a quartet, their popularity blossomed, and he was signed to Liberty Records.

It was only appropriate that Denny and his group recorded their debut album in Honolulu. It took the group just over three hours to cut the entire album at a cost of $850 at the Webley Edwards Studio. "We went overtime 20 minutes and I didn't have enough money," he recalls, "but I pleaded with the engineer and he let us finish it."

All of the material on the album, which featured a unique blend of Asian, Polynesian, and other world music, was perfected by the band in its live set, including "Quiet Village," Denny's best-known song. "When I opened the Shell Bar, it had a very exotic setting—just outside the room was a pond. There were always these frogs croaking when we played, but when we stopped, they stopped croaking," says Denny. "One night, as the frogs started croaking, some of the guys in the band started doing bird calls and it broke everyone up in the room." The following day, one visitor asked Denny to perform the arrangement with the "birds" and the frogs. "At first I thought he was putting me on, but then I realized he was very serious."

In the studio, Denny's band—Arthur Lyman on vibes, John Kramer on string bass, and Augie Colon on percussion—supplied the bird calls, while Denny recreated the sound of the frogs croaking by rubbing a stick over a grooved-wooden instrument.

"Quiet Village," released as a single, became a number four hit. That song, "Stone God," and "Love Dance" were written by Les Baxter, a former arranger for Nat King Cole [see 7]. While no other tracks from the album became hits, some did gain notoriety.

"Some time after the album was released I visited Disneyland," says Denny. "I was waiting outside the Jungle Cruise and I heard this music that sounded vaguely familiar. Suddenly it dawned on me that they were playing 'Lotus Land.' Much to my amazement, that song was used by choreographers and even massage parlors."

Exotica hit the summit of the Best Selling Monophonic LP's chart in its eighth week. The album's cover girl, model Sandy Warner, whose face was featured peering out from behind a bamboo curtain, would go on to grace the cover of 10 more of Denny's albums, but none had the impact of *Exotica*.

THE TOP FIVE
Week of June 22, 1959

1. **Exotica**
   Martin Denny

2. **Gigi**
   Soundtrack

3. **The Music from Peter Gunn**
   Henry Mancini

4. **From the Hungry i**
   The Kingston Trio

5. **Come Dance with Me**
   Frank Sinatra

26 Film Encores LONDON 1700
MANTOVANI

Producer: None listed

Track listing: My Foolish Heart / Unchained Melody / Over the Rainbow / Summertime in Venice / Intermezzo / Three Coins in the Fountain / Love Is a Many Splendored Things / Laura / High Noon / Hi-Lili, Hi-Lo / September Songs / Theme from "Limelight"

July 13, 1959
1 week stereo

Italian-born, British-bred Annunzio Paolo Mantovani was a violinist first and foremost who loved classical music. Yet it was his knack for arranging pop music for a large orchestra that turned him into a unlikely star.

Mantovani, as he was known to his fans, had his first chart hit in 1935 with "Red Sails in the Sunset." Two decades later, the conductor/arranger was a consistent best-seller on the album chart.

In 1955 alone, he had three albums break into the top 20. *The Music of Rudolf Friml* reached number 13, while *Waltz Time* peaked at number 14. *Song Hits from Theatreland* reached number eight.

Two years later Mantovani experienced his greatest success with a similarly themed *Film Encores*. The album, which featured the "cascading strings" of Mantovani's 40-piece orchestra interpreting the movie music, was an interesting choice for Mantovani. As Kenneth Mantovani reveals, his father wasn't "a film buff."

"The idea for the album originated with Decca," says Kenneth. "They suggested he make an album of film music, so he chose the titles on it and they approved it."

THE TOP FIVE
Week of July 13, 1959

1. **Film Encores**
   Mantovani

2. **South Pacific**
   Soundtrack

3. **Gigi**
   Soundtrack

4. **The Music from Peter Gunn**
   Henry Mancini

5. **My Fair Lady**
   Original Cast

The material on the album ranged from "Over the Rainbow" from *The Wizard of Oz* and "September Song" from *Knickerbocker Holiday* to the title themes of *High Noon* and *Intermezzo*. Other selections included "Summertime in Venice" from *Summertime*, "Unchained Melody" from *Unchained*, and the title themes from *My Foolish Heart* and *Three Coins in the Fountain*.

"Since he had classical training and was a violinist by trade, he liked the classics rather than lighter music," Kenneth Mantovani says. "But he was happy doing it, as long as he had his way at the podium."

What made Mantovani stand out was his use of strings. With 40 pieces, the orchestra was considered large, and when performing, the string section produced an unusual "cascading" sound. He was also somewhat of a showman at the podium. "He would always do things differently to make things sound different, like holding notes longer than other conductors," says Kenneth.

Film Encores hit the pole position of the Best Selling Stereophonic LP's in its eighth week on the chart, even though it failed to spawn a hit single. Despite the success, Mantovani remained unaffected. "He really never appreciated just how popular he was," says Kenneth. "He had his job to do, so he went off to work and made records, but then he would come home just like any other father and act like a father, not a pop star."

CAPITOL 1199 **The Kingston Trio at Large**
THE KINGSTON TRIO

Producer: Voyle Gilmore

Track listing: M.T.A / All My Sorrows / Blow Ye Winds / Corey, Corey / The Seine / I Bawled / Good News / Getaway John / The Long Black Rifle / Early Mornin' / Scarlet Ribbons (For Her Hair) / Remember the Alamo

July 27, 1959
15 weeks mono

Although its second album, *From the Hungry i*, stalled at number two, the Kingston Trio would not stay away from the summit of the *Billboard* Top LP's chart for long. *The Kingston Trio at Large* was released in June of 1959. Six weeks later, it became the Trio's second Number One album in less than a year [see 21]. It was a heady period for the group—the week that *At Large* hit the top, *From the Hungry i* and *The Kingston Trio* were still in the top 15.

Recorded in February 1959 in New York with Voyle Gilmore again producing, *At Large* was the group's first stereo album, although, ironically, it topped the mono album chart, not the stereo list. The new technology necessitated some adjustments in the studio. "They separated us a bit more and had three mikes, but they were pretty close together," recalls guitarist/singer Nick Reynolds. "We could still hear the blend in our ears. We didn't use headphones, so we could still hear each other. They also used separate instrument mikes."

Even with the more complex recording process, *At Large*, like its predecessors, was recorded in a whirlwind fashion. "We would come into town, get up in the morning, rehearse, record in the afternoon, and do a show at night,"

recalls Reynolds. The album also marked the first time that the group's touring bassist—David "Buck" Wheat, who the Trio knew from their San Francisco days—joined the group in the studio.

With the release of *At Large*, the Trio was reaching new heights of popularity. Soon after the album hit the top of the chart, the group appeared on the cover of *Life* magazine, making their faces as familiar as their harmonies. "The cover of *Life* at that time was like being in everybody's living room," Reynolds says. "That is when we went from obscure to recognizable."

Then, of course, there was the music. Reynolds describes "M.T.A.," which led off the album, as "a novelty song." The single, a comic *Twilight Zone*–like adventure about a man stuck riding the Boston subway because he didn't have enough money to pay for the new higher fare, reached number 15. "We recorded it and the people in the studio

said, 'Hey, that's going to be your next single.' It wasn't as popular as 'Tom Dooley,' but it was the second- or third-most-requested song we had."

With the push from Capitol to record as many albums as quickly as humanly possible, the Trio had to hunt for new material, such as Jane Bowers's "Remember the Alamo," which closed the album. Also included was a stereo remake of the Trio's first single, "Scarlet Ribbons."

Although many consider *At Large* the Kingston Trio's finest album—including singer/banjo-player Dave Guard and the National Academy of Recording Arts & Sciences, which presented the group with a Grammy for best folk performance of 1959—Reynolds differs. His pick is 1964's *Time to Think*, recorded shortly after President John F. Kennedy's assassination. Says Reynolds, "It was our best musical effort and best emotional effort."

THE TOP FIVE
Week of July 27, 1959

1. **The Kingston Trio at Large**
   The Kingston Trio

2. **Exotica**
   Martin Denny

3. **From the Hungry i**
   The Kingston Trio

4. **Inside Shelly Berman**
   Shelly Berman

5. **The Music from Peter Gunn**
   Henry Mancini

28 Heavenly COLUMBIA 1351
JOHNNY MATHIS

Producers: Mitch Miller, Al Ham

Track listing: Heavenly / Hello, Young Lovers / A Lovely Way to Spend an Evening / A Ride on a Rainbow / More Than You Know / Something I Dream Last Night / Misty / Stranger in Paradise / Moonlight Becomes You / They Say It's Wonderful / I'll Be Easy to Find / That's All

November 9, 1959

5 weeks mono

With the incredible success of *Johnny's Greatest Hits* [see 16], Johnny Mathis became one of the premier recording artists in the country. His follow-up albums, *Swing Softly, Open Fire, Two Guitars,* and *More Johnny's Greatest Hits,* all made the top 10, but it would take *Heavenly* to put Mathis back on top.

For this album—Mathis's first recordings with arranger Glenn Osser—the crooner turned to a mix of show tunes, standards, and contemporary ballads. Many of the song selections were chosen because they had been performed by Mathis's heroes. "I was influenced by Ella Fitzgerald, Sarah Vaughan, and Nat King Cole," he says. "I would listen to their recordings and then go in and sing the same songs." Such was the case with "A Lovely Way to Spend an Evening," a tune performed by Fitzgerald and included in the film *Higher and Higher,* featuring a young Frank Sinatra [see 13].

"A Ride on a Rainbow" was from the NBC-TV show *Ruggles of Red Gap.* "I heard Judy Holiday, who performed it in the Broadway production, sing it.

THE TOP FIVE
Week of November 9, 1959

1. **Heavenly**
   Johnny Mathis

2. **The Kingston Trio at Large**
   The Kingston Trio

3. **Inside Sheley Berman**
   Sheley Berman

4. **South Pacific**
   Soundtrack

5. **From the Hungry i**
   The Kingston Trio

And that was it for me," says Mathis. "I fell in love with her. She was just a fabulous actress. I was a kid and I was very impressionable. Any time I heard anyone sing anything really well, I was influenced by the performance. Then I found out there was a beautiful song there. That's one of my favorite songs of all time."

"Misty," *Heavenly*'s best-known number, almost didn't make it on the album. "We always had two or three extra songs," Mathis says. " 'Misty' was sort of relegated to that second or third spot. I was adamant that we record the song, because I had known Erroll Garner, the composer who wrote it, since I was 13 years old, and I had promised him that I was going to record the song. It would have been very embarrassing if we didn't record it."

Yet Columbia executives had other ideas. They wanted Mathis to record "Love Look Away" from *Flower Drum Song* [see 23]. In the end, Mathis won out—"Misty" made it on *Heavenly*. He still remembers recording the track: "For the high note after the instrumental break, I had to walk across the room, because the engineers didn't know how to make a crescendo. So I walked across the room and sang and then walked straight into the microphone, because I wanted it to sound like my voice was coming out of the oboe solo."

Mathis would later appease the Columbia executives by recording "Love Look Away" in February 1961. The track appeared on the album *I'll Buy You a Star,* which stalled at number 38.

Heavenly hit the summit in its eighth week on the chart. It was one of three Mathis titles in the top 10 at the time—*More Johnny's Greatest Hits* held at number nine, while *Johnny's Greatest Hits* dropped to number 10.

CAPITOL 1258

Here We Go Again!
THE KINGSTON TRIO

29

Producer: Voyle Gilmore

Track listing: Molly Dee / Across the Wide Missouri / Haul Away / The Wanderer / 'Round About the Mountain / Oleanna / The Unfortunate Miss Bailey / San Miguel / E Inu Tatou E / Rollin' Stone / Goober Peas / A Worried Man

December 14, 1959
8 weeks mono; 2 weeks stereo

Here We Go Again! was the name of the Kingston Trio's fourth album, but it may also have been what chart-watchers said to themselves as the album rose to the top of Billboard's Top LP's chart in a mere six weeks, becoming the group's third Number One album in just over a year [see 21 and 27]. Meanwhile, its first three albums, The Kingston Trio at Large, From the Hungry i, and The Kingston Trio remained strong sellers, giving the group an unprecedented four albums in the top 10 at once.

Yet, as is so often the case, the group's enormous popularity inevitably led to a backlash. "It was very hurtful to read the things people would say about us," says guitarist/singer Nick Reynolds. "We were opening up doors for a great myriad of singers who had a place to make some money, rather than work at a Chevron station." One of the reasons

that the Trio was attacked was because it rarely took an overtly political stance, unlike their folk forefathers Woody Guthrie and the Weavers. "We consciously had to say, 'Well, are we going to do the songs that are going to put us on the blacklist or take the middle of the road?' The political climate at that time did not allow you to speak your mind at all," he says.

Here We Go Again! was recorded in May 1959 back at Capitol's Studio B in Los Angeles with producer Voyle Gilmore once again throwing some new technology into the mix. On the album, Gilmore used what he called "double-voicing." Says Reynolds, "It sounded real full and nice, but not as clean as the first one." According to Reynolds, the overdubbing helped cover up the Trio's tired voices. "When you are doing so many albums a year, you're not singing right in pitch all the time," he says.

"A Worried Man," the single released from Here We Go Again!, stalled at number 20, but by that time, the Trio didn't need a hit single to drive its album sales—the group's name alone was enough. Says Reynolds, "At that time, every album we put out was selling a million copies. We were basically album sellers; we didn't have much success with singles, except for 'Tom Dooley.' "

Here We Go Again! marked the first Trio collaboration with John Stewart,

who would eventually replace singer/banjoist Dave Guard in 1961. Stewart contributed "Molly Dee," the album's lead track. "We were working at the Ambassador Hotel at the Coconut Grove in Los Angeles and he came in and said, 'Hey, I got some songs.' Since we were in the middle of doing an album, we said, 'Hey, come down to the studio and teach it to us right there.' He was just a kid in junior college."

Another track, "Olenna" was one of the songs the Trio used in its radio and television commercials for 7-Up, something Reynolds regrets to this day. "I think that's one of the reasons why people labeled us as being too commercial," he says.

THE TOP FIVE
Week of December 14, 1959

1. **Here We Go Again!**
   The Kingston Trio

2. **Heavenly**
   Johnny Mathis

3. **Inside Shelley Berman**
   Shelley Berman

4. **South Pacific**
   Soundtrack

5. **The Lord's Prayer**
   The Mormon Tabernacle Choir

30 The Lord's Prayer COLUMBIA 6068
THE MORMON TABERNACLE CHOIR/THE PHILADELPHIA ORCHESTRA

Director: Dr. Richard P. Condie /
Conductor: Eugene Ormandy

Track listing: The Lord's Prayer / Come,
Come Ye Saints / Blessed Are They
That Mourn / O, My Father / How
Great the Wisdom and the Love / Holy,
Holy, Holy / 148th Psalm / For unto Us
a Child Is Born / David's Lamentation /
Battle Hymn of the Republic

January 11, 1960
1 week stereo

With a membership of 375 and a history dating well over a century, the Mormon Tabernacle Choir is undoubtedly the largest and oldest vocal ensemble ever to top the *Billboard* album chart.

It was in 1847 that the first Mormon Choir sang in its newly settled home of Salt Lake City, Utah. Music has always been a big part of Mormon culture, and is even addressed in the religion's scriptures: "For my soul delighteth in the song of the heart." Yet even Mormon leader Brigham Young likely would have been surprised by the widespread popularity of the Choir in 1960.

The Tabernacle Choir's recording history dates back to 1910, when the vocal group was the subject of recording experiments conducted by the Columbia Phonograph Company and the Victory Company. It wasn't until October 19, 1959, however, that a Mormon Tabernacle Choir landed an album on *Billboard's* album chart. *The Lord's Prayer* featured the Choir, directed by Dr. Richard P. Condie, accompanied by the Philadelphia Orchestra, conducted by Eugene Ormandy, along with organists Alexander Schreiner and Frank W. Asper. It wasn't the first time that the Choir had joined forces with the Philadelphia Orchestra, as Columbia had previously released *The Beloved Choruses.* "We did have a very good working relationship with Eugene Ormandy," says Helen Hillier, who sang in the Choir from 1954 through 1980. "He loved the Choir and we loved Eugene Ormandy."

In its prime, the Choir would record one or two albums a year, Hillier says. *The Lord's Prayer,* like most of the Choir's albums, was recorded in the Tabernacle, the famed auditorium built in 1867. The 6,000-seat building, which is 250 feet long and 150 feet wide and has a ceiling 80 feet high, is known for its fine acoustics.

For material, the Choir drew on a cross-section of Christian music, ranging from Leroy J. Robertson's "The Lord's Prayer" and "Come, Come Ye Saints," to Johannes Brahms's "Blessed Are They That Mourn" and George Frederick Handel's "For unto Us a Child is Born."

The song that would stand out on the album, however, was one of the more unlikely choices to be sung by the Choir, "Battle Hymn of the Republic" by Peter J. Wihousky and Julia Ward Howe. "I remember Ormandy as he conducted and we rehearsed 'Battle Hymn of the Republic,' " says Hillier. "He did it with kind of a smile on his face and rather tongue-in-cheek, because he thought the album would probably sell, because of that particular song. But I don't think anyone, including him, had any idea what it actually would become."

The Tabernacle Choir's version of the song reached number 16 on the pop chart and went on to win a Grammy. "It was a classical recording, but even the teenagers that were listening to rock 'n' roll were buying it," says Hillier. "It became the Choir's signature piece. We always concluded our performances with it. It was what people came to hear."

On January 11, 1960, spiritual themes and imagery seemed to be at an all-time high on the *Billboard* charts. On the Best Selling Pop EP's list, Tennessee Ernie Ford held the Number One and number three positions with *Hymns* and *Spirituals.* At number two on the Stereo Action Albums chart was Johnny Mathis's *Heavenly* [see 28]. It only seemed appropriate that *The Lord's Prayer* was at the summit.

THE TOP FIVE
Week of January 11, 1960

1. **The Lord's Prayer**
   The Mormon Tabernacle Choir/
   The Philadelphia Orchestra

2. **Heavenly**
   Johnny Mathis

3. **Here We Go Again**
   The Kingston Trio

4. **The Sound of Music**
   Original Cast

5. **For the First Time**
   Mario Lanza

Producer: Goddard Lieberson

Track listing: Preludium / The Sound of Music / Maria / My Favorite Things / Do-Re-Mi / Sixteen Going on Seventeen / The Lonely Goatherd / How Can Love Survive / The Sound of Music (Reprise) / Laendler / So Long, Farewell / Climb Ev'ry Mountain / No Way to Stop It / An Ordinary Couple / Processional / Sixteen Going on Seventeen (Reprise) / Edelweiss / Climb Ev'ry Mountain

January 25, 1960
16 weeks: 15 weeks stereo,
12 weeks mono

Mary Martin in *The Sound of Music*.

The songwriting duo of Richard Rodgers and Oscar Hammerstein II were no strangers to the top of the charts prior to the release of the original cast recording of *The Sound of Music*. The soundtrack from their first collaboration, *Oklahoma!*, topped the chart in January 1956. It was followed by the soundtrack of *The King and I* that same year [see 4], *South Pacific* [see 15] in 1958, and the original cast recording of *Flower Drum Song* in 1959 [see 23].

The Sound of Music opened on October 3, 1959, at the Shubert Theatre in New Haven, Connecticut. Mary Martin, a veteran of such Broadway favorites as *Annie Get Your Gun* and *South Pacific*, was cast as Maria Augusta Trapp, a would-be nun who ends up as a governess to seven children. Singer/actor Theodore Bikel, whose non-musical film credits include *The African Queen* and *Moulin Rouge*, played Captain von Trapp, a one-time member of the Austrian Navy.

After rave notices in New Haven,

the production moved to the Shubert Theatre in Boston on October 13, before hitting the big time on November 16, when it opened on Broadway at the Lunt-Fontanne Theatre in New York.

It was in New York, shortly after the production opened its run at the Lunt-Fontanne, that the original cast album was recorded. The session, which was held on a Sunday late in 1959, offered a challenge to some of the cast members. "You couldn't just do your stage performance in the recording studio," says Bikel, a multilingual folksinger who was signed to Elektra Records. "A recording studio was a far more intimate setting. So we didn't have to project so much as we did on stage. Since *The Sound of Music* was the first musical I ever did on stage, I had to be extra careful to adapt to the medium."

While Martin, by then a veteran of the stage and cast recordings, didn't have the same problems, opera singer Patricia Neway, who appeared as the Mother Abbess, also had to make some adjustments in the studio. "An opera singer who belts is not necessarily comfortable with a microphone that sits right next to your nose," says Bikel.

Nonetheless, the entire album was recorded in a little more than a day. "We went back the next day and did a few extra takes," Bikel says. "But not all of us—just Mary Martin, myself, Marion Marlowe, and Pat Neway."

The success of the album was bittersweet to Bikel. "I was surprised by the success and a little bit miffed," he says. Bikel, like most of the cast members, merely received one week's salary for his contribution to the album, and no royalties from its sales. "I received less than $2,000 for making the album, and I was one of the better paid."

Still, by participating in the recording of *The Sound of Music* Bikel was bestowed an honor that money cannot buy. He was the first person to record "Edelweiss," the last song written by Rodgers and Hammerstein. "It was a song written especially for me and it was written only 11 days before we opened on Broadway," Bikel says. "When we were in Boston they decided that something else was needed to utilize whatever talent I had. So they retired to a room at the Ritz-Carlton, which had a piano in it, and they wrote 'Edelweiss.'"

Hammerstein who was terminally ill with pneumonia, died in 1960. "It has always intrigued me as a philosophical and theological notion," says Bikel, "that the very last word that this dying man wrote was 'forever.'"

Indeed, *The Sound of Music* has lived forever as one of the greatest musicals ever recorded. Five years after the cast album hit Number One, the soundtrack [see 79] also landed in the pole position at the height of Beatlemania.

THE TOP FIVE
Week of January 25, 1960

1. **The Sound of Music**
   Original Cast

2. **Here We Go Again**
   The Kingston Trio

3. **Heavenly**
   Johnny Mathis

4. **The Lord's Prayer**
   The Mormon Tabernacle Choir

5. **For the First Time**
   Mario Lanza

32 Persuasive Percussion COMMAND 800
ENOCH LIGHT/TERRY SNYDER AND THE ALL-STARS

Producer: Enoch Light

Track listing: I'm in the Mood for Love / Whatever Lola Wants / Misirlou / I Surrender, Dear / Orchids in the Moonlight / I Love Paris / My Heart Belongs to Daddy / Tabu / The Breeze and I / Aloha Oe / Japanese Sandman / Love Is a Many-Splendored Thing

April 25, 1960
13 weeks (nonconsecutive)

Courtesy of Photofest

When veteran bandleader Enoch Light rounded up a group of session players, including Terry Snyder, Tony Mottola, Willie Rodriguez, Dick Hyman, Jack Lesberg, Teddy Sommer, Artie Marotti, Stanley Webb, and Domonic Cortese for a series of recording sessions in the summer of 1959, the musicians had no idea that the recording would change the way the world listened to music.

"We were all in the dark about it," says guitarist Mottola, who along with Snyder was a member of the band on *The Perry Como Show*. "After we thought it was in the can," Mottola says, "Terry kept telling me that he had gone in the studio again with Enoch to do some more things on xylophone, vibraphone, and bongos. He said, 'I don't know what the hell he's doing, but I'm making a lot of money on these extra dates.'" Light wouldn't even tell the session players the name of the album.

Although the musicians didn't know it, Light, recording engineer Robert Fine, and arranger Lew Davies were on a mission. At the time, stereo technology was already more than a year old, but

Light felt that no musical recording had yet taken full advantage of the two-channel separation of sound. With *Persuasive Percussion*, Light's goal was to change that. For material, Light picked instrumental versions of a number of standards, including Cole Porter's "I Love Paris" and "My Heart Belongs to Daddy."

While *Persuasive Percussion* was in production, Light was also serving as the head of Grand Award Records, a label that he was a partner in that was eventually sold to ABC. Light offered *Persuasive Percussion* to ABC, but the label passed. Undaunted, Light started a new label, Command, whose first release would be *Persuasive Percussion*.

Light's experiments perfecting stereo separation led to more than 30 recording sessions. When the album was finished, Light and Fine had trouble cutting the master recording. The duo went through more than a dozen Westrex cutters, since the machines weren't built to handle stereo recordings. The problems resulted in a six-month delay in the album's release as the master had to be cut 39 times before it met with Light's approval.

The sound wasn't the only atypical aspect of *Persuasive Percussion*. The album's cover features an unusual modern art design consisting of black dots

created by famed German artist Josef Albers.

Upon its release, *Persuasive Percussion* was first embraced by the hi-fi industry, as it became the perfect vehicle to show off stereo equipment. Of course, members of the music community, including the session players who played on the album, were also impressed.

"The end result was fabulous," says Mottola. "You would hear a rhythm section smack in the middle, and then on the left you would hear a bongo roll, and then on the right side you would hear a trumpet."

Just after the release of *Persuasive Percussion*, *Provocative Percussion* by Enoch Light and the Light Brigade was issued. Both albums entered the stereo chart on January 25, 1960, but *Persuasive Percussion* proved to be the favorite. *Provocative Percussion* spent five weeks at number two, but was unable to make it to the top. When *Persuasive Percussion* hit the top spot in its 14th week, *Provocative Percussion* had dropped down to number six.

Both albums spawned successful sequels. Volume 2 of *Persuasive* and *Provocative* reached numbers three and four, respectively, in 1960, while a third *Persuasive* set peaked at number three in 1961.

THE TOP FIVE
Week of April 25, 1960

1. **Persuasive Percussion**
   Enoch Light/Terry Snyder
   and the All-Stars

2. **The Sound of Music**
   Original Cast

3. **Faithfully**
   Johnny Mathis

4. **Theme From a
   Summer Place**
   Billy Vaughn

5. **Mr. Lucky**
   Henry Mancini

DOT 25276

Theme from a Summer Place
BILLY VAUGHN

Producer: None listed

Track listing: Theme from a Summer Place / Tammy / Tracy's Theme / Climb Every Mountain / Que Sera, Sera / The Terry Theme from Limelight / True Love / The Sound of Music / The Three Penny Opera / Some Enchanted Evening / All the Way / Sayonara

May 2, 1960
2 weeks mono
(nonconsecutive)

Randy Wood, the president of Dot Records and producer of most of the label's sides, can still remember the phone call he received from Bud Dentridge, a Dearborn, Michigan–based retailer. "He said, 'Make us an album with "Theme from a Summer Place" on it. You can put some other good songs with it, but be sure you call it "Theme from a Summer Place,"'" Wood recalls. Dentridge sent Wood a copy of Percy Faith's version of the song, which went on to top the Hot 100 on February 22, 1960. "It sounded good and Bud's enthusiasm caused me to believe in it," says Wood.

Excited by the possibilities, Wood took the idea to Dot Records musical director, arranger, and conductor Billy Vaughn, already a star in his own right. Prior to 1960, Vaughn had two top 10 albums to his credit: *Sail Along Silv'ry Moon* and *Blue Hawaii*, which reached number five and number seven in 1958 and 1959, respectively.

Even if Vaughn was less than thrilled about recording the theme from the 1959 film starring Dorothy McGuire, and other film and TV tunes, he trusted Wood's instincts. "Billy and I had a great relationship," Wood says. "If he didn't agree with me, he would cooperate, and vice versa. We believed in each other, so if one felt strongly, the other would go along."

With the project on its way,

Vaughn and Wood selected the other tracks to round out the album, including "Tammy," "Que Sera Sera," and "The Sound of Music." Says Wood, "We got a big orchestra together with lots of strings and English horns. We had as many musicians as we could afford in the big studio at United Recorders." The sessions began on a Saturday morning at 9 A.M. "We finished the full album, all 12 sides, at 4 P.M.," Wood recalls.

In order to get the album to the stores as soon as possible, while Faith's "Theme from a Summer Place" was still hot, Wood had a mastering engineer on standby at the sessions. "Over the weekend he made the masters and sent them out to my house to be approved," Wood recalls, "and by Tuesday, we were shipping records."

It wasn't too big of a surprise that *Theme from a Summer Place* became a hit album. The title track was still lodged in the collective consciousness of record-buyers; Vaughn's trademark "twin saxophones" were a known commodity; and Mantovani, with his *Film Encores* album [see 26], had already proven that there was a healthy appetite for instrumental versions of movie music.

When *Theme from a Summer Place* hit the top in its seventh week on the Mono Action Albums chart, a record retailer named Bud Dentridge, Wood, and Vaughn

THE TOP FIVE
Week of May 2, 1960

1. **Theme from a Summer Place**
   Billy Vaughn

2. **Sixty Years of Music America Loves Best**
   Various artists

3. **The Sound of Music**
   Original cast

4. **Italian Francis**
   Connie Francis

5. **Sold Out**
   The Kingston Trio

34 Sold Out CAPITOL 1352
THE KINGSTON TRIO

Producer: Volye Gilmore

Track listing: El Matador / The Mountains O'Mourne / Don't Cry Katie / Medley: Tanga Tika and Toerau / With Her Head Tucked Underneath Her Arm / Carrier Pigeon / Bimini / Raspberries, Strawberries / Mangwani Mpulele / With You My Johnny / The Hunter / Farewell Adelita

May 9, 1960
12 weeks (nonconsecutive):
3 weeks stereo, 10 weeks mono

The title of the Kingston Trio's fifth album reflected the band's popularity as a live act. With three Number One albums under its belt [see 21, 27, and 29], the Trio could fill concert halls across the country, while the release of a new album would draw crowds at record stores. *Sold Out* shot to the summit of *Billboard*'s Top LP's chart in three short weeks, becoming the group's third consecutive chart-topper and its fastest-rising album to date.

But success and the pressure that goes with it were beginning to take their toll on the group. "We were having some problems internally," admits guitarist/singer Nick Reynolds. "There was just too much pressure." By 1960, all three of the Trio members were married with children and were finding it increasingly difficult to juggle family life with pop stardom. "The record company would want us to do all the promotional things," Reynolds says. "When we would get into town, we couldn't just go to the hotel and get some rest; we would have to go to 25 radio stations."

THE TOP FIVE
Week of May 9, 1960

1. **Sold Out**
   The Kingston Trio

2. **The Sound of Music**
   Original Cast

3. **Theme from a Summer Place**
   Billy Vaughn

4. **Sixty Years of Music America Loves Best**
   Assorted Artists

5. **Italian Favorites**
   Connie Francis

Aside from the obligations, there was also tension brewing within the group over the Trio's musical direction. "Bobby [Shane] and I always just wanted to sing," says Reynolds. "Dave [Guard] wanted to progress to a different level, but we said, 'Hey, we like doing what we are doing. It has worked real well.' "

Sold Out was recorded in New York City during February 1960. According to Reynolds, the group had little choice in deciding where it would record. "The record company would fly people in wherever we were just to get some stuff on tape," Reynolds says. "Most of the stuff we arranged right in the studio. We would rehearse it, work on the harmony parts, decide who was going to sing lead, and then record it."

For material, the group once again relied mostly on outside sources —only three of the 13 tracks on the album are credited to the group. "El Matador," the only single released from the album, was penned by Jane Bowers and Irving Burgess, who each had contributed a song to the Trio's *At Large*. It peaked at number 32.

The Trio also opted to once again re-record an early single for inclusion on an album. "Raspberries, Strawberries" was originally released as a single in early 1959, but made its first stereo appearance on *Sold Out*.

Even with pressure building within the group, the Trio still had a sense of humor during the making of *Sold Out*. That's evident from the inclusion of "With Her Head Tucked Underneath Her Arm," a song about a ghost haunting King Henry VIII. In the song, the King suspects the spirit is one of his former wives. He's just not sure which one.

WARNER BROS. 1379 **The Button-Down Mind of Bob Newhart**
BOB NEWHART

Producer: None listed

Track listing: Abe Lincoln vs. Madison Avenue / The Cruise of the U.S.S. Codfish / Merchandising the Wright Brothers / The Krushchev Landing Rehearsal / Driving Instructor (pilot script for a new TV series) / Nobody Will Ever Play Baseball

July 25, 1960
14 weeks mono (nonconsecutive)

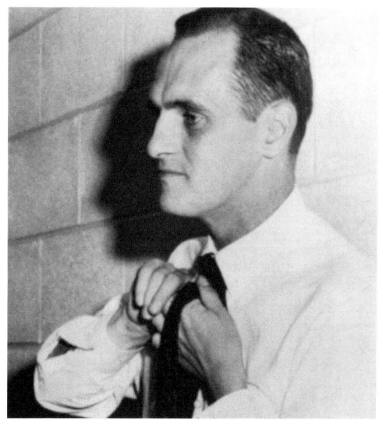

By 1959, Bob Newhart had served in the army, worked as an accountant and an advertising copywriter, hosted an ill-fated syndicated radio show, and written and hosted a local TV show in Chicago. "It was a man-on-the-street show that was on at 8:30 in the morning and watched by no one," Newhart says of the latter endeavor. But then his luck changed, thanks to Dan Sorkin, a disc jockey heard on "Chicago's Morning Show" on WCFL.

"The Warner Bros. people were coming through Chicago," Newhart recalls, "and Dan Sorkin said to them, 'I have this very funny friend of mine. I would like to have you listen to some things he has done.' " Sorkin telephoned his friend and told him to record some of his best comedy bits. "I recorded into a tape recorder, without any audience, 'The Submarine Commander' ['The Cruise of the U.S.S. Codfish'], 'Abe Lincoln,' and the 'Driving Instructor,' because those were the only three routines I had at the time," says Newhart. Sorkin and Newhart played the tape to a few Warner Bros. executives, including George Avakian, head of talent for the label, who offered

Newhart a contract. "To this day, I don't know if they liked it because Dan was an important disc jockey or if they actually liked it," says Newhart.

Once the contract was signed, Avakian suggested that Newhart cut his first album live at a nightclub. The only problem was that Newhart had never played a nightclub before. "I had maybe done five or six individual appearances, but never in a nightclub," says Newhart. That didn't stop Warner Bros., who had the aspiring comedian's agent Sid Bernstein book Newhart into a Houston club called the Tidelands, where he was the opening act.

"I was there for two weeks," says Newhart. "I spent most of the time coming up with material so I could fill up the album. I had a lot of ideas, but I never bothered to expand them." Once Newhart felt he had enough material to fill an album, it was decided that his shows on a Friday and Saturday night in February 1960 would be recorded. "The first night there was a drunken woman in the front row who kept yelling out through my entire set, 'This is a

bunch of crap,' " says Newhart. "So it turned out that the Friday night tape was totally unusable. She was as clear or more clear than I was, so we just had the two shows on Saturday to work with."

Once the recording was completed, Newhart found the subsequent process of turning it into an album a little strange. "I always found it jarring, because whoever edited it took out the silence," he says. "When I would hear it, it would bother me, because it didn't have my timing. Very often the silence was as important as the words."

Even without Newhart's comedic pauses, *The Button-Down Mind of Bob Newhart* became a smash. The album became the first comedy album to hit the summit of the album chart, and its 14 weeks at Number One remains the longest chart-topping run of any comedy album. Its success also helped pave the way for other new comedians, such as Bill Cosby, and helped save the then-floundering Warner Bros. label from closing in the early '60s, before the Bunny discovered rock 'n' roll.

THE TOP FIVE
Week of July 25, 1960

1. **The Button-Down Mind of Bob Newhart**
   Bob Newhart

2. **Sold Out**
   The Kingston Trio

3. **Elvis Is Back**
   Elvis Presley

4. **Can Can**
   Soundtrack

5. **The Sound of Music**
   Original Cast

36 String Along CAPITOL 1407
THE KINGSTON TRIO

Producer: Voyle Gilmore

Track listing: Bad Man's Blunder / The Escape of Old John Webb / When I Was Young / Leave My Woman Alone / This Mornin', This Evenin', So Soon / Everglades / Buddy Better Get on Down the Line / South Wind / Who's Gonna Hold Her Hand / To Morrow / Along the Colorado Trail / The Tattooed Lady

August 29, 1960
10 weeks stereo, 5 weeks mono
(nonconsecutive)

String Along was the last Kingston Trio album to hit Number One, and it also may have been the most important. It marked the group's fifth Number One album [see 21, 27, 29, and 34], making the Kingston Trio the only group in history whose first five studio albums hit the summit of the *Billboard* charts. (The Trio's second album, *From the Hungry i,* which stalled at number two, was recorded live).

Some have suggested that *String Along*'s title was an answer to Mitch Miller, whose series of *Sing Along* albums [see 19, 22, and 50] were frequently competing with the Trio's albums on the charts. Yet the Trio's Nick Reynolds says this was not the case. "It was definitely not meant to be a dig at Mitch," he says. However, the title did express the same sort of do-it-yourself ethic as the Miller series. "That's why we were so popular," says Reynolds. "People could sing along. People could look at us and say, 'Those three guys are playing two chords on 'Tom Dooley.' We could do that.' And they could."

However, things did get a bit more complex on *String Along,* because the Trio used more strings. In fact, it has been reported that the album, which was recorded in April 1960 at Capitol's Studio B in Hollywood, features Dave Guard playing Gibson's very first 12-string guitar. "We played several different instruments that were bizarre," says Reynolds. Frequent Trio accompanist David "Buck" Wheat designed a percussion instrument he called "boo-bams" to lend a tropical feel to "South Wind." "Boo-bams were tuneable tubes made out of fiberglass," recalls Reynolds, who took the instruments on the road for live dates. "You could play them almost like a xylophone or marimba."

The album also showcased the Trio's ability to cover diverse musical terrain, with contributions once again coming from several different songwriters. The bluesy "Leave My Woman Alone," written by Ray Charles [see 53], was a departure from the Trio's usual folk fare, while "South Wind" was penned by fellow folkie Travis Edmonson of the folk duo Bud & Travis.

Two singles were culled from *String Along,* but neither was a big hit. The first single, "Bad Man's Blunder," peaked at number 37. The song's co-writer, Cisco Houston, was terminally ill in the hospital at the time and was having trouble paying his medical bills. "Freddy Hellerman of the Weavers said we would really help Cisco out if we would sing this song. He got a lot of writer's royalties for it. At that time, you'd put an album out and the writer would make $100,000."

The second single, "Everglades," stalled at number 60. "When we listened to it, it started sounding like the Everly Brothers," admits Reynolds. "So we did it sort of as a parody, but we all loved the Everly Brothers."

Producer: Dave Cavanaugh

Track listing: Nice 'n' Easy / That Old Feeling / How Deep Is the Ocean / I've Got a Crush on You / You Go to My Head / Fools Rush In / Nevertheless / She's Funny That Way / Try a Little Tenderness / Embraceable You / Mam'selle / Dream

October 24, 1960
9 weeks stereo (nonconsecutive),
1 week mono

If 1958 was Frank Sinatra's "Very Good Year" [see 20], 1959 wasn't bad either. In that 12-month span Sinatra managed to land three albums in the top 10, including *Come Dance with Me!* and *No One Cares*. Both of those titles spent multiple weeks at number two, but were unable to reach the summit. However, Sinatra did pick up an album-of-the-year Grammy for the former.

Nice 'n' Easy, Sinatra's first and only album release of 1960, came nearly a year after *No One Cares*. For the sessions, held on March 1–3 at Capitol Records studios in Hollywood, Voyle Gilmore was replaced by Dave Cavanaugh in the control room, but Sinatra's longtime conductor/arranger Nelson Riddle was still on board, marking his eighth album collaboration with the crooner.

Aside from the title track, which was a last-minute addition to the album (replacing "The Nearness Of You," which was dropped), *Nice 'n' Easy* was comprised entirely of songs that Sinatra had previously recorded during his 1940–1953 tenure with Columbia Records.

THE TOP FIVE
Week of October 24, 1960

1. **Nice and Easy**
   Frank Sinatra

2. **Kingston Trio**
   String Along

3. **Bongos**
   Los Admiradores

4. **Persuasive Percussion, Vol. II**
   Enoch Light/Terry Snyder and the All Stars

5. **Sold Out**
   The Kingston Trio

The material ranged from "Fools Rush In," which Sinatra initially recorded in 1940 as a vocalist for the Tommy Dorsey Orchestra, to "Day In—Day Out," which the crooner debuted on a radio program in 1953.

The songs were special to Sinatra, and to many of the instrumentalists in Riddle's orchestra as well. "One of the first solos I ever did on a record was on 'How Deep Is the Ocean,'" says bass trombone player George Roberts, who credits Riddle with giving him the additional exposure.

Roberts also has kind words for Sinatra. "He may not know it, but my feeling is that Sinatra is probably one of the greatest trombone teachers in the world," he says. "If you sit down and listen to him sing and try to emulate what he does, you'll be a hell of a trombone player. I try to play trombone like the way he sings."

As evidenced by the relatively quick recording, Sinatra once again was in top form during the sessions for *Nice 'n' Easy*. "The first take was usually the best one," Roberts says. "It was much less pretentious than sitting around for two hours trying to make it better when you really couldn't. The first takes of some of the Sinatra things were fabulous."

The public agreed. In its 10th week on the chart, *Nice 'n' Easy* became Sinatra's third chart-topper, knocking another Capitol album, the Kingston Trio's *String Along*, from the Number One spot.

38 G.I. Blues RCA 2256
ELVIS PRESLEY

Musical directors: Joseph Lilley and Hal Wallis

Track listing: Tonight Is So Right for Love / What's She Really Like / Frankfort Special / Wooden Heart / G.I. Blues / Pocket Full of Rainbows / Shoppin' Around / Big Boots / Didja' Ever / Blue Suede Shoes / Doin' the Best I Can

December 5, 1960
10 weeks (nonconsecutive): 2 weeks stereo, 8 weeks mono

Nine months after Elvis Presley was discharged from the army, the King scored his fifth Number One album with *G.I. Blues*, the soundtrack to his fifth film. Yet *G.I. Blues* wasn't Elvis's official comeback album. That release, recorded shortly after his return to civilian life and appropriately titled *Elvis Is Back!*, spent three weeks at number two, but was unable to unseat the Kingston Trio's *Sold Out* [see 34].

G.I. Blues was recorded on April 27 and 28, 1960, at RCA Studios and at a subsequent session May 6 at Radio Recorders in Hollywood, the studio that Elvis frequently used for recording soundtrack material. As Jimmie Haskell, who played accordion at the sessions, notes, there were guards in front of the studio to keep away any fans who might have discovered Elvis's whereabouts. Presley's crack sidemen—guitarist Scotty Moore and drummer D.J. Fontana—were present at the sessions, but they were augmented by several ace session players, including guitarists Tiny Timbrell and Neal Matthews, bassist Ray Siegel, drummer Bernie Mat-

tinson, and pianist Dudley Brooks.

The movie, co-starring Juliet Prowse, was filmed in April of 1960. It featured Elvis as a young American soldier in the entertainment unit stationed in Germany. In real life, the Army had refused to allow Elvis into the unit, fearing complaints of having given the star preferential treatment.

With both the film and album, Elvis's career continued to take a new turn, as his manager Colonel Tom Parker attempted to mold him into an entertainer who could be appreciated by fans of all ages. This transformation initially didn't sit too well with Elvis and his band. "That kind of material wasn't our normal thing," says Scotty Moore. "A lot of those songs were kind of the same. Those songs like 'Pocket Full of Rainbows' weren't the type of songs Elvis could sink his teeth into."

As Moore recalls, Presley's lack of interest in the material was apparent. "He would fool around and stall and do everything he could not to do the songs,

although he knew he was going to do them, because each one had already been picked for a certain scene and he understood the mechanics. But once he started working on them, he would put his heart and soul into them no matter how goofy they were."

Elvis also kept his sense of humor. Haskell, known for his work with Ricky Nelson [see 12], recalls that at the end of one session, Elvis and the Colonel decided to play a prank on an eager song-plugger who was hoping to have Elvis record one of his songs. "Since it was the end of the day, Elvis and the Colonel agreed that no matter what he played for them, they would say that it was terrible and walk out of the room and they did, but it was all just a joke."

G.I. Blues became Elvis's fifth Number One album in its sixth week on the chart, and enjoyed the longest chart stay of any of his chart-toppers since 1957's *Loving You* [see 9], silencing any suspicions that his popularity may have waned during his time in the service.

THE TOP FIVE
Week of December 5, 1960

1. **G.I. Blues**
   Elvis Presley

2. **The Button-Down Mind of Bob Newhart**
   Bob Newhart

3. **Nice and Easy**
   Frank Sinatra

4. **The Button-Down Mind Strikes Back!**
   Bob Newhart

5. **String Along**
   The Kingston Trio

WARNER BROS. 1393 ## The Button-Down Mind Strikes Back! **39**
BOB NEWHART

Producer: None listed

Track listing: Automation and a Private in Washington's Army / The Grace L. Ferguson Airline (and Storm Door Co.) / Bus Drivers School / Retirement Party / An Infinite Number of Monkeys / Ledge Psychology

January 1, 1961
1 week mono

The success of *The Button-Down Mind of Bob Newhart* [see 35] was a shock to the young comedian. "I saw the album as an adjunct to my new nightclub career. I would go into a town, some people would have heard the album and they would come and see me. So, I was totally unprepared for what happened," he says. "I certainly never expected it to go to Number One and never expected to 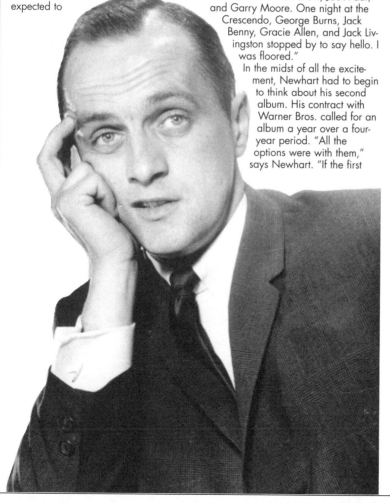 sell as many copies as it did."

Disc jockeys such as Howard Viken at WCCO in Minneapolis and Dan Sorkin at WCFL in Chicago began to play Newhart's routines from *The Button-Down Mind*, and sales of the album exploded. Sorkin, who had helped Newhart land his recording contract with Warner Bros., contributed liner notes to the album, and returned on the sleeve of *Strikes Back!*, boasting that his liner notes on Newhart's debut had sold well over 200,000 copies. KSFO San Francisco DJ Don Sherwood, and WCCO's Viken also wrote humorous tributes to Newhart, who had become a full-fledged star by the time he made his way to Hollywood for an engagement at the Crescendo in the fall of 1960.

"It was like New Year's Eve every night," Newhart says. "All of a sudden I was getting calls from people asking me to do the Ed Sullivan show, Jack Paar, and Garry Moore. One night at the Crescendo, George Burns, Jack Benny, Gracie Allen, and Jack Livingston stopped by to say hello. I was floored."

In the midst of all the excitement, Newhart had to begin to think about his second album. His contract with Warner Bros. called for an album a year over a four-year period. "All the options were with them," says Newhart. "If the first album didn't work, they were under no obligation to record a second one." Of course, Warner Bros. not only wanted a second album, they wanted it as soon as possible.

Strikes Back! was recorded in Freddie's Club in Minneapolis and the Hungry i in San Francisco in the summer and fall of 1960. The latter location was frequented by folk music sensations the Kingston Trio [see 27].

As had been the case when preparing to record his first album, Newhart was faced with a tight deadline and a lack of material. "Before the first album, I was working at a TV station in Chicago with a friend of mine named Bill Daily, who eventually wound up being on my TV show as Howard Borden, the airline pilot. Bill and I were both dabbling in stand-up, but we didn't have much going," Newhart says. "Bill had a date coming up and he asked if he could borrow a piece from me called 'The Grace L. Ferguson Airline (and Storm Door Co.),' and I said sure. But when the deadline came up for the second album, I had to call him up and tell him I needed it back, because I was one cut short. He didn't want to give it up, because he said it was his best routine."

By the time Newhart recorded *Strikes Back!*, he was no longer a novice. His delivery on the follow-up record is noticeably looser than on *The Button-Down Mind*. "By that time I was a little more comfortable in front of an audience," he says. "I had gotten over some of the stage fright. The first one was recorded during my first engagement at a nightclub. By the second one, I had played about 10 different nightclubs."

THE TOP FIVE
Week of Janaury 1, 1961

1. **The Button-Down Mind Strikes Back!**
   Bob Newhart

2. **Music from Exodus, and Other Great Tunes**
   Mantovani

3. **Wonderland by Night**
   Bert Kaempfert

4. **This Is Brenda**
   Brenda Lee

5. **Temptation**
   Roger Williams

40 Wonderland by Night DECCA 74101
BERT KAEMPFERT AND HIS ORCHESTRA

Producer: Bert Kaempfert

Track listing: Wonderland By Night / La Vie En Rose / Happiness Never Comes Too Late / On the Alamo / As I Love You / Dreaming the Blues / Tammy / The Aim of My Desires / This Song Is Your Alone / Drifting and Dreaming / Stay With Me / Lullaby for Lovers

January 16, 1961
5 weeks mono (nonconsecutive)

Although Bert Kaempfert, along with Enoch Light [see 32] and Lawrence Welk [see 42], was one of the premiere instrumental band leaders in the early '60s, today he is perhaps best known for his work with three of the biggest acts in the history of popular music: Elvis Presley, Frank Sinatra, and the Beatles.

Before the German-born multi-instrumentalist exprienced success in America as an artist, Elvis recorded the Kaempfert song "Wooden Heart" for *G.I. Blues* [see 38]. Kaempfert's influence would continue with *Wonderland By Night.*

Long before George Martin worked with the Beatles, Kaempfert worked with them, producing the group's first session in 1961, in which the Beatles backed Tony Sheridan. The date yielded Sheridan's "My Bonnie Lies Over the Ocean" and "When the Saints Go Marching In" and the Beatles' "Ain't She Sweet" and "Cry for a Shadow." (Those recordings, except for "When the Saints Go Marching In," later turned up on the Beatles' *Anthology 1* [see 423].) In 1966, Sinatra's English translation of a Kaempfert

tune became a huge hit called "Strangers in the Night" [see 86].

Kaempfert's own rise to the top began in 1959, when he was hired as a staff producer for Polydor Records in Germany. The move paid off for the label, as Kaempfert produced such hits as "Morgen" by Ivo Robic and "Die Gitarre and Das Meer" by Freddy Quinn.

As a recording star in his own right, Kaempfert first began to experience success with a song called "Wunderland bei Nacht," the instrumental theme of a film about Germany. Kaempfert traveled to New York in late 1959 to secure a publishing deal. Soon after, Decca Records made an agreement with Polydor to distribute the bandleader's releases in America.

When "Wonderland by Night" began to show potential as a hit, Decca worked feverishly to assemble an album. As a result, many of the tracks that rounded out the album, including the Kaempfert original "Lullaby for

Lovers" and his version of the standard "La Vie En Rose," were filler.

"We had to take whatever he had in his catalog to come up with 12 selections and put the album out," says Milt Gabler, the head of artists and repertoire for Decca Records. "Everything was recorded in Europe and we had to take what he had for the LP." The instrumental hit was particularly appealing to more mature listeners, hence the need to issue the album as soon as possible. "People wanted an LP," says Gabler. "Kids bought singles, but not adults."

On January 9, 1961, "Wonderland by Night" topped the Hot 100. A week later, with the single still in the top spot, the album of the same name hit the summit of the mono album chart. It was Kaempfert's first and only album chart-topper and the first of his two albums to crack the top 10 (four years later, his *Blue Midnight* reached number five).

Kaempfert continued to chart albums through 1971. He died at the age of 56 in June 1980 in Switzerland.

THE TOP FIVE
Week of January 16, 1961

1. **Wonderland By Night**
   Bert Kaempfert

2. **Music from 'Exodus' and Other Great Themes**
   Mantovani

3. **Exodus**
   Soundtrack

4. **Last Date**
   Lawrence Welk

5. **This Is Brenda Lee**
   Brenda Lee

Producer: None listed

Track listing: Theme from Exodus / Summer in Cyprus / Escape / Ari / Karen / Valley of Jezreel / Fight for Survival / In Jerusalem / The Brothers / Conspiracy / The Brothers / Conspiracy / Prison Break / Dawn / Fight for Peace

January 23, 1961
14 weeks stereo (nonconsecutive), 3 weeks mono

For the *Exodus* soundtrack album, two great talents joined forces. Prior to *Exodus*, film producer Otto Preminger proved that he knew the importance of a strong score by employing Elmer Bernstein on *The Man with the Golden Arm* and Duke Ellington on *Anatomy of a Murder*. Before being tapped by Preminger to score *Exodus*, Ernest Gold had proven his mettle with the score to Stanley Kramer's *On the Beach*. The work earned him a Golden Globe and his first Oscar nomination. But it was with the *Exodus* soundtrack that Gold would truly shine.

The film, based on Leon Uris's bestselling novel, told the story of Jewish refugees trek to Palestine. It starred Paul Newman and Eva Marie Saint, and was shot on location in Israel and on Cyprus.

To prepare Gold for the job, Preminger asked the composer to visit the film locations to absorb an authentic flavor for the film. Yet Gold was at odds with some of Preminger's ideas. "They do not trust the composer to come up with something original. They wanted Israeli folk songs for *Exodus*," he told William H. Rosar in an interview conducted for *The Cue Sheet*, published by the Society for the Preservation of Film Music.

There was also a tight deadline for the soundtrack, which forced Gold to turn to Gerard Schurmann to orchestrate the project. "I only had four weeks and three days to write 90 minutes of music," Gold told Rosar in *The Cue Sheet*. "That's why I went for an orchestrator. Schurmann is much more than an orchestrator. He is a serious composer and a superb master of the orchestra. He is marvelous. But I've always preferred to orchestrate my own music."

Though he made a living making music for films, Gold joked about the lack of credit composers of film scores receive in a 1961 article he wrote for

Opera News: "...first, in huge letters, the name of the company, those of the stars, and the title. This would be followed by several credit lines, such as 'Adapted from the stage success...' 'Based on the book...' Then a long, long list of all other artists, the set designer, wigmaker, hairdresser and so on. Finally (you had better get your magnifying glass) it would say 'Music by So-and-So.' As a fitting conclusion to the credits, the letters would revert to their former proud size and proclaim the producer and director."

Gold did enjoy his moment in the spotlight, however. *Exodus* reached the top of the stereophonic album chart in its second week on the chart. The title track was covered by Ferrante & Teicher and reached number two on the Hot 100. Versions by such diverse talents as Mantovani (who attempted to cash in on the *Exodus* phenomenon with his own album), Eddie Harris, and Pat Boone were less successful.

The Gold rush continued on April 12, 1961, at the Grammy Award ceremonies. *Exodus* earned Gold the award for best soundtrack album, while "Theme from *Exodus*" was named song of the year.

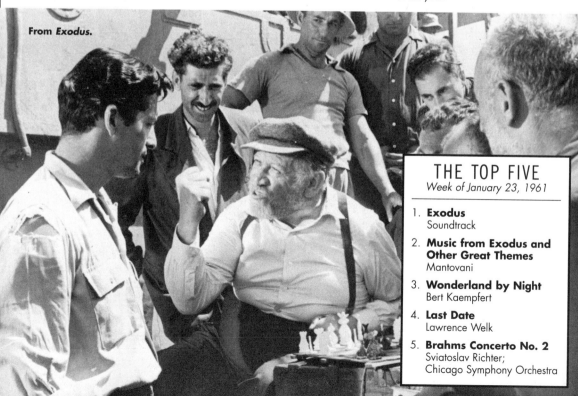

From *Exodus*.

THE TOP FIVE
Week of January 23, 1961

1. **Exodus**
   Soundtrack

2. **Music from Exodus and Other Great Themes**
   Mantovani

3. **Wonderland by Night**
   Bert Kaempfert

4. **Last Date**
   Lawrence Welk

5. **Brahms Concerto No. 2**
   Sviatoslav Richter;
   Chicago Symphony Orchestra

42 Calcutta! DOT 5359
LAWRENCE WELK

Arrangements: Larry Gordon, Bill Fontaine, George Wyle, Bob Ballard, George Cates, Milt Rogers, and Joe Rizzo

Track listing: Calcutta / Sailor (Your Home Is the Sea) / Perfidia / April in Portugal / Humoresque Boogie / Corrine Corrina / Bombay Mam'selle / Mountain King / Blue Tango / Ruby / Save the Last Dance for Me

March 13, 1961
11 weeks stereo, 8 weeks mono (nonconsecutive)

When veteran German-born bandleader Lawrence Welk first heard "Calcutta" he wasn't impressed. "I listened to it and I thought it was interesting, but when I played it for Lawrence, he wasn't so sure," says Welk's musical supervisor, George Cates. When Cates, who was also a recording artist at the time, said that he would record the song, Welk relented. "If it's good enough for you to do, then it's good enough for me," Welk told Cates.

"Calcutta" was a German tune composed by Heino Gaze and originally entitled "Tivoli Melody." It marked a change for Welk, who had been leading bands since the middle of the 1920s. "Instead of the 'champagne music' we decided that we would do something a little different," Cates says. "We decided to use a harpsichord." Originally, the track was set to be the B-side of "My Grandfather's Clock," but then radio picked up on the song, featuring Frank Scott on the harpsichord.

While critics often attacked Welk's music for its blandness, he was certainly popular with the public. Even in the rock era, he had charted 13 albums prior to *Calcutta!* While the majority of his albums peaked in the mid-teens, *Last Date*, his 1960 album peaked at number four.

Undoubtedly contributing to Welk's resurgence was the exposure he received on television. In 1952, Welk made his television debut on KTLA in Los Angeles. Three years later, on July 2, 1955, *The Lawrence Welk Show* was picked up by the ABC television network. Welk's popularity was so great that ABC gave the bandleader a second hour on October 8, 1956, for *Lawrence Welk's Top Tunes and New Talent.*

The TV exposure and radio play of "Calcutta" sent the single climbing the Hot 100. Quick to cash in on his rising popularity, Welk rushed into the studio between TV shows to cut a full album around "Calcutta." As the album's back cover states, "the smash hit single leads a parade of instrumental hits." In keeping with the feel of "Calcutta," harpsichord was prominently featured on the album. "We had to use harpsichord on just about every recording after that," says Cates.

Although none of the other tracks on the album actually became hits, the popularity of "Calcutta" was sufficient enough to drive the album to the top. The single reached Number One on February 13, 1961. Exactly a month later, *Calcutta* simultaneously topped the stereophonic and monophonic album charts.

It was Welk's first and last Number One album and single of the rock era. The bubbly-music bandleader continued to prosper on TV until 1982. A decade later, he died of pneumonia.

THE TOP FIVE
Week of March 13, 1961

1. **Calcutta!**
   Lawrence Welk

2. **Exodus**
   Soundtrack

3. **Great Motion Picture Themes**
   Various Artists

4. **Camelot**
   Original Cast

5. **Sinatra's Swingin' Session**
   Frank Sinatra

COLUMBIA 5620 **Camelot** **43**

ORIGINAL BROADWAY CAST RECORDING

Producer: Goddard Lieberson

Track listing: Overture [Orchestra] / Parade [Orchestra] / I Wonder What the King Is Doing Tonight [Richard Burton] / The Simple Joys of Maidenhood [Julie Andrews] / Camelot [Burton, Andrews] / Follow Me [Marjorie Smith] / C'est moi [Robert Goulet] / The Lusty Month of May [Andrews, ensemble] / Then You May Take Me to the Fair [Andrews, John Cullum, James Gannon, Bruce Yarnell] / How to Handle a Woman [Burton] / The Jousts [Burton, Andrews, Ensemble] / Before I Gaze at You Again [Andrews] / If Ever I Would Leave You [Goulet] / The Seven Deadly Virtues [Roddy McDowall] / What Do Simple Folks Do [Andrews, Burton] / The Persuasion [McDowall, M'el Dowd] / Fie on Goodness! [Knights] / I Loved You Once in Silence [Andrews] / Guenevere [ensemble] / Camelot (Reprise) [Burton]

*June 5, 1961
6 weeks mono*

Nearly five years after the landmark success of *My Fair Lady* [see 2], the team of lyricist Alan Jay Lerner and composer Frederick Loewe had another hit on their hands with their next musical, *Camelot*. And once again Moss Hart staged the production and Julie Andrews was the leading lady. Co-star Robert Coote was another alumnus of *My Fair Lady*, as were musical arrangers Robert Russell Bennett, Philip J. Land, and Trude Rittman, musical director Franz Allers, and album producer Goddard Lieberson.

Julie Andrews in *Camelot*.

Camelot made its Broadway debut on December 3, 1960, at the Majestic Theatre. Prior to its Broadway opening, the musical had brief runs in Boston and Toronto, where it was the first production staged at the O'Keefe Centre. "They were finishing the theater as we were trying to ready our new show for its first out-of-town performance," recalls Andrews.

Andrews portrayed Queen Guenevere, while accomplished British actor Richard Burton made his musical debut as King Arthur. Robert Goulet was cast as Lancelot, and Roddy McDowall as the evil Mordred.

While *Camelot* was a hit, it wasn't quite as successful as *My Fair Lady*. "*Camelot* may not have been as critically successful as *My Fair Lady*, but it did have a magic of its own and people were attracted to that," says Andrews. "Perhaps it was because the original

book by T.H. White [*The Once and Future King*] was so amazing, or that Richard Burton was so compelling as King Arthur."

Musically, the show was loaded with highlights. "The title song is very beautiful and evocative," Andrews says. "And I particularly love 'I Loved You Once in Silence.'"

In its 20th week on the 150 Best Selling Monaural LP's chart, *Camelot* hit the summit. Its six-week reign at the top and its overall chart life of 265 weeks were no match for the legacy of *My Fair Lady*, yet *Camelot* is still the third most successful original cast album of the rock era, behind *My Fair Lady* and *The Sound of Music* [see 31]. Andrews feels timing had a lot to do with the success of the musicals: "I believe that if *Camelot* had been produced before *My Fair Lady*, it would have been an even bigger hit."

THE TOP FIVE
Week of June 5, 1961

1. **Camelot**
   Original Broadway Cast

2. **G.I. Blues**
   Elvis Presley

3. **Calcutta**
   Lawrence Welk

4. **Exodus**
   Soundtrack

5. **Great Motion Picture Themes**
   Various artists

44 Stars for a Summer Night COLUMBIA PMS 1
VARIOUS ARTISTS

Producer: None listed

Track listing: Summertime [Ray Conniff and His Orchestra] / Jeannie with the Light Brown Hair [The Dave Brubeck Quartet] / In the Evening by the Moonlight; Listen to the Mocking Bird; While Strolling Through the Park One Day [Frank DeVol and His Rainbow Strings] / Lazy Afternoon [Les Elgart and His Orchestra] / Bouquet [Percy Faith and His Orchestra] / By the Campfire [Andre Kostelanetz and His Orchestra] / Stairway to the Stars [Bobby Hackett] / Star Eyes [Art Van Damme Quintet] / It's a Wonderful World [Les Brown and His Orchestra] / Just Friends [Billy Butterfield] / Like Love [Andre Previn, His Piano and Orchestra] / Ramona [Jerry Murad's Harmonicats] / March from "The Love for Three Oranges" [Columbia Symphony Orchestra] / "Waltz of the Flowers" from "Nutcracker Suite" [New York Philharmonic] / Second Movement (Scherzando) from "Symphonie Espagnole" [New York Philharmonic] / Russian Sailors' Dance from "The Red Poppy" [Philadelphia Orchestra] / Waltz No. 7 in C-Sharp Minor, Op. 64, No. 2 [Alexander Brailowsky] / "One Fine Day" from "Madame Butterfly" [Columbia Symphony Orchestra] / Can Can [New York Philharmonic] / Fantasia on "Greensleeves" [The Strings of the Philadelphia Orchestra] / Clair de lune [Philippe Entremont] / Londonderry Air [The Mormon Tabernacle Choir and the Philadelphia Orchestra] / Liebestraum [Ivan Davis] / "The Stars Were Shining" from "Tosca" [Columbia Symphony Orchestra] / Hoe Down from "Rodeo" [New York Philharmonic]

July 17, 1961
9 weeks stereo, 4 weeks mono

Leonard Bernstein

Columbia Records was one of the more innovative record companies in the late '50s and early '60s. Its 1958 album *Johnny's Greatest Hits* was the first "best of" package. The label was also one of the first to release specially-priced various-artists compilations in an attempt to boost the individual artists' albums.

Stars for a Summer Night was one such compilation. As the album cover promised, the set featured material from "22 brilliant performers." A special insert inside the package displayed the cover art for the artists' albums where the individual tracks could also be found.

Although the *Stars for a Summer Night* cover claimed that the album was "designed for summer listening," the only hint of a seasonal theme on the album is the opening track, a version of "Summertime" by Ray Coniff and His Orchestra.

Stan Kavin, the popular merchandise director for Columbia Records, was involved in compiling the album. He chose selections from various pop instrumental artists for sides one and two, and reserved classical recordings for sides three and four. Aside from exposing individual artists, Columbia also used the album as a tool to promote stereo. "It was released in the early days of stereo," Kavin says, "so that was another reason why the album was released, to introduce people to the virtues of stereo."

In its seventh week, *Stars for a Summer Night* shot to the top of the 50 Best Selling Stereo LP's chart. The fact that it was a various artists album with no real theme earned it a place in history. It is the only such album to top the album chart in the rock era.

For most of the artists featured, *Stars for a Summer Night* represented their only trip to the summit, but there were a few exceptions: Andre Previn conducted the orchestra on the *Gigi* soundtrack [see 17]; Eugene Ormandy, the Philadelphia Orchestra, and the Mormon Tabernacle Choir reached the pole position with *The Lord's Prayer* [see 30]; and Leonard Bernstein scored one of his greatest triumphs with the soundtrack to *West Side Story* [see 52].

THE TOP FIVE
Week of July 17, 1961

1. **Stars for a Summer Night**
   Various artists

2. **Calcutta**
   Lawrence Welk

3. **Exodus**
   Soundtrack

4. **The Sound of Music**
   Original Cast

5. **Great Motion Picture Themes**
   Various Artists

MGM 39460 **Carnival!**
ORIGINAL CAST

45

Producer: Arnold Maxin

Track listing: Opening—Direct from Vienna / Mire (Can You Imagine That?) / Sword, Rose and Cape / A Very Nice Man / I've Got to Find a Reason / Yes, My Heart / Humming / Theme from Carnival! (Love Makes the World Go 'Round) / Grand Imperial Cirque de Paris / Her Face / Yum, Ticky, Ticky, Tum, Tum / The Rich / Beautiful Candy / Everybody Likes You / I Have Him / Her Face / It Was Always You / It Was Always You (Reprise) / She's My Love / Theme from Carnival!

July 17, 1961
1 week mono

Washington Post drama critic Richard L. Coe ended his March 11, 1961, review of the new musical Carnival! with these words: "Carnival! definitely you must see. I can't wait until the LP album comes along." Coe was not alone, so MGM Records ushered the cast of the musical into a New York recording studio only days after the show opened its Broadway engagement on April 13 at the Imperial Theater.

The show, based on Michael Stewart's book, featured the words and music of Bob Merrill. It told the tale of a shy woman, Lili, who hooks up with a carnival where she falls for a lowly puppeteer rather than a magnificent magician.

Carnival!, inspired by the 1953 film Lili, initially went into rehearsals on February 6, 1961. Prior to its Broadway bow, the musical played 20 performances at the National Theatre in Washington, D.C., and 16 dates at the Forrest Theatre in Philadelphia.

The musical starred Anna Maria Alberghetti as Lili, with Jerry Orbach, who was featured in the off-Broadway production The Fantasticks, as the puppeteer. Other cast members included Kaye Ballard as the Incomparable Rosalie, and James Mitchell as Marco The Magnificent.

The material in the musical ranged from Mitchell and Ballard's "It Was Always You," which Coe called "probably the maddest love song ever staged," to "Mira," performed by Alberghetti. "That was the song that stopped the show every night," says Alberghetti. "It was a simple song, but I managed to carve out some things out of it that made it quite unique." Alberghetti says

she cut the song for the album in one or two takes.

Alberghetti attributes the success of Carnival! to its strong characters. "Although it was a musical, it was really a play, figuratively," she says. "You got a really close-up feeling of Lili's character." The magic of the show was also apparent on the album, Alberghetti says, because "the characters were very alive and very real."

The fact that the album was recorded on a Sunday, which was usually reserved as a day off for the cast, caused a bit of concern. "I thought that vocally, after having done eight shows, that our voices wouldn't be as clean, because we were tired," Alberghetti says. "But all of our energy was so up that the recording went flawlessly. There were no problems."

Carnival! hit the top of the 150 Best Selling Monaural LP's chart in its eighth week on the chart, dislodging another great musical, Camelot, from the pole position.

Anna Maria Alberghetti
in Carnival!

THE TOP FIVE
Week of July 17, 1961

1. **Carnival!**
   Original Cast

2. **Camelot**
   Original Cast

3. **Stars for a Summer Night**
   Various artists

4. **Exodus**
   Soundtrack

5. **Never on Sunday**
   Soundtrack

46 Something for Everybody RCA 2370
ELVIS PRESLEY

Engineer: Bill Porter

Track listing: There's Always Me / Give Me the Right / It's a Sin / Sentimental Me / Starting Today / Gently / I'm Comin' Home / In Your Arms / Put the Blame on Me / Judy / I Want You with Me / I Slipped, I Stumbled, I Fell

August 21, 1961
3 weeks mono

The title of Elvis Presley's second 1961 album effectively summed up his post-Army career. Under the guidance of Colonel Tom Parker, Elvis toned down his rebellious nature and evolved into an entertainer who could be enjoyed by the entire family.

Something for Everybody was released in July 1961, approximately six months after His Hand in Mine. That title, Elvis's first full album of religious songs, reached number 13 in February 1961, and was the first album release of an incredibly active year for Elvis. Between His Hand in Mine and Something for Everybody, several other projects were issued. On March 20, Elvis scored a Number One hit single with the dramatic ballad "Surrender," his adaptation of the Italian standard "Torna a Sorrento" ("Come Back to Sorrento"). Two months later, Elvis by Request, a four-song EP was issued. That disc, including the title song to the film Flaming Star, peaked at number 14. Despite the heavy schedule, guitarist Scotty Moore says the sessions were usually fairly relaxed. "We really didn't rush, but we did have an incredible amount of songs to cut," he says.

Flaming Star, released in December 1960, was a Western that featured Elvis in his first non-singing dramatic role. Since music wasn't an essential part of the film, a full soundtrack album was not released.

Elvis's next film, Wild in the Country, was similar. It featured Elvis in a dramatic role, along with Tuesday Weld and Hope Lange, and only included a few songs.

While Wild in the Country also did not generate a full soundtrack album, its "I Slipped, I Stumbled, I Fell" ended up as a last-minute addition to Something for Everybody. It was the only track on the album that wasn't cut during the March 12–13 sessions held at RCA Studios in Nashville. These sessions featured Elvis's usual crew—guitarist Scotty Moore, bassist Bob Moore, drummer D.J. Fontana, and backing vocalists the Jordanaires. As usual, a number of session players were also present, including guitarist Hank Garland, drummer Buddy Harman, pianist Floyd Cramer, saxophonist Boots Randolph, and backing vocalist Millie Kirkham.

As its title suggests, Something for Everybody was meant to appeal to a wide audience, with side one of the album devoted to ballads and side two consisting of more upbeat rockers. Despite this strategy, the album failed to generate a hit single. ("There's Always Me"/"Judy" wasn't released as a single until 1967, and the two songs stalled at numbers 56 and 78, respectively.)

While Moore is fond of "Judy," not much else on Something for Everybody stands out. It simply doesn't stand up as one of Presley's finest efforts. The fact that it was commercially successful is a tribute to "the man delivering the message," Moore says.

Something for Everybody hit the summit of the 150 Best Selling Monaural LP's chart in its seventh week, becoming Elvis's first non-soundtrack Number One since Elvis' Christmas Album [see 10] — and his last non-soundtrack studio album to top the chart.

THE TOP FIVE
Week of August 21, 1961

1. **Something for Everybody**
   Elvis Presley

2. **Stars for a Summer Night**
   Various artists

3. **Exodus to Jazz**
   Eddie Harris

4. **Never on a Sunday**
   Soundtrack

5. **Goin' Places**
   The Kingston Trio

CAPITOL 1569 **Judy at Carnegie Hall**
JUDY GARLAND

Producer: Andy Wiswell

Track listing: Overture: The Trolley Song / Over the Rainbow / The Man That Got Away / When You're Smiling (The Whole World Smiles with You) / Medley: Almost Like Being in Love / This Can't Be Love / Do It Again / You Go to My Head / Alone Together / Who Cares? (So Long as You Care for Me?) / Puttin' on the Ritz / How Long Has This Been Going On? / Just You, Just Me / The Man That Got Away / San Francisco / I Can't Give You Anything but Love / That's Entertainment / Come Rain or Come Shine / You're Nearer / A Foggy Day / If Love Were All / Zing! Went the Strings of My Heart / Stormy Weather / Medley: You Made Me Love You / For Me and My Gal / The Trolley Song / Rock-A-Bye Your Baby with a Dixie Melody / Over the Rainbow / Swanee / After You've Gone / Chicago

September 11, 1961
9 weeks stereo, 13 weeks mono

At the mere age of 15, Judy Garland was signed to Decca Records in August 1937. Two years later, she starred as Dorothy in the legendary film musical *The Wizard of Oz*. Garland continued as a star of song and the big screen, appearing in several MGM musicals through the mid-'50s, including the original *A Star Is Born* in 1954.

In 1955, Garland moved to Capitol Records and focused on recording and touring. *Miss Show Business*, her first album for the label, reached number five. Her subsequent albums, 1956's *Judy* and 1957's *Alone* both peaked at number 17.

THE TOP FIVE
Week of September 11, 1961

1. **Judy at Carnegie Hall**
   Judy Garland

2. **Never on Sunday**
   Soundtrack

3. **Goin' Places**
   The Kingston Trio

4. **Yellow Bird**
   Lawrence Welk

5. **Camelot**
   Original Cast

After a hiatus, Garland returned to the concert stage in grand style in 1961 with a 16-city tour, which included a stop on April 23, 1961, at Carnegie Hall. A crowd of 3,165 packed the theater beyond its capacity and Capitol captured it all on tape.

To Garland, the recording was an afterthought and she wasn't about to make any concessions that would hurt her performance. "Her attitude was, I'm going to do my concert and if you can make a record out of it, go ahead," recalls orchestra director Mort Lindsey. "At one point the producer was concerned that the drums were going to be too loud on the record, but Judy just said, 'The heck with you. This is my night. We're doing a concert, we're not doing a recording.'"

Any fears on the part of producer Andy Wiswell proved to be unfounded, as Garland put on the performance of her career. Of course, the recording had to be edited. "On the album, they left off about 22 minutes of applause,"

says Lindsey. "She came out to a standing ovation to start with and from then on, she could do no wrong. It was such an exceptional night. Anyone who was there will tell you, it was like a prayer meeting." Among those in attendance were Rock Hudson, Jule Styne, Carol Channing, and Julie Andrews. "No matter where you looked, you saw movie stars and famous people," says Lindsey.

The performance was a career retrospective with Garland performing such notable tunes as "Over the Rainbow" from *The Wizard of Oz* and "The Man That Got Away" from *A Star Is Born*. "They were all songs that almost belonged to her," adds Lindsey. "It wasn't unknown territory."

Record buyers greeted *Judy at Carnegie Hall* as enthusiastically as those who attended the concert. In its seventh week, the album knocked Elvis Presley's *Something for Everybody* from the summit of the 150 Best Selling Monaural LP's chart, becoming the first live music recording to top the album list.

48 Stereo 35/MM COMMAND 826
ENOCH LIGHT AND HIS ORCHESTRA

Producer: Enoch Light

Track listing: Heat Wave / The Man I Love / I've Got a Crush on You / All the Way / My Romance / You Do Something to Me / Zing Went the Strings of My Heart / Someone to Watch Over Me / Love for Sale / I'll See You Again / I See Your Face Before Me / With a Song in My Heart

November 20, 1961
7 weeks stereo

With the release of *Persuasive Percussion* [see 32], Enoch Light revolutionized stereo recording and launched the highly successful Command label. With the subsequent releases *Provocative Percussion, Persuasive Percussion, Volume 2,* and *Provocative Percussion, Volume 2* in 1960, and *Persuasive Percussion, Volume 3* in 1961, the hot streak continued, as all of those albums made the top five. However, Light wasn't just concerned with commercial success. As was the case with *Provocative Percussion,* one of his main motivations was to improve the sound of recorded music. With *Stereo 35/MM,* Light attempted to take his quest to a new level.

Recorded at Carnegie Hall in New York City, the album was named for the material it was recorded on: 35-millimeter magnetic film. Light and recording engineer Robert Fine believed that 35-millimeter film offered better sound reproduction than tape, which was flawed due to possible distortions caused by hiss and flutter. The wider 35-millimeter film, on the other hand, allowed for greater separation of channels and higher running speeds. Since film runs on a closed-circuit loop, it has no flutter and little background noise.

Light's sound innovations didn't come without a price. Carnegie Hall has great natural acoustics, but it was also costly to rent. The film on which the album was recorded was also expensive, running approximately $30 for 10 minutes of recording stock.

While Light and Fine worked on the recording, the group of 60 ace sidemen that made up Light's orchestra were more concerned with the music, says trumpet player Doc Severinsen, who later went on to fame as leader of the *Tonight Show* band. "We didn't care much," he says. "We just thought it was another nice, new recording technique, but it didn't have an effect on the way

we played." The material, ranging from George Gershwin's "I've Got a Crush on You" and "Someone to Watch Over Me" to Irving Berlin's "Heat Wave" and Cole Porter's "Love For Sale," was arranged by Lew Davies.

While the musicians weren't overly concerned with the technology, they were knocked out by the results. "I remember going up into a temporary control room that they set up in one of the dressing rooms," says Severinsen, "and when we heard the stuff back, it was pretty amazing compared to what we were used to." The famed acoustics of Carnegie Hall also contributed to the high-quality recording. "It was a very forward-thinking idea to record in a wonderful hall like that," Severinsen adds. "Most albums like that were done in a studio and they didn't have the feeling of a performance. Although we were recording, we had the feeling that this was a performance, since we were at Carnegie Hall."

The sessions to record the album went fairly smoothly, as Light and Davies plotted out arrangements that would fully exploit the sound capabilities of the film. "Enoch knew exactly what he wanted," says Severinsen. "Everything was recorded very cleanly." There wasn't the need for multiple takes of the songs, because the orchestra rehearsed the material prior to the recording.

The expert musicianship combined with the new technology in sound recording also played well with the public, as *Stereo 35/MM* became Light's second chart-topper and his sixth top five album in less than two years. *Stereo 35/MM, Volume Two* also performed well, peaking at number eight in 1962.

Courtesy of Photofest

THE TOP FIVE
Week of November 20, 1961

1. **Stereo 35/MM**
   Enoch Light and His Orchestra

2. **Judy at Carnegie Hall**
   Judy Garland

3. **The Sound of Music**
   Original Cast

4. **Camelot**
   Original Cast

5. **Never on Sunday**
   Soundtrack

Elvis Presley and Joan Blackman in *Blue Hawaii*.

RCA 2426 **Blue Hawaii**
ELVIS PRESLEY

49

Musical director: Joseph Lilley

Track listing: Blue Hawaii / Almost Always True / Aloha Oe / No More / Can't Help Falling in Love / Rock-a-Hula Baby / Moonlight Swim / Ku-U-I-Po / Ito Eats / Slicin' Sand / Hawaiian Sunset / Beach Boy Blues / Island of Love / Hawaiian Wedding Song

December 17, 1961
20 weeks mono, 4 weeks stereo

Despite the success of such films as *Loving You* [see 9] and *G.I. Blues* [see 38], Elvis Presley's presence in a film wasn't always as good as gold. In December 1960, *Flaming Star*, a Western that featured the King in his first non-singing role, failed to ignite the box office. Another film designed to showcase Elvis the actor, *Wild in the Country*, was also shot in 1960. Elvis recorded songs for both movies, but there were no soundtrack albums released in conjunction with the films. It was Elvis's next film, in which he returned to the film/soundtrack combination, that set the model for much of his output in the 1960s.

Blue Hawaii, originally titled *Hawaii Beach Boy*, co-starred Angela Lansbury as Elvis's mother and Joan Blackman as his girlfriend. It was one of the first of what guitarist Scotty Moore calls "the rubber stamp movies." While some of the songs were as lightweight as the

film's plot, Elvis and his support musicians found *Blue Hawaii* challenging. "It was interesting going from something like *G.I. Blues* to that," says Moore. "We were trying to make it still sound like rock 'n' roll, but add a Hawaiian flavor to things."

With the hopes of giving the songs an authentic Hawaiian feel, a number of additional players were brought in, including steel guitar player Bernie Lewis and ukulele players Fred Tavares and Alvino Rey. In addition to Elvis's usual backing vocalists, the Jordanaires, a group called the Surfers were enlisted.

Expert session drummer Hal Blaine was also called into the sessions, which were held March 21–23, 1961, at Radio Recorders in Hollywood, although Presley's longtime drummer D.J. Fontana and Bernie Mattinson were also present. Blaine says the drummers often decided who would play on a track with a coin toss: "It really didn't matter, because if you didn't play drums you'd shake a tambourine. D.J. usually played a tambourine or shaker."

For *Blue Hawaii*, the percussion went far beyond a standard drum kit. "They told me to bring anything Hawaiian I could find," says Blaine, "so I went to the Professional Drum Shop in Hollywood where I used to do all of my business and I rented about $1,000 a day worth of instruments. I took whatever they had in the store, whether it was from Hawaii or India. I sort of became

the purveyor of Hawaiian sound."

Blue Hawaii hit the top in its eighth week on the chart, giving Elvis his seventh Number One album and second of 1961. Unlike *G.I. Blues*, which failed to yield a hit, *Blue Hawaii* did spawn a successful single. In January 1962, the majestic ballad "Can't Help Falling in Love" peaked at number two. "It's a very simple, very gentle song, but it's a very touching song," says Blaine. The single failed to unseat Chubby Checker's "The Twist" from the Number One spot, but it, its B-side "Rock-A-Hula Baby," and the popularity of the film were enough to make *Blue Hawaii* the longest-running Number One album of Elvis's career.

THE TOP FIVE
Week of December 17, 1961

1. **Blue Hawaii**
   Elvis Presley

2. **Judy at Carnegie Hall**
   Judy Garland

3. **The Kingston Trio Close Up**
   The Kingston Trio

4. **Portrait of Johnny**
   Johnny Mathis

5. **Time Out**
   Dave Brubeck

50 Holiday Sing Along with Mitch COLUMBIA 8501
MITCH MILLER AND THE GANG

Producer: Mitch Miller

Track listing: Santa Claus Is Comin' to Town / Winter Wonderland / Must Be Santa / Jingle Bells / The Twelve Days of Christmas / Sleigh Ride / The Christmas Song / Silver Bells / I Saw Mommy Kissing Santa Claus / Rudolph, the Red-Nosed Reindeer / Let It Snow! Let It Snow! Let It Snow! / Frosty the Snowman / White Christmas

January 13, 1962
1 week stereo

Following the success of *Sing Along with Mitch* [see 19] and *Christmas Sing-Along with Mitch* [see 22], Mitch Miller proceeded to record "sing-along" albums at an astonishing rate and continued to enjoy incredible success.

From 1959 through the fall of 1961, Columbia released 11 more Miller *Sing Along* albums, plus a *Greatest Hits* for good measure. The titles ranged from *Still More! Sing Along with Mitch* and *Folk Songs Sing Along* to *Saturday Night Sing Along* and *Your Request Sing Along.*

"Everyone thought that people wouldn't buy albums if you put them out just three months apart," Miller says. "It was unheard of." Under Miller's contractual agreement, he was required to fund the recording of the albums out of his own pocket. "I would just spend some of my royalties," he says. "So I wasn't screwing up any budgets."

Miller's success wasn't limited to recording. On January 27, 1961, NBC debuted the musical variety show *Sing Along with Mitch*, with the lyrics flashed on the screen so TV viewers could "sing along" at home. The popular show ran through September 2, 1966. It wasn't the first time the concept had been attempted on TV, however—on June 4, 1958, the series *Sing Along* had made its debut. Yet that show, which aired prior to the success of *Sing Along with Mitch*, lasted a mere six weeks.

In the spring of 1961, *TV Sing Along with Mitch*, which was inspired by the NBC show, made it to number three, making it Miller's highest-charting album since *Christmas Sing-Along with Mitch*, which had hit the summit in 1958.

With *Christmas Sing-Along with Mitch* returning to make number eight in 1959 and number six in 1960, it seemed only natural that Miller and the Gang record a holiday sequel. This time around, however, Miller decided on a more modern repertoire, including "Must Be Santa," a relatively new number written by Hal Moore and Bill Fredericks in 1960. Miller even had the nerve to cover Irving Berlin's classic "White Christmas," a song closely linked to his holiday chart rival Bing Crosby [see 11].

In fact, Miller says his holiday albums were more user-friendly than Crosby's classic *Merry Christmas*. "Crosby was one hell of a singer," he says. "But the way he phrases things made it hard to sing along with, although I loved to listen to him."

Holiday Sing Along with Mitch was Miller's fifth album of 1961. Interestingly, it didn't hit Number One until its sixth week on the chart, after the holidays had passed. It remained the last holiday album to top the album chart until Kenny G was able to score a Number One album with *Miracles: The Holiday Album* [see 402] in 1994. Miller still holds another unique spot in chart history, however: he is the only artist ever to have two Number One Christmas albums.

THE TOP FIVE
Week of January 13, 1962

1. **Holiday Sing Along with Mitch**
   Mitch Miller and the Gang

2. **Blue Hawaii**
   Elvis Presley

3. **Stereo 35/mm**
   Enoch Light and
   the Light Brigade

4. **Breakfast at Tiffany's**
   Henry Mancini

5. **Judy at Carnegie Hall**
   Judy Garland

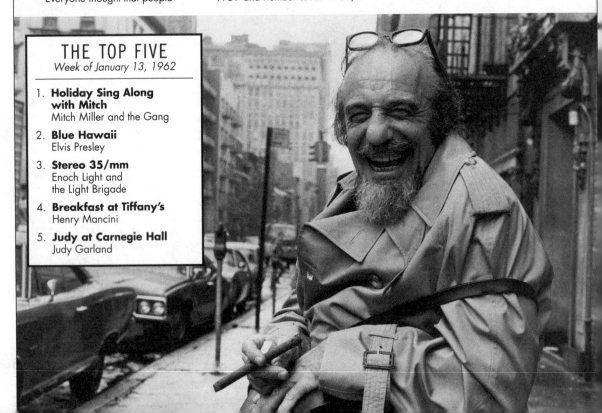

RCA VICTOR 2362 **Breakfast at Tiffany's**
HENRY MANCINI

51

Producer: Dick Peirce

Track listing: Moon River / Something for Cat / Sally's Tomato / Mr. Yunioshi / The Big Blow Out / Hub Caps and Tail Lights / Breakfast at Tiffany's / Latin Golightly / Holly / Loose Caboose / The Big Heist / Moon River Cha Cha

February 10, 1962
12 weeks stereo (nonconsecutive)

With *Breakfast at Tiffany's*, Henry Mancini scored his second Number One album [see 24—*The Music from Peter Gunn*] and his second hit single with "Moon River," the song featured prominently in the movie. Yet despite the success of the album, which knocked Elvis Presley's *Blue Hawaii* from the top of the album chart, Mancini has one regret. "I blew it on 'Moon River,' " he says. "In hindsight I think Audrey Hepburn sang that song as well as it has ever been sung."

Breakfast at Tiffany's features two versions of "Moon River," the album opener performed by a 16-voice chorus and the Latin-flavored "Moon River Cha

Cha," which closes the album. Yet Audrey Hepburn's tender reading of the tune, which was featured in the film, was left off the *Breakfast at Tiffany's* soundtrack album. According to Mancini, the song was inspired by Hepburn and her image on the screen. Moreover, the actress loved the song—when a Paramount executive complained at a preview screening "that fucking song's gotta go," she shot up out of her chair to defend it. Indeed, Hepburn's admiration for Mancini's work went beyond her fondness for that one song. After viewing the film, she sent Mancini a note, which read in part, "A movie without music is a little bit like an aeroplane without fuel. However beautifully the job is done, we are still on the ground and in a world of reality. Your music has lifted us all up and sent us soaring."

As with *The Music from Peter Gunn*, Mancini first recorded the score for the film in mono and later re-recorded the music to be released as the soundtrack album in stereo. "Since we were going to re-record, I just overlooked [Audrey's version]," Mancini admits.

Mancini and lyricist Johnny Mercer

wrote "Moon River" specifically for the film. "It was indicated in the script," he recalls. "In fact it was in the original novella that Truman Capote wrote. [Hepburn's character] Holly Golightly is on the fire escape with a guitar and she's singing this song. I had to figure out what kind of melody she would be singing, then John came up with the lyrics."

Breakfast at Tiffany's was recorded in four sessions. Yet the lush orchestrations on *Tiffany's* were distinctively different than the jazzy big-band sounds of *Peter Gunn*. "We had to do 12 tunes and we would try to get three in each session," he recalls.

Again, as had been the case with *The Music from Peter Gunn*, Mancini was paired with director Blake Edwards, with whom he would continue to collaborate in such notable films and scores as *Days of Wine and Roses*, *Victor/Victoria*, and the *Pink Panther* films, yet *Breakfast at Tiffany's* remains one of their crowning achievements, as "Moon River" has been recorded by every one from Louis Armstrong [see 68] and Andy Williams to R.E.M.

Audrey Hepburn in
Breakfast at Tiffany's.

THE TOP FIVE
Week of February 10, 1962

1. **Breakfast at Tiffany's**
   Henry Mancini

2. **Blue Hawaii**
   Elvis Presley

3. **Stereo 35/MM**
   Enoch Light

4. **The Sound of Music**
   Original Cast

5. **Camelot**
   Original Cast

52 West Side Story COLUMBIA 2070
SOUNDTRACK

Conductor: Johnny Green

Track listing: Prologue / Jet Song / Something's Coming / Dance at the Gym / Maria / America / Tonight / Gee, Officer Krupke / I Feel Pretty / One Hand, One Heart / Quintet / The Rumble / Somewhere / Cool / A Boy Like That; I Have a Love

May 5, 1962
54 weeks (nonconsecutive): 53 weeks stereo, 12 weeks mono

Richard Beymer and Russ Tamblyn in *West Side Story.*

When the original cast album of *West Side Story* was released in March 1958, it didn't set the world on fire. "Unlike most shows, it did not sell a lot of albums right away," says lyricist Stephen Sondheim. "Over a period of years it remained steady, whereas most show albums have an immediate peak and then an immediate falloff. *West Side Story* never really had a peak, because *West Side Story* wasn't a big hit. It just made its money back and a little profit and it received mixed reviews and mixed audience reaction, but the film was the huge hit." Sharing the success of the film was the soundtrack album.

The music of *West Side Story* first began to take shape in the fall of 1955 and was completed by the summer of 1957. The project teamed the relatively young and up-and-coming Sondheim with the veteran composer Leonard Bernstein. "He liked to work together and I liked to work separately," Sondheim says. "When I first came onto the project, he had written the main theme of 'Maria' and 'Cool,' but otherwise we did everything together." During a six-month break in the project, Bernstein went off to work on *Candide.* "A number of songs in *West Side Story* were discards from *Candide,*" says Sondheim. "And, a number of discards from *West Side Story* showed up in the 1956 production of *Candide.*"

Bernstein and Sondheim would usually talk on the phone, write separately for two days, and then meet on the third day. The joint writing sessions were held at Bernstein's residence—the Osborne, at 205 West 57th Street. "He had a 10-room apartment, but the room he chose for his study was the least attractive room. It looked out onto an airshaft. It was about 15 feet square, had minimal lighting, a bar, a piano, a sofa, and bookshelves with a lot of scores. Lenny believed in working in a sort of a monk-like atmosphere without visual and aural distractions."

What Bernstein and Sondheim accomplished in that small room wasn't truly appreciated until the release of the *West Side Story* soundtrack, which included the voices of Marni Nixon as Maria, Jim Bryan as Tony, and Betty Ward as Anita. Russ Tamblyn, who portrayed Riff, was the only lead actor in the film that contributed his own singing to the soundtrack.

In its 28th week on the chart, the *West Side Story* soundtrack album hit the summit of the 150 Best Selling Monaural LP's chart. The same week, the original cast album reached its peak at number five in its 82nd week on the chart. Yet the legacy of *West Side Story* didn't end there. The album spent a total of 54 weeks at the top of one of *Billboard's* album charts (53 weeks on the stereo chart, and 12 on the mono), making it the album with the most weeks at Number One in the rock era.

Although Sondheim doesn't feel that *West Side Story* translated well to the big screen, it did bring the musical to the masses. "What was wonderful about the film was that it introduced the piece to many thousands of people that never had a chance to see the show," he says.

The success of the soundtrack was sweet to Sondheim and Bernstein, whose music initially received a critical beating. "Diana Shore did 'Tonight' and Johnny Mathis did 'Maria,' but up until the release of the film, the score was universally pounced on," Sondheim says. "When the show opened in New York City, they said it's all very exciting, but you can't hum anything. Then the movie came out four years later and suddenly everyone could hum everything."

THE TOP FIVE
Week of May 5, 1962

1. **West Side Story**
   Soundtrack

2. **Blue Hawaii**
   Elvis Presley

3. **College Concert**
   The Kingston Trio

4. **Breakfast at Tiffany's**
   Henry Mancini

5. **Your Twist Party**
   Chubby Checker

ABC-PARAMOUNT 410 # Modern Sounds in Country and Western Music

RAY CHARLES

53

Producer: Sid Feller

Track listing: Bye Bye, Love / You Don't Know Me / Half as Much / I Love You So Much It Hurts / Just a Little Lovin' / Born to Lose / Worried Mind / It Makes No Difference Now / You Win Again / Careless Love / I Can't Stop Loving You / Hey, Good Lookin'

June 23, 1962
14 weeks mono; 1 week stereo

By 1962, Ray Charles was already a 10-year recording veteran who had shown he was adapt at a number of musical styles, from R&B fare, such as his first Number One single, "Georgia on My Mind," to jazz, which he explored on the 1961 album *Genius + Soul = Jazz*. That album, recorded with members of Count Basie's Band, reached number four on the album chart. Yet Charles's musical ambitions stretched far beyond just R&B and jazz. He also loved country music, and planned to make an entire album devoted to the genre. It would be called *Modern Sounds in Country and Western Music.*

"The album was a bit different for me, since it was completely different from rhythm and blues," says Charles. "It was one of the few times when I thought about something I wanted to do and it really worked."

Yet Charles's decision to make a country album caught Sam Clark, the president of ABC-Paramount Records, by surprise. "He didn't fight me on it, but he thought I was making a mistake. He thought I would lose a lot of my fans. He had a legitimate concern, but I felt if I lost any fans I would gain as many as I would lose. He just said, 'It's your

career, so if you want to take a chance, go ahead.' "

Although the record label considered Charles's decision to record a country album a gamble, the singer-pianist didn't think of the project in those terms. "When I do music, I don't think of it as being something risky," he says. "I've always loved country music since I was a child. My mom used to let me stay up late on Saturday nights to listen to the Grand Ole Opry. So, as I musician, I wanted to do a country album, not as a country singer, but do it my way."

The most difficult part of making the album was deciding on material, Charles says. "I had to search through about 150 different tapes looking for songs that would fit me," he says. Charles ended up with a diverse selection of tunes made famous by the likes of Eddy Arnold, Hank Williams, and the Everly Brothers. "When I was choosing the songs, I was not getting into the personalities," says Charles. "I was just trying to choose the songs. I didn't care

who did them, whether it was Hank Williams or George Jones."

Yet Charles didn't just record the songs as straightforward country tracks. Instead, he utilized a string section and a choir. "We had a bunch strings and voices and stuff," says Charles. "So, it was not done like a typical country album. We took country songs and modernized them."

Although it has been reported that Charles didn't want any singles released from the album, he says that was not the case. "I never told ABC how to do marketing," he says. "I always tell record companies, 'Let me do the music and you do the marketing.' " The label did just that, releasing Charles's version of "I Can't Stop Loving You" after actor Tab Hunter began to receive airplay with his cover of the song. Charles's version won out, reaching Number One on the Hot 100 on June 2, 1962. Three weeks later, *Modern Sounds in Country and Western Music* joined the single atop the charts.

THE TOP FIVE
Week of June 23, 1962

1. **Modern Sounds in Country and Western Music**
   Ray Charles

2. **West Side Story**
   Soundtrack

3. **Breakfast at Tiffany's**
   Henry Mancini

4. **Stranger on the Shore**
   Mr. Acker Bilk

5. **Blue Hawaii**
   Elvis Presley

54 Peter, Paul and Mary WARNER BROS. 1449
PETER, PAUL AND MARY

Producer: Albert Grossman

Track listing: Early in the Morning /
500 Miles / Sorrow / This Train /
Bamboo / It's Raining / If I Had My
Way / Cruel War / Lemon Tree / If I
Had a Hammer / Autumn to May /
Where Have All the Flowers Gone

October 20, 1962
7 weeks: 6 weeks mono, 1 week
combined chart

As early as 1958, the Kingston Trio
[see 21] had proven that folk music
could be a chart force. Yet the self-
titled debut by the Greenwich Village,
New York–based trio of Peter Yarrow,
Paul Stookey, and Mary Travers offered
something substantially different than the
Kingstons. "Our voices were not all in
the center," says Peter Yarrow. "Stereo
meant Paul was full left, I was full right,
and Mary was in the center. And the
guitars were separated. It gave people
an absolute intimate sense of what we
were doing. It wasn't a sound. It was
three distinct human beings that were
acoustically completely accessible. It
allowed us to be individuals, rather than
the Kingston Trio."

Peter, Paul and Mary joined forces
in 1961, at the suggestions of manag-
er/producer Albert Grossman. Yarrow
was a solo folk artist who appeared on
the CBS-TV special "Folk Sound U.S.A.,"
Stookey had been in a rock 'n' roll
band in high school and performed
stand-up comedy in Greenwich Village,
while Travers had performed in school

choruses and in The Next President, an
unsuccessful 1957 Broadway musical
with Mort Sahl.

Under Grossman's guidance, the trio
worked with arranger Milt Okun to craft
its sound and cut some demo tapes, but
initially the group generated little interest. "We went to Columbia, and they
said, 'The group can sing very well, but
the material is all wrong.' It was virtually
the repertoire of the first album that we
had sang on a demo, but they didn't
get it. The didn't understand the appeal.
They didn't understand the idiom. They
didn't understand the part that folk
music was inevitably and shortly to play
in the American political, musical, and
cultural landscape," says Yarrow.

Eventually, as Billboard reported in
its February 3, 1962, issue, the trio
found a home at Warner Bros. Their
debut album, Peter, Paul and Mary, was
recorded at Music Makers studio in
New York. It took approximately a
month for the group to complete the 12
tracks. "People were kind of amazed
how much time we took in the studio,"
Yarrow recalls. "Back then, a month
was considered a long time."

The trio opted for a mix of originals,
such as "Early in the Morning," and folk
staples, like Pete Seeger's "If I Had a
Hammer" and "Where Have All the
Flowers Gone."

"If we loved a song, we did it. It did-
n't make a difference if we had written
it or not," says Yarrow. "It was just
about singing something that moved
you. It had nothing to do with trying to
anticipate the public's taste, or trying to

satisfy a publishing company, or a
record company, it was a piece of art,
the people's art."

"Lemon Tree," the first single
released from Peter, Paul and Mary,
stalled at number 35 in June. "If I Had a
Hammer," however, was more successful, eventually reaching number 10. As
"The Hammer Song" climbed the Hot
100, Peter, Paul and Mary nailed down
the top of the 150 Best Selling Monaural LP's chart, temporarily knocking off
West Side Story. It marked the first
music album on Warner Bros. to go to
Number One. However, the album was-
n't truly recognized for its stereo sound
until just over a year later, on October
26, 1963, when it returned to Number
One on the Top LP's chart, which no
longer separated the stereo and monaural versions of albums.

THE TOP FIVE
Week of October 20, 1962

1. **Peter, Paul and Mary**
   Peter, Paul and Mary

2. **West Side Story**
   Soundtrack

3. **Modern Sounds in Country
   & Western Music**
   Ray Charles

4. **The Music Man**
   Soundtrack

5. **Ramblin' Rose**
   Nat King Cole

WARNER BROS. 1475 **My Son, the Folk Singer**

ALLAN SHERMAN

55

Musical Director: Lou Busch

Track listing: The Ballad of Harry Lewis / Shake Hands with Your Uncle Max / Sir Greenbaum's Madrigal / My Zelda / The Streets of Miami / Sarah Jackman (with Christine Nelson) / Jump Down, Spin Around (Pick a Dress o' Cotton) / Seltzer Boy / Oh Boy / Shticks and Stones

December 1, 1962
2 weeks mono

It was at a party that Joe Smith, then the head of promotion and artist & repertoire for Warner Bros. Records, first crossed paths with Allan Sherman. The comedian had served as a producer of *The Steve Allen Show* and helped develop *I've Got A Secret*, but on this night he was displaying another talent. "Allan sat by the piano while someone played Broadway show tunes and he sang great parodies," recalls Smith. So impressed was Smith that he and Sherman began talking about having the comedian record an album called *Gold And Moments on Broadway*.

Although he was better known for his TV endeavors, Sherman began recording song parodies in 1951 for Jubilee Records. It was in 1956 that Sherman recorded a parody of *My Fair Lady* drenched in Jewish humor, yet the publishers of Alan Jay Lerner and Frederick Loewe's music would not give the comedian permission to record their music, so the album was never released.

"We found out very quickly that we could never get permission to do those songs, so we recommended that Allan take a lot of public-domain songs and

do them," says Smith. The result was *My Son, the Folk Singer*. "It was recorded all in one three-hour session after we stopped at the unemployment office, where he picked up a check," says Smith. Approximately 50 of Sherman's show business friends attended the session at Western Studios in Hollywood, hence the liner notation, "Recorded live at a big expensive Hollywood party." Lou Busch played piano and conducted a small band that accompanied Sherman. "We all just cracked up during the session," says Smith, "because Allan had written these lyrics but nobody had heard them before."

Material covered on the album included "The Ballad of Harry Lewis" ("The Battle Hymn of the Republic"), the story of a man who died in a fire at a fabric warehouse set to collect insurance money; "Sarah Jackman" ("Frere Jacques"), a tale of a local yenta; and "Shticks and Stones," a parody that included bits of Harry Belafonte's "Day-O" [see 3] and several other songs.

Testimonials from such top-notch comedic talent as Steve Allen, Jack Benny, Jerry Lewis, and Harpo Marx were featured on the album's back cover, which may have helped the fast-breaking sales.

"When we put it out, it went berserk," says Smith. "I don't think I've been involved with an album by a new artist over all these years that sold so fast and so many records." As a result, *My Son, the Folk Singer* hit the summit in its fifth week on the 150 Best Selling Monaural LP's chart, knocking legitimate folk singers Peter, Paul & Mary from the top position. Ironic, perhaps, but Allan Sherman was likely laughing all the way to the bank.

THE TOP FIVE
Week of December 1, 1962

1. **My Son, the Folk Singer**
   Allan Sherman

2. **Modern Sounds in Country & Western, Vol. 2**
   Ray Charles

3. **Peter, Paul & Mary**
   Peter, Paul & Mary

4. **West Side Story**
   Soundtrack

5. **Jazz Samba**
   Stan Getz / Charlie Byrd

56 The First Family CADENCE 3060
VAUGHN MEADER

Courtesy of PhotoFest

Producer: Robert Mack

Track listing: The Experiment / After Dinner Conversations / The Malayan Ambassador / Relatively Speaking / Astronauts / Motorcade / The Party / The Tour / But Vote!! / Economy Lunch / The Decision / White House Visitor / Press Conference / The Dress / Saturday Night, Sunday Morning / Auld Lang Syne / Bedtime Story

December 15, 1962
12 weeks mono

In early 1962, Vaughn Meader was just another young comedian working the Greenwich Village club scene, at least until his manager suggested he audition for the CBS summer TV series Celebrity Talent Scouts, hosted by Jim Backus. Since Meader wasn't actually discovered by a celebrity, he was billed as "the producer's find." Recalls Meader, "I was doing John F. Kennedy. My impression of Kennedy kind of evolved out of a little political, satirical act I was doing in the Village." With Kennedy's popularity at an all-time high, Meader's impersonation didn't go unnoticed. Earle Doud, a comedy writer for Jack Paar and Johnny Carson, and Bob Booker, a Miami disc jockey, caught Meader's

performance. "They called me up and said it would be a great idea for an album," Meader says.

While Doud and Booker may have been convinced, the record industry wasn't. The pair shopped a demo recording of Meader's Kennedy act to every major label in New York. "A fellow at CBS told Earle Doud that he wouldn't touch it with a 10-foot pole," Meader says. "So for Christmas, Earle sent him a 10-foot pole." New York–based Cadence Records, one of two small labels to express interest in the project, finally agreed to produce the album. The album, featuring Meader as Kennedy, Naomi Brossart making her recording debut as the First Lady, and Doud and Booker as "heads of state and freeloaders and relatives," was recorded at Fine Recording studios in New York City in front of a live audience on October 22, 1962. Ironically, this was the night Kennedy made his famed Cuban Missile Crisis speech. "The audience was in the studio and had no idea of the drama that was taking place," says Meader. "But the cast had heard the speech and our throats almost dropped to our toes, because if the audience had heard the Cuban Missile Speech, we would not have received the reaction we did."

Once the album was completed, Booker used his connections to help gain exposure. "He knew a few airwave personalities," Meader says. "So they sent it over to WINS radio in New York." A disc jockey by the name of Stan C. Burns put it on the air. "It caused so much excitement that the next morning WNEW put it on the air, and so did everyone else."

Meader became an overnight sensation and at the time, The First Family became the fastest-selling album in history. On December 8, 1962, it debuted at number 11. A week later, it shot all the way to the top of the chart, with sales of 1.6 million in two weeks. It sold 3.6 million in a month, 5.5 million in a year, and went on to win a Grammy for Album of the Year.

A sequel, The First Family, Volume Two, reached number four six months later, but Meader's Kennedy impersonations would soon have to end. A Kennedy parody of "The Night Before Christmas" was recorded and set for release as a single when Kennedy was assassinated on November 22, 1963. "It was almost guaranteed to be a million-seller," Meader says of the single. "We printed 100 DJ copies, but then he was assassinated." The record was recalled and The First Family albums were pulled from the shelves. "They dug two graves when they shot the president," fellow comedian Lenny Bruce told Greenwich Village audiences in the days following the tragedy, "one for Kennedy and one for Vaughn Meader." In reality, Meader went on to record other albums, including a 1969 album called The Second Company. It received positive reviews, but failed to chart.

THE TOP FIVE
Week of December 15, 1962

1. **The First Family**
   Vaughn Meader

2. **My Son, the Folk Singer**
   Allan Sherman

3. **Jazz Samba**
   Stan Getz / Charlie Byrd

4. **West Side Story**
   Soundtrack

5. **Modern Sounds in Country & Western Music, Vol. 2**
   Ray Charles

WARNER BROS. 1487 **My Son, the Celebrity** 57
ALLAN SHERMAN

Arranger and conductor: Lou Busch

Track listing: Al 'N Yetta / Barry Is the Baby's Name & Horowitz & Get on the Garden Freeway / Mexican Hat Dance / The Bronx Bird Watcher / The Let's All Call Up AT&T and Protest to the President March / Harvey and Sheila / Won't You Come Home, Disraeli / No One's Perfect / When I Was a Lad / Me / Shticks of One and Half a Dozen of the Other

March 9, 1963
1 week mono

Allan Sherman and Warner Bros. didn't waste much time in capitalizing on the comedian's budding popularity. His second album, *My Son, the Celebrity*, was recorded on November 30, 1962, less than a month after *My Son, the Folk Singer* [see 55] debuted on the charts.

The date also marked Sherman's 38th birthday. Since the session for *My Son, the Folk Singer* had a party-like atmosphere, Sherman opted to record the follow-up live at his birthday party. The liner notes even credited PJ's of Hollywood for providing refreshments for the birthday party recording session.

Initially, Sherman did not want to do a second album, recalls Joe Smith, the head of promotion and A&R for Warner Bros. "He was going to hang us up, so I threatened to give him all of his money at one time, which would have been a terrible tax blow, so he ran and did another album quick," he says.

Despite only months between albums, coming up with new material was no problem for Sherman, says Smith. "He could hear a song and come up with a parody immediately," says Smith, who recalls bringing Sherman to visit future *Hogan's Heroes* star Bob Crane at a Los Angeles radio station. "Crane had a very big morning show at the time and he asked Allan how fast he could come up with a parody. Allan told him he thinks of them when he hears a song. Crane had just played Peggy Lee's 'The Gypsy.' He asked Allan to come up with a parody and he did it on the spot."

For his record, however, Sherman once again parodied songs that were public domain or wrote originals with musical collaborator Lou Busch, because most legitimate songwriters of the day wanted nothing to do with Sherman's parodies and would not give their permission for him to bastardize their work. Some of the distinctively Jewish jokes featured on *Folk Singer* gave way to more mainstream humor on *My Son, the Celebrity*.

The cover once again featured Sherman strumming an acoustic guitar, but this time the comedian was joined by his "genuine" family, including his maid and his pet beagle Jackson B. Sherman. The family members posed wearing various garb, such as a "rented riding habit" and "borrowed mink polo coat."

When *My Son, the Celebrity* hit Number One in its eighth week on the mono chart, *My Son, the Folk Singer* had moved back up to number four. The rise of *My Son, the Celebrity* had to be especially sweet for Sherman, as the album knocked *The First Family* [see 56], by his arch comic rival Vaughn Meader, from the summit. It was Meader's album that had displaced *My Son, the Folk Singer* from the top spot.

Both *Folk Singer* and *The First Family* received Grammy nominations for Album of the Year, the only time two comedy albums have been up for the prize. On May 15, 1963, Meader won the Album of the Year honor. Sherman had already won the battle on the charts.

THE TOP FIVE
Week of March 9, 1963

1. **My Son, the Celebrity**
   Allan Sherman

2. **Songs I Sing on the Jackie Gleason Show**
   Frank Fontaine

3. **The First Family**
   Vaughn Meader

4. **My Son, the Folk Singer**
   Allan Sherman

5. **Moving**
   Peter, Paul & Mary

58 Jazz Samba VERVE 8432
STAN GETZ / CHARLIE BYRD

Charlie Byrd

Producer: Creed Taylor

Track listing: Desafinado / Samba Dees Days / O Pato / Samba Triste / Samba Triste / Samba De Uma Nota So / E Luxo So / Baia

March 9, 1963
1 week stereo

Prior to 1962, tenor saxophonist Stan Getz and guitarist Charlie Byrd had well-respected careers in jazz circles. Getz had played with such jazz luminaries as Stan Kenton, Jimmy Dorsey, Benny Goodman, and Woody Herman before venturing out on his own in the late 1940s, while Byrd studied under the classical guitar master Segovia and played with Woody Herman in 1959. Despite their standing in the jazz world, however, neither Getz nor Byrd had charted a title on the pop album in the rock era. That would change, however, after Byrd returned home from a 1961 South America tour.

"I didn't play with any of the big-name people," says Byrd. "I didn't get to meet any of the composers or prominent stars, but I played with some very good Brazilian musicians who were familiar with these songs," says Byrd. "By the time we got back home, we had included about four or five of these tunes in our repertoire and they were very well received."

In his engagements in the Washington, D.C., clubs, Byrd realized that jazz fans liked the sounds of samba and bossa nova. "I thought maybe I could do a record of that material, but I had no idea it would end up on the pop charts."

When Byrd's acquaintance Getz dropped in to Washington for a club gig, Byrd invited the saxophonist over to his home for lunch. "I played these tapes for him and played some tunes that I knew, and he got very excited," Byrd recalls. "He said, 'Why don't we do it for my label?' I didn't have anything going at the time that was as exciting as doing an album with Stan Getz, so I agreed."

Jazz Samba was recorded in Pierce Hall at All Souls Unitarian Church in Washington, D.C., on February 13, 1962. Getz was on tenor sax, Byrd was on guitar, and they were backed by Byrd's band, consisting of bassist Keter Betts, Byrd's younger brother Gene on bass and guitar, and Buddy Deppenschmidt and Bill Reichenbach on drums. The decision to use two drummers was inspired by the Brazilian jazz combos, Byrd says. Remarkably, Getz did not rehearse with Byrd and his band prior to the recording session. "We just talked about it a little bit in a hotel room and then went and recorded the album," Byrd says.

As for the unusual recording location, Byrd says the room simply had good acoustics. "I recorded with the engineer Ed Green at various places around town, because he didn't like a dull studio sound," Byrd says. In fact, a hall at a Washington Jewish community center was the original location chosen for the sessions. "But there was a bus stop right near it, so we had to move to the other place. There was nothing spiritual in our choice," Byrd quips.

By the time *Jazz Samba* reached the top spot in its 23rd week on the 50 Best Sellers—Stereo chart, the album had inspired a full-blown Latin music craze. Titles such as Joe Harnell and His Piano Orchestra's *Fly Me to the Moon and the Bossa Nova Pops*, Laurindo Almeida and the Bossa Nova All Stars' *Viva Bossa Nova*, and Getz's and Enoch Light and His Orchestra's identically titled *Big Band Bossa Nova* albums were all present on the album chart. *Jazz Samba* also spawned a hit single, as "Desafinado," co-written by Antonio Carlos Jobim, reached number 15.

THE TOP FIVE
Week of March 9, 1963

1. **Jazz Samba**
   Stan Getz / Charlie Byrd

2. **West Side Story**
   Soundtrack

3. **Fly Me to the Moon and the Bossa Nova Pops**
   Joe Harnell and His Piano Orchestra

4. **Moving**
   Peter, Paul and Mary

5. **Moon River and Other Great Movie Themes**
   Andy Williams

Stan Getz

Courtesy of Photofest

ABC-PARAMOUNT 442 **Songs I Sing on the Jackie Gleason Show**

FRANK FONTAINE

59

Producer: Sid Feller

Track listing: When Your Hair Has Turned to Silver / I'm Forever Blowing Bubbles / That Old Gang of Mine / Daddy's Little Girl / If You Were the Only Girl in the World / Mary's a Grand Old Name / (The Gang That Sang) Heart of My Heart / I Wonder Who's Kissing Her Now / Beautiful / If I Had My Way / Always / Easter Parade

March 16, 1963
5 weeks mono

From the early '50s through the '60s, comedian Jackie Gleason was one of the biggest stars on television. His comedy-variety show spawned the enormously popular sitcom *The Honeymooners* and made stars of Art Carney, Buddy Hackett, and Frank Fontaine.

In 1962, Fontaine was cast in the fourth incarnation of Gleason's variety program, *The Jackie Gleason Show: The American Scene*, as Gleason's sidekick. Prior to joining Gleason, Fontaine was already a well-known comedian featured in nightclubs amd films and on TV, and radio, but it was with Gleason that his career thrived.

Fontaine's character "Crazy Guggenheim" was a staple of the show's regular "Joe the Bartender" sketch. One day during rehearsals, Fontaine began to sing an old standard—not in character, but in his own voice. The cast and Gleason were floored by Fontaine's vocal prowess and it was decided that Fontaine should close each episode with his rendition of a different standard. The popularity of

Fontaine's singing led to a contract with ABC-Paramount.

"Jackie broached the idea to ABC," says Sid Feller, who was the director of A&R for ABC. "It sounded like a good idea, so we signed him."

Yet even Feller, who produced the album and arranged several of the songs on the album, was surprised by Fontaine's vocal abilities on the TV show. "He would have this crazy look on his face and would wear this dumb hat and then he would sing and out came this big, booming operatic voice."

Instead of attempting the popular songs of the day, Fontaine stuck mostly to standards, such as Irving Berlin's "Always" and "Easter Parade," for his first album. "We did songs that he knew," says Feller. "It was all old standards from the '20s. He knew these songs as a child." The album, however, did include one original, "Beautiful," which was co-written by Fontaine.

ABC-Paramount operated on a shoestring budget and often cut corners when making orchestral recordings, but for Fontaine's album, says Feller, the company spared no expense. The full orchestra was conducted by Sammy Spear, the musical director of Gleason's show.

Gleason's name wasn't only included in the album's title, he also signed the liner notes, but Feller says the essay was actually written by a label executive, rather than the Great One.

Almost a decade before Fontaine entered the studio to cut his first album, Gleason was a recording star in his own right. *Lonesome Echo*, his 1955 Capitol album that featured instrumental music conducted by Gleason, topped the chart on July 23.

Nearly eight years later, Fontaine joined his boss in the Number One album club, as *Songs I Sing on the Jackie Gleason Show* topped the 150 Best Sellers in its sixth week on the chart.

THE TOP FIVE
Week of March 16, 1963

1. **Songs I Sing on the Jackie Gleason Show**
   Frank Fontaine

2. **My Son, the Celebrity**
   Allan Sherman

3. **Moving**
   Peter, Paul and Mary

4. **The First Family**
   Vaughn Meader

5. **West Side Story**
   Soundtrack

60 Days of Wine and Roses COLUMBIA 8815
ANDY WILLIAMS

Robert Mersey

Track listing: Falling in Love With Love / I Left My Heart in San Francisco / You Are My Sunshine / What Kind of Fool Am I? / When You're Smiling / Days of Wine and Roses / It's a Most Unusual Day / My Coloring Book / Can't Get Used to Losing You / I Really Don't Want to Know / Exactly Like You / May Each Day

May 4, 1963
16 weeks: 11 weeks stereo, 15 weeks mono, 1 week combined chart

In the late '50s, crooner Andy Williams had scored a number of top 10 singles, including the Number One hit "Butterfly," but it wasn't until 1962 that Williams broke into the top 10 of the album chart. That year the singer's *Moon River & Other Great Movie Themes*, which included Williams's take of the Henry Mancini–Johnny Mercer classic, reached number three.

With his star rising, Williams was tapped by NBC for his own musical variety show. During the summer of 1958 and 1959, Williams had hosted one-off TV specials on ABC and CBS, respectively, but this marked the first time he would host a regular-season series.

However, the weekly exposure didn't automatically translate into increased popularity. *Warm and Willing*, Williams's 1962 follow-up to *Moon River* peaked at number 16. Undaunted, Williams opted to record yet another Mancini/Mercer number, "Days of Wine and Roses," which was written for the film of the same name starring Jack

Lemmon and Lee Remick. At the same time, Williams recorded the Doc Pomus–Mort Shuman song, "Can't Get Used to Losing You." Both songs charted, with the later climbing all the way to number two, while "Days of Wine and Roses" made number 26.

With the success of the two-sided single, executives at Columbia persuaded Williams to fill out an album showcasing both hits, along with several of the songs he performed on his TV show. Yet the recordings weren't taken directly from the show itself, despite the fact that Williams regularly sang live, and with a live orchestra, in front of the TV cameras.

"The quality of TV audio at that time wasn't as high as the quality of recordings you could make in a studio," Williams says. "So I had to go into the recording studio and redo them, but we used the same arrangements we used on the show." The recorded version of "You Are My Sunshine," however, was markedly different from the one that

appeared on the album. "On my television show, I did it originally with Peggy Lee and George Gobel," Williams says.

Days of Wine and Roses, which was subtitled *And Other TV Requests*, turned out to be a blockbuster for Williams. "It sold so well because every week I would sing these songs on my show," he says. "The fact that you could see these songs performed live on TV and then go out and buy the album definitely helped sales."

Days of Wine and Roses topped the mono album chart in its third week on the chart. A week later, on May 11, 1963, it rose to the stereo summit and earned its place in history as the last album to top the separate mono and stereo charts. On August 17, *Billboard* combined the stereo and mono lists into one chart, the Top LP's. *Days of Wine and Roses* remained at Number One for one week on the new chart before making way for *Little Stevie Wonder/The 12 Year Old Genius*.

THE TOP FIVE
Week of May 4, 1963

1. **Days of Wine and Roses**
   Andy Williams

2. **West Side Story**
   Soundtrack

3. **Songs I Sing on the Jackie Gleason Show**
   Frank Fontaine

4. **Moving**
   Peter, Paul & Mary

5. **The Kingston Trio #16**
   The Kingston Trio

TAMLA 240 # Little Stevie Wonder/The 12 Year Old Genius

LITTLE STEVIE WONDER

Producer: Berry Gordy

Track listing: Fingertips / Soul Bongo / La La La La La / (I'm Afraid) The Masquerade Is Over / Hallelujah I Love Her So / Drown in My Own Tears

*August 24, 1963
1 week*

When *Little Stevie Wonder/The 12 Year Old Genius* hit the peak in its seventh week on the Top LP's chart, Wonder became the youngest artist ever to score a Number One album and only the second teenager, after Ricky Nelson [see 12], to top the chart. *Little Stevie Wonder/The 12 Year Old Genius* was also the first live album ever to reach Number One.

Some of the album may have been recorded while Wonder was 12, hence its title, but by the time it was released Wonder had celebrated his 13th birthday. And despite his triumph at that tender age, Wonder's success was not immediate. His first album, 1962's *The Jazz Soul of Little Stevie*, and his first three singles had all failed to chart, despite the fact Wonder was backed by ace session players, including Marvin Gaye on piano and drums.

Wonder was signed to the Motown subsidiary Tamla, after his cousin, Ronnie White of the Miracles, convinced a Motown talent scout to give the young musician a listen. It was Motown founder Berry Gordy who decided that Wonder should be recorded live, because despite his lack of chart success, the young musician was knocking out audiences with his live performances on Motown's Motortown Revue showcases.

"It's almost like that was another person," Wonder says of his early success. "But I still remember the shows that we recorded. It was at the Apollo Theatre on a Saturday." He also recorded at the Regal Theatre in Chicago; "Fingertips," which would go on to become Wonder's first charting single, was recorded there.

Motown opted to label Wonder "the 12-year-old genius" in an effort to align him with Ray Charles [see 53], who was also blind and often referred to as a "musical genius." Wonder was flattered but a bit perplexed by the title. "I never thought of myself as a genius," he says. "I couldn't really relate to it. It was a nice compliment, but it wasn't like I was saying, 'Yes, I'm a genius.'"

The top-notch players who accompanied Wonder in the studio and on the road may have helped to keep him humble. "They all used to call me 'hardsocks,'" says Wonder. "I was like their little son or something. When I did a good show, they would say it, but if it was messed up they wouldn't say anything, so I knew that must not have been that good of a show that night."

Although Wonder's sidemen were all seasoned pros, sometimes they had a hard time keeping up with the multi-instrumentalist teen. At one point during "Fingertips," which features Wonder on bongos and harmonica, bassist Larry Moses can be heard frantically shouting, "What key? What key?"

"They probably thought 'Fingertips' was cute," Wonder says of his accompanists. "But they were more into the blues and jazz songs I would do. They used to like when I sang 'Masquerade Is Over.' They could better relate to that kind of song, because most of them were jazz musicians."

Wonder's young age also perplexed some of those who attended his performances. "I remember once I was playing the Apollo and I met this lady from England who said, 'Isn't it strange for a young lad to sing love songs to adults?' I just said, 'I don't know. It's fine to me.'"

It was also fine to the American public. On August 10, 1963, an edited version of the opening track, titled "Fingertips (Pt. II)," hit Number One on the singles chart. Two weeks later, *Stevie Wonder/The 12 Year Old Genius* joined it at the top, marking the beginning of a long career of chart dominance.

THE TOP FIVE
Week of August 24, 1963

1. **Little Stevie Wonder/ The 12 Year Old Genius**
   Little Stevie Wonder

2. **Trini Lopez at PJ's**
   Trini Lopez

3. **Days of Wine and Roses**
   Andy Williams

4. **Moving**
   Peter, Paul & Mary

5. **My Son, the Nut**
   Allan Sherman

62 My Son, the Nut WARNER BROS. 1501
ALLAN SHERMAN

Producer: Jimmy Hilliard

Track listing: You Went the Wrong Way, Old King Louie / Automation / I See Bones / Hungarian Goulash No. 5 / Headaches / Here's to the Crabgrass / Hello Muddah, Hello Fadduh! / One Hippopotami / Ratfink / You're Getting to be a Rabbit With Me / Eight Foot Two, Solid Blue / Hail to Thee, Fat Person

*August 31, 1963
8 weeks*

By the middle of 1963, Allan Sherman's star had risen to the point that he no longer had to turn exclusively to public domain songs for his parodies. For his third album, *My Son, the Nut*, Sherman covered songs by contemporary songwriters, but of course they were all given the unique Sherman twist. "You Came a Long Way from St. Louis," by Jim Benson Brooks and Bob Russell, became "You Went the Wrong Way, Old King Louie"; "C'est Si Bon," by Jerry Seelen, Henri Betti, and Johnny Desmond, was turned into "I See Bones"; and "Rag Mop," by Johnnie Lee Wells and Deacon Anderson, was transformed into "Rat Fink." Says Joe Smith, Warner Bros. head of A&R and promotion, "We had to be very careful to get permission, because once Allan did his parody, it could possibly ruin the copyright of a song forever."

For "Hello Muddah, Hello Fadduh!," the song that would become Sherman's first hit single, the comedian turned to another public domain piece, Ponchielli's "Dance of the Hours." Smith still recalls when he first heard of the song.

THE TOP FIVE
Week of August 31, 1963

1. **My Son, the Nut**
   Allan Sherman

2. **Trini Lopez at PJ's**
   Trini Lopez

3. **Little Stevie Wonder/ The 12 Year Old Genius**
   Little Stevie Wonder

4. **Moving**
   Peter, Paul and Mary

5. **Days of Wine and Roses**
   Andy Williams

"Allan was in New York doing *The Tonight Show* and he called me and woke me up at 2 A.M. to sing me 'Hello Muddah, Hello Fadduh!,' " says Smith. "My wife was real pissed off at the time, because her father was in the hospital and she thought something had happened to him."

Musically, *My Son, the Nut* marked a change for Sherman and his arranger and conductor Lou Busch. As the album cover noted, "Allan Sherman sings nutty things, this time with strings." Horns and other instrumentation were also featured on the album.

On the cover, Sherman was photographed literally up to his neck in 700 pounds of extra fancy mixed nuts, courtesy of the Los Angeles Nut House.

Thanks in part to the success of "Hello Muddah, Hello Fadduh!," *My Son, the Nut* became the fastest-climbing chart-topper of Sherman's career, reaching the summit in a mere three weeks. Its eight-week stay at the top also bested Sherman's previous efforts.

"Hello Muddah, Hello Fadduh!," however, didn't make it to the top of the Hot 100. It spent three weeks at number two, but was unable to unseat such stiff competition as Little Stevie Wonder's "Fingertips (Pt. II)" [see 61] and the Angels' "My Boyfriend's Back."

While *My Son, the Nut* marked Sherman's greatest commercial triumph, it was his third and final chart-topper before a dramatic slide in popularity. Sherman's next four albums failed to crack the top 20. The comedian died of respiratory illness at the age of 49 on November 20, 1973, as he was putting the final touches on an album for Warner Bros.

"Allan was a one-of-a-kind character and a very bright man," says Smith. "If he was still alive and took 10 songs and went in and did parodies, he'd be as popular today as he was back then."

Producer: Albert Grossman

Track listing: Very Last Day / Hush-A-Bye / Long Chain On / Rocky Road / Tell It on the Mountain / Polly Von / Stewball / All My Trials / Don't Think Twice, It's All Right / Freight Train / Quit You Low Down Ways / Blowin' in the Wind

November 2, 1963
5 weeks

Peter, Paul and Mary was important for introducing the American public to the new breed of folk music. However, the trio's third album, *In the Wind*, was even more significant. It featured three songs written by a young, up-and-coming singer-songwriter named Bob Dylan.

Like Peter, Paul and Mary, Dylan was part of the New York folk scene, and he also shared manager Albert Grossman with the trio. Yet in 1962, the same year *Peter, Paul and Mary* went to Number One, his self-titled debut album failed to chart. On September 7, 1963, Dylan made his album chart debut when *The Freewheelin' Bob Dylan* entered at number 125. Less than two months earlier, on October 26, 1963, *In the Wind* had debuted at number 12 on the Top LP's chart. Both albums contained versions of "Blowin' in the Wind."

Says Peter Yarrow, "Bob Dylan was in Greenwich Village when we were,

writing songs at places like the Kettle of Fish and the White Horse. He was a friend. When we heard the songs, it was immediate. We knew they were something we wanted to sing."

However, Peter, Paul and Mary didn't fully realize how important Dylan would become. "When you're living it, you don't look at tomorrow that way," Yarrow says. "We sensed that something exciting was going on, but when you fall in love you don't think about how long it's going to last, you just love every moment. By that same sense, we knew that Bobby Dylan was just about the best writer we had ever heard of that genre."

"Blowin' in the Wind" was just one of three Dylan songs that appeared on the album. Dylan's original of "Don't Think Twice, It's All Right" was also included on *The Freewheelin' Bob Dylan*, but his rendition of "Quit Your Low Down Ways" would not be legitimately released until 1991, when it was included on *The Bootleg Series—Volumes 1–3 (Rare & Unreleased) 1961–1991* boxed set.

Peter, Paul and Mary's versions of "Blowin' in the Wind" and "Don't Think Twice, It's All Right" were released well in advance of *In the Wind*. The former, released as the follow-up to "Puff the Magic Dragon," became the trio's second consecutive single to reach number two, while the latter reached number nine. The success of the two singles, as well as the trio's previous recordings,

were enough to blow *In the Wind* to the top spot in its second week on the chart. Ironically, the album it bumped from the summit was *Peter, Paul and Mary*, which had returned to Number One a year after originally reaching that lofty perch.

Dylan, however, would have to be patient. Despite the exposure he gained from Peter, Paul and Mary's hit cover of "Blowin' in the Wind," not to mention the notoriety he generated from his own work throughout the balance of the 1960s, he would not top the album chart until more than a decade later, with *Blood on the Tracks* [see 170].

THE TOP FIVE
Week of November 2, 1963

1. **In the Wind**
   Peter, Paul and Mary

2. **Peter, Paul and Mary**
   Peter, Paul and Mary

3. **Ingredients in a Recipe for Soul**
   Ray Charles

4. **Elvis' Golden Records, Vol. 3**
   Elvis Presley

5. **The Second Barbra Streisand Album**
   Barbra Streisand

64 The Singing Nun PHILIPS 203
THE SINGING NUN

Producer: None listed

Track listing: Dominique / Soeur Adele / Fleur de Cactus / Complainte Por Marie-Jacques / Je Voudrias / Tous Les Chemins / Plume de Radis / Mets Ton Joli Jupon / Resurrection / Alleluia / J'ai Trouve Le Seineur / Entre Les Etoiles

December 7, 1963
10 weeks

Debbie Reynolds in The Singing Nun.

The Singing Nun was one of the most unlikely pop stars ever to top the album chart. Jeanine Deckers, who was known as Sister Luc-Gabrielle at the Fichermont Monastery, frequently entertained her cohorts at the convent with her songs played on guitar. She called the instrument, which she purchased at a music shop in Brussels before joining the missionary of the Dominican order, Adele.

Her songs were such a hit with the young girls that visited Fichermont that they asked Sister Luc-Gabrielle, whose uplifting demeanor had earned her the nickname "Soeur Sourire" (Sister Smile), if she had a recording that they could acquire. No such recording was available, but Sister Luc-Gabrielle found the idea of recording intriguing.

Initially, Philips politely turned down Sister Luc-Gabrielle's request to use its studios to make a non-commercial recording; it was just before the Christmas season and the studios were too busy. However, Sister Luc-Gabrielle's second request was granted. Once the executives at Philips heard Sister Luc-Gabielle, backed by a chorus of four other nuns and her guitar, Adele, they asked her if the recording could be

released commercially. The album was initially released in Europe under the name Soeur Sourire.

It was that recording that came to the attention of Mercury Records, the Chicago-based label that oversaw Philips. Mercury A&R executive Lou Reizner was the man who suggested the company bring the music of Sister Luc-Gabrielle to America. "Lou was assigned to look through foreign releases, especially those coming out of our sister companies," says Irwin H. Steinberg, who was executive vice president of Mercury Records at the time. "Actually, it wasn't a big record in Belgium, but he listened to it and thought it was unique."

It was Reizner who suggested that "Dominique," a tribute to the founder of the Dominican order, should be released as a single. A disc jockey in Boston jumped on the song and its popularity soon spread. Mercury wanted to release the album in America, but was faced with one minor problem: The European version only had 10 tracks on it. The top brass felt that two additional songs were needed to complete the album for U.S. release. "We went back to Philips in Belgium and told them that

we needed two more songs," says Steinberg. The Singing Nun agreed to the request and recorded two additional tunes.

Once completed, the album was included in "Philips Connoisseur Collection" and packaged in an elaborate gatefold sleeve with a lyric book and a portfolio of watercolor sketches of convent life painted by Sister Luc-Gabrielle. Both the album and the single were surprise hits, as Sister Luc-Gabrielle, better known as the Singing Nun, became the first artist ever to top both charts simultaneously. With the album still at the top of the charts, Sister Luc-Gabrielle appeared, from the convent, on "The Ed Sullivan Show" on January 5, 1964.

Yet Luc-Gabrielle's success was short-lived. A follow-up album, Her Joy, Her Songs "failed miserably," Steinberg says, stalling at number 90 in 1964. Two years later, Debbie Reynolds starred in a biopic about the Singing Nun, but it was too late to resuscitate Luc-Gabrielle's recording career.

Luc-Gabrielle subsequently left the convent and became a missionary. On March 25, 1985, at the age of 52, she committed suicide, leaving a note complaining about tax problems.

THE TOP FIVE
Week of December 7, 1963

1. **The Singing Nun**
   The Singing Nun

2. **In the Wind**
   Peter, Paul & Mary

3. **The Second Barbra Streisand Album**
   Barbra Streisand

4. **Peter, Paul & Mary**
   Peter, Paul & Mary

5. **Trini Lopez at PJ's**
   Trini Lopez

CAPITOL 2047 **Meet the Beatles!**
THE BEATLES

65

Producer: George Martin

Track listing: I Want to Hold Your Hand / I Saw Her Standing There / This Boy / It Won't Be Long / All I've Got to Do / All My Loving / Don't Bother Me / Little Child / Till There Was You / Hold Me Tight / I Wanna Be Your Man / Not a Second Time

February 15, 1964
11 weeks

Beatlemania may have seemingly happened overnight, but before the frenzy hit there was a time when the Beatles couldn't even get a record released in America, despite the fact that the group was a hit in England.

By 1964, the Beatles were already veterans, having gone through several names and lineups. The band's history dates back to the summer of 1957, when John Lennon invited Paul McCartney to join his skiffle group the Quarry Men. In 1958, the group's name was changed to Johnny and the Moondogs, and George Harrison was enlisted. A year later, the group was known as the Silver Beatles. Stuart Sutcliffe, who Lennon knew from art school, became the band's bass player. Pete Best rounded out the group of drums. After settling on simply "the Beatles," the band honed its chops at club engagements in Hamburg, Germany, and its home base of Liverpool. By 1961, Sutcliffe had left the band to focus on his art career, leaving the bass duties for McCartney. (A year later, Sutcliffe died of a brain hemorrhage.)

At the Cavern Club in Liverpool in late 1961, Brian Epstein discovered the band. By 1962, he signed on as the group's manager and began shopping around for a record deal. "When Brian

Epstein came around, he pulled a few strings and caught the ears of some of the people at EMI with his marvelous new group, but I wasn't consulted," says George Martin, then an executive at EMI's Parlophone label. "I wasn't important."

The second time around, however, Martin was in the loop. "At the time I finally met them, in the spring of 1962, I was unaware that literally every record company, including my own, had turned Brian and the Beatles down," he says.

Martin, however, was impressed. "The Beatles then were just very young guys. They were desperate for someone to recognize their talent. Of course, they ignored their lack of success, because they had enormous faith in their own ability," he says. "I was hungry for new blood and I was able to identify the potential greatness when I saw it."

By the summer of 1962, the band was signed by Parlophone and Ringo Starr was recruited to replace Pete Best, who was asked to leave the group. In October 1962, the Beatles scored their first top 20 British hit with "Love Me Do," and in early 1963 they had a number two hit with "Please Please Me." A third single, "From Me to You," brought them to Number One in the U.K. In the midst of all this, they spent one day—February 11, 1963—to record their first album.

The album, Please Please Me, was released a month later and became a hit in Britain, but Capitol, EMI's American label, still wasn't interested. Instead, Please Please Me was licensed to the independent Vee-Jay label, retitled Introducing the Beatles, and released in July 1963. Initially, it failed to crack the album chart.

Finally, Capitol had a change of heart when the label was presented with

"I Want to Hold Your Hand," in late 1963. On December 26, the single was released in the United States.

Capitol released the group's second album, Meet the Beatles!, on January 20, 1964. The record's cover photo was identical to the one used on the group's second U.K. album, With the Beatles, but the track listing was substantially different. Capitol opted to eliminate all the cover versions featured on the U.K. album, save for "Till There Was You," which was familiar to American listeners from its original appearance in The Music Man [see 14]. The label also added the Beatles' "I Want to Hold Your Hand" (which would soon be the group's first American Number One single), "I Saw Her Standing There," and "This Boy."

Although Martin and the Beatles weren't too fond of Capitol's cut-and-paste approach [see 66], the American public didn't mind. Meet the Beatles! hit the summit in its second week on the Top LP's chart. Beatlemania had hit America at last.

THE TOP FIVE
Week of February 15, 1964

1. **Meet the Beatles!**
   The Beatles

2. **The Singing Nun**
   The Singing Nun

3. **In the Wind**
   Peter, Paul & Mary

4. **Little Deuce Coupe**
   The Beach Boys

5. **West Side Story**
   Soundtrack

66 The Beatles' Second Album CAPITOL 2080
THE BEATLES

Producer: George Martin

Track listing: Roll Over Beethoven / Thank You Girl / You Really Got a Hold on Me / Devil in Her Heart / Money (That's What I Want) / You Can't Do That / Long Tall Sally / I Call Your Name / Please Mister Postman / I'll Get You / She Loves You

May 4, 1964
5 weeks

Despite its title, *The Beatles' Second Album* wasn't actually the Fab Four's second American LP. Just as Capitol had taken the liberty to proclaim, "The First Album by England's Phenomenal Pop Combo" on the cover of *Meet the Beatles!* (which was in fact the group's second American album), the label once again attempted a bit of revisionist history with the title of the group's second Capitol Records album.

The Beatles' Second Album was actually the group's fifth American album chart entry. With the success of the Number One single "I Want to Hold Your Hand" and *Meet the Beatles!*, *Introducing...The Beatles*, the Beatles' first American album, finally began to climb the chart. That album, which was licensed to the independent Vee-Jay label, was released in July 1963 and again in January 1964. Before Capitol could rush-release *The Beatles' Second Album*, two other Beatles-related LPs appeared on the chart: early recordings of the band on an MGM album called *The Beatles with Tony Sheridan and Their Guests* and a Vee-Jay compilation album titled *Jolly What! The Beatles & Frank Ifield*. Both of those albums, however, failed to make much of an impact.

The MGM title peaked at number 68, while *Jolly What!* stalled at number 104.

The Beatles' Second Album was another story. With Beatlemania in full effect, the album debuted at number 16 on the Top LP's chart on April 27, 1964. *Meet the Beatles!* was at Number One for the 11th straight week at the time, while *Introducing...the Beatles* was in the number two position. The following week, *The Beatles' Second Album* rocketed to the summit, pushing *Meet the Beatles!* down to the number two position, while *Introducing* fell to number four.

When *The Beatles' Second Album* finished its five-week run at Number One, the Fab Four had racked up a total of 16 consecutive weeks at the top with their first two Capitol albums, the longest run by one act since Andy Williams's *The Days of Wine and Roses* [see 60].

Like *Meet the Beatles!*, *The Beatles' Second Album* was comprised of a hodgepodge of material culled from the group's British albums and singles. "We always objected terribly to what the

Americans did to our recordings, but I had no say in it," says George Martin, the group's producer. "They just did what they wanted to do."

Capitol had chosen to delete five cover versions from the Beatles' second British album, *With the Beatles*, when the label issued it in the U.S. as *Meet the Beatles!* Those songs—"Roll Over Beethoven," "Please Mister Postman," "You Really Got a Hold on Me," "Money," and "Devil in Her Heart"— surfaced on *The Beatles' Second Album*. Also included was the group's second Number One single, "She Loves You," which topped the Hot 100 on March 21, 1964, and its B-side "I'll Get You." Two other B-sides, "You Can't Do That" and "Thank You Girl," were also featured.

Yet *The Beatles' Second Album* did have something special for American fans. It contained the premiere of two new recordings, the Beatles' cover of Little Richard's "Long Tall Sally" and a new John Lennon/Paul McCartney original, "I Call Your Name." Those tracks didn't make their debut in the U.K. until June 19, on the *Long Tall Sally* EP.

THE TOP FIVE
Week of May 4, 1964

1. **The Beatles' Second Album**
   The Beatles

2. **Meet the Beatles**
   The Beatles

3. **Hello Dolly!**
   Original Cast

4. **Introducing...the Beatles**
   The Beatles

5. **Honey in the Horn**
   Al Hirt

RCA VICTOR 1087

Hello, Dolly!

ORIGINAL BROADWAY CAST

67

Producer: Andy Wiswell

Track listing: Prologue / I Put My Hand In / It Takes a Woman / Put on Your Sunday Clothes / Ribbons Down My Back / Motherhood / Dancing / Before the Parade Passes By / Elegance / Hello, Dolly! / It Only Takes a Moment / So Long Dearie / Finale

June 6, 1964
1 week

It's doubtful that anyone would have thought that the first wave of Beatlemania would be temporarily interrupted by a phenomenon inspired by Thornton Wilder's story of a widowed matchmaker secretly looking for love herself. Yet that was the case, thanks to the incredible success of Hello, Dolly!.

The musical, based on Wilder's story The Matchmaker, with music and lyrics by Jerry Herman, opened on Broadway on January 16, 1964, two weeks before the Beatles would score their first Number One single with "I Want to Hold Your Hand." The play's leading lady was Carol Channing, a veteran of the stage whose 1950 performance in Gentleman Prefer Blondes had landed

her on the cover of Time magazine. Channing knew from her first meetings with Herman that Hello, Dolly! would be special. "He had a little apartment down on East 10th Street off of Fifth Avenue," she recalls. "It was like a monastery. It was all white stucco. It had nothing in it but a bed, a piano, and a kitchen table. It looked like good work was done there, like those monks that saved literature in the Dark Ages. I was there every day and he taught me the score and it grew right there in that little monastery."

According to Channing, Herman had some very particular plans for the title song. "He specifically said that he wanted that song to sound very, very relaxed and Mother Earth, but then Phil Lang [who handled the orchestrations] said, 'But my flutes don't go down that far.' And Jerry said, 'Forget your flutes. I want this quality.' " Sure enough it was that earthy quality and the incredible success of the play on Broadway that would catapult Hello, Dolly! to the top of the charts.

In fact, Channing says RCA Victor jumped at the chance of releasing the Original Broadway Cast recording soon after the play opened in New York.

"The reviews were sensational and the lines at the box office went on all day and all night. RCA Victor wanted the album right away," she recalls. With the company performing eight shows a week, the album had to be recorded on Sunday, on their only day off. Channing remembers the sessions at Webster Hall in New York City: "I was doing the actual gestures that went along with all the songs and the producer came rushing in and said, 'Carol, you don't need to do those gestures and the acting. All you have to do is sing it.' But the gestures are what made it happen. When I acted, it was like a real performance, rather than just singing. I couldn't do it any other way."

With the musical a smash, Hello, Dolly! entered the chart on February 22, 1962. Sixteen weeks later, it dislodged The Beatles' Second Album and ended the Fab Four's 16-week run at Number One on the album chart. Channing and the cast of Hello, Dolly!, however, had little chance to enjoy their accomplishment. "When you're in a hit show, you are busy thinking about the next audience," she says. "All right, so we outdid the Beatles, we didn't have the time to think about it."

Carol Channing in Hello, Dolly!

THE TOP FIVE
Week of June 6, 1964

1. **Hello, Dolly!**
   Original Cast

2. **Funny Girl**
   Original Cast

3. **Hello, Dolly!**
   Louis Armstrong

4. **The Beatles' Second Album**
   The Beatles

5. **Call Me Irresponsible and Other Hit Songs**
   Andy Williams

68 Hello, Dolly! KAPP 1364
LOUIS ARMSTRONG

Producer: Michael Kapp

Track listing: Hello, Dolly! / It's Been a Long, Long Time / A Lot of Livin' to Do / A Kiss to Build a Dream On / Someday / Hey, Look Me Over / I Still Get Jealous / Moon River / Be My Life's Companion / Blueberry Hill / You Are Woman, I Am Man / Jeepers Creepers

June 13, 1964
6 weeks

A month before the original cast album of *Hello, Dolly!* ended the Beatles' two-album, 16-week run on top of the album chart, Louis Armstrong's interpretation of "Hello, Dolly!" broke the Fab Four's 14-week run at the top on the Hot 100 single chart. For Armstrong it was a long-overdue triumph that made it possible to record what would be his first charting album in nearly a decade.

Although there is some debate over his birthday (Armstrong liked to claim he was born on July 4, 1900, but a birth certificate unearthed after his death revealed he was actually born on August 4, 1901), few could debate the fact that Louis "Satchmo" Armstrong was one of the most important figures in jazz, pop, and a significant influence on rock 'n' roll. Even in his recording debut in April of 1923 as a sideman for the King Oliver band, Armstrong blew his way into the spotlight, playing the cornet with a force and clarity few could match.

According to producer Michael Kapp, Armstrong got the green light to record *Hello, Dolly!* after the success of

his single of the same name. Says Kapp, "We had to record it in Las Vegas between Louis's dates at the Riviera." Although Armstrong was a living legend when the album was recorded, Kapp says "he was a pussycat to work with." Armstrong was still a masterful musician at the time of the recording, but Kapp says his age was starting to catch up with him. "He needed eight bars between singing the chorus to get the instrument back up to his lips, but he could still play like no one else," he recalls.

While Armstrong's "Hello, Dolly!" single proved to be the hit version, hitting Number One on the Hot 100, the Original Cast album topped the album chart first, only to be knocked out by Armstrong's album of the same name. Of course Armstrong's version of "Hello, Dolly!" was decidedly different from Carol Channing's take. His famed gruff voice accompanied by banjo and brass

made Jerry Herman's tune swing like it had never swung before. Armstrong even named-dropped himself into the opening lines of the song for good measure.

Hello, Dolly! wasn't the only Broadway show Armstrong mined. The album also includes jazzy takes of "A Lot of Livin' to Do" from *Bye Bye Birdie*, "Hey, Look Me Over" from *Wildcat*, "I Still Get Jealous" from *High Button Shoes*, and even the Henry Mancini–Johnny Mercer classic "Moon River" from the film soundtrack to *Breakfast at Tiffany's* [see 51].

While Armstrong had enjoyed chart success during his lengthy career with such albums as *Satch Plays Fats*, his tribute to Fats Waller, which climbed to number 10 in 1955, and *Ella and Louis*, featuring Ella Fitzgerald, which peaked at number 12 in 1956, *Hello, Dolly!* marked a career high point. He died seven years later on July 6, 1971, but his music still lives today.

THE TOP FIVE
Week of June 13, 1964

1. **Hello, Dolly!**
   Louis Armstrong

2. **Funny Girl**
   Original Cast

3. **Hello, Dolly!**
   Original Cast

4. **The Beatles' Second Album**
   The Beatles

5. **Call Me Irresponsible and Other Hit Songs**
   Andy Williams

Producer: George Martin

Track listing: A Hard Day's Night (vocal) / Tell Me Why (vocal) / I Cry Instead (vocal) / I Should Have Known Better (instrumental) / I'm Happy Just to Dance with You (vocal) / And I Love Her (instrumental) / I Should Have Known Better (vocal) / If I Feel (vocal) / And I Love Her (vocal) / Ringo's Theme (This Boy) / Can't Buy Me Love (vocal) / A Hard Day's Night (instrumental)

July 25, 1964
14 weeks

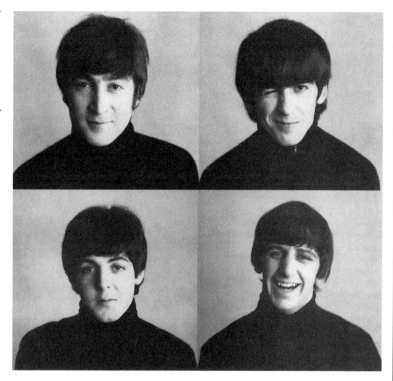

On June 26, 1964 the soundtrack to *A Hard Day's Night* was released. On July 6, the film made its debut at the London Pavilion to rave reviews. Less than three weeks later, the Fab Four had their third Number One album. Even more impressive was the fact it was the third time the group had hit the summit in less than six months.

The title of the Beatles' first foray on to the silver screen was inspired by an expression used by drummer Ringo Starr. "It was typical of Ringo," says producer George Martin. "He was inclined to come up with all sorts of odd ways of putting things. He said, 'God, it's been a hard day's night' when he finished one particular take and was feeling a bit tired. Everyone thought it was a great title. It was just something he said out of the blue and that became the title of the film."

"When the title was decided, John [Lennon] went away and wrote a tune," Martin adds. "The main characteristic of that track, of course, is that it starts off on that clangy guitar chord, which was devised in order to make an impact on

the picture. It was actually written with the idea of it being the opening track of the picture."

A Hard Day's Night, the movie, written by Alun Owen and directed by Richard Lester, was a fictional tale of two days in the life of the group, but it was inspired by the band's real-life rise to superstardom. The Beatles' newfound fame meant that they were often isolated from the public, while being whisked from train to car to hotel room to the stage. *A Hard Day's Night* captured the frenzy, with an ample supply of humor and zaniness.

A Hard Day's Night, the album, was recorded during March and April of 1964. The film's title track, featuring Lennon's double-tracked lead vocal and Paul McCartney on harmony, was cut on April 16. The album was a milestone in the evolution of the Beatles, since it marked the first time an album by the group consisted solely of Lennon and McCartney compositions, even if the American edition of the album was filled out by Martin's instrumental versions of four of their songs. The songs on the second side of the British release later turned up in America on *Something New* and *Beatles '65* [see 73].

While the title track was written

specifically for the film, Martin says most of the others already existed, although legend has it that Lennon and McCartney worked at a feverish pace to write the material for the film. "There may have been other songs which we recorded for the picture, which they happened to have up their sleeves," he says. " 'If I Fell' was one of those, but mostly they were already recorded."

In fact, "Can't Buy Me Love" spent five weeks at Number One more than two months before the soundtrack was released. Martin was a bit concerned about the music being overexposed. "I had to argue with Lester so that he didn't use the music too much. I was a bit worried, because he used 'Can't Buy Me Love' in two different sequences."

In its second week on the chart, *A Hard Day's Night* hit the top of the album chart. A week later, the title track became the group's third straight Number One single, with the album still firmly entrenched in the top position. *A Hard Day's Night* held at Number One until Halloween. All together, the Fab Four spent a total of 30 weeks on top of the album chart in 1964—the most weeks at the top for an artist in a single year since Harry Belafonte racked up a total of 37 weeks at Number One in 1956 [see 3].

THE TOP FIVE
Week of July 25, 1964

1. **A Hard Day's Night**
   The Beatles

2. **Hello, Dolly!**
   Original Cast

3. **Hello, Dolly!**
   Louis Armstrong

4. **Funny Girl**
   Original Cast

5. **Stan Getz & Jose Gilberto**
   Getz/Gilberto

70 People COLUMBIA 9015
BARBRA STREISAND

Producer: Robert Mersey

Track listing: Absent Minded Me / When in Rome (I Do as the Romans Do) / Fine and Dandy / Supper Time / Will He Like Me / How Does the Wine Taste? / I'm All Smiles / Autumn / My Lord and Master / Love Is a Bore / Don't Like Goodbyes / People

October 31, 1964
5 weeks

It's only appropriate that Barbra Streisand became a pop music super-star thanks to her role in the Broadway musical *Funny Girl*, since it was largely because of her performance in such musicals as *I Can Get It for You Wholesale* and *Pins and Needles* that Streisand landed a recording contract with Columbia in 1962.

Despite failing to yield a hit single, *The Barbra Streisand Album*, the singer's 1963 debut album, established Streisand as a hit recording artist, as it reached number eight. *The Second Barbra Streisand Album*, also released in 1963, fared even better, peaking at number two. *The Third Album*, which peaked at number five, was one of three hit albums featuring Streisand that were released in 1964.

Streisand was cast as Fanny Brice in the Broadway musical *Funny Girl* in 1963. The original cast recording, which reached number two, was released by Capitol in the spring of 1964. It was Columbia, however, that issued Streisand's rendition of "People," the Bob Merrill–Jule Styne tune from the musical, as a single. It became Streisand's first hit, reaching number five.

THE TOP FIVE
Week of October 31, 1964

1. **People**
   Barbra Streisand

2. **Everybody Loves Somebody**
   Dean Martin

3. **A Hard Day's Night**
   The Beatles

4. **Something New**
   The Beatles

5. **How Glad I Am**
   Nancy Wilson

In order to capitalize on the success of *Funny Girl* and "People," Columbia assembled an album around the hit single. On the album, Streisand was accompanied by pianist Peter Daniels. Peter Matz, who worked on Streisand's first two albums, handled the arranging on conducting on six of the songs, with Ray Ellis, who worked on *The Third Album*, arranging and conducting the other five.

"We did the single first," Matz says. "Barbra was rehearsing *Funny Girl* when we did 'People' and we had to do it rather quickly, because they wanted to get the song out before the show went on the road. To this date, there remains a wrong note on the French horn part, but we didn't have time to fix it."

For other material, Streisand turned to another Merrill-Styne composition, "Absent Minded Me," along with "I'm All Smiles," from the Broadway musical *The Yearling*, and Rodgers and Hammerstein's "My Lord and Master."

As stipulated in her contract with Columbia, Streisand choose her own material. "She was extremely creative," says Matz. "She had a lot of input about the shape of the songs."

Her voice was also in top form at the time. "She was singing with a lot more passion then," says Matz. "She wasn't so concerned about perfection. She was into more of an emotional performance."

Thanks largely to the success of the single, *People* rose to the top in its fifth week on the chart, knocking the Beatles' *A Hard Day's Night* from Number One. It would be the first of several times that Streisand would reach the summit.

CAPITOL 2198 **Beach Boys Concert** **71**
BEACH BOYS

Producer: Brian Wilson

Track listing: Fun, Fun, Fun / The Little Old Lady from Pasadena / Little Deuce Coupe / Long, Tall Texan / In My Room / Monster Mash / Let's Go Trippin' / Papa-Oom-Mow-Mow / The Wanderer / Hawaii / Graduation Day / I Get Around / Johnny B. Goode

December 5, 1964
4 weeks

With the success of such chart-topping albums as *Meet the Beatles!* [see 65], *The Beatles' Second Album* [see 66], and *A Hard Day's Night* [see 69], Beatlemania swept America. The group's first performances were greeted with near-riotous responses from screaming, adoring fans. But such fervor wasn't limited to the Fab Four. America—or, more specifically, Hawthorne, California—had its own rising stars in the Beach Boys. As *Beach Boys Concert* proved, the surf group's fans thought the Beach Boys were every bit as exciting as the Beatles.

Recorded on August 1, 1964, at the Civic Auditorium in Sacramento, California, *Beach Boys Concert* is as much a recording of the young band in concert as it is a testimonial of the enthused response it generated from its fans. Although Sacramento isn't known for its beaches, the city was a top market for the Beach Boys. "We would play there three times a year," says singer Mike Love. "They even had parades in the town for us, because the Beach Boys were so incredibly hot there. That's why we recorded our first live album in that city."

Proof positive of the group's popularity in Sacramento was the crowd response on *Beach Boys Concert.* "There was this Beatlemania-like wall of screams," says Love. "The album kind of encapsulates the whole mood and feeling." Adds Brian Wilson, "Those girls in the audience were, like, out of their heads. They totally lost it. I got hit right above the eye with a [makeup] compact. We had to tell them to please stop throwing things."

The crowd's response made it difficult for the Beach Boys to perform. "It was tough to even hear what we were singing," he says. It also made it necessary for the band to enter the studio to add overdubs to what was billed on the cover as "the Beach Boys' first 'live' album." Love says, "Otherwise it would be a record with just screams, so we had to fix it up."

Although the album features live versions of five originals written or co-written by Beach Boys mastermind Brian Wilson, including the group's first Number One single, "I Get Around," the majority of *Beach Boys Concert* is comprised of cover versions of some of the group's favorite songs of the day. "In the very early days of the Beach Boys, like the Stones and the Beatles, we had a very limited amount of original songs, so by necessity we did a lot of covers of songs we really liked so we could do an entire show," Love says.

The material covered on *Beach Boys Concert* ranged from Bobby "Borris" Pickett & the Crypt-Kicker's Number One novelty hit "Monster Mash" and Murry Kellum's country-flavored "Long, Tall Texan" to the Dick Dale instrumental "Let's Go Trippin'." Yet the most telling songs covered on *Concert* were Chuck Berry's "Johnny B. Goode" and the Four Freshmen's "Graduation Day." Both acts were a major influence on the Beach Boys.

While Berry's music had a major impact on the group (indeed, it was the inspiration for the Beach Boys' second hit single, "Surfin' U.S.A." [see 182]), Love says the Four Freshmen served as the musical blueprint for the Beach Boys famed vocal arrangements. "That was who Brian studied to learn about four-part harmonies," says Love. "There is quite an art to singing like that."

THE TOP FIVE
Week of December 5, 1964

1. **Beach Boys Concert**
   The Beach Boys
2. **People**
   Barbra Streisand
3. **Everybody Loves Somebody**
   Dean Martin
4. **A Hard Day's Night**
   The Beatles
5. **Roustabout**
   Elvis Presley

72 Roustabout RCA 2999
ELVIS PRESLEY

Musical director: Joseph Lilley

Track listing: Roustabout / Little Egypt / Poison Ivy League / Hard Knocks / It's a Wonderful World / Big Love Big Heartache / One Track Heart / It's Carnival Time / Carny Town / There's a Brand New Day on the Horizon / Wheels on My Heels

January 2, 1965
1 week

With *Roustabout*, Elvis Presley's first Number One album since *Something for Everybody* [see 46], the King proved that he could compete with such new pop forces as the Beatles, the Rolling Stones, and the Beach Boys on the sales charts. Yet while those acts had yet to lay down their most impressive and influential recordings, by the mid-'60s it was clearly apparent that Elvis was past his prime artistically and that his days as a serious chart-topping force were winding down.

Roustabout, Elvis's ninth full-length film soundtrack, was what guitarist Scotty Moore terms a "rubber stamp" effort. Following the success of films and albums like *G.I. Blues* [see 38] and *Blue Hawaii* [see 49], Elvis continued to make albums and films that followed the mold. Aesthetically, the films and the albums were nothing to rave about, but Elvis's legion of fans ate them up, so he continued to crank out the films and soundtrack albums at the rate of two or three a year.

Between *Blue Hawaii* and *Roustabout*, Presley hit the top 10 of the album chart with four soundtracks: *Girls! Girls! Girls* in 1962, *It Happened at the World's Fair* and *Fun in Acapulco* in

1963, and *Kissin' Cousins* in 1964. Only the latter, which stalled at number six, failed to make the top five.

Roustabout was recorded at sessions held February 24–28 and March 2–6, 1964, at Radio Recorders in Hollywood. Elvis's frequent collaborators, guitarist Scotty Moore, drummer D.J. Fontana, pianist Floyd Cramer, and backing vocalists the Jordanaires, were once again joined by an army of session players, including guitarists Tiny Timbrell and Billy Strange, bassists Bob Moore and Ray Siegel, pianist Dudley Brooks, and drummers Buddy Harman, Bernie Mattinson, and Hal Blaine.

As Blaine recalls, the sessions were usually relatively relaxed with Elvis in a playful mood, despite the fact that he wasn't thrilled by the material. Blaine says that songwriters were frequently invited into the studio while Elvis gave their material a go. "They would just be beaming because Elvis was going to sing their song," Blaine says. "But sometimes, maybe halfway into a tune, he would say, 'I don't think I like this song,' and walk away from the mic. Then you would just see this songwriter, or song-

writing team, melt. It was really kind of sad." Presley's dissatisfaction with the material was also apparent in the finished takes. On the CD version of *Roustabout*, Elvis can be heard breaking into mock blues singing, "We gotta end" at the close of "Carny Town."

The influence of Elvis was quite apparent on his entourage, Blaine says. "Elvis was quite heavily into karate at the time and sometimes he would walk across the room and do a karate kick and let out a scream," Blaine says. Eventually, others in Elvis's camp caught the karate bug. "All of a sudden, every one would be into karate and there would be these karate fights in the studio," Blaine says. "Everyone became a karate expert."

The film *Roustabout*, which featured the big-screen debut of a young Raquel Welch, opened on November 11, 1964. Nearly two months later, the album became Elvis's fourth and final Number One soundtrack album during its eighth week on the chart. It was also his final chart-topping album of the '60s. Fittingly, it was knocked from the summit by *Beatles '65*.

THE TOP FIVE
Week of January 2, 1965

1. **Roustabout**
   Elvis Presley

2. **The Beach Boys Concert**
   The Beach Boys

3. **12 x 5**
   The Rolling Stones

4. **Mary Poppins**
   Soundtrack

5. **Where Did Our Love Go**
   The Supremes

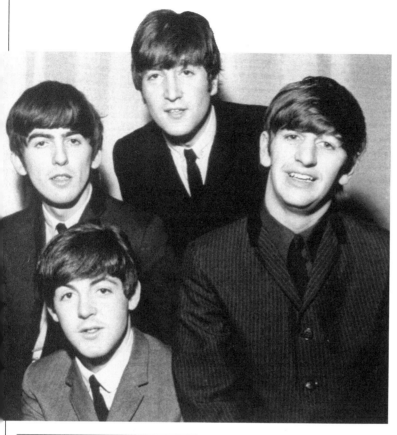

title.' And then we kind of forgot about it. But then we kept seeing the American albums were different. We were trying to be generous by putting 14 tracks on an album, and then we would do singles and extended plays. Those tracks would never be on the album [in the U.K.]. That was like cheating. But in America, people would have a hit single and then make an album of rubbish with just the single on it. Nobody actually told us for ages that in America they would only pay you royalties on 10 tracks. So Capitol would take 10 tracks, keep four tracks, and stick them on a new album with another cover with some singles. We weren't happy about that at all."

While the Beatles may not have been pleased with *Beatles '65*, the album did contain some significant moments, aside from the usual assortment of rip-roaring rock 'n' roll cover versions. "I Feel Fine" opens with a bit of guitar feedback from John Lennon, which is believed to be the first recording of feedback on a pop record. Elsewhere, on songs such as "I'm a Loser," Bob Dylan's influence on Lennon is apparent.

Beatles '65 is also significant for another reason. It became the first Beatles album to knock an Elvis Presley title from the top of the album chart. It was a symbolic event that effectively, albeit belatedly, captured the shift of popularity from the King to the Fab Four. Yet it had to be a bittersweet achievement for the Beatles. "They were very big fans of Elvis," says producer George Martin. "But they weren't very big fans of Elvis's films, and neither was I. Elvis's films were dreadful. Most of the songs that were in them were pretty awful too."

Producer: George Martin

Track listing: No Reply / I'm a Loser / Rock and Roll Music / I'll Follow the Sun / Mr. Moonlight / Honey Don't / I'll Be Back / She's a Woman / I Feel Fine / Everybody's Trying to Be My Baby

January 9, 1965
9 weeks

The Beatles were an incredible success in Great Britain, but they were even more successful in America. And it wasn't just because America had a larger population—it also had a greater number of Beatles albums. With *Beatles '65*, Capitol Records continued the tradition it started with *Meet the Beatles* [see 65]: Instead of issuing the Fab Four's albums as they were released in the U.K., Capitol Records would retitle the albums, resequence the tracks, add British hit singles, and delete other songs so they could be saved for another album.

Something New, the 1964 American album release following *A Hard Day's Night*, for example, included five songs from the British version of *A Hard*

Day's Night. However, it was unable to match the success of that album [see 69]. *Something New* spent nine weeks at number two, but it never made it to the top.

The Beatles returned to the top of the album chart with *Beatles '65*, which featured eight tracks from the British album *Beatles for Sale* and various other odds and gems. "I'll Be Back" was another leftover from the British version of *A Hard Day's Night*, while "I Feel Fine" and "She's a Woman," only available as a single in the U.K., also became a double-sided hit in America. On December 26, 1964, "I Feel Fine" became the Beatles' sixth Number One single, while "She's a Woman" peaked at number four.

For the Beatles, Capitol's reconfigurations of their British albums became a growing annoyance. "In '64, when we first came to America, we noticed that *With the Beatles* was called *Meet the Beatles*," says George Harrison. "If you compared the English copy with the American copy, you could see that it wasn't as good of a cover, but so much was going on, we really didn't get annoyed over that. We just thought, 'Oh that's funny. Look, they changed the

THE TOP FIVE
Week of Janaury 9, 1965

1. **Beatles '65**
   The Beatles

2. **Roustabout**
   Elvis Presley

3. **Mary Poppins**
   Soundtrack

4. **Where Did Our Love Go**
   The Supremes

5. **The Beach Boys Concert**
   The Beach Boys

74 Mary Poppins BUENA VISTA 4026
ORIGINAL MOTION PICTURE SOUNDTRACK

Arranged and conducted by Irwin Kostel

Track listing: Overture / Sister Suffragette / The Life I Lead / The Perfect Nanny / A Spoonful of Sugar / Pavement Artist (Chim Chim Cher-ee) / Jolly Holiday / Supercalifragilistic- expialidocious / Stay Awake / I Love to Laugh / A British Bank (The Life I Lead) / Feed the Birds (Tuppence a Bag) / Fidelity Fiduciary Bank / Chim Chim Cher-ee / Step in Time / A Man Has Dreams (The Life I Lead) (A Spoonful of Sugar) / Let's Go Fly a Kite

March 13, 1965
14 weeks (nonconsecutive)

In 1960, songwriting siblings Richard M. and Robert B. Sherman were working on several different projects for Walt Disney, including *Mary Poppins*, based on a series of short stories written by P.L. Travers.

Disney had stumbled upon the stories one evening back in 1939, when he came home to find his daughter laughing aloud as she read Travers's tales of an English nanny. Although he had tried unsuccessfully to obtain motion picture rights to the stories for nearly two decades, Disney nonetheless put his staff to work on the project, confident that he could eventually sway Travers.

"We were doing five pictures at the same time in different stages of development," recalls Robert Sherman. Among the other projects the Shermans were working on as they composed what would be the greatest work of their career were *Summer Magic, Bon Voyage,* and *In Search of the Castaways.*

From left: Richard Sherman, Julie Andrews, Dick Van Dyke, and Robert Sherman.

What made the task even more difficult was the fact that each project had a distinctive ethnic flavor and time period. "We had to constantly shift gears," Richard explains, "from doing a Mexican type of tune for the *Zorro* television series to *Escapade in Florence.*"

Despite the multiplicity of projects, *Mary Poppins* remained special from the start. Travers finally agreed to sell Disney the film rights in 1962, after reading screenwriter Don DaGradi's story outline and hearing a few of the Shermans' tunes.

"We knew from the very beginning it was going to make a great musical," remembers Robert. "Walt did too," Richard adds. The Sherman brothers actually worked with DaGradi and co-writer Bill Walsh on the screenplay, although they are only credited for the lyrics and music. "We couldn't have written ten songs unless we knew where we were going with them," Robert explains. Richard concurs: "We had to have a reason for telling the audience about this magical word, 'Supercalifragilisticexpialidocious,' or for the wonderful things about being a chimney sweep or about Mary Poppins's formula for having a good attitude, 'A Spoonful of Sugar.'"

The brothers drew on their on experiences for some of the most memorable cuts. "Supercalifragilisticexpialidocious" was a word the brothers and their friends made up at summer camp. "Let's Go Fly a Kite" was also inspired by their childhood, specifically by trips to the park with their father. Another classic, "A Spoonful of Sugar," was inspired by Robert's son Jeff, who upon returning home from school one day told his father how he'd had the Salk vaccine administered.

The latter song came after Julie Andrews, who made her screen debut in *Mary Poppins,* rejected a ballad called "The Eyes of Love," which to this day has only been released as a demo version on the CD reissue of the soundtrack. Although 17 songs appear on the album, the Shermans wrote 35 tunes for *Mary Poppins,* some of which later turned up in different incarnations, including "Trust in Me" from *The Jungle Book* and "The Beautiful Briny" from *Bedknobs and Broomsticks.*

Aside from topping the album chart, *Mary Poppins* also picked up several awards. The soundtrack won Grammys for Best Original Score (over the Beatles' *A Hard Day's Night*) and Best Original Recording for Children, as well as Academy Awards for Best Original Music Score and Best Song, for "Chim Chim Cher-ee."

THE TOP FIVE
Week of March 13, 1965

1. **Mary Poppins**
   Soundtrack

2. **Goldfinger**
   Soundtrack

3. **Beatles '65**
   Beatles

4. **You've Lost That Lovin' Feelin'**
   Righteous Brothers

5. **My Fair Lady**
   Soundtrack

Composer: John Barry

Track listing: Main Title — Goldfinger [Shirley Bassey] / Into Miami / Alpine Drive — Auric's Factory / Oddjob's Pressing Engagement / Bond Back in Action Again / Teasing the Korean / Gassing the Gangsters / Goldfinger (Instrumental Version) / Dawn Raid on Fort Knox / The Arrival of the Bomb and Count Down / The Death of Goldfinger — End Titles

March 20, 1965
3 weeks

No other film series has captured the public's imagination more than the ongoing adventures of a secret agent named Bond—James Bond. And no other movie theme music is as recognizable as the "James Bond Theme." While James Bond film soundtracks would later feature hits from such artists as Paul McCartney & Wings [see 221], Carly Simon, and Duran Duran, the music from Bond films wasn't initially a hit with the public, at least until *Goldfinger.*

Dr. No, the soundtrack from the first Bond film featuring the "James Bond Theme," stalled at number 82 in 1963. The album from the next installment, 1964's *From Russia with Love,* made it to number 27. With the next film and soundtrack album, all of the elements would fall into place.

"It was the first time I was allowed to do the theme song and the entire score," says composer/conductor John Barry. "That was very important to me, so I could integrate the theme with the score." Monty Norman was credited with composing the score and theme for *Dr. No.* For *From Russia with Love,*

Lionel Bart was credited with the theme, while Barry composed the score.

After completing the score for "Goldfinger," Barry turned to singer/actor Anthony Newley for lyrics, unaware that Newley usually composed music, while his songwriting partner Leslie Bricusse wrote the lyrics. Together, Newley and Bricusse were interested in the project, but one question remained. "Anthony wanted to know what the hell 'Goldfinger' was. So I told him, 'It's very simple, it's like "Mack the Knife." It's a song about a villain.' "

Although Newley recorded a demo version of the song, it would remain unreleased until 1992, when it was featured on *The Best of James Bond.* "It was never intended for use in the movie," Barry says. "We wanted someone with real conviction that could sing the song," Barry says. "Shirley Bassey had the conviction."

Goldfinger, like most of Bond material, was recorded at the Cine-Tele Studios in London in approximately four days. Bassey's vocal was cut in one night. "It was like an old converted church hall," Barry says. "It wasn't a tight room, it had a terrific resonance, which made

the whole Bond thing work. The brass shots would go on forever, but it wasn't a good room for rhythm sections."

Despite its later success, the "Goldfinger" theme almost didn't make it in the film or on vinyl. "When Harry Saltzman, who was one of the producers, finally heard it, he thought it was the worst thing he had ever heard in his life," Barry says. "It wasn't going to be in the picture, but we were pressed for time. The director Guy Hamilton said, 'I don't know about the hit parade, but I do know in terms of the mood at the beginning of the picture with the title, I think it's outstanding.' "

In the film, Sean Connery as James Bond can be heard making a wisecrack about the Beatles, which makes it all the more ironic that the early Bond albums suffered the same fate as the early Fab Four releases. Because of the cost of music publishing in the U.S., four tracks, including "Pussy Galore's Flying Circus," were omitted from the U.S. release, yet even that couldn't stop *Goldfinger* from hitting the summit. Says Barry, "From every point of view stylistically, *Goldfinger* is my favorite. That was like the blueprint."

Sean Connery and Honor Blackman in *Goldfinger.*

THE TOP FIVE
Week of March 20, 1965

1. **Goldfinger**
   Soundtrack

2. **Mary Poppins**
   Soundtrack

3. **Beatles '65**
   The Beatles

4. **You've Lost that Loving Feeling**
   Righteous Brothers

5. **Where Did Our Love Go**
   The Supremes

76 Beatles VI CAPITOL 2358
THE BEATLES

Producer: George Martin

Track listing: Kansas City/Hey-Hey-Hey-Hey! / Eight Days a Week / You Like Me Too Much / Bad Boy / I Don't Want to Spoil the Party / Words of Love / What You're Doing / Yes It Is / Dizzy Miss Lizzy / Tell Me What You See / Every Little Thing

July 10, 1965
Six weeks

With the title of *Beatles VI*, Capitol Records once again tried to rewrite history, just as the label attempted to do with the title *The Beatles' Second Album* [see 66]. *Beatles VI* was actually the Beatles' eighth full American album. It was, however, the band's sixth album on Capitol Records (if you don't count *The Beatles' Story*, a late-1964 documentary double album, which included highlights from their songs and interview segments).

Beatles VI was comprised of the remaining six tracks from the British *Beatles for Sale* album (the others had been used on *Beatles' '65*), three songs from the forthcoming British version of *Help!*, and "Bad Boy" and "Yes It Is."

As was the case with the Beatles' other early albums, several of the selections on *Beatles VI*, such as "Kansas City/Hey-Hey-Hey-Hey!," "Bad Boy,"

"Words of Love," and "Dizzy Miss Lizzy," were cover versions of early rock 'n' roll songs that were staples in the band's live shows. These tracks were usually recorded in one or two takes, with producer George Martin occasionally overdubbing a bit of piano. George Harrison says the question of who would sing lead on the cover versions was usually decided by "who had the biggest ego and who shouted the loudest. John [Lennon] was the main man, really. He was the one that started the group. From his point of view, Paul [McCartney] joined his band and then I joined his band. After a point, it became our band, but John was the oldest and he was probably the best vocalist as well. There weren't really any rules. It was just the way things evolved naturally."

Also included on *Beatles VI* is "You Like Me Too Much," one of Harrison's first Beatles' compositions. "It's one of those very early songs that I wrote when I didn't know what I was doing," he admits. "I didn't know how to write songs and I didn't have anyone to help me write them. It's a little naive song that I don't feel particularly attached to."

The Lennon-McCartney composition "Eight Days a Week" became the Beatles' seventh Number One single on March 13, 1965, but it wasn't included on an album until the release of *Beatles*

VI. The song, the first to feature a fade-in, was initially considered as a title track for *Help!*.

The Beatles also employed novel tricks in the studio on a number of other tracks. On the cover of Buddy Holly's "Words of Love," Ringo Starr plays a packing case instead of his drum kit. On "Every Little Thing," Starr plays tympani.

Beatles VI became the Fab Four's fifth Number One album and second chart-topper of 1965 when it jumped from number 48 to the peak in its third week on the chart. The Beatles could do no wrong.

THE TOP FIVE
Week of July 10, 1965

1. **Beatles VI**
   The Beatles

2. **Herman's Hermits on Tour**
   Herman's Hermits

3. **Mary Poppins**
   Soundtrack

4. **My Name Is Barbra**
   Barbra Streisand

5. **The Sound of Music**
   Soundtrack

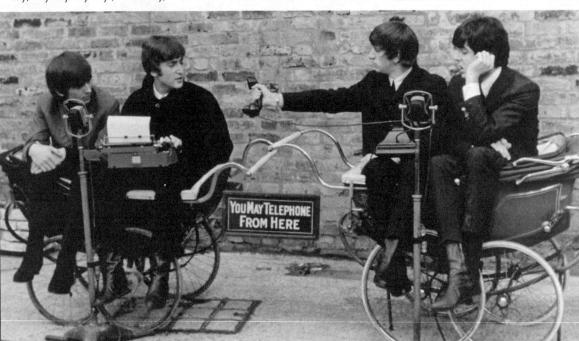

Out of Our Heads
THE ROLLING STONES

77

Producer: Andrew Loog Oldham

Track listing: Mercy Mercy / Hitch Hike / The Last Time / That's How Strong My Love Is / Good Times / I'm All Right / Satisfaction / Cry to Me / The Under Assistant West Coast Promotion Man / Play with Fire / The Spider and the Fly / One More Try

August 21, 1965
3 weeks

It was only fitting that the Rolling Stones scored their first Number One by knocking the Beatles from the summit, since the bands were arch rivals, frequently battling it out on the charts and in debates among music enthusiasts.

The Stones' first three American albums fared well. In late 1964, *England's Newest Hit Makers/The Rolling Stones* reached number 11, while *12 x 5* climbed to number three. In the spring of 1965, *The Rolling Stones, Now!* peaked at number five. Yet the Stones wouldn't truly break through in America until the release of "(I Can't Get No) Satisfaction" and *Out of Our Heads.*

The group's fourth American album marked a few firsts. It was the first to be issued in the U.S. before the U.K. and the band's first album recorded in stereo. The landmark single "Satisfaction" was also released first in America. "It was only because we were actually in America touring," says Stones manager/producer Andrew Loog Oldham. "Once you have a record like 'Satisfaction,' you just want to get it out."

Much has been written about singer

Mick Jagger and guitarist Keith Richards's initial distaste for the song. "I don't think they should be criticized for not being able to see the woods through the trees for a couple of days," Oldham says. "We were making albums in about 10 days. Each song would get 20 to 25 minutes and then it was on to the next one."

The Stones recorded the first take of "Satisfaction" and four other songs for *Out of Our Heads* on May 10, 1965, at the historic Chess studios in Chicago. "It was uptempo, but a more acoustic version," Oldham says. The following day, the final, electric version was cut at RCA Studios in Hollywood. While the Stones may have been turned off by the fact that "Satisfaction" was, in Oldham's words, "so fucking simple," he saw the appeal of the song. "I said, 'This is the National Anthem.' Let's put it out."

Although Oldham's own liner notes boast that *Out of Our Heads* was recorded in London, Chicago, and Hollywood, he admits that he was it stretching a bit. " 'I'm All Right' was recorded live, but it wasn't in London," he says. "It was either in Liverpool or Manchester." Yet Jagger did overdub some of his vocals in a London studio, he says.

The bulk of *Out of Our Heads* was recorded in Los Angles. The Stones covered material recorded by Marvin

Gaye, Sam Cooke, and Solomon Burke, but Jagger and Richards also showed off their budding songwriting talents. The original "The Under Assistant West Coast Promotion Man," credited to fictitious Nanker Phelge, was inspired by a London Records employee. "In England promotion men never left their office, but this guy actually toured with us," Oldham says.

The track "Play with Fire" featured a notable guest. After mixing "The Last Time" during a break in touring, Oldham called producer Phil Spector to the studio for his opinion. "Everyone was very tired," Oldham says. Drummer Charlie Watts, bassist Bill Wyman, and guitarist Brian Jones couldn't stay awake. "But we needed a B-side. So we recorded 'Play with Fire' at 8 A.M. with some portly gentleman cleaning the studio. It was Mick singing, Keith playing acoustic, [Spector's assistant] Jack Nitzsche on harpsichord, and Phil Spector on bass."

On July 10, 1965, "Satisfaction" hit Number One on the Hot 100. Six weeks later *Out of Our Heads* topped the album chart, while the Stones were packing them in on tour. "It was a triple-header—the single, the album, and the tour," Oldham says. "It was the beginning of the period where we were on a roll and no one could stop us."

THE TOP FIVE
Week of August 21, 1965

1. **Out of Our Heads**
   The Rolling Stones

2. **Beatles VI**
   The Beatles

3. **Summer Days (and Summer Nights)**
   The Beach Boys

4. **Herman's Hermits on Tour**
   Herman's Hermits

5. **The Sound of Music**
   Soundtrack

78

Help! CAPITOL 2386
THE BEATLES

Producer: *George Martin*

Track listing: Help! / The Night Before / You've Got to Hide Your Love Away / I Need You / Another Girl / You're Gonna Lose That Girl / Ticket to Ride / The Bitter End / Another Hard Day's Night / The Chase / From Me to You Fantasy / In the Tyrol

September 11, 1965
9 weeks

Just over a year after the Beatles first soundtrack, *A Hard Day's Night* [see 69], hit Number One on the Top LP's chart, the Fab Four was back on top with its second soundtrack, *Help!*

Like *A Hard Day's Night*, *Help!* was directed by Richard Lester. This time Lester chose to film in color at exotic locations, such as the Bahamas, Austria, and the Salisbury Plain in England, as well as on a London soundstage. The soundtrack was similar to *A Hard Day's Night* in that the American version of *Help!* contained Beatles songs used in the film along with score music. The Beatles songs included on Side 2 of the British version of the album turned up on American releases of *Beatles VI* [see 76] and *Rubber Soul* [see 81].

Although longtime Beatles producer George Martin had proven quite adept at scoring with *A Hard Day's Night*, he wasn't used on *Help!* "I had nothing to do with the score," Martin says. "Although the music for the first film was an enormous success, Dick Lester and I didn't get on too well. When it came to the second film, I recorded all the tracks with the Beatles, but that was the end of it. Lester engaged Ken Thorne to do the score and he put the album together in a way I didn't like without my supervision."

The Beatles' tracks on the album were recorded between February and April of 1965. "Ticket to Ride," one of the first tracks recorded for the soundtrack, was released as a single well in advance of the film. *Eight Arms to Hold You*, the original title of the Beatles' second film, was listed in fine print under the Lennon-McCartney writing credit on the single. On May 22, 1965, "Ticket to Ride" became the Beatles' eighth Number One single.

Martin suggests that the song that would later become the title track to the film was written well in advance of the film. "I think ["Help!"] came before the film and they took the title from that," he says. "It didn't matter what they called the film. It could have been anything."

Yet "Help!," with its urgency, was a fitting title track. John Lennon claimed years later that the song was more than just another gem of a song—he was, in fact, crying out for help. "To me it was just a pop song," Martin says. "I didn't see any great significance in it."

Whether "Help!" was really Lennon's personal plea, just another great pop song, or both, it struck a chord with the public. On September 4, 1965, it became the Beatles' ninth Number One single. A week later, with the single still holding fast at the top of the Hot 100, *Help!* hit the summit of the Top LP's chart, rocketing all the way from number 61. It was the group's sixth Number One album in a mere two years.

THE TOP FIVE
Week of September 11, 1965

1. **Help!**
   The Beatles

2. **Look at Us**
   Sonny & Cher

3. **Out of Our Heads**
   The Rolling Stones

4. **The Sound of Music**
   Soundtrack

5. **Summer Days (And Summer Nights)**
   The Beach Boys

RCA 2005 ## The Sound of Music
SOUNDTRACK

79

Julie Andrews in
The Sound of Music.

In early 1964, production on the soundtrack began at 20th Century Fox. Andrews had seen the musical on Broadway, so she was well aware of Mary Martin's performance. However, she never listened to the original cast recording prior to recording the soundtrack. "I didn't consciously try to be different," Andrews says. "I just tried to serve the music and the lyrics as best as I could."

Recording the songs before the actual scenes for the film were shot was a challenge for Andrews. "The things I most remember were the difficulties of trying to convey the correct emotions about mountains, sounds of the countryside, and the joy of what one sees without actually having seen them first," she says.

Yet even before the songs were recorded, the scenes had been painstakingly planned out. "The locales in the musical numbers had been well researched before we recorded the songs," Andrews says. "For example, we knew how many steps we had to climb, or that we would be running along a covered arbor, or dancing around a fountain."

One of Andrews's favorite songs from the soundtrack is the shortest track on the album. "I have always been very fond of 'Edelweiss,' even though I barely sang it in the film," she says.

The soundtrack version of the *The Sound of Music* hit the summit in its 35th week on the chart. Although it only stayed at Number One for two weeks, it went on to become one of the best-selling and most-loved soundtracks of all time, with a total of 233 weeks on the chart.

Producer: Neely Plumb

Track listing: Prelude and the Sound of Music [Maria] / Overture and Preludium (Dixit Dominus) [Orchestra and Nuns Chorus] / Morning Hymn and Alleluia [Nuns Chorus] / Maria [Nuns Chorus] / I Have Confidence [Maria] / Sixteen Going on Seventeen [Rolf and Liesl] / My Favorite Things [Maria] / Do-Re-Mi [Maria and the Children] / The Sound of Music [The Children and the Captain] / The Lonely Goatherd [Maria and the Children] / So Long, Farewell [The Children] / Climb Ev'ry Mountain [Mother Abbess] / Something Good [Maria and the Captain] / Processional and Maria [Organ, Orchestra, and Nuns Chorus] / Edelweiss [The Captain, Maria, the Children, and Chorus] / Climb Ev'ry Mountain (Reprise) [Chorus and Orchestra]

November 13, 1965
2 weeks

More than five years after the original cast recording of *The Sound of Music* [see 31] topped the album chart, the soundtrack from the film version of the classic tale hit the chart.

The Sound of Music wasn't composer Richard Rodgers and Lyricist Oscar Hammerstein II's first chart-topping effort. The team had first hit the summit with the soundtrack to the *The King and I* [see 4] in 1956. That was followed by *South Pacific* in 1958 [see 15] and the original cast album to *Flower Drum Song* a year later.

It also was not the first time Julie Andrews, who replaced Mary Martin in the lead role as Maria in the film version of *The Sound of Music*, had topped the chart. Andrews's vocals were a key element in the Number One original cast albums to *My Fair Lady* [see 2], *Camelot* [see 43], and the soundtrack to *Mary Poppins* [see 74].

Also involved in the soundtrack were director Robert Wise, orchestrator Irwin Kostal, and musical supervisor–associate producer Saul Chaplin, all of whom worked on *West Side Story* [see 52]. Another player involved was screenwriter Ernest Lehman, who spearheaded the plan to bring *The Sound of Music* to the big screen, having proven successful with *The King and I.*

Yet Lehman just didn't want to duplicate the stage version of the musical. He eliminated the songs "No Way to Stop It" and "How Can Love Survive?," moved "My Favorite Things" and "Do-Re-Mi" to other scenes, and replaced the ballad "An Ordinary Couple" with a Rodgers song called "Something Good."

THE TOP FIVE
Week of November 13, 1965

1. **The Sound of Music**
   Soundtrack

2. **Help!**
   The Beatles

3. **The In Crowd**
   Ramsey Lewis Trio

4. **Whipped Cream & Other Delights**
   Herb Alpert & the Tijuana Brass

5. **Highway 61 Revisited**
   Bob Dylan

80 Whipped Cream & Other Delights A&M 110
HERB ALPERT'S TIJUANA BRASS

Producers: Herb Alpert & Jerry Moss

Track listing: A Taste of Honey / Green Peppers / Tangerine / Bittersweet Samba / Lemon Tree / Whipped Cream / Love Potion No. 9 / El Garbanzo / Ladyfingers / Butterball / Peanuts / Lollipops and Roses

November 27, 1965
8 weeks, nonconsecutive

Herb Alpert and Jerry Moss were the "A" & "M," respectively, in A&M Records. The duo scored their first success with "The Lonely Bull," which Alpert, a trumpet player, recorded for a mere $65 in October 1962 under the name of the Tijuana Brass. When the single reached number six and went on to sell more than 700,000, it established both Alpert and A&M as substantial forces in the music industry.

The success of the single inspired Alpert to record a full album, also titled *The Lonely Bull*. It reached number 24. The follow-up, 1963's *Herb Alpert's Tijuana Brass, Volume 2*, eventually reached number 17, while his third long-player, 1965's *South of the Border*, climbed to number six.

With his fourth album, *Whipped Cream & Other Delights*, Alpert and A&M hit the big time. Ironically, it wasn't only the music that gave the album its notoriety. The cover featured model Dolores Erickson, who was three months pregnant at the time, seductively posed wearing a blanket of shaving cream. At first A&M art director Peter Whorf attempted the shot with real whipped cream, but it attracted flies and melted with the heat of the lighting.

THE TOP FIVE
Week of November 27, 1965

1. **Whipped Cream & Other Delights**
   Herb Alpert's Tijuana Brass

2. **My Name Is Barbra, Two...**
   Barbra Streisand

3. **The Sound of Music**
   Soundtrack

4. **Help!**
   Soundtrack

5. **The In Crowd**
   Ramsey Lewis

"More people come up to me and say, 'That *Whipped Cream* album is really something,' " says Alpert. " 'The music is okay, but that cover!' I don't think people bought it for the cover, but it was certainly memorable."

Whipped Cream & Other Delights, much like *The Lonely Bull*, was inspired by a single. Alpert's "Whipped Cream," a catchy instrumental featuring his trademark combination of mariachi music, pop, and jazz, only reached number 68 on the Hot 100, but its success was big enough to give Moss an idea. "My partner got the idea to incorporate a bunch of food titles and sandwich it, if you will, into an album," says Alpert.

At the time, Alpert admits, his career was in "little more than a holding pattern," since he had been unable to duplicate the success of his first single. "Things started to pick up again with *South of the Border* when the Clark Teabury gum company used 'The Mexican Shuffle' in an ad. 'Whipped Cream' came along and made a little noise, but nothing too exciting happened until the *Whipped Cream* album came out and 'A Taste of Honey'

exploded," says Alpert. "That was probably the pivotal song in my career."

Alpert would often spontaneously arrange his material in the studio. "But for 'A Taste of Honey,' I had the idea for the arrangement before I went into the studio, except for that bass drum that stops and starts in the middle. That was a device we used to let the musicians know where the bridge ended and the third verse started. We were originally going to take it out, but the more I heard it on the reference tapes, the more I began to feel it belonged in the arrangement. That bass drum kind of became synonymous with that sound."

By November 1965, "A Taste of Honey" became Alpert's first top 10 single in three years, eventually peaking at number seven. The single went on to take Grammy awards for record of the year, best instrumental performance (non-jazz), best instrumental arrangement, and best-engineered record of 1965. "A Taste of Honey" and *Whipped Cream & Other Delights'* provocative cover were enough to give Herb Alpert and A&M Records its first Number One album.

CAPITOL 2442 # Rubber Soul
THE BEATLES

81

Producer: George Martin

Track listing: I've Just Seen a Face / Norwegian Wood (This Bird Has Flown) / You Won't See Me / Think for Yourself / The Word / Michelle / It's Only Love / Girl / I'm Looking Through You / In My Life / Wait / Run for Your Life

January 8, 1966
6 weeks

On *Rubber Soul* the Beatles were reaching new levels of songwriting expertise, both musically and lyrically. This was evident even in the album's reconfigured American version, released just four months after *Help!* [see 78].

As per Capitol's usual overhaul, four tracks from the British version of *Rubber Soul* were deleted from the American album, while "I've Just Seen a Face" and "It's Only Love," from the British version of *Help!*, opened each side of the American *Rubber Soul*.

The album includes several standouts, including "Michelle," Paul McCartney's followup to the Number One hit "Yesterday" [see 87], John Lennon's heartfelt "In My Life," and "Norwegian Wood (This Bird Has Flown)," which was the first Beatles recording to feature sitar.

"I'd been listening to the sitar and I was getting interested in it," says George Harrison. "One day I went to this little shop in London called India Craft. I was buying some incense and I spotted this sitar in the back of the shop.

It was a pretty cheap one, it wasn't a brilliant one, but I bought it anyway. I brought it to Abbey Road and I tried to play it a little bit, but I didn't have much of a clue about how to hold it and how to tune it."

While Harrison was only vaguely familiar with the sitar, producer George Martin had some experience working with the instrument. "I was no stranger to Indian instruments," he says. "I cut my teeth on doing spoofs with Peter Sellers before the Beatles arrived, so I knew about the sitar and the tabla."

While recording "Norwegian Wood," the sitar came in handy, despite the fact Harrison was still only learning how to actually play it. "John played a six-string, I played a 12-string guitar, we laid down the basic track, but it still seemed to need something else," Harrison says. "So at that point I picked up the sitar and tried to play that lick. It sounded promising, so I just kind of figured it out. Everyone was real happy, because it gave the edge to that song. It made it a little more unique and gave it a little finishing touch." Other instrumental innovations on *Rubber Soul* included McCartney's use of fuzz bass on Harrison's "Think for Yourself," which is believed to be one of the first uses of the distortion tool on record.

Lyrically, the Beatles were also making artistic leaps. Lennon's "Norwegian Wood" delved into his personal life, revealing that he had been unfaithful to his then-wife Cynthia. "He was more or less stating what he felt about her in that," says George Martin. McCartney

also drew upon his personal life—"I'm Looking Through You" was reportedly inspired by a tiff McCartney had with his girlfriend at the time, actress Jane Asher. But it wasn't all negative energy. "Even now, when I hear songs like 'The Word,' they just ooze this sort of energy and optimism," Harrison says.

Rubber Soul hit the summit in its third week on the chart, becoming the Beatles' seventh Number One album in less than two years. But it had one distinction that made it different than all of the group's previous Number One albums: It was the first Beatles chart-topper not to include a Number One single. In fact, there wasn't even a single released from the album.

THE TOP FIVE
Week of January 8, 1966

1. **Rubber Soul**
   The Beatles

2. **The Sound of Music**
   Soundtrack

3. **Whipped Cream & Other Delights**
   Herb Alpert's Tijuana Brass

4. **December's Children (and everybody's)**
   The Rolling Stones

5. **Going Places**
   Herb Alpert and the Tijuana Brass

82 Going Places A&M 112
HERB ALPERT AND THE TIJUANA BRASS

Producers: Herb Alpert and Jerry Moss

Track listing: Tijuana Taxi / I'm Getting Sentimental Over You / More and More Amor / Spanish Flea / Mae / 3rd Man Theme / Walk, Don't Run / Felicia / And the Angels Sing / Cinco de Mayo / A Walk in the Black Forest / Zorba the Greek

March 5, 1966
6 weeks, nonconsecutive

Herb Alpert and A&M Records were so hot by the spring of 1968 that the artist and label scored their second Number One album by knocking out their first, as *Going Places* dethroned *Whipped Cream & Other Delights* [see 80]. Although *Whipped Cream* had been temporarily displaced for six consecutive weeks by no less a force than the Beatles' *Rubber Soul* [see 81], the album rebounded back to Number One for two weeks before being topped by *Going Places*.

While *Going Places* didn't have the immediate impact of *Whipped Cream*'s famed cover art—*Whipped Cream* cover girl Dolores Erickson was in the latter stages of pregnancy and was unable to reprise her role—it did offer more of Alpert's trademark sound, which some compared to mariachi music.

"I never listened to mariachi music," Alpert says. "I was just trying to make the music, for the most part, which was just coming out of me. It had a Latin flavor, probably because I was using some percussion instruments in a non-traditional way. Using the trumpet and having the harmonies sometimes gave one the feeling of that Mexican-flavored music, but it was never a direct attempt on my part. I'm a jazz musician at heart and I tried to be spontaneous and real and respond to what I was feeling."

Unlike *Whipped Cream*, *Going Places* had no thematic thread running through the material. In fact, "3rd Man Theme" first appeared as the B-side of "Taste of Honey," from *Whipped Cream*, but it too charted, reaching number 47 in October 1965. Alpert's arrangement of the film theme, which was a Number One hit in 1950 for Anton Karas, was inspired by another Gold Star Recording Studio regular, Phil Spector.

"I was caught up in the wall of sound Phil Spector was caught up in doing," says Alpert. "I thought that's what I need, I need some heavier artillery, so I got two drummers and seven or eight guitar players, and I loaded up the studio, thinking that would be the answer."

Alpert's cover version of the theme to the film *Zorba the Greek* became the album's biggest hit, reaching number 11 in February 1966. "I knew that was a great song, but with the first recording, I didn't feel we captured the spirit of the composition, so we attempted it three different times," he says. "The last time was at Radio Recorders. The combination of that recording and Larry Levine's excellent engineering put that one over the top."

Although it only reached number 27, "Spanish Flea" is one of the best-known Tijuana Brass tracks. It was written by Julius Wechter, who played marimba on several of the group's songs and recorded with labelmates the Baja Marimba Band. When *The Dating Game* made its debut in October 1966 on ABC-TV, the song was adopted as its theme, which was okay with Alpert. "It was used with the right kind of humor," he says.

THE TOP FIVE
Week of March 5, 1966

1. **Going Places**
   Herb Alpert and the
   Tijuana Brass

2. **Whipped Cream &
   Other Delights**
   Herb Alpert's Tijuana Brass

3. **Rubber Soul**
   The Beatles

4. **The Sound of Music**
   Soundtrack

5. **September of My Years**
   Frank Sinatra

RCA 3547 # Ballads of the Green Berets
SSGT BARRY SADLER

83

Producer: Andy Wiswell

Track listing: *The Ballad of the Green Berets / Letter from Vietnam / I'm a Lucky One / Garet Trooper / The Soldier Has Come Home / Salute to the Nurses / I'm Watching Raindrops Fall / Badge of Courage / Trooper's Lament / Bamiba / Saigon / Lullaby*

March 12, 1966
5 weeks

Elvis Presley was the first artist to top the chart with a military-themed album when *G.I. Blues* hit Number One in 1960 [see 38]. It was mere coincidence that the other military-inspired album to top the chart, SSgt Barry Sadler's *Ballads of the Green Berets*, was also on RCA Records. The two performers however, had substantially different stories. Elvis was a huge pop star who was drafted into the military. Upon his return to civilian life, he starred in the light-hearted musical *G.I. Blues*, which spawned the hit soundtrack album. Sadler, on the other hand, was a member of the U.S. Army Special Forces. Following his leave from the military, after falling victim to a booby trap in Vietnam, the soldier began pursuing a music career.

It was Robin Moore, author of *The Green Berets*, who brought the musical talents of the New Mexico–born soldier to the attention of executives at RCA Records. "A very rough tape was brought to me of Barry singing 'The Ballad of the Green Berets.' We signed Barry for the project and hooked him up with producer Andy Wiswell," says Don

Burkhiemer, then manager of artists and repertoire for RCA Records. The album was recorded relatively quickly, but the label ran into a snag when readying the album for release.

"The package was about to be printed when we found out that it was against Army regulations to use a photograph of a military man in uniform on an album cover without permission from the U.S. government," says Burkhiemer. RCA decided to send the record executive to the Pentagon to seek approval. "I got there early in the morning and started out with a sergeant and worked up through the chain of command," he says. "I went from a lieutenant to majors to colonels. I ended up with a general and I finally convinced him on the steps of the Pentagon that night that it was in the best interest of the Army and the Green Berets that they approve the use

of the photo of Barry Sadler in uniform for the package, because there was a feeling of patriotism in uniform."

From a train station near the Pentagon, Burkhiemer called the printer and the head of RCA to tell them to print the album covers. It turned out to be well worth the trouble, as Sadler became an overnight sensation. "The Ballad of the Green Berets," which was co-written by Moore, hit the top of the Hot 100 on March 5, 1966. A week later, with the single holding in the pole position, Sadler's album also hit the top.

Sadler's success can best be attributed to timing; as Burkhiemer admits, "he wasn't the best singer in the world." In 1966, the majority of the public was still in favor of America's involvement in the Vietnam War. Says Burkhiemer, "It was the correct message at the correct time."

THE TOP FIVE
Week of March 12, 1966

1. **Ballads of the Green Berets**
   SSgt Barry Sadler

2. **Whipped Cream and Other Delights**
   Herb Alpert & the Tijuana Brass

3. **Going Places**
   Herb Alpert & the Tijuana Brass

4. **Rubber Soul**
   The Beatles

5. **The Sound of Music**
   Soundtrack

84 If You Can Believe Your Eyes and Ears DUNHILL 50006
THE MAMAS AND THE PAPAS

Producer: Lou Adler

Track listing: Monday, Monday / Straight Shooter / Got a Feelin' / I Call Your Name / Do You Wanna Dance / Go Where You Wanna Go / California Dreamin' / Spanish Harlem / Somebody Groovy / Hey Girl / You Baby / In Crowd

May 21, 1966
1 week

The Mamas and the Papas' road to the summit of *Billboard*'s album chart began in the summer of 1965. After spending much of the summer camping in the Virgin Islands, the group, which consisted of John Phillips, his wife Michelle, Dennis Doherty, and Cass Elliot, decided to flee their home base of New York for Los Angeles. John Phillips answered a newspaper ad from a man seeking someone to drive his car from New York to L.A. The car, it turned out, was a limousine. "So we all hopped in and headed for L.A.," says John.

The group rehearsed in the car during the cross-country trek. At a stop in Las Vegas, Michelle won some money at the craps tables to help cover the group's expenses. Once in L.A., the group crashed at a friend's apartment near the Sunset Strip. "It was a one-bedroom with 20 people living in it," says John. Low on cash, the group begged for money for food and heated it on a makeshift hot plate made from a converted bathroom heater. It was their friend Barry McGuire, who'd had a Number One hit in the fall of 1965 with "Eve of Destruction," who provided the

Mamas and the Papas with their big break. "We were rehearsing and he came by and said that it sounded great and we should go down and meet Lou Adler, who was producing his album," John Phillips says.

When the group arrived at Sunset Sound Studios a few days later, McGuire wasn't there, but Adler agreed to give the quartet a listen. "He told us to go down the hall into this room to warm up for a few minutes," Phillips says. "We sang about 10 songs. We didn't know that Lou was in the room." Adler was so impressed that he signed the band the following day.

Initially, the group was enlisted as back-up singers for McGuire, who cut the John and Michelle Phillips song "California Dreamin'." Adler loved the song, but wasn't crazy about McGuire's version. He suggested that the Mamas and Papas record it for their own album. "It's the same backing track that's on Barry's album," says Phillips. "We just took his voice off and Denny sang lead."

"California Dreamin'" was the Mamas and the Papas' first hit, but it wasn't the group's first single. Initially, Dunhill released "Go Where You Wanna Go" and distributed it to radio stations along the West Coast. "Then

Lou had a dream one night and realized that it should be 'California Dreamin' ' instead, so they recalled all of those singles," John recalls. "I thought it was a wise choice." The single eventually reached number four.

Aside from recording their own material, the Mamas and Papas paid tribute to some of their favorites artists by covering their songs, including the Beatles' "I Call Your Name." Says John Phillips, "Cass was in love with John Lennon. If you listen closely during the instrumental break, you can hear Cass whisper twice, 'John.' "

It was the John Phillips original, "Monday, Monday," however, that became the Mamas and the Papas' first Number One single, on May 7, 1996. Initially, the track almost didn't make the album. "Everyone hated it except for me," says Phillips. "I really wanted to put it on the album, but everybody couldn't understand what it was about. I don't really know what it's about, but it was cool. We did it as a test recording first, but it came out so well, we used that."

Two weeks after "Monday, Monday" first hit the top of the Hot 100, *If You Can Believe Your Eyes and Ears* reached the summit in its 11th week on the album chart.

THE TOP FIVE
Week of May 21, 1965

1. **If You Can Believe Your Eyes and Ears**
   The Mamas and the Papas

2. **What Now My Love**
   Herb Alpert & the Tijuana Brass

3. **Big Hits (High Tide and Green Grass)**
   The Rolling Stones

4. **Going Places**
   Herb Alpert & the Tijuana Brass

5. **Color Me Barbra**
   Barbra Streisand

Producers: *Herb Alpert & Jerry Moss*

Track listing: *What Now My Love / Freckles / Memories of Madrid / It Was a Very Good Year / So What's New? / Plucky / Magic Trumpet / Cantina Blue / Brasilia / If I Were a Rich Man / Five Minutes More / The Shadow of Your Smile*

May 28, 1966
9 weeks (nonconsecutive)

The week before *What Now My Love* hit Number One, Herb Alpert & the Tijuana Brass had five albums in the top 20 of the Top LP's chart, with *What Now My Love* at number two, *Going Places* [see 82] at number four, *Whipped Cream & Other Delights* [see 80] at number eight, *South of the Border* at number 17, and *The Lonely Bull* at number 20. With the TJB, as they were popularly known, all over the

album chart, it was no surprise that it took Alpert a mere three weeks to rack up his third consecutive Number One.

And Alpert was among the least surprised of all. "I was in the studio and my partner Jerry Moss called and said we had orders for something like 1,300,000 albums while I was still working on *What Now My Love*," he says. "It was a good news–bad news story. It was good news and worthy of getting excited about, but at the same time I felt a little prejudged. I like people to buy the product because they enjoy the record."

The title track was inspired by a walk on the beach in Waikiki, Hawaii. "I heard some horns honking. It sounded like 'toot toot beep beep.' So, I completed the phrase, 'toot toot beep beep bop,' and the arrangement developed itself," Alpert says.

Within three takes, Alpert nailed his trumpet parts on the cut. "I took home

the rough mix of it, which to me was exactly what I was looking for," he says. "We went back to do the master mix for the single and we couldn't get back to the feeling we had on the rough mix, so we actually used the rough mix as the final mix, which appeared on the single and the album. Released as a single, with "Spanish Flea" [see 83] as the B-side, "What Now My Love" reached number 24 on the Hot 100. The song also earned Alpert Grammy awards for best non-jazz instrumental performance and best instrumental arrangement of 1966.

What Now My Love was recorded in less time than the TJB's earlier efforts, with the album completed in less than two months. "I had all the songs, so we were rolling," Alpert says. "My fastball was humming."

The track "So What's New?" was written by TJB guitarist John Pisano and soon became the theme song for *The Lloyd Thaxton Show*, a syndicated pop music show similar to *American Bandstand.*

Alpert recorded "If I Were a Rich Man," from *Fiddler on the Roof*, because it was one of his father's favorite songs. "He liked it a lot," Alpert says. "He was a big fan of the Brass."

The elder Alpert wasn't alone, as the TJB managed to garner a wide demographic of fans, both young and old. "It was pretty amazing to see little kids and older people at the same concert," Alpert says.

It was also amazing that the TJB was one of only two acts to have two Number One albums in 1966. The other? The Beatles, who had three.

THE TOP FIVE
Week of May 28, 1966

1. **What Now My Love**
   Herb Alpert & the Tijuana Brass

2. **If You Can Believe Your Eyes and Ears**
   Mamas and the Papas

3. **Big Hits (High Tide and Green Grass)**
   Rolling Stones

4. **Color Me Barbra**
   Barbra Streisand

5. **The Sound of Music**
   Soundtrack

Strangers in the Night REPRISE 1017
FRANK SINATRA

Producer: Sonny Burke

Track listing: Strangers in the Night / Summer Wind / All or Nothing at All / Call Me / You're Driving Me Crazy! / On a Clear Day (You Can See Forever) / My Baby Just Cares for Me / Downtown / Yes Sir, That's My Baby / The Most Beautiful Girl in the World

July 23, 1966
1 week

If anyone thought the arrival of the Beatles would keep the Chairman of the Board from the top of the charts, they had to think again during the mid-'60s. By 1961, Sinatra already had three Number One albums to his credit in the rock era [see 13, 20, and 37], and a shift in the musical landscape, no matter how revolutionary, wasn't about to render him obsolete.

In 1961 Sinatra launched his own record company, Reprise. With his former label Capitol continuing to issue his material while new albums were released on Reprise, Sinatra titles flooded the market. In 1961 alone, he had six albums in the top 10. In the following years, however, with Capitol throwing together compilation albums, his chart performance became more erratic. For example, 1963's *Tell Her You Love Her* stalled at number 129, while 1965's *September of My Years* reached number five, and earned the crooner a Grammy for album of the year.

Strangers in the Night began to take shape after Sinatra recorded the song of the same name for the film *A Man Could Get Killed*. It was Reprise A&R man Jimmy Bowen and music publisher Hal Fine who enlisted Sinatra for the

project. Fine had played Bowen an instrumental version of the song written by German multi-instrumentalist Bert Kaempfert [see 40]. Bowen promised that if Fine could provide English lyrics to the track, Sinatra would sing it.

Songwriters Charlie Singleton and Eddie Snyder composed the lyrics and Sinatra agreed to sing the song like only he could. Bowen produced the track with Ernie Freeman handling the arrangement, rather than Sinatra's long-time arranger Nelson Riddle, who is credited on the album's other nine tracks. Drummer Hal Blaine, who played on the song, also added his own personal touch. "I stole the Phil Spector thing I used on 'Be My Baby,' except I slowed it down," he says. "It's a slower tempo, so everything just kind of fit."

Also playing on the session was guitarist Glen Campbell [see 109]. "I was sitting about 10 feet from Sinatra's vocal booth," he says. "It was a V-shaped booth aimed out toward the orchestra so he could hear it. I don't even think he had earphones on." Campbell was awed to be in the presence of the legendary crooner. "I was just hoping I wouldn't make a mistake," he says.

Sinatra's recording sessions were

always special, says Blaine. "The mystique of Frank Sinatra is just amazing," he says. "He always booked double sessions. The first three hours were rehearsals for the orchestra and the studio hands would check everything and every seat for squeaks, because once Sinatra would walk in, he would want everything perfect."

After the rehearsals, Sinatra would get down to business. "He would shake a few songs and then he would do everything live with the orchestra in one or two takes," Blaine says. "It was amazing."

After the single was cut successfully, a full album was assembled around the track. Sonny Burke was brought in to produce the rest of the tracks, which ranged from Lerner and Lane's "On a Clear Day (You Can See Forever)" and Rodgers and Hart's "The Most Beautiful Girl in the World" to a cover of Petula Clark's 1965 Number One hit "Downtown," but it was "Strangers in the Night" that stood out.

On July 2, 1966, the song became Sinatra's first Number One single of the rock era. Three weeks later, Ol' Blue Eyes was at the summit of the Top LP's chart for the fourth time in his career.

THE TOP FIVE
Week of July 23, 1966

1. **Strangers in the Night**
   Frank Sinatra

2. **"Yesterday"... and Today**
   The Beatles

3. **What Now My Love**
   Herb Alpert & the Tijuana Brass

4. **Lou Rawls Live!**
   Lou Rawls

5. **Aftermath**
   The Rolling Stones

Producer: George Martin

Track listing: Drive My Car / I'm Only Sleeping / Nowhere Man / Dr. Robert / Act Naturally / And Your Bird Can Sing / If I Needed Someone / We Can Work It Out / What Goes On? / Day Tripper

July 30, 1966
5 weeks

"I personally like *Revolver* [see 88], and *Rubber Soul* [see 81] is still my favorite album," says George Harrison. "I always think of them as a continuation of each other. They could actually be blended into one album, because they have a similar sound." In America, songs from the British version of *Rubber Soul* and the then-forthcoming U.K. edition of *Revolver* actually *were* melded together, along with two songs from the U.K. version of *Help!* and the British hit single "We Can Work It Out"/"Day Tripper," to form the U.S.-only release *"Yesterday"...and Today.*

"Yesterday"...and Today's original cover featured what has become one of the most notorious photos in rock history: a shot of the Beatles in blood-splattered white lab coats, caught in the act of hacking up plastic baby dolls. The album with its original artwork, known as the "butcher block" cover or "Somnambulant Adventure," met with public outcry and was promptly withdrawn from the marketplace. In its place was a sedate photo of John Lennon, George Harrison, and Ringo Starr congregating around a shipping suitcase, with Paul McCartney seated inside the case. Some have suggested that the "butcher block" cover was the Beatles' way of protesting Capitol's "butchering" of their albums, yet the group's producer, George Martin, says that was not the case. "They certainly were pretty upset about the way things were handled in America, as I was, but the 'butcher block' cover was just a result of their rather macabre sense of humor."

While the group's previous album, *Rubber Soul,* had featured no singles, *"Yesterday"...and Today* was virtually a collection of hits. "Yesterday," which wasn't released as a single in the U.K. until 1976,

became the Beatles' 10th Number One hit in America on October 9, 1965. The track was significant because it marked the first time a song credited to the group was actually performed by one Beatle solo. McCartney performed the song on acoustic guitar, backed by a string quartet.

"Yesterday" also became the group's most popular song—at least with other performers. It has been covered more than 2,500 times, making it the most covered song ever, according to *The Guinness Book of World Records.*

The flip side of "Yesterday," which was also featured on *"Yesterday"...and Today,* was a cover version of Buck Owens's "Act Naturally," with Starr on lead vocals. It reached number 47.

The Beatles hit the top of the Hot 100 again with "We Can Work It Out" on January 8, 1966. The single's B-side, "Day Tripper," reached number five. The third single released in advance of *"Yesterday"...and Today* was Lennon's "Nowhere Man," which reached number three. Its flip, "What Goes On," didn't fare nearly as well, peaking at number 81.

Despite the fact that six of the album's 11 tracks were available on singles prior to its release—or maybe because of it—*"Yesterday"...and Today* reached the top of the Top LP's chart in its fourth week, becoming the Beatles' eighth Number One album.

THE TOP FIVE
Week of July 30, 1966

1. **"Yesterday"...and Today**
   The Beatles

2. **Strangers in the Night**
   Frank Sinatra

3. **Aftermath**
   The Rolling Stones

4. **What Now My Love**
   Herb Alpert and the Tijuana Brass

5. **Lou Rawls Live!**
   Lou Rawls

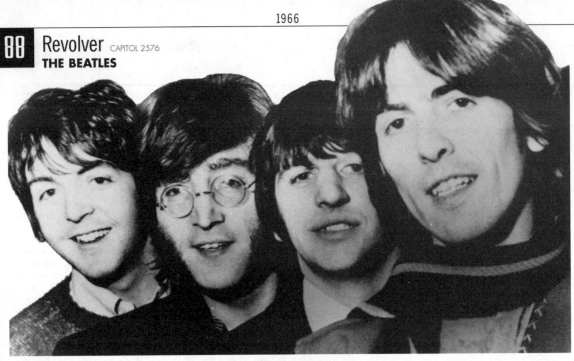

88 Revolver CAPITOL 2576
THE BEATLES

Producer: George Martin

Track listing: Taxman / Eleanor Rigby / Love You To / Here, There and Everywhere / Yellow Submarine / She Said She Said / Good Day Sunshine / For No One / I Want to Tell You / Got to Get You Into My Life / Tomorrow Never Knows

September 10, 1966
6 weeks

On *Revolver*, the Beatles continued the musical evolution that would reach its apex on *Sgt. Pepper's Lonely Hearts Club Band* [see 95]. Most consider *Sgt. Pepper's* to be the band's masterpiece, but when asked about his favorite Beatles album, producer George Martin says, "*Pepper's* is one of them, but not the favorite. I like *Rubber Soul* and I love *Revolver*."

Revolver was the last Beatles album to be altered for American release; three songs that appeared on the British version—"I'm Only Sleeping," "Doctor Robert," and "And Your Bird Can Sing" —had already been plundered for use on the U.S.-only *"Yesterday"...and Today* [see 87], and were therefore deleted from the American *Revolver*. From this point onward, all Beatles albums would have identical tracks on each side of the Atlantic.

The album showcased three writing contributions by George Harrison, his most to date. His "Taxman" was chosen to open the album, marking the first time one of his songs had been used to kick

off a Beatles album. Says Harrison, "That was my dig at the government. In the early days, we were always struggling. We never had money for years, then eventually we started to make some. And in those days, there used to be 20 shillings in the pound, and out of those 20 shillings, they took 19-and-half for tax. They were just bleeding us. I was so pissed off, I wrote that song."

Ringo Starr's lead-vocal contribution, "Yellow Submarine," would later serve as the inspiration for the Beatles' animated film of the same name. The soundtrack album that accompanied the film reached number two on the album chart in February 1969.

Elsewhere on *Revolver*, the Beatles continued their musical experimentation, breaking new ground on tracks such as "Eleanor Rigby" and "Tomorrow Never Knows." None of the Beatles actually played on the former song. Instead, an eight-piece string section was used to provide instrumental support. "Tomorrow Never Knows" included sitar and such psychedelic studio trickery as backward tape loops. "We had gotten really into recording more," says Harrison. "I think our ears had been tweaked up. It may have had something to do with the jazz cigarettes people were smoking in them days. There was something in the air. In California, there was a lot happening with the Byrds. There was just a buzz going on. We were able to hear things we never heard before."

As a result, the Beatles began to experiment more in the studio. "We'd always look for different sounds on

stuff," says Harrison. "If we got stuck there was a cupboard underneath the stairs of the number two studio in Abbey Road. It was full of these weird little drums, percussion things, tambourines, horns, and bells and all kinds of stuff. A lot of the sounds you hear on the records is just because, as they say, necessity is the mother of invention."

The Beatles played their final formal concert on August 29, 1966, at Candlestick Park in San Francisco. The band couldn't have been hotter on the charts than they were at the time: *Revolver* hit the top in a mere two weeks, making it the Beatles' fastest climbing chart-topper since *Beatles '65* [see 73], their second Number One album in less than two months, and their third ace of 1966.

THE TOP FIVE
Week of September 10, 1966

1. **Revolver**
   The Beatles

2. **Doctor Zhivago**
   Soundtrack

3. **What Now My Love**
   Herb Alpert & the Tijuana Brass

4. **Somewhere My Love**
   Ray Conniff & the Singers

5. **The Sound of Music**
   Soundtrack

Producers: Brian Holand, Lamont Dozier

Track listing: Love Is Like an Itching in My Heart / This Old Heart of Mine (Is Weak for You) / You Can't Hurry Love / Shake Me, Wake Me (When It's Over) / Baby I Need Your Loving / These Boots Are Made for Walking / I Can't Help Myself / Get Ready / Put Yourself in My Place / Money (That's What I Want) / Come and Get These Memories / Hang on Sloopy

October 22, 1966
2 weeks

By the fall of 1966, Diana Ross, Mary Wilson, and Florence Ballard were already enjoying huge success as the Supremes. When "You Can't Hurry Love" knocked Donovan's "Sunshine Superman" from the top of the Hot 100 on September 10, 1966, it became the trio's seventh Number One single, yet the group wasn't having the same kind of success on the Top LP's chart.

Where Did Our Love Go, the debut album that shared the name of the Supremes' first Number One single, spent four weeks at number two on the Top LP's chart, but was kept out of the top position by *Beatles '65* [see 73]. Only two of the Supremes' next six albums managed to crack the top 10—*More Hits by the Supremes* hit number six in September 1965, while *I Hear a Symphony* peaked at number eight in April 1966. Yet the Supremes would get their due at the summit of the album chart that same year with their eighth album *Supremes A' Go-Go*.

Unlike some of the trio's early efforts, *Supremes A' Go-Go* had no specific theme. "We had a concept when we did *A Bit of Liverpool*, which had a lot of the British hits on it," says Diana Ross. "We also did an album of Sam Cooke songs [*We Remember Sam Cooke*], and later we did a Rogers and Hart album [*The Sumpremes Sing Rogers & Hart*], but when we did *A' Go-Go*, we would just go in and record a couple of songs and then we would go out on tour, then we would record a few more, and eventually they put it out as an album. Motown was mostly known for its singles."

At the time, the Supremes were still a relatively young act. The group was founded in Detroit in 1959 as a quartet known as the Primettes. Shortly after changing its name to the Supremes in 1961, the group was slimmed down to a trio when Barbra Martin left the quartet.

While the Supremes often paid tribute to their contemporaries by covering their songs, the group's early hits, including their first seven Number One singles, came from the writing team of Brian Holland, Lamont Dozier, and Eddie Holland.

"You Can't Hurry Love," the only hit from *Supremes A' Go-Go*, was one of the eight Holland-Dozier-Holland songs on the album. Other selections included the Supremes' versions of Number One hits by Nancy Sinatra ("These Boots Are Made for Walking") and the McCoys ("Hang on Sloopy"). Also included was the Supremes' take on "Money (That's What I Want)," a song co-written by Motown founder Berry Gordy Jr. for Barrett Strong and best known for the cover version included on *The Beatles' Second Album* [see 66].

The Fab Four may have kept the Supremes' debut album from the top spot with *Beatles '65*, but *Supremes A' Go-Go* turned the tables. Not only did the album end *Revolver's* six-week run at Number One, but "You Can't Hurry Love" kept the Beatles' "Yellow Submarine" out of the top spot on the Hot 100.

THE TOP FIVE
Week of October 22, 1966

1. **Supremes A' Go-Go**
   The Supremes

2. **Revolver**
   The Beatles

3. **Dr. Zhivago**
   Soundtrack

4. **The Mamas and the Papas**
   The Mamas and the Papas

5. **What Now My Love**
   Herb Alpert & the Tijuana Brass

90 Doctor Zhivago MGM 90620
SOUNTRACK

Composer: Maurice Jarre

Track listing: Overture from "Doctor Zhivago" / Main Title from "Doctor Zhivago" / Lara Leaves Yuri / At the Student Cafe / Komarovsky and Lara's Rendezvous / Revolution / Lara's Theme from "Doctor Zhivago" / The Funeral / Sventyski's Waltz / Yuri Escapes / Tonya Arrives at Varykino / Yuri Writes a Poem for Lara

November 5, 1966
1 week

Sir Ralph Richardson and Geraldine Chaplin in *Doctor Zhivago*.

Doctor Zhivago is an epic love story set in Russia during World War I. When director David Lean decided to take Boris Pasternak's 1957 novel to the big screen, he felt it needed a similarly epic soundtrack to enhance the drama, passion, and beauty of the story. He called on Maurice Jarre, a young French composer who picked up an Academy Award for his work on Lean's *Lawrence of Arabia*.

In composing and recording the film's score, Jarre attempted to capture the sound of Russia during the war, which was no easy feat, considering he was living in Los Angeles at the time. "I wanted to find balalaikas, a Russian instrument that has a big sweeping sound, but they were difficult to find," he recalls. "I didn't just want one or two, I wanted 25 or 30." After searching for weeks, Jarre discovered a Russian Orthodox Church located in downtown Los Angeles. "I found 24 people who had balalaikas, but they didn't know how to read music," he says. "So I had to teach them the 16 bars of 'Lara's Theme.' "

The soundtrack was recorded in 10 days at the MGM Studios, featuring a 105-piece, 40-voice orchestra. Aside from the balalaikas, Jarre also utilized a banjo-like instrument called a shamisen, a Japanese harp known as a koto, and an early predecessor of the synthesizer.

To inspire the music, Jarre traveled to the film location near Madrid, where Lean had a huge set of Moscow constructed, but much of the score was written after he returned home to Los Angeles.

Originally, Lean had planned to use an old piece of Russian music as a centerpiece for the score. "He thought it was public domain, but it wasn't. After doing research, MGM found out it was written by three composers, but they couldn't clear the rights to it. So David called me and told me I had to write a new theme for the movie."

Jarre was thus thrust into the hot seat, having to compose the new theme in a matter of weeks before the film's opening. "I played him what I wrote and he said, 'Maurice, I think you can do better.' " Lean also rejected Jarre's next three attempts. "He said, 'Don't think about Doctor Zhivago and Russia. I want you to think about doing a love theme for your girlfriend,' " Jarre says.

Lean's advice paid off. Jarre took his girlfriend to the mountains for the weekend. "On Monday morning, I went in my studio and I wrote the main theme in an hour." He notes that the theme, which appears several times in the film and in different variations on the soundtrack, wasn't particularly Russian-sounding; it was the instrumentation that made the tracks sound that way.

Doctor Zhivago's climb to the top wasn't immediate. It took the soundtrack album 34 weeks to hit Number One and knock *Supremes A' Go-Go* from the summit. And its stay at the top only lasted a mere week, but for many, Jarre's romantic score music would be embedded in their hearts and minds for a lifetime.

THE TOP FIVE
Week of November 5, 1966

1. **Doctor Zhivago**
   Soundtrack

2. **The Monkees**
   The Monkees

3. **Supremes A' Go-Go**
   The Supremes

4. **The Mamas and the Papas**
   The Mamas and the Papas

5. **Revolver**
   The Beatles

COLGEMS 101 **The Monkees**
THE MONKEES

91

Producers: Tommy Boyce, Bobby Hart, Jack Keller, Michael Nesmith

Track listing: (Theme from) The Monkees / Saturday's Child / I Wanna Be Free / Tomorrow's Gonna Be Another Day / Papa Gene's Blues / Take a Giant Step / Last Train to Clarksville / This Just Doesn't Seem to Be My Day / Let's Dance On / I'll Be True to You / Sweet Young Thing / Gonna Buy Me a Dog

November 12, 1966
13 weeks

"The Monkees," a half-hour situation comedy inspired by the Beatles' *A Hard Day's Night* [see 69], made its television debut in September 1966, but by then, the fictitious group put together for the TV show was already on its way to becoming a reality. "After the pilot was sold, we went into frantic and intense rehearsals," says Micky Dolenz. "I had to learn how to play the drums. I was a guitar player at the time, but they cast me as the drummer."

Dolenz was one of more than 400 people who answered an ad in *Daily Variety* that read, "Madness!! Auditions. Folk and Rock Musicians-Singers for Acting Roles in a New TV Series. Running parts for four insane boys, age 17–21." The others cast for the show along with Dolenz were Michael Nesmith, Peter Tork, and Davy Jones. (Among those who auditioned but didn't get the part was Stephen Stills [see 120].) Although the Monkees weren't actually a performing band, they would nonetheless have their own material and records: The TV show's producers Bert Schneider and Bob Rafelson turned to music publisher

Don Kirshner for songwriters and producers for the new "band," and the Monkees' records would be released on Colgems, a new label started by Screen Gems, the Columbia Pictures company that produced the series.

Eventually, Tommy Boyce and Bobby Hart were chosen to produce and write material for the Monkees, but not all the band members made it to the sessions. "Mike Nesmith had already been writing a lot of tunes and he was in quite frequently, as was Peter, who was a rather accomplished musician," says Dolenz. At the time, Jones didn't play an instrument and Dolenz was still trying to master the drums, so a number of studio players, such as Glen Campbell [see 109], Leon Russell, and Hal Blaine were called in to play on the tracks.

"Everything was basically treated as a single," says Dolenz. "The producers were going to their stable of hit writers, which included Carole King [see 133], David Gates, and Neil Diamond."

Although the hit material was important to the Monkees, the success of the

group of TV actors as an actual recording act came as a surprise. " 'The Monkees' was a television show about a rock 'n' roll group. The fact that we became a group, we went on the road, did all the concerts, and recorded all the music was the equivalent of Leonard Nimoy becoming a Vulcan," says Dolenz.

Yet the Monkees' career as a recording act began even before the show debuted. "Last Train to Clarksville" was released on August 16, 1966. By the time the show premiered, it was on the Hot 100. "It was a radio hit with massive promotion behind it," says Dolenz. "A lot of people had a vested interest in 'The Monkees' and made sure it was a hit."

On November 5, the song, penned by Boyce and Hart, went to Number One. A week later, *The Monkees* hit the summit in its sixth week on the Top LP's chart. Monkeemania was in full effect as the TV show "band" had been transformed into a legitimate chart-topping force.

THE TOP FIVE
Week of November 12, 1966

1. **The Monkees**
   The Monkees

2. **Dr. Zhivago**
   Soundtrack

3. **Supremes A' Go-Go**
   Supremes

4. **The Mamas and the Papas**
   The Mamas and the Papas

5. **What Now My Love**
   Herb Alpert & the Tijuana Brass

92 More of the Monkees
THE MONKEES

COLGEMS 102

Music supervision: Don Kirshner

Track listing: She / When Love Comes Knockin' (At Your Door) / Mary, Mary / Hold on Girl / Your Auntie Grizelda / (I'm Not Your) Steppin' Stone / Look Out (Here Comes Tomorrow) / The Kind of Girl I Could Love / The Day We Fall in Love / Sometime in the Morning / Laugh / I'm a Believer

February 11, 1967
18 weeks

Not only was "The Monkees" sitcom inspired by the Beatles' film *A Hard Day's Night* [see 69], but the group's success on the charts was also starting to resemble the Fab Four's, as *The Monkees* was knocked from the summit of the Top LP's chart by its follow-up. The Beatles experienced a similar phenomenon when *Meet The Beatles!* [see 65] was displaced by *The Beatles' Second Album* [see 66]. Most impressively, however, the Monkees first two albums held the top position for a total of 31 weeks, almost twice as long as their British models, whose first two chart-toppers occupied the Number One spot for 16 weeks.

"Comparing the Monkees to the Beatles was a bit like comparing William Shatner to Neil Armstrong," says Monkees drummer Micky Dolenz. "To compare us to the Beatles was like compar-

ing apples to oranges. When John Lennon was asked about it, he said, 'I like the Monkees. I like the Marx Brothers.' That was the closest thing to the truth. The Monkees were more like a Marx Brothers musical than the Beatles."

With Colgems president Don Kirshner frequently bringing in tunes from his songwriters, the Monkees soon found themselves with a backlog of material. "By the time the first album was recorded, there was enough material to do three albums," says Dolenz. "Then, when we started selling all of those albums, everybody wanted in on the act."

In fact, on the liner notes, Kirshner made a point to list the famous songwriters, such as Gerry Goffin and Carole King [see 133], Neil Sedaka, and Carole Bayer, before he wrote about the Monkees' talents.

The reliance on outside songwriters was beginning to frustrate Monkee Mike Nesmith, who was a songwriting talent in his own right. As had been the case on the group's first album, Nesmith was allowed two writing and producing credits on *More Monkees*, but the hits continued to come from outside writers.

"I'm a Believer," penned by Neil Diamond, was released as a single in December of 1966. By the end of the year, the song became the Monkees' second Number One single. Tommy Boyce and Bobby Hart's "(I'm Not Your)

Steppin' Stone," the B-side, also charted, peaking at number 20, and paving the way for *More of the Monkees*. Both tracks were included on the album, creating a pent-up demand for the new Monkees' long-player.

More of the Monkees entered the chart at number 122 on February 4, 1967. A week later, it jumped all the way to the top, displacing *The Monkees* and giving the group its second Number One album. With the one-two punch of *The Monkees* and *More of the Monkees*, the Prefab Four dominated the top spot of the album chart from November 12, 1966, through June 17, 1967.

THE TOP FIVE
Week of February 11, 1967

1. **More of the Monkees**
   The Monkees

2. **The Monkees**
   The Monkees

3. **S.R.O.**
   Herb Albert & the Tijuana Brass

4. **Dr. Zhivago**
   Soundtrack

5. **The Temptations Greatest Hits**
   The Temptations

A&M 124 ## Sounds Like...
HERB ALPERT & THE TIJUANA BRASS

93

Producers: Herb Alpert & Jerry Moss

Track listing: Gotta Lotta Livin' to Do / Lady Godiva / Bo-Bo / Shades of Blue / In a Little Spanish Town / Wade in the Water / Town Without Pity / The Charmer / Treasure of San Miguel / Casino Royale

June 17, 1967
1 week

Herb Alpert & the Tijuana Brass's streak of consecutive Number One albums was cut short at three, as Alpert's seventh album, *S.R.O.*, spent six weeks at number two, but was prevented from hitting the summit by *The Monkees*. But later that same year, the TJB, as the group was known, got revenge by knocking *More of the Monkees* from Number One with *Sounds Like...*.

Alpert, however, wasn't overly concerned about the streak. "I wasn't a chart watcher," he says. "I wasn't going to allow myself to feel good or bad based on the weekly charts."

For *Sounds Like...*, Alpert joined forces with songsmiths Burt Bacharach and Hal David on "Casino Royal," the theme to a 1967 James Bond spoof starring Peter Sellers and Woody Allen, among others. "Bacharach recorded it in London and apparently he didn't like the end result," Alpert says. "He sent me a tape of the song and the arrangement and I liked it a lot. So, he sent me the multitracks and I added in my trumpet. That song has a real special quality." In May 1967, the single reached number 27.

Also featured on the album was Alpert's cover of Gene Pitney's 1961 hit "Town Without Pity." One of Alpert's concert favorites, "Wade in the Water," finally made it on wax with the release of *Sounds Like...* as well. Says Alpert, "I tried to record it a little differently than the way it was normally heard. There is always a challenge to come up with a different twist on a song. One of the things that I always looked for when I recorded a song was how many different ways I could play a song."

Like its predecessor, *Sounds Like...* was recorded at a fairly fast pace. Alpert finished the entire project in approximately two months, while break-

ing for an occasional live date. Recording at Gold Star Recording Studio in Hollywood, Alpert usually went for spontaneity rather than perfection. "On a lot of the tracks I would just have a basic idea of how I wanted it to sound rhythmically and I would go to the studio with the musicians that I felt would best represent the sound I was looking for," he says. "I would develop the sound and a good part of the arrangement right on the spot in the studio."

Similarly, Alpert often refrained from rehearsing his trumpet parts until he was actually ready to cut his tracks in the studio. "I did that to try to keep it as fresh as possible," he says. "I didn't have the need to play the melody over and over. Once I got the rhythm track that I liked, I would be playing the melody the first time when I recorded it. I always felt that by the first take or second take, I had it. By that time, I wanted to turn on the tape machine and play it back."

Alpert's spontaneity paid off, as *Sounds Like...* became his fourth Number One album after only three weeks on the chart.

THE TOP FIVE
Week of June 17, 1967

1. **Sounds Like...**
   Herb Alpert & the
   Tijuana Brass

2. **Revenge**
   Bill Cosby

3. **I Never Loved a Man the Way I Love You**
   Aretha Franklin

4. **More of the Monkees**
   The Monkees

5. **Born Free**
   Andy Williams

94 Headquarters COLGEMS 103
THE MONKEES

Producer: Douglas Farthing Hatlelid

Track listing: You Told Me / I'll Spend My Life With You / Forget That Girl / Band 6 / You Just May Be the One / Shades of Gray / I Can't Get Her Off My Mind / For Pete's Sake / Mr. Webster / Sunny Girlfriend / Zilch / No Time / Early Morning Blues and Greens / Randy Scouse Git

*June 24, 1967
1 week*

With *Sounds Like...* [see 93], Herb Alpert & the Tijuana Brass broke the Monkees' 31-week run at the top of the album chart, but it would only take the Monkees a week to regain the top spot, as their third album, *Headquarters*, became the third Monkees' title in 33 weeks to hit the apex of the Top LP's chart.

Although *Headquarters*'s one-week stay at Number One paled in comparison to the chart-topping power of *The Monkees* [see 91] and *More of the Monkees* [see 92], the group's third album was its most important effort to date. "On *Headquarters* we put our foot down," says drummer/singer Micky Dolenz. "Up to that point the powers that be were more or less dictating what to release. Mike [Nesmith] was always very concerned about this. He wanted to have his own songs recorded and released as singles, but the singles invariably ended up being a song by Neil Diamond, John Stewart, or Boyce and Hart. By then, we felt very confident that we could record as a group, so there was a battle for creative control, which we ultimately won."

While the Monkees began as nothing more than a cast of characters for a TV sitcom, by March 1967 the group had evolved into a legitimate recording band, holed up in RCA Studio C in Hollywood. "We recorded together before that, but that was the first time we went in and did a concept album," says Dolenz. "We buried ourselves in the studio for six to eight weeks. That's all we did. We just recorded that album from start to finish. We lived in there. We slept in there. We had sex in there. It was really down and dirty."

In the liner notes, the Monkees pointed out that they were indeed in control of *Headquarters*: "We aren't the only musicians on this album, but the occasional extra bass or horn player played under our direction, so that this is all

ours." As Dolenz explains, "*Headquarters*, in a way, was the first real Monkees album."

With members of the Monkees writing or cowriting seven of the album's 14 tracks, *Headquarters* showcased the group as songwriters in their own right. Some of the material originated out of in studio jams. "For 'No Time' we just started screwing around doing old rock 'n' roll stuff," says Dolenz. Although it was essentially a group composition, the band gave the songwriting credit to Hank Cicalo as a reward for serving as the engineer during the session.

Another original track, "Randy Scouse Git" was written the night after the Beatles threw the Monkees a party at London's Speakeasy. "I had just fallen in love with the girl that would become my first wife, Samantha" says Dolenz. "I was sitting in my hotel room and I just started musing about everything that was happening—the party, Samantha, and my experiences in London. There's a lyric in the song about 'the four kings of EMI,' and that was obviously the Beatles." The song became the only hit from *Headquarters*. It reached number two in the U.K., where it was issued under the name "Alternate Title," but it wasn't released as a single in the U.S. Says Dolenz, "In England, 'Randy Scouse

Git' is kind of rude. Randy means horny. A scouse is kind of a rascal from Liverpool, and a git is a jerk." Dolenz first heard the expression on "Till Death Do Us Part," the British TV show that inspired "All in the Family."

In an ironic twist, *Sgt. Pepper's Lonely Hearts Club Band* [see 95], by "the four kings of EMI," whose *A Hard Day's Night* movie had been the inspiration for "The Monkees" TV show, would limit *Headquarters*' stay at the top spot to a lone week.

THE TOP FIVE
Week of June 24, 1967

1. **Headquarters**
   The Monkees
2. **Sounds Like...**
   Herb Alpert & the Tijunana Brass
3. **Revenge**
   Bill Cosby
4. **I Never Loved a Man the Way I Love You**
   Aretha Franklin
5. **Born Free**
   Andy Williams

CAPITOL 2653 # Sgt. Pepper's Lonely Hearts Club Band

THE BEATLES

95

Producer: George Martin

Track listing: Sgt. Pepper's Lonely Hearts Club Band / With a Little Help from My Friends / Lucy in the Sky with Diamonds / Getting Better / Fixing a Hole / Being for the Benefit of Mr. Kite! / Within You Without You / When I'm Sixty-Four / Lovely Rita / Sgt. Pepper's Lonely Hearts Club Band (Reprise) / A Day in the Life

July 1, 1967
15 weeks

"Sgt. Pepper's Lonely Hearts Club Band grabbed the world of music by the scruff of the neck and shook it hard," says producer George Martin. "It drove a splitting wedge right through the core of popular music. Many people see it as a watershed...Yet the Beatles themselves never pretended they were creating great art...They just wanted to do something different."

Although the Beatles had scored two Number One albums in 1966 [see *Rubber Soul*—81 and *Revolver*—88], that year "had been a bit of disaster," Martin says. There were death threats following John Lennon's controversial remarks about the Beatles being more popular than Jesus. Also, the band had vowed never to tour again. "By the time we started work on *Pepper*, the Beatles had been on their treadmill for four years. They weren't only sick of the constant attention and media pressure, there were signs that many fans were disenchanted, too," says Martin. So the Beatles decided to get back to what they loved—making music.

One of the first songs recorded by the band when it entered EMI Studios in December 1966 was "Strawberry Fields Forever," which set the tone for *Pepper* but did not make it on the album. Instead, it was released as the flip side to "Penny Lane" in February 1967 and later turned up on the band's *Magical Mystery Tour* album [see 99].

"When I'm Sixty-Four," was the first track recorded that actually made it onto the album, but *Pepper* didn't really begin to take shape until early 1967. McCartney, on a plane ride to America, came up with the *Sgt. Pepper's* concept. The Beatles found that they didn't have to be the Beatles—they could don a new identity, and did so in the title track, which served as an introduction to the first concept album. "The opening track gave John [Lennon] and Paul the opportunity and the idea to write a song for Ringo [Starr]," says Martin. "The Billy Shears character helped make *Pepper* work and gave it a bit of direction."

That song, "With a Little Help from My Friends," was written specifically for Ringo's limited but distinctive vocal style. "Paul actually wrote the song very cleverly, based on no more than five adjacent notes," says Martin.

One night, while in the studio, Lennon began to feel ill. He had taken LSD, but despite the rumors and coincidence of the initials, that wasn't the inspiration for "Lucy in the Sky with Diamonds." Says Martin, "It had absolutely nothing to do with LSD and everything to do with the mind of a child." The song was inspired by a drawing by Lennon's son, Julian, of a classmate named Lucy.

The album's most striking track is "A Day in the Life." While Lennon came up with the initial idea after reading a news clipping about a car accident, it was the collaboration between him and McCartney that made the song a classic. "John had no fixed ideas of the way the song should be arranged," says Martin. "He was stumped in the middle section. He asked his mate if he had anything suitable. Paul had written a scrap of a song. Although it had little to do with the opening lines, it served as an effective counterpoint to John's creation."

Perhaps the most amazing fact about *Pepper* is that it was recorded on a four-track, meaning Martin had to come up with inventive ways to get all of the Beatles, strings, brass, and sound effects on tape.

It took more than 600 hours for the Beatles to complete their masterpiece, but only two weeks for it to top the album chart following its release. Popular music would never be the same.

THE TOP FIVE
Week of July 1, 1967

1. **Sgt. Pepper's Lonely Hearts Club Band**
   The Beatles

2. **Headquarters**
   The Monkees

3. **Sounds Like...**
   Herb Alpert & the Tijuana Brass

4. **I Never Loved a Man the Way I Love You**
   Aretha Franklin

5. **Surrealistic Pillow**
   Jefferson Airplane

96 Ode to Billie Joe CAPITOL 2830
BOBBIE GENTRY

Producer: Kelly Gordon

Track listing: Mississippi Delta / I Saw an Angel Die / Chickasaw County Child / Sunday Best / Niki Hoeky / Papa, Woncha Let Me Go to Town with You / Bugs / Hurry, Tuesday Child / Lazy Willie / Ode to Billie Joe

October 14, 1967
2 weeks

Arranger/conductor Jimmie Haskell, whose first claim to fame was his work with Ricky Nelson [see 12], still remembers the call. "A producer named Kelly Gordon called me and said, 'Come on over, because I just signed a girl and I want you to throw some strings on her record.' " When Haskell reported to Capitol Records studios, he was introduced to a young singer named Bobbie Gentry. "I was told that Capitol had just brought a master from her called 'Mississippi Delta,' which was a gravel-voiced Southern rocker," Haskell says. However, it wasn't that song that would take Gentry to the top of the single and album charts. It was the track that was supposed to be the B-side, "Ode to Billie Joe," which featured Gentry singing and playing a five-string Martin guitar.

Without giving any specific instructions, Gordon asked Haskell to cover the B-side with strings "so we won't be embarrassed to release it." In his previous arranging stints, Haskell was provided with demos to serve as a guide. "So I had to come up with my own thoughts on the song," Haskell says. "To me it sounded like a movie, because the song has a great story. I used the strings like I

THE TOP FIVE
Week of October 14, 1967

1. **Ode to Billie Joe**
   Bobbie Gentry

2. **St. Pepper's Lonely Heart's Club Band**
   The Beatles

3. **Diana Ross and the Supremes Greatest Hits**
   Diana Ross and the Supremes

4. **The Doors**
   The Doors

5. **Aretha Arrives**
   Aretha Franklin

was scoring a film, to heighten the images that she was singing about."

Shortly after the record was finished, the A&R staff at Capitol met and decided that "Ode to Billie Joe" should be an A-side, except there was one minor problem: the song, which ran four minutes and 15 seconds, was longer than the usual single. "Voyle Gilmore [see 36], who was the head of A&R for Capitol Records, asked Kelly why he made the single so long," Haskell recalls. "So Kelly asked him why he decided to make it the A-side."

As it turned out, the length wasn't a problem. On August 26, 1967, less than a month after the song debuted on the Hot 100, "Ode to Billie Joe" hit Number One. Its popularity set the stage for Gentry's hit album, named for the Number One single.

With the single already burning up the charts, the album was recorded quickly. "I did the tracks in a double session in one day," Haskell says. "After I finished conducting the arrangements, Bobbie did the vocals and then Kelly did the mixdowns. The entire album was completed in approximately a week. The artwork took longer than that," Haskell quips.

Ode to Billie Joe hit the top of the album chart in its fifth week, nearly two months after the single first topped the Hot 100. Aside from the unforgettable title track, which inspired a 1976 film based on the song's mysterious lyrics, Ode to Billie Joe is notable for another reason. It's the album that knocked Sgt. Pepper's Lonely Hearts Club Band from the summit after its 15-week stay at the top.

MOTOWN 663 # Diana Ross and the Supremes Greatest Hits

DIANA ROSS AND THE SUPREMES

97

Producers: Brain Holland and Lamont Dozier

Track listing: When the Lovelight Starts / Shining Through His Eyes / Where Did Our Love Go / Ask Any Girl / Baby Love / Run, Run, Run / Stop! In the Name of Love / Back in My Arms Again / Come See About Me / Nothing But Heartaches / Everything Is Good About You / I Hear a Symphony / Love Is Here and Now You're Gone / My World Is Empty Without You / Whisper You Love Me Boy / The Happening / You Keep Me Hangin' On / You Can't Hurry Love / Standing at the Crossroads of Love / Love is Like an Itching in My Heart / There's No Stopping Us Now

October 28, 1967
5 weeks

Diana Ross and the Supremes Greatest Hits wasn't just the second Supremes album to top the album chart—it was also the second greatest-hits set to hit the top (Johnny Mathis's *Johnny's Greatest Hits* [see 16] was the first) and the second two-record set to hit Number One (following Judy Garland's *Judy at Carnegie Hall* [see 47]).

The Supremes went through a lot in the 12 months and one week following their first Number One album. Two more albums by the trio had been released since *Supremes A' Go-Go* [see 89] hit the top of the chart: *The Supremes Sing Holland-Dozier-Holland*, which peaked at number six in March 1967, and *The Supremes Sing Rogers & Hart*, which stalled at number 20 in

July 1967. While the concept albums were only moderately successful, the Supremes couldn't miss on the Hot 100.

Following the success of "You Can't Hurry Love" [see 89], the trio scored three more Number One singles with "You Keep Me Hangin' On," "Love Is Here and Now You're Gone," and "The Happening," giving the Supremes four consecutive and 10 total Number One singles. Their previous Number One singles were "Where Did Our Love Go," "Baby Love," "Come See About Me," "Stop! In the Name of Love," "Back in My Arms Again," and "I Hear a Symphony."

With the incredibly successful string of singles under their belt, a greatest-hits package was a natural. All 10 of the group's Number One singles are featured on the album, but to fill out the two-disc set Motown had to turn to some less popular material. The opening track, "When the Lovelight Starts Shining Though His Eyes," had been the trio's first top 40 hit, peaking at number 23 in January 1964, while while several other

tracks on the set were either previously unissued as singles or had failed to crack the Hot 100. Compiled together, however, the songs were Number One, as *Diana Ross and the Supremes Greatest Hits* hit the top of the album chart in its fifth week on the chart.

Two other items of note: First, although all of the tracks featured on the album were recorded at a time when the group was simply known as the Supremes, the *Greatest Hits* collection was the first Supremes album to carry the group's new name, highlighting Ross.

And perhaps the oddest thing about *Diana Ross and the Supremes Greatest Hits* was that fact that Carol Channing, of all people, wrote the liner notes. Here she pointed out that *Hello, Dolly!* [see 67] had opened in Detroit on November 18, 1963. "And that was just about the time that Diana, Florence and Mary started to make that Motown sound famous around the world," she wrote.

"She really liked us," says Diana Ross, "and she was really sweet and very funny."

THE TOP FIVE
Week of October 28, 1967

1. **Diana Ross and the Supremes Greatest Hits**
   Diana Ross and the Supremes

2. **Sgt. Pepper's Lonely Hearts Club Band**
   The Beatles

3. **The Doors**
   The Doors

4. **Ode to Billy Joe**
   Bobbie Gentry

5. **Aretha Arrives**
   Aretha Franklin

98 Pisces, Aquarius, Capricorn & Jones Ltd. COLGEMS 104
THE MONKEES

Producer: Chip Douglas

Track listing: Salesman / She Hangs Out / The Door into Summer / Love Is Only Sleeping / Cuddly Toy / Words / Hard to Believe / Peter Percival Patterson's Pet Pig Porky / Pleasant Valley Sunday / Daily Nightly / Don't Call on Me / Star Collector

December 2, 1967
5 weeks

By the summer of 1967, the Monkees had gone full circle. "After we gained the creative control from the powers that be, we decided that rather than continue to record as a group as we had on *Headquarters,* we all wanted to become independent. *Pisces, Aquarius, Capricorn & Jones, Ltd.* was the beginning of that, with each of us performing and singing on our own tracks."

With the individual band members taking charge of specific tracks, more outside players were once again called in, including synthesizer player Paul Beaver. "We had the first Moog synthesizer on the West Coast," says Micky Dolenz, who also dabbled with the Moog. In keeping with the times, the use of the synthesizer on "Daily Nightly"

and "Star Collector" helped make *Pisces, Aquarius, Capricorn & Jones, Ltd.* the Monkees' most psychedelic album to date. Dolenz had mastered the instrument enough to play on Mike Nesmith's "Daily Nightly," but for the more complex parts on the Carole King–Gerry Goffin track "Star Collector," Beaver was brought in.

"I got pretty good at playing it eventually," says Dolenz. "I had it set up in my little studio at my house. One night John Lennon sat on the thing for five hours making flying saucer sounds."

The Monkees were also pushing the outer limits of TV by slipping messages into the TV show and their music. Just as "Last Train to Clarksville" from *The Monkees* [see 91] had a subtle anti-war message, "Salesman," written by Nesmith's friend Craig Vincent Smith, had a sly drug reference in it, which made NBC executives uneasy. "We were censored a lot, because we were under the massive corporate banner of NBC and since we had the TV show, there was a lot of concern about influencing the young."

"Pleasant Valley Sunday," written by Goffin and King, was recorded while the group was in Los Angeles to headline two nights at the Hollywood Bowl on June 9 and 10, 1967. "That was truly one of the best tunes we ever did

and one of the best tunes that Carole King ever wrote," says Dolenz, who sang lead vocals on the track. "It's a real classic." The single climbed to number three in August, setting the stage for *Pisces, Aquarius, Capricorn & Jones, Ltd.*

The album's title, conceived by Dolenz, referred to the band member's Zodiac signs. Davy Jones and Nesmith were born on December 30, 1945 and 1943, respectively, making them both Capricorns, so the former's surname was used to complete the album title.

On November 25, 1967, *Pisces, Aquarius, Capricorn & Jones, Ltd.* entered the Top LP's chart at number 29. A week later it became the fourth and final Monkees album to ride atop the album chart. Its five-week run at the top was ended by *Magical Mystery Tour* [see 99], as the Beatles knocked their American counterparts from Number One for the second consecutive time. But for the two-year span between 1966 and 1967, the Monkees spent 37 weeks at the top of the album chart, beating the Beatles' 27.

The 59th and final original episode of "The Monkees" aired on August 19, 1968. By that time the Monkees had evolved from a TV show cast into one of the most successful rock acts of their day.

THE TOP FIVE
Week of December 2, 1967

1. **Pisces, Aquarius, Capricorn & Jones, Ltd.**
   The Monkees

2. **Greatest Hits**
   Diana Ross and the Supremes

3. **Strange Days**
   The Doors

4. **Sgt. Pepper's Lonely Hearts Club Band**
   The Beatles

5. **The Doors**
   The Doors

CAPITOL 2835 # Magical Mystery Tour
THE BEATLES

99

Producer: George Martin

*Track listing: Magical Mystery Tour /
The Fool on the Hill / Flying / Blue Jay
Way /Your Mother Should Know /
I Am the Walrus / Hello Goodbye /
Strawberry Fields Forever / Penny
Lance / Baby You're a Rich Man /
All You Need Is Love*

*January 6, 1968
8 weeks*

The triumph of *Sgt. Pepper's Lonely Hearts Club Band* was soured by the death of the Beatles' longtime manager Brian Epstein, who was found dead on August 27, 1967, in his London flat from an overdose of sleeping pills. He was 32. "We all knew that everything would not be quite the same again," says producer George Martin.

Shattered by Epstein's death, the Beatles buried their sorrow in their artistic endeavors and began work, with Paul McCartney at the helm, on a film called *Magical Mystery Tour*. The title track, recorded prior to Epstein's death in April 1967, while the band was putting the finishing touches of *Sgt. Pepper's* [see 95], was a logical progression.

In the U.K., *Magical Mystery Tour* was released as a six-song double EP, which included "Flying," the Beatles first released instrumental recording and their first song to be listed as a group composition, and "I Am the Walrus," a Lennon song inspired by Lewis Carroll's poem "The Walrus and the Carpenter" from *Alice in Wonderland*. The six songs from the British EP made up the first side of the American album, released in November 1967. The film made its debut on the BBC, which telecast it in black and white on December 26, 1967. It was later released theatrically in the America, but it was panned by critics on both sides of the Atlantic.

While the film may have been little more than an oddity, the music was topnotch, especially when combined with the collection of singles that made up side two of the American album. Two of those tracks, "Strawberry Fields Forever" and "Penny Lane," were recorded during the *Pepper* sessions.

"I've found that my initial gut reaction to a piece of music is almost always right," says Martin. "When I first heard 'Strawberry Fields Forever,' I was captivated." An early, simple version of the track was recorded with John Lennon's vocal and guitar. Later, drums and bass

and a slide guitar played by George Harrison were added, but Lennon wasn't satisfied. A new version had to be recorded. This time it had an introduction played on the mellotron, and it started with the chorus. Eventually the vocals were double-tracked and brass and cello were added.

"Penny Lane," recorded shortly thereafter, was "a curious mirror to 'Strawberry Fields,' " says Martin. "Typical of the way John and Paul's minds worked, it was Paul's reply record to 'Strawberry Fields.' In their usual synchronicity, they had both been working on songs which were very evocative of their childhoods." Both Penny Lane and Strawberry Fields were places in Liverpool frequented by Lennon and McCartney as youths.

The songs never made it on *Sgt. Pepper's* because Epstein was worried about the Beatles' standing on the charts. "He came to me and asked for a good strong single that would bring them back up, so I thought of the best possible coupling I could, I gave him 'Strawberry Fields' and 'Penny Lane' back-to-back, stupid me," says Martin. "With two A-sides, the radio play was split from the start. For the first time in four years, we failed to make it to Number One in England."

Yet "Penny Lane" did hit Number One in America, as did "All You Need Is Love," a *Mystery Tour* track first performed live on June 25, 1967, as part of the international TV special "Our World," which an estimated 400 million people watched. "Hello Goodbye," a third Number One single, was also included on the album, making it a shoo-in as the Fab Four's 11th Number One album.

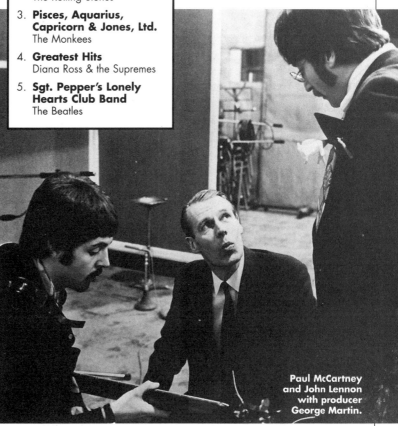

Paul McCartney and John Lennon with producer George Martin.

100 Blooming Hits PHILIPS 248
PAUL MAURIAT AND HIS ORCHESTRA

Producer: None listed

Track listing: Somethin' Stupid / Penny Lane / This Is My Song / Seuls au Monde (Alone in the World) / Inch Allah / (There's a) Kind of Hush / Puppet on a String / L'amour est Bleu (Love is Blue) / Adieu à la Nuit (Adieu to the Night) / Mama

March 2, 1968
5 weeks

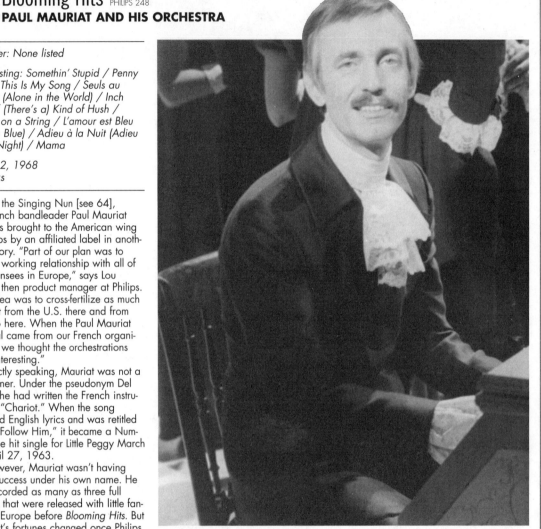

Like the Singing Nun [see 64], French bandleader Paul Mauriat was brought to the American wing of Philips by an affiliated label in another territory. "Part of our plan was to have a working relationship with all of our licensees in Europe," says Lou Simon, then product manager at Philips. "The idea was to cross-fertilize as much product from the U.S. there and from there to here. When the Paul Mauriat material came from our French organization, we thought the orchestrations were interesting."

Strictly speaking, Mauriat was not a newcomer. Under the pseudonym Del Roma, he had written the French instrumental "Chariot." When the song received English lyrics and was retitled "I Will Follow Him," it became a Number One hit single for Little Peggy March on April 27, 1963.

However, Mauriat wasn't having much success under his own name. He had recorded as many as three full albums that were released with little fanfare in Europe before Blooming Hits. But Mauriat's fortunes changed once Philips executives in America heard an instrumental called "L'Amour est Bleu." Says Simon, "We thought it had interesting

melodic content and we were looking for things to sell at the time."

As a test, Philips opted to release the song, with its title translated into English, as a single. "It had not been a hit worldwide," Simon says. "Paul only had moderate success in France up to that point, but then 'Love Is Blue' caught on."

The song, written by Andre Popp and Pierre Cour, had a spotty track record prior to Mauriat's cover. In 1967, it was entered in the Eurovision song contest and placed fourth. The song was recorded by Vicky Leandros in 19 different languages, but it didn't really catch on until Mauriat's instrumental version was released.

When the single began climbing the charts, Philips contacted Mauriat's French label and asked for an entire album. Ironically, Blooming Hits also included a cover of "Puppet on a

String," the song made famous by Sandie Shaw, which won the 1967 Eurovision song contest.

Other songs given the Mauriat treatment on the album included "Penny Lane" by the Beatles [see 99]; "Somethin' Stupid," which had been a Number One hit by Nancy and Frank Sinatra; "Mama," cowritten by Sonny Bono; and "(There's a) Kind of Hush," a hit for Herman's Hermits.

On February 10, 1968, "Love Is Blue" hit the top of the Hot 100. It had already inspired four different cover versions that also hit the chart.

Three weeks later, Blooming Hits hit the summit, ending the eight-week reign of the Beatles' Magical Mystery Tour. Blooming Hits was Mauriat's first and only album chart-topper. He continued to chart albums through 1971, but none of his subsequent efforts cracked the top 50.

THE TOP FIVE
Week of March 2, 1968

1. **Blooming Hits**
   Paul Mauriat and His Orchestra

2. **John Wesley Harding**
   Bob Dylan

3. **Magical Mystery Tour**
   The Beatles

4. **Axis: Bold as Love**
   The Jimi Hendrix Experience

5. **Lady Soul**
   Aretha Franklin

COLUMBIA 3180 **The Graduate** **101**
SOUNDTRACK

Producer: Teo Macero

Track listing: Sounds of Silence / The Singleman Foxtrot / Mrs. Robinson (Version 1 as heard in film) / Sunporch Cha-Cha-Cha / Scarborough Fair/Canticle (Interlude) / On the Strip / April Come She Will / The Folks / Scarborough Fair/Canticle / A Great Effect / The Big Bright Green Pleasure Machine / Whew / Mrs. Robinson (Version 2 as heard in film) / Sounds of Silence

April 6, 1968
9 weeks (nonconsecutive)

The *Graduate* was the album that made Simon & Garfunkel superstars, but it wasn't just a Simon & Garfunkel album. Six of the album's 14 tracks were instrumentals performed and written by jazz pianist Dave Grusin. His compositions would be overshadowed by the songs of Simon & Garfunkel, particularly a new tune called "Mrs. Robinson."

Prior to the spring of 1968, Paul Simon and Art Garfunkel had already enjoyed considerable success. The boyhood friends, who met in sixth grade at a New York City elementary school, first performed together as Tom & Jerry in 1957. Nearly a decade later, the duo found success using their surnames, scoring three consecutive top five hits in 1965: the Number One single "The Sounds of Silence," "Homeward Bound," and "I Am a Rock." The duo's highest-charting album prior to *The Graduate* was *Parsley, Sage, Rosemary and Thyme*, which climbed to number four in December 1966.

The Graduate was Mike Nichols's second film. After earning recognition as a comedian and Broadway theater director, Nichols made his big-screen debut with the film adaptation of *Who's Afraid of Virginia Woolf.* He thought a Simon & Garfunkel score would be perfect for *The Graduate,* a coming-of-age story starring Dustin Hoffman as Ben Braddock and Anne Bancroft as the seductive Mrs. Robinson, the mother of Ben's girlfriend.

"We were working on *Bookends* [see 102] at the time and staying at the Beverly Wilshire," recalls Art Garfunkel. "Mike would pick us up in his Hertz rental car and bring us down to the soundstage."

While Nichols was waiting for the duo to deliver some new material, he temporarily placed existing Simon & Garfunkel songs "The Sounds of Silence" and "Scarborough Fair/Canticle" into the film.

"Mike was beginning to love it just as is," adds Garfunkel. "So he really was fixing on the one new tune he needed to keep the chug-chug rhythm thing going while Dustin's character is racing from Berkeley to Southern California. I knew that Paul was in the middle of writing an up-tempo song, and I was guessing that he wasn't very big on it and it wouldn't get finished, because to Paul it was simple, but I thought it

was very appropriate. It was called 'Mrs. Roosevelt.' I said, 'Mrs. Roosevelt' could easily be 'Mrs. Robinson.'"

With the score all but complete, Grusin was a little perplexed about his involvement in the project. "The hilarious part about *The Graduate* album for me is that I wasn't sure why I was hired," he says. "I got there and Paul had been working on new songs for some time, but Mike almost had the picture cut with existing Simon & Garfunkel material. The few things that I wrote were little source-music pieces."

Grusin knew album producer Teo Macero from his work with jazz great Miles Davis. When Macero called one day asking him to compile his material for a soundtrack album he was shocked. "I said, 'There isn't an album there.' I had barely enough stuff, and most of the Simon & Garfunkel stuff had been previously released." (In those days, soundtracks were usually comprised of new material.)

"So I sent all this stuff and it was a joke," adds Grusin. "When I heard it, it was still a joke, but it went through the roof. I couldn't believe it."

The Graduate hit Number One in its fourth week on the chart and would stay at the top for seven consecutive weeks before being temporarily displaced by Simon & Garfunkel's own *Bookends* [see 102].

THE TOP FIVE
Week of April 6, 1968

1. **The Graduate**
   Soundtrack

2. **Blooming Hits**
   Paul Mauriat & His Orchestra

3. **Lady Soul**
   Aretha Franklin

4. **John Wesley Harding**
   Bob Dylan

5. **Parsley, Sage, Rosemary & Thyme**
   Simon & Garfunkel

Dustin Hoffman in *The Graduate*.

102 Bookends COLUMBIA 9529
SIMON & GARFUNKEL

Producers: Paul Simon, Art Garfunkel and Roy Halee

Track listing: Bookends Theme (Instrumental) / Save the Life of My Child / America / Overs / Voices of Old People / Old Friends / Bookends Theme / Fakin' It / Punky's Dilemma / Mrs. Robinson / Hazy Shade of Winter / At the Zoo

*May 25, 1968
7 weeks (nonconsecutive)*

Paul Simon and Art Garfunkel were working on their fourth album, *Bookends*, when filmmaker Mike Nichols asked them to score his film *The Graduate* [see 101]. "Mrs. Robinson" was the only new Simon & Garfunkel song on the album, and arguably the most popular. It was featured twice in the film and on the soundtrack, but the completed version of the tune wasn't unveiled until April 1968 with the release of *Bookends*.

Following Garfunkel's suggestion, Simon agreed to change his song-in-progress "Mrs. Roosevelt" to "Mrs. Robinson," named after the character portrayed by Anne Bancroft in *The Graduate*. The duo showed Nichols the chorus, with the line, "Jesus loves you more than you will know." Garfunkel recalls, "The sarcastic edge was just right. Mike loved the chorus. Paul never finished writing the verses during that time, so in the movie you just hear the 'dut-da-duts,' but the chorus exists. When the film came out, we were back in the studio finishing the album, so the rest of the song got written after the film's release."

"Punky's Dilemma" was written specifically for *The Graduate*, but wasn't used in the film because Nichols fell in love with the way previously released Simon & Garfunkel songs worked in the film. "That was supposed to be used in the scene when Dustin's character is at home, finished with college, floating in the pool and wondering what to do with his future," says Garfunkel. "Paul wrote, 'Wish I was a Kellogg's Cornflake/Floatin in my bowl. . .,' but Mike didn't quite go for it. I remember him saying, 'Can you make it into a funeral dirge just to give it an odd twist?'"

Instead, "Punky's Dilemma" appears on *Bookends* as a dreamy folk-pop number.

Bookends also includes three previously released singles that hadn't yet appeared on an album: "A Hazy Shade of Winter" climbed to number 13 in December 1966 (a cover by the Bangles would reach number two in 1987); "At the Zoo" reached number 16 in April 1967; and "Fakin' It" stalled at number 23 in August 1967.

Those songs, combined with the full version of "Mrs. Robinson" and a number of new tracks, were enough to push *Bookends* to Number One in its fifth week on the chart, temporarily displacing *The Graduate* for seven weeks. In fact, *Bookends* and *The Graduate* held the top two positions for eight consecutive weeks, while "Mrs. Robinson" reached Number One on the Hot 100 on June 1, and held the top spot for three weeks.

On March 12, 1969, Simon & Garfunkel won three Grammys. "Mrs. Robinson" was named record of the year and best contemporary pop vocal performance by a duo or group, while *The Graduate* won best original score written for a motion picture.

THE TOP FIVE
Week of May 25, 1968

1. **Bookends**
   Simon & Garfunkel

2. **The Graduate**
   Soundtrack

3. **The Birds, the Bees & the Monkees**
   The Monkees

4. **The Best of the Brass**
   Herb Alpert & the Tijuana Brass

5. **Lady Soul**
   Aretha Franklin

A&M 4146 # Beat of the Brass **103**
HERB ALPERT & THE TIJUANA BRASS

Producers: Herb Alpert and Jerry Moss

Track listing: Monday, Monday / A Beautiful Friend / Cabaret / Panama / Belz Mein Shtetele Belz (My Home Town) / Talk to the Animals / Slick / She Touched Me / Thanks for the Memory / The Robin / This Guy's in Love with You

July 26, 1968
2 weeks

By 1968, Herb Alpert had accomplished several notable achievements. He and his partner Jerry Moss had established a successful recording company with the 1962 launch of A&M Records. He also was a successful recording artist, with four Number One albums to his credit [see 80, 82, 85, and 93]. Yet one thing Alpert and A&M had yet to do was score a Number One single. Also, since establishing the Tijuana Brass, all of Alpert's recordings had been instrumentals. That all changed with *The Beat of the Brass.*

"In the real early days, under the name of Dore Alpert, I recorded a few vocals," Alpert says of the brief period in 1959 when he was signed to Dot Records as a vocalist and recorded the song "Tell It to the Birds." Alpert's vocals would make a dramatic return when the trumpet player went to work on his own television special for CBS in 1968. "The producer asked me if I would consider singing a song," Alpert says. "So I called Burt Bacharach and asked him if he had a wonderful song tucked away in his drawer someplace that he finds himself whistling now and then. He sent over a song called 'This Boy Is in Love with You.' I was just crazy about the melody and the feeling of the song, so I met with Hal David and he changed some of the lyrics for the TV show."

During the show, which was broadcast on April 22, 1968, Alpert sang the song to his then-wife Sharon on the beach in Malibu.

"It wasn't recorded to be a single, it was just part of the show," he says. "But when the show was aired, we got an enormous response to it."

In much the same way Alpert recorded his trumpet tracks, his vocal on "This Guy's in Love with You" was recorded in a single take. "The vocal group that backed me on it was in the studio when I recorded it," he says. "We did the track and then I put my voice on it. I got a lot of encouragement, but I didn't know if they were just stroking me or if they were really impressed. They liked it a heck of a lot more than I did."

Yet after several listens to the demo tape at home, Alpert began to like the track. "I realized it had something. There was a certain unpretentious quality I brought to it that worked." The American public agreed—on June 22, 1968, the song become the first Number One single for Alpert, A&M, and writers Bacharach and David.

None of the other tracks on the album fared nearly as well, but there were a few other noteworthy songs, particularly Alpert's version of the Mamas and the Papas "Monday, Monday" [see 84] and covers of "Cabaret" and "Thanks for the Memory," which served as the theme of *The Bob Hope Show.* The album hit the summit of the Top LP's chart in its 12th week on the chart, primarily based on the strength of "This Guy's in Love with You." It was Alpert's fifth and final Number One album as an artist, but his label would go on to score several more.

THE TOP FIVE
Week of July 26, 1968

1. **The Beat of the Brass**
   Herb Alpert & the Tijuana Brass

2. **Wheels of Fire**
   Cream

3. **Bookends**
   Simon & Garfunkel

4. **A Tramp Shining**
   Richard Harris

5. **The Graduate**
   Soundtrack

104 Wheels of Fire ATCO 700
CREAM

Producer: Felix Pappalardi

Track listing: White Room / Sitting on Top of the World / Passing the Time / As You Said / Pressed Rat and Warthog / Politician / Those Were the Days / Born Under a Bad Sign / Deserted Cities of the Heart / Crossroads / Spoonful / Traintime / Toad

August 10, 1968
4 weeks

"**S**itting on Top of the World" was the name of the old Mississippi Sheiks blues standard (popularized by Howlin' Wolf) Cream covered on its third album, but it also summed up the band's position at the time. "We were sort of flying already," recalls Ginger Baker, who played drums in the power trio. "*Fresh Cream* and *Disraeli Gears* were still on the charts when we recorded *Wheels of Fire*. We had this sort of confidence of giants."

Cream was formed in July 1966 after guitarist Eric Clapton left John Mayall's Bluesbreakers, bassist Jack Bruce departed Manfred Mann, and Baker exited the Graham Bond Organisation. The trio was named by Clapton because it was considered "the cream of the crop" of British blues musicians. Despite tremendous commercial success first in England and subsequently in America, all was not well with the supergroup.

"By the time of *Wheels of Fire*, really, the band probably was dead already, but it didn't know it," Baker admits. "There were things going down through those sessions that probably led to the demise of Cream as it turned out. If you notice, Eric didn't do very much

writing, and I didn't do much more."

While Clapton's contribution did not include songwriting, his stamp is all over the two-disc set, particularly on "White Room," which would become a rock classic, and the live version of Robert Johnson's "Crossroads," which became so synonymous with Clapton that his 1988 boxed-set career retrospective and its 1996 sequel were titled after the track.

The first disc of *Wheels of Fire* was recorded during February 1968 at Atlantic Records studios in New York. Cream had recorded its previous album, *Disraeli Gears*, which climbed to number four, at the same studio. In fact, the band even stayed at the same hotel during the sessions. In the studio, Cream and producer Felix Pappalardi continued to experiment with varied instrumentation, including tympani, strings, brass, tubular bells, and glockenspiel. Says Baker, "We were just trying to go for-

ward, so we tried some pretty far-out things. *Wheels of Fire* was probably the most experimental thing we ever did. We broke a lot of new ground."

The second disc, recorded live during the band's two-week stand at the famed Fillmore West in San Francisco, offered the first taste of live Cream on record. By that time, the band had become known for its wildly improvisational performances, which were often incredibly powerful, but sometimes excessive. "We had this E.S.P. thing going where we could change arrangements onstage and everybody knew where everybody was going," Baker explain. "It was a continuing adventure."

Three months after the release of *Wheels of Fire*, Cream played two farewell concerts at London's Royal Albert Hall. After Cream disbanded, Clapton and Baker joined another supergroup, Blind Faith [see 115].

THE TOP FIVE
Week of August 10, 1968

1. **Wheels of Fire**
   Cream

2. **The Graduate**
   Soundtrack

3. **Time Peace/The Rascals' Greatest Hits**
   The Rascals

4. **The Beat of the Brass**
   Herb Alpert & the Tijuana Brass

5. **Aretha Now**
   Aretha Franklin

ELEKTRA 74024 # Waiting for the Sun
THE DOORS
105

Producer: Paul A. Rothchild

Track listing: Hello, I Love You / Love Street / Not to Touch the Earth / Summer's Almost Gone / Wintertime Love / The Unknown Soldier / Spanish Caravan / My Wild Love / We Could Be So Good Together / Yes, the River Knows / Five to One

September 7, 1968
4 weeks (nonconsecutive)

When the Doors entered the studio in early 1968, the band "hit the third album wall," said producer Paul A. Rothchild. The Los Angeles band's 1967 self-titled debut album, which featured the Number One hit "Light My Fire," was recorded in a mere six days. Strange Days, the followup album released later that year, took about two months. Then came Waiting for the Sun, which could have been called Waiting for Jim, as Doors frontman Jim Morrison "frequently didn't show up or showed up late, drunk or uninspired," Rothchild said.

In a short 12 months, Morrison had become a rock star and sex symbol and was beginning to feel trapped by his own image. "He was getting tired of the rock star trip," said Rothchild. "With that much fame, he figured, 'I am the Lizard King, I can do anything,'" as Morrison himself stated at the end of "Not to Touch the Earth." Morrison frequently showed up stoned with various hangers-on in tow. Drummer John Densmore got so disgusted that at one point he quit the band, only to return to the studio the next day. As manager Bill Siddons

noted, "Jim's unpredictable behavior was wearing everyone out."

Morrison's inner struggle, coupled with the band's shortage of new material and Rothchild's perfectionist tendencies, made the sessions difficult. "It didn't have the ease that the other records had," said Rothchild. "Most of it was invented in the studio. They were digging for tunes."

"Five to One" came together from a studio jam, with Morrison chanting his lyrics over Densmore's 4/4 beat, while Robbie Krieger and Ray Manzarek improvised guitar and keyboard parts, respectively.

Yet other songs were extremely tedious to record. Part of "The Unknown Soldier" took up to 60 takes to complete. The track, which Rothchild said was "pieced together in sections like a film," was Morrison's first overtly political song.

"Hello, I Love You" showed the other side of the Doors. The song was discovered by Rothchild after he asked the band if they had any songs that they thought "were not worthy of their dignity." When Densmore brought up the title, Morrison cringed. "Jim said, 'It's just a dumb

little song I wrote out in Venice one day when I saw this black chick walk by,'" Rothchild recalled. "He sang the song and when they hit the chorus the first time, I shit in my pants. I said, ~'That's a Number One record.'"

With a little studio wizardry and experimenting, including a middle section in which Rothchild stacked 10 different recordings of Krieger's guitar recorded at different speeds, the song was completed. Rothchild's hunch also turned out to be correct, as "Hello, I Love You" became the Doors' second Number One single on August 3, 1968.

Just over a month later, Waiting for the Sun would become the Doors' first and only Number One album. Said Rothchild of the difficult sessions, "We knew where the end of the maze was. Sometimes we would rattle around inside, but we knew we would come out the other end."

Yet three years later, Morrison's self-destructive behavior took its final toll. On July 2, 1971, he was found dead in a bathtub in Paris. Medical officials said Morrison, 27, died of a heart attack. He may have suspected his fate as early as Waiting for the Sun, as he sung in "Five to One": "No one here gets out alive."

THE TOP FIVE
Week of September 7, 1968

1. **Waiting for the Sun**
   The Doors

2. **Time Peace/ Greatest Hits**
   The Rascals

3. **Wheels of Fire**
   Cream

4. **Feliciano!**
   Jose Feliciano

5. **Realization**
   Johnny Rivers

106 Time Peace/The Rascals' Greatest Hits ATLANTIC 8190
THE RASCALS

Producer: The Rascals

Track listing: I Ain't Gonna Eat Out of My Heart Anymore / Good Lovin' / You Better Run / Come on Up / Mustang Sally / Love Is a Beautiful Thing / In the Midnight Hour / Lonely Too Long / Groovin' / A Girl Like You / How Can I Be Sure / It's Wonderful / Easy Rollin' / A Beautiful Morning

September 28, 1968
1 week

Time Peace was a bittersweet triumph for the Rascals, as it became the band's highest-charting—and last—album to crack the top 10. It was also the album the group was least involved in, according to singer/keyboardist Felix Cavaliere.

The Young Rascals formed in New York in late 1964, after Cavaliere joined Joey Dee & the Starlighters, a band that included Eddie Brigati and Gene Cornish. Soon the trio opted to leave Dee and form a quartet with the addition of Dino Danelli. The group's first single, "I Ain't Gonna Eat Out of My Heart Anymore," featuring Brigati on lead vocals, stalled at number 52 in February 1966, but a follow-up called "Good Lovin'," with Cavaliere singing, took off, hitting Number One on the Hot 100 on April 30, 1966. In the next few years the group's "blue-eyed soul" sound produced several other hits,

including "Groovin'," which went Number One on May 27, 1967, and "How Can I Be Sure," which climbed to number four later that year. The Young Rascals were also performing fairly well on the album chart. Groovin' reached number five in the fall of 1967.

The success brought the group a certain amount of freedom. Following the release of "It's Wonderful" in late 1967, the group was allowed to change its name to simply "the Rascals," its original choice for a moniker. Once Upon a Dream, which climbed to number 9 in the spring of 1968, was the first album issued under the new moniker. Then came Time Peace.

The band's success put it in a strange dilemma, says Cavaliere. "I was not too enamored with the amount of tax we were paying," he says. "So I took a hiatus to Mexico at the time and the next thing I knew there was a greatest hits album. The selection of the songs was taken on by the company, which was a little strange because we were supposed to have creative control."

Yet Cavaliere understood why the label put the collection together. "The record label wanted product out and didn't have any," he says. "In those days we didn't have the luxury of a year and a half or two years between albums."

While 13 of Time Peace's 14 tracks had been previously released on other albums, "A Beautiful Morning" made its

album debut on the LP. Yet "People Got to Be Free," which went to Number One on the Hot 100 just over a month before Time Peace hit the summit of the album chart, was left off the album, as Atlantic opted save the track for 1969's Freedom Suite.

"It was a mixed bag," Cavaliere says of Time Peace. "The whole concept was something that came from a commercial point of view, rather than an artistic product. The so-called establishment was making its presence felt once again. It was kind of ironic, because that was the reason I took off in the first place."

THE TOP FIVE
Week of September 28, 1968

1. **Time Peace/The Rascals' Greatest Hits**
   The Rascals

2. **Waiting for the Sun**
   The Doors

3. **Feliciano!**
   Jose Feliciano

4. **Cheap Thrills**
   Big Brother and the Holding Company

5. **Realization**
   Johnny Rivers

COLUMBIA 9700 ## Cheap Thrills

BIG BROTHER AND THE HOLDING COMPANY

Producer: John Simon

Track listing: Combination of the Two / I Need a Man to Love / Summertime / Piece of My Heart / Turtle Blues / Oh, Sweet Mary / Ball and Chain

October 12, 1968
8 weeks (nonconsecutive)

Big Brother and the Holding Company formed in January 1966 and served as the house band at San Francisco's Avalon Ballroom as an instrumental ensemble. The band didn't gain significant notice, however, until it found a voice in a charismatic singer from Port Arthur, Texas, named Janis Joplin, who signed on to front the band in June. By August, the band had secured a contract with Mainstream Records.

With Joplin, Big Brother became the surprise hit of the Monterey Pop Festival in June 1967. Bob Dylan's manager Albert Grossman was impressed enough to sign the band. Its self-titled debut on Mainstream reached number 60. That album, along with the band's growing live following, was enough to secure Big Brother a contract with Columbia.

On March 8, 1968, Big Brother played opening night at the Fillmore East in New York, but none of the material featured on Cheap Thrills was recorded at the Fillmore, despite what the album cover states, says Big Brother founder Peter Albin. "We wanted to do a live record and Cheap Thrills was basically a culmination of that desire, but it's not a live record," says Albin. "It was live in the way we recorded in the studio. We didn't do a lot of overdubs, we did vocals at the same time. We played to a small group of friends, but

most of it wasn't concert recordings."

Big Brother's rendition of blues singer Willie Mae "Big Mama" Thornton's "Ball and Chain," recorded at Winterland in San Francisco, is the only concert recording on the album. The rest of the album was recorded between live dates at various studios.

The loose sessions didn't go very well. In fact, Grossman suggested replacing bassist Albin and drummer David Getz. Producer John Simon, unhappy with the sound of the record, left the project before the album was completed and requested that his name be left off of it altogether.

For material, Big Brother turned to a mix of covers and originals, half of which was culled from its live set. "'I Need a Man to Love' was something that [guitarist] Sam [Andrew] threw together in the studio." Albin's "Oh Sweet Mary" was basically a remake of "Coo Coo" from the first album. "We wanted to do it again, but eliminate Mainstream Records from the publishing. So we renamed it

and added other parts to it."

The album's highlights, most notably "Piece of My Heart," showcased Joplin's bluesy vocals. The song, written by Bert Berns and Jerry Ragavoy, was brought to the band's attention by fellow San Franciscan Jack Casady of the Jefferson Airplane [see 202], Albin says. It would go on to become Big Brother's biggest hit single, reaching number 12.

The album's title, originally Dope, Sex and Cheap Thrills, was pared down to the safer moniker for its August 1968 release. A month later, Grossman announced that Joplin, along with Andrews, would be leaving the group by the end of the year. The announcement couldn't have come at a worse time for the remaining members of Big Brother, as Cheap Thrills climbed to Number One in its eighth week on the chart. Joplin went on to a successful but brief solo career prior to her death [see 130], while Big Brother, which reunited with Joplin for a live performance in April 1970, carried on until 1972.

Copyright Lisa Law

108 Electric Ladyland REPRISE 6307
THE JIMI HENDRIX EXPRIENCE

Producer: Jimi Hendrix

Track listing: ...And the Gods Made Love / Have You Ever Been (to Electric Ladyland) / Crosstown Traffic / Voodoo Chile / Little Miss Strange /Long Hot Summer Night / Come On (Let the Good Times Roll) / Gypsy Eyes / Burning of the Midnight Lamp / Rainy Day, Dream Away / 1983...(A Merman I Should Turn to Be) / Moon, Turn the Tides...gently gently away / Still Raining, Still Dreaming / House Burning Down / All Along the Watchtower / Voodoo Chile (Slight Return)

November 16, 1968
2 weeks

In December 1967, Jimi Hendrix began work on his most ambitious album to date. Hendrix had grown tired of being known for onstage antics like burning his guitars. He was a serious musician. To prove his point, he would need a double album to express his musical vision.

Hendrix began his career in the early '60s as a session guitarist with the Isley Brothers [see 208]. By 1965, he formed his own band, Jimmy James and the Blues Flames. A year later, Chas Chandler of the Animals introduced him to bassist Noel Redding and drummer Mitch Mitchell. The trio was dubbed the Jimi Hendrix Experience.

The group's first album, Are You Experienced?, released in May 1967, reached number five. Axis: Bold as Love, released in January 1968, peaked at number three. Hendrix had earned a place next to Eric Clapton [see 104] as one of rock's premiere guitarists.

"On Electric Ladyland Jimi was able to stretch out, expand and bring other musicians in," says Eddie Kramer, who engineered the album. Hendrix had opted to produce the album himself, instead of relying on Chandler, who walked out of the sessions early on.

The initial sessions were recorded on four-track at Olympic Studios in London. Later Hendrix moved to the Record Plant in New York, which had one of the few 12-track machines in the U.S. "'Crosstown Traffic' and 'All Along the Watchtower' were recorded on four-track, but then eventually dubbed over, so Jimi had more tracks to play with," says Kramer. A few months later, a 16-track was used. "The more tracks that became available, the more complex the songs became," Kramer says.

Yet while Hendrix was in the midst of his studio experimentation, he was forced to hit the road. Hendrix had block-booked the Record Plant at a cost of $60,000. "He was definitely frustrated," says Kramer. "He was trying to establish himself as a producer, but he had to keep interrupting the recording to go out on the road and make money."

When Hendrix was able to get a stretch of time in the studio, the results were often mind-boggling. "When Jimi and I mixed '1983,' that was a performance in itself. We mixed it straight through without stopping as if we were performing the song live." The track ran nearly 14 minutes.

Hendrix would often break the sessions to go catch some live music in local clubs. Usually he would return in the wee hours of the morning with several others in tow, and work until the sun came up. Often these hangers-on would be a distraction, but other times, they added to the sessions. That was the case when Hendrix cut "Voodoo Chile." Says Kramer, "That back and forth musical conversation between Jimi and Steve Winwood [see 115] was spine-tingling."

Material written by some of Hendrix's peers was also included. When Hendrix heard Bob Dylan's [see 170] "All Along the Watchtower" in early 1968, he knew he had to record it. Says Kramer, "It started off as a fairly simple song, but by the time we were done it was recorded in 16-track and mixed a half-dozen times. Jimi had a great love for Dylan's material and he wanted to make sure he got it right."

Electric Ladyland was released in October 1968. Five weeks later, it hit the summit, with Are You Experienced? still in the top 10 after 65 weeks on the chart. It was Hendrix's first and only Number One album.

Less than two years later, on September 18, 1970, Hendrix was dead at the age of 27. The cause was inhalation of vomit induced by a barbiturate overdose.

THE TOP FIVE
Week of November 16, 1968

1. **Electric Ladyland**
   The Jimi Hendrix Experience

2. **Cheap Thrills**
   Big Brother and the
   Holding Company

3. **Time Peace/Greatest Hits**
   The Rascals

4. **Feliciano!**
   Jose Feliciano

5. **The Second**
   Stepenwolf

on this big organ that looked like the organ at the Crystal Cathedral and it just blew me away," Campbell recalls.

Yet when Campbell initially recorded the song at Capitol Records Studio A in Hollywood, he wasn't pleased with the results. "We couldn't get the sound we wanted for the record, so we ended up carting that organ down to the studio and we had Jimmy play on it."

The rest of the album was comprised of a diverse selection of songs Campbell simply "wanted to sing," including Otis Redding's "(Sittin' on) the Dock of the Bay," the Bee Gees' "Words," Sonny Bono's "You Better Sit Down Kids," and Tim Hardin's "Reason to Believe." The latter track would later be recorded by Rod Stewart [see 134].

"I didn't have enough time in those days to really look for songs," says Campbell. "The career was going full blast by then." Although Campbell was given songwriting credit for "Fate of Man," the lyrics for the song came from a poem written by Campbell's grandfather, Daniel. The music for the track was also borrowed. "I just played 'Danny Boy' behind it," Campbell says.

Ultimately, not even Campbell's interesting song selection could keep the *Wichita Lineman* down. On the album's jacket, Capitol boasted that it was "Probably one of the best albums you've ever heard...Probably the best album he's ever made..." Although the label may have had trouble backing up the former claim, the latter certainly held true, at least based on its chart performance. In its sixth week on the Top LP's chart, the *Wichita Lineman* climbed to the top, becoming Campbell's first and only Number One album.

Producer: Al De Lory

Track listing: Wichita Lineman / (Sittin' on) the Dock of the Bay / If You Go Away / Ann / Words / Fate of Man / Dreams of the Everyday Housewife / The Straight Life / Reason to Believe / You Better Sit Down Kids / That's Not Home

December 21, 1968
5 weeks (nonconsecutive)

By 1967, Glen Campbell's career had come to life. After recording sessions with the Champs in 1960, playing sessions with Elvis Presley and Frank Sinatra [see 86], and working as a touring replacement for the Beach Boys' Brian Wilson, Campbell became a star in his own right. His 1967 debut album *Gentle on My Mind* climbed to number five. The follow-up *By the Time I Get to Phoenix*, also released in 1967, didn't fare as well on the charts—it stalled at number 15—but earned Campbell a Grammy for album of the year. Although his first two albums of 1968—

Hey, Little One and *A New Place in the Sun*—failed to crack the top 20, Campbell had another hit on his hands with *Bobbie Gentry & Glen Campbell*, an album that paired him with the voice behind *Ode to Billy Joe* [see 96].

Given the number of albums Campbell released in 1968, the singer-guitarist had little time to search for material. Aside from all the recording and live dates, Campbell was also spending time in front of the television camera. After guesting on "The Smothers Brothers Comedy Hour" on CBS, he was asked to host a summer replacement for the show in June 1968, which was so successful that Campbell landed his own series in early 1969.

Wichita Lineman was centered around the title track, written by Jimmy Webb, the same Los Angeles–based songwriter who'd penned Campbell's first top 30 hit, "By the Time I Get to Phoenix." Campbell still recalls the first time he heard the song about a telephone company worker, not a football player, during a visit to Webb's Hollywood Hills home. "He played it for me

---

THE TOP FIVE
Week of December 21, 1968

1. **Wichita Lineman**
   Glen Campbell

2. **The Beatles**
   The Beatles

3. **Cheap Thrills**
   Big Brother & the
   Holding Company

4. **Feliciano!**
   Jose Feliciano

5. **The Second**
   Steppenwolf

110 The Beatles APPLE 101
THE BEATLES

Producer: George Martin

Track listing: Back in the U.S.S.R. /
Dear Prudence / Glass Onion / Ob-La-
Di, Ob-La-Da / Wild Honey Pie / The
Continuing Story of Bungalow Bill /
While My Guitar Gently Weeps /
Happiness Is a Warm Gun / Martha
My Dear / I'm So Tired / Blackbird /
Piggies / Rocky Raccoon / Don't Pass
Me By / Why Don't We Do It in the
Road? / I Will / Julia / Birthday / Yer
Blues / Mother Nature's Son /
Everybody's Got Something to Hide
Except for Me and My Monkey / Sexy
Sadie / Helter Skelter / Long, Long,
Long / Revolution 1 / Honey Pie /
Savoy Truffle / Cry Baby Cry /
Revolution 9 / Good Night

December 28, 1968
9 weeks (nonconsecutive)

The simple title The Beatles suggests a group effort, but that suggestion couldn't have been further from the truth. The two-record set, more than any other Beatles album before it, was more like a collection of solo songs than a group effort. Tension in the group was reaching a new high. The fact that the album came with four individual portraits of the Beatles, rather than a group picture, was fitting.

In a sharp contrast to the covers of Sgt. Pepper's [see 95] and Magical Mystery Tour [see 99], The Beatles was packaged in a plain white sleeve with the group's name tastefully embossed on it. Because of this spartan cover design, most refer to the LP, the band's first on its own Apple label, as The White Album.

"In the beginning of 1968 we went to India," says George Harrison. "We

went to see the Maharishi, so a lot of the songs on The White Album were written in the Himalayas. Donovan was up there and he showed John [Lennon] how to play with this style of finger-picking. A lot of the songs, like 'Goodnight,' 'Julia,' and 'Dear Prudence'—they all basically have that same acoustic, picking background."

Paul McCartney's solo contributions included "Wild Honey Pie," "Blackbird," and "Why Don't We Do It in the Road." Also featured was "Don't Pass Me By," the first Beatles song written by Ringo Starr.

Harrison's "While My Guitar Gently Weeps" was nearly rejected by the other members of the band. "I ran through the song and it wasn't exactly happening, so there wasn't much interest in it," he says. "I felt a little bit pissed off because we really never got into the song." That evening, Harrison spent the night with his friend Eric Clapton. "The next morning we were driving into London and I asked Eric if he would come to the studio and play on the tune." Clapton was hesitant to accept the offer. "He said, 'No, I can't do that. The Beatles never let anyone else play on their records.'" Yet Harrison insisted. "I said, 'It's my tune and I'd like to you play on it.' So I took him into the session and it was a good move, because then everyone started paying a little more attention." With Clapton sitting in

on electric guitar, the Beatles had to rethink their instrumental approach. "I just played acoustic and sang," Harrison says. "John never played on the record and Paul played piano with Ringo on drums." Later, McCartney overdubbed bass onto the track. Yet Clapton wasn't satisfied with the cut. "He said, 'Hang on, it doesn't sound Beatle-y enough.'" To get the trademark finishing touch, a phaser was used to double-track portions of the song. "That's why the guitar sounds the way it does," Harrison explains. Although Clapton played lead, Harrison's use of "My Guitar" in the song's title was appropriate: "Eric played my cherry-red Les Paul, which he had actually given me as a present," says Harrison.

Two of the album's tracks, "Piggies" and "Helter Skelter," took on an eerie added meaning following the Manson family's Tate-LaBianca slayings. At the murder sites, Manson family members scrawled the words "POLITICAL PIGGY" and "HELTER SKELTER."

Says Harrison, "It was mentioned as if we were sending him messages. It's just sick. It just shows that everyone is on their own trip, but they can attribute their actions to someone else. The famous one is God told 'em to do it. But it's such a lot of bullshit. The Beatles never told anyone to do anything, and I don't suppose God told anyone to do anything either."

THE TOP FIVE
Week of December 28, 1968

1. **The Beatles**
   The Beatles

2. **Wichita Lineman**
   Glen Campbell

3. **Cheap Thrills**
   Big Brother and the
   Holding Company

4. **The Second**
   Steppenwolf

5. **Wild Flowers**
   Judy Collins

DIANA ROSS & THE SUPREMES WITH THE TEMPTATIONS

Producer: Motown Productions in association with George Schlatter–Ed Friendly Productions

Track listing: T.C.B. / Stop! In the Name of Love / Introduction of Diana Ross and the Supremes / You Keep Me Hangin' On / Introduction of the Temptations: Get Ready / Introduction of Diana Ross: The Way You Do the Things You Do / Medley: A Taste of Honey / Eleanor Rigby / Do You Know the Way to San Jose / Mrs. Robinson / Respect / Somewhere / Ain't Too Proud to Beg / Introduction to the Temptations / Hello, Young Lovers / For Once in My Life / (I Know) I'm Losing You / With a Song in My Heart / Without a Song / Medley: Come See About Me / My World Is Empty Without You / Baby Love / I Hear a Symphony / The Impossible Dream

February 8, 1969
1 week

In 1959, the vocal trio of Mary Wilson, Florence Ballard, and Betty Travis was put together by manager Milton Jenkins to back up his male singing group the Primes. The female group, which was later rounded out by Diana Ross, was known as the Primettes, but would rise to fame as the Supremes. The Primes would also change their name. They would become known as the Temptations.

Nearly a decade later, the pairing of Motown's star male and female vocal groups was a natural. While the Temp-

THE TOP FIVE
Week of February 8, 1969

1. **TCB**
   Diana Ross & the Supremes with the Temptations

2. **The Beatles**
   The Beatles

3. **Wichita Lineman**
   Glen Campbell

4. **Greatest Hits, Vol. 1**
   The Association

5. **Diana Ross & the Supremes Join the Temptations**
   Diana Ross & the Supremes with the Temptations

tations weren't as successful as the Supremes, they were stars in their own right. The quintet scored several hits, including "My Girl," which topped both the Hot 100 and R&B singles chart in 1965. On the Top LP's chart, the Temptations' highest-charting album was 1966's *The Temptations Greatest Hits*, which peaked at number five. Ironically, it would take a reunion with their old backing vocalists to take them to the top of the album chart.

By the time the two groups joined forces for *Diana Ross and the Supremes Join the Temptations* in 1968, each group had gone through personnel changes following their initial breakthroughs. In July 1967, Ballard was officially dismissed from the Supremes and replaced by Cindy Birdsong, who had been filling in for Ballard during tour dates. Also in 1967, David Ruffin quit the Temptations, to be replaced by Dennis Edwards.

Diana Ross and the Supremes Join the Temptations, which showcased the combined forces of the groups, climbed to number two on January 11, 1969, but was denied the top spot by *The Beatles*.

TCB was an NBC-TV special featuring both groups. The soundtrack album entered the chart at number 134 on

December 28, 1968. Six weeks later, it temporarily dislodged *The Beatles* from the top spot, becoming the first album from a TV special to hit Number One.

The television special required plenty of preparation. "We had a lot of rehearsals, because we switched songs," says Diana Ross. For example, the Supremes reworked the Temps' "My Girl" as "My Guys" for the first "Introduction of the Temptations."

Although the album is full of musical highlights, including Ross's covers of Simon & Garfunkel's "Mrs. Robinson" and the Beatles' "Eleanor Rigby," Ross recalls the TV show more fondly than the audio recording. "Visually it was more fun," she says. "We did silly things and got to make fools of ourselves. We were dressed in these costumes and we did a lot of dancing and comedy."

One of those comic bits did make it onto the album. In the "Introduction of Diana Ross," in which the Temps sing "Our Girl," the group's members pretend they can't remember the singer's name. "The name is Ross," Diana responds in her best James Bond impersonation, "Betsy Ross."

With her solo career about to take off [see 155], it's unlikely anyone ever had trouble remembering Ross's name again.

112 Blood, Sweat & Tears COLUMBIA 9720
BLOOD, SWEAT & TEARS

Producer: *James William Guercio*

Track listing: *Variations on a Theme by Eric Satie (1st and 2nd Movements) / Smiling Phases / Sometimes in Winter / More and More / And When I Die / God Bless the Child / Spinning Wheel / You've Made Me So Very Happy / Blues—Part II / Variations on a Theme by Eric Satie (1st Movement)*

March 29, 1969
7 weeks (nonconsecutive)

Blood, Sweat & Tears' 1968 debut album, *Child Is Father to the Man*, was a hit with critics but a commercial disappointment. It stalled at number 47 as tensions were heating up within the band.

Al Kooper, formerly of the Blues Project, founded BS&T, but following the release of *Child Is Father to the Man*, his relationship with the band's other members was beginning to deteriorate. "The view of the band at that time was that since Al Kooper had arranged most of the material, he was singing lead, that it was solely his invention. But that was not the case, it was combined effort," says drummer Bobby Colomby.

In fact, the original line-up's sound was equal parts Kooper's keyboard, Steve Katz's guitar, Jim Fielder's bass, and Colomby's drumming, combined with a horn section featuring Fred Lipsius, Jerry Weiss, and Randy Brecker.

"Al left the band acrimoniously," says Colomby. "No one had a smile on their face. He felt that he had to be the lead singer, and many of us felt that he did not have enough power in his voice to carry what we had envisioned for the band."

THE TOP FIVE
Week of March 29, 1969

1. **Blood, Sweat & Tears**
   Blood, Sweat & Tears

2. **Wichita Lineman**
   Glen Campbell

3. **Goodbye Cream**
   Cream

4. **Ball**
   Iron Butterfly

5. **The Beatles**
   The Beatles

BS&T broke up after Kooper's departure but reunited at the insistence of Columbia Records president Clive Davis. The band found its new lead singer at a small club in New York called Steve Paul's Scene. "Steve and I were at this club. We weren't paying attention to the stage, but we were sitting right under this large speaker. We heard this unbelievable voice coming out of it, like Ray Charles or Bobby Blue Bland. When I looked on the stage, it seemed as if the singer was lip-synching, because he did not look like what I was hearing," says Colomby. But Colomby and Katz remembered that voice. After initial auditions for a new lead singer left them empty-handed—and Colomby's dream frontmen Stephen Stills [see 120] and Stevie Wonder [see 61] were unattainable—BS&T called on that voice from the club. It belonged to David Clayton-Thomas.

Kooper wasn't the only original member to leave prior to the recording of *Blood, Sweat & Tears*. Horn players Brecker and Weiss also departed, and were replaced by Chuck Winfield, Lew Soloff, and Jerry Hymann. Kooper's absence gave the group, now nine members strong, a newfound freedom, says Colomby. "We were allowed to express more of our individual qualities as players. We had some really excellent jazz musicians in the band."

BS&T recorded its self-titled album at Columbia studios in New York with producer James William Guercio, who would soon rise to fame with his work with Chicago.

The horn-based, big-band rock sound was the basis for BS&T's musical approach, but its influences came from across the board, as the material the band covered suggested. *Blood, Sweat & Tears* featured arrangements of material ranging from French composer Erik Satie and jazz great Billie Holiday to contemporary songwriters such as Laura Nyro and Steve Winwood [see 321].

Blood, Sweat & Tears contained three big hits—"You Made Me So Very Happy," "And When I Die," and "Spinning Wheel"—all of which climbed to number two and went gold, making *Blood, Sweat & Tears* the first album ever to spawn three gold singles. The album outdid the chart performance of the singles, nailing down the top spot in its ninth week on the chart.

Courtesy of Photofest

Scene from *Hair*.

Ragni and Rado played the lead characters George Berger and Claude Hooper Bukowski, respectively, yet singer/actress Melba Moore and actress Diane Keaton are the cast members who became *Hair's* most well-known alumni. Moore is featured on "Ain't Got No," "Air," "White Boys," "Good Morning Starshine," and "The Flesh Failures," while Keaton sings on "Black Boys."

Hair wasn't only a hit with theatergoers and the critics—many of the era's pop stars were also tapping into "the age of Aquarius." The Fifth Dimension's Billy Davis Jr. was so knocked out by the play's opening number "Aquarius," he and his group covered the song and album-closer "The Flesh Failures (Let the Sunshine In)." The Fifth Dimension's version of "Aquarius/Let the Sunshine In" topped the Hot 100 on April 12, 1969. Two weeks later, the original cast album hit Number One in its 39th week on the Top LP's chart.

The success of the album came to a shock to MacDermot. "I was surprised. I was so involved in what I was doing that I had no time to look at the charts, and then a guy from RCA called me and said we were Number One."

Hair's chart triumph continued on May 10, 1969. With the original cast album and the Fifth Dimension single still the top album and single in the country, the Cowsills' version of "Hair" hit number two. Other *Hair* hits included Oliver's "Good Morning Starshine," which reached number three, and Three Dog Night's "Easy to Be Hard," which made it to number four.

Hair is also notable for another reason: It is the last original cast recording to have topped the album chart.

Producer: Andy Wiswell

Track listing: Aquarius / Donna / Hashish / Sodomy / Colored Spade / Manchester England / I'm Black / Ain't Got No / Air / Initials / I Got Life / Hair / My Conviction / Don't Put it Down / Frank Mills / Be-In / Where Do I Go? / Black Boys / White Boys / Easy to Be Hard / Walking in Space / Abie Baby / Three-Five-Zero-Zero / What a Piece of Work Is Man / Good Morning Starshine / The Flesh Failures (Let the Sunshine In)

April 26, 1969
13 weeks

Hair began its life as a story written on scraps of paper by two actors named Gerome Ragni and James Rado. Within a few years, those bits and pieces were turned into a story worthy of a musical. To write the music to accompany their story of "the age of Aquarius," Ragni and Rado tracked down composer Galt MacDermot.

"They had a complete book and lyrics when I met them," MacDermot recalls. "And I worked from the lyrics." MacDermot composed the score to the musical in a mere three weeks in order

to make a deadline for the New York Shakespeare Festival Public Theater. *Hair* opened there on October 29, 1967. But by the time the musical made it to Broadway, on April 29, 1968, MacDermot had composed additional material.

Only days after *Hair* became the first rock musical to open on Broadway, the cast was ushered into RCA's Studio B to record the original cast album. RCA executives suspected that they had a hit on their hands, as the musical was drawing huge crowds at the Biltmore Theatre and had received a rave review from the *New York Times*.

"Actually, I think we went into the studio a little too soon," admits MacDermot. "After about a month or so, the cast and the band would have known it much better." As is the case with most original cast albums, the sessions were squeezed in between performances. "We just did one song after another," MacDermot says. "We worked well into the night, but we did it all in one day. Most of the numbers were done live, just like we did them in the theater. But, then at the very end we did a little bit of overdubbing."

The music wasn't the only thing memorable about *Hair*, as the cast featured a few notable performers. Writers

THE TOP FIVE
Week of April 26, 1969

1. **Hair**
   Original Cast

2. **Blood, Sweat & Tears**
   Blood, Sweat & Tears

3. **Galveston**
   Glen Campbell

4. **Greatest Hits**
   Donovan

5. **Cloud Nine**
   Temptations

114 Johnny Cash at San Quentin COLUMBIA 9827
JOHNNY CASH

Producer: Bob Johnston

Track listing: Wanted Man / Wreck of the Old 97 / I Walk the Line / Darling Companion / Starkville City Jail / Folsom Prison Blues

August 23, 1969
4 weeks

Johnny Cash, Sun Records labelmate of Elvis Presley [see 1], Carl Perkins, and Jerry Lee Lewis, played his first prison in 1956. It seemed like a natural thing for him to do. "Because of my song 'Folsom Prison Blues,' the cons thought that I was one of them," says Cash.

In reality, though, Cash's only time in prison was served as a performer, but the gravelly-voiced country singer did have a reputation as an outlaw for his often-wild behavior and his style of dress. Good guys wore white; Cash was the Man in Black.

After Cash played Huntsville Texas state prison in 1956, word spread and he was deluged with requests to perform at prisons around the country. In 1968, a decade after Cash's first charting album, the singer recorded Johnny Cash at Folsom Prison with producer Bob Johnston. It climbed to number 13 and became his highest-charting album to date, while the song "Folsom Prison Blues" went on to top the country singles chart.

On February 24, 1969, Cash paid his fourth visit to California's San Quentin Prison. This time Cash wasn't only making a live album, the show was also filmed for a British TV special by Granada Television. He also came armed with several songs that woud

make their recorded debut on Live at San Quentin, including "A Boy Named Sue" and a tune named after the prison, which Cash wrote the night before the engagement. In "San Quentin," Cash put himself in the prisoner's shoes, expressing the frustration, isolation, and rage the convicts felt for the fortress they called home.

When Cash performed the song that day, even he was taken aback by the response. "Everyone was a little bit uneasy with the excitement following the song 'San Quentin,'" Cash says. "The prisoners stood up on the tables and started stomping their feet. They demanded that I sing it again, which I did. We were all a little uneasy, because they were really overly excited."

Another new song, "A Boy Named Sue," a hilarious tale about a young man seeking revenge on the deadbeat dad who'd given him a woman's name, was also well received. "I didn't know the lyrics to the song, so I had them on a piece of paper on the stand in front of me," Cash says. Three days before the performance, Cash had received the song from Shel Silverstein. The song

connected with the general public as well as the cons, as it rose to number two on the Hot 100 and topped the country chart.

Yet the prisoners didn't respond only to Cash's songs of rebellion. "They had the same reaction to the spiritual 'Peace in the Valley,'" says Cash. Although the song, which was also recorded by Elvis [see 8], is included on the album between "A Boy Named Sue" and "Folsom Prison Blues," it is not listed on the record sleeve.

Even after Cash left the stage that evening, the show wasn't over. "I remember when we were walking out past Death Row, the inmates were yelling at me from their cells asking me to sing a song," Cash says. "So I took out my guitar and sang 'Folsom Prison Blues' down on the pavement outside of the prison."

Despite the possible risk in playing for an audience of dangerous criminals, Cash never felt threatened. "Maybe I should have, but I always felt safe," he says. "I felt that the inmates would have protected me as much as the guards did."

THE TOP FIVE
Week of August 23, 1969

1. **Johnny Cash at San Quentin**
   Johnny Cash

2. **Blood, Sweat & Tears**
   Blood, Sweat & Tears

3. **Hair**
   Original Cast

4. **Best of Cream**
   Cream

5. **Blind Faith**
   Blind Faith

Producer: Jimmy Miller

Track listing: Had to Cry Today / Can't Find My Way Home / Well All Right / Presence of the Lord / Sea of Joy / Do What You Like

September 20, 1969
2 weeks

Following the dissolution of Cream [see 104], guitarist/vocalist Eric Clapton and drummer Ginger Baker joined forces with Steve Winwood, the boy-wonder keyboardist/vocalist formerly of the Spencer Davis Group and Traffic. Winwood had played with Clapton briefly in the 1966 studio group Powerhouse. Rick Grech, from the popular British folk-rock outfit Family, rounded out Blind Faith.

"Eric and I put the band together, because musically we thought we had something to offer," says Winwood. "But things started to escalate a little out of our hands. I still think the album was a great album and it stands up by itself as a great album, by a great band."

The material recorded at the sessions, held in February, May, and June of 1969 at Morgan and Olympic Studios in London, alternated between well-rehearsed material and free-form jams. The former resulted in such tracks as Winwood's "Can't Find My Way Home" and Clapton's "Presence of the Lord," the first non-instrumental recording he'd ever written alone; the latter was most evident in Baker's 15-minute "Do What You Like," most notable for

the drummer's percussive attack. As Winwood puts it, "Ginger Baker's drumming tends to be rather unforgettable."

Following the completion of the album, the band played its only U.K. date on June 7, 1969, at London's Hyde Park, where it was joined onstage by Donovan. On July 12, the band made its American debut at Madison Square Garden in New York, kicking off its U.S. tour.

Blind Faith wasn't only known for the instrumental prowess of the group's players. The album's cover was one of the most controversial in rock history. It featured a photo of a nude 11-year-old girl, falsely rumored to be Baker's daughter, holding a phallic-shaped metallic model of an futuristic airplane. The cover was deemed too controversial for the American market, but was later reinstated on a subsequent reissue. "At the time I didn't think anything of it at all," admits Winwood. "But now I can see how controversial it is, because I have children of my own."

Six weeks after *Blind Faith*'s August release, the album hit the peak of the Top LP's chart, but by that time the band, which was wrapping up its first and only tour, was ready to call it quits. Says Winwood, "I don't think it could have gone on beyond that. There was a lot of pressure on the band to play in various different ways. There was too much business pressure. We probably should have stuck to our guns a little tighter than we did. We tended to do Cream songs and Traffic songs when we played live, rather than forging our own identity. We called it quits because

we didn't feel we were able to continue on with the same integrity that we had when we started."

Following the band's split, Winwood reformed Traffic with Jim Capaldi and Grech, before emerging as a successful solo artist [see 321]; Clapton worked as a session player for Delaney and Bonnie, the opening act on the Blind Faith tour, and for George Harrison [see 128], before forming Derek and the Dominos and later launching an acclaimed solo career [see 179]. Following the demise of Ginger Baker's Airforce in 1970, which included Winwood and Grech, the drummer moved to Lagos, Nigeria, where he built a recording studio later used by Paul McCartney & Wings [see 173]. Baker resurfaced in the early 1990s as a member of blues-rock outfit Masters of Reality.

THE TOP FIVE
Week of September 20, 1969

1. **Blind Faith**
   Blind Faith

2. **At San Quentin**
   Johnny Cash

3. **Blood, Sweat & Tears**
   Blood, Sweat & Tears

4. **Hair**
   Original Cast Recording

5. **Green River**
   Creedence Clearwater Revival

116 Green River FANTASY 8393
CREEDENCE CLEARWATER REVIVAL

Producer: John Fogerty

Track listing: Green River / Commotion / Tombstone Shadow / Wrote a Song for Everyone / Bad Moon Rising / Lodi / Cross-Tie Walker / Sinister Purpose / The Night Time is the Right Time

October 4, 1969
4 weeks

Green River was only Creedence Clearwater Revival's third album, but by its August 1969 release, the band had been playing together for a

THE TOP FIVE
Week of October 4, 1969

1. **Green River**
   Creedence Clearwater Revival

2. **Johnny Cash at San Quentin**
   Johnny Cash

3. **Blind Faith**
   Blind Faith

4. **Through the Past Darkly (Big Hits Vol. 2)**
   Rolling Stones

5. **Blood, Sweat & Tears**
   Blood, Sweat & Tears

decade. CCR had its origins in 1959 in El Cerrito, California, a suburb of San Francisco. Guitarist John Fogerty, bassist Stu Cook, and drummer Doug Clifford were all in the eighth grade when they formed the Blue Velvets. The band was rounded out by John's older brother Tommy on vocals and rhythm guitar. By 1964, Tommy Fogerty and the Blue Velvets landed a recording contract with Fantasy Records.

Following a name change to the Golliwogs—the label thought it made the band sound British—and the release of seven singles, the quartet was re-christened Creedence Clearwater Revival, with John assuming the role of frontman. It found success with a cover of Dale Hawkins's "Suzie Q" in the summer of 1968. The group's self-titled debut album stalled at number 57, but the number two single "Proud Mary" would help Bayou Country, its second album, climb to number seven in March 1969.

By then, the group's popularity had earned it spots at high-profile festivals in Denver, Atlanta, Atlantic City, and Woodstock, where it shared the stage with the likes of Jimi Hendrix [see 108], Led Zeppelin [see 118], and Janis Joplin [see 130].

Soul and R&B cover versions were the standout tracks on the band's 1968 self-titled debut, but by Bayou Country, John Fogerty had developed into a

skilled songsmith in his own right. His songs would soon be covered by such artists as Ike & Tina Turner and Elvis Presley.

On Green River, CCR was more focused than ever. "'Suzie Q' was a cover. 'Proud Mary' was kind of an uptown sophisticated thing, and some of the other stuff was a little more R&B-flavored," says John Fogerty. "When we got into Green River it was a little more rockabilly. It was more in the middle where R&B and country meet, and that's my favorite place.

"Out of all the albums I've done, Green River is my favorite," adds Fogerty. "The philosophical and musical place where it seemed to be resting was at the very center of my soul. I felt that way in 1969 and I feel that way now."

Part of Fogerty's emotional closeness to the album may be because the title track was inspired by his childhood memories. "There was a river up in Northern California that I always referred to as the Green River," Fogerty says. "From the time I was four until I was about nine, I would go there in the summertime. Many of my childhood memories come from my time spent at that creek. As life went on I just sort of melded everything else into that place."

Green River was the first CCR album recorded at Wally Heider Studio in San Francisco with engineer Russ Gary. The band would use that same combination for all of its future studio albums. Like CCR's first two albums, Green River was recorded fairly quickly, as it was the second of three CCR studio albums Fantasy released in 1969, amidst frequent live performances. "We were well-rehearsed when we went in," says Doug Clifford. "We knew exactly what songs we were going to do, so we could finish in a week."

A pair of double-A-side singles were issued in advance of the album. "Bad Moon Rising" climbed to number two in June, while the flipside, "Lodi," stalled at number 52. "Green River" became CCR's third number two single, while its flipside, "Commotion," reached number 30 in September.

In its fourth week on the chart, Green River hit Number One, marking the first time CCR had hit the top of any Billboard chart. "In the back of my mind, I knew the game is to try to be Number One and try to be as popular as you can be," admits Fogerty. With Green River, Creedence Clearwater Revival finally achieved that goal.

The latter song, which Harrison composed on piano, turned out to be one of the Beatles' finest ballads.

Ringo Starr also contributed material. His "Octopus's Garden" was composed during the *Let It Be* sessions. Starr can been seen working on the song with Harrison and McCartney in the *Let It Be* film documentary. Yet the song sounds like an outtake from the *Yellow Submarine* era.

The cover photo of *Abbey Road*, named after the studio where the Beatles recorded 191 songs, features the band members crossing the street in front of the building. The Beatles' attire—McCartney barefoot but wearing a suit, Harrison dressed in the dungarees of a gravedigger, Lennon looking like a priest, and Starr like an undertaker—further fueled speculation that McCartney had been killed in a car crash in 1969.

Fittingly, *Abbey Road* winds down with "The End," a track that features solos by all four members of the band, followed inexplicably by McCartney's 23-second "Her Majesty." For the Beatles, *Abbey Road* truly marked the end. Says producer George Martin, "It was the last thing they ever did together, so *Abbey Road* has a special place for me." The rest of the public agreed, as *Abbey Road* hit the top in its third week on the chart. Five weeks later, the double-A-side single "Something"/"Come Together" reached the top of the Hot 100, giving the group another double crown. The Beatles would go on to rack up three more Number One albums, but *Abbey Road* was their real swan song.

Producer: George Martin

Track listing: Come Together / Something / Maxwell's Silver Hammer / Oh! Darling / Octopus's Garden / I Want You (She's So Heavy) / Here Comes the Sun / Because / You Never Give Me Your Money / Sun King / Mean Mr. Mustard / Polythene Pam / She Came in Through the Bathroom Window / Golden Slumbers / Carry That Weight / The End / Her Majesty

November 1, 1969
11 weeks (nonconsecutive)

"*Abbey Road* was an enjoyable album to make after the bad time we had with *Let It Be*" [see 122], says George Harrison. "It was good to go back to the studio and do a new record, because the songs were good and everyone was happy."

Although *Let It Be* would be the last Beatles album of new material to be released, *Abbey Road* was in fact the last album the Beatles recorded. The band had put aside the bad vibes that had surfaced during the *Let It Be* sessions and came together to record one of their finest albums. The material on the album varied from John Lennon's basic rocker "Come Together" and his avant-garde ode to Yoko Ono, "I Want You (She's So Heavy)," to the complex suite of songs, mostly written by McCartney, that closes the album. "We actually rehearsed," says Harrison. "We did arrangements for those songs like 'Polythene Pam' and 'She Came in Through the Bathroom Window,' which were just bits and pieces of songs that were tacked together, learned them, and played it as one performance."

By that time, Harrison's confidence as a writer had grown. "'Something' and 'Here Comes the Sun' were great, because I knew they were good songs, but I was a bit worried when John wrote a song called 'Here Comes the Sun' as well," Harrison says. Eventually, Lennon altered his song's title to "Sun King."

Harrison recalls writing his two tracks: "I wrote 'Here Comes the Sun' in Eric Clapton's garden and I wrote 'Something' while we were making *The White Album* in number one studio at Abbey Road, which was an enormous studio they used for orchestras. I used to just go in there and kind of hang out."

THE TOP FIVE
Week of November 1, 1969

1. **Abbey Road**
   The Beatles

2. **Green River**
   Creedence Clearwater Revival

3. **Through the Past Darkly (Big Hits, Vol. 2)**
   The Rolling Stones

4. **Blind Faith**
   Blind Faith

5. **Johnny Cash at San Quentin**
   Johnny Cash

118 Led Zeppelin II ATLANTIC 8236
LED ZEPPELIN

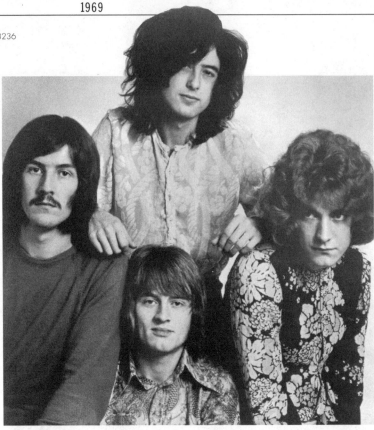

Producer: Jimmy Page

Track listing: Whole Lotta Love / What Is and What Should Never Be / The Lemon Song / Thank You / Heartbreaker / Living Loving Maid (She's Just a Woman) / Ramble On / Moby Dick / Bring It on Home

December 27, 1969
7 weeks (nonconsecutive)

With its 1969 self-titled debut, Led Zeppelin knocked the rock world on its backside with an innovative mix of hard rock and heavy blues. Led Zeppelin rose out of the ashes of the Yardbirds, a seminal British blues-rock group whose lineup at various times boasted the talents of Eric Clapton [see 104], Jeff Beck, and finally Jimmy Page. Previously a session player, Page joined the Yardbirds in 1968, just as the band began to disintegrate. Undaunted, the young guitar whiz opted to recruit his own lineup, dubbed the New Yardbirds. John Paul Jones, a bassist/keyboardist also known for his session work, was first to sign on. The vocalist spot was filled by Robert Plant, a blues singer from Birmingham, England, who in turn suggested drummer John Bonham, who had played with Plant in the Band of Joy, to round out the quartet.

The group soon adopted a new moniker inspired by a joke by the Who's drummer, Keith Moon, who suggested the mix of hard rock and heavy blues would go down like a lead balloon. Instead, Led Zeppelin, which featured a photo of the Hindenburg on the cover, soared up the Top LP's chart. The album, recorded three weeks after the band formed, was released on January

12, 1969. It climbed to number 10 and the band hit the road to play in front of its growing legion of fans in America.

Rather than waiting until they finished their maiden voyage to America, the members of Zeppelin opted to write and record most of the band's second album while they were on tour. "It was recorded every spare moment that we were on the road," says John Paul Jones. "We literally wrote the album on the road and whenever there were a couple of hours between shows we booked a studio and went in and recorded. It had great spontaneity and urgency."

Some of the tracks, such as "Whole Lotta Love," were spawned from Zeppelin's explosive live shows. In concert, the band played extended versions of its songs, such as the Led Zeppelin epic "Dazed and Confused," allowing plenty of room of improvisation and the creation of new songs. "We were very hot," says Jones. "We realized that it was going to be a very successful band. We were getting across, we were doing what we wanted, and we were very free. It was a very exhilarating time."

Led Zeppelin was so brazen, in fact, that it borrowed heavily from some of its blues heroes without feeling the need to share songwriting credits. "The Lemon

Song" was inspired by Howlin' Wolf's "The Killing Floor," and "Whole Lotta Love" was based on a Willie Dixon song. Nearly 20 years after the fact, the band acknowledged the debt, reaching an out-of-court settlement with Dixon.

Yet there was much more to Led Zeppelin than a bunch of borrowed blues riffs. The band's instrumental prowess and no-holds-barred approach paved the way for nearly every hard rock band to follow. Led Zeppelin II would eventually become known as the quintessential heavy metal album. Aside from Jimmy Page's incredible guitar and inventive riffing, there was Bonham's drumming, notably showcased on "Moby Dick." Says Jones, "He used his hands as well as sticks. That's what he used to do onstage. He started off with his hands and then he would pick up sticks. On occasion there would be blood all over the drums."

Led Zeppelin II made it to Number One in its eighth week on the chart. Fittingly, it was the last Number One album of the '60s, and the album it dislodged from the peak position was the Beatles' Abbey Road. Although Abbey Road would return to the top spot for three more weeks, the '60s were indeed over. The revolutionary Fab Four sounded tame compared to the mighty Led Zeppelin.

THE TOP FIVE
Week of December 27, 1969

1. **Led Zeppelin II**
   Led Zeppelin

2. **Abbey Road**
   The Beatles

3. **Let It Bleed**
   The Rolling Stones

4. **Live in Las Vegas**
   Tom Jones

5. **Willie and the Poor Boys**
   Creedence Clearwater Revival

COLUMBIA 9914 **Bridge Over Troubled Water**
SIMON AND GARFUNKEL   **119**

Producers: Paul Simon, Arthur Garfunkel, and Roy Halee

Track listing: Bridge Over Troubled Water / El Condor Pasa / Cecilia / Keep the Customer Satisfied / So Long, Frank Lloyd Wright / The Boxer / Baby Driver / The Only Living Boy in New York / Why Don't You Write Me / Bye Bye Love / Song For the Asking

March 7, 1970
10 weeks

One of the ironies of the music business is that success often leads to an act's demise. Such was the case with Simon and Garfunkel. After scoring their second consecutive Number One album with *Bookends* [see 102] and their second Number One single with "Mrs. Robinson," Paul Simon and Art Garfunkel began to drift apart.

Bridge Over Troubled Water was a perfect title for the duo's follow-up album, as Simon and Garfunkel were finding it increasingly difficult to work with each other. At times when the album was being recorded, the duo didn't work together, as Garfunkel was in Mexico acting in Mike Nichols's war comedy/drama *Catch-22*.

Simon addressed Garfunkel's absence in the song "The Only Living Boy in New York." Says Garfunkel, "Paul would say he wrote it with me in mind. I was down in Guaymas, Mexico, making this film." As Garfunkel notes,

Simon makes reference to the duo's early stage name, Tom and Jerry, by using Tom in the opening line. "It's very dear and very affectionate," he says. "It's a song about somebody missing his colleague."

While Simon may have missed Garfunkel, there were likely other times when he was happy he was gone. Garfunkel objected to Simon's politically charged "Cuba Si, Nixon No," so the track was left off the album, much to Simon's displeasure. That dispute and Garfunkel's film commitments raised tensions between the two childhood friends.

"It was a tough album to make, but tough is one of the words that leads to great results," says Garfunkel. "Tough leads to wanting to take a rest. Neither of us expected that rest to mean the dissolution of Simon and Garfunkel."

In *Bridge Over Troubled Water* and its title track, Simon and Garfunkel issued a fitting swan song. Simon originally wrote the tune on guitar as a gospel hymn with two verses. He opted to let Garfunkel sing lead, a decision he later regretted when it became one of the duo's most popular songs. Simon added the third verse in the studio at Garfunkel's request, as the song was transformed into a majestic piano ballad, complete with a sweeping string arrangement and Garfunkel's alternating chilling and bombastic vocals.

Garfunkel says "Bridge Over Troubled Water" remains one of the duo's crowning achievements. "The song is so

damn strong. It constantly lives for me as a tender expression of 'if you are hurting, I will try to provide some strength.' It's a little tough to sing '59th Street Bridge Song (Feelin' Groovy)' today, but not 'Bridge Over Troubled Water,' because I didn't grow beyond that sentiment. All I have to do is put my mind there and the hurt goes on. And the need to be soothed when things hurt is timeless."

"Bridge Over Troubled Water" hit Number One on the Hot 100 on February 28, 1970. A week later, the album hit the top spot. The album and single also simultaneously topped the British charts.

"The Boxer," released well in advance of the album, reached number seven in May 1969, while "Cecilia" reached number four in May 1970. A fourth single, "El Condor Pasa," Simon's adaptation of a Peruvian folk song, stalled at number 18 in October 1970.

On March 16, 1971, Simon and Garfunkel swept the 13th annual Grammy Awards as *Bridge Over Troubled Water* won album of the year and the title track took record of the year, song of the year, best contemporary song, best arrangement accompanying vocalists, and best-engineered record.

By that time, however, the Simon and Garfunkel partnership was history. Art Garfunkel continued to pursue acting, landing a role in *Carnal Knowledge*, while Paul Simon's solo career was just beginning [see 208].

THE TOP FIVE
Week of March 7, 1970

1. **Bridge Over Troubled Water**
   Simon and Garfunkel

2. **Led Zeppelin II**
   Led Zeppelin

3. **Abbey Road**
   The Beatles

4. **Willie and the Poorboys**
   Creedence Clearwater Revival

5. **Chicago II**
   Chicago

120 Déjà Vu ATLANTIC 7200
CROSBY, STILLS, NASH & YOUNG

Producers: David Crosby, Stephen Stills, Graham Nash & Neil Young

Track listing: Carry On / Teach Your Children / Almost Cut My Hair / Helpless / Woodstock / Déjà Vu / Our House / 4 + 20 / Country Girl (a) Whiskey Boot Hill (b) Down, Down, Down (c) Country Girl (I Think You're Pretty) / Everybody I Love You

*May 16, 1970
1 week*

When Crosby, Stills & Nash joined forces in the summer of 1968, each member brought with him an impressive rock resume. David Crosby was a member of the Byrds until he was ousted, Stephen Stills was fresh from Buffalo Springfield's breakup, and Graham Nash had quit the Hollies. Together the trio recorded a self-titled debut album, which reached number six in late 1969. Singer/guitarist Neil Young [see 141], another former Buffalo Springfield member, joined the band onstage at Woodstock [see 123], its second live appearance. By the fall of 1969, it was decided that Young would be featured on the next album, *Déjà Vu*, which would be credited to the four singer-songwriters.

In the months between the recording of *Crosby, Stills & Nash* and *Déjà Vu*, there were major changes. "During the first album we were all in love with each other," says Nash. "We were in love with the music, and we were in love with beautiful, bright, funny, unique women—Stephen with Judy Collins, myself with Joni Mitchell, and David

with Christine Hinton. When we started to make *Déjà Vu*, I had broken up with Joni, Stephen had broken up with Judy Collins, and Christine had been killed. It was a very different feeling for us. It was a much darker album in general, but there are some bright, up things, like 'Teach Your Children.'"

On the same day that Crosby's girl-friend was killed in a head-on collision, the group's first album was certified gold for sales of more than 500,000 copies. Hinton's death made it difficult for Crosby to continue. "I was having a lot of trouble functioning in the studio," Crosby says. "I would go in some times and be in tears, unable to work. The other guys carried me a lot during that record."

Even with his terrible personal pain, Crosby was able to contribute the title track and "Almost Cut My Hair," which was recorded live in the studio. "We used to try to get a live vocal with the track as much as possible, but that was completely live. That's just a moment of time snipped off the end of the tape and stuck on the record," he says.

The addition of Young to the group also shook things up, as he contributed the achingly beautiful "Helpless" and "Country Girl," and co-wrote "Every-body I Love You" with Stills. "Neil changed the chemistry," says Crosby. "He's a tremendously powerful musical force, and anytime he's involved, believe me, you know it."

For the members of Crosby, Stills, Nash & Young, working on *Déjà Vu* was an escape form their personal pain. "The music saved our ass," says Nash. "We could at least unite and feel great

about that. We looked forward to going into the studio every night."

Yet even the sessions, held at Wally Heider's Studio III in Los Angeles, became a pain, as the members' distinct visions led to arguments. "It became a project that went on longer than it should have," Nash says of the album, which required more than 800 hours of studio time. "Tempers got a little flared there toward the end."

Nonetheless, Crosby, Stills, Nash & Young realized that through the time and pain they were creating one of their finest efforts. Says Crosby, "We knew that we were doing some of the best work of our lives." Some of the material was so good that it would help drive the band's next two albums to the top as well [see 131 and 186].

THE TOP FIVE
Week of May 16, 1970

1. **Déjà Vu**
   Crosby, Stills, Nash & Young

2. **Bridge Over Troubled Water**
   Simon & Garfunkel

3. **McCartney**
   Paul McCartney

4. **Hey Jude**
   The Beatles

5. **Band of Gypsys**
   Jimi Hendrix, Buddy Miles & Billy Cox

Club Sandwich that his self-titled effort, recorded on a four-track machine in his living room at home, was his most enjoyable solo album to record. "Linda and I were newlyweds, and we had a baby, so we had that golden glow that you get in the first year of marriage," he said. That happiness was reflected in songs such as "The Lovely Linda" and "Maybe I'm Amazed," which would become a hit when it was revived as a live recording years later [see 221].

"I felt a certain relief at not being tied into the Apple situation, because along with a regret about the break-up of the Beatles there was also a good side to it, which was the feeling of a new start...even if it was a little bit terrifying," McCartney told *Club Sandwich*.

The album also found McCartney in an experimental mode, recording material ranging from the Beatles' outtake "Teddy Boy" to some new instrumentals. "It was so intimate, it was just me, and, listening to it now, I think that I did stuff that I wouldn't normally have done," McCartney told *Club Sandwich*. "Some of the instrumentals I like a lot. They may not mean much — 'Momma Miss America' doesn't really add up to much — but I like them."

Fans also responded. The record, known as "The Cherry Album" because of its cover art, reached the top of the album chart in its third week, despite the fact it failed to spawn a hit single.

While *McCartney* was displaced from the pole position, ironically, by *Let It Be* after a three-week run at the top, it did accomplish what McCartney set out to do: establish the former Beatle as a solo force.

Producer: Paul McCartney

Track listing: The Lovely Linda / That Would Be Something / Valentine Day / Every Night / Hot as Sun Glasses / Junk / Man We Was Lonely / Oo You / Momma Miss America / Teddy Boy / Singalong Junk / Maybe I'm Amazed / Kreen — Akrore

May 23, 1970
3 weeks

Possibly the most signficant thing about Paul McCartney's first solo album, simply known as *McCartney*, was that it officially confirmed the demise of the Beatles.

The album was set for release on April 17, 1970, just two weeks before the Beatles' *Let It Be* was to hit the street. Yet a week prior to the album's release, a mock interview McCartney conducted with himself, which was to be included with promotional copies of the album, was leaked to the press. In the interview, McCartney asked and answered three questions that seemingly put the

Beatles to rest for good.

"Are you planning a new album or single with the Beatles?," McCartney asked, only to answer, "No." "Do you foresee a time when Lennon-McCartney become an active songwriting partnership again?," McCartney asked, answering again with a "No." "Do you miss the Beatles and George Martin? Was there a moment, e.g., when you thought, 'Wish Ringo was here for this break?'" Once again the answer was "No."

Missing the Beatles seemed to be the furthest thing from McCartney's mind. Indeed, he seemed to relish his new solo status, writing, performing, and producing the whole album by himself in Campbelltown, England, in late 1969. In fact, the only other person to receive a credit on the album was McCartney's wife, Linda, who contributed vocal harmonies and shot the photos of McCartney and his family that graced the album's gatefold.

As the gatefold photos suggest, McCartney was enjoying a period of domestic bliss. Twenty-five years later, McCartney told his fanclub newsletter

THE TOP FIVE
Week of May 23, 1970

1. **McCartney**
   Paul McCartney

2. **Bridge Over Troubled Water**
   Simon & Garfunkel

3. **Déjà Vu**
   Crosby, Stills, Nash & Young

4. **Chicago**
   Chicago

5. **Band of Gypsys**
   Jimi Hendrix, Buddy Miles & Billy Cox

122 Let It Be APPLE 34001
THE BEATLES

Producer: Phil Spector

Track listing: Two of Us / Dig a Pony / Across the Universe / I Me Mine / Dig It / Let It Be / Maggie Mae / I've Got a Feeling / One After 909 / The Long and Winding Road / For You Blue / Get Back

June 13, 1970
4 weeks

THE TOP FIVE
Week of June 13, 1970

1. **Let It Be**
   The Beatles

2. **McCartney**
   Paul McCartney

3. **Woodstock**
   Soundtrack

4. **Déjà Vu**
   Crosby, Stills, Nash & Young

5. **Bridge Over Troubled Water**
   Simon & Garfunkel

Let It Be was the final Beatles album of new material to hit the summit of the Top LP's chart, but it wasn't the final album they recorded. Although the bulk of Let It Be was originally recorded for an album, then to be titled Get Back, in January, February, March, and April of 1969, before the band began recording Abbey Road [see 117], the project was subsequently shelved. When the album was finally released as Let It Be on May 18, 1970, the Beatles were already history.

The original concept of Get Back was to capture the Beatles performing live with no overdubs for a television special. The group began rehearsing for the show on January 2, 1969, but eight days later George Harrison walked out, temporarily quitting the group. Plans for the TV show gave way to a film capturing the making of the album.

"It wasn't like being in a recording studio with a band making an album," says Glyn Johns, who served as engineer on the bulk of the sessions and was also originally slated to produce the shelved Get Back album. "There were so many other aspects of what they were trying to achieve other than the record, and they went through some pretty serious changes while it was going on. There were some internal problems and external problems while it was going on."

As Harrison explains, "It wasn't very much fun. Everyone was fed up and everyone wanted to leave the band. Although we salvaged it and we did some good tracks, it generally was done in a depression. It was done in a trough."

To augment the band, Harrison recruited keyboard player Billy Preston, who was featured so prominently on the track "Get Back" that he received co-billing on the single. Released on May 5, 1969, "Get Back" became the Beatles' 17th Number One single. However, it would take nearly a year before the album containing the track would be released.

The single of "Get Back" contained no production credit. Both Johns and longtime Beatles producer George Martin worked on the sessions, but their efforts would be overshadowed by another great producer, Phil Spector, known for his work with Ike and Tina Turner, the Crystals, and the Ronettes, and for his legendary "wall of sound" approach.

Although promotional copies of the Get Back album were pressed, the Beatles weren't happy with the project. It was yanked from the release schedule, as the group concentrated on another album of new material, Abbey Road.

Eventually, however, much of the material recorded during the Get Back sessions would see the light of day as Let It Be.

"About 18 months later, after the band had split up, John decided he was going to take the tapes and give them to Phil Spector and make an album from the tapes that I had recorded, which was basically all rehearsal tapes," says Johns. "Phil Spector turned it into this sugary, syrupy piece of shit with strings and choirs all over it."

While rock historians to this day debate the Spectorization of the Beatles' "live in the studio album," the public ate it up, and never mind the fact that the album's release came a month after Paul McCartney announced the band had officially split up.

Indeed, the legend of the Beatles would be hard to live down. Spector was remixing portions of Let It Be at Abbey Road unbeknownst to McCartney, while McCartney [see 121] was being mastered at the same studio. And, somehow fittingly, it was Let It Be that knocked McCartney's solo debut from the summit.

Let It Be hit Number One as "The Long and Winding Road"/"For You Blue" hit the top of the Hot 100. It would be the last time the Fab Four scored simultaneous Number Ones.

COTILLION 500 # Woodstock
SOUNDTRACK

Producer: Eric Blackstead

Track listing: I Had a Dream [John B. Sebastian] / Going Up the Country [Canned Heat] / Freedom [Richie Havens] / Rock & Soul Music [Country Joe & the Fish] / Coming to Los Angeles [Arlo Guthrie] / At the Hop [Sha-Na-Na] / The "Fish" Cheer / I-Feel-Like-I'm-Fixin-to-Die Rag [Country Joe McDonald] / Drug Store Truck Drivin' Man [Joan Baez featuring Jeffrey Shurtleff] / Joe Hill [Joan Baez] / Suite: Judy Blue Eyes [Crosby, Stills & Nash] / Sea of Madness / Wooden Ships [Crosby Stills, Nash & Young] / We're Not Gonna Take It [The Who] / With a Little Help from My Friends [Joe Cocker] / Soul Sacrifice [Santana] / I'm Going Home [Ten Years After] / Volunteers [Jefferson Airplane] / Medley: Dance to the Music/Music Lover/I Want to Take You Higher [Sly & the Family Stone] / Rainbows All Over Your Blues [John B. Sebastian] / Love March [Butterfield Blues Band] / Star Spangled Banner / Purple Haze & Instrumental Solo [Jimi Hendrix]

July 11, 1970
4 weeks

"The crowd was the real star, not the music." That sentiment has been frequently voiced by those who attended Woodstock and even by some of the musicians who played the massive three-day rock festival. The sea of humanity, which consisted of more than 400,000 people camped out on Max Yasgur's farm in Bethel, New York, may have upstaged the music. Yet dozens of memorable musical moments occurred on the weekend of August

THE TOP FIVE
Week of July 11, 1970

1. **Woodstock**
   Soundtrack

2. **Let It Be**
   The Beatles

3. **McCartney**
   Paul McCartney

4. **ABC**
   Jackson 5

5. **Live at Leeds**
   The Who

15–17, 1969, as Michael Wadleigh's film *Woodstock* and the subsequent soundtrack albums proved.

Although the concert, billed officially as the Woodstock Music and Arts Festival, took place in August, it has been said that Woodstock marked the end of the '60s. With that in mind, it's worth noting that the album knocked the Beatles' *Let It Be* from the apex of the Top LP's & Tapes chart. The Beatles were at Woodstock in spirit only—a stage announcement mimicked "Revolution No. 9" and Joe Cocker covered "With a Little Help from My Friends"—but it's doubtful the festival would have happened in the first place had the Fab Four not changed the face of popular music.

By the time *Woodstock* hit Number One, the Beatles had officially split. A few months later, two of festival's biggest stars—Jimi Hendrix and Janis Joplin—were dead. The dream had turned into a nightmare.

But during that weekend in upstate New York, the dream was alive and well. *Woodstock* captures that optimism. The three-record set was compiled from 64 reels of eight-track tape recorded over the festival's three-and-half days. For legal reasons, some acts on the bill—Creedence Clearwater Revival [see 116], Blood, Sweat & Tears [see 112],

the Band, and Janis Joplin [see 130]—weren't included on the album or its 1971 sequel, *Woodstock Two*, which peaked at number seven. The inclusion of the Who's "We're Not Gonna Take It," meanwhile, marked the legendary British band's only appearance on a Number One album. Aside from the music, the album also includes stage announcements, such as the famed warning about the bad "brown acid" circulating at the festival.

Crosby, Stills & Nash were joined by Neil Young at Woodstock, where they were making only their second public performance [see 120]. "I remember there being a real powerhouse of energy when we played," says David Crosby. "The audience reaction was completely nuts."

Santana landed a recording contract with Columbia Records thanks to their show-stopping performance at Woodstock [see 126]. "There was a lot of excitement, energy, hopes, and dreams," says Carlos Santana. "It was like a real climax."

Although there were several top acts of the day sharing the bill, Santana says there was no competition between them. "It wasn't like the NFL," he says. "Woodstock was basically peace, love, and music."

124 Blood, Sweat & Tears 3
BLOOD, SWEAT & TEARS
COLUMBIA 30090

Producers: Bobby Colomby, Roy Halee

Track listing: Hi-De-Ho / The Battle / Lucretia Mac Evil / Lucretia's Reprise / Fire and Rain / Lonesome Suzie / Symphony for the Devil/Symphony for the Devil 1. Emergence — A. Fanfare II. Devil's Game — A. Labyrinth; B. Satan's Dance; C. The Demand III. Submergence — A. Contemplation; B. Return / He's a Runner / Somethin' Comin' On / 40,000 Headmen

August 8, 1970
2 weeks

Just as the commercial failure of The Child Is Father to the Man brought on the departure of Al Kooper, the success of Blood, Sweat & Tears also brought about changes in the band. And, those changes were reflected on Blood, Sweat & Tears 3.

"Instead of keeping the same spirit we had on the first two albums—'Music is not brain surgery and let's have fun'—we thought everything out to the maximum degree," says drummer Bobby Colomby. Part of the problem was that the group's incredible success had led it to go out on the road to bask in its new-found fame. "We weren't a band that could write arrangements and rehearse on the road," says Colomby. "When all expectations for a third album were highest, we had not even begun to assemble an album. And by the time we did, it was, in a sense, too late."

Blood, Sweat & Tears 3 was released in June 1970, more than 16 months after the release of the band's self-titled breakthrough album. "In 1970, there was a different sentiment," Colomby says. "The public was used to seeing a new album by their favorite artists every eight months."

While BS&T toured and worked on 3, Chicago [see 147], another rock group that employed horns, also began to increase in popularity. The two groups were often compared to each other, a pairing that Colomby says was off the mark. "The whole nature of the music was different. We were much more jazz-oriented. They had a lot of lead singers and harmonies. We had one lead singer, David [Clayton Thomas], who had an unmistakable voice."

Yet there was a disadvantage to that voice, Colomby admits. "When you hear that kind of voice, with a horn section, with such repetition on radio, it tends to wear on you." A backlash against BS&T had begun. The group lost favor with critics, who had initially embraced the group's original Al Kooper–fronted lineup. "The same critic who wrote that 'Spinning Wheel' was 'a pop gem' was now writing it was 'pop drivel,'" Colomby says.

On Blood, Sweat & Tears 3, the group once again kept the song selection diverse with material from Gerry Goffin and Carole King [see 133], Steve Winwood [see 321], James Taylor, Laura Nyro, and Joe Cocker. There were also some originals, including an ambitious concept piece, "Symphony for the Devil," which was combined with a cover of the Rolling Stones' "Sympathy

for the Devil" [see 132].

"[Keyboardist] Dick Halligan wrote 'Symphony for the Devil,' which was based on the devil's interval. In medieval times priests did not allow any composers to use that particular interval of music, because it sounded way too devilish. He took that concept and wrote an arrangement around 'Sympathy for the Devil.' It was a lofty and ambitious piece of work, but looking back, it was a big mistake. People didn't like the fact we covered 'Sympathy for the Devil,' since it was so elite. They were like, 'How dare you fuck with the Stones?'"

Blood, Sweat & Tears 3 featured two top 30 hits—"Hi-De-Ho" and "Lucretia Mac Evil"—and the album hit Number One in its fourth week on the chart. Yet it was evident that the group's better days had already passed.

THE TOP FIVE
Week of August 8, 1970

1. **Blood, Sweat & Tears 3**
   Blood, Sweat & Tears

2. **Cosmo's Factory**
   Creedence Clearwater Revival

3. **Woodstock**
   Soundtrack

4. **Let It Be**
   The Beatles

5. **McCartney**
   Paul McCartney

FANTASY 8402 **Cosmo's Factory**
CREEDENCE CLEARWATER REVIVAL

Producer: John C. Fogerty

Track listing: Ramble Tamble / Before You Accuse Me / Travelin' Band / Ooby Dooby / Lookin' Out My Back Door / Run Through the Jungle / Up Around the Bend / My Baby Left Me / Who'll Stop the Rain / I Heard It Through the Grapevine / Long as I Can See the Light

August 22, 1970
9 weeks

Following the success of *Green River* [see 116], Creedence Clearwater Revival scored another double-sided hit single. "Down on the Corner" climbed to number three, while the flip side "Fortunate Son" reached number 14 in November 1969. Both songs were included on *Willy and the Poor-boys*, the band's fourth album, which peaked at number three in January 1970.

CCR previewed its next album with more double-sided hits. In March 1970, "Travelin' Band," backed with "Who'll Stop the Rain," became the band's fourth number two single in March 1970. "Up Around the Bend," featuring "Run Through the Jungle" as its flip side, reached number four. All four tracks were included on CCR's fifth album, *Cosmo's Factory*, released in July 1970.

"What I was trying to achieve at that point was to make an album that served as the culmination of Cree-

dence's growth or output," says singer-songwriter John Fogerty. "It was supposed to be one more grand moment of that phase before moving on."

Put simply, Fogerty felt it was time for Creedence to change. "It was the middle of 1970 and I was a very hard-driven AM radio commercial animal," he says. "I thought we had done a lot of similar stuff. I didn't want to bore anybody or start repeating myself."

The title of the album referred to the band's Berkeley, California, rehearsal space in drummer Doug Clifford's back yard. Clifford's interest in ecology and nature earned him the nickname "Cosmo" back in his college days. The band's space became known as "the factory" after Clifford complained about the cramped and smoky conditions of the rehearsal space, but admitted that it "beat working at a factory."

By 1970, Fogerty had become a spokesman for the common man. "Who'll Stop the Rain," a subtle allegory about the Vietnam War, was one of his finest moments. "Protest songs were always kind of done with a real loud approach vocally and a harmonica, à la Bob Dylan," says Fogerty. "I really wanted to do a song about the times, but I didn't want to be so obvious. I wanted to say what I wanted to say and come to people in layers, so they were absorbing the beauty of it and enjoying the song, before it ever occurred to them what it was actually about."

Elsewhere, CCR stuck to basic rock 'n' roll themes in tracks such as "Travelin' Band," which was meant as a trib-

ute to rock 'n' roll pioneer Little Richard. CCR may have done too good a job. In October 1971, Fogerty and his publishing company were sued by the owner of Little Richard's "Good Golly Miss Molly," but the suit was later dropped.

Creedence also took time to stretch out on *Cosmo's Factory*, as the band known for its three-minute hit singles included two unusually long songs on the album. Opener "Ramble Tamble" clocked in at seven minutes and nine seconds, while the band's cover of the R&B classic "I Heard It Through the Grapevine" ran over 11 minutes. "We used to jam out on that when we played it in the clubs and people loved it," Clifford says. "It was a nice, long dance track."

Cosmo's Factory became CCR's second Number One album in its fifth week on the chart. By September, the group had yet another number two single with "Lookin' Out My Back Door," but the tensions between the Fogerty brothers were increasing. By January 1971, Tom left the group, which continued as a trio until late 1972. John Fogerty would find success again during his solo career [see 285].

THE TOP FIVE
Week of August 22, 1970

1. **Cosmo's Factory**
   Creedence Clearwater Revival

2. **Woodstock**
   Soundtrack

3. **Blood, Sweat & Tears 3**
   Blood, Sweat & Tears

4. **Live at Leeds**
   The Who

5. **John Barleycorn Must Die**
   Traffic

126 Abraxas COLUMBIA 30130
SANTANA

Producers: Fred Catero & Santana

Track listing: Singing Winds, Crying Beasts / Black Magic Woman/Gypsy Queen / Oye Como Va / Incident at Neshabur / Se a Cabo / Mother's Daughter / Samba Pa Ti / Hope You're Feeling Better / El Nicoya

October 24, 1970
6 weeks, nonconsecutive

By the time Santana's self-titled debut album was released in September 1969, the San Francisco–based band had already made a name for itself on the festival circuit, playing such high-profile gigs as the Woodstock Festival.

The band, lead by singer-guitarist Carlos Santana, was originally known as the Santana Blues Band when it was founded in 1967. By 1968, the band had shortened its name to Santana and was headlining the Filmore West in its hometown of San Francisco. Santana's popularity on the San Francisco scene helped the group land a place on the Woodstock bill. And a knockout performance at that historic festival [see 123] helped the group secure a deal with Columbia Records.

Santana reached number four in November 1969, thanks to the buzz surrounding the band's Woodstock performance and tracks such as "Jingo," and "Evil Ways," which went on to become a top 10 hit.

By the time the band was ready to record its follow-up, things had changed drastically for the group. "All of a sudden we went from the streets of San Francisco to arenas," says Carlos Santana. "It was kind of like riding the rapids with everything going by so fast."

Santana was constantly reminded of its newfound fame while recording Abraxas at Wally Heider Recording Studio in San Francisco. "I remember in between songs, the phone would ring and Miles Davis would be calling to see how things were going. We had become part of a circle that was very prestigious."

Proof of Santana's immense popularity with its peers and the public is the fact that Abraxas entered the Top LP's chart at number eight on October 10, 1970. A week later, it was number two. In its third week, it hit the peak, ending the nine-week reign of Creedence Clearwater Revival's Cosmo's Factory.

One of the highlights of Abraxas was Santana's cover of Fleetwood Mac's [see 218] "Black Magic Woman." Says Santana, "We decided to record it after Gregg Rolie, the keyboard player and singer at the time, started playing it at a soundcheck in Fresno. If you listen to Fleetwood Mac's, it's very different than ours, even though it is the same song. We arranged it differently and put our own fingerprints on it, and it became our 'Black Magic Woman' even though they get the royalties." Backing up Santana's statement is that fact that his band's version of the song reached number four on the Hot 100 in January 1971, while the Fleetwood Mac original never charted in the U.S. and stalled at number 37 in the U.K.

Another cover version standout was Sanatana's version of salsa musician Tito Puente's "Oye Como Va." Says Santana, "When I was in San Francisco, I used to listen to this radio station that played all-night party music. When that one came on, I said, 'Wow, that's not so different from "Voodoo Chile" [see 108] or "Purple Haze."' There's some songs that you can play in Jerusalem or Japan or Mexico and people are going to get up and dance."

With Abraxas, Santana's hybrid of Afro-Latin rhythms and rock likewise proved to be universal.

THE TOP FIVE
Week of October 24, 1970

1. **Abraxas**
   Santana

2. **Cosmo's Factory**
   Creedence Clearwater Revival

3. **Led Zeppelin III**
   Led Zeppelin

4. **Third Album**
   Jackson 5

5. **Sweet Baby James**
   James Taylor

ATLANTIC 7201 **Led Zeppelin III**
LED ZEPPELIN

127

Producer: Jimmy Page

Track listing: Immigrant Song / Friends / Celebration Day / Since I've Been Loving You / Out on the Tiles / Gallows Pole / Tangerine / That's the Way / Bron-Y-Aur Stomp / Hats Off to (Roy) Harper

October 31, 1970
4 weeks

After establishing itself as the premiere hard-rock outfit in the world on *Led Zeppelin II* [see 118], Led Zeppelin made a left turn, going the acoustic route for much of its third album. The album was given a critical beating on both sides of the Atlantic, but to the members of Led Zeppelin, the change made perfect sense.

"All the different directions we took were just part of the way we heard it," says bassist/keyboardist John Paul Jones. "It was all part of our musical experience. Nobody said, 'Oh let's go in this direction or that direction.' Somebody would just have an acoustic guitar or a mandolin and start playing

something, the others would pick up on it, and it would develop into a number. Or some of us would come in with an idea."

In the case of *Led Zeppelin III*, most of the material was brought in by vocalist Robert Plant and guitarist Jimmy Page, and later completed with contributions by Jones. After more than two years of continuous touring, Plant and Page decided to retreat to a small cottage in the mountains of Wales called Bron-Y-Aur. As a result of the relaxed atmosphere, the duo wrote mostly acoustic numbers that reflected Plant's love of such California-based acts as the Byrds, the Buffalo Springfield, Moby Grape, Joni Mitchell, and Crosby, Stills, Nash & Young [see 131].

Undoubtedly adding to the relaxed vibe of *Led Zeppelin III* was the fact that much of the album was not recorded in a studio. Instead, the group rented a mansion in Hampshire called Headley Grange and recorded the bulk of the album during the late spring and early summer of 1970 with the Rolling Stones mobile unit and engineer Andy Johns [see 145]. "It was nice and relaxed,"

says Jones. Since the band was living where it was recording, it was able to stretch out and record in a pressure-free environment without worrying about hourly studio rates. "We all sat out on the grass a lot and played acoustic guitars and mandolins," says Jones. "It was very pleasant." Some of the album was even recorded outdoors. "You can hear the odd airplane," says Jones.

Yet *Led Zeppelin III* wasn't just an acoustic love-in. On such tracks as "The Immigrant Song," "Celebration Day," and "Out on the Tiles," the band rocked as hard as it ever had. It also continued to pay tribute to its blues heroes. The traditional "Gallows Pole" was widely associated with Leadbelly. Another traditional tune was reworked into "Hats Off to (Roy) Harper," named for a British folk eccentric.

It was those two songs and the rest of the acoustic numbers featured on side two of the album that garnered the most heat from the critics. "Part of Robert's lyrics may have come from California, but nothing else," says Jones. "Jimmy, Robert, and I were very interested in folk music like the Incredible String Band. We all had this diverse musical taste and we liked to draw on it. A lot of people made a big deal that there was a lot of acoustic numbers on the third album, rather conveniently forgetting that there were some acoustic numbers on the first album. People had decided we were a heavy rock band by the second album. When we did some more acoustic numbers, they were like, 'Wow, they changed directions,' when in fact, we hadn't. We probably changed direction on the second album, if anything, by not doing so many acoustic numbers."

THE TOP FIVE
Week of October 31, 1970

1. **Led Zeppelin III**
   Led Zeppelin

2. **Abraxas**
   Santana

3. **Cosmo's Factory**
   Creedence Clearwater Revival

4. **Third Album**
   Jackson 5

5. **Sweet Baby James**
   James Taylor

128 All Things Must Pass APPLE 639
GEORGE HARRISON

Producer: George Harrison and Phil
Spector

Track listing: I'd Have You Anytime /
My Sweet Lord / Wah-Wah / Isn't It a
Pity (Version One) / What Is Life / If
Not for You / Behind That Locked Door
/ Let it Down / Run of the Mill /
Beware of Darkness / Apple Scruffs /
Ballad of Sire Frankie Crisp (Let It Roll)
/ Awaiting on You All / All Things Must
Pass / I Dig Love / Art of Dying / Isn't
It a Pity (Version Two) / Hear Me Lord
/ Out of the Blue / It's Johnny's
Birthday / Plug Me In / I Remember
Jeep / Thanks for the Pepperoni

January 2, 1971
7 weeks

"I've always looked at *All Things Must Pass* like somebody who has had constipation for years and then finally they get diarrhea," says George Harrison. "And that's what happened. I was only allowed to do my one or two [tunes] on Beatle albums, so I had a backlog of songs. When I did *All Things Must Pass*, it was just good to get them out of the way."

George Harrison was actually the first Beatle to record an album outside the group. In 1968, his soundtrack to the film *Wonderwall* reached number 49. Another album, the experimental *Electronic Sound*, featured Harrison dabbling on a Moog synthesizer. That album, released on the Zapple imprint, stalled at number 191 in 1969. Yet Harrison didn't record his official solo debut until 1970 with *All Things Must Pass*, and what a debut it was.

"I was nervous, because I had really

never done a solo album before with me as an artist," says Harrison. "Yet I was very happy. The Beatles had finished. We were all tired of that. The fact that I had all these songs that had been collecting, and that I was be able to put an album out and release all this stuff, was very exciting. Most of these songs were written a couple years prior to 1970."

In fact, Beatles sideman Billy Preston, who appeared on *Let It Be* [see 122] actually beat Harrison to the punch with a few of Harrison's songs. Preston's versions of "My Sweet Lord" and "All Things (Must) Pass" (as it was titled on Preston's album), appeared on Preston's Harrison-produced *Encouraging Words* months before the release of *All Things Must Pass*. There were even plans for the release of a single of Preston's version of "My Sweet Lord," but the plan was scrapped, so that it would not compete with Harrison's single.

Harrison was inspired to write the song by the Edwin Hawkins Singers' version of "Oh Happy Day." Says Harrison, "Basically all I did was rewrite that song. I switched the chord sequence around a bit." When the song was recorded for Preston's album, the Edwin Hawkins Singers actually appeared on the track. Ironically, Harrison was sued for plagiarizing another song—the Chiffons' Number One hit "He's So Fine." He was later found to have committed copyright infringement, but a United States District Court judge ruled that

Harrison had not intentionally plagiarized the Chiffons' hit.

"My Sweet Lord" became the first solo Beatle Number One hit on December 26, 1970, but it was only a small part of the sprawling, three-LP *All Things Must Pass*. "It was really only a double album," says Harrison. "The third album, which was called *Apple Jam*, was supposed to be a free record. The price of the boxed set was supposed to be the price of the two records, because the third pressing was just a jam session, not a proper album."

All Things Must Pass, recorded in the familiar confines of Abbey Road Studios, includes several guest collaborators. Although he does not appear on the album, Bob Dylan cowrote "I'd Have You Anytime" with Harrison on Thanksgiving Day in 1969. Harrison also covered Dylan's "If Not For You" on the album. Among the featured guest players were Ringo Starr, Billy Preston, Dave Mason, Badfinger, and an uncredited Eric Clapton. "Eric was on the whole album," says Harrison. "I did a tour of Europe with Delaney & Bonnie with Eric. After they split up, the guys in the band were hanging out with Eric in London, and that's when Eric started to put together what became Derek & the Dominoes."

All Things Must Pass hit the summit a week after "My Sweet Lord" first hit the top of the Hot 100, making Harrison the first Beatle to score a simultaneous Number One album and single.

THE TOP FIVE
Week of January 2, 1971

1. **All Things Must Pass**
   George Harrison

2. **Abraxas**
   Santana

3. **Stephen Stills**
   Stephen Stills

4. **The Partridge Family Album**
   The Partridge Family

5. **Live Album**
   Grand Funk Railroad

Producers: Tim Rice and Andrew Lloyd Webber

Track listing: Overture / Heaven on Their Minds / What's the Buzz / Strange Thing Mystifying / Everything's Alright / This Jesus Must Die / Hosanna / Simon Zealotes / Poor Jerusalem / Pilate's Dream / The Temple / Everything's Alright / I Don't Know How to Love Him / Damned for All Time / Blood Money / The Last Super / Gethsemane (I Only Want to Say) / The Arrest / Peter's Denial / Pilate and Christ / King Herod's Song / Judas' Death / Trial Before Pilate (Including the 39 Lashes) / Superstar / Crucifixion / John Nineteen: Forty-One

February 20, 1971
3 weeks (nonconsecutive)

In 1966, on the eve of the Beatles' first American tour, John Lennon said that the Beatles were "more popular than Jesus." That may have been true at the time, or of the band as a whole, but apparently it was not the case with one Beatle as a solo artist. Five years after Lennon's controversial comment, *All Things Must Pass*, George Harrison's first Number One solo album [see 128], was knocked from the top spot on the chart by Jesus—*Jesus Christ Superstar*, that is.

In the same interview, Lennon also said, "I don't know which will go first—rock and roll or Christianity." Ironically, it was a combination of the two that made *Jesus Christ Superstar* a success.

The album, billed as "a rock

opera," was the brainchild of Tim Rice and Andrew Lloyd Webber, two struggling young British composers who met in 1965. "I was writing pop songs and I was a law student," says Rice. "Andrew was a very enthusiastic theater supporter and wanted to write for the musical theater."

The duo's first effort of note, *Joseph and the Amazing Technicolor Dream-*

Andrew Lloyd Weber

Tim Rice

coat, also combined elements of the Bible, rock music, and theater, but it wasn't especially well-received.

"*Joseph* was not any commercial success at all at that point," says Rice. "It was only successful in England as kind of project in schools. It really hadn't made any money or given us a track record or any status. We were starting from scratch with *Jesus Christ Superstar*."

Yet *Joseph and the Amazing Technicolor Dreamcoat* did garner the attention of an agent named David Land, who signed the duo. "He gave us 30 pounds a week to give up our day jobs and concentrate on writing a musical," says Rice. "I had this idea that the story of Jesus would be a good idea for a musical. It would be different."

Yet once the project was completed, Land had a hard time finding interested parties in staging the work as a musical. "The only interest he could get on *Superstar* was as a record," says Rice. "So as second-best, we agreed we would do it as an album for MCA."

"Since it was going to be a record, we turned it into sort of an operatic format, but we wanted it to be contemporary with rock music," Rice adds.

To record the album, the duo enlisted a combination of rock stars and unknowns. Deep Purple lead singer Ian Gillan played the lead role of Jesus Christ. Some of the then-unknowns included Murray Head, who played Judas Iscariot, and Yvonne Elliman, who was featured as Mary Magdalene. Head would have a hit more than a decade later with the Rice-penned "One Night in Bangkok," while Elliman rose to fame on the *Saturday Night Fever* soundtrack [see 226].

"Most people wanted session fees rather than royalties , which they would regret later," says Rice. "We wanted to give them royalties because we were working on a tight budget, but they wanted session fees because they reckoned the record would not be a hit."

Some were outraged by the very concept of a two-record rock album telling the story of the last seven days of Jesus' life. "It was quite controversial, which undoubtedly helped the album," says Rice. "A lot of people thought it was blasphemous, but they were usually people who hadn't heard it."

THE TOP FIVE
Week of February 20, 1971

1. **Jesus Christ Superstar**
   Various artists

2. **Chicago III**
   Chicago

3. **All Things Must Pass**
   George Harrison

4. **Abraxas**
   Santana

5. **Tumbleweed Connection**
   Elton John

130 Pearl COLUMBIA 30322
JANIS JOPLIN

Producer: Paul A. Rothchild

Track listing: Move Over / Cry Baby / A Woman Left Lonely / Half Moon / Buried Alive in the Blues / My Baby / Me and Bobby McGee / Mercedes Benz / Trust Me / Get It While You Can

February 27, 1971
9 weeks

Janis Joplin was in top form during the recording sessions for her second solo album, *Pearl*, recalled producer and longtime friend Paul A. Rothchild. "She was up, healthy and happy and seemingly not using [drugs] at all," he said. "We learned subsequently that two or three weeks prior to her death, she had been chipping, which is junkie talk for taking tiny hits, but she didn't want to die."

Joplin certainly had everything to live for. Although her first solo album, *I Got Dem Ol' Kozmic Blues Again Mama!*, which peaked at number five, failed to match the commercial success of Big Brother and the Holding Company's *Cheap Thrills* [see 107], Joplin was primed for her next career step. After exiting Big Brother, Joplin formed the Kozmic Blues Band, which backed her for one album and tour. For her next album, she decided to turn to a group of unseasoned players, who would become known as the Full-Tilt Boogie Band. "She intentionally wanted these pure kids," Rothchild said. "She didn't want any too-hip, too-wise, or too-stoned guys in the band."

The new blood invigorated Joplin, as did some advice from Rothchild. "I told her to sing like she sang in church

choir," he said. "And she sang pure like an angel. You can hear that voice throughout the album, like in 'Me and Bobbie McGee.' She starts off with that sweet girl voice and ends up kicking major butt by the end of the song. She got cranked up even a little harder than Jim Morrison did [see 105], and Jim could really get cranked up."

Since Rothchild preferred the acoustics of Sunset Sound studios, he persuaded Columbia president Clive Davis to allow Joplin to become the first CBS act to record in an independent studio. The atmosphere was loose and upbeat when the sessions began in September 1970. When searching for additional material, Joplin sung a verse she wrote over drinks with Bobby Neuwirth at the No Name bar in Sausalito. Rothchild liked the verse enough to encourage her to write additional lyrics. The following day, Joplin cut "Mercedes Benz." Said Rothchild, "She told me she had to stomp her foot when she sang it and we recorded it just like that."

Another tune, "Buried Alive in the Blues" was written by Nick Gravenites, after he spent some time in the studio with Joplin. On October 3, 1970, the

band cut the instrumental track. Pleased with the sessions, Joplin headed for the local watering hole Barney's Beanery for a few drinks before returning to her room at the Landmark Hotel in Hollywood.

She never had a chance to cut a vocal. The following evening, she was found dead in her room of a heroin overdose. She was 27. Rothchild, Joplin's manager Albert Grossman, and the band gathered to decide whether to complete the album or scrap the project. "We knew it was going to be an emotionally difficult situation, trying to do a Janis Joplin album without Janis there, but everyone voted to finish as kind of a monument to Janis herself and to the greatness that she was putting down," Rothchild said. "We decided that this record should not die with her."

Two weeks later, *Pearl* was complete. "Buried Alive in the Blues" would appear on the album as an instrumental track. As a testament to Joplin's popularity and talent, *Pearl* climbed to Number One in a mere seven weeks. With the album still in the top position, "Me and Bobby McGee," written by Kris Kristofferson, hit the summit of the Hot 100, giving Joplin her first Number One single.

Producers: David Crosby, Stephen Stills, Graham Nash & Neil Young

Track listing: Suite: Judy Blues Eyes / On the Way Home / Teach Your Children / Triad / The Lee Shore / Chicago / Right Between the Eyes / Cowgirl in the Sand / Don't Let It Bring You Down / Bye-Byes/America's Children / Love the One You're With / Pre-Road Downs / Long Time Gone / Southern Man / Ohio / Carry On / Find the Cost of Freedom

May 15, 1971
1 week

Almost a year to the day after Crosby, Stills, Nash & Young scored their first Number One album with *Déjà Vu* [see 120], the band found itself atop the charts again with *4 Way Street*. The two-record live set featured performances recorded during the summer of 1970 at the Fillmore East in New York, the Chicago Auditorium in Chicago, and the Forum in Los Angeles. Yet it wasn't the first time that a CSN&Y live performance had been featured on a Number One album. *Woodstock* [see 123] captured songs from the band's second-ever live performance.

By the time *4 Way Street* was released in April 1971, the members of Crosby, Stills, Nash & Young were flying solo. Stephen Stills's self-titled album, released in late 1970, eventually climbed to number three, thanks to the hit single "Love the One You're With." Crosby followed suit with *If I Could Only Remember My Name*, which stalled at number 12. Young, who was recording solo before joining the band, continued with *After the Gold Rush*, which reached number eight in late 1970.

Appropriately, *4 Way Street* featured a mix of material the group recorded together and songs the band members recorded on their solo albums. The studio version of Young's "Southern Man" was featured on *After the Gold Rush*. Crosby's "Triad" was a Byrds reject that was recorded by the Jefferson Airplane [see 202]. Nash's "Chicago" was featured on his then-forthcoming solo debut, *Songs for Beginners*, released in June 1971. Stills took the spotlight with a live rendition of "Love the One You're With."

For Nash, a live album made perfect sense. "We were obviously very capable of doing perfect harmonies," he says. "So we allowed ourselves the luxury of live recording on *4 Way Street*. There are no overdubs on it. Consequently, there are some flat notes and some slightly off harmonies, but I think it is completely overwhelmed by the spirit of the piece."

Stills, on the other hand, wasn't so sure a pure live recording was the right approach for CSN&Y. "It's really out of tune," says Stills, who suggested that the group overdub some vocal parts. "I said, 'Graham, it ain't cheating, it's just making it so I can bear to listen to it.' But he said, 'No, we don't want to destroy the purity of it.'"

Crosby sides with Nash. "There was a real powerhouse energy when we performed together," he says. "And *4 Way Street* captured that."

THE TOP FIVE
Week of May 15, 1971

1. **4 Way Street**
   Crosby, Stills, Nash & Young

2. **Jesus Christ Superstar**
   Various artists

3. **Up to Date**
   Partridge Family

4. **Pearl**
   Janis Joplin

5. **Golden Bisquits**
   Three Dog Night

132 Sticky Fingers ROLLING STONES 59100
THE ROLLING STONES

Producer: Jimmy Miller

*Track listing: Brown Sugar / Sway /
Wild Horses / Can't You Hear Me
Knocking / You Gotta Move / Bitch /
I Got the Blues / Sister Morphine /
Dead Flowers / Moonlight Mile*

*May 22, 1971
4 weeks*

The world had changed dramatically since the Rolling Stones scored their first Number One album in the United States with *Out of Our Heads* [see 77], and so too had the Stones. On July 3, 1969, the body of founding member Brian Jones was found at the bottom of his swimming pool, less than a month after he'd left the band. On December 6, 1969, as Mick Jagger was onstage singing "Sympathy for the Devil," a young fan was stabbed to death by Hell's Angels working as security guards at a free concert at Altamont Raceway in Northern California. Yet despite this adversity, or maybe even because of it, the Stones were reaching new creative heights in their recorded work.

Sticky Fingers marked the debut of Rolling Stones Records, the band's own label, distributed through Atlantic's Atco imprint. It was also guitarist Mick Taylor's first full studio album as a member of the Stones—Taylor, formerly of John Mayall's Bluesbreakers, had played on only part of 1969's *Let It Bleed.*

"Mick [Jagger] was very up," recalls Andy Johns, one of the engineers who worked on the sessions. "Mick Taylor was very much a part of the proceed-

ings and the vibes weren't that heavy. It was just a good time and quite a creative period for them."

Adding to the good vibes was the fact that a portion of the album was recorded at Jagger's Stargroves estate. "The Rolling Stones had just finished building a mobile unit, which was the first proper audio truck in Europe," says Andy Johns. "It was a lot more fun than being in a studio. We were all living together and we used different rooms for different sounds. There was a very communal sort of vibe."

One of the first songs cut during the sessions at Stargroves was "Bitch." Says Johns, "The horn players, Jim Price and Bobby Keys, were recorded from the cloak room, because it had a really good sound."

Sticky Fingers marked a departure for the Stones. Aside from the rockers "Brown Sugar" and "Bitch," which opened on each side, the album was the band's most low-key and introspective effort to date. The album-closing ballad "Moonlight Mile" reflected the mood. "That was recorded live except for the strings and the vocals," says Johns. "We got that done at about 5:30 A.M. and the sun was just coming in the windows. It's got that early-in-the-morning feel to it, where everyone has been up all night having a good time after a nice dinner and then got down to work. I don't think we would have gotten that feel if we had been at Olympic."

The band did return to Olympic Studios in London to record "Can't You Hear Me Knocking" and several other cuts. Tracks such as "Brown Sugar" and "Wild Horses" were cut at the leg-

THE TOP FIVE
Week of May 22, 1971

1. **Sticky Fingers**
   The Rolling Stones

2. **Jesus Christ Superstar**
   Various artists

3. **4 Way Street**
   Crosby, Stills, Nash & Young

4. **Up to Date**
   Partridge Family

5. **Mud Slide Slim and the Blue Horizon**
   James Taylor

endary Muscle Shoals Sound in Alabama during the band's 1969 American tour.

The former track stirred controversy. Some critics complained Jagger's lyrics were racist and sexist, and also could be interpreted as a reference to heroin. Nonetheless, on May 29, 1971, "Brown Sugar" became the Stones sixth Number One single on the American charts.

"Brown Sugar" wasn't the only controversial aspect of *Sticky Fingers.* The cover, designed by Andy Warhol, featured a close-up shot of a male model, from the waist to the knees, in a pair of tight jeans, complete with a working zipper, and a pair of bulging briefs on the inner sleeve.

Fittingly, *Sticky Fingers* zipped up the charts in a mere two weeks. After debuting at number 10 on May 15, the album nailed down the top spot a week later.

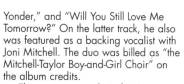

ODE 77009 **Tapestry** **133**
CAROLE KING

Producer: Lou Adler

Track listing: I Feel the Earth Move / So Far Away / It's Too Late / Home Again / Beautiful / Way Over Yonder / You've Got a Friend / Where You Lead / Will You Love Me Tomorrow? / Smackwater Jack / Tapestry / (You Make Me Feel Like) a Natural Woman

June 19, 1971
15 weeks

Tapestry was Carole King's first chart-topping album as an artist, but as a songwriter, with her first husband, Gerry Goffin, she had contributed songs to such Number One albums as The Monkees [see 91], More of the Monkees [see 92], and Blood, Sweat & Tears 3 [see 124].

King didn't have much initial success as a vocalist. Her first single, 1959's "Baby Sittin'," failed to catch on. A year later, "Oh Neil," King's answer song to

Neil Sedaka's "Oh Carol," also went nowhere. After a decade of constructing such hits as "The Loco-Motion" with Goffin at the famed Brill Building, King was encouraged to record her own songs again by her friend James Taylor. Writer: Carole King, released in 1970, was a commercial disappointment, but it inspired King to begin work on a follow-up.

"I did not think about commercial success at that time," King says. Since Taylor inspired King to record her own material again, it was only fitting that he was featured on several tracks, and King returned the favor by playing piano on his Mud Slide Slim and the Blue Horizon album, which included a cover of King's "You've Got a Friend."

Says King, "We would record my songs and then we would go to another studio where James was recording his album. It was one kind of continuous album in our minds." On Tapestry, Taylor played acoustic guitar on "So Far Away," "Home Again," "Way Over

Yonder," and "Will You Still Love Me Tomorrow?" On the latter track, he also was featured as a backing vocalist with Joni Mitchell. The duo was billed as "the Mitchell-Taylor Boy-and-Girl Choir" on the album credits.

The sessions, conducted in January of 1971 at A&M Studios B & C in Hollywood, went smoothly, King recalls. Producer Lou Adler had first worked with King back in 1962. Aside from producing her most successful albums, Adler owned the Ode label and served as King's manager. King named the album after a piece of needlepoint that would be featured on the album's cover photo and later given to Adler as a gift.

On February 10, Tapestry was released. The first single, a double-A-side featuring "It's Too Late" and "I Feel the Earth Move," was released on April 16. Two months later, it topped the Hot 100 as Tapestry pried the Rolling Stones' Sticky Fingers from the Number One position of the Top LP's chart. Yet King had other things on her mind. "I was very much more involved with my family," says King. "I had experienced Number One records before as a writer and I was about to have my third child."

On July 31, with Tapestry still holding firm at the top, Taylor scored his first Number One single with his version of King's "You've Got a Friend."

Tapestry's 15-week reign atop the chart marked the most weeks spent at Number One by an album since the Beatles' Sgt. Pepper's Lonely Hearts Club Band in 1967 [see 95]. The album's entire chart run was even more impressive—it stayed on the chart for an incredible 302 weeks, making it the longest-charting album by a female solo artist.

THE TOP FIVE
Week of June 19, 1971

1. **Tapestry**
   Carole King

2. **Sticky Fingers**
   The Rolling Stones

3. **Ram**
   Paul and Linda McCartney

4. **Jesus Christ Superstar**
   Various artists

5. **Carpenters**
   Carpenters

134 Every Picture Tells a Story MERCURY 609
ROD STEWART

Producer: Rod Stewart

Track listing: Every Picture Tells a Story / Seems Like a Long Time / That's All Right / Tomorrow Is Such a Long Time / Maggie May / Mandolin Wind / (I Know) I'm Losing You / Reason to Believe

October 2, 1971
4 weeks

With stints with the Jeff Beck Group, as a solo artist, and as the frontman of the Faces, Rod Stewart's gravel-throated singing made him one of the most distinctive rock voices of the late '60s. Yet despite that fact, Stewart, a former gravedigger, was still looking for a commercial breakthrough in 1971. His first solo effort, *The Rod Stewart Album*, stalled at number 139 in 1969. *Gasoline Alley*, released in 1970, fared significantly better, reaching number 27, but Stewart still wasn't satisfied. "I was getting desperate," he says. "I had seen so many of the bands that I used to go see make it—the Stones, the Yardbirds, Manfred Mann, Eric Burdon & the Animals. I would think, 'I can sing as good or better than most of these guys. When is it going to be my turn?'"

Stewart's turn came with *Every Picture Tells a Story*. "We had no preconceived ideas of what we were going to do," Stewart says. "It was such an innocent time. We would have a few drinks and strum away and play." The looseness paid off, as Stewart and company—Faces guitar player Ron Wood, drummer Mick Waller, pianist Pete Sears, and acoustic guitar player Martin Quittenton—worked extremely fast. "Maggie May," "Reason to Believe,"

and "Every Picture Tells a Story" were cut in a mere two days, even though Stewart and his mates frequently strayed from the studio to visit the local pub.

Waller would turn up for the sessions with just a snare drum and a stick. "He would go around to the rest of the studios and borrow stuff from Simon Kirke of Free or whoever else was around," says Stewart. Yet Waller's minimalist approach, combined with a mix of acoustic guitars and mandolin, helped make *Every Picture Tells a Story* an intimate affair. "If you listen to 'Maggie May,' there's only half a drum kit on there. I don't think there are any cymbals on there whatsoever," Stewart says.

For material, Stewart opted for a mix of originals and proven classics, including a cover of "That's All Right," a song made famous by Elvis Presley; a take of the traditional "Amazing Grace," which is tacked onto the end of "That's All Right" and not listed on the label or sleeve; the Temptations' "(I Know) I'm Losing You"; and Tim Hardin's ballad "Reason to Believe."

The latter track was released as a single with "Maggie May," a song almost left off the album, as the B-side. "A mate that I was living with at the time didn't think it had any melody to it, and I nearly believed him," Stewart recalls. "I said, 'Yeah, you're right. It does ramble on a bit, doesn't it.'" Yet Stewart didn't have a choice. He'd only recorded nine songs (including "Amazing Grace") and if he pulled "Maggie May," the album would be too short.

Although "Maggie May" was hardly a traditional single with its classical guitar intro and mandolin break at midsong, at least one listener found it more immediately appealing than "Reason to Believe." As Stewart recalls, "It was a disc jockey in Cleveland who took the initiative and turned it over and that was it—all hell broke loose." With "Maggie May" as the A-side, the single soared up the chart, hitting Number One on the Hot 100 and on the British singles chart the same week that *Every Picture Tells a Story* topped the album chart on both sides of the Atlantic. Says Stewart, "If it wasn't for that disc jockey, I could still be digging graves."

THE TOP FIVE
Week of October 7, 1971

1. **Every Picture Tells a Story**
   Rod Stewart

2. **Tapestry**
   Carole King

3. **Every Good Boy Deserves Favour**
   Moody Blues

4. **Shaft**
   Isaac Hayes

5. **Ram**
   Paul & Linda McCartney

and piano, was fleshed out by co-producer Phil Spector's use of strings.

Lennon had been a big supporter of Spector's involvement in the Beatles' troubled *Let It Be* project. "There's a myth about Phil," says Ono, referring to the producer's famed mad-genius tendencies, "but he's actually a very professional person in the studio. He knew exactly how to deal with an artist like John. His sensitivity level was very similar [to Lennon's], so they got along very well."

While *Imagine* may be best known for its optimistic title track, it also featured some scathing attacks in the songs "Give Me Some Truth," "Crippled Inside," and "How Do You Sleep?," the latter of which, littered with Beatles references and featuring George Harrison on slide guitar, was aimed at Paul McCartney. "It was all done in fun, but people took it very seriously," Ono says. "They both appreciated black humor and when they talked they would always come up with some snappy and witty remarks and they understood that it wasn't meant to hurt each other. It was more of a witticism, rather than John really trying to hurt Paul. John was laughing when he was making it." Still, the song contributed to the widespread impression of serious acrimony between Lennon and McCartney, the latter of whom took the matter seriously enough to respond to it a decade later, following Lennon's death, in the song "Here Today" [see 270].

In its seventh week on the chart *Imagine* hit the top spot, making Lennon the third Beatle, after McCartney [see 120] and Harrison [see 128], to score a Number One solo album. Ringo Starr's highest-charting album, 1973's *Ringo*, peaked at number two.

Producers: John & Yoko and Phil Spector

Track listing: Imagine / Crippled Inside / Jealous Guy / It's So Hard / I Don't Want to Be a Soldier / Give Me Some Truth / Oh My Love / How Do You Sleep? / How? / Oh Yoko!

October 30, 1971
1 week

Following the breakup of the Beatles [see 122], John Lennon initially generated more notice for his various activities than he did for his post-Beatles music. *Unfinished Music No. 1: Two Virgins*, his first album with his then-girlfriend and future wife Yoko Ono, created controversy with a cover design that featured Lennon and Ono naked. The album of experimental music, as well as the subsequent avant-garde follow-ups *Unfinished Music No. 2: Life with the Lions* and *The Wedding Album*, were commercial and critical disappointments. All three albums, released in 1969, failed to crack the top 100 of the album chart, but Lennon and Ono still made headlines with their eight-day bed-in for peace in a Canadian hotel room.

With the 1969 single "Give Peace a Chance" and *The Plastic Ono Band—Live Peace in Toronto 1969*, which reached number 10, Lennon was back on track artistically. *John Lennon/Plastic Ono Band*, released in late 1970, was hailed by critics and fans alike and reached number six.

For the follow-up album, Lennon opted to take even more of a commercial approach. "*Plastic Ono Band* was basically guitar, bass, and drums, and some piano" says Ono. "With *Imagine*, John wanted to put on strings and make more of a pop album."

The album was recorded at Lennon's Ascot Sound Studios located in his Tittenhurst Park mansion. "It was a very laid-back nice time," says Ono. "There were people dropping in all the time and we'd have little jam sessions." Notable players on the album include bassist Klaus Voorman (Lennon's old chum from the Beatles' Hamburg days), George Harrison, drummer Jim Keltner, and pianist Nicky Hopkins.

The peace-themed title track became Lennon's biggest solo hit to date when it peaked at number three. Lennon wrote the lyrics of the song on the back of a hotel bill while traveling on an airplane and composed the music at home. "John was very elated about that particular song," says Ono. "He felt that it was really important for the world to hear, and he was right. It became a very important song. He wanted to keep it very simple and easy, so even children could sing and the message would get across." The song's sparse arrangement, centered around Lennon's vocals

THE TOP FIVE
Week of October 30, 1971

1. **Imagine**
   John Lennon

2. **Every Picture Tells a Story**
   Rod Stewart

3. **Shaft**
   Isaac Hayes

4. **Santana**
   Santana

5. **Tapestry**
   Carole King

136 Shaft ENTERPRISE 5002
ISAAC HAYES

Producer: Isaac Hayes

Track listing: Theme from Shaft /
Bumpy's Lament / Walk from Regio's /
Ellie's Love Theme / Shaft's Cab Ride /
Cafe Regio's / Early Sunday Morning /
Be Yourself / A Friend's Place /
Soulsville / No Name Bar / Bumpy's
Blues / Shaft Strikes Again / Do Your
Thing / The End Theme

November 6, 1971
1 week

Initially, Isaac Hayes thought Shaft was
going to be more than a musical
opportunity. "I wanted to act," says
Hayes. "It was a secret passion of mine
and I was told by someone involved in
the film that they would give me a try. I
committed to the music, but by then they
had already cast Richard Roundtree."
Although he didn't get a chance to audition for the role as the smooth-talking
private detective, Hayes was still thrilled
to be involved in the project. "It was a
concept designed to go after the black
consumer market with a black leading
man, a black director, and a black composer," he says. This genre of cheesy
action pictures, designed to appeal to
the black moviegoer, would soon earn
the title "blaxploitation," but as Hayes
notes, it also provided black artists an
avenue to express themselves.

By 1971, Hayes was already a success. He had co-written (with partner
David Porter) the 1967 Sam & Dave hit
"Soul Man," which was later covered
by the Blues Brothers [see 235], and
had scored top 10 albums with 1969's
Hot Buttered Soul and 1970's The Isaac
Hayes Movement. Nonetheless, he still
had to audition to land the job to compose the musical score to Shaft.

THE TOP FIVE
Week of November 6, 1971

1. **Shaft**
   Isaac Hayes

2. **Santana**
   Santana

3. **Every Picture Tells a Story**
   Rod Stewart

4. **Imagine**
   John Lennon

5. **Tapestry**
   Carole King

"The film's producers wanted to see
if I had a handle on what I was going
to do," he says. "I was given footage
from three scenes and I wrote the music
for those three scenes." Hayes laid
down a stripped-down rhythm track for
the main theme. Another piece wound
up being "Ellie's Love Theme," named
for the John Shaft character's love interest. "The third piece was used for a
montage of shots when Shaft was going
through Harlem. That tune wound up
being 'Soulsville,'" Hayes says.

Even during the first day of recording on the soundstage, the sessions for
Shaft went incredibly smoothly. "The
engineer came out from the studio and
said, 'Okay, are you guys ready?
Where's your charts?' We said, 'What
charts? We don't have any charts. It's
all in our heads already.' There was
some serious concern on his face." Yet
Hayes and his band, which included
members of the Bar-Kays, had it down,
and completed the basic tracks well
ahead of schedule.

It took Hayes approximately six
weeks to score the film and an additional month to finish the soundtrack for
record release. "I had to extend some
parts," he says. "There were some cues
in the movie that lasted maybe a minute
or so, but for the record I had to extend
those out into entire songs."

The composer never dreamed that
the soundtrack and title theme would go
on to become huge hits. "I was just trying to make it work within the context of
the film," he says. "When I finished on
the soundstage with the film, I was just
so relieved that the producer and the
director were pleased with my work."

Two weeks after the two-record
soundtrack album hit the summit of the
Top LP's chart, "Theme from Shaft"
reached Number One on the Hot 100.
The album and single also earned
Hayes Grammy Awards for Best Instru-
mental Arrangement, Best-Engineered
Recording, and Best Original Score
Written for a Motion Picture, as well as
an Oscar for Best Song.

Perhaps more importantly, Shaft
opened the film scoring world to other
black composers, including Curtis Mayfield [see 148].

Producer: Santana

Track listing: Batuka / No One to Depend On / Taboo / Toussaint L'Overture / Everybody's Everything / Guajira / Jungle Strut / Everything's Coming Our Way / Para Los Rumberos

October 13, 1971
5 weeks

The success of *Abraxas* [see 126] brought changes for Santana. Most notably, Carlos Santana opted to add a second guitarist, hiring on Neal Schon, who was being hailed by San Francisco locals as "the Eric Clapton of the Bay Area." Clapton himself had tried to recruit Schon for Derek and the Dominoes, but Schon chose Santana.

Says Santana, "I heard a duet sound, like on 'Jungle Strut.' I wanted two guitars synchronized, like the Allman Brothers." Yet the new personnel failed to defuse tensions brewing in the band. "We would fight like cats and dogs to create that chemistry. You could hear us cussing at each other between takes," he says. Yet while the members of Santana were having trouble relating to each other, making it difficult to work as a group, "the chemistry was still there," Santana says.

"Most bands, with the exception of the Rolling Stones or the Grateful Dead, cannot stay together after the first two or three albums," he adds. "Some people are not equipped to deal with success and all of a sudden they become unreliable or inconsistent."

While Santana was having personnel problems, the 1971 self-titled album was a reunion of sorts, as several associates, including percussionist Coke Escovedo, were featured. Escovedo, who was recovering from a brain aneurysm, co-wrote the album's "No One to Depend On" with Santana percussionist Michael P.R. Carabello.

Originally, Santana recorded what was set to be the group's third album with engineer Eddie Kramer. "We cut some tracks live at Hammersmith Odeon and we also went into Trident Studios in London, but it didn't work out," Santana says. "We wanted to work with Eddie, because he worked with Jimi Hendrix [see 108], but it just wasn't our sound."

Instead, the band returned to San Francisco and recorded the album at Columbia Studios with engineer Glen Kolotkin. Upon its release, the album was dubbed simply *Santana*, like the band's 1969 debut album. For convenience's sake, some referred to it as *Santana III*, since it was the band's third album.

With Santana still basking in the success of *Abraxas*, the third album entered the Top LP's chart at number 13 on October 16, 1971. A week later, it climbed to number four, where it stayed for two weeks. On November 6, it hit number two, before reaching the summit a week later.

The album spawned two singles. "Everybody's Everything" reached number 12 in December 1971, while "No One to Depend On" stalled at number 36 in March 1972.

But 1971's *Santana* would be the final album released by that incarnation of the band and the last Santana album to top the charts. Following the album's release, keyboardist Gregg Rolie and Schon left the group and eventually formed Journey [see 263]. "We all knew it was becoming disjointed and we had to split," says Santana. "We disintegrated."

THE TOP FIVE
Week of October 13, 1971

1. **Santana**
   Santana

2. **Shaft**
   Isaac Hayes

3. **Every Picture Tells a Story**
   Rod Stewart

4. **Imagine**
   John Lennon

5. **Teaser & the Firecat**
   Cat Stevens

138 There's a Riot Goin' On EPIC 30986
SLY & THE FAMILY STONE

Producer: Sylvester Stewart

Track listing: Luv N' Haight / Just Like a Baby / Poet / Family Affair / Africa Talks to You "The Asphalt Jungle" / There's a Riot Goin' On / Brave & Strong / (You Caught Me) Smilin' / Time / Spaced Cowboy / Runnin' Away / Thank You for Talkin' to Me Africa

December 18, 1971
2 weeks

Initially, the future didn't hold much promise for the psychedelic soul group Sly & the Family Stone. *Dance to the Music,* the group's 1968 debut album stalled at number 142, even though the title track became a top 10 hit. The group's follow-up album, *Life,* fared even worse, stalling at number 195 in late 1968. However, the group's fortunes changed dramatically with the single "Everyday People." The single, which topped the Hot 100 in February 1969, helped propel 1970's *Stand!* to number 13. The band scored its second Number One single a year later with "Thank You (Falettin Me Be Mice Elf Again)." By the time Epic released Sly & the Family Stone's *Greatest Hits,* the group's popularity was sufficient enough to drive the album all the way up to number two in November 1970.

Yet the pressure of newfound stardom was catching up with the group's leader, Sylvester Stewart, who went by the name of Sly Stone. The former San Francisco area radio personality drew from his own bloodline to form a band. He had recruited his brother Freddie to play guitar, his sister Rosemary to sing and play piano, and his cousin Larry

Graham to handle the bass duties. Trumpet player Cynthia Robinson had been with Stone in an earlier group called the Stoners. The lineup of Sly & the Family Stone was rounded out by drummer Greg Errico.

"We really were a family," says Graham. "The other members who were added to the group felt like family, too." The ties in the band were such that when one member got into something new, the others would follow. "When someone got into dogs, everyone got into dogs," says Graham. "When we got into motorcycles and T-Birds, we all had motorcycles and T-Birds. We did things together."

However, that family feeling didn't carry on through the recording of *There's a Riot Goin' On.* "[Sly] recorded a good portion of the album by himself," says Graham. "There was more overdubbing of our parts. Before, on the earlier albums, we would play live in the studio."

Since Stone was working on the album in his home studio in Bel Air, California, and the band members still lived in the San Francisco area, there was little interaction between the members of the band during the sessions. "It wasn't often that we were all in the studio together at the same time; we

would just basically come in and do our part."

And often, rather than waiting for the other members to come to the studio, Stone would lay down the tracks himself. Graham, for instance, did not play bass on a few of the songs that made the album.

At the time, Stone's reputation had begun to sour. He frequently showed up late or not at all for concert dates and continued to work on *There's a Riot Gonna On* long after the proposed deadline. Eventually, he was thrown out of his home for defaulting on his mortgage payments. As a result, Stone took up residence in a camper outside of a studio so he could finish the album.

When *There's a Riot Gonna On* was finally released, more than two years after the band's last studio effort, the Family and the fans weren't disappointed. "There were a lot of new ideas being exposed on that album," says Graham. "It was a big progression from the last album."

On December 4, 1971, "Family Affair," became Sly & the Family Stone's third Number One single. Two weeks later, the group scored its first Number One album, as *There's a Riot Gonna On* hit the summit in its sixth week on the chart.

THE TOP FIVE
Week of December 18, 1971

1. **There's a Riot Goin' On**
   Sly & the Family Stone

2. **Led Zeppelin**
   Led Zeppelin

3. **Santana III**
   Santana

4. **Teaser & the Firecat**
   Cat Stevens

5. **Chicago**
   Chicago at Carnegie Hall

ODE 77013

Music
CAROLE KING

139

Producer: Lou Adler

Track listing: Brother, Brother / It's Going to Take Some Time / Sweet Seasons / Some Kind of Wonderful / Surely / Carry Your Load / Music / Song of Long Ago / Brighter / Growing Away from Me / To Much Rain / Back to California

January 1, 1972
3 weeks

Following the tremendous and surprising success of Tapestry, Carole King returned to the A&M studios in August and September of 1971 with many of the same musicians and Lou Adler once again producing. "I didn't feel any pressure," says King. "Other people around me felt some pressure. The people made all the money off selling Tapestry, but I didn't feel pressure to repeat the success. I was surprised by it in the first place."

For King, the making of Music wasn't much different than her previous recordings. "I've always done the same thing," she says. "Written a song, put it on demo, record, or tape, and then gone on to do whatever was up next. To me if it was successful, it was kind of a miracle. I just do what I do without worrying if it is going to be commercial."

For Music, King once again wrote with Toni Stern, co-author of Tapestry's Number One hit "It's Too Late." Stern and King collaborated on "It's Going to Take Some Time," "Sweet Seasons," and "Too Much Rain." "Some Kind of Wonderful" was a Goffin-King oldie that was a R&B hit in 1961 for the Drifters. The remaining eight tracks were King solo compositions.

Musically, King and Adler took a more jazz-oriented approach on Music, with a full horn section replacing the single horns that were featured on some tracks on Tapestry. James Taylor was once again featured, playing guitar on "Too Much Rain," "Some Kind of Wonderful," and "Song of Long Ago." On the latter track, he also contributed backing vocals.

King was also beginning to become more involved in politics. Although none of the songs are overtly political, she used the liner notes to send a message— "use the power, register and vote"—to the millions of people buying her records. "I have always been an advocate of people getting involved and doing the right thing with their lives," she says.

On August 18–21, in the middle of the Music sessions, King, who had overcome a bad case of stage fright, celebrated with a triumphant stand at the Greek Theatre in Los Angeles. All four nights were sold out.

Music was released on November 30, 1971, just weeks before King gave birth to her third child (and first with her second husband Charles Larkey, who played bass on Tapestry and Music). On the album cover, King, several months pregnant, was photographed behind the piano.

Music became King's second Number One album in seven months. It hit the top spot after a mere four weeks on the chart while Tapestry was still in the top 10, holding at number nine. King's first solo album, Writer, which had been repromoted following the success of Tapestry, had climbed to number 84.

"Sweet Seasons," the first single from Music, was released on January 11, 1972. Less than two months later, it peaked at number nine.

THE TOP FIVE
Week of January 1, 1972

1. **Music**
   Carole King

2. **Led Zeppelin**
   Led Zeppelin

3. **Teaser & the Firecat**
   Cat Stevens

4. **Chicago at Carnegie Hall**
   Chicago

5. **E Pluribus Funk**
   Grand Funk Railroad

140 American Pie UA 5535
DON MCLEAN

Producer: Ed Freeman

Track listing: American Pie / Till Tomorrow / Vincent / Crossroads / Winterwood / Empty Chairs / Everybody Loves Me, Baby / Sister Fatima / The Grave / Babylon

January 22, 1972
7 weeks

By 1971, the career of singer-songwriter Don McLean was looking up. In 1968, he had fallen approximately $20,000 in debt, largely because he refused to sign away his publishing royalties to prospective record labels. Finally, a fledging filmmaker, who wanted to make a movie about the young singer-songwriter, hooked McLean up with a company called Mediarts. The film project was scrapped, but the label funded the recording of his debut album, *Tapestry*. Although the album, released in April 1970, initially failed to chart, Mediarts allowed McLean to go to work on a second album.

"Everyone thought they had this sweet-singing young man who writes these pretty tunes," McLean says. "Then I came up with this nine-minute rock 'n' roll thing. They actually fought it a little bit. They said, 'We don't want to put that out as a single, let's put out a slow ballad.'"

The song in question was "American Pie," a tune chronicling McLean's days as a paperboy and the history of rock 'n' roll. The epic track stretched from "the day the music died" (February 3, 1959, when Buddy Holly, Ritchie Valens and the Big Bopper died in an airplane crash) to references to the Beatles, Mick Jagger, and Bob Dylan.

Yet there was a time when "American Pie" almost didn't see the light of day at all. "We were about halfway through making the record and one day [Mediarts executive] Ed Freeman came to me and said, 'I've got bad news for you, the record company is going to fold.' I thought, 'Great, here we go again.'" Fortunately for McLean, the label was purchased by United Artists. Executives at UA, unlike the powers-that-be at Mediarts, loved "American Pie." There was just one problem: They thought the song was too long to be released in its entirety as a single. So the label put out an edited version as a single. "It got a lot of airplay, but radio stations began to get a lot of phone calls from people who had bought the album, who said that they wanted to hear the whole song," McLean says.

To help remedy the situation, UA issued another version of the single. This time it included the entire song with one part on each side of the 45. Still, the hardcore fans wouldn't accept the single and went out and bought the uninterrupted album version.

On January 15, 1972, "American Pie" hit the top of the Hot 100. A week later, the album, dedicated to Buddy Holly, joined the single at Number One. Although *American Pie* featured other memorable tracks, such as "Vincent," a tribute to Van Gogh, and "Babylon," a traditional tune that was taught to McLean by the Weavers' Lee Hays, they were all overshadowed by "American Pie." Says McLean of his signature song, "The first job I ever had was as a paperboy. That's my story."

THE TOP FIVE
Week of January 22, 1972

1. **American Pie**
   Don McLean

2. **Concert for Bangla Desh**
   George Harrison & Friends

3. **Music**
   Carole King

4. **Chicago at Carnegie Hall**
   Chicago

5. **Led Zeppelin**
   Led Zeppelin

REPRISE 2032 # Harvest
NEIL YOUNG

141

Producers: Elliot Mazer, Neil Young, Jack Nitzsche, and Henry Lewy

Track listing: Out on the Weekend / Harvest / A Man Needs a Maid / Heart of Gold / Are You Ready for the Country / Old Man / There's a World / Alabama / The Needle and the Damage Done / Words (Between the Lines of Age)

March 11, 1972
2 weeks

By 1971, Neil Young had already enjoyed artistic success as a member of pioneering folk-rock outfit Buffalo Springfield, as a solo artist, and with Crosby, Stills, Nash & Young [see 131], but Young had yet to experience his greatest commercial triumph.

Buffalo Springfield, which included Stephen Stills, never cracked the top 40 of the album chart, but scored a top 10 single in 1967 with "For What It's Worth (Stop, Hey What's That Sound)." "Mr. Soul," perhaps Young's finest contribution to the group, was not issued as a single.

Following the breakup of Springfield, Young began his solo career in 1969, but ironically it didn't take full flight until he joined Crosby, Stills, Nash & Young. *After the Gold Rush*, Young's third solo album, released while he was touring with CSN&Y, garnered critical acclaim and reached number eight in September 1970.

Although he was plagued by chronic back problems, Young would go on to make the most successful album of his career in 1971. "It was very spontaneous," says co-producer Elliot Mazer. Much of the album was cut at Quadrafonic Sound Studios in Nashville, Tennessee, which Mazer co-owned. "I was working on an album by a guy named Jay Coles and we had heard that a bunch of artists from New York and Los Angeles were coming to Nashville to do the last Johnny Cash TV show." Mazer was introduced to Young by Young's manager Elliot Roberts. Young told Mazer he was impressed with a band of local Nashville musicians called Area Code 615, so Roberts suggested that Young visit the studio and play with some of the musicians. "We went into the studio and Neil played a couple of songs and we were stunned by how beautiful his songs were and how incredible he was," says Mazer. "It was magic."

Most of what would become *Harvest* was cut live in the studio at brisk pace on 16-track. "We did 'Heart of Gold' and five other songs in two days," says Mazer, "Then Neil had to go on the road." The sessions were a departure for Young, who was backed by the group of Nashville musicians dubbed the Stray Gators, rather than his usual backing band Crazy Horse.

One song in particular stood out. "When Neil did 'Heart of Gold,' we all knew it was a hit. It was just a question

of recording it." Backing vocals by James Taylor and Linda Ronstadt [see 192] were overdubbed "in the control room on the playback of the take," adds Mazer. "It was pretty obvious that we had the right take."

Young also called upon his CSN mates for backing vocals on "Are You Ready for the Country," "Alabama," and "Words," which were recorded at Young's Broken Arrow Studio #2, located at his Northern California ranch.

Aside from those songs and the cuts recorded in Nashville, *Harvest* includes "A Man Needs a Maid" and "There's a World," which feature accompaniment by the London Symphony Orchestra, and "The Needle and the Damage Done," recorded live at UCLA's Royce Hall in Los Angeles. The latter track was inspired by Crazy Horse guitarist Danny Whitten's heroin problem. It proved prophetic when Whitten died of a heroin overdose in late 1972.

With Young's back problems requiring surgery, *Harvest* took nearly a year to complete. "We were concerned about Neil's health," says Mazer, "but we weren't too worried about the album, because we had already cut 'Heart of Gold,' which everyone thought would be a huge single."

Harvest became Young's first and only Number One album in its second week on the chart. A week later, with *Harvest* still holding at the summit, "Heart of Gold" hit the top of the Hot 100.

THE TOP FIVE
Week of March 11, 1972

1. **Harvest**
   Neil Young

2. **American Pie**
   Don McLean

3. **Concert for Bangla Desh**
   George Harrison and Friends

4. **Fragile**
   Yes

5. **Music**
   Carole King

142 America
AMERICA
WARNER BROS. 2576

Producers: Ian Samwell, Jeff Dexter, and America

Track listing: Riverside / Sandman / Three Roses / Children / A Horse with No Name / Here / I Need You / Rainy Day / Never Found the Time / Clarice / Donkey Jaw / Pigeon Song

March 25, 1972
5 weeks

Although the band's three members came together in Great Britain at London's Central Park High School, they were known collectively as America. Dewey Bunnell, Gerry Beckley, and Dan Peek were the sons of American military men based in London. When the trio got together, little did its members know that they would take both the U.S. and the U.K. by storm.

After graduating from high school in 1969, Peek went back to the U.S. to attend college. After a six-month stint, he returned to London to find that his high school chums Bunnell and Beckley were writing their own songs. While doing a little studio work on the side, Beckley met the booking agent for the popular London nightspot known as the Round-house. "They booked us in there to play shows," says Bunnell. "It was just three of us, acoustic guitars, and we did 20 minutes. We ended up opening for some pretty big acts—the Who, Pink Floyd [see 157], and Elton John [see 146]. Then we took it on the road for

about six months."

The club tour worked. America soon garnered coverage in the British music weeklies and developed a small but loyal following. "The fact that we were Americans in London helped us," says Bunnell. Jeff Dexter, a DJ who liked the band, hooked the trio up with Warner staff producer Ian Samwell, who was impressed enough to set up an audition for America with the president of the Warner Bros. London office. "We played acoustic guitars right in his office," he says. "We had these songs worked out to perfection, three-part harmonies, and we all had our guitar parts. We could play them in our sleep."

Several of the songs America played that day, including "Riverside" and "I Need You," ended up on America.

The trio recorded the majority of the album at Trident Studios in London. Ken Scott, who was also producing sessions for David Bowie, served as engineer. "We laid everything down loosely," Bunnell says.

Once the album was completed, it was delivered to Warner Bros. Beckley's ballad "I Need You" was penciled in as the first single. But the Warner executives asked if the trio had any more songs. "They sent us down to Morgan Studios in London—it was a live-in farm demo studio. Led Zeppelin [see 118] had worked there, so there were some pretty heavy vibes." America went on to record four more songs. One was "A Horse with No Name."

America was originally released without that track, which first appeared as a single in England. When "A Horse with No Name" became a hit there, it was decided the song would be included on all future pressings of the album. Says Bunnell, "'I Need You' [which also became a top 10 hit] was much more in the pocket as a traditional ballad. 'A Horse With No Name' had the quirkiness that put us on the map."

After six weeks on the chart, America hit the apex of the Top LP's & Tapes chart, while "A Horse with No Name" topped the Hot 100. The album knocked out Harvest while the single displaced "Heart of Gold." Both were recorded by Neil Young [see 141], one of America's major influences.

THE TOP FIVE
Week of March 25, 1972

1. **America**
   America

2. **Harvest**
   Neil Young

3. **Baby I'm-a Want You**
   Bread

4. **Nilsson**
   Nilsson Schmilsson

5. **Paul Simon**
   Paul Simon

ATLANTIC 8230 **First Take 143**
ROBERTA FLACK

Producer: Joel Dorn

Track listing: Compared to What /
Angelitos Negros / Our Ages or Our
Hearts / I Told Jesus / Hey, That's No
Way to Say Goodbye / The First Time
Ever I Saw Your Face / Tryin' Times /
Ballad of the Sad Young Men

April 29, 1972
5 weeks

Roberta Flack's first album was released in June 1969, but didn't crack the Top LP's & Tape chart until January 31, 1970. It spent two weeks at number 195, before falling off the chart altogether, but that wouldn't be the last time First Take would grace the pages of Billboard.

Following the initial disappointing showing of First Take, Flack, a North Carolina–bred former school teacher, experienced some success with her second album, 1970's Chapter Two, which peaked at number 33. Her third effort, 1971's Quiet Fire. made number 18. Yet her career didn't really begin to take off until 1972, when her smoldering version of the folk song "The First Time Ever I Saw Your Face," an album cut on First Take, was included in Play Misty for Me, the 1972 suspense thriller starring Clint Eastwood as a disc jockey.

"My mom answered the phone and said, 'Clint Eastwood is on the phone.' She didn't know who he was by name, but I did and I was shocked, chagrined, mortified," Flack says. "He said he wanted to use this song. That was three years later, and everybody had been telling me that it was too slow, so I had started to pick up the tempo when I played it live. People responded to it live, but it

hadn't been released as a single. It didn't have any commercial importance to me, but I was in love with it. When he said he wanted to use it, I said, 'I would like to do it again, because it's too slow.' But he said, 'It's perfect, I love it, it's just the right length. I want to use every note just the way it is.'"

After the film became a hit, Atlantic released "The First Time Ever I Saw Your Face" as a single, and it and First Take began to climb the charts. The album re-entered the chart on March 18, 1972, with the single already racing up the Hot 100. "The First Time Ever I Saw Your Face" hit Number One on April 15. Two weeks later First Take also hit the peak, with the single still holding the Number One position.

The album's title was literal. First Take was recorded in a mere 10 hours over a two-day period. For Flack, who had 600 songs in her repertoire when she auditioned for Atlantic, narrowing the field for the album was difficult. "I

did about 16 or 17 songs," she says, "and we took the best ones, which were usually the first takes."

Among the other tracks included on First Take were a cover of Leonard Cohen's "Hey, That's No Way to Say Goodbye" and "Angelitos Negros." The latter tune was inspired by Flack's desire to make a pro-black statement, but also by her boyfriend at the time, who spoke fluent Spanish. "I used to sing 'The Impossible Dream' and 'We Shall Overcome' in my live set and dedicate it to Dr. King," Flack says. "People would come up to me and say that they liked the way I sung these songs of protest, because I sang them with such love." In "Angelitos Negros," which means "Black Angels," Flack introduces the song by asking, "Painters, why do you always paint white virgins? Paint beautiful black angels." Says Flack, "That song makes a very beautiful statement." Thanks to Clint Eastwood, that statement was finally heard.

THE TOP FIVE
Week of April 29, 1972

1. **First Take**
   Roberta Flack

2. **America**
   America

3. **Harvest**
   Neil Young

4. **Eat a Peach**
   Allman Brothers

5. **Fragile**
   Yes

144 Thick as a Brick REPRISE 2072
JETHRO TULL

Producer: Jethro Tull

Track listing: Thick as a Brick / Thick as a Brick

June 3, 1972
2 weeks

Jethro Tull's back-to-back Number One albums, 1972's *Thick as a Brick* and 1973's *A Passion Play* [see 164], are arguably the most uncommercial and uncompromising albums ever to top the Billboard album chart.

Named after the 18th-century inventor of the seed drill, Jethro Tull was formed in 1968 in Blackpool, England. After its initial success in the U.K., the group began to establish a following in America with its third album, 1970's *Benefit*, which climbed to number 11 and went gold. The follow-up, 1971's *Aqualung*, featured several tracks, such as "Locomotive Breath," which became standards on the burgeoning album rock radio format. The album went on to sell more than two million copies in America, setting the stage for *Thick as a Brick*.

"It was the first time Jethro Tull really did a concept album," says singer/flautist Ian Anderson. "We were wrongly accused of having made a concept album with *Aqualung*. To me it was

just a song collection. However, we got this sort of tag as being a concept-album group. My reaction to that was to come up with the material for the follow-up album *Thick as a Brick*, as almost a parody of what a concept album might be."

Thick as a Brick was conceived and recorded as one piece of music nearly 44 minutes long, broken into two parts to accommodate the two sides of an album. The cover featured a mock newspaper called the St. Cleve Chronicle with stories relating to the album, including a lead piece on Gerald (Little Milton) Bostock, a fictitious eight-year-old boy who shared writing credits with Anderson.

"It was definitely a conceptualized piece of music and lyric, but it was done with a sense of fun," Anderson explains. "Lyrically, a lot of the ideas and sentiments expressed are my own somewhat contradictory views and emotions I had as a child or young teenager. It kind of added to the humor of it for me to pretend that these were the sentiments of a rather precocious eight-year-old."

The album was written, composed, and arranged over a grueling month-long period with a lineup that included Anderson taking on violin, sax, and trumpet chores, as well as his usual lead vocals, flute, and acoustic guitar;

Martin Barre on electric guitar and lute; John Evan on organ, piano, and harpsichord; Jeffrey Hammond-Hammond on bass; and Barriemore Barlow on percussion. "Everyday I would write a new piece of music," Anderson recalls. "I would meet the guys at the rehearsal room and we would build up the song from the day before. We always finished rehearsal around tea time and I would have the evening and a couple of hours the next morning to work on the next piece of music."

Yet the actual recording process went fairly quickly. Says Anderson, "After we had the whole piece organized, we went in and recorded it, which only took about two weeks. In fact, it took longer to do the album cover than to record the album."

THE TOP FIVE
Week of June 3, 1972

1. **Thick as a Brick**
   Jethro Tull

2. **First Take**
   Roberta Flack

3. **Harvest**
   Neil Young

4. **Crosby & Nash**
   Crosby & Nash

5. **Manassas**
   Stephen Stills

Exile on Main St. 145
THE ROLLING STONES

Producer: Jimmy Miller

Track listing: Rocks Off / Rip This Joint / Casino Boogie / Tumbling Dice / Sweet Virginia / Torn & Frayed / Black Angel / Loving Cup / Happy / Turd on the Run / Ventilator Blues / Just Wanna See His Face / Let it Loose / All Down the Line / Stop Breaking Down / Shine a Light / Soul Survivor

June 17, 1972
4 weeks

When the Rolling Stones were recording *Sticky Fingers* [see 132], "the vibes weren't too heavy," says Andy Johns, one of the engineers who worked on the album. Yet the Stones' next album, *Exile on Main St.*, "was a whole other trip altogether," he says, as hard drug use began to take its toll on the band. Nonetheless, the Stones continued to roll through a creative high point, even if it was through a drug-induced haze.

As the title suggests, the album was recorded while the Stones were in exile in the South of France to escape high taxes in their native U.K. Most of *Exile* was recorded in basement of guitarist Keith Richard's Nellcote villa with the Rolling Stones mobile unit. "It was not easy to record there," says Andy Johns. "There were these funny little rooms and the vibe there was very weird. The electricity kept going on and off and everything kept going out of tune, because it was so humid. It was recorded during the spring, summer, and fall."

Toward the end of the sessions, Johns discovered what may have been causing some of the bad vibes. "The house had been the headquarters of the

Gestapo when the South of France had been occupied," he says. "The air-conditioning ducts in the floor were in the shape of swastikas. I imagine that downstairs in the basement, where we recorded, was where they would interrogate prisoners."

A few songs were left in the can from previous sessions, including "Sweet Black Angel," which was recorded during the *Sticky Fingers* sessions at singer Mick Jagger's Stargroves estate. Says Andy Johns, "At the time, the working title was 'Bent Green Needles,' which I'm sure was Keith's idea of a joke." That track was recorded in a large room. "I remember putting Mick Taylor's amp in the fireplace with microphones up the chimney."

The album opener, "Rocks Off," was "particularly good. That one really worked," Johns says. "'Stop Breaking Down' was one of the best blues things they ever did," he adds. "[Mick] Taylor played brilliantly on that."

The biggest hit from *Exile*, "Tumbling Dice" which reached number seven, was also one of the most difficult songs to record. "That was a marathon tracking date," Johns says. "That went on for about two weeks. They would just sit and play the intro riff over and over for

hours and hours trying to get the groove right. We must have done 150 or 200 takes."

In all, *Exile*, the Stones' first two-record set, took a year to complete—six months to record and another six months of mixing at Sunset Sound in Hollywood. "At that time, nobody took a year to make a record," says Andy Johns. "We were supposed to start at 6 P.M. every day, but nobody would even plug anything in until midnight. Because it went on for so long, there was a feeling of being in the trenches."

Jagger's wife Bianca was pregnant during the sessions. She gave birth to her daughter Jade on October 21, 1971. "She kept calling and hassling Mick, and Keith was pissed off about that," Johns says. "And Anita [Pallenberg] and Keith were fighting, because everyone was at their house for months and months. It drove her up the wall."

Adding to the complications and tension was the drug use. "There were a lot of drugs," says Johns. "But there was also a lot of fun. We had a blast. We were living in the South of France, everyone had plenty of money, everyone was young, and the Stones were making amazing music at the height of their powers."

THE TOP FIVE
Week of June 17, 1972

1. **Exile on Main St.**
   The Rolling Stones

2. **Thick as a Brick**
   Jethro Tull

3. **First Take**
   Roberta Flack

4. **Manassas**
   Stephen Stills

5. **Joplin in Concert**
   Janis Joplin

146 Honky Chateau UNI 93135
ELTON JOHN

Producer: Gus Dudgeon

Track listing: Honky Cat / Mellow / I Think I'm Going to Kill Myself / Susie (Dramas) / Rocket Man (I Think It's Going to Be a Long, Long Time) / Salvation / Slave / Amy / Mona Lisas and Mad Hatters / Hercules

July 15, 1972
5 weeks

Elton John (right) with lyricist Bernie Taupin.

By 1971, Elton John had recorded six albums in a two-year span. John's 1969 debut album, *Empty Sky*, wouldn't be released in America until 1975, but half of those six—*Elton John*, released in 1970, and *Tumbleweed Connection* and *Madman Across the Water*, both released in 1971—had broken into the top 10. It was under this hectic schedule that John recorded his seventh album, *Honky Chateau*, named for Chateau d'Herouville in France, where the album was recorded.

"We were doing two albums a year, because he was contractually obliged to do two albums a year," says producer Gus Dudgeon. "Elton never at any time wanted to get to the end of his contract and find that he owed the record company any product at all."

Honky Chateau marked the recording debut of former Magna Carta guitarist Davey Johnstone in John's band. Elsewhere, John stuck with Dudgeon, who had worked on all of his previous efforts, but he opted to ditch the string arrangements by Paul Buckmaster, which had been featured on his previous albums. "That was never a conscious decision," says Dudgeon. "Any-

thing we ever used on any album at any time, was purely based on the composition." If there was a change, Dudgeon adds, it would come from John's longtime lyricist Bernie Taupin. "Every album began with Bernie, the lyric came first, then the songs."

While the strings were left off, horns were added to the mix on "Honky Cat." It marked the first time Dudgeon had handled horn arrangements, which proved to be quite troublesome. "They took a hell of a long time," he says, "not so much to do the arrangements, but to explain to four Frenchmen, who didn't speak much English, by an Englishman that didn't know much French. They had never heard of Muscle Shoals. So when I tried to explain how the Muscle Shoals people played, it just went right by them." The sessions for the horn arrangements at Strawberry Studios began at about 5 P.M. in the evening and ran through the night. "We finally got it done at seven in the morning," Dudgeon says.

"Rocket Man," which would go on to become John's biggest hit to date when it reached number six in July, came together quickly. "It was written in literally a half an hour at breakfast time," Dudgeon says. "By the time he was doing *Honky Chateau*, Elton was writing entire albums on the spot, in the studio, in about five days."

Honky Chateau contained one surprise for John that Dudgeon added to the final mix. "Elton was never around for any overdubs," Dudgeon says. "He figured we knew what we were doing, so he just let us get on with it. On 'I Think I'm Going to Kill Myself,' I was going to use his stepfather playing spoons, but he was on holiday. So I called up 'Legs' Larry Smith from the Bonzo Dog Band. He was a tap-dancer and that was the nearest thing I could think of to spoons, so I dubbed him on. The first time Elton heard it was when he got a pressing of the album."

When "Rocket Man" was released as a single, critics compared it to David Bowie's 1969 track "Space Oddity," which was also produced by Dudgeon. "That was unfortunate," he says. "That was my career-opener and it directly led to me working with Elton, because he liked the record. But I wasn't aware of doing anything similar to 'Space Oddity' on 'Rocket Man.' In fact, I think it's a very different kind of record. If he had been singing about anything else, I don't think there would have been any kind of comparison."

Thanks in part to "Rocket Man" shooting up the Hot 100, *Honky Chateau* became John's first Number One album in its fifth week on the chart. It was the beginning of one of the greatest chart runs of the '70s.

THE TOP FIVE
Week of July 15, 1972

1. **Honky Chateau**
   Elton John

2. **Exile on Main St.**
   Rolling Stones

3. **Roberta Flack & Donny Hathaway**
   Roberta Flack & Donny Hathaway

4. **Thick as a Brick**
   Jethro Tull

5. **Joplin in Concert**
   Janis Joplin

COLUMNS 31102 **Chicago V**
CHICAGO **147**

Producer: James William Guercio

Track listing: A Hit By Varese / All Is Well / Now That You've Gone / Dialogue (Part I) / Dialogue (Part II) / While the City Sleeps / Saturday in the Park / State of the Union / Goodbye / Alma Mater

August 19, 1972
9 weeks

Chicago V marked a few firsts for the seven-piece band named after the windy city. It was the group's first single-disc set and it was the first time the band, formerly known as the Chicago Transit Authority, hit Number One on the Top LP's & Tapes chart.

The jazz-rock combo, formed in 1967, went through a number of names, including the Missing Links and the Big Thing, before it arrived at the Chicago Transit Authority. That named was shortened simply to Chicago after the city's mayor, Richard Daley, threatened a lawsuit.

With its blend of jazz and rock elements, Chicago was often compared to Blood, Sweat & Tears [see 112], which also worked with Columbia staff producer James William Guercio. The group's trademark instrumental breaks resulted in lengthy songs, so its first three albums were two-disc sets. *Chicago Transit Authority*, released in 1969, stalled at number 17. *Chicago II*, released a year later, reached number four, thanks to the top 10 singles "Make Me Smile" and "25 or 6 to 4." *Chicago III* didn't have any big hit singles but still managed to reach number two in 1971, while *Chicago at Carnegie Hall*, a four-record set, climbed to number three later that same year.

THE TOP FIVE
Week of August 19, 1972

1. **Chicago V**
   Chicago

2. **Honky Chateau**
   Elton John

3. **School's Out**
   Alice Cooper

4. **A Song for You**
   The Carpenters

5. **Greatest Hits**
   Simon & Garfunkel

Much of Chicago's success came from the band's virtually nonstop touring. By fall of 1971, "we had cut back a bit, but we were still touring 200 days a year," says drummer Danny Seraphine. In fact, several of the songs featured on the album were fine-tuned on the road. "We rehearsed a lot of the songs on the road, instead of learning it in the studio and then cutting it," Seraphine says.

The band, which also included keyboardist/vocalist Robert Lamm, trombone player James Pankow, trumpet player Lee Loughnane, guitarist Terry Kath, horn player Walt Parazaider, and bassist/vocalist Peter Cetera, opted to break its tradition and go the single-disc route on *Chicago V* for a few reasons. "We were touring so much and it just became too much weight on us to try and do double albums all the time," he says.

Also, the band, which had initially made a name for itself with its loose fusion of jazz and rock, had changed its direction. "We became more singles-oriented," Seraphine says. "That in itself made the songs shorter. We got sick and tired of our songs getting chopped

up, and decided to try and condense things. I don't know whether that was good or bad. It worked to a certain degree, but we may have left a little bit of our artistic integrity behind." Nonetheless, Seraphine says, "musically, we were still doing some things that were turning people's heads."

While many appreciated Chicago for its members' musical prowess, others flocked to the band for the pop appeal of tracks like "Saturday in the Park," which became the band's highest-charting single when it reached number three on September 23, 1972. The second single, "Dialogue," only made number 24, after radio shied away from the track because of its anti-war political sentiments.

Overall, the band managed to find a balance on *Chicago V*. "It managed to show the artistic, musical side of the band, yet it had that commercial accessibility that made it successful. It wasn't self-indulgent, but we didn't turn our backs on the purists."

Chicago V hit the top spot in its fourth week on the chart when it became the group's first of five consecutive albums [see 163] to hit Number One.

148 Superfly CURTOM 8014
CURTIS MAYFIELD

Producer: Curtis Mayfield

Track listing: Little Child Runnin Wild / Pusherman / Freddie's Dead / Junkie Chase / Give Me Your Love / Eddie You Should Know Better / No Thing on My / Think / Superfly

October 21, 1972
4 weeks

By 1972, Curtis Mayfield had already earned his place in the pop music history books as one of the most important forces in R&B. Originally a gospel singer, Mayfield formed the Impressions with friend Jerry Butler in 1957. During the mid-'60s Mayfield led the Impressions through several classic hits, such as "We're a Winner" and "People Get Ready," which were innovative both musically and lyrically. While leading a new soul movement known as the Chicago Sound, Mayfield simultaneously managed to capture the trials, tribulations, and hopes of the civil rights movement.

In 1970, Mayfield went solo, as the Impressions carried on. Mayfield's first three solo efforts, *Curtis, Curtis/Live!,* and *Roots,* were fairly successful, each cracking the top 40, yet it would take *Superfly* to put him on top.

In late 1971, after performing the first of two nights at Lincoln Center in New York, Mayfield was approached by screenwriter Phillip Fenty and film producer Sig Shore. Backstage, Fenty showed Mayfield his script for *Superfly.* "At that point in my life I was ready for anything. Anything positive," Mayfield says. "I was more than happy to read over the script."

After more than a decade in the music business, Mayfield had a pretty impressive list of credits. Aside from his work with the Impressions, he'd produced and written material for several acts. In 1970, he launched his third record company, Curtom.

"Having done so many things in the business, it was a challenge for me to possibly score a movie," Mayfield says. "I was all into it. Within the script itself, I wrote in areas where music should be, what song should be taken from parts of the dialogue. I was very turned on about doing it."

Isaac Hayes's *Shaft* [see 136] had already proven that contemporary soul music tied into a blaxploitation film blockbuster could make for a huge hit record. Yet Mayfield's *Superfly* was hardly a carbon copy of *Shaft.*

The lyrics in songs such as "Freddie's Dead" and "Pusherman" were a stark contrast to the glitzy images of violence and drugs featured in the film. "Even though I loved the script and the way it read, I chose to not ride along the glitter and the surface of the movie itself," Mayfield says. "I didn't want it to appear as a Coke commercial. I wanted to write in depth and maybe those who watched it would understand."

Mayfield's message was received as alarming. "Freddie's Dead," centered around a character who served as a fall guy for a drug dealer in the film, became an unlikely hit single. It climbed to number four with a unique sound that combined Latin-flavored percussion, funky guitar, and Mayfield's trademark falsetto.

Buoyed by the single and the buzz surrounding the film, *Superfly* hit Number One in its ninth week on the chart.

"I am still very proud of that work," says Mayfield, who went on to score several other films. "We showed the industry that music was very important to lock in with the dialogue and that you didn't need a football lot and $250,000 to do it."

THE TOP FIVE
Week of October 21, 1972

1. **Superfly**
   Curtis Mayfield

2. **Carney**
   Leon Russell

3. **Days of the Future Passed**
   Moody Blues

4. **Never a Dull Moment**
   Rod Stewart

5. **Chicago V**
   Chicago

A&M 4365 # Catch Bull at Four 149
CAT STEVENS

Producer: Paul Samwell-Smith

Track listing: Sitting / Boy with a Moon & Star on His Head / Angelsea / Silent Sunlight / Can't Keep It In / 18th Avenue / Freezing Steel / O Caritas / Sweet Scarlet / Ruins

November 18, 1972
3 weeks

Thanks in part to the top 10 hit single "Peace Train," Cat Stevens's fifth album, 1971's *Teaser and the Firecat*, climbed all the way to number two. Yet Stevens's popularity was so widespread that he didn't need a hit single to fuel his greatest chart triumph, which occurred a year later with the release of *Catch Bull at Four.*

Born Steven Georgiou, Stevens began his career in 1967 and scored several British hits on the Deram imprint. Some of his early material, including "The First Cut Is the Deepest," would become hits for other performers, including Rod Stewart. A bout with tuberculosis in 1968 led the singer to rethink his musical direction, and he ultimately abandoned his initial heavily produced pop style in favor of more straightforward and stripped-down folk music.

"When I first met him, he basically played me three albums of material," says guitarist Alun Davies. "We all met at [producer] Paul Samwell-Smith's apartment and Steve proceeded to play about 50 songs, most of which would appear on the first three [A&M] albums."

Yet following the release of *Teaser and the Firecat*, Stevens's backlog of material was depleted. "He was then forced to write on the road," says Davies, "because he was a heavily tour-ing musician by then." The fact that much of *Catch Bull at Four* was written on the road is reflected in some of the music, particularly in "18th Avenue (Kansas City Nightmare)." Says Davies, "That had something to do with getting wasted in Kansas one night. He went on the missing list for 12 hours." To this day, Davies isn't sure if Stevens ingested some sort of drug or just had "a few too many brandies."

Catch Bull at Four marked a turning point musically for Stevens. "It's quite a piano-dominated album, where the first three were led by guitar," Davies says. "It moved away from the folkier side of things."

The album was recorded at Richard Branson's Manor Studio in Oxfordshire and Chateau d'Herouville in France in a fairly business-like manner. "With a number two album, we were touring a lot," Davies says. "It had to be done between touring schedules, so the sessions were pretty efficient and pretty happy."

Although he didn't play on the track, Davies calls "Sweet Scarlet," a song featuring Stevens's singing backed only by his own piano playing, "the gem of the album. That shines head and shoulders above everything else on there. It was an amazing one-off performance."

"Sitting," the only charting single from *Catch Bull at Four*, stalled at number 16, but at that point in his career, Stevens didn't need a top 10 single to drive his album sales. In its sixth week on the chart, *Catch Bull at Four* became Stevens's first and only Number One album.

THE TOP FIVE
Week of November 18, 1972

1. **Catch Bull at Four**
   Cat Stevens

2. **Superfly**
   Curtis Mayfield/Soundtrack

3. **Days of Future Passed**
   Moody Blues

4. **All Directions**
   The Temptations

5. **Ben**
   Michael Jackson

150 Seventh Sojourn THRESHOLD 7
THE MOODY BLUES

Producer: Tony Clarke

Track listing: Lost in a Lost World / New Horizons / For My Lady / Isn't Life Strange / You and Me / The Land of Make-Believe / When You're a Free Man / I'm Just a Singer (in a Rock and Roll Band)

December 9, 1972
5 weeks

"It was quite a traumatic time for the group," says Moody Blues singer-guitarist Justin Hayward of the months the veteran British act spent making its seventh album, appropriately titled *Seventh Sojourn*. "We were going through a lot of personal anxiety and that's reflected in the material." Indeed, the lyrics and even the song titles on *Seventh Sojourn* suggest that the Moodies did in fact have the blues.

Formed in Birmingham, England, in 1964, the band was originally fronted by singer-guitarist Denny Laine, who was featured on its top 10 hit "Go Now!" Laine, who left the group along with bassist Clint Warwick in 1966, went on to join Paul McCartney & Wings in 1971 [see 161]. With Hayward and singer bassist John Lodge recruited, the Moodies, who also included Ray Thomas (flute, vocals), Mike Pinder (keyboards, vocals), and Graeme Edge (drums), became known for a grandiose, orchestrated sound and spacey lyrics. Their third album, 1968's *Days of Future Passed*, featured live

string accompaniment, but often the group relied on a Mellotron—a keyboard instrument that reproduces string sounds—to create its symphonic sound.

Yet for *Seventh Sojourn*, the Moodies opted for some new technology. "We dumped the Mellotron and discovered an instrument called the Chamberlain, which gave us a much better orchestral sound," says Hayward.

Although the Moodies had failed to crack the top 20 of the singles chart after the early success of "Go Now!," their popularity was increasing with each album release. By 1972, they were one of the premiere rock acts in the world.

"There was a lot of pressure," Hayward recalls. "The nature of the business then was that every record you made was tremendously important." With stress and heightened expectations mounting, the Moodies had tentative plans that *Seventh Sojourn* would be their last hurrah.

Ironically, just as the Moody Blues were preparing to go on hiatus, they experienced the biggest success of their career. "Isn't Life Strange," released in advance of *Seventh Sojourn*, stalled at number 29 in June 1972. Then something strange happened. Disc jockeys picked up on the Moodies' four-year-old epic "Nights in White Satin" from *Days of Future Passed*. The single hit number two in November, while *Days of Future Passed* climbed to number 3, paving the way for *Seventh Sojourn*. The new album shot to the top spot of the *Bill-*

board Top LP's & Tape chart in four weeks. "It was almost as if 'Nights in White Satin' was the single from *Seventh Sojourn*," Hayward says. "The record company was trying to stop it by suggesting to radio stations that they shouldn't play it, but it didn't matter."

A second single from *Seventh Sojourn*, "I'm Just a Singer (In a Rock and Roll Band)," peaked at number 12 in March.

After completing an extensive world tour, the Moodies began recording their eighth album, but it was quickly aborted, leaving the band members free to dive into outside projects. The band would not regroup until 1978 [see 259]. As Hayward puts it, "*Seventh Sojourn* closed a particular part of the book."

THE TOP FIVE
Week of December 9, 1972

1. **Seventh Soujourn**
   The Moody Blues

2. **All Directions**
   Temptations

3. **Rhymes & Reasons**
   Carole King

4. **Catch Bull at Four**
   Cat Stevens

5. **Close to the Edge**
   Yes

ELEKTRA 75049 **No Secrets** 151
CARLY SIMON

Producer: Richard Perry

Track listing: The Right Thing to Do / The Carter Family / You're So Vain / His Friends Are More Than Found of Robin / We Have No Secrets / Embrace Me, You Child / Waited So Long / It Was So Easy / Night Owl / When You Close Your Eyes

January 13, 1973
5 weeks

Even before Carly Simon released her debut album, she was surrounded by good company. In 1966, Bob Dylan's manager Albert Grossman arranged recording sessions with the Band's [see 170] Robbie Robertson, Rick Danko, and Richard Manuel. Dylan even rewrote the lyrics to "Baby Let Me Follow You Down" specifically for Simon. However, the sessions were aborted after Simon and Grossman had a disagreement.

It took several years for Simon to resurface, but it turned out to be worth the wait. Her self-titled 1971 debut, featuring the top 10 hit "That's the Way I've Always Heard It Should Be," reached number 30. Her follow-up, *Anticipation*, included the title track, which reached number 13, while that album also clocked in at number 30. In March 1972, Simon picked up a Grammy for best new artist and was poised to record the best album of her career.

It happened at Trident Studios in London during September and October of 1972. Richard Perry was enlisted to produce *No Secrets* by Elektra Records founder Jac Holzman. "Since her first album came out, I had always wanted to produce her," says Perry. "So, when Jac called me, it was kind of like fate." Initially, Simon began working on an album with Paul Buckmaster, known for his string arrangements on Elton John's albums, but the project was shelved at Holzman's insistence and Perry was hired on. At first, Simon was hesitant to work with Perry. She feared that the producer, primarily known for his work with Barbra Streisand [see 234] and Nilsson, would make her

record sound too slick. Perry, however, did just the opposite, giving Simon more of a rock edge.

The album featured several noted session players, including Beatles associate Klaus Voorman, who played bass on every track. "Everyone was very upbeat," says Perry. "We had a very homogeneous group of musicians and Carly was in great form and happy to be there. We all had the feeling that we were in the middle of making a record that had enormous potential and lasting significance."

"You're So Vain," which would turn out to be the album's best-known song, was also the most difficult to complete. "We had to cut that on three separate occasions until we got it right, each time with a different drummer" says Perry. "It's a very unique piece of material, because it starts out very quietly and slowly builds leading up to the chorus. It was a little tricky to achieve that."

The uncredited backing vocalist on the song is Rolling Stones frontman Mick Jagger [166]. Originally, Harry Nilsson was also featured, but he had a change of heart. "Harry just said, 'I don't think the two of you need me,' so he backed out," Simon says.

Adds Perry, "Carly suggested that Mick sing backing vocals on it, but after we had the track complete, we temporarily abandoned the idea, because we all felt it was a hit the way it was. But then, one afternoon he just showed up in the studio. After Carly and Mick did the backing vocals together, Carly went out and recut her lead vocal again. She

had already sung it, but she was so inspired by the backing vocal session, she just went out and did it in one or two takes and surpassed her original."

Even today, the question of who Simon is addressing in the song remains a mystery, although actor Warren Beatty and Jagger are often mentioned as possible subjects. "It's kind of funny and it proves the point that if you leave a question unanswered, people stay much more interested," Simon says. "I'm perfectly aware that it would be anticlimactic to tell."

No Secrets also included a song written by James Taylor, who Simon married on November 3, 1972. "Carly wanted to record one of James's songs and I suggested 'Night Owl,' because I knew it was a funkier, bluesier tune than his more folk-oriented material," says Perry. "It turned out to be a great track." The song features the McCartneys on backing vocals, who were credited merely as "Paul and Linda" on the album's sleeve. "They had been recording the title song for *Live and Let Die* in the room next door," he adds.

On January 6, 1973, "You're So Vain" hit the top of the Hot 100. The following week, *No Secrets* topped the album chart, while the single was still locked in at Number One.

THE TOP FIVE
Week of January 13, 1973

1. **No Secrets**
   Carly Simon

2. **Seventh Sojourn**
   Moody Blues

3. **Rhymes & Reasons**
   Carole King

4. **One Man Dog**
   James Taylor

5. **Living in the Past**
   Jethro Tull

152 The World Is a Ghetto UNITED ARTISTS 5652
WAR

Producer: Jerry Goldstein

Track listing: The Cisco Kid / Where Was You At / City, Country, City / Four Cornered Room / The World Is a Ghetto / Beetles in the Bog

February 17, 1973
2 weeks

War was on the map as the backing band for former Animals vocalist Eric Burdon. While Burdon was initially part of the British invasion, War was uniquely American, and a definite product of Southern California. After two albums with Burdon, the singer left, but the seven-member-strong War continued.

At first, things were shaky. *War*, released in 1971, barely dented the albums chart, topping out at number 190. But the follow-up, 1972's *All Day Music*, fared significantly better, reaching number 16, proving that War could indeed stand on its own and setting the stage for *The World Is a Ghetto*.

War's ability to find commercial acceptance without Burdon gave the group a newfound confidence and freedom, says producer Jerry Goldstein, who first experienced success as co-producer of the Angels' 1963 Number One hit "My Boyfriend's Back," and later as a member of the Strangeloves.

Sensing that the band was at a creative high, Goldstein booked Crystal Studios in Los Angeles for 30 straight days, so that War's momentum wouldn't be interrupted. Although some of the material was rehearsed before entering the studio, most was created on the spot with spontaneous grooves, he says.

The World Is a Ghetto came at a turning point in War's career. "*War* was really an accumulation of the past," Goldstein says. "On *All Day Music*, they started to create things, but on *The World Is a Ghetto* they were forced to be spontaneous. They needed to make an album and they needed to be creative."

The opening track, "The Cisco Kid," was inspired by the late-'50s TV show of the same name. Guitarist Howard Scott came up with the concept on the steps of his Compton apartment. "It was really based on the fact that he was the only non-Anglo hero in late '50s and '60s that they could relate to," Goldstein says. "Every other superhero was white."

The public not only related to the sentiments of "The Cisco Kid," but also to its infectious Latin groove, as the single became War's biggest hit, reaching number two. The band later presented Duncan Renaldo, the man who portrayed the Cisco Kid on TV, with a gold record.

Although six out of the seven members of War were African-American and the seventh Danish, the group specialized in Latin rhythms and would later score a hit with "Low Rider," a song that would become an anthem for the Latino car culture.

War was also known for its social commentary in such cuts as "The World Is a Ghetto" and "Four Cornered Room." Yet for many, the music was as important as the message. Goldstein still remembers recording the title track. An edited version of the 10-minute song was released as a single and reached number seven. Says Goldstein, "When Charles Miller played that sax solo, I cried. I had never heard anybody with that kind of feeling and soul. I sat in the studio at the end of the night and listened to it over and over again until the morning."

THE TOP FIVE
Week of February 17, 1973

1. **The World Is a Ghetto**
   War

2. **No Secrets**
   Carly Simon

3. **Talking Book**
   Stevie Wonder

4. **Rhymes & Reasons**
   Carole King

5. **Hot August Night**
   Neil Diamond

MCA 2100 **Don't Shoot Me I'm Only the Piano Player** `153`

ELTON JOHN

Producer: Gus Dudgeon

Track listing: Daniel / Teacher I Need You / Elderberry Wine / Blues for Baby and Me / Midnight Creeper / Have Mercy on the Criminal / I'm Going to Be a Teenage Idol / Texan Love Song / Crocodile Rock / High Flying Bird

March 3, 1973
2 weeks

Less than six months after scoring his first Number One album with *Honky Chateau* [see 146], Elton John returned with "Crocodile Rock," a rollicking slab of nostalgia that preceded the release of his next album, *Don't Shoot Me I'm Only the Piano Player*.

The fact that the album was recorded virtually on the heels of *Honky Chateau* was nothing out of the ordinary for John. "Every time we were making an album, the previous one was just coming out," says producer Gus Dudgeon, "so we were able to gauge the reaction to what had just been released against what we were working on."

Once again, John and company opted to record at Strawberry Studios in France. The album's title was inspired by a meeting between John and legendary comedian Groucho Marx, as was the cover art, which features a movie theater entrance with a *Go West* poster on display. The nostalgic feel also seeped into the music, particularly in "Crocodile Rock."

Says Dudgeon, "The song could have gone any one of several ways. It could have been done as a serious, out-and-out rock tune, but for some reason, as soon as Elton sang that 'la, la la la, la' 'Speedy Gonzales' bit, I realized what we were talking about was more of a silly, throwaway kind of novelty thing. Once we cut the rhythm track, we decided that we should go for a Johnny and the Hurricanes kind of cheesy organ sound. We kept trying things, because of the throwback in the lyric. We put in the 'Dream Lover' guitar and all kinds of throwback things. We even tried a Duane Eddy bit, which didn't quite come off."

By the time *Don't Shoot Me I'm Only the Piano Player* debuted on the album chart, "Crocodile Rock" had already hit Number One on the Hot 100. But *Don't Shoot Me* wasn't just an exercise in nostalgic frivolity.

The album-opened with "Daniel," a bittersweet ballad about a war veteran heading off for Spain and leaving behind America and a younger brother. John's recording, however, left some unanswered questions. "There's this mystical missing verse," says Dudgeon. "The die-hard fans always ask if we recorded it and then cut it out, but the fact is, we never recorded the third verse." Dudgeon recalls a recent conversation with guitarist Davey Johnstone. "He remembered that the third verse had something about 'a ship's dog named Paul.' They all just cracked up when they saw it, so Elton said, 'That's obviously got to go.' And it went."

In its fourth week on the chart, *Don't Shoot Me I'm Only the Piano Player* became John's second Number One American album, and first to top the album charts in both the States and England. And "Daniel," even with the missing verse, managed to climb all the way to number two on the Hot 100.

THE TOP FIVE
Week of March 3, 1973

1. **Don't Shot Me I'm Only the Piano Player**
   Elton John

2. **No Secrets**
   Carly Simon

3. **The World Is a Ghetto**
   War

4. **Soundtrack**
   Deliverance

5. **Hot August Night**
   Neil Diamond

154 "Dueling Banjos" from the Original Sountrack Deliverance WARNER BROS. 2683

ERIC WEISSBERG AND STEVE MANDELL

Producer: None listed

Track listing: Dueling Banjos / Little Maggie / Shuckin' the Corn / Pony Express / Old Joe Clark / Eight More Miles to Louisville / Farewell Blues / Earl's Breakdown / End of a Dream / Buffalo Gals / Reuben's Train / Riding the Waves / Fire on the Mountain / Eighth of January / Bugle Call Rag / Hard Ain't It Hard / Mountain Dew / Rawhide

March 17, 1973
3 weeks

Eric Weissberg

By 1972, Eric Weissberg, a onetime member of folk group the Tarriers, had become a much in-demand session player known for his banjo and bass-playing. When he received a call to play a traditional bluegrass tune called "Dueling Banjos" for a film, he figured it was just another gig.

"They asked me if I could play that song and they wanted a guitar and a banjo, so I called Steve Mandell," says Weissberg. "We went to this office and auditioned. We must have played it 25 ways—sad, slow, fast." After passing the audition, Weissberg and Mandell were invited to go on the film's location in Clayton, Georgia. "Then I found out that it was directed by John Boorman."

Once on location, Weissberg discovered Boorman's plan. "He wanted to shoot the scene to the music, because it was a pivotal scene in the beginning of the picture," says Weissberg. The duo worked on the song on location with Boorman and the film's cast for two days. Once Boorman had effectively choreographed the scene, Weissberg and Mandell traveled to nearby Atlanta to record the track. "We must have recorded 10 different closely related versions of the song," says Weissberg.

When Boorman heard the completed tapes, he invited the duo to record the entire soundtrack for the film, an adaptation of a James Dickey novel called Deliverance. The film about four men on a canoe trip gone awry starred Burt Reynolds, Jon Voight, Ned Beatty, and Ronny Cox.

"We went back to the studio the next weekend and did 'Dueling Banjos' 50 different ways," Weissberg says.

With the sessions completed, Weissberg moved onto other projects. "About a year later, I was doing a jingle session and one of the singers told me he heard my record on the radio," Weissberg says. "And I said, 'What record?,' because it had been 10 years since I did my own record." The singer reminded Weissberg of the soundtrack gig, but as far as Weissberg knew, it did not exist as a record.

After some investigation, Weissberg learned that "Dueling Banjos" had been pressed as a single to be used as a musical bed for live commercial spots for the film. In Minneapolis, one disc jockey began receiving requests for the song. Soon Warner Bros. decided to release the track as a single.

"When it was obvious that it was going to be a big hit, I happened to be sitting in my lawyer's office and I told him that in three days I could record an entire album to go with the single," Weissberg says. The attorney put in a call to Warner Bros. president Joe Smith. "All of a sudden his eyes got real wide. He put his hand over the mouthpiece and said, 'Joe says the album's already out.' I said that's impossible. What album?" says Weissberg.

Quick to jump on a hot record, Warner Bros. added "Dueling Banjos" and "End of a Dream" to New Dimensions in Banjo and Bluegrass, a 1963 album Weissberg had recorded with Marshall Brickman for Elektra Records. "Elektra was bought by Warner Bros., so they had the album in their catalog," says Weissberg. "So they took off the first cut on each side and put both sides of the 'Dueling Banjos' single on the album."

The single made number two, and Dueling Banjos hit the summit in its eighth week on the chart. Nonetheless, even to this day, Weissberg is still slightly annoyed. "They never told me anything about this, which really ticked me off, because one of the cuts they took off was a tune I wrote. I could have been getting publishing royalties for it."

THE TOP FIVE
Week of March 17, 1973

1. **"Dueling Banjos" from the Original Soundtrack Deliverance**
   Eric Weissberg and Steve Mandell

2. **Don't Shoot Me I'm Only the Piano Player**
   Elton John

3. **Lady Sings the Blues**
   Diana Ross

4. **Rocky Mountain High**
   John Denver

5. **No Secrets**
   Carly Simon

MOTOWN 758 **Lady Sings the Blues**
DIANA ROSS

155

Executive producer: Berry Gordy

Track listing: The Arrest / Lady Sings the Blues / Baltimore Brothel / Billie Sneak into Dean & Dean's, Swingin' Uptown / T'ain't Nobody's Bizness If I Do / Big Ben, C.C. Rider / All of Me / The Man I Love / Them There Eyes / Gardenias from Louis / Cafe Manhattan, Had You Been Around, Love Theme / Any Happy Home / I Cried for You (Now It's Your Turn to Cry Over Me) / Billie & Harry, Don't Explain / Mean to Me / Fine and Mellow / What a Little Moonlight Can Do / Louis Visits Billie on Tour, Love Theme / Cafe Manhattan Party / Persuasion, T'ain't Nobody's Bizness If I Do / Agent's Office / Love Is Here to Stay / Fine and Mellow / Lover Man (Oh, Where Can You Be?) / You've Changed / Gimme a Pigfoot (and a Bottle of Beer) / Good Morning Heartache / All of Me / Love Theme / My Man (Mon Homme) / Don't Explain / I Cried for You (Now It's Your Turn to Cry Over Me) / Strange Fruit / God Bless the Child / Closing Theme

April 7, 1973
2 weeks

Billie Holiday never had a Number One album, but she was nonetheless one of the greatest jazz vocalists of all time. Her career might have been even more storied had she lived longer—she died of heart and liver disease exacerbated by years of drug abuse on July 15, 1959, at the age of 44.

Thirteen years later, Diana Ross faced one of the biggest challenges of her career. She had found success fronting the Supremes [see 89] and as a solo artist, but could Ross also make good as Billie Holiday? Lady Sings the Blues was a film biography of Holiday presented by Motown founder Berry Gordy. Ross made her major film debut in the picture starring as Holiday opposite Billy Dee Williams, with Richard Pryor co-starring.

For Ross, singing Holiday's songs on Motown's first motion picture soundtrack was as challenging as portraying the singer in the film. "I had to prepare myself ahead of time," she says. "I had to know when I'm doing this song is Billie Holiday on drugs, off drugs, going off drugs, or is she straight. I couldn't sing the songs in the normal way, because there were a lot of other things

that needed to be considered."

While preparing for the part and filming the picture, Ross listened to nothing but Billie Holiday's music, but she wasn't trying to copy her singing style. "I had decided absolutely and completely not to try to sing like Billie Holiday, because I thought that would be wrong and I would be criticized if I tried to do that. The most important thing that I could do as an actress was to know what kind of pain she was going through at the time when she was singing those songs. I hoped to have the feeling there, rather than trying to sound like her, which I never did."

Despite Ross's popularity, there were those who were skeptical about her ability to play Holiday. "There were a lot of people who felt that I couldn't do it,

because I didn't have enough pain in my life to sing jazz and blues and portray someone as extraordinary as Billie Holiday," she says.

Ross prepared for the role by interpreting Holiday's songs. "When she was singing 'You've Changed,' it didn't have to be directed at another person. She could have been thinking of herself. To me, the message was that she was looking at herself."

Although Ross received mixed reviews, she earned an Oscar nomination for her performance. The only single released from the album, "Good Morning Heartache," stalled at number 34 in March, but by April, Lady Sings the Blues, which also includes score music by Michael LeGrand, fought its way to the top in its 20th week on the chart.

THE TOP FIVE
Week of April 7, 1973

1. **Lady Sings the Blues**
   Diana Ross

2. **Don't Shot Me I'm Only the Piano Player**
   Elton John

3. **Prelude/Deodato**
   Eumir Deodato

4. **Deliverance**
   Soundtrack

5. **Rocky Mountain High**
   John Denver

156 Billion Dollar Babies
ALICE COOPER

WARNER BROS. 2685

Producer: Bob Ezrin

Track listing: Hello Hooray / Raped and Freezin' / Elected / Billion Dollar Babies / Unfinished Sweet / No More Mister Nice Guy / Generation Landslide / Sick Things / Mary-Ann / I Love the Dead

*April 21, 1973
1 week*

With the 1972 album *School's Out* and the single of the same name, Alice Cooper, the man and the band, could no longer be dismissed as a rock 'n' roll freak show. The album, Cooper's fourth, held the number two position on the album chart for three weeks, while the single climbed to number seven and would live on for years as a teen anthem. It would also set the stage for Cooper to deliver the most successful album of his career.

"*School's Out* was the album no one ever expected," says Cooper. "We were the band that everyone called the flavor of the month. So it was fun to smear it in those people's faces. That's why we called the next album *Billion Dollar Babies*. We thought the best thing to do was to make fun of ourselves and flaunt the whole thing."

Cooper's band formed in Phoenix in 1965 and underwent several name changes before opting for Alice Cooper, a name frontman Vincent Furnier also adopted as his own. The band became widely known for its outrageously theatrical stage shows, but its recordings went largely unnoticed until *School's Out*.

For the follow-up album, Cooper and company holed up in Morgan Studios in London in December 1972 where they were frequently visited by some famous friends. "One night when we were cutting the basic tracks, Marc Bolan came in with Harry Nilsson, Keith Moon, Rick Grech, Ringo, and Donovan. We ended up doing an hour version of 'Jailhouse Rock,'" says Cooper. Yet only Donovan, who was recording in the studio next door, actually made it onto *Billion Dollar Babies*. His voice was featured reciting lyrics along with Cooper on the title track. "Getting him to rock out on a song was really pretty cool," says Cooper. "After that, his career was never the same."

Although none of the album's four singles cracked the top 20, they were hits on album rock radio and several would become staples of Cooper's live set. "Elected," the first single, was actually a rewrite of the song "Reflected" from the band's 1969 debut album, *Pretties For You*. "The '72 election was coming up and everyone was saying, 'Elvis for President,' so we said, 'Why not Alice for President?'"

Another Cooper favorite was "No More Mister Nice Guy." Says Cooper, "That has a Who open-chord feel to it. It was a real basic pop song with a funny lyric. Every time we came into a different town, there were new rumors about us. We figured everyone hated us so much, we would take it to the extreme— 'You think we are bad now, wait until you see what's coming.'"

The album's finale, "I Love the Dead," cemented Cooper's position of rock's most notorious ghoul. "It was such a funny song. Certainly it was scary, but it was like any good horror movie, which is initially very scary, but then it becomes really funny."

America apparently got the joke. Cooper wasn't elected President, but *Billion Dollar Babies* hit Number One after six weeks on the chart. Says Cooper, "We were there with the Rolling Stones, the Beatles, the Who, and Led Zeppelin—all of those people we looked up to. Then, all of a sudden we weren't just on the charts with them, but ahead of them. It was an unbelievable dream."

THE TOP FIVE
Week of April 21, 1973

1. **Billion Dollar Babies**
   Alice Cooper

2. **Lady Sings the Blues**
   Diana Ross

3. **The Dark Side of the Moon**
   Pink Floyd

4. **Aloha from Hawaii Via Satellite**
   Elvis Presley

5. **The World Is a Ghetto**
   War

HARVEST 11163 # The Dark Side of the Moon
PINK FLOYD
157

Producers: Pink Floyd

Track listing: Speak to Me / Breathe in the Air / On the Run / Time / The Great Gig in the Sky / Money / Us and Them / Any Colour You Like / Brain Damage / Eclipse

April 28, 1973
1 week

Prior to 1973, Pink Floyd had established itself as the most innovative British psychedelic group both in the studio and on the stage. Their albums featured surrealistic sound-scapes, highlighted by a bevy of aural effects, while their performances featured cutting-edge lighting and staging. However, the Floyd's musical innovation only brought it moderate success in America, at least initially. Its highest-charting album prior to *The Dark Side of the Moon* was its sixth U.S. release, 1972's *Obscured by the Clouds*, a soundtrack to the film *The Valley*, which reached number 46.

The title *The Dark Side of the Moon* first surfaced in 1971 when Floyd bassist/vocalist Roger Waters wrote a song with that title in 1971 for the *Meddle* album. Although the song did not make the LP, the idea didn't die. At a meeting in drummer Nick Mason's kitchen, the group, which also included guitarist David Gilmour and keyboardist Rick Wright, agreed to take the theme of lunacy, examined in the song, and expand it into a concept album that touched upon such pressures of modern life as work, aging, death, and money.

Alan Parsons, who had worked as an assistant engineer on chart-toppers like the Beatles' *Abbey Road* [see 117] and *Let It Be* [see 122], was tapped to

engineer the album, which the group began recording on June 1, 1972. By the time Floyd entered Abbey Road Studios, the material was well-rehearsed.

"One of the interesting things about *The Dark Side of the Moon* is that it was toured before it was recorded, and it was toured while it was being recorded," says Parsons. Pink Floyd first performed *The Dark Side of The Moon* material on January 20, 1972, at the Brighton Dome in England, more than a full year before the album was released.

Since "quadraphonic was all the rage" at the time, says Parsons, he and Floyd incorporated various sound effects to exploit the new technology. For example, the album opens with the sounds of a heartbeat (actually a heavily processed bass drum), clocks ticking, alarms and a cash register ringing, and several disembodied voices rambling. The various sound effects reappear several times on the album, most notably on "Money" and "Time."

"The clock sounds I had lying around, as the result of a sound-effects recording I had done a few months before," says Parsons. Adding to the effect was a "damped bass guitar trying to sound like a clock ticking," he says.

To produce the various voices, Waters made a series of questions on flash cards and presented them to friends and acquaintances. Among those participating were Paul and Linda McCartney, but their voices didn't make the album. However, Wings guitarist Henry McCulloch is heard on the album. "One of the questions was, 'When did you last thump somebody?' and he said, 'It was New Year's Eve.' The next card said, 'Do you think you were in the right?' And he said, 'I don't know, I was really drunk at the time,'

which you hear on the album," says Parsons. When McCulloch's wife came in and was asked the first question, she also responded, "New Year's Eve."

By the time *The Dark Side of the Moon* was completed in January 1973, the members of Pink Floyd and Parsons were pleased with their work. "It was their best album to date," says Parsons. "Everyone felt it was a winner, because it had such strength in its compositions, in its performance, and in its sounds."

Yet the members of Pink Floyd and Parsons couldn't possibly have anticipated the impact that *The Dark Side of the Moon* would have. It hit the top spot in its seventh week on the chart, and while it only managed to hold the top position for a week, its overall durability proved to be remarkable. It remained on the album chart for an incredible 741 weeks, beating the previous record of 490 weeks held by Johnny Mathis's *Johnny's Greatest Hits* [see 16], and it remains one of the best-selling albums of all time.

THE TOP FIVE
Week of April 28, 1973

1. **The Dark Side of the Moon**
   Pink Floyd

2. **Aloha From Hawaii Via Satellite**
   Elvis Presley

3. **Billion Dollar Babies**
   Alice Cooper

4. **The Best of Bread**
   Bread

5. **Houses of the Holy**
   Led Zeppelin

158 Aloha from Hawaii Via Satellite RCA 6089
ELVIS PRESLEY

Producer: Joan Deary

Track listing: Introduction: Also Sprach Zarathustra (There from 2001: A Space Odyssey) / See See Rider / Burning Love / Something / You Gave Me a Mountain / Steamroller Blues / My Way / Love Me / Johnny B. Goode / It's Over / Blue Suede Shoes / I'm So Lonesome I Could Cry / I Can't Stop Loving You / Hound Dog / What Now My Love / Fever / Welcome to My World / Suspicious Minds / Introductions by Elvis / I'll Remember You / Medley: Long Tall Sally/Whole Lotta Shakin' Goin' On / American Trilogy / A Big Hunk O' Love / Can't Help Falling in Love

May 5, 1973
1 week

Following the success of *Roustabout* [see 72], Elvis Presley continued to make what his onetime guitarist Scotty Moore calls "rubber-stamp movies," yet the films and their accompanying soundtracks began to decline in popularity. In fact, *Girl Happy* and *Harum Scarum*, both released in 1965, were the only two post-*Roustabout* soundtracks to crack the top 10.

The King had to wait more than three years for his next top 10 hit, which was simply titled *Elvis*. The LP, culled from a December 1968 NBC-TV program, often referred to as the "comeback special," was Presley's first live album. It reached number eight in February 1969. On July 26 of that year, Elvis played his first live date in eight years at the International Hotel in Las Vegas. Joining Elvis in his band was guitarist James Burton, who, like Elvis, was

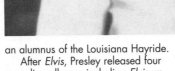

an alumnus of the Louisiana Hayride.

After *Elvis*, Presley released four more live albums, including *Elvis as Recorded at Madison Square Garden*, which peaked at number 11 in August 1972. While most artists are lucky if they can release one successful live album, Elvis hadn't grown tired of the format yet.

In January 1973 Elvis and his entourage flew to Hawaii for a special event—a TV show to be beamed live via satellite from the Honolulu International Center to Japan and the Far East. Fans in America would have to wait for a taped version to air on April 4 on NBC-TV.

On January 13, Elvis and his band went in for a rehearsal session to make sure the cameras were in the proper position. "We rehearsed a bunch of things," Burton recalls. "While everyone else was taking a break, I was just playing around, messing with some tunes and I started playing the old Hank Williams song 'I'm So Lonesome I Could Cry.' Elvis came over and said, 'What's that? It sounds real familiar.' I told him and then he started singing it. He loved it so much he put it in the show."

Although the two-record *Aloha from Hawaii via Satellite* featured six songs that were included on the Madison Square Garden live album, it did offer something new for Elvis's fans. "I'm So

Lonesome I Could Cry" was one of eight songs that had never appeared on an Elvis album. Others included covers of the Beatles' "Something," Paul Anka's "My Way," and James Taylor's "Steamroller Blues."

The show, held on January 14, was beamed to an estimated 1 billion viewers. Elvis was ready. "He was in great form, looking great, and in great health," says Burton. Presley was on such a high that a special matinee benefiting the Kuiokalakaini Lee Cancer Fund was held the day of the worldwide telecast. The benefit raised $75,000 and Elvis performed Lee's best-known song, "I'll Remember You" during both shows.

After the show was completed, all agreed it was a triumph. "Everyone felt so good about it, including the crew members, the staff, and the television people," says Burton. "We had a great get-together after the show that night and Elvis was very happy. Everyone was inspired by the whole thing."

In its 11th week on the chart, *Aloha from Hawaii Via Satellite* became Elvis's first Number One album since *Roustabout* in 1965. It was the King's ninth and final album chart-topper.

On August 16, 1977, Presley was found unconscious in a Graceland bathroom. He was rushed to a hospital, but it was too late. The King was gone at the age of 42.

THE TOP FIVE
Week of May 5, 1973

1. **Aloha from Hawaii Via Satellite**
   Elvis Presley

2. **Houses of the Holy**
   Led Zeppelin

3. **The Best of Bread**
   Bread

4. **The Dark Side of the Moon**
   Pink Floyd

5. **Billion Dollar Babies**
   Alice Cooper

ATLANTIC 7255 # Houses of the Holy
LED ZEPPELIN

159

Producer: Jimmy Page

Track listing: The Song Remains the Same / The Rain Song / Over the Hills and Far Away / The Crunge / Dancing Days / D'yer Mak'er / No Quarter / The Ocean

May 12, 1973
2 weeks

As Led Zeppelin prepared to record *Houses of the Holy*, they were rolling on a creative high. The band's fourth album, which was officially untitled but is commonly referred to as *Led Zeppelin IV*, was the band's masterpiece. Along with such rockers as "Black Dog" and "Rock and Roll," it contained "Stairway to Heaven," which successfully fused the band's acoustic and electric sides into one eight-minute epic. Despite the track's length, it became the most-played song in the history of album rock radio during the '70s. Yet strangely enough, *Led Zeppelin IV* never made it to the top of the charts. The album, which didn't feature the band's name on its cover, spent four weeks at number two, but it was unable to knock Sly & The Family Stone's *There's a Riot Goin' On* [see 138] or Carole King's *Music* [see 139] from Number One.

Led Zeppelin remained undaunted. Although *Led Zeppelin IV* didn't reach the top, it went on to become the group's best-selling album (and by 1996 had become the fourth-best-selling album of all time). The creative high continued on *Houses of the Holy*, recorded primarily during February and March of 1972. Again, the band opted to bypass tradition and recorded the album at a mansion, rather than a recording studio. Instead of Headley Grange, this time the band chose Mick Jagger's summer home, Stargroves [see 132].

"The vibe was much the same," says bassist/keyboardist John Paul Jones. "We would do the tours, we would do the recordings, then we wouldn't see each other at all. We weren't a band that socialized."

During the period prior to the *Houses of the Holy* sessions, Page and Jones, who by then both had home studios, used the down time to work up some material. "I worked on 'No Quarter' at home," says Jones. "That was right after I set up my home studio. I started off with an electric piano with some interesting effects. I had most of the song worked out before they heard it, the melody and everything. Then Jimmy came up with a guitar part and Robert put some lyrics to it." The final version featured Jones on grand piano, synthesizer piano, and synthesized bass.

On other tracks, Jones also experimented with the instrumentation. "The Rain Song" featured mellotron, "The Crunge" had synthesizer, and "Dancing Days" had organ. Yet Zeppelin was generally most effective with the traditional guitar/bass/drums lineup, featured at its most explosive on the unforgettably catchy riff of "The Ocean."

While Plant's otherworldly lyrics were often criticized, the band showed it still had a sense of humor on a reggae tune mysteriously titled "D'yer Mak'er." Says Jones, "It's from an old joke. I was telling a friend I took my wife on holiday and he said, 'D'yer mak'er?' and I said, 'No, she went on her own free will.'"

The album's opening track, "The Song Remains The Same," would later serve as the title track for the band's 1976 album and concert film. A song called "Houses of the Holy" was also cut during these sessions, but the band opted to keep it in the can until the release of *Physical Graffiti* [see 196].

Zeppelin scored its fourth Number One album at the expense of one of Plant and Page's heroes—Elvis Presley. The duo had met Presley in Las Vegas in 1972. A year later, in its second week on the chart, *Houses of the Holy* knocked Presley's *Aloha from Hawaii Via Satellite* from Number One. Elvis had left the peak of the album chart for the final time.

THE TOP FIVE
Week of May 12, 1973

1. **Houses of the Holy**
   Led Zeppelin

2. **The Best of Bread**
   Bread

3. **Aloha from Hawaii Via Satellite**
   Elvis Presley

4. **The Beatles/1962–1966**
   The Beatles

5. **The Beatles/1967–1970**
   The Beatles

160 The Beatles/1967–1970 APPLE 3403
THE BEATLES

Producer: George Martin

Track listing: Strawberry Fields Forever / Penny Lane / Sgt. Pepper's Lonely Hearts Club Band / With a Little Help from My Friends / Lucy in the Sky with Diamonds / A Day in the Life / All You Need Is Love / I Am the Walrus / Hello, Goodbye / The Fool on the Hill / Magical Mystery Tour / Lady Madonna / Hey Jude / Revolution / Back in the USSR / While My Guitar Gently Weeps / Ob-La-Di, Ob-La-Da / Get Back / Don't Let Me Down / The Ballad of John and Yoko / Old Brown Shoe / Here Comes the Sun / Come Together / Something / Octopus's Garden / Let It Be / Across the Universe / The Long and Winding Road

May 26, 1973
1 week

More than three years after the Beatles officially called it quits, the group scored its 15th Number One album with the two-disc greatest hits set The Beatles/1967–1970. The album, which covered the second phase of the band's career, was released simultaneously with another two-record set, The Beatles/1962–1966. The two albums were released primarily to combat the growing market for Beatles "greatest hits" bootlegs.

The collections are often referred to as the "Red" and "Blue" albums, because of the colored borders adorning their front-cover photos. The Beatles/1962–66, or the Red Album, featured the photo that originally graced the cover of the band's first British album, Please Please Me, while The Beatles/1967–1970, or the Blue Album, featured the foursome posed at the same location, approximately eight years later, only the once–clean-cut moptops had grown their hair (and, in some cases, mustaches and beards) and changed their overall look considerably. The second photo had originally been slated to run on the LP cover of the troubled Get Back project, which eventually saw the light of day as Let It Be [see 122].

The album contains songs from such chart-topping albums as Sgt. Pepper's Lonely Hearts Club Band [see 95], Magical Mystery Tour [see 99], The Beatles [see 110], Abbey Road [see 117], and Let It Be, as well as assorted singles first compiled on Hey Jude. That album, featuring various tracks from 1964 to

1969, peaked at number two in March 1970. However, most of its later-day offerings were also included on The Beatles/1967–1970.

The single "Hey Jude" is notable for several reasons. It was the first release on the Beatles' Apple imprint and was the group's longest-running Number One single by two different measures: The single, which hit Number One on the Hot 100 on September 28, 1968, stayed at the peak for nine weeks, longer than any other Beatles hit; and at seven minutes and 11 seconds, it's the longest single ever to top the Hot 100.

The single's B-side, "Revolution," is a sped-up version of "Revolution 1," which appeared on The Beatles. The single version of "Revolution" also was included on the Hey Jude album.

In all, The Beatles/1967–1970 includes eight Number One singles and a total of 13 top 10 hits, spanning the group's incredibly impressive body of work. Yet John Lennon was never quite

satisfied with the Beatles' recordings, says George Martin, who produced all but three of the tracks on The Beatles/1967–1970. Says Martin, "Many years after we did [Sgt. Pepper's] I was with John in his Dakota apartment and he suddenly turned to me and he said, 'If we possibly could, I would love to record everything we did all over again.'"

The Beatles/1967–1970 outperformed The Beatles/1962–1966, which peaked at number three. Yet the Blue Album didn't have the chart potency of the group's previous Number Ones. It only stayed at the pole position for a week—the shortest stay of any of the group's previous chart-toppers—before it was knocked out of the top spot. Yet Paul McCartney couldn't feel too bad about this turn of events: It was his Red Rose Speedway that dethroned the Beatles' 15th Number One, and that album, was in turn knocked from the top spot by George Harrison's Living in the Material World.

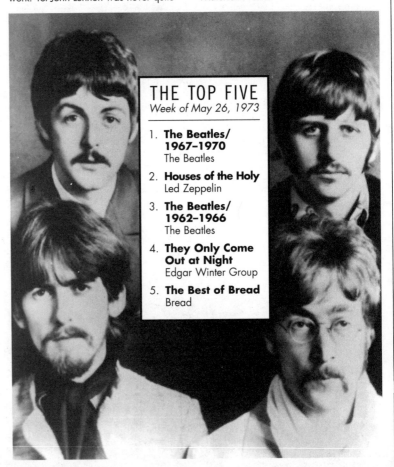

THE TOP FIVE
Week of May 26, 1973

1. **The Beatles/ 1967–1970**
   The Beatles

2. **Houses of the Holy**
   Led Zeppelin

3. **The Beatles/ 1962–1966**
   The Beatles

4. **They Only Come Out at Night**
   Edgar Winter Group

5. **The Best of Bread**
   Bread

THE TOP FIVE
Week of June 2, 1973

1. **Red Rose Speedway**
   Paul McCartney and Wings

2. **House of the Holy**
   Led Zeppelin

3. **The Beatles/1967–1970**
   The Beatles

4. **They Only Come
   Out at Night**
   Edgar Winter Group

5. **The Beatles/1962–1966**
   The Beatles

Producer: Paul McCartney

*Track listing: Big Barn Bed / My Love /
Get on the Right Thing / One More
Kiss / Little Lamb Dragonfly / Single
Pigeon / When the Night / Loup
(1st Indian on the Moon) / Medley:
(a) Hold Me Tight (b) Lazy Dynamite
(c) Hands of Love (d) Power Cut*

*June 2, 1973
3 weeks*

Paul McCartney had to feel a certain satisfaction when his fourth post-Beatles album, *Red Rose Speedway*, knocked the Fab Four's *1967–1970* [see 160] from the top spot on the albums chart. After all, McCartney was attempting to establish his new group, Wings, as a viable entity, distinct from his notoriety with the Beatles.

After becoming the first Beatle to hit the top of the album chart as a solo artist [see *McCartney*—121], the singer-songwriter recorded an album with his wife, Linda. *Ram*, which contained McCartney's first post-Beatles Number

One single, "Uncle Albert/Admiral Halsey," spent two weeks at number two. For his third album, McCartney formed a band called Wings, consisting of Linda on keyboards, former Moody Blues [see 150] member Denny Laine on guitar, and New York session player Danny Seiwell, who had played on *Ram*, on drums. Without the benefit of a hit single, Wings' *Wild Life* stalled at number 10 in early 1972.

Prior to recording *Red Rose Speedway*, guitarist Henry McCullough was added to the lineup. But despite McCartney's ambitions to make Wings into a legitimate band, he didn't quite pull it off on *Red Rose Speedway*. "He was less than secure, really," says Glyn Johns, who served as an engineer on the album. "I admired him for what he was trying to do, but I think he was confused. He didn't know if he wanted to be the bass player in the band or Paul McCartney. He ended up with a bunch of sycophantic musicians who were all climbing up his backside. It wasn't a band, although he was constantly saying he wanted it to be one."

Red Rose Speedway was spotty at best. "The band itself was not very good," adds Johns. Yet the album did include one gem, the ballad "My Love," which McCartney wrote for Linda.

The same week that "My Love" hit the summit on the Hot 100, McCartney scored his second post-Beatles' Number One album with *Red Rose Speedway*. The album hit the top in its fourth week on the chart.

While McCartney may have slipped artistically, he still showed signs of brilliance and continued to have commercial success. *Red Rose Speedway* was the first of five consecutive Number One albums for McCartney and Wings [see 173].

Says Johns, "There were a couple of songs that I thought were a bit iffy, but it never crossed my mind for a minute that Paul McCartney was not going to carry on with the same sort of standing he'd established for himself with the Beatles. I felt that the material that was less than what one expected was just him trying to explore new territory because he was on his own."

162 Living in the Material World APPLE 3410
GEORGE HARRISON

Producer: George Harrison

Track listing: Give Me Love (Give Me Peace on Earth) / Sue Me, Sue You Blues / The Light That Has Lighted the World / Don't Let Me Wait Too Long / Who Can See It / Living in the Material World / The Lord Loves the One (That Loves the Lord) / Be Here Now / Try Some, Buy Some / The Day the World Gets 'Round / That Is All

June 23, 1973
5 weeks

With All Things Must Pass [see 128], George Harrison and Phil Spector "tended to produce everything to the max, with strings, voices, and horns," says Harrison. "For Living in the Material World I felt people had already heard that type of album, so what I did was reduce it down to something more simple."

For the album, Harrison cut the cast of guest players considerably, but still called on the talents of a number of noted musicians, including keyboardists Nicky Hopkins and Gary Wright, bassist Klaus Voorman, and drummers Jim Keltner and Ringo Starr. The album's title track featured Harrison returning to his Eastern musical influences. "I had Zakir Hussein playing tabla on the bridge," he says.

Phil Spector was once again slated to co-produce with Harrison, as he did on All Things Must Pass, but this time he had trouble making the sessions. In the end, Spector's involvement on Living in the Material World was limited to a co-producer credit on "Try Some, Buy Some." Says Harrison, "At that point in time I was just chanting, 'Hare Krishna'

all the time, and Phil and a couple of musicians that wanted to take drugs were in the toilet hiding from me, because I was so straight."

Rather than return to Abbey Road Studios, Harrison opted to record Living in the Material World at the Apple Studio located at 3 Saville Row in London. "We recorded some of Let It Be [see 122] in there and up on the roof, but the studio was a problem and they had to change a lot of the equipment. Living in the Material World was one of the first things recorded there after the studio had been changed around a bit," Harrison says.

Yet the problems in the studio persisted during the Living in the Material World sessions. "It turned out the control room was bass-light," Harrison says. "So we kept adding low end to everything and not any highs. When I played it, it was really woolly, it sounded like there was about 18 sheets of cotton wool in front of the speakers. I got quite depressed, because right around that time Stevie Wonder's Talking Book came out and it sounded so brilliant and my record sounded so dull."

Harrison temporarily abandoned Living in the Material World while he went to work on the benefit concerts for Bangladesh, which featured Bob Dylan,

Eric Clapton, Ringo Starr, and Ravi Shankar. The three-album The Concert for Bangladesh, which featured live recordings from the benefit, peaked at number two in early 1972.

When Harrison went back to work on Living in the Material World, he decided to have the album remastered for the European and American release. "For the one in Europe, I just let the bloke in Apple Studio master it," says Harrison. "I didn't give him any instructions. I just said, 'Do what you can.'" For the American remastering, Harrison turned to Doug Sax. "He was the hot guy at the time," Harrison says. "I spent a long time with him and we mastered the shit out of that record. But in retrospect, I think we went over the top, we actually changed the mix a little. For the English version, they cleaned it up a bit and it was fine."

The album opener, "Give Me Love (Give Me Peace on Earth)," went on to become Harrison's second Number One single on June 30, 1973, a week after Living in the Material World became Harrison's second chart-topping solo album. Ironically, in order to reach the summit a second time, Harrison had to knock Red Rose Speedway, by his former bandmate Paul McCartney, from the Number One position.

THE TOP FIVE
Week of June 23, 1973

1. **Living in the Material World**
   George Harrison

2. **Red Rose Speedway**
   Paul McCartney & Wings

3. **Houses of the Holy**
   Led Zeppelin

4. **There Goes Rhymin' Simon**
   Paul Simon

5. **The Beatles/1967–1970**
   The Beatles

Producer: James William Guercio

Track listing: Critics' Choice / Just You 'n' Me / Darlin' Dear / Jenny / What's This World Comin' To / Something in This City Changes People / Hollywood / In Terms of Two / Rediscovery / Feelin' Stronger Every Day

July 28, 1973
5 weeks (nonconsecutive)

Chicago VI was a change for the band named after a major metropolis. The group had recorded all of its previous albums in New York or Los Angeles, but following the huge sales of *Chicago V* [see 147], the band was enjoying the rewards of its success. Producer/manager Jim Guercio had built a studio at his recently purchased Caribou Ranch in Colorado, and the band opted to seek refuge there to record its sixth album.

"New York was a real aggressive city-type atmosphere and it was reflected in the music," says drummer Danny Seraphine. "When we got to Colorado, it was kind of a new beginning. It was basically a new world for us city boys." The band lived at the ranch during February 1973 while cutting the album. "Jimmy had renovated all of the cabins. There was a real family atmosphere," Seraphine adds. "I kept a horse up there. When I finished recording or before the sessions, I would go riding up in the mountains."

Yet there were some drawbacks. "The downside was the lack of oxygen [because of the high altitude]," Seraphine says. "Some of the singers lost a note off their top range, because they weren't used to it." Also, the ranch location was isolated. "Eventually, we would get kind of stir crazy. We would have to jump in a car and run down to Boulder for the last call in a nightclub to feel like human beings."

The new studio wasn't the only change for Chicago. The band's success altered their personal relationships. "Feelin' Stronger Every Day," which went on to become a top 10 hit, had a special meaning for bassist/vocalist Peter Cetera. "Peter wrote that song [with trombonist/percussionist James Pankow] about his marriage falling apart. He gone through a real hard time and was starting to feel stronger again." Its anthemic nature also served as a theme of sorts for the band, as Chicago was on a roll.

While the band was experiencing great commercial success, it was often the target of critical barbs. The band responded with "Critics' Choice." Says Seraphine, "In those days when they discovered you, you were the fair-haired golden boys, but when you became successful, they just slammed the shit out of you." The song was written by keyboardist Robert Lamm. "He was just really pissed off, because some of his

work had gotten slammed, so that was his protest."

While Cetera was writing about feeling stronger after his breakup, Pankow penned a tune, sung by Cetera, called "Just You 'n' Me," about his new love. "He wrote that for his wife-to-be," Seraphine says. The song also went on to become a hit, reaching number four. "What I loved about that song is we could be very commercial and then throw in a jazz section and pull it off," he adds.

The public loved that song and the album too, as *Chicago VI* hit Number One in its third week on the chart, becoming the band's second consecutive chart-topper. In just over a year, Chicago would make it three straight [see 174].

THE TOP FIVE
Week of July 28, 1973

1. **Chicago VI**
   Chicago

2. **The Dark Side of the Moon**
   Pink Floyd

3. **Living in the Material World**
   George Harrison

4. **Now & Then**
   The Carpenters

5. **There Goes Rhymin' Simon**
   Paul Simon

164 A Passion Play CHRYSALIS 1040
JETHRO TULL

Producer: Jethro Tull

Track listing: "A Passion Play"

August 18, 1973
1 week

Fueled by the success of *Thick as a Brick* [see 144], Jethro Tull decided to have another go at making an album that featured one extended piece running the length of the album, rather than traditional rock songs.

To capitalize on the band's popularity, Chrysalis released *Living in the Past*, a compilation of Tull's early works, in late 1972. The title track became its first hit single, climbing to number 11, while the album reached number three.

A Passion Play, however, was the true follow-up effort to *Thick as a Brick*. Tull leader Ian Anderson says the album was a response to the success of *Thick as a Brick*. Yet the group was unable to recapture the magic that made *Thick as a Brick* a surprise hit.

"When we came to *A Passion Play*, we probably fell into the trap and made that slight error in judgment of coming up with something that took itself much too seriously," he says. "The follow-up concept album probably lacked the little element of humor and self-parody which was apparent on *Thick as a Brick*."

According to Anderson, the album was troubled from the start. The initial sessions, held at Chateau D'Herouville in France, located on the outskirts of Paris, were aborted after six weeks due to health and technical problems. "Unfortunately I don't think a week went by without somebody in the band being really seriously ill with some sort of gastrointestinal problem," he says. "The

food and catering was not what we were used to."

After ditching the French sessions, the band returned to England and went back into the studio. "We had overworked that music to the point that it was really easy to start again with a completely clean sheet and move on to something else."

The album, which lyrically offers a vague attack on religion coupled with the fairy-tale–like "The Story of the Hare Who Lost His Spectacles," featured an elaborate musical soundtrack, with the Tull members once again taking on a number of different instruments, ranging from soprano saxophone to glockenspeil and marimba. Yet while *Thick as a Brick* won praise from some critics, *A Passion Play* was almost universally panned as

excessive nonsense. "That certainly did the album a lot of harm," Anderson says, noting that while the album climbed to Number One in a mere five weeks, it quickly plummeted back down the charts.

"*A Passion Play* was a product of a move that was afoot to try to extend pop and rock music, if not to the limits, to push it into the area where it went as far as it could in terms of composition and musical complexity," Anderson says. Yet he admits that Jethro Tull "pushed things perhaps a little bit past the point where they weren't as accessible as they ought to have been." Nonetheless, Anderson says many of the Tull faithful hail *A Passion Play* as the band's finest album, even if it's a view that he doesn't personally share.

THE TOP FIVE
Week of August 18, 1973

1. **A Passion Play**
   Jethro Tull

2. **VI**
   Chicago

3. **The Dark Side of the Moon**
   Pink Floyd

4. **Diamond Girl**
   Seals & Croft

5. **Foreigner**
   Cat Stevens

CAPRICORN 0111 **Brothers and Sisters** **165**
THE ALLMAN BROTHERS BAND

Producers: Johnny Sandlin and the Allman Brothers Band

Track listing: Wasted Words / Ramblin' Man / Come and Go Blues / Jelly Jelly / Southbound / Jessica / Pony Boy

September 8, 1973
5 weeks

Brothers and Sisters was truly a bittersweet triumph for the Allman Brothers Band. After several false starts as the Allman Joys, the Hour Glass, and the 31st of February, Duane and Gregg Allman formed the Allman Brothers Band in March 1969.

Duane, the elder Allman, had become an acclaimed session player, working for the likes of Percy Sledge, Aretha Franklin, and Wilson Pickett. The Allman Brothers Band teamed the guitarist and his brother, singer/keyboardist/guitarist Gregg, with second guitarist Dickie Betts, bassist Berry Oakley, and drummers Butch Trucks and "Jaimoe" Johnson.

The group's distinctive blend of rock, R&B, and blues was captured on its self-titled debut and *Idlewood South*, released in 1969 and 1970 on Atco.

At Fillmore East, released on Capricorn in 1971, captured the feel of the band's acclaimed live performances. It peaked at number 13, while critics hailed the Allmans as America's best rock 'n' roll group.

Then tragedy struck. On October 29, 1971, Duane was killed in a motorcycle accident in Macon, Georgia. *Eat A Peach*, which combined three tracks recorded in the studio before Duane's death along with live material from the Fillmore East concerts, reached number four.

Just as the band was getting back on its feet, tragedy struck again. On November 11, 1972, bassist Oakley was killed in a motorcycle crash, three blocks away from the site of Duane's accident.

"We had just gotten through the thing with Duane the previous album. It took a year or so to just to get straightened out, because that was such a shock to us all. Then we lost Berry in the middle of *Brother and Sisters*," recalls Betts. "That whole period was really tough on all of us."

The band opted not to replace Duane with another guitarist. Instead, keyboardist Chuck Leavell filled out the sound, while bassist Lamar Williams replaced Oakley.

One of the last tracks recorded with Oakley was "Ramblin' Man," a tune that Betts penned but wasn't sure was right for the Allmans. "I thought it was a little bit too country for our band," recalls Betts. "I knew it was a good song, but I thought someone else would cut it, but the band loved it." So it wouldn't be mistaken for a country tune, Betts composed a stacked ending with layered guitars, giving it a definitive rock 'n' roll feel. The song, which reached number two, became a blueprint for what would be known as "Southern rock." That distinctive sound was also heard on the instrumental "Jessica," which was named for Betts's daughter.

With Gregg Allman's backlog of songs drying up, Betts rose to the forefront, writing four of the album's seven tracks, and handling the lead vocals on "Ramblin' Man" and "Pony Boy."

The influence of the fallen Allmans lived on as well. On "Pony Boy," Betts played Duane Allman's 1932 Dobro guitar, which was given to him by the Allman family after Duane's death. And the final words in the liner notes state, "Dedicated to a brother—Berry Oakley."

THE TOP FIVE
Week of September 8, 1973

1. **Brothers and Sisters**
   The Allman Brothers Band

2. **VI**
   Chicago

3. **The Dark Side of the Moon**
   Pink Floyd

4. **Foreigner**
   Cat Stevens

5. **We're an American Band**
   Grand Funk

166 Goats Head Soup ROLLING STONES 59101
THE ROLLING STONES

Producer: Jimmy Miller

Track listing: Dancing with Mr. D / 100 Years Ago / Coming Down Again / Doo Doo Doo Doo Doo (Heartbreaker) / Angie / Silver Train / Hide Your Love / Winter / Can You Hear the Music / Star Star

October 13, 1973
4 weeks

On *Exile on Main St.* [see 145], the Rolling Stones were able to make one of their finest albums, in spite of heavy drug use. On the follow-up, *Goats Head Soup*, the drugs began to take their toll on the band, which continued to experience commercial success, even after losing favor with critics.

"It was getting a little more bizarre by then," says Andy Johns, who served as chief engineer and mixed the record. "That album suffered from drugs and alcohol. You can hear it in the music. Just about everyone was getting high, except for Bill [Wyman, the bassist] and Charlie [Watts, the drummer]."

"Heroin was now playing a bigger factor in what was going on," he adds. "It definitely was not helping. It was very negative." The primary user was guitarist Keith Richards, but "Mick [Jagger] wasn't exactly straight and I definitely wasn't," Johns says.

To make matters worse, Richard was to face charges for use, supply, and traf-

ficking of cannabis and heroin in Nice, France, while Wyman's wife, Astrid, was raped in her Jamaican hotel room. "That stuff was definitely on their minds," says Johns.

With the exception of "Silver Train," which was recorded in Ireland, *Goats Head Soup* was recorded at Dynamic Sound Studios in Kingston, Jamaica. "There was an attitude of 'Let's get it done,'" says Johns. "It was just pure momentum. I don't know that there was much of a direction at all. It was like, 'Let's do an album,' and those were the songs that came out during the four or five months."

And, as was the case on the previous albums, the Stones spent days attempting to perfect the recordings. Johns recalls that Richards had a particularly rough time with "Doo Doo Doo Doo (Heartbreaker)," which went on to become a number 15 hit. "The track was really out of tune," says Johns. "Everyone was so out of it that instead of recutting the track, Keith spent four days trying to get the bass in tune, and there was no way to make it work, because the electric piano and the guitar were out of tune with each other. Things were getting a little fuzzy there."

In all, *Goats Head Soup* simply wasn't up to par with the Stones' previous few efforts. "There weren't as many good songs and the recording was pretty shabby," Johns admits. "It's not their greatest effort, although there are some

gems on it." Johns's personal favorites are "Winter," which he calls "one of the best things that they ever did," and the coyly titled "Star Star," (better known as "Starfucker") which he says "is a classic rock 'n' roll song."

The big hit from *Goats Head Soup* was "Angie," an acoustic ballad that became the Stones' seventh Number One single on October 20, 1973. It's rumored that David Bowie's wife, Angela, inspired the song.

The week before "Angie" went to Number One, *Goats Head Soup* hit the top in its third week on the chart. It wasn't the Stones' finest hour, but it was good enough to give the band its third straight Number One album of new material and fourth chart-topping LP overall.

THE TOP FIVE
Week of October 13, 1973

1. **Goats Head Soup**
   The Rolling Stones

2. **Brothers & Sisters**
   Allman Brothers Band

3. **Let's Get It On**
   Marvin Gaye

4. **Los Cochinos**
   Cheech & Chong

5. **Innervisions**
   Stevie Wonder

MCA 10003

Goodbye Yellow Brick Road

ELTON JOHN

167

Producer: Gus Dudgeon

Track listing: Funeral for a Friend / Love Lies Bleeding / Candle in the Wind / Bennie and the Jets / Goodbye Yellow Brick Road / This Song Has No Title / Grey Seal / Jamaica Jerk-Off / I've Seen That Movie Too / Sweet Painted Lady / The Ballad of Danny Bailey (1909–34) / Dirty Little Girl / All the Girls / Your Sister Can't Twist (But She Can Rock 'n' Roll) / Saturday Night's Alright for Fighting / Roy Rogers / Social Disease / Harmony

November 10, 1973
8 weeks

"We had decided years before that we would never even attempt to make a double album," says producer Gus Dudgeon, "because we could count the number of double albums we thought were worth diddley-shit on one hand. We more or less felt it was kind of an ego trip that very seldom paid off. You're asking people to pay more money and if you are going to do that, you really have to justify it."

Yet that vow never to release a double album would soon be broken due to an unusual set of circumstances. Initially, John and company began work on their new album in Jamaica, where the Rolling Stones had just completed their *Goats Head Soup* album [see 166], but things didn't go as planned. "When we went to Jamaica, Elton wrote the songs he needed for what became *Yellow Brick Road*, including the song 'Yellow Brick Road,'" says Dudgeon. But then, due to severe technical problems in the studio, the Jamaican sessions were aborted.

It was decided that the session would resume at Strawberry Studios in France, where John had recorded his two previous albums. "At the Chateau he sat down and wrote some more songs, because that was what he was used to doing. It was like, 'Blimey, I'm here, it's five days before we start recording, we'll do some rehearsals, and I'll write some songs.' So all of a sudden, we actually had a bunch more songs, which made it more than a single album and there was no way we wanted to throw anything away. We thought everything was good. If the Jamaican sessions hadn't cancelled out, it would have been a single like all of the others."

The two-record set included a diverse selection of material, ranging from the all-out rocker "Saturday Night's Alright for Fighting" and the R&B-styled "Bennie and the Jets" to the epic title ballad and Marilyn Monroe–inspired "Candle in the Wind." "Saturday Night's Alright" was particularly difficult to cut. "The biggest problem was that Dee [Murray, the bassist]] and Nigel [Olsson, the drummer] hated playing rock 'n' roll. They loved playing ballads, so they really weren't playing very well," says Dudgeon. John, who was frustrated with their performance, decided to cut his vocal standing up, without playing piano, to get his sidemen into the groove. "We actually got a good take as a result," Dudgeon says. "And then we just put a bit of piano in afterwards."

"Bennie and the Jets" was a pseudo-live recording. "But I did use audience reaction from an Elton concert, which he had done in London," says Dudgeon. The producer was inspired to add the crowd noise while mixing the record. "That opening chord, that 'chink,' it reminded me of something someone would do in concert, to remind the band what comes next."

The song was never intended to be released as a single until it started picking up airplay at an R&B station in Detroit. Dudgeon still recalls when John received a phone call from the female DJ, who had a knack for picking hits. "She insisted on telling Elton that if he put out 'Bennie and the Jets' as a single, he would have a Number One black hit." Although the single stalled at number 15 on the R&B chart, it did go on to top the Hot 100 on April 13, 1974. By that time, however, *Goodbye Yellow Brick Road* had already completed its two-month stay atop the album chart, and John had already recorded his next album, *Caribou* [see 177].

THE TOP FIVE
Week of November 10, 1973

1. **Goodbye Yellow Brick Road**
   Elton John

2. **Goats Head Soup**
   Rolling Stones

3. **Brothers and Sisters**
   Allman Brothers Band

4. **Los Cochinos**
   Cheech & Chong

5. **Angel Care**
   Art Garfunkel

168 The Singles 1969–1973 A&M 3601
CARPENTERS

Producers: Richard & Karen Carpenter, Jack Daugherty

Track listing: We've Only Just Begun / Top of the World / Ticket to Ride / Superstar / Rainy Days and Mondays / Goodbye to Love / Yesterday Once More / It's Going to Take Some Time / Sing / For All We Know / Hurting Each Other / (They Long to Be) Close to You

January 5, 1974
1 week

By 1974, Richard and Karen Carpenter, a pair of musical siblings from Downey, California, had experienced a great deal of success. The duo, known simply as the Carpenters, had scored Number One hit singles with "(They Long to Be) Close to You" and "Top of the World," while "We've Only Just Begun," "Rainy Days and Mondays," "Superstar," "Hurting Each Other," and "Yesterday Once More" had all peaked at number two. On the album chart, however, the Carpenters couldn't get past number two. Their second album, 1970's Close to You, 1971's self-titled effort, and 1973's Now & Then all peaked one position shy of the summit. It wasn't until A&M decided to collect the Carpenters' greatest hits on one album that the duo was truly on top of the world, or at least on top of the album chart.

When A&M began compiling The Singles 1969–1973, Richard Carpenter was adamant about one thing. "I didn't want to call it Greatest Hits, because most of those things are the act's only hits. They're not the greatest hits, they're the only hits. Since we were doing quite well, I figured this would be Volume 1." In hindsight, Richard Carpenter says he is convinced that the album, which sold more than four million copies in America alone, would have even been more successful had he gone with the Greatest Hits title and a photograph of the duo on the cover. "The whole thing was my idea," he says. "The dark cover, with the logo, having it looking kind of understated. It almost looks like a damn tombstone."

Yet the music on the album, featuring Richard's sparkling arrangements and Karen's unforgettable voice, more than made up for its bland cover art. The Singles 1969–1973 was certainly an accurate title, since it ranged from the duo's first single, a slowed-down version of

the Beatles' "Ticket to Ride" [see 78], which stalled at number 54, to "Top of the World," the final single released by the group in 1973. "Karen was more of a ballad singer, so I slowed it down," says Richard of the Beatles cover. "That remains one of my favorite Carpenter recordings." For the Singles album, Karen re-recorded her vocal and drum tracks and guitars were added.

Often Richard knew when the duo had recorded a hit track long before its release. "'Superstar,' 'We've Only Just Begun,' 'Hurting Each Other,' and 'Sing,' I thought were hits right off the bat, but I couldn't say that about 'Close to You' or 'Top of the World,'" he says.

The latter track was written by Richard and his longtime friend John Bettis, who was a member of the pre-Carpenters group Spectrum. "We

thought it was a pleasant little album cut," Richard says. "But then the public let us know. The Japanese let us know by releasing it as a single in Japan, and country singer Lynn Anderson recorded it. Her version was almost the same as ours and it became a country hit that started to cross over to top 40. Finally, we saw the light."

"Top of the World" hit Number One on the Hot 100 on December 1, 1973. Just over a month later, the Carpenters scored their first and only Number One album. "I remember Karen saying, 'It's about time that an album of ours went to Number One in Billboard,'" says Richard.

Tragically, less than a decade later, on December 4, 1983, Karen Carpenter died from heart problems brought on by anorexia nervosa. She was 32.

THE TOP FIVE
Week of January 5, 1974

1. **The Singles 1969–1973**
   Carpenters

2. **Goodbye Yellow Brick Road**
   Elton John

3. **You Don't Mess Around with Jim**
   Jim Croce

4. **The Joker**
   Steve Miller Band

5. **Jonathan Livingston Seagull**
   Neil Diamond

ABC 756 # You Don't Mess Around with Jim 169

JIM CROCE

Producers: Terry Cashman and Tommy West

Track listing: You Don't Mess Around with Jim / Tomorrow's Gonna be a Brighter Day / New York's Not My Home / Hard Time Losin' Man / Photographs and Memories / Walkin' Back to Georgia / Operator (That's Not the Way It Feels) / Time in a Bottle / Rapid Roy (The Stock Car Boy) / Box # 10 / A Long Time Ago / Hey Tomorrow

January 12, 1974
5 weeks

In the late '60s, the career of an aspiring songwriter named Jim Croce didn't hold much promise. An album he recorded for Capitol with his wife Ingrid, appropriately titled Jim and Ingrid Croce, failed to chart in 1969. "Jim was a mediocre writer in the '60s," says his friend and co-producer Tommy West. "He was a great folk singer and great performer, but he wasn't a great writer."

Two things happened in Croce's life that would greatly affect his career. First he met guitarist Maury Muehleisen. Then, in February 1971, he found out that Ingrid was pregnant with their first child. "All of a sudden his writing changed," says West. "He decided to tell the truth."

West first noticed the change in Croce's writing when he received a new demo tape containing such songs as "Time in a Bottle" and "Operator." West was so impressed, he shared his enthusiasm with his partner Terry Cashman. "I played it for him and he said, 'Jesus,

this is better than anything he has done.'" The pair invited Croce into the studio to cut more demos in hopes of landing Croce a new record deal. "We cut some demos and nobody liked them," West says. "Then we went back into the studio and cut some more and nobody liked those. We couldn't get a deal. Nobody saw what we thought we saw." Finally, with financial assistance from a friend, West and Cashman took Croce to the Hit Factory in New York on October 5, 1971, without a record deal.

The album, which was cut in three weeks, was shopped to nearly every major label. "Every label in the business turned it down," says West. "The only way we got it released on ABC Records was because Cashman and I were signed to the label as artists."

The sessions were done totally live, says West. "We would cut it as an ensemble and Jim did the final vocal right then and there." The track "Time in a Bottle" was originally cut on an eight-track, West says. "We bumped it up to 16 tracks, but I couldn't figure out what to put on the other tracks." Then West noticed a harpsichord in the studio that was lying around from an earlier session. "In the back of my mind, I grafted a line from a doo-wop record by the Jesters called 'The Wind' and I put that in there on harpsichord and doubled that," West says. The combination of harpsichord, guitar, and bass led many

to assume that a string section had played on the track.

Initially, the album spawned two hit singles. The title track reached number eight in September, while "Operator (That's Not the Way It Feels)" peaked at number 17 in December. Croce's success continued with his second solo album, Life and Times, which included the Number One single "Bad, Bad Leroy Brown."

You Don't Mess Around with Jim took on a second life after the album cut "Time in a Bottle" was featured prominently in an ABC Movie of the Week called She Lives. Says West, "It was like a ripoff of Love Story, but the song was all over it." Croce, who was already experiencing tremendous success, now had another hit on his hands. Yet on September 20, 1973, only eight days after the TV movie telecast, the 30-year-old singer-songwriter was killed in a plane crash in Louisiana. Five others on the chartered plane, including Muehleisen, were also killed.

"Time in a Bottle" became Croce's second Number One single on December 29, 1973. Two weeks later Croce scored his posthumous album chart-topper with You Don't Mess Around with Jim, which had been on the chart for 47 weeks. On January 26, 1974, with You Don't Mess Around with Jim still at the summit, Croce's final album, I Got a Name peaked at number two.

THE TOP FIVE
Week of January 12, 1974

1. **You Don't Mess Around with Jim**
   Jim Croce

2. **The Singles, 1969–1973**
   The Carpenters

3. **Goodbye Yellow Brick Road**
   Elton John

4. **I've Got a Name**
   Jim Croce

5. **The Joker**
   Steve Miller Band

170 Planet Waves ASYLUM 1003
BOB DYLAN

Producer: None listed

Track listing: On a Night Like This /
Going Going Gone / Touch Mama /
Hazel / Something There Is About You
/ Forever Young / Forever Young /
Dirge / You Angel You / Never Say
Goodbye / Wedding Song

February 16, 1974
5 weeks

By the mid-'60s, Bob Dylan had become the most influential singer-songwriter of the rock era. His songs were covered by Peter, Paul & Mary [see 63], and his work had influenced such rock icons as the Beatles [see 73] and Jimi Hendrix [see 108]. Yet despite the admiration of his peers and the acclaim of rock critics, more than a decade into his career, Dylan had yet to top the album chart. He had come close, though—Highway 61 Revisited, his landmark 1965 album, had reached number three, and John Wesley Harding, his 1968 "comeback" album, spent four weeks at number two, but was unable to top the Beatles' Magical Mystery Tour [see 99] or Paul Mauriat's Blooming Hits [see 100].

By the time Dylan's contract with Columbia Records expired in 1973, he had amassed eight top 10 albums. With Dylan freed from Columbia, record executive David Geffen quickly made a verbal deal with the singer-songwriter to record for his Asylum Records label. The album would be Dylan's first recorded collaboration with the Band, Dylan's former backing group, a star attraction in its own right with three top 10 albums.

Planet Waves, which would be Dylan's first new recording in nearly three years, came together quickly. Initially, Dylan and the Band were rehearsing in Malibu, California, for a forthcoming tour, when they decided to go into the Village Recorder in West Los Angeles and cut an album. "The guy that was managing the studio was also one of Dylan's accountants," says engineer Rob Fraboni. "He offered them a secrecy situation where nobody would know that they were there. Based upon that, they came in." Fraboni, the chief engineer at the studio, was scheduled to work on another project, but found the combination of Dylan and the Band too much to resist.

Although the liner notes state that the album was recorded on November 5,

6, and 9, 1973, the sessions actually began on November 4 without the Band's drummer, Levon Helm. "On the first day they came in and did a bunch of songs like 'House of the Rising Sun,' which didn't make the record," says Fraboni. "The only one that made the record was 'Never Say Goodbye.' Then Levon came and three days later, that was the whole record.

"It was striking to do something that powerful that quickly," Fraboni adds. Dylan wrote "Wedding Song" while lying on his back in the control room. The album was mostly recorded live in the studio. "There were only two overdubs," Fraboni adds. "One piano overdub and one harmony vocal." Initially, Dylan attempted to overdub part of his vocal on "Going Going Gone." Says Fraboni, "After trying one overdub he just stopped and said, 'I could do this all day long and I don't even know if it's the right thing to do.'"

The sessions were conducted in an extremely loose and improvisational manner, with the Band naturally following Dylan's lead. "They had been rehearsing together before, but when they went into the studio, the Band prob-

ably only knew about four of the songs," says Fraboni. "What was incredible was that they were so in tune with Bob, such great musicians, and so intuitive, they were able to basically just watch Bob's hands on the chord changes and play along. It might have taken a take or two for them to learn the songs, but these were songs that they had never played before."

One such song was "Forever Young," which appears on the album in two different versions. "Bob said to me that he had carried this song around in his head for several years and he had never written it down, and now he wasn't quite sure how to record it," Fraboni says. As a result, five different versions were cut. The slow version, which ended up closing side one of the album, was recorded in one take. Ken Lauber played congas on the track, although he is not credited on the sleeve. "I remember sitting behind the board thinking, 'My God, I've never witnessed anything like this in my life,'" says Fraboni. "The sheer, emotional intensity and musicianship was amazing." After the track was complete, all of the musicians, including Dylan, piled into the control room for the playback. "At the end, no one said a word and everyone kind of wandered out of the control room," Fraboni says.

In spite of the sheer brilliance of the performance, Dylan considered leaving the track off the album during the mastering phase, but Fraboni convinced him to keep the track.

Planet Waves entered the chart on February 9, 1974, at number 19. A week later, it shot up to the top, finally giving Dylan that elusive Number One.

THE TOP FIVE
Week of February 16, 1974

1. **Planet Waves**
   Bob Dylan

2. **Greatest Hits**
   John Denver

3. **Under the Influence of Love Unlimited**
   Love Unlimited

4. **You Don't Mess Around with Jim**
   Jim Croce

5. **Goodbye Yellow Brick Road**
   Elton John

COLUMBIA 32801

The Way We Were

BARBRA STREISAND

171

Producer: Tommy LiPuma

Track listing: Being at War with Each Other / Something So Right / The Best Thing You've Ever Done / The Way We Were / All in Love Is Fair / What Are You Doing the Rest of Your Life? / Summer Me, Winter Me / Pieces of Dreams / I've Never Been a Woman Before / Medley: My Buddy/How About Me

March 16, 1974
2 weeks

Following the success of *People* [see 70], Barbra Streisand had to wait nearly a decade until her next chart-topper. Streisand remained on a hot streak in the two years immediately after *People*, as her next four albums made the top five. Yet during the period from 1967 to 1974, 1971's *Stoney End* was the only one out of dozen Streisand albums to crack the top 10.

Although *The Way We Were* was released in conjunction with the film of the same name (which starred the singer/actress and Robert Redford), it was not a soundtrack album. The soundtrack, which was also titled *The Way We Were* and included the title track, peaked at number 20.

Pianist/composer Marvin Hamlisch co-wrote the theme song with the husband-and-wife songwriting team of Alan and Marilyn Bergman. "I loved the film and it spoke to my strength as a songwriter, which is love songs," says Hamlisch. "And, I was thrilled to work with the Bergmans." Although Streisand didn't receive a songwriting credit, she too had suggestions. It was her idea to replace the original opening lyric, "Day-

dreams," with the word "Memories," which was originally only included in the final verse. "She was very helpful," Hamlisch adds. "She knew what was good for her and her voice. It was a wonderful collaboration."

With the single and film complete, it was hastily decided that a Streisand album, in addition to the film soundtrack, should be released in conjunction with the film. Blue Thumb Records co-founder Tommy LiPuma was called in to put together the album.

"Basically what we did was take 'The Way We Were' and several things that had not been released on an album, like 'Summer Me, Winter Me' and a few other Alan and Marilyn Bergman tunes," LiPuma says. He also recorded three new tracks with Streisand—cover versions of Carole King's "Being at War with Each Other," Paul Simon's "Something So Right," and Stevie Wonder's "All in Love Is Fair."

Says LiPuma, "The challenge for me was to get the tracks that I wasn't involved in and remix them to make everything sound uniform." Yet that was not an easy task. "A million multitracks

came over to me and there were no ledgers, so I had no idea which vocal was used," he says. LiPuma had to listen to the two-track recordings and compare them to the multitracks to figure out what was the final vocal. "It was a nightmare putting the thing together," he says, "because there were numerous performances. I had to listen to all of them to find the right take."

The new recordings with Streisand, however, were a breeze. "She's such a pro," LiPuma says. "All of the things that I did were live performances with the orchestra. She just got up and knocked them over." The new material was recorded in a single day. "Ultimately, I spent more time on the things that I didn't produce than I did on the new material," LiPuma says.

On February 2, 1974, "The Way We Were" became Streisand's first Number One single. Six weeks later, she scored her second Number One album when *The Way We Were* hit the peak in its fifth week on the Top LP's & Tapes chart. The song also went on to win a Grammy and an Oscar for songwriters Hamlisch and Alan and Marilyn Bergman.

Barbra Streisand and Robert Redford.

THE TOP FIVE
Week of March 16, 1974

1. **The Way We Were**
   Barbra Streisand

2. **Court and Spark**
   Joni Mitchell

3. **Planet Waves**
   Bob Dylan

4. **Greatest Hits**
   John Denver

5. **Hotcakes**
   Carly Simon

172 John Denver's Greatest Hits RCA 0374
JOHN DENVER

Producer: Milton Okun

Track listing: Take Me Home, Country Roads / Follow Me / Starwood in Aspen / For Baby (For Bobbie) / Rhymes and Reasons / Leaving on a Jet Plane / The Eagle and the Hawk / Sunshine on My Shoulders / Goodbye Again / Poems, Prayers and Promises / Rocky Mountain High

March 30, 1974
3 weeks (nonconsecutive)

It may have been a bit presumptuous for John Denver to collect the best songs from his first six albums for a compilation called John Denver's Greatest Hits. By November 1973, when the album was released, Denver had only had two top 10 hits: "Take Me Home, Country Roads," his first chart single, which had climbed to number two in August 1971, and "Rocky Mountain High," which had reached number nine in March 1973.

Denver's earliest success came as a songwriter. Peter, Paul & Mary [see 54] scored a Number One hit in December 1969 with their interpretation of Denver's "Leaving on a Jet Plane." Denver's version of the song appeared on his first solo album, Rhymes and Reasons. For Greatest Hits, he opted to re-record some of the early tracks, such as "Leaving on a Jet Plane" and "Rhymes and Reasons."

"By the time we did Greatest Hits, I had my own band," says Denver. "On those original recordings, I didn't have a band, I was just playing with session players."

The singer-songwriter felt strongly about including "Rhymes and Reasons"

on Greatest Hits, even though the song was not a hit. "It's one of my favorite songs, because it speaks to people about where we are in the world and where we are going."

Although Denver had only scored a few legitimate hits, he had found a significant audience with his feel-good songs about the virtues of home and nature, such as "Take Me Home, Country Roads" and "Rocky Mountain High." Says Denver, "I'm the kind of person who looks on the bright side, and people can relate to that. 'Country Roads' is not so much about West Virginia—it's about going home, and a lot of people have memories about that sort of thing."

A number of factors helped propel Greatest Hits to the top of the charts. For one, Denver had begun to develop a high profile on television. "I had appeared on the 'Tom Jones Show,' 'The Smothers Brothers' show, and as a guest on Bob Hope, and all that exposure

helped create an audience for me," he says.

Adding to Denver's momentum was the release of "Sunshine on My Shoulders" as a single. The track had first appeared on the 1971 album Poems, Prayers and Promises. "We knew that it was getting a whole lot of airplay up in the Northwest, so RCA decided to release it as a single," Denver recalls.

At approximately the same time, NBC broadcast a television movie about a young woman who was dying of leukemia, using the song as its theme. "All of those things kind of happened at once," Denver says. "They were all mutually supportive."

As "Sunshine on My Shoulders" was burning up the Hot 100, Greatest Hits climbed up the Top LP's & Tapes chart. On March 30, both the single and album hit the summit simultaneously. Denver had truly reached a "Rocky Mountain High."

THE TOP FIVE
Week of March 30, 1974

1. **John Denver's Greatest Hits**
   John Denver

2. **Court and Spark**
   Joni Mitchell

3. **Tubular Bells**
   Mike Oldfield

4. **The Way We Were**
   Barbra Streisand

5. **Band on the Run**
   Paul McCartney & Wings

Producer: None listed

Track listing: Band on the Run / Jet / Bluebird / Mrs. Vandebilt / Let Me Roll It / Mamunia / No Words / Helen Wheels / Picasso's Last Words (Drink to Me) / Nineteen Hundred and Eighty Five

April 13, 1974
4 weeks (nonconsecutive)

With two albums under their belt—1971's *Wild Life* and 1973's *Red Rose Speedway* [see 161]—Paul McCartney must have felt that he had hit his stride with his post-Beatles combo Wings. The band had just scored a number two hit with "Live and Let Die," the theme to a James Bond film. Then something went wrong. Denny Seiwell and Henry McCullough opted to leave the group on the eve of the band's trip to Nigeria to record a new album. "It was going to be a normal Wings album, but then our drummer and guitarist never showed up—left us in the lurch at the last minute," McCartney told Vic Garbarini in *Musician*. "It was literally an hour before we were getting into the plane to go on this trip to Africa...so we ended up just the three of us in Lagos, and I played a lot of the stuff myself."

Singing, handling bass, drums, some guitars, and producing was no problem for McCartney, as he had already proven on his self-titled solo effort [see 121], yet the *Band on the Run* sessions, held at Ginger Baker's studio in Lagos, would offer other challenges. McCartney and his wife were held up at knifepoint. And to add insult to injury, McCartney was accused by local musicians of attempting to rip off their music. But in spite of this adversity, McCartney and his group somehow managed to produce what many call his finest post-Beatles effort.

For inspiration, McCartney turned to some of his ex-bandmates and acquaintances. The line, "If we ever get out of here" in "Band on the Run," for example, was inspired by George Harrison, who used the phrase out of frustration during an Apple Records board of directors meeting. "Picasso's Last Words (Drink to Me)" was the result of a dinner McCartney had in Jamaica with Dustin Hoffman. The actor, who was in the middle of filming *Papillon*, asked McCartney how he wrote songs and proceeded to hand him a copy of *Time* magazine with Picasso's obituary. Hoff-

man watched in amazement as McCartney crafted a song about the late artist.

Some of the sounds were also inspired by McCartney's former mates. The track "Let Me Roll It" was reminiscent of John Lennon's Plastic Ono Band. "My use of tape echo did sound more like John than me," McCartney admitted in his fan newsletter *Club Sandwich*. "But tape echo was not John's territory exclusively! And you have to remember that, despite the myth, there was a *lot* of commonality between us in the way that we thought and the way that we worked."

Two other songs, "Jet" and "Helen Wheels," were written about subjects closer to home. "Helen Wheels," which was a top 10 hit in January 1974, was named after the singer's Land Rover, which he affectionately referred to as

"hell on wheels." Another top 10 hit, "Jet," was named after the McCartney's black Labrador puppy.

Band on the Run, aided by the one-two punch of "Helen Wheels" and "Jet," strode to the pole position in its 17th week on the chart, becoming McCartney's third Number One solo album. Less than two months later, the title track topped the Hot 100.

Perhaps more importantly to McCartney, the album got the thumbs-up from one of his harshest critics. Lennon told *Rolling Stone* that "*Band on the Run* is a great album. Wings is almost as conceptual a group as Plastic Ono Band is. Wings keeps changing all the time. I mean the backup men for Paul. It doesn't matter who's playing, you can call them Wings, but it's Paul McCartney music. And it's good stuff."

THE TOP FIVE
Week of April 13, 1974

1. **Band on the Run**
   Paul McCartney & Wings

2. **Greatest Hits**
   John Denver

3. **Tubular Bells**
   Mike Oldfield

4. **Court and Spark**
   Joni Mitchell

5. **Love Is the Message**
   MFSB

174 Chicago VII COLUMBIA 32810
CHICAGO

Producer: James William Guercio

Track listing: Prelude to Aire / Aire / Devil's Sweet / Italian from New York / Hanky Panky / Life Saver / Happy Man / (I've Been) Searchin' So Long / Mongonucleosis / Song of the Evergreens / Byblos / Wishing You Were Here / Call on Me / Woman Don't Want to Love Me / Skinny Boy

April 27, 1974
1 week

For Chicago's seventh album, the band returned to Jim Guercio's Caribou Ranch, and returned musically to the jazz roots and multi-disc format that had launched the group's greatest successes. The band also spent its longest stretch ever recording an album, as the sessions ran from August until December of 1973.

"Some of the purest jazz we ever did is one that album," says drummer Danny Seraphine, who wrote or co-wrote the album's first three tracks, all of which are instrumentals. "Aside from the first record, I think that may be the best album we ever made. It was the best combination of jazz and pop we recorded."

Jazz and pop weren't the only kinds of music that Chicago mined on its seventh album. The track "Mongonucleosis" was a salsa number. "Happy Man," written and sung by bassist/vocalist Peter Cetera, was a bossa nova–type ballad. The Latin influence in Chicago's sound was expanded with the addition of Brazilian percussionist Laudir De Oliveria, who appeared as a session player on *Chicago VI* [see 163]. In 1974, prior to recording *Chicago VIII* [see 197], De Oliveria became the band's eighth member. "The Latin groove was evident on some of the earlier albums, but Laudir solidified it," Seraphine says.

With multiple songwriters in the band, there was often competition between band members to land their compositions on the albums. "It was like a big family sitting at a dinner table grabbing for food," Seraphine says. "Usually the best songs got on the record." Six of the band's seven members had songwriting credits on the album.

Chicago VII hit the summit of the Top LP's & Tapes chart in its fifth week on the chart, but only held the spot for one week, the shortest span of any of group's five Number One albums. Yet *Chicago VII* did spawn three hit singles. "(I've Been) Searchin' So Long" peaked at number nine on May 1, 1974. "Call on Me," the second single from the album, reached number six on August 10, and "Wishin' You Were Here" climbed to number 11 on November 30, 1974.

Al Jardine and Carl and Dennis Wilson of the Beach Boys [see 71], who were also managed by Guercio, dropped by the Caribou Ranch during the sessions and sang backing vocals on "Wishin' You Were Here." The use of the Beach Boys was quite appropriate, as the ballad opens with the sounds of the ocean. Says Seraphine, "It turned out great, and it was the start of a relationship that went on for years," as the two groups would often tour together in the following years.

"Skinny Boy," the album's closing track, featured guest vocals by the Pointer Sisters. The song also served as the title track of keyboardist Robert Lamm's solo album, which was released in August 1974 but failed to chart. While Lamm wasn't able to achieve solo success, the hits kept right on coming for Chicago [see 197].

THE TOP FIVE
Week of April 27, 1974

1. **Chicago VII**
   Chicago

2. **John Denver's Greatest Hits**
   John Denver

3. **The Sting**
   Soundtrack

4. **Band on the Run**
   Paul McCartney & Wings

5. **Tubular Bells**
   Mike Oldfield

Producer: Marvin Hamlisch

Track listing: Solace / The Entertainer / Easy Winners / Hooker's Hooker / Luther / Pine Apple Rag / Gladiolus Rag / The Entertainer / The Glove / Little Girl / Pine Apple Rag / Merry-Go-Round Music / Solace / The Entertainer / Rag Time Dancer

May 4, 1974
5 weeks

When ragtime pianist Scott Joplin wrote "The Entertainer" in 1902, *The Billboard,* as it was called back then, had yet to include charts of the hottest hits of the day. Seventy-two years later, Joplin and "The Entertainer" finally got their due, thanks to pianist/composer Marvin Hamlisch and a film starring Robert Redford and Paul Newman as a pair of con men.

Hamlisch became involved in *The Sting* at the request of director George Roy Hill. The pair had been friends for years, dating back to Hill's days as a director of Broadway plays for which Hamlisch would occasionally serve as a rehearsal pianist. But a lot had changed for Hamlisch since those days of warming up the piano stool. On February 2, 1974, Barbra Streisand scored her first Number One single with "The Way We Were," a song co-written by Hamlisch, and Alan and Marilyn Bergman. The song would be featured as the title track of Streisand's second Number One album [see 171], and would garner the Bergmans and Hamlisch a Grammy for song of the year and an Oscar for best song in a motion picture.

Writing for Streisand, however, was a lot different than working on *The Sting.* For one thing, Hamlisch wasn't a particularly big fan of Joplin's music. Yet Hamlisch had to choose which Joplin pieces would work the best in the context of the film. "The way George cut the film was very musical," Hamlisch says. "But Joplin's music wasn't always a perfect fit, so I had to do things to make it fit."

Initially, a soundtrack album wasn't even planned. "It was an afterthought," Hamlisch admits. "I don't think anyone realized that it would be a big hit." Since the music was recorded with a relatively small band of 10 or 11 players, an album could be recorded inexpensively, even if it wasn't a big seller.

While performing the music for the film, Hamlisch grew to have a greater appreciation for Joplin's music. "We really used the creme de la creme of Scott Joplin," Hamlisch says. Included on the album were three different takes of "The Entertainer." To fill in the places in the film where Joplin's music didn't work, Hamlisch wrote originals such as "Luther" and "The Glove." Says Hamlisch, "Anything I wrote was written in a very Scott Joplin manner, and hopefully no one could tell my originals from his music."

It was the success of the film, which went on to win an Oscar for best picture, and the single, "The Entertainer," that propelled *The Sting* to Number One in its 15th week on the chart, making it the first instrumental album to hit the summit since the similarly left-field soundtrack album *"Dueling Banjos" from the Original Soundtrack Deliverance* [see 154]. "The Entertainer," like "Dueling Banjos," did not hit the top of the Hot 100—it stalled at number three—but the fact that it was a hit at all was a shock to Hamlisch.

"We were totally surprised when 'The Entertainer' became a hit single," he says. "We had no idea that in the midst of all the rock 'n' roll that was dominating the charts, we could have a hit with some Scott Joplin ragtime."

THE TOP FIVE
Week of May 4, 1974

1. **The Sting**
   Soundtrack
2. **Chicago VII**
   Chicago
3. **Greatest Hits**
   John Denver
4. **Buddah & the Chocolate Box**
   Cat Stevens
5. **Shinin' On**
   Grand Funk

176 Sundown REPRISE 2177
GORDON LIGHTFOOT

Producer: Lenny Waronker

Track listing: Somewhere U.S.A. / High and Dry / Seven Island Suite / Circle of Steel / Is There Anyone Home / The Watchman's Gone / Sundown / Carefree Highway / The List / "Too Late for Prayin'

June 22, 1974
2 weeks

When Sundown knocked Paul McCartney & Wings' Band on the Run from the Number One spot, it was a particularly sweet victory for Gordon Lightfoot. "That kind of bemused me, because in 1963, when I was just starting out, along come the Beatles and boy, they just blew everybody away," he says.

Born on November 17, 1938, in Orillia, Ontario, Lightfoot began singing at the age of eight. By 11, he was a soloist for his church choir. Although confident with his singing, Lightfoot felt his piano playing could be better. In 1958, while reading a copy of down beat, he saw an ad for a course in contemporary jazz music theory at the Los Angeles–based Westlake college and soon journeyed to California.

Upon returning to Canada, a live recording of the Weavers spurred Lightfoot to trade the piano and romantic jazz for an acoustic guitar and folk music. Influenced by Pete Seeger, Bob Gibson, and Bob Dylan, Lightfoot took to performing with a renewed vengeance. Albert Grossman, who managed Dylan and Peter, Paul, & Mary, soon took Lightfoot on as a client.

In 1966, he was signed to United Artists Records, but at this stage Lightfoot was known primarily as a songwriter, as Peter, Paul & Mary had scored a top 30 hit in 1965 with his "For Lovin' Me."

In February 1971, he scored his first hit under his own name, "If You Can Read My Mind," which climbed to number five and propelled his first Reprise album, Sit Down Young Stranger, to number 12. Three albums followed over the next three years, but all failed to top that success.

For Sundown, Lightfoot recalls: "I had pretty good working conditions. I was living on a farm north of Toronto and I had a real good go at writing. I wrote the whole album in two or three months. But I kind of wondered at that point if we were going to have another big album. I was working away, but it was always tough."

Making things even tougher was Lightfoot's personal life. "It was a really strange time in my life," he recalls. "I was in a really difficult relationship with a woman." It was that relationship that inspired the title track.

Recorded at Eastern Sound Studios in Toronto in approximately a week, Sundown featured a group of musicians that had been playing together for five years, but it also marked a change. "We hadn't used a drummer very much up to that point," he says. "We were still real folky."

Drummer Jim Gordon traveled up north with producer Lenny Waronker and engineer Lee Herschberg. As Lightfoot explains, "It was their turn to travel. We were like a couple of hockey teams getting together and we were on home ice."

With Sundown complete, Lightfoot hit the touring circuit. While performing in Belfast, Ireland, "The promoter announced from the stage at the end of the show that the album had just gone Number One in Billboard," he recalls. "I just couldn't believe it." A week later, the title track topped the Hot 100 as the album held at Number One. "Carefree Highway," also from Sundown, made the top 10 as well.

THE TOP FIVE
Week of June 22, 1974

1. **Sundown**
   Gordon Lightfoot

2. **Band on the Run**
   Paul McCartney & Wings

3. **The Sting**
   Soundtrack

4. **Buddha & the Chocolate Box**
   Cat Stevens

5. **Maria Muldaur**
   Maria Muldaur

Producer: Gus Dudgeon

Track listing: The Bitch Is Back / Pinky / Grimsby / Dixie Lily / Solar Prestige a Gammon / You're So Static / I've Seen the Saucers / Stinker / Don't Let the Sun Go Down on Me / Ticking

July 13, 1974
4 weeks

The week that *Caribou* went to Number One, MCA Records announced that it had signed Elton John to an $8 million, five album contract. It made the singer-pianist the highest-paid performer in pop music and few could contend that John's talent and commercial clout weren't worth the money. *Caribou* was John's fourth consecutive Number One album in a mere two years. Certainly there was no other artist hotter than Elton John.

. The success of *Caribou* leaves no hints that the sessions were riddled with problems, but that was the case, says producer Gus Dudgeon. The album was recorded and named for James Guercio's Caribou Ranch studio, which was frequented by Chicago [see 163] and the Beach Boys [see 182]. "The reason why we went to Caribou was that we heard 'Rocky Mountain Way' by Joe Walsh. We found out it was recorded there and we all agreed that it was a brilliantly recorded record," says Dudgeon. While the serene, mountainous setting of the Caribou Ranch may

have provided a nice atmosphere, the high elevation created difficulties for Dudgeon.

"I checked it out and it seemed fine, but when we got there I was using a desk I had never used before and I was having a major problem with the monitors, because we were 8,500 feet up in the Rockies. The pressure the speakers had to work against was not ground level, so they didn't work the same way." The recording was also rushed. John had only 10 days to record in mid-February 1974 before he departed on a tour of Japan, Australia, and New Zealand.

Dudgeon is the first to admit that "technically, *Caribou* is not a great album. However, by some sort of miracle, some of the songs, like 'Don't Let the Sun Go Down on Me,' turned out extremely well." The majestic ballad featured some well-known backing vocalists, including Beach Boys Carl Wilson and Bruce Johnston, and Toni Tennille. "Every time I hear it I get such a buzz off it," says Dudgeon. "I can still remember the session. There's something about that record that is really special. Everybody did a great job on that one, everything is right on the money." Released as a single in advance of the album, "Don't Let the Sun Go Down on Me" peaked at number two.

Aside from "Don't Let the Sun Go Down on Me," Dudgeon doesn't have much good to say about the rest of *Caribou*, including lyricist Bernie Taupin's tongue-in-cheek ode to his writing partner's occasional foul moods, "The Bitch Is Back." Says Dudgeon, "It's an okay track. It was a hit, but not one that I would call a favorite," he says. "This is the first time that we had a couple of weak or shit songs on an album. 'Grimsby' is the worst thing. It was supposed to be a joke, but it's neither funny enough nor good enough." Dudgeon also singles out "Solar Prestige a Gammon" as one of John's weakest moments. "I suppose there is an element of stupidity and probably blase-ness coming in."

Even with the weak material, John was more popular than ever, as *Caribou* became his fastest chart-topper to date, reaching Number One in a mere two weeks.

THE TOP FIVE
Week of July 13, 1974

1. **Caribou**
   Elton John

2. **Back Home Again**
   John Denver

3. **Sundown**
   Gordon Lightfoot

4. **Band on the Run**
   Paul McCartney & Wings

5. **The Sting**
   Soundtrack

178 Back Home Again RCA 0548
JOHN DENVER

Producer: Milt Okun

Track listing: Back Home Again / On the Road / Grandma's Feather Bed / Matthew / Thank God I'm a Country Boy / The Music Is You / Annie's Song / It's Up to You / Cool An' Green An' Shady / Eclipse / Sweet Surrender / This Old Guitar

August 10, 1974
1 week

"I was raised on country music," says John Denver. "My dad was a big fan of country music. *Back Home Again* was meant to be my country album. 'Back Home Again' was very much a country song, as were 'Grandma's Feather Bed,' and 'Thank God I'm a Country Boy.' The other ones weren't necessarily country, but they came out of a sense of being in the country or being on the farm."

Denver also went with acoustic instrumentation to give the album a down-home feel. "There's not an electric guitar on the album," he notes. For Denver, who toured frequently, the title track was literal. "It's about coming home from the road and having all the things that I ever longed for as an Air Force brat," he says. "It was epitomized by a woman, a partner in life."

That woman was Denver's wife and college sweetheart Ann Martel, who inspired "Annie's Song," another track on the album, which turned out to be a hit. The song came to Denver while he was skiing. The couple had gone through a rough period in their relationship but had emerged closer than ever. "I skied down this run and right back onto the lift," Denver recalls. "As I was on the lift, my heart was pounding, my thighs were burning, and then I started to notice how great it is to be alive. The air was so fresh and smelled so great and the color of the sky was so blue. It filled up my senses. And then I began to think about what other things fill up your senses and I thought of our relationship, how it was like a night in the forest and the mountains in springtime."

By the time Denver reached the top of the lift, he had the song almost completely written in his head. "I skied straight to the car, walked upstairs to get my guitar and started singing this song," he recalls. On July 27, 1974, "Annie's Song" became Denver's second Number One single. Two weeks later, *Back Home Again* became his second consecutive album chart-topper.

"Annie's Song" wasn't the only deeply personal track on *Back Home Again*. Denver calls "This Old Guitar" the "story of my life in three minutes."

"Thank God I'm a Country Boy" was another track that some Denver fans might assume was autobiographical, but it wasn't written by Denver. The song was written by John Martin Sommers, a friend of Denver's from Aspen who led a bluegrass group called Liberty. "I had heard the song and invited them on tour with me as an opening act," Denver says. "But when I heard the song, I knew it was made for me. It had so much energy and it was a great song for concerts."

Denver's original version of "Thank God I'm a Country Boy" appeared on *Back Home Again*. "I never thought of it as a single," Denver admits. However, the song didn't become a hit until nearly a year later, after RCA released a live version of the song, culled from the 1975 album, *An Evening with John Denver*. The live version of "Thank God I'm a Country Boy" became Denver's third Number One single on June 7, 1975, and later that year, he would once again top the album chart [see 206].

THE TOP FIVE
Week of August 10, 1974

1. **Back Home Again**
   John Denver

2. **Caribou**
   Elton John

3. **Before the Flood**
   Bob Dylan / The Band

4. **461 Ocean Blvd.**
   Eric Clapton

5. **On Stage**
   Loggins & Messina

461 Ocean Boulevard **179**
ERIC CLAPTON

the *Layla* sessions. Dowd was initially hesitant to let Terry play guitar during the *461* sessions, but agreed to try him out. "After about a week, George was a vital part of the team," Dowd says. Yvonne Elliman, featured on *Jesus Christ Superstar* [see 129], and later *Saturday Night Fever* [see 226], contributed backing vocals and co-wrote "Get Ready" with Clapton.

While not in the studio, Clapton and company holed up at a white, tiled-roof house, whose address served as the title of the album. Recorded in April and May of 1974, *461 Ocean Boulevard* recast Clapton from a guitar-slinging hotshot to a singer-guitarist more interested in songs than musical virtuosity.

For material, Clapton opted for a mix of traditional blues numbers, like "Motherless Children" and "I Can't Hold Out," and Clapton originals, such as "Get Ready" and "Let It Grow." Terry contributed "Mainline Florida" and turned Clapton on to the album's gem, "I Shot the Sheriff," originally recorded by Bob Marley and the Wailers.

After Clapton cut the track, he was hesitant to include it on the album. "Eric wasn't trying to upstage a record he revered, but when we got it ready to put it out, he started to protest, because he didn't feel that his was as good as the original," Dowd says. After some discussion, however, "I Shot the Sheriff" was included. *461 Ocean Boulevard* hit Number One in its fifth week on the chart, becoming Clapton's first chart-topping solo album. A month later, "I Shot the Sheriff" topped the Hot 100, the first reggae song to go to Number One. Its success would pave the way for such artists as the Police [see 276] in the coming years.

Producer: Tom Dowd

Track listing: Motherless Child / Give Me Strength / Willie and the Hand Jive / Get Ready / I Shot the Sheriff / I Can't Hold Out / Please Be with Me / Let It Grow / Steady Rollin' Man / Mainline Florida

August 17, 1974
4 weeks

Following his commercial and artistic triumphs with Cream [see 104] and Blind Faith [see 115], Eric Clapton spent 1969 as a member of the Delaney and Bonnie band. With assistance from many of the players in that group, Clapton cut his self-titled debut album, which was released in March 1970. Later that year, Clapton formed Derek and the Dominos, which included Duane Allman [see 165] on guitar. The group cut the classic album *Layla and Other Assorted Love Songs* before splintering in 1971, with Clapton battling his heroin addiction.

Various live recordings were released as compilations during Clapton's 1972 and 1973 hiatus. But Clapton wouldn't make his true comeback until the spring of 1974, when he returned to Criteria Studios in Miami with producer Tom Dowd to work on his second solo studio album. In the fall of 1970, Derek and the Dominos had cut *Layla* with Dowd at Criteria, but a lot had changed in those four years. Clapton was attempting to get his feet back on the ground, but to do that he needed to make a musical shift. "He knew he had to reach out and find something he hadn't been doing to get back on the healthier side of doing things," says Dowd, who also served as an engineer on the three Cream albums. "Eric and I were good friends," says Dowd. "He knew I was sensitive to where he was coming from."

To cut the album, Dowd and Clapton auditioned several rhythm sections before opting to go with former Domino Carl Radle on bass and Jamie Oldaker on drums. While Radle played on all the tracks, a few other drummers made appearances on *461 Ocean Boulevard*. Jim Fox from the James Gang is featured on "Steady Rollin' Man" and Al Jackson, on loan from Booker T. & the MG's, played on "Give Me Strength." Says Dowd, "Everyone wanted to play with Eric."

Also on hand was George Terry, who had frequented the studio during

---

THE TOP FIVE
Week of August 17, 1974

1. **461 Ocean Boulevard**
   Eric Clapton

2. **Back Home Again**
   John Denver

3. **Caribou**
   Elton John

4. **Before the Flood**
   Bob Dylan / The Band

5. **On Stage**
   Loggins & Messina

180 Fulfillingness' First Finale TAMLA 332
STEVIE WONDER

Producer: Stevie Wonder

Track listing: Smile Please / Heaven Is 10 Zillion Light Years Away / Too Shy to Say / Boogie on Reggae Woman / Creepin' / You Haven't Done Nothin' / It Ain't No Use / They Won't Go When I Go / Bird of Beauty / Please Don't Go

September 14, 1974
2 weeks

By 1974, Stevie Wonder had completed the transition from young musical genius to one of the most innovative and independent composer/musicians on the pop scene. In 1971, after reaching his 21st birthday, Wonder made a bold move by renegotiating his contract with Motown and establishing his own Taurus Productions and Black Bull publishing company. And Wonder wasn't just breaking the mold on the business side—with his early-'70s albums Music of My Mind, Talking Book, and Innervisions, Wonder played virtually all the instruments, taking the synthesizer in particular to new heights. The latter two albums, which reached number three and four, respectively, also marked the first time Wonder had hit the

top 10 of the album chart since Little Stevie Wonder/The 12 Year Old Genius [see 61].

"Boogie on Reggae Woman," one of the best-known songs from Wonder's next album, Fulfillingness' First Finale, was originally slated for Innervisions. "But it just didn't feel right for that album," Wonder says. "I went back and I had a demo of 'Golden Lady,' which was originally called 'Oh Little Lady,' and that felt better in that spot on Innervisions, so I ended up saving 'Boogie on Reggae Woman' for the next album."

While "Boogie on Reggae Woman" was propelled by Wonder's joy, another memorable track on Fulfillingness' First Finale was fueled by his rage. In "You Haven't Done Nothin'," Wonder took aim at President Richard Nixon and other politicians who weren't making good on their campaign promises. "It wasn't just about Nixon," Wonder says. "It was about the political climate at the time. Many politicians were promising things and after a while it's like, 'Come on.' I was thinking of the whole Vietnam situation, what happened with that, the soldiers who had gone over, and Agent Orange."

The track "They Won't Go When I Go" actually dated back to the summer

of 1971. "I was sad, because I had left Motown, but I hadn't signed with anyone. A lot of people were bugging me, asking me what I was going to do. I just went back to the studio and put the basic melody and idea down. Years later, Yvonne Wright came up with a great lyric for it."

Fulfillingness' First Finale became Wonder's second album chart-topper in its sixth week on the chart. "You Haven't Done Nothin'," featuring the Jackson 5 on backing vocals, was the first single released from the album. On November 2, 1974, it became Wonder's fourth Number One single.

"Boogie on Reggae Woman" hit the top of the R&B chart, becoming Wonder's 10th R&B Number One, and peaked at number three on the Hot 100.

The use of the word Finale in the album's title was appropriate, because Fulfillingness' First Finale did mark the end in a chapter of Wonder's career. It concluded Wonder's four-year, four-album working relationship with associate producers Malcolm Cecil and Bob Margouleff. "We didn't lose our friendship," Wonder says. "We were just at a place where we decided it was time for us to grow."

THE TOP FIVE
Week of September 14, 1974

1. **Fulfillingness' First Finale**
   Stevie Wonder

2. **Bad Company**
   Bad Company

3. **461 Ocean Boulevard**
   Eric Clapton

4. **Endless Summer**
   Beach Boys

5. **Rags to Rufus**
   Rufus

SWAN SONG 8501 **Bad Company**
BAD COMPANY

181

Producer: Bad Company

Track listing: Can't Get Enough / Rock Steady / Ready for Love / Don't Let Me Down / Bad Company / The Way I Choose / Movin' On / Seagull

September 28, 1974
1 week

When former Free vocalist Paul Rodgers and drummer Simon Kirke got together with ex–Mott the Hoople guitarist Mick Ralphs and one-time King Crimson bassist Boz Burrell in the summer of 1973, some called it a supergroup. "We were very excited and very hot with the new material," recalls Rodgers. "All of us had come from very much live playing bands, so there was an instant live feel."

Bad Company was born out of a series of backstage conversations in the early '70s between Rodgers and Ralphs. Rodgers's post-Free group Peace was the support act on a tour with British glam-rockers Mott the Hoople when he met Ralphs. "We jammed on the tuning amps backstage," Rodgers recalls. "He was a little frustrated with what he was doing, so we started getting into material. Some of the stuff was really good, like 'Can't Get Enough,' but they weren't being played by his band."

Although the seeds were planted for

Bad Company, Rodgers went back and recorded two albums with the reunited Free before that band once again fell apart. When Ralphs left Mott, he, Rodgers, and Kirke formed Bad Company. Burrell rounded out the quartet a few months later.

With the lineup complete, Bad Company became the first act signed to the Swan Song label, owned by Led Zeppelin and its manager Peter Grant, who also took on Bad Company as a client. "There was immediate interest in the band and it was a great door-opener for us," Rodgers says of the Led Zeppelin connection. "It meant love us or not, everybody would at least give us a listen."

Bad Company was recorded in November 1973 in Ronnie Lane's Mobile Studio at Headley Grange, Hampshire, in a mere 10 days, virtually live, although the band had not performed together onstage at that point. "We did it in this really old haunted house with the mobile studio outside," Rodgers recalls. "We had the drums set up in the hallway, because it added a lot of nice echo, and the vocal in this big room with a huge log fire, because that was a nice vibe." On "Bad Company," the band's theme song, Rodgers took to the great outdoors. "We set up a microphone in the middle of a field. I did the vocal for that song right out there at midnight with the moon," he says.

While Ralphs's power-chord–driven "Can't Get Enough" was beyond the vocal range of Mott the Hoople singer Ian Hunter, and therefore rejected by that band, it was the perfect vehicle for Rodgers's husky blues-soaked vocals. "As soon as I heard it, I knew it was a song I could sing and deliver," Rodgers says.

Soon after the album was released, the band hit the road in America with the Edgar Winter Group. Manager Grant had learned with Led Zeppelin that touring drives album sales. "At the start of the tour the album was number 99," Rodgers recalls, "and at the end of the tour, the album was Number One."

THE TOP FIVE
Week of September 28, 1974

1. **Bad Company**
   Bad Company

2. **Endless Summer**
   Beach Boys

3. **Fulfillingness' First Finale**
   Stevie Wonder

4. **If You Love Me,
   Let Me Know**
   Olivia Newton-John

5. **Caribou**
   Elton John

182 Endless Summer CAPITOL 11307
THE BEACH BOYS

Producer: Brian Wilson

Track listing: Surfin' Safari / Surfer Girl / Catch a Wave / The Warmth of the Sun / Surfin' U.S.A. / Be True to Your School / Little Deuce Coupe / In My Room / Shut Down / Fun, Fun, Fun / I Get Around / The Girls on the Beach / Wendy / Let Him Run Wild / Don't Worry Baby / California Girls / Girl Don't Tell Me / Help Me Rhonda / You're So Good to Me / All Summer Long

October 5, 1974
1 week

Nearly a decade after the Beach Boys first topped the Top LP's chart with *Beach Boys Concert* [see 71], the group returned to the summit with *Endless Summer*, an appropriately titled two-record compilation spanning the group's 13-year career.

Prior to the release of *Endless Summer*, the Beach Boys already had three greatest-hits albums to their credit: *Best of the Beach Boys*, released in 1966, climbed to number eight; a year later, *Best of the Beach Boys, Vol. 2* stalled at number 50; *Best of the Beach Boys, Vol. 3*, released in 1968, only reached number 153. When Capitol Records began discussions about another Beach Boys hits package, the band had one request—don't call it *Best of the Beach Boys, Vol. 4.*

"We suggested *Endless Summer*,

because that was the name of a surfing movie back in the '60s and it also gave the connotation of timelessness, which the Beach Boys' music certainly had," says Beach Boys vocalist Mike Love.

Endless Summer is comprised primarily of hits, including obvious choices like the top 10 hits "Surfer Girl," "Be True to Your School," the Number One singles "I Get Around" and "Help Me Rhonda," and the group's first top five hit "Surfin' U.S.A." The latter track, reissued as a single to create additional interest in *Endless Summer*, reached number 36 during its second chart run. But the re-released "Surfin' U.S.A." was no longer credited to Brian Wilson and Mike Love. Instead, the credit read "by Chuck Berry" ("Sweet Little Sixteen"). The song's music was certainly inspired by that Berry song, but the Beach Boys composed original lyrics for their tune. "Chuck Berry didn't write 'Surfin' U.S.A.,'" says Love. "He didn't surf too much." Love says Murry Wilson, the father of Beach Boys Brian, Carl, and Dennis, felt it was so close to Berry's song that he feared the rock pioneer would sue the band if he wasn't given a songwriting credit. "Brian actually did the arrangement and I helped write the words, but we were not credited. I was not thrilled with the situation," Love says.

Endless Summer wasn't limited to the hits, however. "The Warmth of the Sun" was never issued as a single, but it held a special place in the hearts of the Beach Boys. "Brian and I wrote that

song in the early morning hours of the day that President Kennedy was assassinated. We stayed up to 2 or 3 A.M. and we awoke the next morning to the news that Kennedy had been shot in Dallas," Love says. "We had just finished writing this song about losing someone you loved. We didn't change it, but the impact and the emotions of that event intertwined with creating that song and the actual performance in the studio."

The music of *Endless Summer* also made an emotional impact on a new generation of Beach Boys fans. Not only did the album hit Number One in its fifth week on the chart, it rode the Top LP's & Tape list for an impressive 155 weeks—that's three years.

THE TOP FIVE
Week of October 5, 1974

1. **Endless Summer**
   The Beach Boys

2. **If You Love Me, Let Me Know**
   Olivia Newton-John

3. **Bad Company**
   Bad Company

4. **Not Fragile**
   Bachman-Turner Overdrive

5. **Caribou**
   Elton John

MCA 411 # If You Love Me, Let Me Know

OLIVIA NEWTON-JOHN

183

Producers: John Farrar and Bruce Welch

Track listing: If You Love Me (Let Me Know) / Mary Skeffington / Country Girl / I Honestly Love You / Free the People / The River's Too Wide / Home Ain't Home Anymore / God Only Knows / Changes / You Ain't Got the Right

October 12, 1974
1 week

Olivia Newton-John's solo career did not get off to a promising start. *If Not For You*, her 1971 debut album, peaked at number 158 and only stayed on the chart for four weeks. By 1974, however, the British-born, Australian-bred singer's luck began to change. The title track from her second album, *Let Me Be There*, climbed all the way to number six, but the album didn't fare as well, stalling at number 54. Still, the single represented an artistic breakthrough for Newton-John.

"I was kind of establishing a style for myself up to that point," she says. "In England there wasn't a country chart and a pop chart, there was just one chart. My producers and my manager were trying to establish a style for what we they thought suited my voice best. It seemed to be country and folk." On Newton-John's third album, *If You Love Me, Let Me Know,* the singer continued to explore those genres.

The breakthrough track was a song written by Peter Allen and Jeff Barry called "I Honestly Love You." Says Newton-John, "That came to me with a pile of demos that were sent to my producer John Farrar. We used to sit and wade through them and one day John said, 'I found this song and I think it's great.' I remember the first time I heard it. I thought, 'This is a knockout song, I've got to do it.'"

If You Love Me, Let Me Know was recorded at EMI Studios and CSS London. "I Honestly Love You" was recorded at the latter studio. "It was such a small studio," Newton-John says. "John and the engineer were sitting above my head and they couldn't move while we were recording, because you could hear the squeaking of the floorboards, through the microphones." Although John sang the song three times, it was the first take that made the album.

For other material, Newton-John turned to some of her favorite writers, including the Beach Boys' Brian Wilson, represented with "God Only Knows," and Gerry Rafferty, whose "Mary Skeffington" is featured.

The album also includes "Changes," a Newton-John original. "That was the first song I ever wrote that I recorded," she says. "John [Farrar] taught me a few open-tuning things and I was playing around with a guitar and the song came to me. I had a girlfriend next door who was going through a divorce. I played it to Bruce Welch and he liked it a lot."

The public was also taken by Newton-John. On June 29, 1974, the album's first single, "If You Love Me (Let Me Know)," reached number five, becoming the biggest hit of her fast-rising career. That was only the beginning. The second single, "I Honestly Love You," reached Number One on October 5, 1974. A week later, *If You Love Me, Let Me Know* went to Number One as well.

THE TOP FIVE
Week of October 12, 1974

1. **If You Love Me, Let Me Know**
   Olivia Newton-John

2. **Not Fragile**
   Bachman-Turner Overdrive

3. **Can't Get Enough**
   Barry White

4. **Bad Company**
   Bad Company

5. **Caribou**
   Elton John

184 Not Fragile MERCURY 1004
BACHMAN-TURNER OVERDRIVE

Producer: Randy Bachman

Track listing: Not Fragile / Rock Is My Life, and This Is My Song / Roll on Down the Highway / You Ain't Seen Nothing Yet / Free Wheelin' / Sledgehammer / Blue Moanin' / Second Hand / Givin' It All Away

October 19, 1974
1 week

"**W**e were on an upward curve," says Randy Bachman. "This was going to be our third album. We knew we had a consistency and we were getting better, as far as writing and playing, so we did have high hopes for the album. I really wanted success badly after the Guess Who."

As a guitarist for the Guess Who, Bachman had tasted success with hits like the Number One "American Woman," yet he left the band in 1970 after converting to the Mormon faith. After releasing a solo album, Bachman joined forces with his brother Robbie and fellow Guess Who founder Chad Allan in a new band called Brave Belt. After the release of a few albums, guitarist Tim Bachman and singer/bassist C. Fred Turner were enlisted to replace Allan, and the group changed its name to Bachman-Turner Overdrive. Initially, no record companies were interested. "I received about 25 or 26 refusals," says Bachman, who financed the band's first album and paid the band members a salary with royalties he earned with the

Guess Who. "Once I hit the $100,000 mark, I had to tell everyone that would be their last paycheck." Later that week, however, Bachman received a phone call from Charlie Fach at Mercury Records.

In 1973, the label released the band's debut album, which stalled at number 70. The band's luck changed with *Bachman-Turner Overdrive 2*, which was released later that same year. The album climbed to number four, thanks in part to the hit single "Taking Care of Business," which reached number 12.

The title of *Not Fragile* was inspired by an album by the art-rock band Yes, who had released an album called *Fragile* in 1971. "We were sort of the anti-Yes," says Bachman. "*Fragile* was a very delicate and symphonic and kind of classical in a way. Ours was the exact opposite. It was just blunt, hit them over the head with a guitar and drum beat kind of a thing. But it wasn't a slam against Yes."

Bachman intended *Not Fragile* to be an eight-song album with four tracks on each side, totaling approximately 20 minutes a side. That changed, however, shortly after the band played the record back to Fach. "He said, 'I don't hear the magical song. We've got the FM radio thing happening, now we're looking for a big hit single.'"

When Bachman told Fach that the

band had only recorded eight songs, engineer Mark K. Smith suggested they play Fach the guide track, which the band used to warm up with and set various mike levels. At first Bachman was hesitant. The track was a joke, meant only for his brother. "I'm stuttering on it and guitar is out of tune," Bachman says. Yet Fach liked the song.

Bachman said the band would include the song on the album, if he could recut his vocal, without the stuttering. "But it ended up sounding like Bill Murray doing Frank Sinatra," says Bachman, who kept the original vocal and re-sequenced the album to make room for the track, called "You Ain't Seen Nothing Yet."

Once the album was released, the track began to generate requests. "Charlie kept calling me telling me that it was receiving top 10 phone requests in Oregon and Detroit," Bachman says. "He wanted to release it as a single, but I wouldn't give him permission. It was in the days of Led Zeppelin, when it wasn't good for rock acts to have singles."

Finally, Bachman agreed to give the label the go-ahead to release the single. As "You Ain't Seen Nothing Yet" climbed the Hot 100, *Not Fragile* hit the summit. It was truly a triumph for Bachman, as the Guess Who had never topped the album chart. Less than a month later, "You Ain't Seen Nothing Yet," also hit Number One.

THE TOP FIVE
Week of October 19, 1974

1. **Not Fragile**
   Bachman-Turner Overdrive

2. **Can't Get Enough**
   Barry White

3. **Back Home Again**
   John Denver

4. **If You Love Me Let Me Know**
   Olivia Newton-John

5. **Welcome back, my friends, to the show that never ends—Ladies and Gentlemen Emerson, Lake & Palmer**
   Emerson, Lake & Palmer

Producer: Barry White

Track listing: Mellow Mood (Pt. I) /
You're the First, the Last, My Everything
/ I Can't Believe You Love Me / Can't
Get Enough of Your Love, Babe / Oh
Love, Well We Finally Made It / I Love
You More Than Anything (in This World
Girl) / Mellow Mood (Pt. II)

October 26, 1974
1 week

In 1974, Barry White was happening,
as a writer, producer, arranger, and
star in his own right. Under the Influence of..., by Love Unlimited, a group
managed and produced by White, and
featuring his wife, Glodean James, had
just climbed to number three on the
album chart. Another album, Rhapsody
in White, by the Love Unlimited Orchestra, whose recordings were conducted
and arranged by White, reached number eight.

White wasn't doing too shabbily as
a solo artist either. I've Got So Much to
Give, his 1973 debut, climbed to number 16 and spent more than a year on
the chart. The follow-up, Stone Gon'
reached number 20. However, these
early successes would pale compared to
Can't Get Enough.

"It was a very creative and explosive
time," says White. "I was very proud of
the work I was doing as a producer,
songwriter, singer, and arranger." Yet
White's involvement in other projects
and his own solo career put a strain on
the songwriter. "There was pressure to
come up with songs for Can't Get
Enough," White says. "I was coming off
of two hit albums, so I had to do everything I could to be consistent."

As with White's previous releases,
love continued to be a favorite topic,
but this time around he drew on his own
personal experiences. "I just got through
making love to my wife and she fell off
to sleep, so I went into the kitchen and
wrote 'I Just Can't Get Enough of Your
Love, Babe,'" White recalls. "It came to
me instantly."

To record the album, White chose
Whitney Studios in Glendale, California, for a number of reasons. "I always
like to go where no one else goes," he
says. "The only people that were recording at Whitney was Hanna-Barbera, for
some of their cartoons, and different
choirs, like the Mormon Tabernacle
Choir [see 30]. And it was away from
Hollywood. I used to love the scenic

drive to and from the studio."

While writing "Can't Get Enough of
Your Love, Babe" was easy, recording
the track proved to be a challenge. "We
had finished the track and I was the
only one who wasn't satisfied," says
White. "Everyone else thought it was a
hit. But I knew that there was something
missing in the song." White listened to
the track again and again for 30 minutes. "Then I told everyone to take a 15-
minute legal union break and I sat down
at the piano and I worked that bass
line." When White's backing band
came back into the studio, he taught
bass player Wilton Felder the new riff.
"When we recorded it that way, the
record popped. What they thought was
a great song turned out to be an incredible song."

"Can't Get Enough of Your Love,
Babe" turned out to be a Number One
R&B and pop single. It wasn't the only
hit on the album, but it was enough to
push Can't Get Enough to the summit.

White also topped the R&B singles
chart with "You're the First, the Last, My
Everything." Co-writer Sterling Radcliffe
had written the song 21 years earlier,
before White added his own special
touch to the song and agreed to record
it.

Yet Can't Get Enough was more
than a showcase for a few hit singles—
it was an album introduced and concluded by a pair of appropriately
named instrumental pieces, "Mellow
Mood (Pt. I)" and "Mellow Mood (Part
II)." As White puts it, "The whole thing
was structured."

THE TOP FIVE
Week of October 26, 1974

1. **Can't Get Enough**
   Barry White

2. **So Far**
   Crosby, Stills, Nash & Young

3. **Back Home Again**
   John Denver

4. **Welcome back my
   friends, to the show that
   never ends—Ladies and
   Gentlemen, Emerson,
   Lake & Palmer**
   Emerson, Lake & Palmer

5. **Wrap Around Joy**
   Carole King

186 So Far ATLANTIC 18100
CROSBY, STILLS, NASH & YOUNG

Producers: Crosby, Stills, Nash & Young, Bill Halverson

Track listing: Deja Vu / Helplessly Hoping / Wooden Ships / Teach Your Children / Ohio / Find the Cost of Freedom / Woodstock / Our House / Helpless / Guinnevere / Suite: Judy Blue Eyes

November 2, 1974
1 week

It may have seemed like a silly idea for Atlantic Records to compile an album of Crosby, Stills, Nash & Young's greatest hits, given the fact that the band had only recorded two studio albums at the time. Even Stephen Stills says the album's release was premature. Yet So Far did have something to offer besides the best tracks from 1969's Crosby, Stills & Nash and 1970's Deja Vu [see 120].

The album is notable for the inclusion of "Ohio" and "Find the Cost of Freedom," which were issued as a single on June 4, 1970. Live versions of both tracks were featured on 4 Way Street [see 131], but So Far marked the first time the studio versions of the songs appeared on an album.

"Ohio" is arguably the most important track the group ever recorded. On May 4, 1970, four students were killed by National Guardsmen during an anti-war rally at Kent State University. "Neil wrote it one night after watching the news coverage and we went in and recorded it next day," Stills says, adding that the session was one of the most emotional moments of the band's career, with the horrible TV news images of the catastrophe still fresh in everyone's mind. Although the entire band was credited with vocals, Stills didn't actually sing on the track. "There wasn't really a fourth part, so I just played the guitar, which I kind of liked," he says. Despite its political significance and timeliness, or maybe because of it, "Ohio" stalled at number 14 on August 8, 1970. Also on the chart at the time was Nash's upbeat "Teach Your Children," which featured the Grateful Dead's Jerry Garcia on pedal steel guitar.

Another highlight on So Far was "Woodstock," the band's highest-charting single at the time. The track, originally featured on Deja Vu, reached number 11. It was written by Nash's one-time live-in girlfriend Joni Mitchell, who penned the song as a tribute of sorts to the band's appearance at Woodstock [see 186].

"Woodstock" wasn't Mitchell's only contribution to So Far—her painting of the band graced the album's cover. "We've always disliked photographs of ourselves, because we aren't the great-est-looking people," says Nash. "It's not like we are Clark Gable or something. Since my relationship with Joni, I knew she had this image of the four of us, so I called her up and asked if we could use it and she agreed."

The release of So Far coincided with a 30-date U.S. tour, which some termed a reunion. "It's odd to talk about splitting up and reforming, because we have never really been together," says Nash. "We have always been four people or three people who make music. Sometimes we do it singularly, sometimes in pairs or in a trio, and sometimes in a quartet."

THE TOP FIVE
Week of November 2, 1974

1. **So Far**
   Crosby, Stills, Nash & Young

2. **Wrap Around Joy**
   Carole King

3. **Can't Get Enough**
   Barry White

4. **Walls and Bridges**
   John Lennon

5. **Not Fragile**
   Bachman-Turner Overdrive

ODE 77024 **Wrap Around Joy** 187
CAROLE KING

Producer: Lou Adler

Track listing: Nightingale / Change in Mind, Change of Heart / Jazzman / You Go Your Way, I'll Got Mine / You're Something New / We Are All in This Together / Wrap Around Joy / You Gentle Me / My Lovin' Eyes / Sweet Adonis / A Night This Side of Dying / The Best Is Yet to Come

November 9, 1974
1 week

Following the success of *Music* [see 139], Carole King's second consecutive Number One album, her fortunes dipped slightly. *Rhymes & Reasons* stayed at number two for five weeks, but couldn't knock the Moody Blues' *Seventh Sojourn* [see 150] from the top spot. *Fantasy*, King's next album, made number six in 1973. Both albums failed to yield a hit single. However, King would hit the top one more time with her sixth solo album, *Wrap Around Joy*, thanks largely to "Jazzman," which became the second-highest-charting single of her career.

Like *Music*, *Wrap Around Joy* was recorded with Lou Adler at the helm at A&M studios, and once again King was pregnant. The album was cut during April 1974. On April 29, less than a week after finishing the album, King gave birth to her fourth child, Levi.

Although there were similarities to her previous albums, *Wrap Around Joy* also marked some substantial changes. King composed the entire album with a new writing partner, David Palmer. "I like writing with partners," King says. "It gives the material a different dynamic."

Also, there were changes with her backing band. Noted session drummer Andy Newmark, who would later work with Bryan Ferry, was featured on the album. A second guitarist, Dean Parks, joined Danny "Kootch" Kortchmar, who returned to the King fold. Kortchmar had played on *Tapestry* [see 133], *Music*, and *Rhymes & Reasons*, but not on *Fantasy*. In addition, noted saxophone player Tom Scott was featured on "Jazzman."

That cut was released as the first single from *Wrap Around Joy* on August 9, 1974. Three months later, "Jazzman" reached number two on the Hot 100, but was kept from the top spot by Bachman-Turner Overdrive's "You Ain't Seen Nothing Yet" [see 184]. Although

"Jazzman" wasn't able to reach Number One, its popularity helped King score her third and final Number One album.

"I never imagined that so many people would come to hear my music and love my music," King says. "To this day, I meet people who tell me how much it has affected them. I'm very grateful that I have had that opportunity."

With *Tapestry*, *Music*, and *Wrap Around Joy*, King became a huge star in her own right. However, she was still first and foremost a songwriter. "For me, it's a joy to hear other people do my material," King says. "When I make my demos, I get to do my own material. It's a lot more fun to hear someone like Aretha Franklin or someone like Mariah Carey [see 345] sing a song of mine."

THE TOP FIVE
Week of November 9, 1974

1. **Wrap Around Joy**
   Carole King

2. **Walls and Bridges**
   John Lennon

3. **Photographs & Memories, His Greatest Hits**
   Jim Croce

4. **Not Fragile**
   Bachman-Turner Overdrive

5. **Holiday**
   America

188 Walls and Bridges APPLE 3416
JOHN LENNON

Producer: John Lennon with the Plastic Ono Nuclear Band / Little Big Horns / and The Philharmanic Orchestrange

Track listing: Going Down on Love / Whatever Gets You Thru the Night / Old Dirt Road / What You Got / Bless You / Scared / #9 Dream / Surprise, Surprise (Sweet Bird of Paradox) / Steel and Glass / Beef Jerky / Nobody Loves You (When You're Down and Out) / Ya Ya

November 16, 1974
1 week

Imagine [see 135], John Lennon's first solo commercial triumph, came during a time of harmony and happiness in his personal life. Lennon's next chart-topper, Walls and Bridges, occurred when he was close to hitting bottom.

Following the success of Imagine, Lennon once again made a stylistic left turn. His 1972 double-album Some Time in New York City, which had him backed by Elephants Memory in the studio and the Mothers of Invention in concert, stalled at number 48 and featured some of the weakest material of his career,

while Mind Games, his 1973 album, marked a return to Imagine-styled sounds and reached number nine, but was still not fully up to par artistically.

In March 1973, Lennon began battling with the U.S. Immigration Service, which was attempting to deport him because of a five-year-old British drug conviction. Months later, he split from his wife Yoko Ono and went on what he termed "a lost weekend," a period in which Lennon lived the rock 'n' roll excesses to the hilt, often drinking heavily. The temporary split was supposed to last six months, but ended up lasting three times that long. During this period Lennon's constant companion was May Pang, who had formerly worked as a personal assistant for him and Ono. Pang even received the credit "production coordinator" on Walls and Bridges.

Although Lennon and Ono were separated at the time, they spoke on the phone daily. In fact, their separation fueled much of the material on Walls and Bridges, including the track "Going Down on Love" and "Scared." Says Ono, "It had a lot to do with us being separated. There were a lot of messages to me in those songs."

Lennon recorded Walls and Bridges at the Record Plant in New York during the summer of 1974. "It was a rough period for John," Ono adds. "But it showed that even though he was going through a period of personal trauma, it didn't effect him creatively."

Lennon's desperation is apparent in "Whatever Gets You Thru the Night," which featured a guest appearance by Elton John

[see 177] on keyboards and backing vocals. (The British rocker also sang harmony on "Surprise, Surprise.") "John promised Elton that if 'Whatever Gets You Thru the Night' went to Number One, then he would perform with him at Madison Square Garden," Ono says.

Sure enough, Lennon scored his first Number One single (becoming the last of the ex-Beatles to do so) with "Whatever Gets You Thru the Night" just as Walls and Bridges ascended to the summit of the album chart. On Thanksgiving Night 1974, Lennon joined Elton John onstage, where they performed "Whatever Gets You Thru the Night," "Lucy and the Sky with Diamonds," and "I Saw Her Standing There." (The latter track was released as the B-side of Elton John's 1975 Number One single "Philadelphia Freedom.") It would turn out to be Lennon's final concert performance.

Elton John wasn't the only guest on Walls and Bridges. Harry Nilsson contributed backing vocals to "Old Dirt Road" (Lennon had produced Nilsson's 1974 album Pussycats) and Lennon's son Julian played drums on "Ya Ya."

The cover art of Walls and Bridges consisted of paintings Lennon had made at the age of 11. "That was very important to John," says Ono, "because that had a lot to do with the music on the album. He was really delving into his youth and bringing out emotions from it."

THE TOP FIVE
Week of November 16, 1974

1. **Walls and Bridges**
   John Lennon

2. **Photographs & Memories, His Greatest Hits**
   Jim Croce

3. **It's Only Rock 'N Roll**
   Rolling Stones

4. **Holiday**
   America

5. **Not Fragile**
   Bachman-Turner Overdrive

Willie Weeks on bass, rather than Bill Wyman.

However, the other tracks on the album featured the core Stones lineup, often augmented by the usual assortment of outside players. For example, Billy Preston, known for his work with the Beatles [see 122], played on "If You Can't Rock Me," "Ain't Too Proud to Beg," and "Fingerprint File." Says Johns, "Billy was fantastic. He had been touring with them as an opening act previous to that record, so he ended up playing on those sessions." Other outside players featured on the album included keyboardists Nicky Hopkins and longtime Stones session player Ian Stewart, as well as percussionist Ray Cooper from Elton John's band.

In addition to the nine originals on the album, the Stones opted to cover the 1966 Temptations [see 111] hit "Ain't Too Proud to Beg," but it wasn't Richards's first choice. "Keith kept wanting to do the Dobie Gray song 'Drift Away,'" says Johns. "They tried it for four or five days, but it never quite worked. Ronnie was there for that and Mick Taylor wasn't, so I just kind of assumed that Ronnie was going to be in the band."

In its fourth week on the chart, *It's Only Rock 'N Roll* reached Number One, becoming the Stones' fifth career chart-topper. Its one-week stop at the summit gave it the dubious distinction as the Stones' shortest stay at the top.

On December 12, less than a month after *It's Only Rock 'N Roll* hit Number One, the Stones officially announced that Taylor had left the group due to creative differences.

Producers: The Glimmer Twins

Track listing: If You Can't Rock Me / Ain't Too Proud to Beg / It's Only Rock'n Roll (But I Like It) / Till the Next Goodbye / Time Waits for No One / Dance Little Sister / If You Really Want to Be My Friend / Short and Curlies / Fingerprint File

November 23, 1974
1 week

It's Only Rock 'N Roll is important for several reasons. One, it marked the last Stones album featuring guitarist Mick Taylor and featured the Stones debut of his eventual replacement, Ronnie Wood of the Faces. It was also the first album produced by the Glimmer Twins, the pseudonym adopted by vocalist Mick Jagger and guitarist Keith Richards.

It wasn't a particularly happy time in the Stones camp when the sessions began in November 1973 at Munich's Musicland Studios. "A lot of drugs were going on, which made it kind of difficult," says Andy Johns, who split the engineering duties with Keith Harwood. "It was not the most fun I had working with those guys. It certainly wasn't as fun as *Exile on Main St.* [see 145], and the material was not as good."

The title track, which would eventually join the ranks of "Satisfaction" and "Brown Sugar" as one of the band's best-known anthems, was credited to Jagger-Richards, but rumor has it that the song was actually written by Jagger and Wood in the latter's basement. In the album's liner notes, Wood is credited with the "inspiration" for the song. The track featured the Faces' Kenny Jones on drums, rather than the Stones' Charlie Watts, and R&B great

THE TOP FIVE
Week of November 23, 1974

1. **It's Only Rock 'N Roll**
   The Rolling Stones

2. **Photographs & Memories, His Greatest Hits**
   Jim Croce

3. **Holiday**
   America

4. **Not Fragile**
   Bachman-Turner Overdrive

5. **Cheech & Chong's Wedding Album**
   Cheech & Chong

190 Greatest Hits MCA 2128
ELTON JOHN

Producer: Gus Dudgeon

Track listing: Your Song / Daniel / Honky Cat / Goodbye Yellow Brick Road / Saturday Night's Alright for Fighting / Rocket Man / Bennie and the Jets / Don't Let the Sun Go Down on Me / Border Song / Crocodile Rock

November 30, 1974
10 weeks

With nine top 10 hits in a mere five years, Elton John was at the height of his popularity when MCA Records suggested he take a break from his hectic recording schedule while the company issued his first *Greatest Hits* collection, just in time for the holiday buying season.

Greatest Hits was compiled by John's longtime producer Gus Dudgeon. As its title suggests, *Greatest Hits* features the highest-charting singles from John's four Number One albums—*Honky Chateau* [see 146], *Don't Shoot Me I'm Only the Piano Player* [see 153], *Goodbye Yellow Brick Road* [see 167], and *Caribou* [see 177]. "The Bitch Is Back" from *Caribou*, which was climbing the Hot 100 while *Greatest Hits* was being assembled, didn't make John's first best-of collection, but would surface on *Greatest Hits Vol. II*.

Also included is "Your Song," John's first top 10 hit, and "Border Song," the only track on the collection that wasn't a hit. "Border Song," John's first charting single, stalled at number 92 in August 1970. Both songs were originally featured on John's 1970 self-titled album, which reached number four.

"Your Song" marked a turning point in John's early career. "That was the song that Steve Brown brought to me when he introduced me to Elton," says Dudgeon. Brown produced John's first album, 1969's *Empty Sky*, which reached number six when it was released in America for the first time in early 1975. "Steve didn't feel he was up for the job," Dudgeon adds. "And I admire him for doing that, for having the guts to admit that maybe he wasn't a good enough producer for Elton." While Dudgeon was incredibly impressed with the song, he wasn't sure it would be a hit. "I was concerned, because compared to what was on the charts at the time, it was very sophisticated. So we cheated a bit. We decided we would open the door slowly."

In England, John's 1969 single "Lady Samantha" had received substantial airplay, although it failed to become a hit. "The door was a bit open, but we felt we might blow it with 'Your Song' if it came too early." So, "Border Song" was released as a single first, serving as a primer for "Your Song." John's career received a boost when legendary soul diva Aretha Franklin covered "Border Song." Says Dudgeon, "That immediately gave Elton tremendous credibility in America as a writer."

In January 1971, "Your Song" became a belated hit, reaching number eight. Nearly four years later, John's *Greatest Hits* accomplished one of his greatest album chart triumphs, as it stayed at the summit for 10 weeks, a feat none of his previous or future releases would match.

THE TOP FIVE
Week of November 30, 1974

1. **Greatest Hits**
   Elton John

2. **It's Only Rock 'N Roll**
   Rolling Stones

3. **Not Fragile**
   Bachman-Turner Overdrive

4. **Walls and Bridges**
   John Lennon

5. **Photographs & Memories, His Greatest Hits**
   Jim Croce

Producer: Ohio Players

Track listing: Fire / Together / Runnin' from the Devil / I Want to Be Free / Smoke / It's All Over / What the Hell / Together / Feelings

February 8, 1975
1 week

In 1974, the veteran R&B group the Ohio Players signed to Mercury Records and scored their greatest commercial triumph up to that time with *Skin Tight*. The album reached number 11, thanks in part to the title track, which was a number two hit on the Hot R&B Singles chart.

Skin Tight wasn't the Ohio Players' first taste of success. In 1973, the band had scored a Number One R&B hit with "Funky Worm" on the Westbound label. Yet the group's albums on that imprint had failed to break the top 50. Prior to *Skin Tight*, their high-water mark on the album chart had been 1973's *Pleasure*, which had peaked at number 63.

The history of the Ohio Players dates back to 1959, when the group was known as the Ohio Untouchables and served as a backing band for the Falcons, a group led by Wilson Pickett. Back then the group included guitarist Robert Ward, who would later be "rediscovered" as a notable blues artist in the early 1990s.

The band, led by singer/guitarist Leroy "Sugarfoot" Bonner, had gone through numerous lineup changes by 1974, but was primed for success. *Skin Tight* was recorded in a mere nine days and had to be sandwiched into the band's touring schedule, says bassist Marshall Jones: "We would be playing nights in Buffalo and then we would get up in the morning and fly to Chicago to record."

For *Fire*, the band opted to spend an entire month recording. "We wanted to do *Fire* right, so we took off from the road," he says. The seven-member band recorded the album at Paragon Studios in Chicago. "It kind of reminded us of the basement we used to practice in," says Jones, "and it had a real good sound. We recorded at several studios, but for some reason Paragon was the most comfortable."

Fire, like most of the group's previous LPs, featured a racy album cover—something of an Ohio Players trademark by this time. The woman featured on the album cover was photographed naked, save for a fire helmet and a clear fire hose, which was strategically wound around her body. "It's like the media says, 'Sex sells,'" says Jones.

Musically, the funky title track incorporated fire engine sirens and other sound effects. On January 25, 1975, the track became the Players' second Number One R&B single, and was racing up the pop charts as well.

By February 8, both the album and the single had reached the summit. The "No. 1" featured on the cover model's fire helmet had turned out to be prophetic.

Yet *Fire* wasn't just about fun and games. On "I Want to Be Free," the Players offered some social commentary. "There was a lot of racial oppression at the time," says Jones. That track made number six on the Hot R&B Singles chart, amplifying the triumph the Players had scored with *Fire*. Says Jones, "We were pumped up. Having a Number One album and single was like getting a Super Bowl ring to us."

THE TOP FIVE
Week of February 8, 1975

1. **Fire**
   Ohio Players

2. **Miles of Aisles**
   Joni Mitchell

3. **Heart Like a Wheel**
   Linda Ronstadt

4. **Average White Band**
   Average White Band

5. **Greatest Hits**
   Elton John

192 Heart Like a Wheel CAPITOL 11358
LINDA RONSTADT

Producer: Peter Asher

Track listing: You're No Good / It Doesn't Matter Anymore / Faithless Love / Dark End of the Street / Heart Like a Wheel / When Will I Be Loved / Willin' / I Can't Help It if I'm Still in Love with You / Keep Me from Blowing Away / You Can Close Your Eyes

February 15, 1975
1 week

By 1974, Linda Ronstadt had a respectable following for her mix of country and rock. But it wasn't until *Heart Like a Wheel* that she found a producer who shared her creative vision.

Ronstadt, who grew up singing traditional Mexican songs with her family, graduated to the local clubs in Tucson before hooking up with Bob Kimmel and Kenny Edwards to form the Stone Poneys in 1965. The trio's performances at the Troubadour in Los Angeles led to a contract with Capitol. After three albums and one hit—a cover of "Different Drum," written by Mike Nesmith of the Monkees [see 98]—Ronstadt went off on her own.

Linda Ronstadt, the singer's third solo album, featured a backing band of future Eagles [see 201] Glenn Frey, Don Henley, Bernie Leadon, and Randy Meisner. However, it wasn't until 1973's *Don't Cry Now* that Ronstadt began to reach a larger audience. That album peaked at number 45, but stayed on the chart for 56 weeks, eventually selling more than half a million copies and earning Ronstadt her first gold record.

On the verge of her commercial breakthrough, Ronstadt ran into problems as she prepared to record her final album for Capitol Records. She had become smitten with "Heart Like a Wheel," a song written by Canadian folksinger Anna McGarrigle. "[Texas folksinger] Jerry Jeff Walker had sung it for me in a taxicab at dawn in New York, and I thought it was the most beautiful thing I had ever heard," Ronstadt says. "But I took it around to a lot of producers and they thought it was corny."

Finally, Ronstadt turned to her manager Peter Asher, once half of the British pop duo Peter & Gordon. Asher had taken over as Ronstadt's manager in 1973, and had helped salvage *Don't Cry Now* after a year of costly sessions. "I played it for Peter and he loved it. He thought it was beautiful. I was so glad, we worked on the record together," Ronstadt says. Under Asher's guidance, Ronstadt began a tradition of covering a mix of proven classics and contemporary songs, enhanced by Asher's studio wizardry.

The two biggest hits from *Heart Like a Wheel* were staples of Ronstadt's live set. "You're No Good," originally recorded by Betty Everett, became Ronstadt's first Number One single. Studio musician Andrew Gold and Ronstadt's former Stone Poneys partner Kenny Edwards played most of the instruments on the track. Edwards's involvement was most appropriate, since the Stone Poneys performed the song in their live sets. Says Ronstadt, "We never had a song to close with because we were an acoustic band and played all these ballads." When the Stone Poneys plugged in, Edwards suggested the R&B nugget "You're No Good."

Heart Like a Wheel also included Ronstadt's version of Buddy Holly's "When Will I Be Loved," which climbed to number two. "That was an afterthought," she says. "That was something we had in our club set and we needed one more uptempo song."

THE TOP FIVE
Week of February 15, 1975

1. **Heart Like a Wheel**
   Linda Ronstadt

2. **Average White Band**
   Average White Band

3. **Miles of Aisles**
   Joni Mitchell

4. **Blood on the Tracks**
   Bob Dylan

5. **Dark Horse**
   George Harrison

ATLANTIC 7308 **AWB**
AVERAGE WHITE BAND

193

Producer: Arif Mardin

Track listing: You Got It / Got the Love / Pick Up the Pieces / Person to Person / Work to Do / Nothing You Can Do / Just Wanna Love You Tonight / Keepin' It to Myself / I Just Can't Give You Up / There's Always Someone Waiting

February 22, 1975
1 week

In 1973, the Average White Band was in danger of living up to its ironic moniker. The Scottish sextet, which concocted an interesting brew of funk, jazz, and soul, was signed in Britain to MCA, which released its debut album, *Show Your Hand*. Although the album wasn't issued in America, the group crossed the Atlantic set on conquering the States and recording their second album in Los Angeles. "We started recording the second album and we were practically finished with it when we went to MCA, and we said, 'How do you like it?' And they said, 'We don't. Who are you guys?' They didn't know us because we were signed to MCA in England," says rhythm guitarist Onnie McIntyre.

Down but not out, the group remained in Los Angeles with hopes of securing another record deal. At a party held at the home of a friend, AWB (which also included singer/bassist Alan Gorrie, singer/guitarist Hamish Stuart, keyboardist/sax player Roger Ball, sax player Malcolm [Molly] Duncan, and drummer Robbie McIntosh), ran into legendary Atlantic A&R executive Jerry Wexler. "We took the tapes over there,

because we knew he was going to be there," says McIntyre. "We played them for him and everyone fell about. Jerry was knocked out by them." Wexler signed the band to Atlantic, which was a dream come true for the band, since the label had a reputation for working with such R&B legends as Aretha Franklin, Wilson Pickett, and Otis Redding. Atlantic was far more understanding of AWB's creative vision than MCA.

After securing the tapes of its aborted second album from MCA, the group was flown to Criteria Sound Studios in Miami. "They said, 'We like the material, but we want you to record two new songs,'" says McIntyre. The group came up with "You Got It" and "Nothing You Can Do." Other tracks, including "Pick Up the Pieces," were altered a bit during the sessions. "We changed the bass line and some of the drum parts," McIntyre says.

The sessions at Criteria were a dream come true for the band. "The very first day we went to the studio, Aretha was in recording and Jerry, Arif Mardin, and Tom Dowd were behind the desk," says McIntyre. "All our heroes were there. I remember Alan was trying to take a photograph and he was visibly shaking."

The Miami sessions went so well, the band opted to re-record the entire album, traveling to Atlantic's New York Studios to complete the project. *AWB*, says McIntyre, "captured the band at its peak. The creative juices were all flowing and the chemistry was right."

Unfortunately, AWB's success didn't come without tragedy. With the album starting to move up the charts, the band

was booked for a week at the Troubadour in Los Angeles. "The buzz was happening. It was sold out every night," says McIntyre. "On the last night, a lot of stars turned up, like Cher, Elton John [see 190], and Martha Reeves, and they joined us onstage." On September 23, 1974, at a party to celebrate the triumphant final night of the engagement, McIntosh died of a heroin overdose. The drummer thought he was snorting cocaine.

The group was devastated by McIntosh's death, but vowed to carry on, with McIntosh's friend Steve Ferrone serving as a replacement. Appropriately enough, it was the instrumental entitled "Pick Up the Pieces" that began to catch on. The dance hit crossed over to top 40 as the album began climbing the chart. On February 22, 1975, both the single and the album hit the top simultaneously.

THE TOP FIVE
Week of February 22, 1975

1. **AWB**
   Average White Band

2. **Blood on the Tracks**
   Bob Dylan

3. **Heart Like a Wheel**
   Linda Ronstadt

4. **Miles of Aisles**
   Joni Mitchell

5. **War Child**
   Jethro Tull

194 Blood on the Tracks COLUMBIA 33235
BOB DYLAN

Producer: None listed

Track listing: Tangled Up in Blue /
Simple Twist of Fate / You're a Big Girl
Now / Idiot Wind / You're Gonna
Make Me Lonesome When You Go /
Meet Me in the Morning / Lily,
Rosemary and the Jack of Hearts / If
You See Her, Say Hello / Shelter from
the Storm / Buckets of Rain

March 1, 1975
2 weeks

Following his stint with the Band and Asylum Records [see 170], Dylan returned to the Columbia Records fold. The result was one of his finest albums of the '70s, with the veteran singer-songwriter showing new maturity in his work. Although no producer was credited, legendary Columbia staff producer John Hammond was present at the sessions, while Phil Ramone, who had worked with Dylan and the Band on their 1974 live album, Before the Flood, was credited as engineer.

"They were very quiet, unassuming sessions," says Ramone. "John Hammond was there, but if anyone takes credit for producing Dylan, it's an interesting concept...Never turning off the tape machines was part of the way you recorded Dylan. The notes just poured out of him. He would go from one song to another, almost like a medley. After the first night, John and I sat and tried to figure out what the real album was."

The album ended up being Blood on the Tracks, which many consider Dylan's finest post-'60s work. For Dylan, it was a bittersweet time. The album was recorded in three or four days at A&R Recording in New York. "He was

extremely happy to be in that room, which had originally been owned by Columbia," says Ramone. "He had just come back to Columbia Records and he was going through hell with Sarah, his former wife, at the time."

While Dylan denied that the songs were autobiographical, many believe that they were, including Ramone, who says "You're a Big Girl Now" was written about Sarah. Dylan, however, has suggested that the songs on Blood on the Tracks, including the album-opener "Tangled Up in Blue," were influenced more by his interest in painting.

Whatever the case, Dylan "was loaded with songs," says Ramone. Accompanying Dylan on the album were bassist Tony Brown, steel guitarist Buddy Cage, organist Paul Griffin, and banjo player Eric Weissberg [see 154]. "They were all natural players who could shift with the wind, and that is what Dylan does—he is totally a man who is free musically. Dylan had never met the bass player before the sessions, which was not untypical of Dylan."

Such spontaneous methods of recording made it difficult for the session

players, Ramone says. "He doesn't telegraph what chords he is going to play. Sometimes he will have several bars and in the next version, he will change his mind about how many bars there should be in between a verse, or eliminate a verse, or add a chorus when you don't expect it. He is truly spontaneous in all ways of life."

Dylan, unhappy with an early version of Blood on the Tracks recorded in 1974, recut several tracks in Minneapolis in December of that year. However, Ramone says, "75 percent of Blood on the Tracks is the original album" that was cut in New York.

Blood on the Tracks also included such Dylan gems as "Simple Twist of Fate" and "Lily, Rosemary and the Jack of Hearts." But like many of Dylan's classic albums, it did not spawn a hit single. "Tangled Up in Blue," the only charting single from the album, stalled at number 33. Still, Blood on the Tracks made Number One in its fourth week on the chart, becoming Dylan's second chart-topper and second consecutive Number One studio album. Says Ramone, "It was a major turnaround in his life."

THE TOP FIVE
Week of March 1, 1975

1. **Blood on the Tracks**
   Bob Dylan

2. **AWB**
   Average White Band

3. **Heart Like a Wheel**
   Linda Ronstadt

4. **War Child**
   Jethro Child

5. **Do It ('Til You're Satisfied)**
   B.T. Express

MCA 2133 # Have You Never Been Mellow **195**
OLIVIA NEWTON-JOHN

Producer: John Farrar

Track listing: Have You Never Been Mellow / Loving Arms / Lifestream / Goodbye Again / Water Under the Bridge / I Never Did Sing You a Love Song / It's So Easy / The Air That I Breathe / Follow Me / And in the Morning / Please Mr. Please

March 15, 1975
1 week

With *If You Love Me, Let Me Know* [see 183], Olivia Newton-John became a pop sensation, but her appeal wasn't limited to the pop market. That album also topped the country chart, and Newton-John had scored top 10 country singles with "Let Me Be There," "If You Love Me (Let Me Know)," and "I Honestly Love You." She had also collected a Grammy Award for best female country vocal and a Country Music Association award for female country vocalist of the year in 1974.

Newton-John's victories raised the ire of some country performers, who didn't consider her music authentic country. "I created a controversy in Nashville, because I was an Australian girl, produced by an Englishman and an Australian, singing country music that wasn't written by me," she says. At the time, however, the singer was sheltered from the controversy. "I was on the road in a bus with my band touring the midwest, kind of getting established on the college circuit. I didn't really hear about it for a long time. My manager didn't tell me about it, which was good, because it would have been upsetting to me. I don't like people to think badly of me when I didn't do anything wrong."

Newton-John's third album, *Have You Never Been Mellow,* was recorded at EMI and Abbey Road studios in London with Beatles engineer Tony Clark, but it had little to do with the Fab Four. Instead, the singer continued to mine the country-pop field. "Goodbye Again" and "Follow Me" were penned by fellow country-pop crossover artist John Denver. Newton-John had scored a 1973 British hit with her version of Denver's "Take Me Home Country Roads," and in 1975 she would duet with Denver on his "Fly Away" [see 206].

Newton-John's longtime friend John Farrar once again served as producer and wrote the album's title track. "He played it for me on guitar. He always wrote on guitar," she says. "He has always written incredible melodies and lyrics. That song is a classic. It would still work now."

The singer first worked with Farrar when she was only 15 on the Australian TV program "Go Show." Farrar played guitar in the band, while Newton-John and Pat Carroll were featured singers. Newton-John and Carroll later performed together as Pat & Olivia. Eventually, Carroll and Farrar married.

Following the success of *If You Love Me, Let Me Know,* Newton-John and Farrar had a newfound confidence. "We started doing more of John's material," she says. Farrar also co-wrote the song "It's So Easy."

It was the title track, however, that helped Newton-John garner her second consecutive Number One album. On March 8, 1975, "Have You Never Been Mellow" became her second Number One single. A week later, Newton-John had another chart-topping album.

The album that *Have You Never Been Mellow* replaced at the top was Bob Dylan's *Blood on the Tracks.* Ironically, Newton-John's first American chart single, peaking at number 25 in 1971, had been a cover of Dylan's "If Not For You."

THE TOP FIVE
Week of March 15, 1975

1. **Have You Never Been Mellow**
   Olivia Newton-John

2. **Blood on the Tracks**
   Bob Dylan

3. **Physical Graffiti**
   Led Zeppelin

4. **Phoebe Snow**
   Phoebe Snow

5. **What Were Once Vices Are Now Habits**
   Doobie Brothers

196 Physical Graffiti SWAN SONG 200
LED ZEPPELIN

Producer: Jimmy Page

Track listing: Custard Pie / The Rover / In My Time of Dying / Houses of the Holy / Trampled Under Foot / Kashmir / In the Light / Bron-Y-Aur Stomp / Down by the Seaside / Ten Years Gone / Night Flight / The Wanton Song / Boogie with Stu / Black Country Woman / Sick Again

March 22, 1975
6 weeks

High on the success of *Houses of the Holy* [see 159], Led Zeppelin returned to the Headley Grange mansion where the band had recorded much of *Led Zeppelin III* [see 127] and *IV*. The band came armed with so much material, it was decided that the next album, *Physical Graffiti*, would be a two-record set. It was also set to be the debut release on Swan Song, Led Zeppelin's own Atlantic-distributed label.

The centerpiece of the album was a song called "Kashmir." Vocalist Robert Plant was inspired to write the lyrics for the song after completing a lengthy drive in southern Morocco. Guitarist Jimmy Page originally came up with the riff for the track with drummer John Bonham. Bassist John Paul Jones added the finishing touches.

"We had real strings and brass on that," says Jones. "On the main riff, I did all the Arabic parts on mellotron." Despite the fact that "Stairway to Heaven" is the band's best-known song, "Kashmir" is generally considered the ultimate Zeppelin track. "I'm inclined to agree with that," says Jones. "It was definitely one of my favorites."

The choice to record most of the album at Headley Grange, rather than at a traditional recording studio, once again gave Zeppelin's recorded material a loose, live feel. "In My Time of Dying," for example, ended with nearly a half-minute of conversation and laughter. "The tape tended to be running a lot," says Jones. "That was the vibe. It was recorded at a house, so there was a pretty relaxed vibe about the whole thing. It wasn't like we went in the studio everyday—we kind of lived in the studio. That captured the atmosphere, so we decided to leave it on the tape. There was always lots of laughing. It was like a boys' club. Everyone had a good time."

Another standout track was "Trampled Under Foot." Says Jones, "The instruments were set up all the time in the house. For 'Trampled Under Foot' I was playing the clavinet and just came across the riff while playing and I made it into a song."

A few of the tracks on *Physical Graffiti* were left over from previous album sessions, including "Houses of the Holy," "Down by the Seaside," and "Boogie with Stu." The latter cut featured Rolling Stones keyboardist Ian Stewart and was originally cut during the *Led Zeppelin IV* sessions. "Jimmy and Robert had worked that out," says Jones. "I was away for the day and Ian Stewart was there jamming along with them. It was a fantastic jam, because Stewart [was] a great boogie-woogie player. I came back the next day and added my bass part." The liner notes of the album credited the song to Bonham, Jones, Page, Plant, Stewart, and Mrs. Valens. The members of Led Zeppelin wanted to give a portion of the royalties to the mother of Richie Valens [see 312], since the song's lyrics were borrowed from Valens's "Ooh My Head."

Although *Physical Graffiti* was originally scheduled to be the debut release on Swan Song, the album's elaborate cover art, which features a New York City tenement with interchangeable images visible through the building's die-cut windows, forced a delay. Bad Company's self-titled debut [see 181] became the first Swan Song release and the label's first chart-topper. Within six months, *Physical Graffiti* also hit the peak, giving Led Zeppelin its fourth Number One album.

THE TOP FIVE
Week of March 22, 1975

1. **Physical Graffiti**
   Led Zeppelin

2. **Have You Never Been Mellow**
   Olivia Newton-John

3. **Blood on the Tracks**
   Bob Dylan

4. **What Were Once Vices Are Now Habits**
   Doobie Brothers

5. **Perfect Angel**
   Minnie Riperton

Producer: James William Guercio

Track listing: Anyway You Want /
Brand New Love Affair — Pt. I / Brand
New Love Affair — Pt. II / Never Been
in Love Before / Hideaway / Till We
Meet Again / Harry Truman / Oh,
Thank You Great Spirit / Long Time No
See / Ain't It Blue? / Old Days

May 3, 1975
2 weeks

With its eighth album, Chicago became an eight-piece band as percussionist Laudir de Oliveira, who was featured as a sideman on *Chicago VI* and *Chicago VII*, became a full-fledged member of the band. In September 1974, the band once again returned to Jim Guercio's Caribou Ranch to cut the album, which ended up as a single disc.

Success was beginning to take its toll on Chicago. "We were kind of tired and burned out," says drummer Danny Seraphine. "That's one of my least favorite albums." Nonetheless, the album featured two hit singles. "Harry Truman" was released in February, well in advance of the album. The song, written and sung by keyboardist Robert Lamm, peaked at number 13 on April 5, 1975, but didn't go over well in Japan, a country in which the band had been enjoying considerable success. While Truman may have been one of America's most trusted leaders, in Japan there was no love for the man who had ordered the atomic bombing of Hiroshima during World War II. "I could never figure out to this day why the record

company released 'Harry Truman' in Japan," Seraphine says. "I think it ruined our career for a long time there."

Still, there was no stopping Chicago in America. *Chicago VIII* hit Number One in its fourth week on the chart, knocking Led Zeppelin's *Physical Graffiti* [see 196] from the top spot. It was Chicago's fourth consecutive chart-topper. To celebrate the triumph, Chicago hit the road with the Beach Boys on a 12-city American tour during which the bands played to more than 700,000 people, who paid more than $7.5 million.

"Old Days," the second single from the album, was substantially less controversial than "Harry Truman," but it did raise tempers within the band. The song, written by trombonist/percussionist James Pankow, reached number five on June 7, 1975. Yet bassist/vocalist Peter Cetera, who sang lead on the track, wasn't a particularly big fan of the song filled with Pankow's childhood remembrances. "Peter hated the line 'Howdy Doody,'" says Seraphine. "We used to have arguments about that song. While it was a hit, we performed it live, but later we dropped it from the set. Musically, it's a neat song, but Peter thought the words were wimpy."

A third single from the album, "Brand New Love Affair (Pt. 1 & 2)," stalled at number 61, on September 20, 1975. But that's not to suggest that Chicago's popularity was beginning to wane—witness the success of their next album, *Chicago IX—Chicago's Greatest Hits* [see 209].

198 That's the Way of the World COLUMBIA 33280
EARTH, WIND & FIRE

Producer: Maurice White

Track listing: Shining Star / That's the Way of the World / Happy Feelin' / All About Love / Yearnin', Learnin' / Reasons / Africano / See the Light

May 17, 1975
3 weeks

In 1972, Curtis Mayfield scored his first Number One album with his soundtrack to Sig Shore's *Superfly* [see 148]. Nearly three years later, Earth, Wind & Fire recorded *That's the Way of the World*, a soundtrack to another Shore film. This time the success of the album by far overshadowed that of the movie, which quickly vanished from theaters.

That's the Way of the World, the movie, featured Harvey Keitel as an A&R man and Earth, Wind & Fire playing a role that came naturally to them: a credible R&B act on the rise. By the mid-'70s, the group scored a handful of soul hits and was beginning to make a serious dent on the album chart. Their 1973 album *Head to the Sky* reached number 27 and was later certified gold for sales of more than 500,000 copies, while 1974's *Open Our Eyes* reached number 15 and eventually surpassed sales of a million copies.

Vocalist/percussionist Philip Bailey says the time was right for Earth, Wind & Fire to hit the big time when they began working on their sixth album, *That's the Way of the World*. "We were at the point in the evolution of a band where you really begin to feel your legs and know who you are," he says. "We were on the road a lot in those days and very much in touch with the people."

To write and record the album, the band, led by singer Maurice White, holed up at the Caribou Ranch in Nederland, Colorado, the same studio where Chicago had recorded many of its Number One albums [see 163]. "At that time, Caribou was not open to everyone," says Bailey. "It was very prestigious to work there." EW&F rose to the occasion. "Since we were pretty

much isolated, we really focused and made one of our more intense records. In terms of concentration on the album, it was 24 hours a day."

The band also jelled as songwriters. Says Bailey, "Maurice and I were writing the same thing at the same time. There was a real feeling of camaraderie. It felt like everyone was on the same page."

The songs on the album were proof that the band was experiencing a creative high. "Shining Star," the first track on *That's the Way of the World* helped the group make history. On March 22, 1975, it topped the Hot R&B Singles chart. A week after *That's the Way of the World* hit the peak of the album

chart, "Shining Star" topped the Hot 100, making EW&F the first R&B act to simultaneously top the pop albums and singles charts.

While the album's title track went on to become a top five R&B hit, "Shining Star" became EW&F's signature tune. It was so popular that Shore decided to retitle the movie after the song, but even the new moniker couldn't help the ill-fated film.

Despite the flop at the box office, there was no stopping Earth, Wind & Fire. Says Bailey, "*That's the Way of the World* epitomized the energy and flair of Earth, Wind & Fire's glory days. That's really when we came into our own identity."

THE TOP FIVE
Week of May 17, 1975

1. **That's the Way of the World**
   Earth, Wind & Fire
2. **Chicago VIII**
   Chicago
3. **Tommy**
   Soundtrack
4. **Physical Graffiti**
   Led Zeppelin
5. **Straight Shooter**
   Bad Company

MCA 2142 # Captain Fantastic and the Brown Dirt Cowboy

ELTON JOHN

199

Producer: Gus Dudgeon

Track listing: Captain Fantastic and the Brown Dirt Cowboy / Tower of Babel / Bitter Fingers / Tell Me When the Whistle Blows / Someone Saved My Life Tonight / (Gotta Get a) Meal Ticket / Better Off Dead / Writing / We All Fall in Love Sometimes / Curtains

June 7, 1975
7 weeks (nonconsecutive)

Following the artistic disappointment of *Caribou* [see 177], Elton John and his longtime lyricist Bernie Taupin returned in peak form with the autobiographical *Captain Fantastic and the Brown Dirt Cowboy*. The former part of the title refers to the flamboyant singer-pianist, while the latter is a reference to the lyricist, whose words often invoke tales of the old West. "There's no doubt about it," says producer Gus Dudgeon. "*Captain Fantastic*, technically, musically, and compositionally, [is] the most cohesive Elton John album. It was very obviously going to be something special from the minute we first heard the songs."

To ensure that the album was a success, Taupin took extra pains to write the lyrics as a cohesive set, rather than just cranking out a series of songs. John wrote the music on an ocean liner during a trip from France to New York. John and company took a full month to record the album, rather than a mere week or two, as had been their usual practice. Once again, John chose to work at the Caribou Ranch in Colorado, but by this time Dudgeon had overcome the hurdles that had hampered the *Caribou* sessions. "By then, I had it all sussed out," says Dudgeon. "I basically recorded it completely flat and did all the work on the mix."

Although Dudgeon is not a big fan of concept albums, *Captain Fantastic* worked, with the lyrical concept providing a guideline for the actual recording of the album. "We recorded the songs in running order," says Dudgeon. "In most cases, I did the overdubs in running order, and I mixed them in running order. All the time we were doing it, we knew exactly what was going to occur in the running order, so we knew how to make everything adjust to what came before and what came after."

Captain Fantastic also captured the Elton John Band—bassist Dee Murray, guitarist Davey Johnstone, drummer Nigel Olsson, and percussionist Ray Cooper—in prime form. "The band was in its absolute peak," says Dudgeon. "They played and sang the best they ever had done." The material was also top-notch. "There's hardly a song I don't like," says Dudgeon.

Of particular note is "Someone Saved My Life Tonight," a heartfelt ballad about John's failed suicide attempt and his near-marriage to his old girlfriend Linda Woodrow. "That's an absolutely stunning song and I love the performance of it," says Dudgeon. "It's got a great atmosphere. The only thing I hate about it is the awful string-synthesizer that comes in a quarter of the way through, but that's the only thing that was available at the time." The record-buying public and radio programmers, however, didn't seem to mind, as the single eventually reached number four on the Hot 100.

The album's closing tracks, "We All Fall in Love Sometimes" and "Curtains," were recorded as one long piece of music, although they were separated on the album. The session wowed studio guest Neil Sedaka. "He was just sitting there saying, 'Oh my God, are they really going to do that all in one go?'," recalls Dudgeon.

Upon its release, *Captain Fantastic and the Brown Dirt Cowboy* made an equally shocking impact on the Top LP's & Tapes chart. It was not only John's sixth Number One album, it was the first album ever to *enter* the chart at Number One.

THE TOP FIVE
Week of June 7, 1975

1. **Captain Fantastic and the Brown Dirt Cowboy**
   Elton John

2. **That's the Way of the World**
   Earth, Wind & Fire

3. **Tommy**
   Soundtrack

4. **Blow By Blow**
   Jeff Beck

5. **Hearts**
   America

200 Venus and Mars CAPITOL 11419
WINGS

Producer: Paul McCartney

Track listing: Venus and Mars / Rock Show / Love in Song / You Gave Me the Answer / Magneto and Titanium Man / Letting Go / Venus and Mars—Reprise / Spirits of Ancient Egypt / Medicine Jar / Call Me Back Again / Listen to What the Man Said / Treat Her Gently—Lonely Old People

July 19, 1975
1 week

Venus and Mars is significant to Paul McCartney's career for a number of reasons. Most notably, it became McCartney's third consecutive Number One album (and fourth overall) since leaving the Beatles. Two other factors suggested that McCartney was willing to leave the Beatles behind him: *Venus and Mars* was credited simply to "Wings," rather than "Paul McCartney and Wings," and it was the first effort by a former Beatle not to be issued on Apple, the label the Beatles founded in 1968.

McCartney said giving the group a supporting credit, as was the case on *Red Rose Speedway* [see 161] and *Band on the Run* [see 173], "was an embarrassment to me" in Jeremy Pascall's *Paul McCartney and Wings*. "It was never Paul McCartney and the Beatles, Paul McCartney and the Quarrymen, or Paul McCartney and the Moondogs. Wings is quicker and easier to say and everybody knows I'm in the group anyway."

By early 1975, even before *Band on the Run* had hit the top of the chart, Wings was once again a quintet with

THE TOP FIVE
Week of July 19, 1975

1. **Venus and Mars**
   Wings

2. **Captain Fantastic and the Brown Dirt Cowboy**
   Elton John

3. **One of These Nights**
   The Eagles

4. **Love Will Keep Us Together**
   The Captain & Tennille

5. **Cut the Cake**
   Average White Band

the addition of guitarist Jimmy McCulloch, formerly of Thunderclap Newman and Stone the Crows, and drummer Geoff Britton. Britton's stay, however, was brief. Although the band recorded "Love in Song," "Letting Go," and "Medicine Jar" with the drummer at Allen Toussaint's Sea Saint houseboat studio in New Orleans, he was replaced by Joe English in February 1975, when the band moved to Wally Heider Studios in Los Angeles.

While the personnel change was an annoyance, as was a minor brush with the law (Linda McCartney was busted for carrying a small amount of marijuana in her purse while the band was recording in Los Angeles), those troubles were minor compared to the *Band on the Run* sessions.

With little adversity, McCartney emerged with another fine album. The anthem "Rockshow" made references to triumphant moments in McCartney's career, including the Concertgebow in Amsterdamn, which Wings had played in 1972, and the Hollywood Bowl, where the Beatles had performed a string of historic dates. The album's title track was reprised on side two, much like the Beatles' "Sgt. Pepper's Lonely Hearts Club Band."

Former Traffic member Dave Mason

was featured playing guitar on the album's first single, "Listen to What the Man Said," McCartney's favorite song on the album. But McCartney reserved his praise for another guest musician. "I really liked what Tom Scott did on there with the sax," he told Timothy White in the book *Rock Lives*. "We just went for it live."

The public also took a liking to the song, which hit the top of the Hot 100 just as *Venus and Mars* rose to the summit of the album chart.

Another track on *Venus and Mars*, "Medicine Jar," which was written by McCulloch and his friend Colin Allen from Stone the Crows, would take on an ominous meaning following McCulloch's death from heart failure in September 1979. "Jimmy wanted to write an anti-drug song," McCartney told White. "As to *why*, I'm not sure, but I'd say he'd seen the personal warning signs. That song, I think, was Jimmy talking to himself. Listening to it now and knowing the circumstances of how he died, I'm sure that's what it is. He's really saying to himself, 'Get your hand out of the medicine jar.' I don't think he managed to. He was a great guitar player, but he was into a little too much heavy stuff. But if I'm reading too much into it, then let's just say I'm just as bad as the fucking critics, okay?"

ASYLUM 1039 # One of These Nights
EAGLES
201

Producer: Bill Szymczyk

Track listing: One of These Nights / Too Many Hands / Hollywood Waltz / Journey of the Sorcerer / Lyin' Eyes / Take It to the Limit / Visions / After the Thrill is Gone / I Wish You Peace

July 26, 1975
5 weeks

After initially making their mark as Linda Ronstadt's backing band [see 192], the Eagles took flight in 1972 with their self-titled debut album, which reached number 22. The band's subsequent efforts, 1973's *Desperado* and 1974's *On the Border*, clocked in at number 41 and 17, respectively, but it was the band's fourth album, *One of These Nights*, that put the Eagles among the ranks of pop music's superstars.

Although the Eagles were based in Los Angeles, *One of These Nights* marked the first full album the band recorded in America. The group's first two albums were recorded in England with producer Glyn Johns, known for his work with the Rolling Stones [see 132]. With *On the Border*, says drummer/ vocalist Don Henley, "We cut two tracks over there and we got homesick, basically. We were tired of England. That's also when we changed producers."

For *One of These Nights*, the band (which also included singer/guitarist Glenn Frey, guitarists Bernie Leadon and Don Felder, and bassist Randy Meisner), opted to stay with producer Bill Szym-czyk, who had taken over *On the Border*, and returned to Criteria Studios in Miami. At the close of the *On the Border* sessions, Felder had been asked to become a full member of the band.

At the time, Henley and Frey were roommates in a house that overlooked the Sunset Strip and was built in 1942 for Dorothy Lamour. "It had a music room in it and we converted it to a recording studio and rehearsal space," says Henley. "Glenn and I would go home and listen to Ohio Players [see 191] and Al Green records. We called that period our occult/country-rock/R&B period."

The latter genre isn't usually associated with the Eagles, but Henley insists it was an influence. " 'One of These Nights' is a rhythm & blues track as far as I'm concerned," he says. "The drum style, when you hit the snare and the tom at the same time, was heavily influenced by Al Green records."

The song was written during a particularly productive period. "We wrote 'One of These Nights' and 'Lyin' Eyes' in the same afternoon," says Henley. "We were very excited when we wrote those songs. We knew we had something good. 'Lyin' Eyes' wrote itself. We just sat down and it came pouring out."

Although the group was "growing out of country-rock," Henley nonetheless calls "Lyin' Eyes" the band's "quintessential country-rock song." Part of the reason for the change in producers was the band's shift in direction. "We were excited about getting more hard-edged and more rock 'n' roll oriented," says Henley. "We knew we were headed somewhere. Things were getting better and the band was getting better. We were defining a direction for ourselves."

The album closer, "I Wish You Peace" was written by Leadon and his then-girlfriend, Patti Davis, daughter of future President Ronald Reagan. Davis's songwriting credit annoyed Henley, who felt she hadn't contributed much to the song. This put him at odds with Leadon. "There was a lot of tension in the band at that point," Henley says.

Tension or not, the Eagles jelled on *One of These Nights*. In its fifth week on the chart, the album made Number One. A week later, the title track hit Number One on the Hot 100.

THE TOP FIVE
Week of July 26, 1975

1. **One of These Nights**
   Eagles

2. **Venus and Mars**
   Paul McCartney & Wings

3. **Love Will Keep Us Together**
   The Captain & Tenille

4. **Captain Fantastic and the Brown Dirt Cowboy**
   Elton John

5. **Cut the Cake**
   Average White Band

202 Red Octopus GRUNT 0999
JEFFERSON STARSHIP

Producers: Jefferson Starship, Larry Cox

Track listing: Fast Buck Freddie / Miracles / Git Fiddler / Al Garimasu / Sweeter Than Honey / Play on Love / Tumblin / I Want to See Another World / Sandalphon / There Will Be Love

September 6, 1975
4 weeks (nonconsecutive)

Jefferson Starship had gone through a decade, numerous lineups, and a name change, but the band had yet to score a Number One album when it went into the studio to record its 14th LP, *Red Octopus*.

Formed in San Francisco in early 1965, the band, then known as Jefferson Airplane, was one of the forerunners of the Haight-Ashbury psychedelic scene. Its first album, *Jefferson Airplane Takes Off*, only reached number 128, but the group's fortunes changed with the addition of singer Grace Slick. *Surrealistic Pillow*, released in early 1967, reached number three, propelled by the hits "Somebody to Love" and "White Rabbit." It would take the group nearly a decade to chart that high again.

By 1974, the band had changed its lineup and its name to the more modern-sounding Jefferson Starship and enlisted 19-year-old lead guitar player Craig Chaquico, formerly of the band Steelwind. Original member Marty Balin, who had left the group, rejoined in early 1975 alongside co-founder/guitarist Paul Kantner. Other members included 58-year-old violinist Papa John Creach, bassist/keyboard player Pete Sears, bassist/keyboardist David Freiberg, and drummer John Barbata. "There was definitely a band feeling," says Chaquico, "because it was a big band."

Although some accused the Starship of moving in an overly commercial direction on *Red Octopus*, Chaquico says that wasn't the intent. "Everybody was doing music based solely on their artistic, creative inspiration and intuition. Nobody thought for a second about the charts. That was the furthest thing from our minds.

"We really didn't think about it as a record with commercial top 40 singles," he adds. Indeed, the most accessible track on the album, the Balin ballad "Miracles," clocked in at nearly seven minutes. "It wasn't until later that all of us and our producer thought about doing a shorter version of it." The edited version, which reached number three and became the band's biggest hit to date, also omitted some of the suggestive lyrics on the original that might possibly have hindered its chances for top 40 airplay.

The fact that the Starship had several writers from diverse backgrounds was reflected in the album's material. "The styles ranged from my hard-rock roots to Marty's Airplane folk roots, to Grace's and Paul's styles," Chaquico says.

Red Octopus contains two instrumental tracks, "Git Fiddler" and "Sandalphon." A third track, "Sweeter Than Honey," was originally an instrumental. "When we first played that song live at a big benefit show in San Francisco, Marty was caught in traffic, so we had to go onstage before he was there. We played 'Sweeter Than Honey.' After a couple minutes, Marty came running onstage and started singing the lyrics he was working on."

Although the band recorded the album in approximately three months at Wally Heiders studio in San Francisco, the finishing touches were applied while the Starship was touring. "Our tour was already booked, so we were still mixing and reviewing mixes while we were on the road," says Chaquico.

Red Octopus hit Number One a total of three separate times over a 12-week period, but Chaquico couldn't enjoy the festivities the first time around. "The first time it went to Number One, we were on the road and I wasn't old enough to get into the hotel bar to celebrate," he says.

THE TOP FIVE
Week of September 6, 1975

1. **Red Octopus**
   Jefferson Starship

2. **Captain Fantastic and the Brown Dirt Cowboy**
   Elton John

3. **Between the Lines**
   Janis Ian

4. **One of These Nights**
   The Eagles

5. **The Heat Is On**
   Isley Brothers

The Heat Is On
THE ISLEY BROTHERS
T-NECK 33536

203

Producer: The Isley Brothers

Track listing: Fight the Power (Part 1 & 2) / The Heat Is On (Part 1 & 2) / Hope You Feel Better Love (Part 1 & 2) / For the Love of You (Part 1 & 2) / Sensuality (Part 1 & 2) / Make Me Say It Again Girl (Part 1 & 2)

September 13, 1975
1 week

Ernie Isley can still remember the words of CBS Records executive Ronald Alexenberg during a party where the Isley Brothers were being presented with a gold single for "That Lady" and gold albums for *3 + 3* and *Live It Up*. "He said if the next album has the same quality as the last two, it'll go platinum. We felt that was astounding," says Ernie, "because only the biggest groups were going platinum at that time."

The Isleys were certainly on a roll. The group's 1973 album, *3 + 3*, which had featured younger brothers Ernie, Marvin, and cousin Chris Jasper on an album cover for the first time, had marked the veteran R&B act's album chart high when it had reached number eight. While the Isleys, founded by brothers Ronald, Rudolph, and O'Kelly in the early '50s, weren't necessarily an album chart force, the group was a virtual pop and R&B hit machine, churning out such '60s and '70s classics as "Shout," "Twist and Shout," "It's Your Thing," and "That Lady."

It was almost immediately following the completion of 1974's *Live It Up* that Ernie came up with "Fight the Power." He recalls, "We decided to stay in L.A. for an extra couple days and fly out our

mother, my brothers' wives, and the kids. We could have done a commercial. 'The Isley Brothers have just finished their latest album, what are you going to do now?' 'We're going to Disneyland.' " With his family flying in, the album completed, and his first trip to Disneyland on the horizon, Ernie was in an upbeat mood. "I stepped into the shower and started singing this song. The inspiration was like a bolt of lightning. After I sang the first few lines, I realized that it was a song. I jumped out of the shower, soap and water flying everywhere. I grabbed a piece of paper, wrote it down, and stuffed it inside my guitar case."

By the fall of 1974, the group had recorded a demo version of "Fight the Power" and several other tracks that would round out *The Heat Is On* on a four-track machine in the basement of their mother's home in Inglewood, New Jersey.

Yet the demo session didn't make it much easier to record the album once the group entered Kendun Recorders in Los Angeles. "In a basement setting we could get a full sound with four tracks musically with bass, drums, keyboards, and guitar," Ernie says. "In a professional recording studio, that was hardly

even a skeleton. So we had to create other parts that had to be created virtually on the spot to fill out the songs."

But within a week, the instrumental half of the Isleys—guitarist/drummer Ernie, bassist Marvin, and keyboardist Jasper—were able to complete the basic tracks, leaving Ronald, Rudolph, and O'Kelly to work their vocal magic.

Following a long-established Isleys tradition, each track on the album was presented in a lengthy version, subtitled "part 1 & 2." When the songs were released as singles, they were edited down and billed simply as "part 1."

Each side of the album had a distinctive mood. "It has a dance side, or a fast side, and a slow side or love-making side," says Ernie. "We were told by numerous people how much they dug that concept." One of the tracks on the slow side, "For The Love of You," would later be recorded by Whitney Houston [see 311].

On July 19, 1975, "Fight the Power" became the Isley's second Number One R&B hit. Two months later, *The Heat Is On* hit the summit of the Top LPs & Tapes chart, becoming the Isley's first and only Number One album. And, as Alexenberg predicted, the album did go platinum.

204 Between the Lines COLUMBIA 33394
JANIS IAN

Producer: Brooks Arthur

Track listing: When the Party's Over / At Seventeen / From Me to You / Bright Lights and Promises / In the Winter / Water Colors / Between the Lines / The Come On / Light a Light / Tea & Sympathy / Lover's Lullaby

September 20, 1975
1 week

Success came early for Janis Ian. At the age of 14, she wrote and recorded "Society's Child (Baby, I've Been Thinking)," a controversial tale of an interracial romance that was too hot for 22 record companies. Eventually, Verve Folkways Records signed Ian and released the track, but radio wouldn't touch it. However, the song caught the ear of Leonard Bernstein, who invited Ian to appear on the CBS television special "The Pop Arts." Following the TV exposure, radio stations finally began playing the song. More controversy ensued as the single climbed to number 14 in July 1967, while Ian's self-titled debut album reached number 29.

Another album, *For All the Seasons of the Mind,* followed in 1968, but it failed to repeat Ian's early success. Growing tired of the sexism she was encountering in the music business, Ian announced her retirement in 1968. Three years later, however, she returned, signing to Capitol Records, which released an album to disappointing sales.

The Ian-penned ballad "Jesse" became a top 30 hit for Roberta Flack in October 1973, but Ian's debut album for Columbia Records, *Stars,* which fea-

tured her own version of the song, stalled at number 83 in 1974. Then came *Between the Lines.*

"Nobody thought I would do anything again," Ian says. "A lot of people were surprised." Ian herself didn't have time to be surprised by her second career success. "I was on the road for seven months, I would write for two months, then I would go into the studio and record for three months," she says.

The album was produced by Brooks Arthur, who mixed "Society's Child." Ian says that the sessions, held at 914 Sound Studios in Blauvelt, New York, went so well that she "kept pushing to do six more tracks for the next album, but I couldn't find anyone to agree with me."

Before *Between the Lines* became a hit, Ian struggled playing the club circuit and living on whatever money she made at gigs. While recording the album, a struggling artist by the name

of Bruce Springsteen was laying down "Born to Run" at the same studio. "We hung out at the diner together," Ian recalls. "We were both starving."

The song that helped propel *Between the Lines* to the top of the album chart was "At Seventeen," a confessional ballad about teenage isolation and insecurity, which climbed to number three. "I realized it was a hit when it was sold out all the time," she says. "And when I performed the song, people started clapping after the first few bars. I never thought it would endure the way it has. It is an amazing thing to tap into something that universal."

Between the Lines garnered five Grammy nominations, which at the time was the most ever a female artist had received in one year. Ian won for best female pop vocal performance, while the album was honored as the best-engineered non-classical recording.

THE TOP FIVE
Week of September 20, 1975

1. **Between the Lines**
   Janis Ian

2. **The Heat Is On**
   The Isley Brothers

3. **Honey**
   Ohio Players

4. **Red Octopus**
   Jefferson Starship

5. **Captain Fantastic and the Brown Dirt Cowboy**
   Elton John

COLUMBIA 33453 **Wish You Were Here** **205**
PINK FLOYD

Engineer: Brian Humphries

Track listing: Shine on You Crazy Diamond (Part I–V) / Welcome to the Machine / Have a Cigar / Wish You Were Here / Shine on You Crazy Diamond (Part VI–IX)

October 4, 1975
2 weeks

Following the massive success of *The Dark Side of the Moon*, perhaps it was only appropriate for Pink Floyd to take a look back and pay tribute to Syd Barrett, their original guiding force. Barrett not only christened the band Pink Floyd Sound (after a blues record by Pink Anderson and Floyd Council), he also wrote much of the band's early material, including the 1967 British hits "Arnold Layne" and "See Emily Play." Barrett was also chiefly responsible for the band's psychedelic sound, but by 1968 his drug use had gotten the best of him and he left the band. He later made two influential but commercially unsuccessful solo albums before vanishing into seclusion.

Nearly a decade later, Pink Floyd saluted its former leader with "Shine On You Crazy Diamond," which served as the opening and closing track to *Wish You Were Here*. The album's title also suggested a tribute to Barrett. In fact, many Floyd fans suggested that the band had been thinking of Barrett on "Brain Damage" from *The Dark Side of the Moon*, but Floyd singer/bassist Roger Waters has said that was not the case.

" 'Shine On You Crazy Diamond' was especially about Syd, because he had re-emerged at that point and had started coming to sessions again," Waters once said. "But all that stuff in 'Brain Damage' about 'if the band you're in starts playing different tunes,' I think this was more for me than Syd."

While Waters said he was not "very conscious" of Barrett during the making of *The Dark Side of the Moon*, Barrett served as a definite inspiration for *Wish You Were Here*, which the band began recording in January 1975 at Abbey Road studios.

In fact, one day while the band was putting the finishing touches on "Shine On You Crazy Diamond," Barrett appeared at the studio. The story of Barrett's mysterious reappearance is detailed in *Pink Floyd: Shine On*, a book included with a boxed set containing seven of the band's albums: "He just arrived unannounced, looking fat, bald and haunted. Some of the band didn't immediately recognise him, others were close to tears. Roger confided later that he cried. Syd asked at one point if there was anything he could do and that he was available if needed. He hadn't been seen for seven years. He wasn't seen again."

The period in which the album was made wasn't a particular high point for Pink Floyd. "I definitely think that at the beginning of *Wish You Where Here* recording sessions most of us didn't wish we were there at all, we wished we were somewhere else," Waters told Nick Sedgewick. "I wasn't happy being there because I got the feeling we

weren't together, the band wasn't at all together."

The band's disillusionment was also expressed in "Have a Cigar" and "Welcome to the Machine," which attacked the music industry.

With *The Dark Side of the Moon* having secured Pink Floyd's reputation, *Wish You Were Here* shot to the pole position in only its second week on the chart. As Waters explained to Nick Sedgewick, the band's name alone was enough to secure a hit. "The name 'Pink Floyd,' the name, not us, not the individuals in the band, but the name Pink Floyd is worth millions of pounds. The name is probably worth one million sales of an album, any album we put out. Even if we just coughed, a million people will have ordered it simply because of the name."

THE TOP FIVE
Week of October 4, 1975

1. **Wish You Were Here**
   Pink Floyd

2. **Windsong**
   John Denver

3. **One of These Nights**
   The Eagles

4. **Born to Run**
   Bruce Springsteen

5. **Between the Lines**
   Janis Ian

206 Windsong RCA 1183
JOHN DENVER

Producer: Milton Okun

Track listing: Windsong / Love Is Everywhere / Spirit / Looking for Space / Shipmates and Cheyenne / Late Nite Radio / Cowboy's Delight / Two Shots / I'm Sorry / Fly Away / Calypso / Song of Wyoming

October 18, 1975
2 weeks

"The country album *Back Home Again* [see 178] was to a large degree about how people live in the country," says John Denver. "*Windsong* is on a more spiritual level. Some of the songs are a little further out there. It's more about the environment."

The title track was written one night at Denver's home in Aspen, Colorado, with frequent Denver collaborator Joe Henry. "One night he was at my house and we were talking about the wind," Denver says. "I went to bed that night and the next morning Joe had left, but laying on the kitchen cabinet was this poem. It was beautiful. I sat with that poem and found music there. I ended up changing a few words and a phrase here and there and we ended up having a song. It was a wonderful way to open the album and concerts."

Other songs, such as "Looking for Space," had a deep philosophical bent. "It's about looking for the definition of who you are, by finding out where you are, not only physically, but mentally and emotionally."

In 1975, Denver was still one of the top male pop singers, so popular that many of his peers were inspired by his music. Olivia Newton-John had covered Denver's "Take Me Home Country Roads" in 1973. Denver was so taken

by Newton-John's version that when he decided his song "Fly Away" needed a female voice on it, he called her and asked her to guest on the cut. "I gave her a tape and she took it home and came up with a number of complex vocal parts that were beautiful," Denver says.

"Calypso" was inspired by one of Denver's heroes, famed marine specialist Jacques Cousteau. For one of Denver's TV specials, the singer spent six days on Cousteau's ship called the *Calypso*. Denver had hoped to write a song to serve as backdrop for the piece when it was broadcast on television, but he developed writer's block. "Moments after coming aboard the ship I had the chorus and a great idea for this song, but I couldn't finish it and it was driving me crazy. I had in my mind that I wanted it to be a cowboy's version of a sea chantey."

Frustrated, Denver returned home to

Aspen and hit the ski slopes. "I skied two or three runs, but then I knew I had to go back home to finish the song," he says. In a burst of creativity that mirrored the writing of "Annie's Song" [see 178], Denver returned home and finished "Calypso" in 20 minutes. It was three weeks after the first chorus had come to him aboard Cousteau's ship.

"Calypso," the flip of a double-A-side single that also included "I'm Sorry," became Denver's fourth and final Number One single on September 27, 1975. Today, Denver says that putting two songs on one single was a big mistake. "I got a little arrogant," he says. "I wanted a two-sided hit to go to Number One." Denver is convinced that *Windsong* would have even been more successful had "I'm Sorry" and "Calypso" been released as two separate singles. Nonetheless, *Windsong* became Denver's third and final album to hit the top in its third week on the chart.

THE TOP FIVE
Week of October 18, 1975

1. **Windsong**
   John Denver

2. **Wish You Were Here**
   Pink Floyd

3. **Born to Run**
   Bruce Springsteen

4. **Red Octopus**
   Jefferson Starship

5. **Win, Lose or Draw**
   Allman Brothers Band

MCA 2163 # Rock of the Westies
ELTON JOHN

207

Producer: Gus Dudgeon

Track listing: Medley (Yell Help / Wednesday Night / Ugly) / Dan Dare (Pilot of the Future) / Island Girl / Grow Some Funk of Your Own / I Feel Like a Bullet (in the Gun of Robert Ford) / Street Kids / Hard Luck Story / Feed Me / Billy Bones and the White Bird

November 8, 1975
3 weeks

On the eve of the release of *Captain Fantastic and the Brown Dirt Cowboy* [see 199], Elton John made a surprise move, firing his longtime rhythm section of bassist Dee Murray and drummer Nigel Olsson. Lead guitarist Davey Johnstone and percussionist Ray Cooper stayed on, but the rest of John's band was comprised of new and old faces. Drummer Roger Pope and guitarist Caleb Quaye both had worked with John in the past—Pope played on *Empty Sky*, John's first album, which was belatedly released in 1975 in America; Quaye had played with John in Bluesology in 1966 and on John's self-titled 1970 album—while the new bass player, Kenny Passarelli, was featured on Joe Walsh's "Rocky Mountain Way," one of John's favorite songs. Rounding out the new group was a second keyboardist, James Newton Howard, known for his work with Melissa Manchester.

The new lineup, however, wasn't necessarily a good thing, as *Rock of the Westies*, like *Caribou* before it, turned out to be another commercial triumph but a major artistic disappointment, at least in the eyes of producer Gus Dudgeon. "It was a bit tricky," he says, "because we were dealing with a different bunch of people. It's not

one of my favorite albums."

For the third straight album, John and company opted to record at the Caribou Ranch. As was the case with *Caribou*, there were problems in the studio during the *Rock of the Westies* sessions, but this time it wasn't the equipment. "I remember a dreadful session with LaBelle [who were singing backing vocals]," says Dudgeon. "In the control room they were fine, you could teach them their harmonies, but as soon as they went into the studio they forgot their harmonies and blamed each other for singing the wrong parts. It was just a nightmare." Dudgeon was in such a rush to get through the session, he accidentally forgot to record their part on the last chorus of "Medley." Says Dudgeon, "I made myself an enormous joint, walked into the studio, and imitated LaBelle. If you hear the multi-tracks, it sounds like some Duchess singing, but

nobody's ever spotted it. Not even Elton."

The Caribbean-flavored "Island Girl" went on to become John's third Number One single of 1975 and the fifth of his career, but Dudgeon says it is his least favorite of John's chart-toppers. "Street Kids" has "a good vibe," says Dudgeon. "It's kind of smelly, like it should be." But there were problems—guitarist Davey Johnstone's role was minimized due to a personality conflict with some of the new band members. "There was some weirdness going on," Dudgeon says. "And it's reflected on the album."

Turmoil or no, *Rock of the Westies* had the same commercial clout as its predecessors. Like *Captain Fantastic and the Brown Dirt Cowboy* had done six months earlier, it entered at Number One, making John the first and only artist to score two Number One debuts in one calendar year.

THE TOP FIVE
Week of November 8, 1975

1. **Rock of the Westies**
   Elton John

2. **Red Octopus**
   Jefferson Starship

3. **Wish You Were Here**
   Pink Floyd

4. **Prisoner in Disguise**
   Linda Ronstadt

5. **Windsong**
   John Denver

208 Still Crazy After All These Years WARNER BROS. 25591
PAUL SIMON

Producers: Paul Simon and Phil Ramone

Track listing: Still Crazy After All These Years / My Little Town / I Do It For Your Love / 50 Ways to Leave Your Lover / Night Game / Gone at Last / Some Folks' Lives Roll Easy / Have a Good Time / You're Kind / Silent Eyes

December 6, 1975
1 week

After the dissolution of Simon & Garfunkel [see 119], Paul Simon launched a successful solo career. His self-titled 1972 debut reached number four, as did the single "Mother and Child Reunion." His 1973 follow-up album, There Goes Rhymin' Simon, spent two weeks at number two, but was unable to knock George Harrison's Living in the Material World from the top. While 1974's Paul Simon in Concert/Live Rhymin' stalled at number 33, Simon's third studio effort would prove to be historic on two counts: It would go on to become his first Number One solo album and it contained his first record-

ing with Art Garfunkel since the duo's split in 1969.

The song, titled "My Little Town," was included on both Simon's Still Crazy After All These Years and Garfunkel's Breakaway. "It was at a time when there had been enough separation and time between the two of them," says co-producer Phil Ramone. "The competition was not important, and as it has been proved over and over again, they have always been friends. Artie wanted a more up tune on his album. He and Paul had met and talked about it and Paul felt that this was the tune that could be shared well between the two of them."

Garfunkel wasn't the only special guest to turn up on Still Crazy. Phoebe Snow and the Jessy Dixon Singers were featured on the gospel-flavored "Gone at Last," a track originally written as a duet for Bette Midler. Says Ramone, "That was a great lesson for me and for Paul. It started out as a song that had been recorded too slow. We tried to fix it and fix it, then finally he looked at me and said, 'We should never do this. We

should just recut that track.' And that was the method in which Paul and I worked from there on out. We went back and recut it live, but we laugh at that now, because we both knew that we cut it too fast, after struggling with it being too slow."

Another guest was saxophonist Michael Brecker on the jazz-oriented "Some Folks' Lives Roll Easy." Says Ramone, "Everyone in the world on the musical side knows about that solo. It was one of those great first-take things. Both Paul and I came from the school of immediacy."

The album's best-known track, however, is "50 Ways to Leave Your Lover," Simon's own darkly humorous take on his divorce from his first wife, Peggy, and his first Number One solo single. It began as a series of rhymes Simon sang to his son Harper in the bathtub. Later, in the studio, "Paul was screwing around with a little drum machine, mixing a samba with some other beat," says Ramone. "At the time, [drummer] Steve Gadd was out in the studio warming up, doing military paradiddles and Paul just loved it. That just changed the whole groove of the song."

The album's title ballad and "Have a Good Time" were written for the Warren Beatty film Shampoo, but Beatty passed on them. Missing out on the film tie-in didn't hurt Simon's record sales, however. The inclusion of Simon & Garfunkel tracks in The Graduate may have been a key in launching his career, but by 1975 Simon was a huge star in his own right, and Still Crazy After All These Years hit the summit in its seventh week on the chart.

THE TOP FIVE
Week of December 6, 1975

1. **Still Crazy After All These Years**
   Paul Simon

2. **Red Octopus**
   Jefferson Starship

3. **Windsong**
   John Denver

4. **Rock of the Westies**
   Elton John

5. **Chicago IX—Chicago's Greatest Hits**
   Chicago

Chicago IX—Chicago's Greatest Hits

COLUMBIA 33900

CHICAGO

209

Producer: James William Guercio

Track listing: 25 or 6 to 4 / Does Anybody Really Know What Time It Is? / Colour My World / Just You 'n' Me / Saturday in the Park / Feelin' Stronger Every Day / Make Me Smile / Wishing You Were Here / Call On Me / (I've Been) Searchin' So Long / Beginnings

December 13, 1975
5 weeks

Chicago never wanted to be known as a singles band, so it must have been a bit ironic when Columbia compiled the band's popular singles for a greatest-hits album in late 1975.

As it happens, Chicago was ambivalent about singles on a number of levels. In particular, they were never crazy about the way their songs were often edited for a single release. In fact, Chicago started recording shorter songs because they "got sick and tired of

songs getting chopped up," says drummer Danny Seraphine. When Seraphine first heard the edited version of "Make Me Smile" on his car radio while driving on the Ventura Freeway in Los Angeles, he almost drove right off the road.

Even with the band at the height of its popularity, its songs were still being edited. The versions of "Make Me Smile" and "Does Anybody Really Know What Time It Is?" included on Chicago's Greatest Hits are the edited single versions. The rest of the tracks on the album, however, are presented as full-length album cuts, including "Beginnings," which clocks in at nearly eight minutes.

"25 or 6 to 4," the band's second hit and the lead track on Chicago's Greatest Hits, is perhaps the most misunderstood Chicago track. "It's a song about writing a song," explains Seraphine. Keyboardist Robert Lamm, who penned the song, was having trouble writing a song. " '25 or 6 to 4' in the morning is the time in which the

song was written," Seraphine says.

Chicago's Greatest Hits features songs from the band's 1969 debut, Chicago Transit Authority, which peaked at number 17, through 1974's Chicago VII [see 174]. Since Chicago VIII [see 197] had been released earlier in 1975, Columbia opted to leave that album's hits off of Chicago's Greatest.

Chicago's Greatest Hits, like its predecessors, sports the band's trademark Roman numerals in its title. Seraphine says it was producer/manager Jim Guercio's idea to number the LPs. "He felt if there were numbers on them, it would give them a sense of timelessness, like volumes of encyclopedias." While the band occasionally strayed from the concept for an album, the following LP would then pick up the numerical sequence.

Chicago's Greatest Hits shot to the top of the album chart in a mere three weeks. It was the group's fifth consecutive Number One album, a feat matched only by Paul McCartney [see 221] and Elton John [see 190], and surpassed only by the Beatles [see 95].

Although the band had managed to top the album chart five consecutive times, Chicago didn't have as much luck on the Hot 100. As of late 1975, the highest-charting Chicago single was "Saturday in the Park," which reached number three on September 23, 1972. Chicago would finally land the elusive Number One single with "If You Leave Me Now," which hit the top of the Hot 100 on October 23, 1976. However, Chicago X, the album from which that single was culled, made it only to number three, snapping the group's streak of Number One albums at five.

THE TOP FIVE

Week of December 13 , 1975

1. **Chicago IX—Chicago's Greatest Hits**
   Chicago

2. **Red Octopus**
   Jefferson Starship

3. **Rock of the Westies**
   Elton John

4. **Windsong**
   John Denver

5. **KC & the Sunshine Band**
   KC & the Sunshine Band

210 Gratitude COLUMBIA 33694
EARTH, WIND & FIRE

Producers: Maurice White, Joe Wissert, and Charles Stepney

Track listing: Introduction / Medley: Africano/Power / Yearnin' Learnin' / Devotion / Sun Goddess / Reasons / Sing a Message to You / Shining Star / New World Symphony / Musical Interlude #1 / Sunshine / Singasong / Gratitude / Celebrate / Musical Interlude #2 / Can't Hide Love

January 17, 1976
3 weeks

As the title suggests, Earth, Wind & Fire's Gratitude was meant as a present for its fans. After five albums, the band experienced tremendous success with the 1975 release That's the Way of the World [see 198] and the single "Shining Star." Gratitude, a two-record set released in late 1975, featured three sides of live material, plus a side of new studio tracks.

A live album made perfect sense for Earth, Wind & Fire at the time, says singer/percussionist Philip Bailey. "We had released Open Our Eyes and That's the Way of the World and both of those records had become very big. We were playing those songs on the tour and when we performed them live, they took on a whole other characteristic. We were a hot live band, so it was the most logical thing to do in our career."

Indeed, Earth, Wind & Fire emerged as one of the premiere live attractions in the music world by incorporating special effects usually reserved for huge rock acts, including stunts designed by magician Doug Henning. "We were big fans of theater," Bailey says. "If people came to our shows, we wanted to give them more than just the songs. We began to add different things to the stage production. We were the first black group to do that, before the Jacksons and when a lot of that stuff became the standard. It was a trademark of Earth, Wind & Fire."

While the visual part of Earth, Wind & Fire's show became a big draw, the band never forgot about the music, as evidenced by Gratitude's sparkling live renditions of such hits as "Shining Star" and "Reasons." The album was recorded during the band's 1975 headlining arena tour of such cities as Chicago, Los Angeles, St. Louis, Atlanta, Boston, New York, Philadelphia, and Washington.

Gratitude also included some new studio tracks, which Bailey says was just "good marketing sense. If you do a live album with a couple of new tracks on it that people haven't heard, it gives them more incentive to go out and buy the album." The songs also fit in with the "tour" feel of the album. "Those songs epitomized the feeling of being on the road and they were written on the road," he says.

THE TOP FIVE
Week of January 17, 1976

1. **Gratitude**
   Earth, Wind & Fire

2. **Chicago IX—Chicago's Greatest Hits**
   Chicago

3. **History—America's Greatest Hits**
   America

4. **The Hissing of Summer Lawns**
   Joni Mitchell

5. **Helen Reddy's Greatest Hits**
   Helen Reddy

Among the new studio songs were the title track and "Singasong," which was printed as one word on the album jacket, but later broken into a three-word title when it was released as a single. On January 10, 1976, "Sing a Song" became Earth, Wind & Fire's second Number One R&B single. A week later, Gratitude hit Number One in its seventh week on the album chart. Not only did it represent EW&F's second chart-topping album, it also set the stage for the success of other live Number One albums in the mid-'70s, including Peter Frampton's Frampton Comes Alive! [see 213], Wings Over America [see 221], Barry Manilow Live [see 224], and Donna Summer's Live and More [see 232], which even borrowed Gratitude's format of three live sides with one side of new studio material.

COLUMBIA 33893 # Desire

BOB DYLAN

211

Producer: None listed

Track listing: Hurricane / Isis / Mozambique / One More Cup of Coffee / Joey / Romance in Durango / Black Diamond Bay / Sara

February 7, 1976
5 weeks

For *Desire*, the most important singer-songwriter of the rock era tried something new: he turned to a collaborator. In the summer of 1975, Bob Dylan shared a new song called "Isis" with Jacques Levy, an Off-Broadway director and songwriter who had collaborated with Roger McGuinn, formerly of the Byrds. Levy offered the feedback that Dylan was searching for and a partnership was struck up.

Levy wasn't the only newcomer to the Dylan camp on *Desire*, as a number of musicians, most of whom the singer-songwriter had never played with, appeared at the Columbia Studios in New York in July 1975 when the *Desire* recording sessions commenced. Among those present were Eric Clapton [see 179], Dave Mason, Yvonne Elliman [see 226], a British R&B band called Kokomo, Emmylou Harris, and Scarlet Rivera. The latter was a violinist who hooked up with Dylan purely by chance. "I met him while walking down the street in the East Village," says Rivera. "He saw me walking with my violin case and he struck up a conversation with me." It was a thrill for Rivera, a longtime Dylan fan, who found herself accompanying her idol in the studio a few weeks after that meeting.

One of the first cuts Dylan and company attempted to tackle for the album was "Hurricane," an ode to boxer and convicted murderer Rubin "Hurricane" Carter. Says Rivera, "It was approached several different ways, with back-up singers and without." But Dylan still wasn't happy with the results. "There was a decision made about which way to go, with a big-group sound or a small-band approach," Rivera recalls. Ultimately, Dylan went with the small unit, which included Rivera, bassist Rob Stoner, drummer Andrew Wyeth, and back-up singer Emmylou Harris.

"The sessions were outrageous," Rivera says. "There were really no rehearsals. There was just a rundown of the songs and once the strong structure was understood, the red [recording] light went on."

Once again Dylan was going for feel, rather than studio polish. In fact, there is no producer credit on the album, although Dylan's longtime Columbia Records A&R man Don DeVito was present. "It was all very spontaneous," says Rivera. "He wanted very unpolished and unaffected performances. He was really looking for lots of heart and genuine expression, as opposed to precison playing and a flawless performance."

The material on the album ranged from "Joey," written about notorious New York mobster Joey Gallo, to "Sara," a last-minute addition to the album that was performed live in the studio and directed toward Dylan's estranged wife, possibly in an attempt to reconcile with her.

While Sara may not have been swayed by the song and *Desire*, the public was. In its third week on the chart, the album became Dylan's third chart-topper.

THE TOP FIVE
Week of February 7, 1976

1. **Desire**
   Bob Dylan

2. **Still Cray After All These Years**
   Paul Simon

3. **Gratitude**
   Earth, Wind & Fire

4. **Chicago IX—Chicago's Greatest Hits**
   Chicago

5. **Tryin' to Get the Feelin'**
   Barry Manilow

212 Their Greatest Hits 1971–1975 ASYLUM 1052
EAGLES

Producers: Glyn Johns and Bill
Szymczyk

Track listing: Take It Easy / Witchy
Woman / Lyin' Eyes / Already Gone /
Desperado / One of These Nights /
Tequila Sunrise / Take It to the Limit /
Peaceful, Easy Feeling / Best of My
Love

March 13, 1976
5 weeks (nonconsecutive)

Their Greatest Hits was more than
just a contractual obligation for the
Eagles. The album effectively
summed up the group's first four years
while giving their newfound fans a
chance to catch up on the band's work
prior to their commercial breakthrough
with One of These Nights [see 201].

"We thought it would be good to
bridge the time between albums," says
drummer/vocalist Don Henley. "We
knew it was going to take a while to
make the next one." The album featured
three tracks from the band's 1972 self-
titled debut: "Witchy Woman," "Peaceful, Easy Feeling," and "Take It Easy."
Henley explains the origins of the latter
song, written by Eagles singer/guitarist
Glenn Frey and Jackson Browne [see
250]: "That was a Jackson Browne
song originally, but he shelved it,

because he decided he didn't like it and
didn't want to finish it. Glenn remembered the song and went to Jackson
and said, 'If you don't like that song,
could I finish it, because I think we
would like to record it?" Browne agreed
to let the Eagles have the song, and it
became the band's first hit during the
summer of 1972.

Also included on Their Greatest Hits
is "Best of My Love," a song written by
Frey, Henley, and J.D. Souther, who, like
Frey, had belonged to the country-rock
band Longbranch Pennywhistle. The
song went on to become the Eagle's first
Number One single on March 1, 1975.
" 'Best of My Love' was a song that
Glenn had begun, then I started working on it, and then J.D. Souther came
in," says Henley. "That was when I first
became good friends with J.D. He came
over to my house one day in 1974 and
we wrote the bridge."

Their Greatest Hits also captures the
evolution of Henley the songwriter. "On
the first Eagles album, I really didn't do
any songwriting," says Henley. "
'Witchy Woman' was my only contribution and I only wrote half of that. I had-
n't really found my place yet as a songwriter. I was just sort of hanging on for
the ride at that point."

It was on the Eagles' second album,
1973's Desperado, that Henley truly

found his songwriting voice. The title
track and "Tequila Sunrise," both cowritten by Henley, are included on Their
Greatest Hits.

Also present on the album are "One
of These Nights," "Lyin' Eyes," and
"Take It to the Limit," all of them top five
hits from One of These Nights, the
band's first Number One album. With
such hit-packed fire power, Their Greatest Hits hit the summit in its second
week, giving the Eagles their second
consecutive Number One album and
paving the way for Hotel California [see
220].

THE TOP FIVE
Week of March 13, 1976

1. **Their Greatest Hits**
   Eagles

2. **Frampton Comes Alive!**
   Peter Frampton

3. **Desire**
   Bob Dylan

4. **Fleetwood Mac**
   Fleetwood Mac

5. **Station to Station**
   David Bowie

A&M 3703 **Frampton Comes Alive!** **213**
PETER FRAMPTON

Producer: Peter Frampton

Track listing: Something's Happening / Doobie Wah / Show Me the Way / It's a Plain Shame / All I Want to be (Is by Your Side) / Wind of Change / Baby, I Love Your Way / I Wanna Go to the Sun / Penny for Your Thoughts / (I'll Gve You) Money / Shine On / Jumping Jack Flash / Lines on My Face / Do You Feel Like We Do

April 10, 1976
10 weeks (nonconsecutive)

As a member of early-'70s British hard-rock group Humble Pie, Peter Frampton experienced his greatest success with *Performance—Rockin' the Fillmore*, a two-record set that captured the band's raucous live set in May 1971. Later that year, as the album peaked at number 21, Frampton left the group to pursue a solo project.

Frampton's first three solo albums failed to crack the top 100, leading even Frampton to conclude that he may have miscalculated in leaving Humble Pie. Yet things began to change with 1975's *Frampton*, which reached number 32. Frampton had a growing legion of fans and was on his way to becoming a premier concert attraction. A live album was a natural.

Half of *Frampton Comes Alive!* was recorded at Winterland in San Francisco. "The event was far more important than the recording of it, because it was our first time headlining," says Frampton. "I was far more nervous about having to play for an hour and a half instead of 45 minutes, which was what we were used to doing." Yet Frampton was pumped up at the prospect of headlining. "It was a realization of all those years touring, including the Humble Pie years. I was able to go out, even without a huge hit record, and play to nearly 8,000 people. It was a combination of excitement, nervousness, and relief all in the same breath."

Initially, *Frampton Comes Alive!* was slated to be a single disc. *Frampton* had sold more than 350,000, more than his first three albums combined, yet the singer/guitarist wasn't feeling too secure about his future with A&M Records. "I didn't want to push my luck with A&M, because I thought maybe this might be my last record," he says. "So we only mixed enough for a single record."

The early version didn't include the anthemic rocker "Show Me the Way" or the ballad "Baby, I Love Your Way," two standout tracks from *Frampton*, as the band was still mastering the new material on those early tour dates.

With the recording complete, Jerry Moss—the "M" in A&M Records—flew to New York for the mixing sessions. "After the end of the second side," recalls Frampton, "he stood up and said, 'Where the hell is the rest? We can't have a live album without 'Wind of Change' and 'Show Me the Way.' So he gave the go ahead to record half a dozen more songs."

"Show Me the Way" was recorded at the Island Music Center in Commack, Long Island, and "Baby, I Love Your Way" was culled from a show at the State University of New York at Plattsburgh. The former song became Frampton's first hit single, reaching number 6, while the later peaked at 12. "Do You Feel Like We Do," the third single, reached number 10.

On "Show Me the Way" and "Do You Feel Like We Do," Frampton utilized a talkbox, a guitar effect that mimics vocals. He was introduced to the device by Pete Drake during Frampton's days as an uncredited session player on George Harrison's *All Things Must Pass* [see 128].

Frampton Comes Alive! reached the top spot in its 11th week on the chart and went on to become one of the most popular live albums of all time, selling over six million copies.

THE TOP FIVE
Week of April 10, 1976

1. **Frampton Comes Alive!**
   Peter Frampton

2. **Their Greatest Hits 1971–1975**
   Eagles

3. **Thoroughbred**
   Carole King

4. **Desire**
   Bob Dylan

5. **Run with the Pack**
   Bad Company

214 Wings at the Speed of Sound CAPITOL 11525
WINGS

Producer: Paul McCartney

Track listing: Let 'Em In / The Note You Never Wrote / She's My Baby / Beware My Love / Wino Junko / Silly Love Songs / Cook of the House / Time to Hide / Must Do Something About It / San Ferry Anne / Warm and Beautiful

April 24, 1976
7 weeks (nonconsecutive)

With the release of *Venus and Mars* [see 200], Paul McCartney & Wings became known simply as Wings. Perhaps to prove the point that McCartney, his wife and keyboardist Linda, guitarists Denny Laine and Jimmy McCulloch, and drummer Joe English truly were a group, each was given a moment in the spotlight.

McCartney wrote eight and handled the lead vocal on six of the album's 10 songs, but the other members of the band were also participating. Laine, formerly of the Moody Blues, sang his own "Time to Hide" as well as McCartney's "The Note You Never Wrote." The tracks marked the first time a Laine lead vocal had been featured on a Wings album. His previous lead vocal with the group, "I Lie Around," had been available only as the B-side to the 1973 hit "Live and Let Die."

McCulloch, who had sung "Medicine Jar" on *Venus and Mars*, handled lead vocals on "Wino Junko." Like "Medicine Jar," the song would take on an ominous meaning following McCulloch's drug-related death in September 1979.

On a much lighter note, Linda McCartney was featured on "Cook of the House," while English laid down the vocal on "Must Do Something About It."

While the more democratic operation of Wings may have created harmony in the group, even Linda McCartney admitted in retrospect that perhaps it was a mistake. She told Joan Goodam in *Playboy* that "None of Wings were good enough to play with [McCartney]—including me, for sure. I mean, how do you go out with Beethoven and say, 'Sure, I'll sing harmony with you,' when you've never sung a note? It was *mad*."

Overall, *Wings at the Speed of Sound* featured much lighter fare than its two predecessors. As early as 1971, McCartney's former Beatles mate John Lennon took aim at McCartney's pop sensibilities in the song "How Do You Sleep?," which featured the line, "The

sound you make is Muzak to my ears." In "Silly Love Songs," McCartney seemed to mock his critics, while delivering just what the song title promised. "I *liked* that song," McCartney told Paul Gambaccini in *Rolling Stone*, "but I listen to people and I just get *crackers*. All someone has to say is, 'A bit poppy,' or 'That was a bit sickly, that one,' and I expect the song to flop. Someone says, 'It's a bit too cute.' Well, I *know* that. What do you think goes through my mind when I'm writing a song about *silly* love songs? I'm flashing on all this."

Still McCartney admitted that he was bothered by the critics. "Unfortunately , it still tends to get to me! I still hear them saying it's no good. I wonder if they're right. I wonder if I'm right. And it's great when something wins a poll and you can say, 'Nyahh, nuts to you. I thought I was right.' It's vindication."

Of course, McCartney had to feel vindicated when *Wings at the Speed of Sound* reached the pole position in its third week on the chart. With the album still holding the Number One spot, "Silly Love Songs" topped the Hot 100 on May 22, 1976. Vindication, indeed.

THE TOP FIVE
Week of April 24, 1976

1. **Wings at the Speed of Sound**
   Wings

2. **Presence**
   Led Zeppelin

3. **Their Greatest Hits 1971–1975**
   Eagles

4. **A Night at the Opera**
   Queen

5. **Eargasm**
   Johnnie Taylor

Producer: Jimmy Page

Track listing: Achilles Last Stand / For Your Life / Royal Orleans / Nobody's Fault But Mine / Candy Store Rock / Hots on for Nowhere / Tea for One

May 1, 1976
2 weeks

Prior to 1975, the recording of Led Zeppelin's albums had been generally pleasurable affairs. The band often recorded in houses, such as Headley Grange and Stargroves, using mobile units instead of traditional recording studios. That all changed, however, when the band regrouped to record its seventh album, *Presence*.

On August 5, 1975, singer Robert Plant and his wife were seriously injured in a car accident in Rhodes, Greece. The accident forced the second leg of the *Physical Graffiti* tour to be scrapped. Plant traveled to Malibu, California, to recover and soon the rest of the band joined Plant in California for rehearsals there and at S.I.R. Studios in Hollywood. "It was just after Robert's car accident," says bassist/keyboardist John Paul Jones. "It was really very hard to get the group working. We were in Los Angeles and nobody seemed to want to turn up for rehearsals and for writing sessions."

Eventually, the band opted to pack its bags and headed to Germany, where they convened at Musicland Studios in Munich to record *Presence*. "There's some good stuff on the album, but it was hard going," says Jones.

The difficulties the band was going through at the time were reflected in the music, as *Presence* was Zeppelin's hardest-rocking album to date, with no acoustic tracks. Once the band did settle into the recording process, it recorded *Presence* in just 18 days, with guitarist/producer Jimmy Page putting in 18- and 20-hour sessions to complete the album. The driving work ethic wasn't just expedient — it was necessary: Zeppelin was facing a deadline, as the Rolling Stones had booked the studio to begin work on *Black and Blue* [see 216]. "When we entered the studio we were focused," says Jones. "Whatever happened, we were all professionals, and when the studio is booked, we tended to settle down and do our thing, but that was probably our hardest album to make." Some tracks, such as "For Your Life," were written in the studio. "Royal Orleans," named for a hotel in the French Quarter in New Orleans, was the only group composition on the album. On the album's other six tracks, Plant and Page shared writing credits.

Returning to a regular recording studio wasn't a big problem, Jones says, because he and Page had cut their teeth doing extensive session work with Jeff Beck and the Rolling Stones prior to the formation of Led Zeppelin.

Still recovering from the car accident, Plant recorded most of his vocals sitting in a wheelchair. During an early attempt at recording his vocal for "Achilles Last Stand," Plant fell to the ground and was rushed to the hospital.

In what may have been a testament to Led Zeppelin's power to overcome adversity, *Presence* hit the summit in its second week on the chart, giving the band its fifth career chart-topper.

THE TOP FIVE
Week of May 1, 1976

1. **Presence**
   Led Zeppelin

2. **Wings at the Speed of Sound**
   Wings

3. **Their Greatest Hits 1971–1975**
   Eagles

4. **A Night at the Opera**
   Queen

5. **Eargasm**
   Johnnie Taylor

216 Black and Blue ROLLING STONES 79104
THE ROLLING STONES

Producer: The Glimmer Twins

Track listing: Hot Stuff / Hand of Fate / Cherry Oh Baby / Memory Motel / Hey Negrita / Melody / Fool to Cry / Crazy Mama

May 15, 1976
4 weeks (nonconsecutive)

By the time the Rolling Stones settled down to record their 24th album, they had lost their second guitarist, but this time he lived to tell the tale. "The last five-and-half years with the Stones have been very exciting and proved to be a most inspiring period," said the prepared statement from Mick Taylor. "And as far as my attitude to the other four members is concerned, it is one of respect for them, both as musicians and people. I have nothing but admiration for the group, but I feel now is the time to move on and do something new."

Yet Taylor's statement was only part of the truth, as it has been reported that he was upset that he didn't receive co-writing credits on the Stones songs and was not allowed to fully express himself creatively in the band.

THE TOP FIVE
Week of May 15, 1976

1. **Black and Blue**
   The Rolling Stones

2. **Wings at the Speed of Sound**
   Wings

3. **Frampton Comes Alive!**
   Peter Frampton

4. **Presence**
   Led Zeppelin

5. **I Want You**
   Marvin Gaye

Glyn Johns, who along with his brother Andy worked as engineers on such Stones albums as Sticky Fingers [see 132] and Exile on Main St. [see 145], was called to produce the session with Stones Mick Jagger and Keith Richards, who once again received credit under the pseudonym "the Glimmer Twins." Johns recalls, "I agreed to go in with them and produce the album under the condition that if I didn't finish the album with them, I wouldn't receive a co-producer credit." By this time Johns had an extensive history with the band — he was actually the first to record them, although those early sessions were never released.

"The night before we left for Munich to start making the record, Mick Taylor resigned, so they turned up in Germany without a second guitar player," Johns recalls. "As a result, we got on tremendously well and we cut an immense amount of material in an extremely short period of time. It was great for me to be back with them."

In Munich, Johns found that the Stones actually worked better without Taylor. "He is a brilliant guitar player and he did contribute tremendously when he was in the band, but as his career with the band progressed, he became more difficult and was contributing as much as Keith to the length of time it took to record things."

After breaking for Christmas, the Stones decided to take the mobile unit to Rotterdam, Holland, to complete the album. "They got this hall that was suitable for symphony orchestras, but it was certainly not the right place to make a record, and then they started auditioning people. They were using the recording time to audition guitar players."

Three guitarists who auditioned for the Stones are featured on Black and Blue. Harvey Mandel, from John Mayall's Blues Band, played on "Hot Stuff" and "Memory Motel." Noted session player Wayne Perkins was also featured on the latter track, as well as on "Hand of Fate" and "Fool to Cry," the latter of which went on to become a top 10 hit. It was ex-Faces guitarist Ronnie Wood, however, who played on "Cherry Oh Baby," "Hey Negrita," and "Crazy Mama," who eventually became Taylor's replacement,

The Stones' lax approach to recording soon wore Johns down. "There was an argument between me and Keith, and I lost my rag. I said my piece and told the Rolling Stones they could go fuck themselves. As far as I was concerned, the record was nearly finished, but then they spent nine months finishing it off." Despite such hassles, Johns still has respect for the Stones. "When they did get it together, they were fantastic and unbeatable," he says.

The record-buying public agreed. In its second week on the chart Black and Blue became the Stones' sixth Number One album.

Producer: Tommy LiPuma

Track listing: Breezin' / This Masquerade / Six to Four / Affirmation / So This Is Love? / Lady

July 31, 1976
2 weeks

On *Breezin'* producer Tommy LiPuma helped George Benson rediscover his voice. Benson's jazz/R&B guitar stylings had won him widespread acclaim, including a Grammy nomination for his 1973 album *White Rabbit* and recording contracts from Columbia and Creed Taylor's CTI label. Yet his voice was usually absent from his recordings. That changed, however, when Warner Bros. signed him in 1976 and Benson went to work with Warner Bros. staff producer LiPuma on *Breezin'*.

"When I met Tommy he said, 'George, I heard you sing five years ago in San Francisco and I never could understand why no one had exploited your voice,' " says Benson. "He brought this one song to me called 'This Masquerade' and he said, 'George, you can tear this up.' " Yet Benson had his doubts. "I thought it was a nice song. I liked Leon Russell's version of it, but I didn't think I could improve on it, so I

was kind of reluctant to commit myself to it. What convinced me to do the song is that when I played it for a couple of guys in the band, their wives said, 'Wow, that's my favorite song.' "

The song marked a return to the microphone for Benson, who had started his career in the '50s singing and playing guitar. By the late '60s, however, disc jockeys were telling him they would not play his vocals. "But I didn't let that bother me, because I knew basically people accepted me as a guitar player," he says.

Benson's vocals on "This Masquerade" were compared to Stevie Wonder's. "I knew Stevie. We were good friends and the comparison actually helped the record get airplay," Benson says. "Stevie was one of the top vocalists in the world at the time and I was a guitar player being compared to him. How could I be unhappy?"

Even while in the studio, "This Masquerade," which went on to become a top 10 hit, garnered exceptional responses. Bobby Womack was called in to contribute a reworked version of "Breezin' " as the album's title track, Benson recalls. "Bobby walked in while we were playing back 'This Masquerade.' He said, 'Wow, who in here has a voice like that?' He didn't know that I sang. That was the first indication that

we had something special."

Breezin' was recorded on January 6, 7, and 8, 1976, at Capitol Records in Hollywood. The studio was actually booked for four days, Benson recalls, so with the album complete, Benson and company hung out and partied on the fourth day. Working at Capitol made the sessions extra special for Benson. "That's the studio that Nat [King Cole] built. For me it was a very historic moment being in the studio that so many greats had recorded in. There is so much history there."

THE TOP FIVE
Week of July 31, 1976

1. **Breezin'**
   George Benson

2. **Frampton Comes Alive!**
   Peter Frampton

3. **Wings at the Speed of Sound**
   Wings

4. **Chicago X**
   Chicago

5. **Spitfire**
   Jefferson Starship

218 Fleetwood Mac REPRISE 2225
FLEETWOOD MAC

Producers: Fleetwood Mac and Keith Olsen

Track listing: Monday Morning / Warm Ways / Blue Letter / Rhiannon / Over My Head / Crystal / Say You Love Me / Landslide / World Turning / Sugar Daddy / I'm So Afraid

September 4, 1976
1 week

In its nearly decade-long career, Fleetwood Mac had survived numerous lineup changes while enjoying steady but unspectacular album sales. That would change, however, when the group's co-founder and drummer Mick Fleetwood went searching for a new guitarist to replace Bob Welch in December 1974. By the new year, Fleetwood had found not only a guitar player in Lindsey Buckingham, but also another vocalist for the band in Buckingham's musical partner and girlfriend Stevie Nicks.

"It reminded me of how it felt when we first formed Fleetwood Mac," says Fleetwood of the new lineup. The first incarnation of the group was formed in the summer of 1967 by British singer/guitarist Peter Green, Fleetwood, and bassist John McVie. "There were moments when we got a little lost after Peter left [in 1971]. We made some good music, but we never quite had the focus until we met Stevie and Lindsey."

The duo of Buckingham and Nicks, formerly of the San Francisco group Fritz, had recorded a self-titled album for Polydor in 1973. Fleetwood discov-

ered them when engineer Keith Olsen played him a few cuts off Buckingham Nicks to demonstrate the sound capabilities of Sound City in Van Nuys, California. Fleetwood was impressed not only by the sound of the studio, but by Olsen and the guitar player.

The latest incarnation of Fleetwood Mac, with new members Buckingham and Nicks, recorded Fleetwood Mac at Sound City, with Olsen serving as co-producer and engineer. The new blood instantly had an effect on the band. "It changed the way we wrote," says Fleetwood. "We all came from a blues background, and Stevie and Lindsey came from a country background mixed with a little West Coast Janis Joplin stuff."

Yet there was some tension between the band's veterans and newcomers. "Lindsey didn't understand the way that John and I worked," says Fleetwood. "He had made some demos where he played the bass parts. They were good parts, but they were his parts. He was thinking that was what we were going to use. So John and Lindsey had what we call in the business a friendly musician-to-musician confrontation, and John said, 'Hey, I'm the bass player and this is the way I'm going to play your songs. I can't just copy what you have done.' Lindsey very quickly realized that we were a band and that was the way we worked."

Once that misunderstanding was cleared up, the sessions went fairly smoothly. Fleetwood Mac was completed in three months, a flash compared to the band's future endeavors [see 223]. The album spawned three top 20 hits: Christine McVie's "Over My Head" and "Say

You Love Me" and Nicks's "Rhiannon." Another Nicks composition, "Crystal," originally included on Buckingham Nicks, was rerecorded and included on Fleetwood Mac.

After 58 weeks on the chart, Fleetwood Mac knocked Frampton Comes Alive from the top spot. The album went to sell more than 5 million copies. "It was like pipe dream," Fleetwood says of the success. "We would sell maybe 200,000 or 300,000 copies at the most of each album. The joke was that Warner Bros. made enough to pay the electricity bill for the east wing." Yet Fleetwood had a feeling that the new lineup would finally make Fleetwood Mac a hit in America. "I won't say I knew it was going to be successful, because that would be out of line," he says. "But I had a very, very strong feeling that we did something right."

THE TOP FIVE
Week of September 4, 1976

1. **Fleetwood Mac**
   Fleetwood Mac

2. **Frampton Comes Alive!**
   Peter Frampton

3. **Spitfire**
   Jefferson Starship

4. **Breezin'**
   George Benson

5. **Silk Degrees**
   Boz Scaggs

Producer: Stevie Wonder

Track listing: Love's in Need of Love Today / Have a Talk with God / Village Ghetto Land / Contusion / Sir Duke / I Wish / Knocks Me Off My Feet / Pastime Paradise / Summer Soft / Ordinary Pain / Saturn / Ebony Eyes / Isn't She Lovely / Joy Inside My Tears / Black Man / Ngiculela - Es Una Historia / I Am Singing / If It's Magic / As / Another Star / All Day Sucker / Easy Goin' Evening (My Mama's Call)

October 16, 1976
14 weeks (nonconsecutive)

Initially, Stevie Wonder had no plans to make his follow-up album to *Fulfillingness' First Finale* a two-record set. "I knew that I wanted the album to be different than the previous things that I had done. I knew that I had a lot of material and I was still writing stuff," he says. When Wonder came to the realization that the album would have to be a two-record set, he discussed it with Motown founder Berry Gordy. "He said, 'You're crazy. That's ridiculous, but go ahead and do it.' "

With Gordy's approval, Wonder went wild. He didn't just stop with a two-album set. Upon its completion, the double-album was packaged with a bonus four-song, 7-inch EP. In all, the album included 21 new original songs. For *Songs in the Key of Life*, the music just flowed from Wonder. "It was a case of me living life and letting life encourage music," he says.

With Wonder approaching a career-high level of popularity, the completion of *Songs in the Key of Life*, which was two years in the making, was eagerly

anticipated, even by those involved in the recording process. "Gary Olazabal and John Fischbach, the two engineers who worked on it with me, were very patient," Wonder says. "Everyone kept asking us when were we going to be finished and I just kept saying, 'We're almost finished.' One day Gary went out and had a T-shirt made that said, 'We're almost finished.' "

While the album was in the making, Wonder signed a new seven-year pact with Motown, reportedly worth $13 million. At the time, Wonder was the highest-paid performer in pop music.

And Wonder worked hard for the money. At times, he spent as many as 48 hours straight in the studio. "That's not really that hard to do," Wonder says. "I'd start on a Sunday afternoon and I'd be on a roll and before I knew it, it would be Tuesday."

When the album was finally completed, fans and critics agreed it was worth the wait. One track, "Sir Duke" was a homage to Duke Ellington and other artists who paved the way for Wonder. "There's just so many great musicians who have made a contribution," he says. "I called the track 'Sir Duke' because Duke Ellington was so progressive and innovative."

Another track, "Isn't She Lovely,"

was written for a child Wonder's second wife, Yolanda, was carrying at the time. "We kept talking about what sex the baby would be and I just knew it would be a girl," he says. "I wrote that on the Dream Machine, which was one of the first keyboards that had eight voices."

Ironically, "I Wish," the first single released from the album, was the last song Wonder completed for the album. "I wrote that on a Saturday in the summer of 1976 right after the Motown picnic," he says. "The song was inspired by the fact we were having so much fun. I came back to the studio and wrote that song. When I laid it down, it felt really good. I knew that it was the hit for the album."

Wonder's hunch that the autobiographical song would be a hit was correct. The track, featuring Wonder's sister Renee Hardaway calling him a "nasty boy," went on to become Wonder's fifth number Number One single on January 22, 1977.

Songs in the Key of Life didn't need a hit single to push it to the summit. On October 16, 1976, it became only the third album—after Elton John's *Captain Fantastic and the Brown Dirt Cowboy* [see 199] and *Rock of the Westies* [see 207]—to debut at Number One. It was also Wonder's third Number One album.

THE TOP FIVE
Week of October 16, 1976

1. **Songs in the Key of Life**
   Stevie Wonder

2. **Silk Degrees**
   Boz Scaggs

3. **Frampton Comes Alive!**
   Peter Frampton

4. **Fly Like an Eagle**
   Steve Miller Band

5. **Hasten Down the Wind**
   Linda Ronstadt

220 Hotel California ASYLUM 1084
EAGLES

Producer: Bill Szymczyk

Track listing: Hotel California / New Kid in Town / Life in the Fast Lane / Wasted Time / Wasted Time (Reprise) / Victim of Love / Pretty Maids All in a Row / Try and Love Again / The Last Resort

January 15, 1977
8 weeks (nonconsecutive)

With the success of *Their Greatest Hits 1971–1975* [see 212] giving the band the luxury of time, the Eagles had more than a year and a half to write material for their fifth album. It was the first with guitarist Joe Walsh, formerly of the James Gang. Walsh replaced Bernie Leadon, who had become disenchanted with the band's more rock-oriented direction.

"Bernie had left the group and we left the country-rock material even further behind with his departure," says drummer/vocalist Don Henley. It was producer Bill Szymczyk who introduced Walsh to the band. "Joe had a great influence on the group," says Henley. "The party line on his joining the group was that it made us a strong rock 'n' roll band, but in fact Joe didn't present that much rock 'n' roll to the group. He presented ballads with a lot of harmonies in them." In fact, Walsh's main contribution to *Hotel California* was "Pretty Maids All in a Row," a song Henley calls "a homage to the Beach Boys."

"We wanted Joe to play rock 'n' roll," adds Henley, "which he did onstage, and he did contribute some of the music to 'Life in the Fast Lane,' including the signature lick, which is the introduction of the song."

Hotel California was recorded from March through October 1975 at Criteria Studios in Miami and the Record Plant in Los Angeles. "It was a very difficult and very exciting," Henley says, "because we knew that we were reaching another level in our songwriting and production." To record the album, the Eagles showed a newfound dedication. "We basically just camped out in the studio, we just locked ourselves in," Henley says. "We had a refrigerator, a ping-pong table, roller skates, and a couple of cots. We would go in and stay for two or three days at a time."

The title track began as a demo by guitarist Don Felder. "He would give me cassette tapes with tracks on them. That was on a tape with about five or six other songs," Henley says. The drummer would listen to the tapes in his car when he drove around L.A. "That was the only one of the entire tape that stuck out. I liked it because it was a nice synthesis of cultures. In a sense it was a reggae record rhythmically, but musically it was Spanish. It was sort of a Latin reggae song."

Lyrically, however, the song, along with much of *Hotel California*, focused on the narcissistic Los Angeles lifestyle of the late '70s, a lifestyle critics often accused the Eagles of living. "At first I couldn't understand it," Henley says. "I couldn't understand how people could be so mean-spirited even if they didn't like the music. We never resented criticism per se, unless it got personal. When critics started writing about our personal lives or what kind of people we were, then it got offensive. If they'd just stuck to the music, everything would have been fine."

Yet even the Eagles' harshest critics had to acknowledge that *Hotel California* was the band's masterpiece, artistically and commercially. The album soared to the pole position in its second week on the chart and spawned two Number One singles, "New Kid in Town" and the title track. Henley still considers *Hotel California* the band's finest effort. "Every band has their peak," he says. "That was ours."

THE TOP FIVE
Week of January 15, 1977

1. **Hotel California**
   Eagles

2. **Songs in the Key of Life**
   Stevie Wonder

3. **Wings Over America**
   Wings

4. **Boston**
   Boston

5. **A New World Record**
   Electric Light Orchestra

CAPITOL 11593 # Wings Over America
WINGS **221**

Producer: Paul McCartney

Track listing: Venus and Mars / Rock Show / Jet / Let Me Roll It/ Spirits of Ancient Egypt / Medicine Jar / Maybe I'm Amazed / Call Me Back Again / Lady Madonna / The Long and Winding Road / Live and Let Die / Picasso's Last Words / Richard Cory / Bluebird / I've Just Seen a Face / Blackbird / Yesterday / You Gave Me the Answer / Magneto and Titanium Man / Go Now / My Love / Listen to What the Man Said / Letting Go / Band on the Run / Hi, Hi, Hi / Soily

January 22, 1977
1 week

With the 1976 *Wings Over America* tour, Paul McCartney was trying to come to terms with his past *and* break away from it. The tour, part of a 13-month, 10-country trek, marked McCartney's first American concert appearance in a decade. It also featured McCartney performing several Beatles songs never previously performed onstage.

"They're great tunes...I just decided in the end, this isn't such a big deal. I'd do them," McCartney said in Chet Flippo's *Yesterday: The Unauthorized Biography of Paul McCartney.* To document the occasion, McCartney opted to record every show on the tour, the best of which turned up on the three-record *Wings Over America.*

Even if McCartney was including Beatles material in his set, part of his motivation for hitting the road with Wings was to debunk some of the magic surrounding his former group. "The whole idea behind Wings is to get a touring band so that we are just a band," McCartney told Ben Fong-Torres in *Rolling Stone,* "instead of the whole Beatles myth."

By the time Wings hit the road, that band was a well-polished machine. "With the Beatles," McCartney told *Rolling Stone,* "we might rehearse for three days. We've spent months rehearsing with Wings."

Included in the band's live set were such Wings hits as "Live and Let Die," "My Love," "Listen to What the Man Said," "Band on the Run," and "Silly Love Songs." But the real news was the inclusion of such Beatles classics as "Lady Madonna," "The Long and Winding Road," "I've Just Seen a Face," "Blackbird," and "Yesterday." If performing the songs live with Wings didn't make enough of a statement, McCartney took the additional step of reversing the songs' songwriting credits on the album to read "P. McCartney-J. Lennon," rather than the traditional "Lennon-McCartney."

Wings also threw in some outside material and unfamiliar songs, including a cover of Paul Simon's "Richard Cory,"

the Moody Blues' "Go Now," which Wings guitarist Denny Laine had sung when he was a member of that band, and the McCartney original "Soily," which made its album debut on *Wings Over America.*

In its fifth week on the chart, *Wings Over America* soared to the top, becoming the fifth consecutive and final Wings chart-topper. The band went on to record two more studio albums—1978's *London Town* (which made number two) and 1979's *Back to the Egg*—before McCartney officially went the solo route again.

"It's very difficult for me to assess Wings because they came after the Beatles," McCartney told his fan newsletter *Club Sandwich.* "So, to me, there was always a feeling of let-down because the Beatles had been so big that anything I did had to compare directly with them...I would have felt much better about Wings if it had just happened on its own, either before the Beatles or with a decent interval afterwards. But it happened straight after the Beatles, which was unfortunate. I know why, though—I needed to continue in music. I didn't want to retire or do anything else."

THE TOP FIVE
Week of January 22, 1977

1. **Wings Over America**
   Wings

2. **Hotel California**
   Eagles

3. **Songs in the Key of Life**
   Stevie Wonder

4. **Boston**
   Boston

5. **The Best of the Doobies**
   Doobie Brothers

222 A Star Is Born COLUMBIA 34403
BARBRA STREISAND/KRIS KRISTOFFERSON

Producers: Barbra Streisand and Phil Ramone

Track listing: Watch Closely Now / Queen Bee / Everything / Lost Inside of You / Hellacious Acres / Love Them from "A Star Is Born" (Evergreen) / The Woman in the Moon / I Believe in Love / Crippled Crow / Finale: With One More Look at You/Watch Closely Now / Reprise: Love Them from "A Star Is Born" (Evergreen)

February 12, 1977
6 weeks

A *Star Is Born* was no stranger to the summit of the *Billboard* album chart. Prior to the rock era, in 1954, Judy Garland [see 47] had a Number One album with the soundtrack to the first remake of the 1937 film classic. To remake the film yet again would be a risky move for most, but not for Barbra Streisand. By 1977, Streisand had starred on Broadway and in films, hosted her own TV specials, and scored two Number One albums [see 70 and 171].

Yet Streisand's version of *A Star Is Born* would not be a mere remake. It would feature new music, including two songs co-written by Streisand herself. Despite her enormous talent, songwriting was unusual for Streisand. Prior to

A Star Is Born, she'd had only one other composing credit.

One song, "Lost Inside of You" was written by Streisand and Leon Russell. The pair were introduced through the actor Gary Busey, who was a mutual friend. Streisand wrote "Love Theme from 'A Star Is Born' (Evergreen)" on the acoustic guitar after learning how to play the instrument for a scene in the film. Although the scene was cut from the film, the song survived and went on to become one of Streisand's biggest hits.

The music wasn't the only thing different from the film's two earlier incarnations. "From the very beginning, Barbra and the film's producer Jon Peters wanted to record live," says Phil Ramone. "Every shot was edited to fit the vocal that was performed and it certainly added a dimension to the picture."

Many of the live scenes and songs in the film were recorded at Sun Devil Stadium in Tempe, Arizona, during a concert headlined by Peter Frampton [see 213]. "We had originally gone into the studio to pre-record songs," says Ramone. "But Barbra knew that me and my little team would be able to record the live material right. It would not just feel like Woodstock, it would feel bigger than that."

A Star Is Born also marked a technological first. "Barbra allowed me to

explore the usage of a Dolby four-track," says Ramone. "The film company actually paid for the installation of the system in 25 or 30 theaters across America."

Although Kris Kristofferson, who played an alcoholic rocker in the film, was featured on five of the album's 12 songs, including three solo tracks, Streisand was clearly the star. In its 10th week on the Top LPs & Tapes chart, *A Star Is Born* shot to Number One. It was still holding there when "Love Theme from 'A Star Is Born' (Evergreen)" hit Number One on the Hot 100, giving Streisand simultaneous Number Ones.

THE TOP FIVE
Week of February 12, 1977

1. **A Star Is Born**
   Barbra Streisand/
   Kris Kristofferson

2. **Hotel California**
   Eagles

3. **Songs in the Key of Life**
   Stevie Wonder

4. **Wings Over America**
   Wings

5. **A Day at the Races**
   Queen

WARNER 3010 **Rumours**
FLEETWOOD MAC

223

Producers: Fleetwood Mac, Richard Dashut, and Ken Caillat

Track listing: Second Hand News / Never Going Back Again / Don't Stop / Go Your Own Way / Songbird / The Chain / You Make Loving Fun / I Don't Want to Know / Oh Daddy / Gold Dust Woman

April 2, 1977
31 weeks (nonconsecutive)

With *Fleetwood Mac* [see 218], the veteran band finally found success in America but entered a world of chaos in the process. The new-found fame put pressure on the personal lives of the band's members. Before the band entered the studio to begin recording *Rumours*, all the band members' personal relationships hit the skids. Christine and John McVie divorced, Stevie Nicks and Lindsey Buckingham broke up, and Mick Fleetwood and his wife Jenny (not a member of the band) split. "It was a complete disaster zone," says Fleetwood of the 1976 period during which the album was written and recorded. "It was emotional hell laced with musical pleasure. A lot of people on the outside of the band felt that we were never going to make it through."

The naysayers had their reasons. "Those days were crazy," says Fleetwood. "It's no secret that we were defi-nitely abusing drugs in those days. It was one major lunatic party."

The sessions for *Rumours* began in February 1976 at the Record Plant in Sausalito, California, at a time when some of the band members were hardly speaking to each other. After nine weeks of insanity, the band returned to Los Angeles, where they continued recording at Wally Heider Recording Studio for three more months of work. After a break for a summer tour, the band returned to the studio in the fall to complete the project.

The songs written for the album were deeply personal. "If you listen to the words, you can see there was a lot of pain in songs like 'Go Your Own Way.' Chris wrote 'Oh Daddy' for me," says Fleetwood. "I was the father of two children and my wife had gone off with someone we both knew very well. I was in pieces."

While some tracks were overdubbed so much that the master tapes began to wear thin, others were kept simple. Christine McVie's "Songbird" was recorded live at the vacant Zellerback Auditorium at the University of California at Berkeley. With *Fleetwood Mac* hitting the top spot on September 4, 1976, the band had added incentive to finally complete the follow-up album, and John McVie had a perfect title to replace the tentative *Yesterday's Gone*, which was taken from a line in the track

"Don't Stop." Says Fleetwood, "John McVie had the best phrase. He said it was literally like living through a musical soap opera, and that's why we called the album *Rumours*. You couldn't have written a better plot and you wouldn't believe it if you watched it happening."

Fleetwood Mac not only survived, but thrived. *Rumours* shot to the summit of the Top LPs & Tapes chart in a mere six weeks, displacing longtime rivals the Eagles from the top spot. The album spawned the top 10 hits "Go You Own Way," "Don't Stop," and "You Make Loving Fun," as well as the group's first Number One single, "Dreams." *Rumours* also picked up a Grammy in 1977 for Album of the Year.

THE TOP FIVE
Week of April 2, 1977

1. **Rumours**
   Fleetwood Mac

2. **Hotel California**
   Eagles

3. **Songs in the Key of Life**
   Stevie Wonder

4. **A Star Is Born**
   Barbra Streisand

5. **Leftoverture**
   Kansas

224 Barry Manilow/Live ARISTA 8500
BARRY MANILOW

Producers: Barry Manilow and Ron Dante

Track listing: Riders to the Stars / Why Don't We Live Together / Looks Like We Made It / New York City Rhythm / A Very Strange Medley/Jump Shout Boogie/Avenue C / Jumpin' at the Woodside/Cloudburst/Bandstand Boogie / This One's for You / Beautiful Music (Part I) / Daybreak / Lay Me Down / Weekend in New England / Studio Musician / Beautiful Music (Part II) / Could It Be Magic/Mandy / It's a Miracle / It's Just Another New Year's Eve / I Write the Songs / Beautiful Music (Part III)

July 16, 1977
1 week

In January 1975, Barry Manilow became a star when "Mandy" topped the Hot 100. A year later, Manilow scored his second Number One single with "I Write the Songs." While the Brooklyn-born singer scored three top 10 albums with 1974's *Barry Manilow II*, 1975's *Tryin' to Get the Feeling,* and 1976's *This One's for You,* he didn't reach the peak of the Top LPs & Tapes chart until Arista released an album of some of his best-known songs recorded live.

Recorded primarily at New York's Uris Theatre in December 1976, *Live* captured Manilow in the middle of a 98-city tour at the height of his new-found fame. Yet despite his enormous popularity, Manilow was having trouble dealing with the success. "I remember it being the worst time of my life, and the best of times," he says. "It was the first peak of this pop career of mine and it

was a very confusing and unnatural thing to go through at the time."

Live features in-concert versions of the big hits "Looks Like We Made It," "This One's for You," "Could It Be Magic," "Mandy," and "I Write the Songs." Yet Manilow also turned to some other familiar material. "A Very Strange Medley (V.S.M.)" featured commercial jingles from Kentucky Fried Chicken, State Farm insurance, Stridex facial pads, Band-Aids, Dr. Pepper, Pepsi, Bowlene toilet cleaner, and McDonald's. Manilow had written some of the jingles, but compiled his own creations and the others into "V.S.M." for its campy appeal.

Says Manilow, "Before 'Mandy,' I didn't feel that I could keep the audience's attention with a whole hour of original material, so in desperation I put that together and the crowd went nuts. It was still in the stage show when we

recorded *Live.*"

Also included on *Live* was "Jump Shout Boogie Medley," another collection, which featured a Manilow original from *This One's for You,* covers of a few standards, and "Bandstand Boogie," better known as theme to Dick Clark's *American Bandstand,* which Manilow also co-wrote.

The combination of hits, jingles, and TV themes, all recorded live, proved to be potent. *Live* entered the chart at number 10 on May 28, 1977. It wasn't the only Manilow title on the list that week, as all four of the singer-songwriter's previous albums were still on the album chart.

Eight weeks after its impressive debut, *Live* hit the top, becoming Manilow's first and only chart-topping LP and the second live album of 1977 to hit Number One [see *Wings Over America* — 221].

THE TOP FIVE
Week of July 16, 1977

1. **Barry Manilow Live**
   Barry Manilow

2. **I'm in You**
   Peter Frampton

3. **Rumours**
   Fleetwood Mac

4. **Book of Dreams**
   Steve Miller

5. **Superman**
   Barbra Streisand

ASYLUM 104 **Simple Dreams**
LINDA RONSTADT

225

Producer: Peter Asher

Track listing: It's So Easy / Carmelita / Simple Man, Simple Dream / Sorrow Lives Here / I Never Will Marry / Blue Bayou / Poor Poor Pitiful Me / Maybe I'm Right / Tumbling Dice / Old Paint

December 3, 1977
5 weeks

Some dubbed 1977 the year of Linda Ronstadt. Her face appeared on the cover of everything from *Rolling Stone* and *People* to *Time*, and she was among the performers to be featured at an Inaugural Eve Gala for President-elect Jimmy Carter. Following the breakthrough success of *Heart Like a Wheel* in 1974 [see 192], Ronstadt had racked up three more platinum albums and hit singles with her covers of Martha & the Vandellas' "Heat Wave," Smokey Robinson's "Tracks of My Tears," and Buddy Holly's "That'll Be The Day." In 1977, Linda Ronstadt was pop music's premiere female vocalist.

Simple Dreams, with manager Peter Asher once again serving as producer, was recorded at the Sound Factory in Los Angeles from May 23 to July 22, 1977. Ronstadt opted for her usual eclectic mix of proven classics and contemporary compositions by some of her favorite songwriters. She once again turned to the Buddy Holly songbook with "It's So Easy," which became a top five hit. She also paid tribute to some of her contemporaries, including the Rolling Stones, whose "Tumbling Dice" became a top 40 hit for Ronstadt. She performed the song live with Mick Jagger at a Stones concert at the Community Center in Tucson, Arizona on July 21, 1977, a day before she completed *Simple Dreams*.

"Carmelita" and "Poor Poor Pitiful Me" were penned by Warren Zevon, the American singer-songwriter whose "Hasten Down the Wind" had served as the title track to Ronstadt's 1976 album. "I just loved Warren Zevon's music, but it wasn't very good for singers," says Ronstadt. "It doesn't give you the vocal range. There isn't the opportunity for real singing like there is in a Burt Bachrach song or something like that, but I just love his point of view, and his sort of journalistic way of writing."

The biggest hit off *Simple Dreams* was Ronstadt's version of the Roy Orbison's 1963 classic "Blue Bayou," which climbed to number three. But Ronstadt didn't record it as a tribute to Orbison. Says Ronstadt, "I was trying to sing like a Mexican singer with that falsetto thing at the end. I really wanted to do a traditional Mexican record, but I couldn't. The record company really didn't want me to, and the band didn't know how to play it. We were on the road all of the time, so I couldn't find some way to get off the bus and go down to Mexico to find a band to help me do it."

Ronstadt wouldn't fulfill her dream of recording an album full of traditional Mexican songs until 1987 with *Canciones de mi Padre*, which translates to *My Father's Songs*. However, the success of "Blue Bayou" led to a step in that direction, as she also recorded a Spanish-language version of the song. Says Ronstadt, "I got my dad to write lyrics for it in Spanish, so I could sing it in Spanish. I wanted to do traditional Mexican music, but that was the closest I could get at the time."

THE TOP FIVE
Week of December 3, 1977

1. **Simple Dreams**
   Linda Ronstadt

2. **Rumours**
   Fleetwood Mac

3. **Aja**
   Steely Dan

4. **Live**
   Commodores

5. **Foot Loose &
   Fancy Free**
   Rod Stewart

226 Saturday Night Fever RSO 4001
SOUNDTRACK

Compiled by: Bill Oakes

Track listing: Stayin' Alive / How Deep Is Your Love [Bee Gees] / If I Can't Have You [Yvonne Elliman] / A Fifth of Beethoven [Walter Murphy] / Jive Talkin' [Bee Gees] / K-Jee [M.F.S.B.] / Calypso Breakdown [Ralph MacDonald] / More Than a Woman [Tavares] / Night Fever [Bee Gees] / Boogie Shoes [K.C. & the Sunshine Band] / Disco Inferno [The Trammps] / You Should Be Dancing [Bee Gees] / Open Sesame [Kool & the Gang] / More Than a Woman [Bee Gees] / Manhattan Skyline / Night on Disco Mountain / Salsation [David Shire]

January 21, 1978
24 weeks

John Travolta in *Saturday Night Fever.*

Al Coury will never forget the day he received a call at his New York hotel room from Robert Stigwood. At the time, Coury was an executive at Capitol Records and Stigwood was attempting to woo him to his recently established RSO Records. "He called me and told be to go down to the lobby and pick up *New York* magazine with an article by Nik Cohn in it called 'Tribal Rites of Saturday Night.' I went down to the lobby to get it and he called me back and said, 'I'm going to take that story and make a movie and you are going to have the biggest soundtrack ever.'"

Stigwood's predictions were not too far off the mark. *Saturday Night Fever* topped *Billboard*'s Top Pop Albums chart for a whopping 24 weeks and spawned four Number One singles: the Bee Gees' "How Deep Is Your Love," "Night Fever," and "Stayin' Alive," and Yvonne Elliman's "If I Can't Have You."

THE TOP FIVE
Week of January 21, 1978

1. **Saturday Night Fever**
   Soundtrack

2. **Foot Loose & Fancy Free**
   Rod Stewart

3. **All 'n' All**
   Earth, Wind & Fire

4. **Out of the Blue**
   Electric Light Orchestra

5. **Rumors**
   Fleetwood Mac

According to Coury, a large part of the success was due to the unique collaborative effort between Stigwood's record and film companies. "We were part of the same company," he says. "We worked hand in hand. There wasn't some big corporate umbrella we had to pierce."

Then, of course, there was the music. The Bee Gees would serve as the centerpiece of *Saturday Night Fever*, performing six of the album's 17 tracks and penning "If I Can't Have You" for Elliman. Two versions of "More Than a Woman" would be included—the Bee Gees' original and a remake by another group of singing brothers known as Tavares. Also included were "Disco Inferno" by the Trammps, "Boogie Shoes" by K.C. & The Sunshine Band, and "A Fifth of Beethoven" by Walter Murphy.

By 1977, the Bee Gees were primed for major success. After a slump in the early '70s, the Gibb brothers racked up several hits, including Number Ones "Jive Talkin' " and "You Should Be Dancin'," both of which would be included on *Saturday Night Fever*. The movie would also inspire new material such as

"Stayin' Alive" and "Night Fever."

The Bee Gees recorded the new material for the soundtrack at Chateau D'Herouville in France. Stigwood, who had managed the group since 1967, guided the sessions with the film in mind. "Robert would tell them what the scene was about and what tempo and rhythm to use and the boys would write it the way they wanted it."

Says Coury, "The music was so strong and it perfectly suited what it was depicting. It became one of the major stars of the film." Yet *Saturday Night Fever* was more than just a soundtrack—it was the ultimate disco album, taking a pulsating beat and subculture that grew out of the urban gay nightclub scene to middle America. Ironically, the album's incredible popularity also led to a backlash that ultimately spelled disco's demise. And, although the Bee Gees would go on to have two more Number One albums [see 237, 245], *Saturday Night Fever* was a mixed blessing. "It gave them *too* much exposure," says Coury. "We had to wait more than a year before they came out with a new album."

Producers: Hugh Murphy and Gerry Rafferty

Track listing: The Ark / Baker Street / Right Down the Line / City to City / Stealin' Time / Mattie's Rag / Whatever's Written in Your Heart / Home and Dry / Island / Waiting for the Day

July 8, 1978
1 week

By the time Stealers Wheel first gained notice in America with the top 10 hit single "Stuck in the Middle with You," trouble was already brewing in the band. Although singer/guitarist Gerry Rafferty, who had quit the group, rejoined following the success of the single, things were never quite the same. "Stealers Wheel had great potential," says Rafferty. "Unfortunately its potential was never fulfilled, so I pretty much decided I was going to pursue a solo career."

It wasn't Rafferty's first attempt at going it alone. Following the split of an earlier group, the folk-based Humblebums, Rafferty recorded *Can I Have My Money Back?* in 1971 (it wasn't released in America until 1973). Rafferty's second stab at a solo career took a while to get off the ground. Following the dissolution of Stealers Wheel, he found himself entangled in a web of legal hassles surrounding the band. "After Stealers Wheel finished, I was living in Scotland with my wife and child, and I would have to make frequent visits to London to sort out the legal mess," he recalls. These problems prevented Rafferty from recording for a few years, but his

frequent travels to London would serve as the inspiration for some of his new material. "I used to stay in London for four or five nights at a time. I spent a lot of time wandering around London, wondering if I was going to be able to get out of this terrible mess," says Rafferty.

Although Rafferty wrote "Baker Street" back home in Scotland, the song was about his experiences in London. "It's about the feeling of being alone in a city and how huge a city can be and how small and insignificant a person can feel in the face of it," he says.

The trademark riff of the song, played by Raphael Ravenscroft on saxophone, was always part of the song, but Rafferty didn't initially have saxophone in mind. "I felt at one point I would write lyrics for that part and I would sing it," Rafferty says, "but once the actual song structure came together, I realized it would make a good instrumental passage, but I didn't know what instrument would be appropriate." Rafferty tried guitar and piano, before deciding on the sax.

The track "Right Down the Line," written for Rafferty's wife at the time, was also inspired by the legal problems. "She had stood by me through some

really heavy times," he says. "It was just my way of saying thanks."

The ballad "Whatever's Written in Your Heart" is "one of my favorite songs I've written over the past 25 years," Rafferty says, while the album opener, "The Ark," which features fiddles and mandolin, reflects his background in Scottish and Irish folk music.

City to City was recorded "pretty much live," says Rafferty, at Chipping Norton Studios in London, except for some guitar overdubs. "It was a good band with a really gifted bunch of people," Rafferty says. "There was something about the chemistry that just really clicked."

In June 1978, "Baker Street," the second single from the album, climbed all the way to number two on the Hot 100, but was unable to dethrone Andy Gibb's "Shadow Dancing." Yet Rafferty would eventually have his revenge on the Gibbs, as *City to City* ended the six-month chart-topping reign of *Saturday Night Fever*, featuring Andy's older brothers, the Bee Gees. "It was an incredible surprise to me," says Rafferty. "I would have been happy if the album had sold 200,000 in the U.K. and Europe."

THE TOP FIVE
Week of July 8, 1978

1. **City to City**
   Gerry Rafferty

2. **Saturday Night Fever**
   Soundtrack

3. **Natural High**
   Commodores

4. **Some Girls**
   The Rolling Stones

5. **Stranger in Town**
   Bob Seger & the Silver Bullet Band

228 Some Girls ROLLING STONES 39108
THE ROLLING STONES

Producers: The Glimmer Twins

Track listing: Miss You / When the Whip Comes Down / Just My Imagination (Running Away with Me) / Some Girls / Lies / Far Away Eyes / Respectable / Before They Make Me Run / Beast of Burden

July 15, 1978
2 weeks

Though the Rolling Stones scored their sixth Number One album in 1976 with Black And Blue [see 216], the band was beginning to have trouble living up to its legacy as "the world's greatest rock 'n' roll band." For starters, punk rock had exploded in England with bands such as the Sex Pistols and the Clash targeting the Stones as washed-up dinosaurs. Worse still, guitarist Keith Richards was arrested on February 27, 1977, at the Harbour Castle hotel in Toronto for possession of 22 grams of heroin and five grams of cocaine. A charge of trafficking in heroin would loom over Richards's head for the next year and a half.

In spite of the misfortune, or maybe because of it, when the Stones regrouped at Pathe-Marconi studios in Paris in September 1977, the group

was re-energized. Perhaps the potential of a Richards prison term gave the group the urgency of knowing that this could be their last album for a long time; perhaps they just wanted to show the punks that they could still rock. In any event, the result was Some Girls, the band's finest album since Exile on Main St. [see 145].

"It was a great time," says engineer and mixer Chris Kimsey, who first worked with the Stones engineering Sticky Fingers [see 132] with Glyn Johns. Adding to the mood was the studio environment. The Stones started working on the album in the demo studio and opted to stay in that room because Kimsey and Richards preferred the sound, even though it only had a 16-track soundboard and Mick Jagger favored the main studio.

"The atmosphere was more like a live show," says Kimsey, "because a lot of people would come down to the studio and mill around. The studio was actually like a big soundstage with a whole bar area set up, so it was a very relaxed informal atmosphere."

During the sessions, which ran approximately six months, more than 42 songs were recorded. Several of the songs that didn't make Some Girls would later surface on such subsequent

albums as Emotional Rescue [see 249] and Tattoo You [see 264]. For example, on the same day the Stones cut "Miss You," they also laid down "Start Me Up," which showed up on Tattoo You.

" 'Start Me Up' was canned because we all liked 'Miss You' better," says Kimsey. "It was a great song with Sugar Blue playing Mick's harp riff."

As Some Girls was the band's first full effort with Ronnie Wood, his guitar became more integrated into the overall sound of the band. "Ronnie was quite diverse in his playing," says Kimsey. "He played pedal steel on 'Faraway Eyes' and played a lot of slide guitar, too."

Since the Stones were more interested in songwriting than production, they gave Kimsey a relatively free hand to edit and mix the material. "The title track was actually 24 minutes long, originally," says Kimsey, "but after we finished cutting it, Mick asked me to chop it down to three-and-half, four minutes."

The album's original cover, featuring the faces of Lucille Ball, Raquel Welch, and Farrah Fawcett-Majors on the sleeve, had to be withdrawn after legal action was threatened. Some lyrics on the title track raised some ire as well, especially the line that found Jagger opining that "black girls just wanna get fucked all night."

The controversies, however, didn't hurt the Stones. In its fourth week on the chart, Some Girls hit the summit, becoming the Stones' seventh chart-topper. Three weeks later, "Miss You," the group's answer to the disco craze, topped the Hot 100. The Stones had proven once again that they could survive and even thrive through the fads of the day.

THE TOP FIVE
Week of July 15, 1978

1. **Some Girls**
   Rolling Stones

2. **City to City**
   Gerry Rafferty

3. **Natural High**
   Commodores

4. **Saturday Night Fever**
   Soundtrack

5. **Stranger in Town**
   Bob Seger & the Silver Bullet Band

Compiled by: Bill Oakes

Track listing: Grease [Frankie Valli] / Summer Nights [John Travolta, Olivia Newton-John & Cast] / Hopelessly Devoted to You [Newton-John] / You're the One That I Want [Travolta, Newton-John] / Sandy [Travolta] / Beauty School Drop-Out [Frankie Avalon] / Look at Me, I'm Sandra Dee [Stockard Channing] / Greased Lightnin' [Travolta, Jeff Conaway] / It's Raining on Prom Night [Cindy Bullens] / Alone at a Drive-In Movie / Blue Moon [Sha-Na-Na] / Rock n' Roll Is Here to Stay / Those Magic Changes / Hound Dog / Born to Hand-Jive / Tears on My Pillow / Mooning [Louis St. Louis & Bullens] / Freddy My Love [Bullens] / Rock n' Roll Party Queen [St. Louis] / There Are Worse Things I Could Do [Channing] / Look at Me I'm Sandra Dee (Reprise) [Newton-John] / We Go Together [Travolta, Newton-John & cast] / Love Is a Many Splendored Thing / Grease (Reprise) [Valli]

July 29, 1978
12 weeks (nonconsecutive)

Olivia Newton-John and John Travolta in *Grease*.

RSO Records was enjoying the incredible success of *Saturday Night Fever* [see 226] while preparing to launch *Grease*, which would turn out to be its second huge soundtrack hit of 1978. The project had all the right ingredients for success. The film version, based on the hit Broadway musical, starred *Saturday Night Fever* sensation John Travolta and pop sweetheart Olivia Newton-John [see 183]. The story, set in the late '50s, centered around the love affair between a greaser (Travolta) and a prim-and-proper high school girl (Newton-John). Like the musical, the film featured several remakes of rock 'n' roll classics, but RSO wanted something new as well, so they called on the Bee Gees' Barry Gibb to compose the title track.

Gibb was sitting at home in Miami the day he got the call. "Robert Stigwood called up and said he and [film co-producer] Allan Carr had everything they wanted for the film *Grease*, but the strangest thing is that they didn't have a song called 'Grease.' They asked me if I would write a song for the movie. I went and sat back in the lounge and basically sketched the song out while I was watching television. I didn't think that much of it." An hour later, Gibb called up Stigwood and sang him the song over the phone. "The word was that Allan Carr didn't really like it, but Robert Stigwood did," Gibb says.

Stigwood had the final word, and Gibb's "Grease" was in. It would be performed by Frankie Valli of the Four Seasons. "It was real smart casting, because they found someone to sing it who reflected that era," says Gibb, who also produced the track. "I was a big Four Seasons fan in my childhood, so making the record with one of my heroes was real special to me."

"Grease" became the second Number One hit from the soundtrack. "You're the One That I Want," a duet featuring Travolta and Newton-John, which was also written specifically for the film, also hit the top spot. "*Grease* revived Olivia Newton-John's career," says RSO Records executive Al Coury. Travolta was not known for his singing skills, despite the fact he had released two albums on Midland International Records. Yet Coury says he had the right stuff for a hit record. "He was young, beautiful, and had a great deal of appeal to young audiences, both male and female."

Initially, executives at Paramount Pictures, which distributed the film, wanted to use an illustration on the album cover. "I went crazy," Coury says. "With Olivia Newton-John and John Travolta, we had two of the prettiest people in America, maybe in the world." In the end, Coury won, a photo of Newton-John and Travolta graced the LP cover, and *Grease* went on to become one of the best-selling soundtracks of all time, moving over eight million copies.

THE TOP FIVE
Week of July 29, 1978

1. **Grease**
   Soundtrack

2. **Some Girls**
   Rolling Stones

3. **Natural High**
   Commodores

4. **Stranger in Town**
   Bob Seger & the Silver Bullet Band

5. **Darkness at the Edge of Town**
   Bruce Springsteen

230 Don't Look Back EPIC 35050
BOSTON

Producer: Tom Scholz

Track listing: Don't Look Back / The Journey / It's Easy / A Man I'll Never Be / Feelin' Satisfied / Party / Used to Bad News / Don't Be Afraid

September 16, 1978
2 weeks (nonconsecutive)

Don't Look Back was the album that Boston never really quite finished. "We really rushed to complete that one," says Tom Scholz, the band's founder and creator of its trademark guitar sound. "The second side is only 15 minutes long. I would have liked to have another six months to work on a fifth song on that side."

Boston was launched into orbit following the release of its 1976 self-titled debut. Buoyed by the track "More Than a Feeling," which became an album-rock staple, the album climbed to number three by December of that year.

In support of Boston, the band toured extensively. Upon its return, Scholz went to work on his home studio, dubbed Hideaway, to record a follow-up album. Don't Look Back was approximately 18 months in the making, including a few months for construction of Scholz's studio, which he describes as "the size of a lavatory." The entire album was recorded at Hideaway, save for the piano on the power ballad "A Man I'll Never Be." Says Scholz, "The studio was so small, it was impossible to get the piano in there."

Just as the album's guitar-as-spaceship cover art was a variation of the graphic that graced the band's debut effort, the music on Don't Look Back was strikingly similar to that on Boston. "That is rock 'n' roll the way I like it, so it's always going to sound that way," says Scholz.

On Boston and Don't Look Back, Scholz and company used no synthesizers or computers, something Scholz felt he had to point out in the liner notes of the latter album. "There was a rumor that I wrote the entire first album with a computer program," he says. "There was even an article in Newsweek that had me denying it."

The rumors were generated by Scholz's background. "Someone at CBS glanced at my bio and discovered I was a graduate of MIT, so they tried to market us as modern-day robots," he says. "For a while they even ran radio spots that said, 'Boston, better music through science.' "

While Boston did have an unusual high-tech guitar sound, the songs on Don't Look Back came together organically. " 'Don't Look Back' was the last song I wrote and recorded for the album," says Scholz. "It was just one of those things where everything clicked. I didn't even record a demo for that song. I came up with chord changes, melody, and the arrangement and put it right on the master tape."

Another of Scholz's favorites is "The Journey," a spacey instrumental that follows the title track. "I always wanted to edit that and loop it and make it last for about an hour and put it on when I wanted to go to sleep or relax," says Scholz.

Even without that fifth track on side two, Don't Look Back rocketed up the Top LP's & Tape chart. In its third week on the chart, Don't Look Back hit the top spot.

THE TOP FIVE
Week of September 16, 1978

1. **Don't Look Back**
   Boston

2. **Some Girls**
   The Rolling Stones

3. **Double Vision**
   Foreigner

4. **Grease**
   Soundtrack

5. **Sgt. Pepper's Lonely Hearts Club Band**
   Soundtrack

ASYLUM 155 **Living in the USA**
LINDA RONSTADT

231

Producer: Peter Asher

Track listing: Back in the U.S.A. /
When I Grow Too Old to Dream / Just
One Look / Allison / White Rhythm &
Blues / All That You Dream / Ooh
Baby Baby / Mohammed's Radio /
Blowing Away / Love Me Tender

November 4, 1978
1 week

Following the success of *Simple
Dreams* [see 225], Linda Ronstadt
was on top of the world. On April
3, 1978, the film *FM* premiered with
Ronstadt featured performing a cover
version of Elvis Presley's "Love Me Tender." The song was also featured on *Living in the USA*, which like Ronstadt's

previous hit albums featured a mix of
covers of proven hits and newer compositions by some of Ronstadt's favorite
contemporary songwriters.

Yet there were changes evident as
well. For one, as the album's cover photo
showed, Ronstadt had cut her trademark
long hair. She also traded in her usual
country-style dresses for hot pants, and
her high heels for roller skates.

Living in the USA was recorded at
the Sound Factory in Los Angeles from
May 5 through July 3, 1978. "I remember I wanted to bring my roller skates
into the studio," Ronstadt says. "My
friend Nicolette Larson and I used to
skate everywhere. She used to bring her
skates into the studio because it was
really big and she could skate around in
between takes. My studio wasn't that

big. It had too much carpet, so I wanted
them to take it out so I could skate."

While Ronstadt paid tribute to the
King with a cover of "Love Me Tender,"
she also acknowledged the influence of
the burgeoning British new wave movement by covering the other Elvis. "Allison" had first appeared on Elvis Costello's debut LP, *My Aim Is True*, and
remains his best-known tune today. "I
had a friend at the time and that song
reminded me of her, so I sang it for
her," Ronstadt says. "She was a really
sweet girl, but kind of a party-girl type. I
felt like she needed somebody to talk to
her in a stern voice, because she was
getting married and she would have to
change." Ronstadt's version was
released as a single in the U.K. but
stalled at number 66, and was dismissed in interviews by the acid-tongued
Costello. (Nonetheless, Ronstadt's 1980
album *Mad Love* would include three
songs by Costello.)

Although Ronstadt's attempt at new
wave wasn't initially a commercial success, she continued to score with her
updates of oldies. The album's first single, a remake of Chuck Berry's "Back in
the U.S.A.," climbed to number 16. A
take of Doris Troy's "Just One Look"
stalled at number 44, but Ronstadt was-
n't happy with the recorded version. "It
took me years to learn how to really
sing that, but I could nail it now," she
says, 15 years later.

The biggest hit from *Living in the
USA* was Ronstadt's cover of Smokey
Robinson's "Ooh Baby Baby," which
climbed to number seven. "We used a
live vocal from the rough mix," Ronstadt
says. "We tried to go in and add things
to it, but it never sounded as good as
that live vocal."

THE TOP FIVE
Week of November 4, 1978

1. **Living in the USA**
   Linda Ronstadt

2. **Grease**
   Soundtrack

3. **Live and More**
   Donna Summer

4. **Who Are You**
   The Who

5. **Double Vision**
   Foreigner

232 Live and More CASABLANCA 7119
DONNA SUMMER

Producers: Giorgio Moroder and Pete Bellotte

Track listing: Once Upon a Time / Fairy Tale High / Faster and Faster / Spring Affair / Rumor Has It / I Love You / Only One Man / I Remember Yesterday / Love's Unkind / May Man Medley: The Man I Love/I Got It Bad and That Ain't Good/Some of These Days / The Way We Were / Mimi's Song / Try Me, I Know We Can Make It / Love to Love You, Baby / I Feel Love / Last Dance / MacArthur Park Suite / MacArthur Park / One of a Kind / Heaven Knows / MacArthur Park (Reprise)

November 11, 1978
1 week

By the summer of 1978, Donna Summer was the queen of disco, scoring such hits as the sexy "Love to Love You Baby," "I Feel Love," and "Last Dance." Summer even starred as an aspiring singer in the 1978 disco-themed film Thank God It's Friday, which featured the latter track.

Yet despite her success on the Hot 100 Singles chart, Summer's albums didn't fare as well. Up to that point, her highest-charting album was her 1975 debut, Love to Love You Baby, which reached number 11 in February 1976. There were also those who assumed the singer was nothing more than a puppet of producer Giorgio Moroder, the mas-

termind behind her early hits.

Summer and Casablanca Records devised a plan to prove her naysayers wrong. She would record a live album that would prove her vocal prowess and put to rest the claims that she was nothing more than a studio creation. "It was always rumored that disco singers can't sing," Summer says. "It was all hype from studios, the engineers, and the producers. It's all producers' magic. I just felt that having come from a real history of theater and music, it was time for me to get up there and sing."

Although Summer first gained fame for her work in the recording studio, her first big gig was as a cast member in a production of Hair that played in Munich. While in Germany, Summer was discovered by Pete Bellote and Moroder in 1973.

Recorded at the Universal Amphitheatre in Los Angeles, Live and More featured in-concert recordings of several of Summer's big hits and album tracks. There were also some surprising selections, including a cover of "The Way We Were," a song made popular by Barbra Streisand [see 171].

Yet Live and More, as the title suggests, wasn't just a live album. Summer's concert performance filled three sides of the album, leaving the fourth side open. "But they didn't want me to go in and fake a live performance of something that wasn't real," Summer says. "So they said, 'Let's call it Live and More and the More will be new songs and

that will be good, because that will push the record too."

Side four centered around a discofied cover of Jimmy Webb's "MacArthur Park." Says Summer, "Giorgio thought it would be a great track for me to sing, because it would show more of my range. He felt I needed to sing something more demanding."

Moroder's idea did the trick, as the edited version of "MacArthur Park" hit the top of the Hot 100 the same week that Live and More reached Number One on the album chart. In March 1974, Live and More's studio side yielded another hit, "Heaven Knows" (credited to Summer and a trio of backing vocalists called Brooklyn Dreams), which reached number four.

THE TOP FIVE
Week of November 11, 1978

1. **Live and More**
   Donna Summer

2. **Living in the USA**
   Linda Ronstadt

3. **Grease**
   Soundtrack

4. **Double Vision**
   Foreigner

5. **52nd Street**
   Billy Joel

35609 COLUMBIA **52nd Street**
BILLY JOEL

233

Producer: Phil Ramone

Track listing: Big Shot / Honesty / My Life / Zanzibar / Stiletto / Rosanlinda's Eyes / Half a Mile Away / Until the Night / 52nd Street

November 18, 1978
8 weeks (nonconsecutive)

Success certainly didn't come overnight for Billy Joel, but when it came, it came big. Joel's recording career began in the late '60s as a member of the Hassles, who released two albums that failed to chart. Next was a duo called Attila, which recorded one album in 1970 that also failed to garner notice.

After a solo misstep with 1971's non-charting *Cold Spring Harbour* on the Family label, Joel arrived with his 1974 Columbia debut, *Piano Man*, which reached number 27. However, his follow-ups—1974's *Streetlife Serenade* and 1976's *Turnstiles*—didn't fare as well, peaking at 35 and 122, respectively. It was 1977's *The Stranger* that truly put Joel on the pop map. The album, which included the number three single "Just the Way You Are," spent six weeks at number two but was unable to break *Saturday Night Fever's* [see 226] stranglehold on the Number One spot. "I wasn't a big fan of John Travolta for a while," Joel quips.

With a hit album under his belt, Joel entered A&R Recording in New York to record the follow-up album. "There was a certain amount of pressure to do an album somewhat like *The Stranger*," says Joel. "But my instinct was to not try to do an album like that and just do what I felt like doing."

To that end, Joel incorporated jazz elements into his sound. The album's title refers to the jazz influences and the fact that the album lacks one defining theme. "I was told after the album was done, when I was looking for a title, that 52nd Street [where A&R Recording studio was located] used to be known as Swing Street, because that's where all the jazz guys had their clubs," he says. The title was also a nod to one of Joel's favorite acts, the Beatles. "I was thinking of *Abbey Road* [see 117]," he says. "If you listen to that album, there is really no cohesion, except for George Martin sewing everything together. I looked at my album and I thought, 'What do these songs have in common? Nothing, except they were all recorded at the 52nd Street studio.'"

With material ranging from the pop-rockers "My Life" and "Big Shot" to the ballad "Honesty" and the jazz-infused "Zanzibar," *52nd Street* was Joel's most diverse effort to date. Although this was Joel's fifth solo album, it marked only the third time he had recorded with his own touring band. "They didn't have a lot of finesse, they didn't know how to read sheet music, but they knew how to play the way I wanted to play," he says. "It was rough-and-tumble, performance-oriented rock 'n' roll, and also they could play the softer pieces."

Joel's band, billed as the Lords of 52nd Street, were also able to play with special guests, such as jazz great Freddie Hubbard, whose trumpet solo was featured on "Zanzibar." Says Joel, "That was a special treat for me, because I've always admired and respected jazz players. I remember after we finished the instrumental break that Freddie played on, Liberty DeVitto, my drummer, looked over at me and said, 'Now, I feel like a grown-up.'"

With *52nd Street*, Joel and company did reach a new level in musical maturity and commercial success. The album climbed to Number One in its fourth week on the chart. Even *Grease* [see 229], another soundtrack from a film starring John Travolta, couldn't keep the Piano Man from the pole position.

THE TOP FIVE
Week of November 18, 1978

1. **52nd Street**
   Billy Joel

2. **Live and More**
   Donna Summer

3. **Double Vision**
   Foreigner

4. **Living in the USA**
   Linda Ronstadt

5. **Grease**
   Soundtrack

234 Barbra Streisand's Greatest Hits, Volume 2 COLUMBIA 35679
BARBRA STREISAND

Producers: Barbra Streisand, Phil Ramone, Gary Klein, Charlie Calello, Bob Gaudio, Marty Paich, Tommy LiPuma, and Richard Perry

Track listing: Love Theme from "A Star Is Born" (Evergreen) / Love Theme from "Eyes of Laura Mars" (Prisoner) / My Heart Belongs to Me / Songbird / You Don't Bring Me Flowers / The Way We Were / Sweet Inspiration/Where You Lead / All in Love Is Fair / Superman / Stoney End

January 6, 1979
3 weeks

Barbra Streisand's first *Greatest Hits* album, released in February 1970, may have been a bit premature. While the singer/actress's first nine albums, released from 1963 to 1966, all made the top 10 of the album chart, Streisand didn't enjoy as much success on the Hot 100. In fact, "People" [see 70], which reached number five in 1964, was her only single to break into the top 40 prior to "Stoney End" in 1970.

Barbra Streisand's Greatest Hits Volume 2, however, lived up to its title. The album, which includes songs recorded from 1972 through 1978, features Streisand's first three Number One singles—"The Way We Were" [see 171], "Love Theme from 'A Star Is Born' (Evergreen)" [see 222], and "You Don't Bring Me Flowers," a duet with Neil Diamond. It also chronicles Streisand's success on the silver screen, as two of those three hits were from blockbuster films starring Streisand. She did not appear in the 1978 film *The Eyes of Laura Mars*, but she did have a hit with the theme song, which reached number 21.

Some of the most memorable songs among the other tracks on *Greatest Hits Volume 2* were culled from the 1972 album *Live Concert at the Forum*, which reached number 19. The concert was a benefit for Democratic presidential candidate George McGovern. Streisand originally recorded the song "Where You Lead," written by Carole King and Toni Stern, in 1971 on *Barbra Joan Streisand,* the second album she recorded with producer Richard Perry. It was only appropriate that she performed it at the McGovern concert at the Forum, since King was also on the bill. Instead of doing the song straight, however, Streisand turned it into a medley with Dan Penn and Spooner Oldham's "Sweet Inspiration."

At the concert, Streisand also performed "Stoney End," but initially she was hesitant to perform the song live. "She was afraid to do it, because it had been two years, approximately, since it was a hit," recalls Perry. "She didn't think people would remember it. She wanted to do 'Second Hand Rose' instead." The producer tried to talk Streisand into performing the song and even volunteered to write the lyrics, which Streisand had forgotten, on the floor. "So I was there on my hands and knees for about an hour scrawling in chalk on the stage the verses to 'Stoney End.'" At the concert, Streisand asked the crowd if they wanted to hear the song; the response was overwhelming. "She performed it brilliantly," says Perry.

The studio version of "Stoney End," included on the 1971 album of the same name and on *Greatest Hits Volume 2*, holds a special place in Perry's heart. "That was the first session we had ever done together and it was the longest session in the history of the Los Angeles Musicians Union. It started a 7 P.M. and ended at 5:30 A.M., and not one string player complained." The song was cut with a full orchestra and background singers live in the studio. "'Stoney End' was the third track that we cut that night and it was the one that was the riskiest, but also the one that had the most potential to become a hit." Although the song wasn't in the Streisand mold, the singer was able to adapt to the material. "She came there to sing," says Perry. "When we did the first take, it was a real thrilling moment."

Streisand undoubtedly had another thrilling moment when *Greatest Hits Volume 2* became her fourth Number One album in its sixth week on the chart.

THE TOP FIVE
Week of January 6, 1979

1. **Barbra Streisand's Greatest Hits, Volume 2**
   Barbra Streisand

2. **A Wild and Crazy Guy**
   Steve Martin

3. **52nd Street**
   Billy Joel

4. **C'Est Chic**
   Chic

5. **Grease**
   Soundtrack

ATLANTIC 19217 # Briefcase Full of Blues
BLUES BROTHERS **235**

Producer: Bob Tischler

*Track listing: Hey Bartender / Messin'
with the Kid / Almost / Rubber Biscuit
/ Shot Gun Blues / Groove Me / I
Don't Know / Soul Man / "B" Movie
Box Car Blues / Flip, Flop & Fly*

February 3, 1979
1 week

Much like the Monkees [see 91], the Blues Brothers began as characters on a TV show before developing into a recording act. By the fall of 1977, NBC's two-year-old "Saturday Night Live" had become one of the best-rated late-night shows on television. Funnymen Dan Aykroyd and John Belushi were among the most popular of the show's "Not Ready for Prime-Time Players," but the duo also had other ambitions.

"The Blues Brothers were born when John and Danny decided to play a little blues to warm up the audience before the 'Saturday Night Live' show," says Paul Shaffer, the musical director of both "SNL" and, later, the Blues Brothers Band. For the performances, Aykroyd and Belushi would slip into the alter egos of Elwood Blues and Jake Blues, respectively, complete with black '50s-styled suits, skinny ties, fedoras, and Ray-Bans.

The warm-up performances became so popular that they were soon included on the actual "Saturday Night Live" broadcasts, and Aykroyd and Belushi decided to cut an album. Shaffer helped Belushi put together a band. "We hired each person one by one," says Shaffer. "Sort of like the way it was depicted in the [1981 *Blues Brothers*] movie." This wasn't just any band, though — Belushi and Shaffer turned to some of the most acclaimed session players in the business, including guitarist Steve Cropper and bassist Donald Dunn of Booker T. & the MG's.

Despite Aykroyd and Belushi's comedic backgrounds and the often humorous songs performed by the Blues Brothers, the duo's love for the blues was no joke. "Danny had considerable experience playing harmonica in a Canadian blues band," says Shaffer. "John was in a rock band in high school. He fell in love with the blues while filming *National Lampoon's Animal House*." While working on the 1978 film, Belushi met bluesman Curtis Salgado, who fronted a band led by guitarist Robert Cray. "It was Curtis, in some all-night sessions after filming, who really turned John onto the blues," Shaffer says. "By the time we met to pick the material, John was quite an expert on the seminal blues musicians."

With the all-star crew backing up Belushi's Jake and Aykroyd's Elwood, the Blues Brothers rehearsed before hitting the road to record *Briefcase Full of Blues*. "Everyone knew that John and Danny were so hot that there would be a lot of attention paid to what they did," says Shaffer. "But once the band started rehearsing, you couldn't deny the energy. The first time we ran through 'Soul Man,' [drummer] Steve Jordan and I were so excited that we grabbed each other and started to jump up and down. This was the ultimate soul band."

With enthusiasm from within the band overflowing, the group hit the road in support of comedian and frequent "Saturday Night Live" host Steve Martin. *Briefcase Full of Blues* was recorded live at the Universal Amphitheatre in Los Angeles during a multinight stand in September 1978.

Seven weeks after its December release, *Briefcase Full of Blues* hit Number One, spurred by the top 20 hit cover of Sam & Dave's "Soul Man." For Cropper and Dunn it was déjà vu, since both had played on the 1967 original as members of the Stax house band.

The Blues Brothers' subsequent releases failed to match the success of their debut, and the band's career came to a close when Belushi died of a drug overdose in March 1982. Still, it wouldn't be the last time a "Saturday Night Live" spin-off hit Number One [see *Wayne's World*—359].

THE TOP FIVE
Week of February 3, 1979

1. **Briefcase Full of Blues**
   Blues Brothers

2. **Blondes Have More Fun**
   Rod Stewart

3. **52nd Street**
   Billy Joel

4. **You Don't Bring Me Flowers**
   Neil Diamond

5. **Barbra Streisand's Greatest Hits, Vol. 2**
   Barbra Streisand

236 Blondes Have More Fun WARNER BROS. 3261
ROD STEWART

Producer: Tom Dowd

Track listing: Do Ya Think I'm Sexy? / Dirty Weekend / Ain't Love a Bitch / The Best Days of My Life / Is That the Thanks I Get? / Attractive Female Wanted / Blondes (Have More Fun) / Last Summer / Standin' in the Shadows of Love / Scarred and Scared

February 10, 1979
3 weeks

By 1978, more than seven years after his first Number One album, *Every Picture Tells a Story* [see 134], things had changed dramatically for Rod Stewart. In late '75, the Faces officially split and Stewart left Mercury Records for Warner Bros. He relocated to Los Angeles, partly to escape the U.K. taxman but also to spend time with his latest flame, actress Britt Ekland. Stewart had gone from his humble London beginnings to the glitz and glamour of Beverly Hills, and it soon became reflected in his music. On *Blondes Have More Fun* the earthy sounds of acoustic guitars and mandolins featured on his first Number One single, "Maggie May," gave way to the hedonistic disco beat of "Do Ya Think I'm Sexy?," which would become his best-selling single ever.

While many rock critics looked on in horror as Stewart transformed himself from credible rocker to pop-trendhopper, the public ate it up. Yet Stewart's evolution didn't happen overnight. Following the split of the Faces, Stewart hooked up with veteran American producer Tom Dowd for his 1975 Warner Bros. debut album, *Atlantic Crossing*. The album was moderately successful, paving the

way for his full-fledged comeback on 1976's *A Night on the Town* and 1977's *Foot Loose & Fancy Free*, which included such hits as "Tonight's the Night (Gonna Be Alright)" and "You're in My Heart," respectively.

With the release of *Blondes Have More Fun*, Stewart was primed for his biggest success. He recorded the album with Dowd once again handling the production chores, and with a veteran band, including ex–Vanilla Fudge drummer Carmine Appice. It was with Appice that Stewart co-wrote "Do Ya Think I'm Sexy?," which became the fastest-selling single in the history of Warner Bros. Records—loved by his legions of fans, loathed by most rock critics, and misunderstood by nearly everyone.

"I suppose you could say I was jumping on a bandwagon, really," Stewart says of his disco hit. "But I think it still has some nice lyrics to it. It's not banal. Everybody thought I was singing about myself. Of course I'm not, I'm singing in the third person." While there may have been some confusion about

who was asking the musical question "Do Ya Think I'm Sexy?," there was little question of what Stewart's favorite topic was. "Sex," he says. "I'm a very horny lad." That was not only reflected in his previous hits "Tonight's the Night" and "Hot Legs," but on several tracks on *Blondes Have More Fun*, including "Dirty Weekend," in which the song's protagonist runs away with his best friend's girl for a few days of fun.

Yet it was "Do Ya Think I'm Sexy?" that drove *Blondes Have More Fun* to the top. The album and single hit Number One on their respective charts the same week, marking the second time that Stewart had topped both charts simultaneously.

Although *Blondes* went on to become Stewart's best-selling album, he considers *Foot Loose & Fancy Free*, which peaked at number two, much better. As for the single, "I'm only just about being forgiven," he quips. "It was a bit of tripe, really, when you look at it, but in saying that, it's still our most popular song when we do it live."

THE TOP FIVE
of February, 10 1979

1. **Blondes Have More Fun**
   Rod Stewart

2. **Briefcase Full of Blues**
   Blues Brothers

3. **52nd Street**
   Billy Joel

4. **You Don't Bring Me Flowers**
   Neil Diamond

5. **Barbra Streisand's Greatest Hits, Vol. 2**
   Barbra Streisand

RSO 3041 **Spirits Having Flown**
BEE GEES **237**

Producers: Bee Gees, Karl Richardson, and Albhy Galuten

Track listing: Tragedy / Too Much Heaven / Love You Inside Out / Reaching Out / Spirits Having Flown / Search, Find / Stop (Think Again) / Living Together / I'm Satisfied / Until

March 3, 1979
6 weeks (nonconsecutive)

"**W**e had three or four songs in the top 10 when we were recording Spirits Having Flown," says Bee Gees singer/guitarist Barry Gibb. "We went to pop heaven for about two years. There's a good side and bad side to that. The good side is that you get a hit no matter what, which can be unhealthy. The bad side is you can't answer your own phone, you can't go to the cinema or a restaurant, and you have people climbing over your walls. That's not the life I wanted to lead."

Indeed things had changed dramatically for the Brothers Gibb with the incredible success of Saturday Night Fever [see 226]. Between March and November 1978, while the group was recording Spirits Having Flown, five singles recorded by or written by one of the group's members hit the top spot on the Hot 100, including Andy Gibb's "(Love Is) Thicker Than Water," the Bee Gees' own "Night Fever," Yvonne Elliman's "If I Can't Have You," Andy Gibb's "Shadow Dancing," and Frankie Valli's "Grease" [see 229]. Meanwhile Saturday Night Fever occupied the

Number One spot on the album chart from January 21 until July 8.

"We were just reflecting what was going on around us," Barry Gibb says. "We were suddenly living in a goldfish bowl and we couldn't perceive real life. We couldn't go and hang out like we used to and go sit in a club where we used to get our ideas...Writing became different."

On Spirits Having Flown, the Bee Gees attempted to sidestep disco, which had exploded into a worldwide phenomenon with the success of Saturday Night Fever. "It was at the time of when we had discovered the falsettos and we were experimenting with that," Barry Gibb says. "It was really an experimentation of us trying to move away from Saturday Night Fever. We were trying to follow up such a mammoth album, but not really knowing how to do that, and we were trying to get back to the mindset we had before Saturday Night Fever. It was sort of a scatterbrained scenario. We were looking for a focus and Spirits Having Flown as a title reflects that."

By 1979, the Bee Gees had already been veterans on the roller coaster of fame. The group of brothers—Barry, and twins Robin and Maurice—first performed publicly in 1955. Their 1967 debut album, Bee Gees 1st, climbed to number seven, fueled by the top 20 hits "New York Mining Disaster 1941" and "To Love Somebody." In the late '60s, the band temporarily split. A series of hits and misses followed until the group staged a successful comeback in the mid-'70s with the Number One single

"Jive Talkin'." Says Barry Gibb, "We had been written off by the early '70s as being has-beens. By 1975, we were looking at making a comeback. If Eric Clapton hadn't suggested that we try to make an album in Miami, we might not have come back at all."

The group returned to Miami to record Spirits Having Flown at Criteria Recording Studios. Apparently, the city once again reignited the group's creative spark. "Too Much Heaven," was released as a single to benefit UNICEF in advance of the album. It climbed to the top in seven weeks, setting the stage for Spirits Having Flown. The second and third singles, "Tragedy" and "Love You Inside Out" also hit the top spot, giving the Bee Gees six consecutive Number One singles, tying a record set by the Beatles.

THE TOP FIVE
Week of March 3, 1979

1. **Spirits Having Flown**
   Bee Gees

2. **Blondes Have More Fun**
   Rod Stewart

3. **Cruisin'**
   Village People

4. **Dire Straits**
   Dire Straits

5. **Briefcase Full of Blues**
   Blues Brothers

238 Minute by Minute WARNER BROS. 3193
THE DOOBIE BROTHERS

Producer: Ted Templeman

Track listing: Here to Love You / What a Fool Believes / Minute by Minute / Dependin' on You / Don't Stop to Watch the Wheels / Open Your Eyes / Sweet Feelin' / Steamer Lane Breakdown / You Never Change / How Do the Fools Survive?

April 7, 1979
5 weeks (nonconsecutive)

"We had just come off a record that everyone was a little disappointed with," says keyboardist/vocalist Michael McDonald. "So with *Minute by Minute*, in some ways there was a little more tension, but in some other ways the tension was kind of relieved, because the worst was over."

Simply put, the Doobie Brothers were one of the most successful American rock acts of the '70s. Following the release of 1972's *Toulouse Street*, the group's second album, each subsequent Doobies album cracked the top 10 of the album chart, with 1976's *Takin' It to the Streets*, reaching number eight and going on to sales of more than a million copies. *Best of the Doobies*, a hits collection released later that same year, reached number five.

However, the Doobies' fortunes soured with 1977's *Livin' on the Fault Line*. "Going into that album we were really anxious, because of the success of *Takin' It to the Streets*," says McDonald. "But with *Minute by Minute*, even though there was some anxiety, we had kind of suffered the blow already, so we had a little more of a relaxed attitude about the music."

By 1977, the Doobie Brothers had

gone through significant lineup changes. In 1974, guitarist Jeff "Skunk" Baxter, formerly of Steely Dan, joined the band. A year later, McDonald, who had also worked with Steely Dan, joined. As a result, the band's musical direction began to change from rock to a more polished R&B approach. On *Minute by Minute*, the lead vocals and songwriting credits were split between McDonald and Doobies co-founder guitarist/vocalist Patrick Simmons. Yet McDonald says Simmons was still considered the leader of the band. "If anyone was the leader of the band, it was Patrick," says McDonald. "We all tended to look to him and he had the demeanor for it."

While Simmons remained the leader, McDonald was emerging as the band's creative force, as both of the big hit singles were tracks he co-wrote and sang.

The Doobies spent approximately a year working on *Minute by Minute*, occasionally breaking for a string of live dates. Ted Templeman, who produced all of the Doobie's albums, was again at the helm when the band cut the album at Warner Bros. Studios in North Hollywood.

"What a Fool Believes" was written

by McDonald with Kenny Loggins [see 279] sitting at the piano in his home in Studio City, California. A few days following the writing session, the duo came up with the song's chorus on the telephone. Recording the track was a bit more difficult. "We must have cut 25 takes in the course of a few days," McDonald recalls. When tensions began to rise between the band members who were becoming increasingly frustrated, Templeman intervened. "He said, 'We got it. I'll use take eight and splice it right at the first bridge with take 22 and it'll work,' " McDonald says. "It was great. It worked fine. It was the take we were trying to do, but for some reason, it eluded us."

The title track also did not come easily. "I remember emotionally brutalizing [drummer] Keith Knudsen," says McDonald. "It was a difficult song to play, because it was a 6/8 shuffle, but it was important to get it right, because it was just me on keyboards, Tiran Porter on bass, and Keith on drums. I was so focused on getting the track to feel right that by the time we were finished, Keith was probably close to suicide, but he hung in there until we got it right."

A&M 3708 **Breakfast in America**
SUPERTRAMP

239

Producer: Supertramp and Peter Henderson

Track listing: Gone Hollywood / The Logical Song / Goodbye Stranger / Breakfast in America / Oh Darling / Take the Long Way Home / Lord Is It Mine / Just Another Nervous Wreck / Casual Conversations / Child of Vision

May 19, 1979
6 weeks (nonconsecutive)

Success for Supertramp certainly didn't happen overnight. The British group was founded in 1969, after Dutch millionaire Stanley August Miesegeaes caught singer/keyboardist Rick Davies's band the Joint at a gig in Munich, Germany. The Joint fell apart, but Miesegeaes offered financial support to Davies to start another band. Supertramp was formed with the players who responded to Davies's ads in a British music paper.

The band went through numerous personnel changes as its first few albums failed to chart. Finally, in 1974, the group landed its first chart album with *Crime of the Century*, which reached number 38. The 1975 followup, *Crisis? What Crisis?*, only reached number 44, but the band rebounded with 1977's *Even in the Quietest Moments*, which peaked at number 16, thanks in part to the top 20 single "Give a Little Bit."

With its newfound success, the group relocated to America, and A&M re-released the band's 1970 self-titled album. "We were pretty much settled in Los Angeles at that time," says Davies. "We had a little bit of success with *Quietest Moments*, but we had no idea that *Breakfast* would do what it did."

To record the album, the group took its time, first booking Southcombe Studios in Burbank, California, for weeks of extensive rehearsals before moving into the Village Recorder in Los Angeles for approximately six months. "[Guitarist] Roger [Hodgson] and I had our own demo setups to write with four-track recorders," Davies says.

"It was the first time we came in with a little more arrangement ahead of time."

With a 10-year history under their collective belt, the band members worked like a fine-tuned machine during the making of *Breakfast in America*. "Supertramp at that time was a very easy band to be in," Davies says. "Everyone had their own function and part. We still weren't that big saleswise to start causing the usual friction when the songwriter gets more money than the drummer."

With continued touring and increasing acceptance on FM radio, Supertramp was primed for a breakthrough. "Somehow people seemed to know it was going to be big, I don't know how," Davies says. "We got a tremendous amount of advance orders before the thing was even finished."

Highlights included "The Logical Song." Says Davies, "It was all so easy. The saxophone solo was done at the time of the backing track. John [Helliwell] used to respond to the other players. If there was a good rhythm track, the solo was almost always there."

Breakfast in America was a group effort in the truest sense. "I insisted that we shouldn't have an orchestra on the album, that it should be the band, so whatever noises are on the album, they were produced by the five guys in the band." The only exceptions to that rule were the tuba and trombone played by "Slide" Hyde on the title track.

The title track and concept of the album originated years before the formation of Supertramp. "It was from a song that Roger had written when he was about 15, long before he had seen America," says Davies. "We were just looking for songs and that one came up. It made sense with us moving to America in 1975. We started to bend some of the other songs to that theme, like the track 'Gone Hollywood.'"

Fans ate up *Breakfast in America*, as the album became Supertramp's first and only chart-topper in its eighth week on the chart.

THE TOP FIVE
Week of May 19, 1979

1. **Breakfast in America**
   Supertramp

2. **2-Hot**
   Peaches & Herb

3. **Desolation Angels**
   Bad Company

4. **Minute by Minute**
   The Doobie Brothers

5. **Spirits Having Flown**
   Bee Gees

240 Bad Girls CASABLANCA 5007
DONNA SUMMER

Producers: Giorgio Moroder and Pete Bellotte

Track listing: Hot Stuff / Bad Girls / Love Will Always Find You / Walk Away / Dim All the Lights / Journey to the Centre of Your Heart / One Night in a Lifetime / Can't Get to Sleep at Night / On My Honor / There Will Always Be a You / All Through the Night / My Baby Understands / Our Love / Luck / Sunset People

June 16, 1979
6 weeks (nonconsecutive)

Less than a year after Donna Summer had landed her first Number One album with *Live and More* [see 232], the queen of disco was back at Number One with *Bad Girls*, her third consecutive double-LP set.

Hot on the heels of her first chart-topping single "MacArthur Park" and the number four hit "Heaven Knows" from *Live and More*, Summer likely could have continued her hit streak if she stayed true to the disco grooves that made her a star. Yet on *Bad Girls*, Summer and producers Giorgio Moroder and Pete Bellotte decided to shake things up a bit by inviting other writers to collaborate on the project and incorporating elements of rock 'n' roll in the disco mix.

Bad Girls was recorded at Rusk Sound Studios in Los Angeles, a fitting locale considering that "Bad Girls" and "Sunset People" were inspired by life in the City of Angels.

"Hot Stuff," the single released in advance of *Bad Girls* and the album's opening track, showed off Summer's new direction. The song was co-written by Bellotte, a longtime Summer collabo-

rator, but there was also some new blood involved. Keith Forsey, who had played drums on *Live and More*, and Harold Faltermeyer, credited with arranging *Bad Girls*, also had a writing credit on the song. Doobie Brothers guitarist Jeff "Skunk" Baxter laid down a guitar solo on the track. Summer says that the personnel involved in making the album would often splinter into different camps. "On that day, Keith, Harold, and Pete got together and I could hear them banging away in the studio," she says.

The new writing team proved successful, as "Hot Stuff" became Summer's second Number One single on June 2, 1979.

The follow-up single, "Bad Girls," wasn't a new song. "When [Casablanca president] Neil Bogart heard the song, he said, 'This song is not for you. The audience will never accept this song from you.' He thought it was too rock 'n' roll and that I should give the song to Cher, but I refused to give the song up," Summer says.

Nearly two years later, an engineer working for Moroder stumbled across a

demo of the tune, written by Summer and the trio of backing vocalists—Summer's husband Bruce Sudano, Eddie Hokenson, and Joe "Bean" Esposito—known as Brooklyn Dreams. Moroder said the song was a "stone hit." His prediction became reality when "Bad Girls" topped the Hot 100 on July 14, 1979, becoming Summer's second consecutive Number One single.

The song was inspired by a secretary at Casablanca Records who was accosted by police while walking down Sunset Boulevard. "This women in no way looked like a streetwalker," Summer says. "Merely because of color or because she was in the wrong place, she was harassed by the police. It made me irate."

Bad Girls also allowed Summer to break away from the sexy disco queen image she had been stuck with since her first hit, "Love to Love You Baby." Says Summer, "I was becoming more sassy. The original image was like a feminine victim type with no independence. That character was not who I wanted to be forever. With *Bad Girls*, I was able to make other statements. I was able to be other women."

THE TOP FIVE
Week of June 16 , 1979

1. **Bad Girls**
   Donna Summer

2. **Breakfast in America**
   Supertramp

3. **We Are Family**
   Sister Sledge

4. **Rickie Lee Jones**
   Rickie Lee Jones

5. **Cheap Trick at Budokan**
   Cheap Trick

CAPITOL 11948 **Get the Knack** 241
THE KNACK

Producer: Mike Chapman

Track listing: Let Me Out / Your Number or Your Name / Oh Tara / (She's So) Selfish / Maybe Tonight / Good Girls Don't / My Sharona / Heartbeat / Siamese Twins (The Monkey and Me) / Lucinda / That's What the Little Girls Do / Frustrated

August 11, 1979
5 weeks

When Knack singer/guitarist Doug Fieger was finally inspired to write lyrics to one of guitarist Berton Averre's two-year-old riffs, Averre was a bit concerned. As the two worked at Fieger's apartment on the song, which would be titled "My Sharona" after a girl Fieger was lusting after, Averre questioned the move. "I started singing 'My Sharona,' and Burton said, 'You can't do that. You're living with someone else.' " Yet Fieger couldn't help himself. "After I met Sharona, I knew the feeling I had for her would translate well with the rhythm of that song." Fieger was right. The song became *the* summer hit of 1979, eventually climbing to Number One, and Sharona became his new girlfriend.

The Knack was formed in May 1978. Fieger had recorded a few albums in the early '70s for RCA as a member of a Detroit trio known as Sky, but the Knack would put him on the map. Performing at such Los Angeles clubs as the Troubadour, the Starwood, and the Whisky, the Knack became a top draw. By the end of 1978, more than a dozen record labels were inter-ested in signing the band. The Knack chose Capitol, not because they were offering the most money, but because "they understood what we wanted to do," says Fieger.

What Fieger wanted to do was write and record songs about "his remembered adolescence." The band, which also included drummer Bruce Gary and bassist Prescott Niles, entered MCA-Whitney studios with producer Mike Chapman, known for his work with Blondie and Pat Benatar [see 260], on April 1, 1978. By April 13, the album was completed. "We would come in at noon and leave by 6 P.M.," says Fieger. " 'Maybe Tonight' we did in three takes, but every other song was in one or two takes. We were a live band, so we really didn't have to fix anything." The Knack spent only $17,000 making the album. "It actually cost about $13,000 and we spent about $4,000 on wine. Mike [Chapman] likes really good wine," says Fieger.

The cover photo of *Get the Knack* was taken long before the band was signed to Capitol. "It was among the first 24 exposures we ever took as a band," Fieger says. "But it captured what the band was about." It also recalled *Meet the Beatles*. The back cover shot, in which the Knack struck a Beatle-esque pose performing in front of a white backdrop, and the fact that the band was signed to Capitol, only reinforced the comparisons. "Capitol hadn't had a huge act since the Beatles, so they brought it up a lot," says Fieger. "The back cover was an intentional tongue-in-cheek joke. We never expect-ed to sell more than 25,000 or 50,000 copies of the album and we thought the people that bought it would get the joke."

Of course, *Get the Knack* went on to sell more than two million copies in America, and not everyone got the joke. Some were offended by the band's use of Beatle-like imagery; others disliked their suggestive lyrics. Yet even a backlash couldn't stop *Get the Knack*.

In its seventh week on the chart, *Get the Knack* hit Number One. When the band heard the news, they rushed over to the Capitol Records tower and danced on the desk of then–label president Don Zimmerman. "We told him if the album went to Number One we would do it, so we did," says Fieger. Two weeks later "My Sharona" hit the summit of the Hot 100. The follow-up single, "Good Girls Don't," peaked at number eleven.

THE TOP FIVE
Week of August 11, 1979

1. **Get the Knack**
   The Knack

2. **Bad Girls**
   Donna Summer

3. **Breakfast in America**
   Supertramp

4. **Candy-O**
   The Cars

5. **Teddy**
   Teddy Pendergrass

242 In Through the Out Door SWAN SONG 16002
LED ZEPPELIN

Producer: Jimmy Page

Track listing: In the Evening / South Bound Saurez / Fool in the Rain / Hot Dog / Carouselambra / All of My Love / I'm Gonna Crawl

September 15, 1979
7 weeks

Following the success of *Presence*, Led Zeppelin's long-awaited concert film–live album *The Song Remains the Same* was released. Although neither the band nor its fans were particularly pleased with the film and soundtrack, the album reached number two in November 1976. However, the two-record set was unable to knock Stevie Wonder's *Songs in the Key of Life* from the top spot.

On July 27, 1977, Plant's five-year-old son died of a stomach infection. A devastated Plant remained in seclusion for nearly a year, forcing the cancellation of the second leg of an American tour. When the band finally began working on its eighth and final studio album, their sound was altered dramatically. With guitarist/producer Jimmy Page battling a drug problem, bassist/keyboardist John Paul Jones rose to the forefront, with writing credits on six of the album's seven songs.

"I had gotten a brand new keyboard, a big Yamaha," says Jones. "Basically, Robert and I got to rehearsals first and by the time Jimmy turned up, we had written a number of songs."

The party atmosphere that had characterized the recording of the band's previous albums no longer existed. Like on *Presence*, the band opted for a traditional recording studio rather than a mansion. This time, they chose Abba's Polar Studios in Stockholm, Sweden. "It seemed to be continually nighttime in Stockholm," says Jones. "The sun was out for maybe three hours a day, so if you got up late you'd miss all the daylight, and it was really cold. So we were kind of lethargic."

The change in the band's sound was a natural evolution, Jones says. "Technology was beginning to advance more and we were beginning to use it more," Jones says. "We used synthesizers on some of the early records; it just got more interesting."

"Fool in the Rain" is one of Jones's favorite tracks from the album. "I really liked the Latin influences on that song and that whole sort of swing style," he says. " 'In the Evening' was quite an epic track. I wrote it all on this huge keyboard, and when I played keyboard I played bass as well with the foot pedals, so out of guitar, keyboards, bass, and drums, I was playing two of them."

By this point Led Zeppelin had become one of the most obvious targets of the punk rock movement. Nonetheless, the members of the band liked what they heard and were influenced by their young rivals. "We were quite excited by the energy of punk," says Jones. "So we had begun to tighten up a bit. There was a period when our

things were a little longer and perhaps a little more overblown, but then punk kicked everybody up the ass a little bit, and what we were doing needed stripping down a bit."

Even with the change in the musical climate and the alteration of the Zeppelin sound, *In Through the Out Door* didn't disappoint. The album, which was released in a brown paper bag with six different covers, became Led Zeppelin's sixth and final Number One album in its second week on the chart.

On September 25, 1980, while the band was rehearsing for a long-awaited U.S. tour, drummer John Bonham was found dead in his bed after an afternoon of heavy drinking. In December, Led Zeppelin announced that it was officially calling it quits.

THE TOP FIVE
Week of September 15, 1979

1. **In Through the Out Door**
   Led Zeppelin

2. **Get the Knack**
   The Knack

3. **Candy-O**
   The Cars

4. **Breakfast in America**
   Supertramp

5. **Million Mile Reflections**
   Charlie Daniels Band

ASYLUM 508 **The Long Run** **243**
EAGLES

Producer: Bill Szymczyk

Track listing: The Long Run / I Can't Tell You Why / In The City / The Disco Strangler / King of Hollywood / Heartache Tonight / Those Shoes / Teenage Jail / The Greeks Don't Want No Freaks / The Sad Cafe

November 3, 1979
9 weeks

Before the Eagles entered the Bayshore Recording Studio in Coconut Grove, Florida, to record their sixth studio album, there was yet another personnel change in the band. Following the success of Hotel California [see 220], bassist Randy Meisner left the group. He was replaced by Timothy B. Schmit, who had also replaced Meisner in Poco.

"We kept striving to have more harmony in the band, and I don't mean musical harmony—I mean personal harmony," says drummer/vocalist Don Henley. "Things were a little easier with Timothy in the band. It lowered the drama quotient a great deal."

Yet even the new blood couldn't save the Eagles. "We were just tired," says Henley. "Spiritually, mentally, and physically." The band attempted to break up the monotony of the sessions by recording a cover of Charles Brown's "Please Come Home for Christmas" as a holiday single, with the original "Funky New Year" on the flip side. The band also went on a short tour in July 1978, but that only made things worse. "There was a lot of pressure to top Hotel California, and the touring was relentless," says Henley. "We should have taken about a 12- or 18-month vacation

at that point, but record companies don't really allow you to do that. They want more and more product. They have to keep the big wheels turning at all costs."

Despite the strain of near-constant touring and the pressure of attempting to live up to their previous effort, The Long Run was another success. Though not up to par with Hotel California, the album did have its moments. "I think it's kind of innovative and it's actually kind of a quirky album," says Henley.

"Heartache Tonight," the first single released from the album, was written by Henley, J.D. Souther, Frey, and his old pal from Detroit, Bob Seger [see 247].

Although it wasn't released as a single, the album closer "The Sad Cafe" holds a special place in Henley's heart. "It was kind of our farewell," he says. "Los Angeles and music were beginning to change at that point. Disco was still around and the punk movement had begun. 'The Sad Cafe' was an ode to the Troubadour and Dan Tanna's restau-

rant, which was next door. It was kind of a farewell to our old stomping grounds."

By 1979, however, while making The Long Run, the Eagles were no longer having fun. "It became a very arduous, tedious process making that album," he says. Longtime collaborators Henley and Frey began to fight. "Even though things got easier in some ways with Timothy's arrival, there were other problems in other areas," Henley says. "There was still some factionalism. I have some very dark memories of making that album. There were a few moments of fun, but basically it was very difficult."

After two years and a reported $1 million in studio time, The Long Run was completed. In its third week on the chart, it became the Eagles' fourth consecutive Number One album in just over four years. It would take more than three times that long and a reunion before the Eagles returned to the summit [see 401].

THE TOP FIVE
Week of November 3, 1979

1. **The Long Run**
   Eagles

2. **In Through the Out Door**
   Led Zeppelin

3. **Midnight Magic**
   Commodores

4. **Cornerstone**
   Styx

5. **Head Games**
   Foreigner

244 On the Radio—Greatest Hits—Volumes I & II CASABLANCA 5008
DONNA SUMMER

Producers: Giorgio Moroder and Pete Bellotte

Track listing: On the Radio / Love to Love You Baby / Try Me, I Know We Can Make It / I Feel Love / Our Love / I Remember Yesterday / I Love You / Heaven Knows / Last Dance / MacArthur Park / Hot Stuff / Bad Girls / Dim All the Lights / Sunset People / No More Tears (Enough Is Enough) / On the Radio (Long Version)

January 5, 1980
1 week

A greatest-hits album was a natural for Donna Summer. After all, the disco diva had racked up nine top 10 hits by 1980, including four Number One singles. Yet On the Radio—Greatest Hits—Volumes I & II was unusual: it included two different versions of a new song along with the hits. "[Casablanca Records president] Neil Bogart was a genius at packaging," says Summer.

Like Summer's 1978 hit "Last Dance," which was included in the disco film Thank God It's Friday, "On the Radio" was written specifically for the film Foxes. The former film also generated a hit soundtrack, which reached number 10. But Summer fans turned either to her single or Greatest Hits for a copy of "On the Radio." The single reached number five in March 1980.

While Live and More [see 232] featured concert recordings of Summer's hits, On the Radio offered fans the first chance to obtain a collection of the studio versions. The album runs the gamut from Summer's first hit, "Love to Love You Baby," to "No More Tears (Enough Is Enough)," her duet with Barbra Streisand. "Love to Love You Baby" was recorded in Munich, Germany, with Peter Bellotte and Giorgio Moroder, the production duo that scored several European hits with the singer. Summer came up with the idea and sang the melody to Moroder. "When I came in the next day, Giorgio had already recorded the track and he wanted me to put down my vocal, so I ad-libbed," Summer says. "Those vocals weren't intended for the real record. I was just goofing around. I was lying on the floor when I was doing it. We were hysterical, because it was just too funny." Yet no one else was laughing. When licensed to Casablanca Records in the U.S., the song, featuring Summer's orgasmic sighs and groans, climbed to number two in February 1976 and earned Summer a sex-kitten image she would try to live down for much of her career.

On the other end of the spectrum was "No More Tears (Enough Is Enough)," Summer's duet with Streisand. "It was fun, she's a funny girl," says Summer. The song was recorded the day after Summer wrapped up an eight-night stand at the Universal Amphitheatre in Los Angeles. "Barbra and I were in the studio singing and we were holding the high note, but I didn't breathe right. I just held the note too long and I fell off my stool. Barbra kept holding her note. It was the height of professionalism. Then, at end of the note, she said, 'Are you alright?' It was hysterical, because by the time she asked me, I was coming to. She thought I was playing around."

"No More Tears" became Summer's fourth Number One single on November 24, 1979. A few months later, On the Radio—Greatest Hits—Volumes I & II became Summer's third consecutive Number One album and fourth straight two-record set. She remains the only artist to top the album chart with two consecutive double-albums.

THE TOP FIVE
Week of January 5, 1980

1. **On the Radio–Greatest Hits–Volumes I & II**
   Donna Summer

2. **Greatest**
   Bee Gees

3. **Cornerstone**
   Styx

4. **Journey Through the Secret Life of Plants**
   Stevie Wonder

5. **The Long Run**
   The Eagles

RSO 4200 **Bee Gees Greatest** `245`
BEE GEES

Producers: The Bee Gees, Karl Richardson, Albhy Galuten, and Arif Mardin

Track listing: Jive Talkin' / Night Fever / Tragedy / You Should Be Dancing / Stayin' Alive / How Deep Is Your Love / Love So Right / Too Much Heaven / (Our Love) Don't Throw It All Away / Fanny (Be Tender with My Love) / If I Can't Have You / You Stepped into My Life / Love Me / More Than a Woman / Rest Your Love on Me / Nights on Broadway / Spirits (Having Flown) / Love You Inside Out / Wind of Change / Children of the Word

January 12, 1980
1 week

Bee Gees Greatest, which included the best-known tracks from the Gibb Brothers' incredibly successful mid-'70s comeback, became the trio's third consecutive and final Number One album. It succinctly tied up the '70s, a decade in which the Bee Gees became a dominant force in pop music.

Bee Gees Greatest includes key tracks from 1975's Main Course, which climbed to number 14; 1976's Children of the World, which peaked at number eight; and the trio's Number One albums, Saturday Night Fever [see 226] and Spirits Having Flown [see 237]. Yet despite its title, the two-disc album is more than just a greatest-hits package—

three songs were making their Bee Gees album debuts on the set.

The Bee Gees' version "(Our Love) Don't Throw It Away" had never been released before Greatest. "I wrote it with our keyboard player Blue Weaver during the Fever sessions in France," says Barry Gibb. "It was written along with 'If I Can't Have You.' " Although the cut didn't make Saturday Night Fever, the youngest Gibb, Andy, who had become a successful solo artist, liked the song enough to record it. "In Miami, the Bee Gees recorded it, and then Andy recorded it as well. That was my demo vocal for Andy, so he could learn the song, but then we put it on the shelf." Andy Gibb's version of the song became a top 10 hit in 1978.

Yvonne Elliman's version of "If I Can't Have You," featured on Saturday Night Fever, became a Number One single. The Bee Gees' version, released as the B-side of "Stayin' Alive," wasn't included on the Saturday Night Fever soundtrack. "It was not intended to be in the film," says Barry Gibb. "It was intended to be recorded by somebody else."

The third non-album track included on Greatest, "Rest Your Love on Me," showed another side of the Bee Gees. The country-flavored track had previously been available only as the B-side to "Too Much Heaven." Says Barry Gibb, "It's a country song written with Conway Twitty in mind." The track became the

Bee Gees' first and only song to chart on the country chart. After country disc jockeys flipped over "Too Much Heaven" and began playing "Rest Your Love on Me," it climbed to number 39 on the country singles chart in 1979. Brother Andy and Olivia Newton-John also recorded the track, but the ultimate thrill for Barry Gibb came when Twitty covered the song and his version became a Number One country hit in 1981. While country music and the Bee Gees seem like an odd pair, Barry Gibb says, "Our love of country is still there, so you never know when it's going to pop out."

THE TOP FIVE
Week of January 12, 1980

1. **Bee Gees Greatest**
   Bee Gees

2. **On The Radio–Greatest Hits–Volumes I & II**
   Donna Summer

3. **The Wall**
   Pink Floyd

4. **The Long Run**
   Eagles

5. **Journey Through the Secret Life of Plants**
   Stevie Wonder

246 The Wall COLUMBIA 36183
PINK FLOYD

Producers: Bob Ezrin, David Gilmour, and Roger Waters

Track listing: In the Flesh? / The Thin Ice / Another Brick in the Wall (Part 1) / The Happiest Days of Our Lies / Another Brick in the Wall (Part 2) / Mother / Goodbye Blue Sky / Empty Spaces / Young Lust / One of My Turns / Don't Leave Me Now / Another Brick in the Wall (Part 3) / Goodbye Cruel World / Hey You / Is There Anybody Out There? / Nobody Home / Vera / Bring the Boys Back Home / Comfortably Numb / The Show Must Go On / In the Flesh / Run Like Hell / Waiting For the Worms / Stop / The Trial / Outside the Wall

January 19, 1980
15 weeks

With the success of *The Dark Side of the Moon* [see 157] and *Wish You Were Here* [see 205], Pink Floyd had secured its place as one of the most popular rock acts on the planet. Although *Animals*, the group's 1977 album, stalled at number three, Pink Floyd's popularity had grown to such proportions that the band members began to feel trapped by their own success. While riding in a limo to the final date of Floyd's *Animals* tour, bassist Roger Waters began to talk about his feelings of alienation. "He said he felt that there was a wall between himself and the audience and he would love to one day erect a real one on stage," recalls producer Bob Ezrin. "We kind of laughed about it at the time, but that was the germ for *The Wall*."

More than a year later, Waters invit-ed Ezrin to his home in the country to listen to what Ezrin calls an "inter-minable demo." The 95-minute "song" was the groundwork for *The Wall*, con-taining an embryonic version of "Moth-er." Other bits and pieces would later turn up on Waters's solo albums, *The Pros and Cons of Hitch Hiking* and *Radio K.A.O.S.*

When Floyd settled into Super Bear studios in Miravel, France, in April 1979, the demo had been refined into *The Wall*. "We worked together focus-ing it into a more gestalt personality, a kind of everyman called 'Pink,' " says Ezrin. "We also refined the pacing musi-cally, and basically wrote a show. We built a model for the show at the same time we were actually recording the album on tape, so the album truly is a representation of a fully conceived work. We knew not only how it sound-ed, but what it looked like and how it played."

The band worked tirelessly between April and November 1979, constructing *The Wall* and often second-guessing their work. " 'Comfortably Numb' was the synthesis of the music that David Gilmour had written and a lyric that Roger Waters that had written," says Ezrin. "Dave Gilmour overdubbed his electric guitar to the guide track on the first take and played that famous solo." Yet Gilmour wasn't happy with his per-formance. "He spent nearly six months trying to make it better," Ezrin says. In the end, Gilmour went with one of his last attempts.

As was the case with *The Dark Side of the Moon*, part of *The Wall* sessions were devoted to recording sound effects. "That was an adventure in itself," says Ezrin. "We took sledgeham-mers to televisions, busted through door-ways, and went out to Edwards Air Force Base to record helicopters."

At one point, the band had two stu-dios rented at once in France. "We would have to drive back and forth for two and a half hours on these little wind-ing roads," says Ezrin, "so one team could overdub on the tape we had just completed, while we continued recording."

Aside from Floyd's core members, several additional players and singers were featured on the album, including an orchestra arranged by Michael Kamen, drummer Jeff Porcaro, guitarist Lee Ritenour, Toni Tenille from the Cap-tain & Tenille, and Bruce Johnston from the Beach Boys.

During the sessions, a wall began to develop between the members of the band, as Waters literally forced Rick Wright from the band. "It was really intense and tough on everyone," says Ezrin.

In the end, however, the emotional turmoil produced a gem. *The Wall*, a two-album set, reached Number One in its sixth week, becoming Floyd's third chart-topper. It also spawned the band's first Number One single, "Another Brick in the Wall," which features a chorus of school children on backing vocals. The album also went on to inspire the 1982 film starring Bob Geldof.

THE TOP FIVE
Week of January 19, 1980

1. **The Wall**
   Pink Floyd

2. **On the Radio–Greatest Hits–Volumes I & II**
   Donna Summer

3. **The Long Run**
   Eagles

4. **Bee Gees Greatest**
   Bee Gees

5. **Damn the Torpedoes**
   Tom Petty & the Heartbreakers

Against the Wind 247

CAPITOL 12041

BOB SEGER & THE SILVER BULLET BAND

Producers: Bob Seger, Punch, the Muscle Shoals Rhythm Section, and Bill Szymczyk

Track listing: The Horizontal Bop / You'll Accomp'ny Me / Her Strut / No Man's Land / Long Twin Silver Line / Against the Wind / Good for Me / Betty Lou's Gettin' Out Tonight / Fire Lake / Shinin' Brightly

May 3, 1980
6 weeks

A decade into his career, Detroit native Bob Seger finally found success with *Live Bullet,* a two-disc set featuring the singer and his Silver Bullet Band performing in front of his hometown fans at Cobo Hall. The album only reached number 34, but it set the stage for Seger's commercial breakthrough with his next two studio albums: 1976's *Night Moves* and 1978's *Stranger in Town.* Those albums climbed to numbers eight and four, respectively, and made Seger a star.

Against the Wind was a bit more subdued than *Night Moves* and *Stranger in Town,* which were generally hard-rocking affairs. "Both of those albums were huge hits, but I got kind of into a more laid-back thing for *Against the Wind,*" says Seger. "There were a lot of ballads that I had sitting around. 'Fire Lake' was nine years old when I finally cut that at Muscle Shoals. There was a lot of mid-tempo stuff that I wanted to do, like 'Shining Brightly,' 'No Man's Land,' 'You'll Accomp'ny Me,' and 'Good for Me'...I sensed that if I took just a little bit of the edge off, I might have a shot at Number One, so I

went for it."

The album was recorded over a two-year period at various studios, including Criteria Studios in Miami, the famed Muscle Shoals studios in Sheffield, Alabama, and Bayshore Studios in Coconut Grove, Florida. "During that two-year period, we were on the road for about a year and a half," says Seger. "We would cut a track here and there and then go play concerts for two or three months."

As was the case on his previous two hit albums, Seger was not solely backed by his Silver Bullet Band. The Muscle Shoals Rhythm Section, consisting of pianist Barry Beckett, organist Randy McCormick, guitarists Pete Carr and Jimmy Johnson, bassist David Hood, and drummer Roger Hawkins, was featured on five tracks.

The singer also called on his long-time friend and fellow Detroit native Glenn Frey and Frey's fellow Eagles Don Henley and Timothy B. Schmit [see 243] to contribute backing harmonies to "Fire Lake." Says Seger, "That was great. They really went out of their way. They spent about five hours on it. We

thought they did it good in the first take, but they're perfectionists."

It turned out to be time well spent, as "Fire Lake" climbed to number six on the Hot 100 the same week that *Against the Wind* hit the top spot.

Reaching Number One was no easy feat for Seger, however, as the album had to topple *The Wall* [see 246], a massive hit for Pink Floyd. In its third week on the album chart, *Against the Wind* rose to number two, but it stayed there for the next eight weeks before dethroning the mighty Floyd. "I remember my manager calling me up every week while we were on tour and saying, 'We're Avis,' which meant we were still number two," Seger says, referring to the Avis car-rental firm, whose advertising slogan at the time was, "We're number two, but we try harder."

"Then," says Seger, "one week my manager called and said, 'Hertz,'" a reference to Avis's longtime competitor. That one word, "Hertz," was enough for Seger and his band band to start the celebration. Says Seger, "We just ran into the hall and started screaming and jumping up and down."

THE TOP FIVE
Week of May 3, 1980

1. **Against the Wind**
   Bob Seger & the Silver Bullet Band

2. **The Wall**
   Pink Floyd

3. **Glass Houses**
   Blly Joel

4. **Mad Love**
   Linda Ronstadt

5. **Light Up the Night**
   The Brothers Johnson

248 Glass Houses COLUMBIA 36384
BILLY JOEL

Producer: Phil Ramone

Track listing: You May Be Right / Sometimes a Fantasy / Don't Ask Me Why / It's Still Rock and Roll to Me / All For Leyna / I Don't Want to Be Alone / Sleeping with the Television On / C'Etait Toi (You Were the One) / Close to the Borderline / Through the Long Night

June 14, 1980
6 weeks

THE TOP FIVE
Week of June 14, 1980

1. **Glass Houses**
   Billy Joel
2. **Against the Wind**
   Bob Seger & the Silver Bullet Band
3. **Just One Night**
   Eric Clapton
4. **The Wall**
   Pink Floyd
5. **Mouth to Mouth**
   Lipps Inc.

Following the success of *52nd Street,* Billy Joel hit the road with a tour that found him headlining huge outdoor stadiums. Playing before such large audiences was bound to have an affect on his music, and it can be heard on *Glass Houses.*

"I wanted to write bigger songs that had a lot of energy in them," Joel says. "By the time I started writing songs for *Glass Houses,* I felt I needed to do songs that were bigger, could be louder, a lot faster, shorter, and punchier."

By 1980, the influence of new wave and punk couldn't be denied, even by Joel, a superstar who was primarily considered to be a pop crooner prior to *Glass Houses.* "There was a new wave influence, but I wasn't trying to do new wave," says Joel, who thought the new wave acts were little more than an update of the bands that he grew up listening to, including the Standells, Them, the Shadows of the Knight, and ? & the Mysterians. "That was really where my inspiration came from, not so much from the new wave bands in 1980, but the mid-'60s power-pop bands." Joel expressed those sentiments in "It's Still Rock and Roll to Me," the album's second single, which became Joel's first Number One hit. The tune also found Joel taking aim at rock critics and at the very relevance of rock criticism.

If that doesn't sound like an earthshaking subject, Joel would be the first to agree. "A lot of the subject matter is fairly juvenile," Joel says. "A song like 'All For Leyna' could have been written by a 16-year-old. I was actually thinking like a 16-year-old when I did write that."

The album wasn't an all-out rockfest, however, as it closed with the ballad "Through the Long Night." Says Joel, "That was a departure from most everything else that is on the album. That's all me doing the harmonies." While Joel says cutting that track was a "pain in the ass,"

Glass Houses was generally a pleasant experience. "That was one of the most fun albums I've ever made," he recalls. "Not so much that it was fun to write, but it was fun to record and play. It was very simple and the production aspects on that album were very noticeable."

On some tracks, Joel's vocals go from a double-tracking effect to completely dry, a feel that veteran producer Phil Ramone was initially hesitant to employ. "It was kind of Elvis Presley-ish in a way," says Ramone. "It was a side of Billy that people really hadn't seen

before. He wasn't this overproduced, lush artist. His statement 'It's Still Rock and Roll to Me' is very much about what *Glass Houses* was about. It was a good turning point. It kept his career and his momentum in a very direct line with his audience."

Glass Houses hit the top in its 13th week on the chart, becoming Joel's second consecutive Number One album. While Joel's other '80s studio albums would continue to make the top 10, it would take him nearly a decade to return to the top [see 338].

Producers: The Glimmer Twins

Track listing: Dance (Pt. 1) / Summer Romance / Send It to Me / Let Me Go / Indian Girl / Where the Boys Go / Down in the Hole / Emotional Rescue / She's So Cold / All About You

July 26, 1980
7 weeks

High on the success of *Some Girls* [228], Keith Richards flew to the Bahamas in January 1970 to begin work on the the Rolling Stones' follow-up album at Compass Point Studios. While Richards laid down the groundwork for *Emotional Rescue* in the Bahamas, the rest of the Stones returned to Pathe-Marconi in Paris to cut the bulk of the album. Engineer Chris Kimsey was once again on hand, this time with the additional title of associate producer. "I had more responsibility and helped choose the songs, rather than just sitting behind the board," he says.

The success of *Some Girls* allowed the Stones to stretch out in the studio. "The material on *Emotional Rescue* was a little more diverse than what had come before," says Kimsey. "It was a little more soul-oriented and laid-back, and a lot more relaxed than *Some Girls*." Yet there were similarities. "Because we went back to Paris, *Emotional Rescue* was almost like a continuation of *Some Girls*," says Kimsey.

But while the Stones had plenty of time to write the songs for *Some Girls*, they went to work on *Emotional Rescue* only six months after the completion of its predecessor. "That's why the songwriting is a little more experimental," says Kimsey.

Before the band began working on the album, Richards's drug charges had been resolved. On October 28, 1978, he pleaded guilty to heroin possession, received a one-year suspended sentence, and was ordered to play a special concert for the Canadian National Institute for the Blind. The gig, featuring the Stones and the New Barbarians (a spin-off featuring Richards and Ron Wood), took place on April 22, 1979.

Back in the studio, Wood, the newest Stone, was taking a more active role. He even received a rare co-writing credit on "Dance (Pt. 1)." Kimsey recalls, "It was a big thing for Ronnie to try to get it on there—he had to do it rather carefully and cautiously. There was a pact between Mick and Keith that everything had to be 'Jagger and Richards,' " says Kimsey, "but that slowly changed over the years."

The album ranged from the plaintive ballad "All About You," featuring Richards on lead vocals and trademark Stones rockers like "She's So Cold" and "Let Me Go" to the soul-flavored title track. "Emotional Rescue," which reached number three on the Hot 100, features Jagger singing in a falsetto. "I always found it a bit twee," says Kimsey, "but it was a novel idea. There were a lot of experimental things on that album going on." As was the case with *Some Girls*, some of those experiments were left off the album but later turned up on *Tattoo You* [see 264].

The album's release was soured when tensions began to rise within the group. Richards wanted to tour, but Jagger wasn't interested. Bassist Bill Wyman announced that he planned to leave the group in 1982 on the group's 20th anniversary (he actually remained for another decade after that). And then in February 1980, Wood lived up to the Stones' rebel image when he was arrested for cocaine possession in the Dutch Antilles.

Again, none of these issues hurt record sales. *Emotional Rescue* followed the same path to the summit as *Black and Blue* [see 216]. Like that album, *Emotional Rescue* entered the chart at number eight and then climbed to Number One the following week. And in another telling comparison, *Emotional Rescue*, like *Black and Blue*, wasn't one of the Stones' finest efforts. "I don't think they thought it was as good as *Some Girls*," says Kimsey. "I know I didn't."

THE TOP FIVE
Week of July 26, 1980

1. **Emotional Rescue**
   The Rolling Stones

2. **Just One Night**
   Eric Clapton

3. **Glass Houses**
   Billy Joel

4. **The Empire Strikes Back**
   Soundtrack

5. **Empty Glass**
   Pete Townshend

250 Hold Out ASYLUM 511
JACKSON BROWNE

Producers: Jackson Browne and Greg Ladanyi

Track listing: Disco Apocalypse / Hold Out / That Girl Could Sing / Boulevard / Of Missing Persons / Call It a Loan / Hold On Hold Out

September 13, 1980
1 week

Jackson Browne first made his name as a songwriter whose work had been covered by a wide range of artists, including Nico, the Nitty Gritty Dirt Band, and Tom Rush. In 1972, his self-titled debut album stalled at number 53 but spun off the top 10 hit single "Doctor My Eyes." That same year, the Eagles scored their first hit with "Take It Easy" [see 250, 401] written by Browne and Glenn Frey. It was with his fourth album, however, that Browne scored his critical and commercial breakthrough, 1976's *The Pretender*, which reached number five.

But Browne's triumph was marred by tragedy. In March 1976, his wife Phyllis committed suicide. Perhaps to help himself cope with the grief, he hit the road in 1977 and recorded *Running on Empty*. The album, featuring new material recorded in concert, in hotel rooms, and on Browne's tour bus, was the singer-songwriter's biggest success to date, climbing all the way to number three.

For the follow-up album, Browne opted to return to the recording studio. *Hold Out*, Browne's sixth album, was recorded at the Sound Factory and Record One in Los Angeles and took nearly a year to complete. Greg Ladanyi, who had engineered *Running on Empty*, was enlisted to co-produce

THE TOP FIVE
Week of September 13, 1980

1. **Hold Out**
   Jackson Browne

2. **Emotional Rescue**
   The Rolling Stones

3. **Urban Cowboy**
   Soundtrack

4. **The Game**
   Queen

5. **Diana**
   Diana Ross

the album with Browne.

Although the album included only seven songs, four of the tracks clocked in at more than five minutes. Much of the album was written in the studio. "A good 60 percent of it was in Jackson's mind, but a lot of the lyrics were finished as we were recording the songs in the studio," says Ladanyi. "That's just the way Jackson works sometimes. Some songs just don't get finished unless he is working on them in the studio."

The opening track, "Disco Apocalypse," was Browne's response to the dance-music craze. "At that time, disco music was really a big, big deal," says Ladanyi. "Lyrically, it was a song about what was going on with that scene. That was something that we worked on for a long time, because it was a special song for Jackson."

Another stand-out track was "That

Girl Could Sing," which would go on to become a top 30 hit in the fall of 1980. "The guitar solo on that kind of sounds like a seal," says Ladanyi. "That was something David Lindley did with a slide guitar that was really incredible when it happened. On that record there were a lot of things that David Lindley played once that he never played again, but we managed to get them on tape."

"Boulevard," the first single from *Hold Out*, reached number 19. But *Hold Out* was more than just a collection of singles. "When we were done making *Hold Out*, Jackson was as confident about that record as he was about any other record he has put out." That confidence was justified. In its ninth week on the chart, *Hold Out* hit the top spot, knocking no less a chart power-house than the Rolling Stones from the pole position.

Producer: Queen/Mack

Track listing: Play the Game / Dragon Attack / Another One Bites the Dust / Need Your Loving Tonight / Crazy Little Thing Called Love / Rock It (Prime Jive) / Don't Try Suicide / Sail Away Sweet Sister / Coming Soon / Save Me / Dragon Attack

September 20, 1980
5 weeks

"It was very much a period of change," drummer Roger Taylor says of the months in 1979 and 1980 that Queen devoted to working on *The Game*, their eighth studio album and first to top the American album chart.

After forming in 1971 in England, the band, fronted by the flamboyant vocalist Freddie Mercury, became known for its mix of glam, melodic hard rock, and complex vocal harmonies. Queen's first hit single was "Killer Queen" from the band's third album, 1974's *Sheer Heart Attack*, but their commercial breakthrough came a year later with the aptly titled *A Night at the Opera* and the top 10 single "Bohemian Rhapsody." That song, a mini-opera in itself, would become a hit again 17 years later, thanks to its inclusion on the *Wayne's World* soundtrack [see 352].

Two albums and a few hit singles fol-

lowed *A Night at the Opera*, including "We Are the Champions" from *News of the World*, which climbed to number three. But by 1978's *Jazz*, Queen was desperately searching for something new. "We felt *Jazz* was not one of our finest hours," admits Taylor. "It had its moments, but on the whole, it was rather unsatisfying."

To shake things up, the group decided to record at Musicland Studios in Munich, Germany, although the band had its own studio in Montreaux, Switzerland. They also enlisted the aid of a new producer, simply known as Mack. "We had explored that sort of multi-layered, very complex harmony thing, we wanted to do something stripped-down and basic, but it was still quite eclectic."

The first track recorded for the album was a rockabilly-flavored number penned by Mercury, "Crazy Little Thing Called Love." Since guitarist Brian May wasn't present for the first session, Mercury, Taylor, and bassist John Deacon recorded the basic track as a trio. "Freddie wrote it in the bath," Taylor recalls. "Since it was just the three of us, he said, 'I'll play rhythm [guitar].' I threw the drums up in the corner, and John played bass. We had this backing track that sounded and felt great." May would later overdub some tasty leads to the track, which was first released as a single in the U.K. in late 1979 and

began receiving airplay on American radio stations. On February 23, 1980, "Crazy Little Thing Called Love" went to Number One in the States, while Queen was still working on *The Game*. "There we were with a Number One in America and no album," recalls Taylor.

Some of the other tracks on *The Game*, including "Another One Bites the Dust," which would also top the Hot 100, and "Dragon Attack," were inspired by the Munich nightlife. "We never even considered doing a dance-styled track before," Taylor says. "Being in a different place did stimulate us. We were very much influenced by what was going on in the clubs. A lot of that was assimilated and put into the record."

THE TOP FIVE
Week of September 20, 1980

1. **The Game**
   Queen

2. **Hold Out**
   Jackson Browne

3. **Diana**
   Diana Ross

4. **Emotional Rescue**
   The Rolling Stones

5. **Panorama**
   The Cars

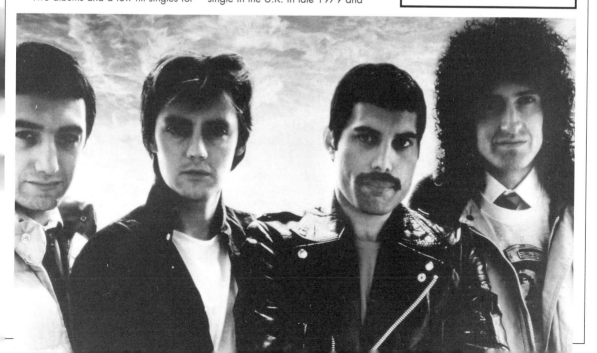

252 Guilty COLUMBIA 36750
BARBRA STREISAND

Producers: Barry Gibb, Albhy Galuten, and Karl Richardson

Track listing: Guilty (Duet with Barry Gibb) / Woman in Love / Run Wild / Promises / The Love Inside / What Kind of Fool (Duet with Barry Gibb) / Life Story / Never Give Up / Make It Like a Memory

October 25, 1980
3 weeks (nonconsecutive)

Following the success of *Barbra Streisand's Greatest Hits, Volume 2* [see 234], the singer's fortunes dipped with her two final albums of the '70s. The soundtrack to *The Main Event* stalled at number 20 in the summer of 1979. *Wet*, also released that year, climbed to number seven, thanks largely to the Number One duet "No More Tears (Enough Is Enough)," with Donna Summer [see 244]. To usher herself into the '80s, Streisand called on the Bee Gees, one of the hottest acts of the '70s [see 245].

Yet Barry Gibb was initially less than enthused about working with Streisand. "I was a little nervous," he says. "She intimidated me to some extent. In fact, if it hadn't been for my wife, I don't think I would have done it. She said, 'If you don't do it, I'll divorce you.' So I had to do it."

But Gibb didn't just go into the project blind. He called on Neil Diamond, who had scored a Number One hit with Streisand in 1978 with "You Don't Bring Me Flowers" [see 234]. "He said that she is an absolute pleasure. Don't be concerned about it, just go ahead and do it."

He was also aware that Streisand had a proven track record with collabo-

rators and that the project would likely benefit him and his brothers Robin and Maurice, who were asked to contribute five songs for the album. "It was a good career move for both us and her," says Gibb. "Barbra has a knack of making it a point to work with someone who is hot at the time. She asked to work with us because she realized we were doing particularly well and it was a good combination." The combination worked so well, in fact, that after the first five songs were presented to Streisand, she requested that the Gibb brothers compose the entire album.

It took approximately six months for the project to be completed. "If there is one thing to say about Barbra, it's that she is the perfectionist everyone says she is," says Gibb. Before Gibb signed on to write, co-produce, and duet with Streisand, the pair laid down some ground rules. "We had an agreement at the beginning that we would all be able

to be critical," says Gibb. "If she wasn't happy, she would be able to say so, and so would I, so there would be no arguments. From day one, we left our egos at the front door."

The pairing of Streisand with the elder Gibb brother, masterminded by executive producer Charles Koppelman, proved to be a winner. Yet the duets weren't played up initially. Streisand was a bit concerned that the public might be growing tired of her star-studded musical pairings, so Columbia chose to release "Woman in Love" as the first single. That track alone was enough to bring Streisand back to Number One, as the single and *Guilty* reached the top simultaneously and held there together for three consecutive weeks. The duets with Gibb, which were subsequently released as singles, didn't fare quite as well. "What Kind of Fool" stalled at number 10, while "Guilty" peaked at number three.

THE TOP FIVE
Week of October 25, 1980

1. **Guilty**
   Barbra Streisand

2. **The Game**
   Queen

3. **One Step Closer**
   The Doobie Brothers

4. **Diana**
   Diana Ross

5. **Crimes of Passion**
   Pat Benatar

COLUMBIA 36854 The River 253

BRUCE SPRINGSTEEN

Producers: Bruce Springsteen, Jon Landau, and Steve Van Zandt

Track listing: The Ties That Bind / Sherry Darling / Jackson Cage / Two Hearts / Independence Day / Hungry Heart / Out in the Street / Crush on You / You Can Look (But You Better Not Touch) / I Wanna Marry You / The River / Point Blank / Cadillac Ranch / I'm a Rocker / Fade Away / Stolen Car / Ramrod / The Price You Pay / Drive All Night / Wreck on the Highway

November 8, 1980
4 weeks

By the turn of the decade, Bruce Springsteen had been called the future of rock 'n' roll and his face had graced the covers of *Time* and *Newsweek* simultaneously. Yet the one thing the Boss had yet to achieve was a Number One album.

Springsteen, a critics' favorite since his 1973 debut, *Greetings from Asbury Park, New Jersey*, began winning over the public in the mid-'70s. His third album, *Born to Run*, featuring the anthemic title track, reached number three in 1975. The follow-up, 1978's *Darkness on the Edge of Town*, was a smash as well, peaking at number five, and Springsteen's loyal fan base continued to grow.

With his next album, *The River*, Springsteen would climb to new artistic and commercial heights. In what was becoming a tradition, Springsteen and his backing unit, the E Street Band, worked tirelessly on the album. "We rehearsed a lot of material in Bruce's house for several months before the recording sessions began," says drummer Max Weinberg. With some 60 songs from which to choose, it was decided that the album would be a two-record set. The recording sessions began in earnest in February 1979 at the Power Station in New York. Weinberg had worked at the studio as a session player on Ian Hunter's *You're Never Alone with a Schizophrenic* a year earlier. "I was very impressed with the facility, particularly in regard to the drums. They really got an incredible sound and it was a fabulous room to play in. I conveyed my excitement to Bruce and we moved from the Record Plant to the Power Station."

Eventually, the months of rehearsing gave way to months of recording. "Five days a week, for about a year and a half, I drove into New York," says Weinberg. "The sessions started at 7 or 8 P.M. and went to 4 or 5 A.M. I saw the sun come up almost every day." Even with the relentless schedule, there were occasional moments of spontaneity when songs were recorded quickly.

"Some things came real fast," says Weinberg. "Bruce would be in the studio writing and we would be in the lounge waiting for him to finish. About a half-hour later, he would call us in and we would record the song he just wrote right there and then."

In the studio, Springsteen remained the focal point. "Instead of the rhythm section playing off each other, everyone played off of Bruce," says Weinberg. "He was literally in the center of the room and all of us played off him. We all just kind of hooked up to his energy."

The River, an ambitious and diverse effort, showed new maturity in Springsteen's songwriting, with songs devoted to dreams ("I Wanna Marry You" and "Crush on You") and the harsh realities of life ("The River" and "Wreck on the Highway"). "There's tremendous scope to that record," confirms Weinberg. "It was both light and dark in tone."

The progress wasn't limited to Springsteen's lyrical vision. "There was a lot of growth on that record," says Weinberg. "It was the first record where we really started to play as a band, all live in the studio, all of us playing simultaneously."

The River quickly became Springsteen's first chart-topper, moving to Number One in its second week on the chart. *The River* also spawned Springsteen's first top 10 single, the rollicking "Hungry Heart," which peaked at number five.

THE TOP FIVE
Week of November 8, 1980

1. **The River**
   Bruce Springsteen

2. **Guilty**
   Barbra Streisand

3. **One Step Closer**
   The Doobie Brothers

4. **The Game**
   Queen

5. **Greatest Hits**
   Kenny Rogers

254 Greatest Hits LIBERTY 1072
KENNY ROGERS

Producers: Larry Butler, Kenny Rogers, and Lionel Richie

Track listing: The Gambler / Lady / Don't Fall in Love with a Dreamer / Ruby Don't Take Your Love to Town / She Believes in Me / Coward of the County / Lucille / You Decorated My Life / Reuben James / Love the World Away / Every Time Two Fools Collide / Long Arm of the Law

December 13, 1980
2 weeks

Veteran country singer Kenny Rogers scored nine top 40 pop hits with producer Larry Butler from 1977 through 1980, but the collaboration was beginning to get a little stale. "The time had come for me to do something totally different," Rogers says. "We realized that the songs were beginning to sound the same and we were living off past glories."

Rogers was searching for something fresh to add to his planned *Greatest Hits* album. "I heard 'Three Times a Lady' by the Commodores on the radio. I happened to know the owner of Motown Records, Berry Gordy, and I asked him if he thought Lionel Richie [see 278] would be interested in writing something for me." Gordy passed the message over to Richie, who agreed to meet Rogers in Las Vegas. "We talked and I told him what I wanted," Rogers recalls. "He came back a week later and said, 'Here's what I had written for you.' The only word he had was 'Lady,' but the music was so beautiful. I agreed to do the song off of that one word."

Rogers had a specific reason for wanting to work with Richie. "I had

remembered that Ray Charles had sung R&B to country tracks [see 53]. I thought that was so clever, because there is such a finite difference between country and R&B. What I wanted to do was sing country to R&B tracks. I went to Lionel and said, 'Don't change your tracks, but just let me sing it my way.' And we were very successful with that approach."

So successful that on November 15, 1980, "Lady" became Rogers's first Number One single. It was still at the top of the Hot 100 a month later when *Greatest Hits* knocked Barbra Streisand's *Guilty* from the Number One spot on the album chart. "I think the single and the album kind of cross-fed each other," Rogers says. "The album was such a huge success because we introduced a new song and it turned out to be Number One. And part of the reason the single ended up going to Number One was because it was part of a greatest-hits album, which was a big package."

Indeed, there was much more to *Greatest Hits* than just "Lady." The

album spanned Rogers's career from 1969 through 1980, going back to the number six hit "Ruby, Don't Take Your Love to Town," written by Mel Tillis and recorded by Rogers and the First Edition. By 1973, Rogers had gone solo. He went on to experience his greatest success with such hits as 1977's "Lucille," which peaked at number five, and 1978's "The Gambler," which climbed to number 16. "That's one song that is so strongly associated with me that I'm known as 'the Gambler' when I go to foreign countries," Rogers says. The song also inspired a series of TV movies starring Rogers.

Much like Johnny Cash [see 114] and later Garth Brooks [see 354], Rogers proved that country music had mainstream appeal. "My intent always was to do country songs that would sell pop, with the understanding that when the market got big enough and the pie got larger, I would then do pop songs that would sell country," Rogers says. "I've always had this theory that country music is what country people will buy."

THE TOP FIVE
Week of December 13, 1980

1. **Greatest Hits**
   Kenny Rogers

2. **Guilty**
   Barbra Streisand

3. **Hotter Than July**
   Stevie Wonder

4. **The River**
   Bruce Springsteen

5. **Back in Black**
   AC/DC

GEFFEN 2001 **Double Fantasy**

JOHN LENNON / YOKO ONO

255

Producers: John Lennon, Yoko Ono, and Jack Douglas

Track listing: (Just Like) Starting Over / Kiss Kiss Kiss / Cleanup Time / Give Me Something / I'm Losing You / I'm Moving On / Beautiful Boy (Darling Boy) / Watching the Wheels / I'm Your Angel / Woman / Beautiful Boys / Dear Yoko / Every Man Has a Woman Who Loves Him / Hard Times Are Over

December 27, 1980
8 weeks

Following the success of *Walls and Bridges* [see 188], former Beatle John Lennon recorded *Rock 'n' Roll*, an album of his interpretations of his favorite early rock classics. The album, released in March 1975, reached number six. Later that year, on October 9 (Lennon's 35th birthday), Sean Ono Lennon was born. The birth of his second son, and his first with Yoko Ono, had such an impact on Lennon that he opted to retire from the music business. He became a househusband, raising Sean at his Manhattan apartment building, the Dakota, while Ono looked over the family's business affairs.

It was only as Lennon's 40th birthday approached that he decided it was time to make music again. Sean was nearing five and was beginning to wonder what his father did aside from being "Daddy." While vacationing with Sean in Bermuda, Lennon began writing songs, which he then played to Ono over the telephone. She responded by writing her own reply songs.

On August 4, 1980, Lennon began recording his first album in five years at the Hit Factory in New York. *Double*

Fantasy was a concept album with Lennon and Ono each contributing seven songs. "It was a dialogue between men and women," says Ono. "When we came up with that idea, John was really panicking, saying, 'We have to make the album right away. It's such a good idea that maybe another couple might do it before we can.' "

The Lennons recorded the album quickly, and without a recording contract. It was truly a labor of love. "It was just a beautiful, beautiful time for us," says Ono. "Every moment was exciting." Once the album was completed, David Geffen offered to release *Double Fantasy* without hearing a note.

Double Fantasy was released on November 17 and debuted at number 25 on the Top LPs & Tapes chart during the week ending December 6, while the album's first single, the mid-tempo "(Just Like) Starting Over" began to climb the Hot 100. The album was receiving favorable reviews, Lennon was speaking happily about making music again, and the couple even began working on another album. Then the unthinkable occurred.

On December 8, 1980, Lennon and Ono returned home from the studio after working on a new song called "Walking on Thin Ice." Waiting for Lennon in the courtyard of the Dakota was an

obsessed fan named Mark David Chapman. Just before 11 P.M., Chapman shot Lennon five times. He was rushed to Roosevelt Hospital, where he died from a massive blood loss.

Lennon's death affected people around the world and gave an ironic twist to much of the material on *Double Fantasy*. " 'I'm Losing You,' when I play it now, it really hits me," says Ono. " 'Starting Over' is really a very happy song, but because of John's death, it's ironic. We felt like we were going to be together for another 50 years or something. We didn't know we weren't meant to be together."

Understandably, "all of the *Double Fantasy* songs are hard for me to listen to," Ono adds. "When we made it, it was just such a happy time and our joy is reflected in the album, literally, but because of that, it is even sadder. It just shows that we didn't know our fate at all."

But the album also had healing powers. The song "Beautiful Boy (Darling Boy)" was inspired by Sean Lennon. "When Sean was a little boy, he used to listen to that song a lot," says Ono. "So he did get something from his dad."

Less than two weeks after Lennon's death, *Double Fantasy* and "(Just Like) Starting Over" both went to Number One.

THE TOP FIVE
Week of December 27, 1980

1. **Double Fantasy**
   John Lennon / Yoko Ono

2. **Guilty**
   Barbra Streisand

3. **Hotter Than July**
   Stevie Wonder

4. **Back in Black**
   AC/DC

5. **Crimes of Passion**
   Pat Benatar

256 Hi Infidelity EPIC 36844
REO SPEEDWAGON

Producers: Kevin Cronin, Gary Richrath & Kevin Beamish

Track listing: Don't Let Him Go / Keep on Loving You / Follow My Heart / In Your Letter / Take It on the Run / Tough Guys / Out of Season / Shakin' It Loose / Someone Tonight / I Wish You Were There

February 21, 1981
15 weeks (nonconsecutive)

REO Speedwagon had been around the block and back more than a few times prior to the release of *Hi Infidelity*. The band formed in Champaign, Illinois, in 1968 with Terry Lutrell as the lead singer, but he was replaced by Kevin Cronin following the band's 1971 self-titled debut. Cronin stuck around for 1972's *REO TWO* but left prior to the 1973 album *Ridin' the Storm Out*, only to rejoin for 1976's *REO*. "We had already gone through the ego thing when one guy wants to do a solo album," Cronin says. "We already tried that and it didn't work very well, so there was a lot of respect between us. We really did need each other."

In the midst of all this maneuvering, the band had enjoyed only limited commercial success. Their highest-charting album had been 1978's *You can Tune a piano, but you can't Tuna fish*, which peaked at number 29. "We were the perennial underdog, which was a position that we felt comfortable in, because

we had grown used to it," says Cronin. "We were the up-and-comer, a band that had something to prove and had a message to get across and that wasn't getting across. We had a real fighter-type attitude." Although REO had been together for more than a decade, they were still basically a support act, not a headliner.

Part of the problem was that the band had fallen into a cyclical rut. "We had been in the habit of making an album every year since 1971," says Cronin. "Every year we would make an album and do a tour and it kind of got to be a cycle." However, with *Hi Infidelity*, the band broke that cycle. In the spring of 1980, Epic released *A Decade of Rock and Roll 1970 to 1980*, a greatest-hits compilation, although the band had few legitimate hits at the time. "We had an extra nine months of time, which gave me the chance to think and write," Cronin says. "I wasn't going to put out another record until I was satisfied with my writing and until we were rehearsed enough."

The band members' love lives at the time were "traumatic," Cronin says, causing him to take a new approach to songwriting. Instead of just focusing on a male point of view, Cronin wrote songs that offered a feminine perspective, like "Keep on Loving You." Also, the band had found a balance between the hard rock that guitarist Gary Richrath favored and the more folk-influenced sound preferred by Cronin. "There weren't any other hard rock bands that were as folk music–oriented as us," Cronin says. "We really played

hard folk-rock, music about people how people feel and how they get along."

The mix of hard-rock and syrupy ballads proved to be a winning combination for REO, as *Hi Infidelity* rose to the peak in its 12th week on the chart, unseating John Lennon and Yoko Ono's *Double Fantasy* [see 255]. "It was really a success on all kinds of levels," says Cronin. "We played all the biggest halls. It was incredible to be able to headline the Astrodome and the Superdome." If there was a thorn in REO's success, it was that the band never gained the respect of rock critics, who lumped the band together with other big mainstream rock attractions of the day. Says Cronin, "We were often compared to Journey [see 263] and Styx [see 257], and usually in a less than complimentary fashion."

THE TOP FIVE
Week of February 21, 1981

1. **Hi Infidelity**
   REO Speedwagon

2. **Double Fantasy**
   John Lennon / Yoko Ono

3. **The Jazz Singer**
   Neil Diamond

4. **Crimes of Passion**
   Pat Benatar

5. **Paradise Theater**
   Styx

Producer: Styx

Track listing: A.D. 1928 / Rockin' the Paradise / Too Much Time on My Hands / Nothing Ever Goes as Planned / The Best of Times / Lonely People / She Cares / Snowblind / Half-Penny, Two-Penny / A.D. 1958

April 4, 1981
3 weeks (nonconsecutive)

The Chicago-based quintet Styx was one of the prime American purveyors of progressive rock in the '70s, but as the band moved into the '80s it began to shift gears. "We tried to be more of a song-based band, one that didn't rely as much on long musical passages," says singer Dennis DeYoung. The results of this stylistic shift were "Babe," the band's first Number One single, and Cornerstone, the 1979 album that spawned the single and climbed to number two. That success set the stage for Paradise Theatre.

The concept of Styx's 10th album was inspired by a painting DeYoung saw hanging in a Chicago art gallery. "It was a painting of the Paradise Theatre, with the words 'temporarily closed' on the marquee. I bought a copy of the painting and I took it home to conceptualize an idea about an album with 'paradise' being the metaphor for America. It just struck me as the perfect metaphor for urban decay, America, and American culture."

The Paradise Theatre was built in 1928. Thirty years later it was leveled after falling on financial hard times. Fittingly, Paradise Theatre opens with "A.D. 1928" and closes with "A.D. 1958." Says DeYoung, "It starts out with hope and promise and ends up run down in complete decay, so that gave us plenty of room to say what we felt about America, growing up in the '60s, coming to grips with the end of Vietnam and Watergate and the oil embargo."

In "Rockin' the Paradise," DeYoung warned Americans not to go for the fast

buck. "That was the first song written for the album. With the Paradise Theatre I had this vision of doing something theatrical," DeYoung says. "Not just because of the title, but something that tried to take the more interesting aspects of the Broadway theater and incorporate them into a rock show."

By the '80s, Styx was a well-tuned machine maintaining an album-a-year schedule. For Paradise Theatre, the band returned to Pumpkin Studios in Oak Lawn, Illinois, the same room they'd used to record Cornerstone. "I don't recall any real snafus," DeYoung says of the sessions, which were completed in approximately three months. "It was a wonderful time creatively for the band."

DeYoung composed "The Best of Times," the album's first single, on the grand piano at his Chicago-area home. "I remember thinking, 'This ain't too bad. This might be okay,' " he says. His hunch proved correct—in March 1981, the single reached number three on the Hot 100.

"Too Much Time on My Hands," the album's other big hit single, was written by lead guitarist Tommy Shaw. "He was having a little bit of writer's block during the Paradise Theatre period. Three days before we went into the studio he played me 'Too Much Time on My Hands,' which he had just written the night before. I knew that was a good one," DeYoung says. DeYoung was right again, as the tune became the album's second top 10 hit, climbing to number nine in May. Meanwhile, Paradise Theatre had debuted on the album chart on January 31. Ten weeks later it knocked REO Speedwagon's Hi Infidelity from the top spot to become Styx's first and only Number One album.

THE TOP FIVE
Week of April 4, 1981

1. **Paradise Theatre**
   Styx

2. **Hi Infidelity**
   REO Speedwagon

3. **Moving Pictures**
   Rush

4. **Arc of a Diver**
   Steve Winwood

5. **Double Fantasy**
   John Lennon / Yoko Ono

258 Mistaken Identity EMI-AMERICA 17052
KIM CARNES

Producer: Val Garay

Track listing: Bette Davis Eyes / Hit and Run / Mistaken Identity / When I'm Away from You / Draw of the Cards / Break the Rules Tonite (Out of School) / Still Hold On / Don't Call It Love / Miss You Tonite / My Old Pals

June 27, 1981
4 weeks

"It was a very optimistic time," recalls Kim Carnes. "We were all anxious to get in the studio. We had just come off a summer tour with James Taylor, playing all the really great outdoor places, so we were in a great frame of mind to go in and cut an album." That album, Carnes' sixth, was *Mistaken Identity*.

Born July 20, 1945, in Los Angeles, Carnes knew she wanted to become a singer-songwriter when she was three. By junior high, she had begun performing. Her first break came when blues singer Big Mama Thornton recorded one of her songs for the 1971 film *Vanishing Point*. Although other artists, such as Barbra Streisand, Frank Sinatra, and Rita Coolidge, covered her songs (often co-written with her husband Dave Ellingson), Carnes's four 1970s albums were released largely without notice.

With the new decade came the success that had been eluding Carnes. She became the first artist signed to EMI-America, a new label owned by Capitol/EMI. Kenny Rogers, a member of the New Christy Minstrels with Carnes and Ellingson in the late '60s, covered the couple's songs on *Gideon*. Then Rogers's duet with Carnes, "Don't Fall in Love with a Dreamer," climbed to number four. A few months later, Carnes had a hit of her own with "More Love," which reached the top 10. Then came *Mistaken Identity*.

Recorded in two week-long sessions at Record One in Los Angeles during December 1980 and January 1981, *Mistaken Identity*, says Carnes, may have been credited to her as a solo artist, but it was very much a group effort. "I had the best band in the world," Carnes says. "This album was a complete collaborative effort. There was such joy in the whole recording process, because we had all been on the road a bunch, this was our album to make together."

For the most part, *Mistaken Identity* was recorded live in the studio. "We would usually get it on the second or third take," Carnes says. That method of working led to some magical moments, particularly in recording the title track, which in its original incarnation was uptempo. "It didn't feel right at all, so we went on to another song. Then, at about 3 A.M., Bill Cuomo, who was one of my keyboard players, started playing it with this slow, wonderful groove, and one by one the band went out and started playing. I started singing and Val put a mike in the middle of the room, and turned on the tape recorder."

The combination of Cuomo's haunting keyboards and Carnes's husky vocals were also the signature of "Bette Davis Eyes," which would become the album's big hit. "I fought real hard to have it released as the first single," Carnes says. "I was as sure as I could be about anything." Sure enough, "Bette Davis Eyes" topped the singles chart on May 16, 1981, and stayed there for nine weeks. It was holding steady in the middle of that run when *Mistaken Identity* made it to Number One on June 27.

THE TOP FIVE
Week of June 27, 1981

1. **Mistaken Identity**
   Kim Carnes

2. **Hi Infidelity**
   REO Speedwagon

3. **Dirty Deeds Done Dirt Cheap**
   AC/DC

4. **Paradise Theatre**
   Styx

5. **Fair Warning**
   Van Halen

THRESHOLD 2901 ## Long Distance Voyager

THE MOODY BLUES

Producer: Pip Williams

Track listing: The Voice / Talking Out of Turn / Gemini Dream / In My World / Meanwhile / 22,000 Days / Nervous / Painted Smile / Reflective Smile / Veteran Cosmic Rocker

July 25, 1981
3 weeks

Following the success of its first Number One album, 1972's *Seventh Sojourn* [see 150] and two years of touring, the Moody Blues went on a four-year hiatus. The compilation *This Is the Moody Blues* and *Caught Live Plus Five*, released in 1974 and 1977, respectively, proved there was still an audience for the veteran British band. But it was 1978's *Octave*, the band's first studio album in six years, that showed the Moodies were still a significant creative force. As singer/guitarist Justin Hayward explains, "A lot of people thought we were finished, but it did surprisingly well."

Octave climbed to number 13 and went on to sell more than a million copies. If that success surprised some, *Long Distance Voyager* had to be a shock. Nearly a decade after the Moodies first reached the top of the *Billboard* album chart, the veteran British act proved its staying power by doing it for a second time.

Long Distance Voyager marked a few firsts for the Moodies. It was the group's first album without producer Tony Clarke, who stopped working with the Moodies during *Octave* after a decade-plus association with the band. It was the first Moodies appearance by former Yes member Patrick Moraz, who replaced founding member Mike Pinder after the completion of *Octave*. It also marked the first and last time the Moody Blues recorded as a group at their own Threshold Studios in West Hampstead, London. "Although I made *Blue Jays* with John Lodge and made my own solo albums in the studio, we'd never actually recorded a Moody Blues album in this wonderful studio," Hayward recalls.

Although the album credits the string performance on *Long Distance Voyager* to the New World Orchestra, Hayward admits that no such troupe really exists. "The album wasn't recorded with an orchestra at all," he adds. "There were some string overdubs, so we just made up the name."

The group's changing lineup and experimentation with drum machines gave them "a slightly different dimension" and updated the Moodies' trademark sound for the '80s. "Mike leaving opened the door for myself and John to play a lot more keyboards," Hayward says. In addition, working with new producer Pip Williams also changed the group's dynamic. "Pip is a detail man," Hayward says. "He would tell us exactly the right notes to play," whereas Clarke had been known as a big-picture man but didn't get into the details.

Two singles were released off *Long Distance Voyager*: "Gemini Dream" peaked at number 12, while "The Voice" reached number 15. "The material on *Long Distance Voyager* was very strong and stands up today, much more so than some of the other material that we have done," Hayward says.

In addition, the album also marked a spiritual rebirth for the Moodies. "We had a lot of fun and a lot of laughs," he recalls. "It was like being in a gang again. Most people join groups so they can be in a gang. With *Long Distance Voyager* we had that feeling again of all being together."

THE TOP FIVE
Week of July 25, 1981

1. **Long Distance Voyager**
   The Moody Blues

2. **Mistaken Identity**
   Kim Carnes

3. **Hi Infidelity**
   REO Speedwagon

4. **Street Songs**
   Rick James

5. **Hard Promises**
   Tom Petty & the Heartbreakers

260

Precious Time CHRYSALIS 1346
PAT BENATAR

Producers: Keith Olsen and Neil Geraldo

Track listing: Promises in the Dark / Fire and Ice / Just Like Me / Precious Time / It's a Tuff Life / Take It Any Way You Want It / Evil Genius / Hard to Believe / Helter Skelter

August 15, 1981
1 week

With the success of her second album, 1980's *Crimes of Passion*, Pat Benatar became a star. The album spent five weeks at number two in early 1981, but was unable to unseat John Lennon and Yoko Ono's *Double Fantasy* [see 255] from the top spot.

Following the album's release, Benatar toured extensively while attempting to come up with new songs for her third album. "I was freaking out," she says. "We were doing most of the writing for *Precious Time* on the road. Then we came home, took two weeks off, and then we went right into the studio, so we were pretty fried."

While Benatar had proven that she was a songwriter in her own right with "Hell Is for Children" from *Crimes of Passion*, she was still just dabbling in songwriting around the period of *Precious Time*. "I really wasn't that confident," she says. Benatar, guitarist Neil Geraldo, guitarist Scott Sheets, and drummer Myron Grombacher all had songwriting credits on *Precious Time*, but they also brought in some hired guns. Tom Kelly co-wrote "Fire and Ice," which went on to become Benatar's third top 20 hit, and Billy Steinberg penned the title track. The album closed with Benatar's version of the Beatles' "Helter Skelter" [see 110]. Says

Benatar, "My mother even knew the lyrics to that song, because I was such a big Beatles fan when I was growing up. That song was something that rocked, sounded dark, and it was a lot of fun to scream to."

"Promises in the Dark," one of two songs Benatar wrote with her longtime boyfriend Geraldo, is a particularly memorable song for the singer. "I wrote it on tour when we were on a plane," she says. "When we got back home I wanted to play it for Neil, but I was still kind of shy about writing lyrics, especially when they were about him. One night I slipped them under the door, because I was too embarrassed to show it to him face-to-face."

On *Precious Time*, Geraldo was credited as co-producer for the first time. "Neil really co-produced *Crimes of Passion*, but he didn't get the credit for it. This was a little more relaxed, because there wasn't that tension that he was doing all this work and not getting credit for it." The sessions, at Sound City

and Goodnight L.A., went fairly quickly. "We just went in there, drank lots of coffee, and went for it," Benatar says. "We didn't do lots of tracking or use a drum machine. We just went in there and played."

While the album was in progress, Benatar picked up a Grammy Award for best female rock performance, for *Crimes of Passion*. With the momentum of the Grammy win, *Precious Time* was able to hit Number One in its fourth week on the chart.

While Benatar went on to win another Grammy, this time for "Fire and Ice," she says that *Precious Time* wasn't her best shot. "If we could have combined some of the songs from the third album with some of the songs from *Get Nervous* [Benatar's fourth album], we would have the correct record, but we made the record too soon," she says. "I really think *Precious Time* went to Number One on the strength of *Crimes of Passion*. That's the record that should have gone to Number One."

THE TOP FIVE
Week of August 15, 1981

1. **Precious Time**
   Pat Benatar

2. **4**
   Foreigner

3. **Long Distance Voyager**
   Moody Blues

4. **Street Songs**
   Rick James

5. **Escape**
   Journey

ourselves, because of the standards we set," Gramm says. "We had a number of extremely diverse ideas and we wanted to keep the creative spark of those ideas intact while we continually crafted songs. It was really painstaking, because the songs went through so many changes."

"Urgent," which climbed to number four, was the album's first single. "It was very uptempo when we first wrote it," Gramm recalls. "It sounded more akin to 'Papa Was a Rolling Stone' by the Temptations. But we tried it several different ways before we finally settled into this really hot and nasty groove that was just screaming for the type of sax that Junior Walker played. Leafing through the *Village Voice*, we found him playing at the Lone Star, where we buttered him up and asked him to play with us."

The four-man lineup also allowed Foreigner room for other guests, including keyboardist Thomas Dolby, who became a successful solo artist a year later. Dolby's keyboards graced several tracks, including "Urgent" and the ballad "Waiting for a Girl Like You," which spent 10 weeks at number two.

One of the most memorable songs on *4* was not a hit. During the recording sessions, held mostly during late 1980 at Electric Lady Studios in New York, Gramm was stricken by a virus, which left his voice sounding ragged on the song "Girl on the Moon." Says Gramm, "We were going to do it again, but it sounded so haunting and so weird, we decided to keep it. On that night John Lennon was assassinated. I drove by and saw the sirens and had not a clue what it was all about. Now when I hear that song, I think of him and that night."

Producer: Robert John "Mutt" Lange and Mick Jones

Track listing: Night Life / Juke Box Hero / Break It Up / Waiting for a Girl Like You / Luanne / Urgent / I'm Gonna Win / Woman in Black / Girl on the Moon / Don't Let Go

August 22, 1981
10 weeks (nonconsecutive)

The title of Foreigner's *4* didn't only refer to the band's fourth album—it also reflected the band's pared-down ranks, says singer Lou Gramm.

Formed in early 1976 by guitarist Mick Jones (a member of Nero & the Gladiators in the early '60s, and later Spooky Tooth and the Leslie West Band), Foreigner's original lineup was six members strong. The band went on to tremendous success with its hard-rock-

ing self-titled 1977 debut, which peaked at number four and spawned the top 10 singles "Feels Like the First Time" and "Cold as Ice." Its follow-up, 1977's *Double Vision*, fared even better, climbing to number three with two top five singles, "Hot Blooded" and the title track. Yet by 1979's *Head Games*, Foreigner had seemingly run out of gas.

"After *Head Games*, we all felt we needed to do something a little different and a little more quirky," Gramm says. "No one was really satisfied with *Head Games*. That was the album that got away." Original bassist Ed Gagliardi had left the band in 1979 and was replaced by Rick Wills, and after early sessions for *4*, guitarist/keyboardist Ian MacDonald and keyboardist Al Greenwood also departed.

With drummer Dennis Elliot still on board, Foreigner worked on *4* for eight long months. "We were very hard on

THE TOP FIVE
Week of August 22, 1981

1. **4**
   Foreigner

2. **Precious Time**
   Pat Benatar

3. **Bella Donna**
   Stevie Nicks

4. **Escape**
   Journey

5. **Long Distance Voyager**
   Moody Blues

262 Bella Donna MODERN 139
STEVIE NICKS

Producer: Jimmy Iovine

Track listing: Bella Donna / Kind of Woman / Stop Draggin' My Heart Around / Think About It / After the Glitter Fades / Edge of Seventeen / How Still My Love / Leather and Lace / Outside the Rain / The Highwayman

September 5, 1981
1 week

For Stevie Nicks, being one-fifth of one of the most successful rock acts of the '70s wasn't enough. As a member of Fleetwood Mac, Nicks had enjoyed incredible success with the group's 1976 self-titled album [see 218] and *Rumours* [see 223], which had emerged as one of the best-selling albums of all time. Yet Nicks was growing increasingly frustrated with life in the supergroup.

"I was in a very big band, very popular, very successful, and making a lot of money," says Nicks. "The only problem was that there were three writers for each album. It took a year for us to do an album and then there were two or three years between albums. So for me as a songwriter, there was hardly a reason to bother to write. I started to feel that I was not being allowed to do the thing I love most, which was writing."

To remedy the situation, Nicks decided it was time to record her own album. However, it wasn't an easy decision to make. "Nobody wanted me to do it and possibly risk the future of Fleetwood Mac," she says. "It was difficult, because I knew that everyone else in the band was going to be angry with me, and they were."

Once Nicks was able to overcome the guilt and the doubt, she found working on *Bella Donna* a creative boon. "I used a completely different set of people," she says. "So from the very beginning, I knew it was going to be real successful, because it was too much fun, it was too interesting, and all the people were totally fascinating. I knew that it couldn't be wrong if I was standing in a room with that many people who were looking forward to coming to work, as opposed to the usual rock 'n' roll attitude."

Bella Donna only took about three and a half months to record, which was a breeze for Nicks, having spent up to a year on some Fleetwood Mac albums. "We were very prepared," she says. "Jimmy Iovine and I knew which songs we were going to use," says Nicks. Before going into the studio, Nicks rehearsed at home with Benmont Tench of Tom Petty & the Heartbreakers, who served as the album's musical director, and back-up singers Sharon Celani and Lori Perry.

The album also featured other special guests, including Petty, Don Henley and Don Felder of the Eagles [see 243], E Street Band member Roy Bittan [see 253], and Davey Johnstone of Elton John's band [see 146].

When Nicks asked Iovine to produce *Bella Donna*, he was completing work on Petty's *Hard Promises*. "When I decided I wanted to do a solo album, I wanted it to sound like Tom Petty," Nicks says. "I met Tom through Jimmy and I got to hear some songs he didn't use that he agreed to share with me."

One of those songs was "Stop Draggin' My Heart Around," which Nicks and Petty recorded as a duet. The track, released as a single, eventually climbed to number three. "That was just an extra gift I got during the recording of the album," says Nicks.

While "Stop Draggin' My Heart Around" was written by Petty and Heartbreaker Mike Campbell, the other nine tracks on the album were written or co-written by Nicks.

Bella Donna was a major accomplishment for Nicks, but she couldn't bask in her solo success for long. She was still a member of Fleetwood Mac, and the band was preparing to record *Mirage* [see 271]. "I had to go back because they were waiting for me," she says. "That was the only drag."

THE TOP FIVE
Week of September 5, 1981

1. **Bella Donna**
   Stevie Nicks

2. **4**
   Foreigner

3. **Escape**
   Journey

4. **Precious Time**
   Pat Benatar

5. **Don't Say No**
   Billy Squier

COLUMBIA 37408 **Escape** 263
JOURNEY

Producers: Mike Stone and Kevin Elson

Track listing: Don't Stop Believin' / Stone in Love / Who's Crying Now / Keep on Runnin' / Still They Ride / Escape / Lay It Down / Dead or Alive / Mother, Father / Open Arms

September 12, 1981
1 week

"I knew we were going to do good," says guitarist Neal Schon. "I knew we were going to sell at least a million records. I felt like we had good songs that were right in line with radio. We had worked hard to build quite a fan base. Even if we put out a terrible record, it would have sold."

Escape wasn't a terrible record, but "one of the best records Journey ever made," Schon says. Journey was formed in February 1973 in San Francisco, when Schon, formerly of Santana, recruited Steve Miller Band bassist Ross Valory, future Tubes drummer Prairie Prince, and guitarist George Tickner. Keyboardist Gregg Rolie, also of Santana fame, joined a few months later. Yet after three albums and multiple personnel changes, Journey still hadn't taken off.

Then, in late 1977, vocalist Steve Perry joined the band. With Perry and new drummer Steve Smith, Journey became an album-rock radio favorite and racked up a string of four consecu-

tive platinum albums, including the 1981 live double-album Captured. Next up was Escape.

Before the album was recorded, road-weary Rolie was replaced by former Babys member Jonathan Cain. "It was a breath of fresh air," Schon recalls. "He had a lot of really great songwriting ability and he kind of rounded out the whole project."

Recorded in approximately a month at Fantasy Studios in Berkeley, California, Escape was one of the least expensive Journey albums. "Everyone basically did their homework and had their shit together," Schon says. "We were in and out of the studio."

Much of the material on the album, including "Stone in Love" and the title track, was born out of Schon's practice of running a tape recorder when he experimented with his guitar. "I came up with 'Stone in Love' in one day," Schon recalls. "I had taken some mushrooms and turned on the cassette recorder. I had no idea what I played until I listened to the tape the next day." Another track, the appropriately titled "Mother, Father," was co-written with Schon's father.

Newcomer Cain also contributed heavily. "He brought 'Don't Stop Believin'.' I came up with a couple chords and jammed them out and then he and Steve finished it." It was the combination of Perry and Cain that led to what would become the band's two biggest hits, the radio-friendly ballads

"Who's Crying Now" and "Open Arms." The former would help propel Escape to the top of the album chart and into the hearts of millions, although the band was despised by rock critics. "The critics never liked us," Schon admits. "But we didn't give a shit. The fans loved us and radio loved us, and we sold a ton of records."

Journey would go on to score with two other multi-platinum albums, 1983's Frontiers and 1986's Raised on Radio, but even during the making of Escape, tension was brewing within the band. "Steven and I used to butt heads a lot," Schon admits. "There was a lot of friction going on between him and me, but it made for better music."

THE TOP FIVE
Week of September 12, 1981

1. **Escape**
   Journey

2. **Bella Donna**
   Stevie Nicks

3. **4**
   Foreigner

4. **Precious Time**
   Pat Benatar

5. **Don't Say No**
   Billy Squier

264 Tattoo You ROLLING STONES 21003
THE ROLLING STONES

Producers: The Glimmer Twins

Track listing: Start Me Up / Hang Fire / Slave / Little T&A / Black Limousine / Neighbours / Worried About You / Tops / Heaven / No Use in Crying / Waiting on a Friend

September 19, 1981
9 weeks

Following the release of *Emotional Rescue* [see 249], the animosity between Rolling Stones frontman Mick Jagger and guitarist Keith Richards had become so acute that the pair, known as the "Glimmer Twins," had stopped speaking to each other. "*Tattoo You* really came about because Mick and Keith were going through a period of not getting on," says associate producer and engineer Chris Kimsey. "There was the need to have an album out, so I suggested that I could go in and make an album of what I knew was still there in the vaults."

During the *Some Girls* [see 228] and *Emotional Rescue* sessions, the Stones cut dozens of additonal tracks that didn't appear on the albums. For example, Richards's "Litte T&A," an ode to his girlfriend Patti Hansen, was originally cut during the *Emotional Rescue* sessions. Kimsey also turned to some earlier sessions. " 'Waiting on a Friend' and 'Tops' were from *Goats Head Soup* [see 166], 'Slave' was from the *Black and Blue* period [see 216], and 'Start Me Up' was recorded on the same day as 'Miss You' [from *Some Girls*—see 228]," he says. "Mick or Keith thought it sounded famiIar, like something on the radio at the time, so it was just sort of forgotten about," Kimsey says of the latter track, which would eventually become a number two hit.

Jagger and Richards may have forgotten about the early version of "Start Me Up," but not Kimsey. "I knew that was there in the vaults," he says. "That was me groundbase for the album. On all the albums I worked on, I would keep a comprehensive log and I always made a point that if anything was happening I would record it, even if it was old Jimmy Reed blues covers."

Despite the fact that the album was mostly comprised of material culled from the vaults, it took several months to put together. The Stones had to regroup to finish some of the songs, but Jagger was busy pursuing his film career, appearing on location for a film called *Fitzcarraldo* that was shot on location in Peru. "Mick was doing the movie, so it was difficult to pin him down," Kimsey says. "It must have taken us a good nine months to do the album."

When the Stones did finally regroup, they returned to Pathe-Marconi Studios in Paris. "Paris was a very good environment for them and a great place for them to work," says Kimsey. "When they did get back together, they were all happy."

When the album was completed, Bob Clearmountain was called in to remix several tracks, including "Start Me Up." Although much of the material was old, the Stones sounded rejuvinated on *Tattoo You*, which may have said more about the faltering state of the band's artistry than was intended. In any event, *Tattoo You* was certainly a better album than *Emotional Rescue*, and fans responded accordingly. While the album followed the same path as *Black and Blue* and *Emotional Resue* to the peak—debuting at number eight before hitting the Number One spot in its second week on the chart—it had more staying power. Its nine-week run at the top represented the longest stay of any Stones album.

ATLANTIC 11111 # For Those About to Rock We Salute You
AC/DC **265**

Producer: Robert John "Mutt" Lange

Track listing: For Those About to Rock (We Salute You) / Put the Finer on You / Let's Get It Up / Inject the Venom / Snowballed / Evil Walks / C.O.D. / Night of the Long Knives / Spellbound

December 26, 1981
3 weeks

Five years of hard work was finally paying off for the Australian heavy metal quintet known as AC/DC. The group's 1979 album, *Highway to Hell*, produced by Robert John "Mutt" Lange, proved to be the group's breakthrough. It climbed to number 17, putting AC/DC in the league of such American hard-rock acts as Aerosmith and Ted Nugent. Then, on February 19, 1980, singer Bon Scott was found dead after a night of drinking. He had choked on his own vomit. The band's road to success had seemingly hit a dead end.

But AC/DC, led by guitarist Angus Young, refused to give up. Scott soundalike Brian Johnson, formerly of the band Geordie, was recruited, and with Lange once again manning the board, the band recorded the triumphant *Back in Black*, which saluted Scott while simultaneously ushering in his successor. The album, buoyed by Young's power chords and Johnson's throaty vocals, climbed all the way to number four, securing the band's position as one of the most popular hard-rock groups in the world.

AC/DC's popularity was now so great that in 1981 Atlantic Records dug into their vaults and released the 1976 album *Dirty Deeds Done Dirt Cheap*, which had previously been issued in the U.K. but not in America. Although the album, featuring Scott on vocals, was five years old, it became AC/DC's highest-charting album to date, reaching number three. Another 1976 album, *High Voltage*, which had failed to chart upon its initial U.S. release, finally did so and made number 146—quite respectable for a five-year-old record. But AC/DC was primed for the biggest album of its career with its third charting album of 1981.

AC/DC initially had a hard time settling down to work on *For Those About to Rock We Salute You*. The band had decided to go to Paris to record the album but couldn't find the right studio. "There was lots of moving about from studio to studio," says recording engineer Mark Dearnley, who had also worked on *Back in Black*. "We tried a few different studios, but it didn't work out. In one, Mutt was happy with the guitar sound but wasn't happy with the way the drums were working, and vice versa in the other."

The solution was to record the band at H.I.S. Studio, which was not a full-fledged recording studio but rather a rehearsal room the band was using to prepare for the recording sessions in Paris. "Everyone was happy with the way they set up in the rehearsal room," says Dearnley, "so eventually they decided to cut their losses and record it there using Mobile One from London."

The space lent itself to an uncommon configuration. "It was a huge stone building," says Dearnley. "We set up the guitars in one room and the drums up in another. We also had a P.A. feeding drums as well, so it was quite an unusual set up."

The album was recorded in about two months in a relaxed environment that favored feeling over studio perfection. "There was a lot of time spent sitting around and chatting, but when the mood was right, they would get up and fire off a couple of takes," says Dearnley. "They are not a band that can just keep plugging at a take until it's right. The mood has to be right for them."

The title track, which features cannon explosions, ended up being one of the most difficult songs to record. "We had a lot of fun trying to find the right cannon sounds for it," says Dearnley. "But in the end it was sorted out in London on the remix."

When *For Those About to Rock We Salute You* was released in late November 1981, the band's growing legion of fans heeded the call. The album entered the chart in the top 10. Two weeks later, it hit Number One.

THE TOP FIVE
Week of December 26, 1981

1. **For Those About to Rock We Salute You**
   AC/DC

2. **Ghost in the Machine**
   The Police

3. **4**
   Foreigner

4. **Escape**
   Journey

5. **Raise**
   Earth, Wind & Fire

266 Freeze-Frame EMI AMERICA 17062
THE J. GEILS BAND

Producer: Seth Justman

Track listing: Freeze-Frame / Rage in the Cage / Centerfold / Do You Remember When / Insane, Insane Again / Flamethrower / River Blindness / Angel in Blue / Piss on the Wall

February 6, 1982
4 weeks

No one could say that the J. Geils Band hadn't worked hard to reach the apex of the *Billboard* album chart—the Boston-based band had been together for 13 years and released 12 albums without a lineup change before finally making it to the top. "We put in years of hard work," says vocalist Peter Wolf. "It was exciting because we spent so many years where people would say, 'J. Who?' It was great to finally have people recognize the band."

The J. Geils Blues Band, named for guitarist J. (Jerome) Geils, was formed in 1967 as an acoustic trio featuring bassist Danny Klein and harmonica player Magic Dick Salwitz. Future frontman Wolf relocated to Boston to attend art school, where he roomed with future film director David Lynch, but his love for music led him to a gig as a disc jockey on radio station WBCN. But spinning records was not enough. Wolf soon joined the Hallucinations, a rock 'n' soul band that included drummer Stephen Jo Bladd.

When Wolf caught the J. Geils Blues Band in action, he and Bladd left the Hallucinations to join forces with Geils and company. A year later, keyboardist Seth Justman signed on.

Before signing with Atlantic Records in 1969, the band opted to drop "Blues" from its name, but the influence remained firmly implanted in its music. With constant touring, the band's rabid following soon expanded beyond the New England area and to the rest of the country. Their third album, 1972's *Full House*, stalled at number 54 but went gold. *Bloodshot*, released in 1973, climbed to number 10 and likewise moved over 500,000 units.

Although the band's subsequent mid-'70s efforts failed to equal their early commercial success, the J. Geils Band remained undaunted and continued to record albums and tour at a relentless pace. A move from Atlantic to the fledging EMI-America label seemed to stoke the band's creative juices: With *Sanctuary*, released in 1978, the band struck gold again, and the follow-up, 1980's *Love Stinks*, climbed to number 18. The stage was now set for the release of *Freeze-Frame*.

As Wolf sees it, time was on the band's side. " 'Love Stinks' was greeted with a great amount of resistance at top 40 radio," he recalls. "People thought it was too hard or too rock, but by the time *Freeze-Frame* came out, disco was waning and people were getting into more traditional and more primal rock."

Freeze-Frame, like the two J. Geils Band albums before it, was recorded near the group's home base of Boston at Long View Farm. And despite modern-day additions such as synthesizers, the J. Geils Band continued to mine the R&B tradition. "Flamethrower," which featured soul belters Luther Vandross and Cissy Houston on backing vocals, picked up airplay on R&B stations. The album's big hits, however, were the title track and "Centerfold." The latter topped the Hot 100 for six weeks, thanks in part to a sexy video that garnered heavy airplay on MTV, which at the time was just beginning to become a powerful force.

THE TOP FIVE
Week of February 6, 1982

1. **Freeze-Frame**
   The J. Geils Band

2. **Escape**
   Journey

3. **4**
   Foreigner

4. **Hooked on Classics**
   The Royal Philharmonic Orchestra

5. **Tattoo You**
   The Rolling Stones

Producers: Richard Gottehrer & Rob Freeman

Track listing: Our Lips Our Sealed / How Much More / Tonite / Lust to Love / This Town / We Got the Beat / Fading Fast / Automatic / You Can't Walk in Your Sleep (If You Can't Sleep) / Skidmarks on My Heart / Can't Stop the World

March 6, 1982
6 weeks

In 1978, with the do-it-yourself ethic of the punk movement sweeping Los Angeles, fashion design student Jane Wiedlin and former high school cheerleader Belinda Carlisle decided they too could form a band. Wiedlin had left her parents' San Fernando Valley home for an old building in Hollywood called the Canterbury, which was a dormitory of sorts for punk rockers. "That was when we decided to form the Go-Go's," Jane

says. "It didn't matter if you'd never picked up an instrument in your life. Everyone was in a band."

Wiedlin and Carlisle traveled separately to San Francisco to see what would turn out to be the final show by the Sex Pistols on January 14, 1978. The Go-Go's, however, didn't want to be like the Sex Pistols. "We didn't really want to be a punk band," Carlisle says. "We wanted to play melodic pop, more like the Buzzcocks or one of those type bands."

After creating a buzz on the L.A. club scene, the Go-Go's traveled to London to record a one-off single for the independent Stiff label. Upon the band's return to L.A., Miles Copeland, the head of I.R.S. Records and manager of the Police, signed them. "He was the only one interested," recalls Carlisle. "Everyone else was afraid to take a chance."

By the time the Go-Go's recorded Beauty and the Beat, the band had settled on a lineup that included Carlisle

on vocals, Wiedlin on rhythm guitar, Charlotte Caffey of the Eyes on lead guitar, Kathy Valentine of the Textones on bass, and Gina Schock of the Baltimore band Miss Edie & the Eggs on drums. The album was recorded at Pennylane Studios in New York. "We did it for fun," Carlisle recalls. "Our priority was not the record; it was more or less having a good time." However, no session players were called in during the recording. "We did a lot of takes and we wouldn't get it. Then we would order a large pizza, eat it, and do another take. We weren't the most proficient musicians and singers, so it took a while to get it right," Carlisle recalls.

When the Go-Go's heard the finished product, they were a bit shocked as the band's punk influences had been airbrushed by Richard Gottehrer's slick production. "We were all horrified," says Carlisle. "We were used to sounding much rawer, the way we did in the clubs. Listening to this pop record at first was a little scary, but it grew on us."

The Go-Go's had differing expectations of how Beauty and the Beat would be accepted. "I remember saying, 'Wow, if we sell 150,000 copies that would be so cool.'" Carlisle recalls. Wiedlin, however, expected bigger things: "I said to one of the record company executives, 'We are going to go platinum,' and he just laughed in my face."

But the Go-Go's had the last laugh. They became the first all-female rock group playing their own instruments to score a Number One album, as Beauty and the Beat, helped along by the hit single "We Got the Beat," reached the top spot after 32 weeks on the album chart.

THE TOP FIVE
Week of March 6, 1982

1. **Beauty and the Beat**
   The Go-Go's

2. **Escape**
   Journey

3. **Freeze-Frame**
   The J. Geils Band

4. **4**
   Foreigner

5. **I Love Rock-n-Roll**
   Joan Jett and the Blackhearts

268 Chariots of Fire POLYDOR 6335
VANGELIS

From *Chariots of Fire.*

Producer: Vangelis

Track listing: Titles / Five Circles / Abraham's Theme / Eric's Theme / 100 Metres / Jerusalem / Chariots of Fire

April 17, 1982
4 weeks

On March 25, 1982, Greek-born Evangelos Papathanassiou celebrated his 39th birthday in London and then went to bed. Hours later, at 4 A.M., he received a phone call. The keyboardist/composer, better known as Vangelis, had just won an Academy Award for his majestic soundtrack to *Chariots of Fire.* Less than a month later, Vangelis also had a Number One album.

Although Vangelis was a relatively new phenomenon in America, by 1982 he was a seasoned veteran of the music business, having experienced his first success as a teenager as a member of the Greek band Formynx. "I was very fortunate that I tasted success early with Formynx—playing in front of 10,000 people in stadiums, all the hysteria. It was great fun, but I wasn't interested in that," Vangelis told Kurt Loder in *Rolling Stone.*

His next project was a collaboration with Dennis Roussos called Aphrodite's Child, a group that scored a 1969 European hit with "Rain and Tears." After that combo broke up, Vangelis went the solo route, scoring such films as *L'Apocalypse des Animaux* and recording solo albums like *Heaven and Hell,* which gained exposure on "Cosmos," the PBS series hosted by Carl Sagan.

In 1974, veteran progressive-rock act Yes asked Vangelis to replace keyboardist Rick Wakeman. He declined the offer, but his friendship with Yes vocalist Jon Anderson led to the release of several collaborative albums, including *The Friends of Mr. Cario,* which yielded the top 10 British hit "I'll Find My Way Home."

The composer, who does not read or write music, explained his composing method to *People*'s Jerene Jones: "I work like a bridge between nature and what comes out through my fingers," he said. "With my synthesizers, I have a lover relationship."

Vangelis's early success allowed him the freedom to build his own recording studio in London near Marble Arch. "In order to do what I'm doing today, you have to go through this music business—to make enough money to build your own studio and then do whatever you like," Vangelis told Loder. "Which is much more healthy, more creative, than to go through singles and chart positions. I'm not against that, but it's not my target."

Chart positions were likely the furthest thing from Vangelis's mind in 1980, when producer David Puttnam signed him on to compose his first score for a major motion picture. The film, *Chariots of Fire,* chronicled the true story of two long-distance runners training for the 1924 Paris Olympic Games. "It's a nice, healthy, pure film,'" Vangelis told Jones in *People.* "I like the Olympic Games and I did it for fun." Vangelis dedicated the soundtrack album to his father Ulysses.

When the film became a hit, so did Vangelis's soundtrack. But *Chariots of Fire* didn't exactly sprint to the pole position of the album chart—it took 27 weeks for the album to reach the peak. On May 8, 1982, the album's opening track, "Titles," which was renamed "Chariots of Fire" for its release as a single, climbed to Number One on the Hot 100. The charts may not have been Vangelis's target, but with *Chariots of Fire* he hit the top anyway.

THE TOP FIVE
Week of April 17, 1982

1. **Vangelis**
   Chariots of Fire

2. **I Love Rock-n-Roll**
   Joan Jett and the Blackhearts

3. **Beauty and the Beat**
   The Go-Go's

4. **Success Hasn't Spoiled Me Yet**
   Rick Springfield

5. **Freeze-Frame**
   The J. Geils Band

Producer: Mike Stone

Track listing: Heat of the Moment / Only Time Will Tell / Sole Survivor / One Step Closer / Time Again / Wildest Dreams / Without You / Cutting It Fine / Here Comes the Feeling

May 15, 1982
9 weeks (nonconsecutive)

"Extremely bizarre" is how drummer Carl Palmer describes it. Palmer had enjoyed a lengthy career with Emerson, Lake & Palmer. His mates—guitarist Steve Howe and keyboardist Geoff Downes—were members of the equally successful group Yes. But when the three joined forces with singer/bassist John Wetton, who'd played in King Crimson and Uriah Heap, they accomplished something that had eluded their previous groups: They had a Number One album.

Asia was formed in January 1981, after Wetton contacted Howe following his departure from Yes. "John and myself had been keen on playing together, and then John started talking to Steve Howe," Palmer says. The trio jammed together for a few days and then enlisted Downes, who had worked with Howe in Yes, as a frontman.

"It was interesting that we all had similar musical backgrounds and we all had a certain amount of success in what we had done," Palmer says. "It seemed like a very natural existence as a group. We were very comfortable with each other from the word go." The group opted to rehearse and write material for approximately six months before entering Townhouse Studio in London to record what would become *Asia*.

"It went fairly easy," Palmer says of the sessions. "It was a very joyful time. Sometimes everything goes so smoothly you can't believe it. We had a lot of good ideas and an awful lot of material." And most of that material, which focused on the most commerical elements of the band members' progressive-rock roots, was well-rehearsed before entering the studio.

But the band opted to tackle one song it had not played in its practice sessions. "The track 'Heat of the Moment' was never ever rehearsed, and was recorded at about 2 A.M.," Palmer says. "It was the last thought of the day. We said, 'Let's just lay this one down and we'll listen to it in the morning.' We just did it as an afterthought, really. It was something in passing and it became a hit single."

The band experimented with the latest technology in making the album, but also turned to ancient instruments. "Steve used a koto on the middle-eight section of 'Heat of the Moment.' It gave the track an unusual sound," Palmer says.

To record the drums, Palmer set up in a room whose walls were lined with tin plates. "It was almost like a fishbowl," he says. "Once the doors were closed, I was in there on my own. It got very warm in there, but the drum sound was incredibly live. It gave it an extra brightness and aggressiveness."

Yet Palmer credits much of Asia's success to timing. "It was the beginning of MTV and it was the beginning of David Geffen's record company, Geffen Records. So we had a lot going for us. MTV was right behind the band and David was well behind the band because he was trying to make a point in the industry."

THE TOP FIVE
Week of May 15, 1982

1. **Asia**
   Asia

2. **Chariots of Fire**
   Vangelis

3. **Beauty and the Beat**
   The Go-Go's

4. **Success Hasn't Spoiled Me Yet**
   Rick Springfield

5. **I Love Rock-n-Roll**
   Joan Jett and the Blackhearts

270 Tug of War COLUMBIA 37462
PAUL McCARTNEY

Producer: George Martin

Track listing: Tug of War / Take It Away / Somebody Who Cares / What's That You're Doing? / Here Today / Ballroom Dancing / The Pound Is Sinking / Wanderlust / Get It /Be What You See / Dress Me Up as a Robber / Ebony and Ivory

May 29, 1982
3 weeks

More than a decade after the breakup of the Beatles, Paul McCartney reunited with the band's famed producer to work on their first full album together since *Abbey Road* [see 117].

It wasn't the first time George Martin had worked with McCartney since the Beatles days—the two shared the production credit of McCartney and Wings' 1973 hit single "Live and Let Die"—but the collaboration couldn't have had come at a better time. Although McCartney had continued to have commercial success with such albums as 1980's number three hit *McCartney II*, critics pointed out that the former Beatle was sorely missing a sounding board.

"My role in the album was to goad Paul a bit," Martin told *Billboard*'s Paul Grein. "I think when he and John Lennon split up, he missed John's goading enormously...I think Paul missed that spur."

Both McCartney and Martin knew that fans would expect a lot from the pairing. "We both tried very hard on this one," Martin told Grein. "Paul and I knew that people would be looking at it

because it was the first time we'd worked together in so long. We talked about it for a couple of months before we went into the studio. We decided early on the general theme of life as a tug of war, a constant struggle of pluses and minuses."

While McCartney and Martin were working on *Tug of War*, Lennon was assassinated on December 8, 1980. "We were already halfway through the album when John died," Martin told Grein. "I remember I rang Paul that morning when I heard the news and said, 'I don't suppose you want to come in today,' and he said, 'Yes, I must come in today; we must work as usual.' Well, we didn't work; we chatted most of the day, but at least he got out of his home. It was a tremendous shock for him."

"If You Were Here Today" was written for Lennon and expressed many of McCartney's feelings that he hadn't previously verbalized. "It was always a very difficult question after John died, to deal with the finality of it," McCartney told his fan newsletter *Club Sandwich*. "He had been making digs at me, in 'How Do You Sleep' and all of that stuff, and I'd not really addressed any of those comments...So I addressed them in 'Here Today,' saying, in effect, 'If you were here today you might say that

such and such a thing is a lot of bullshit, but you and I both know that it isn't.' "

The making of *Tug of War*, which included guest appearances by Stevie Wonder, McCartney's former Beatles mate Ringo Starr, and rock pioneer Carl Perkins, was quite a protracted process. McCartney recounted the recording of "Ebony and Ivory" in *Club Sandwich*: "We started it off in Montserrat, with Stevie Wonder, and then had various sessions in England, without Stevie, to finish it off, including one at Strawberry Studios South, in Dorking. We spent a lot of time fixing and polishing but it was worth it, not only because it was a good track, but because it became Stevie's first Number One single in Britain."

In fact, McCartney told Timothy White that the albums he spent the most time making were *Tug of War*, from 1980 to 1982, and its followup, *Pipes of Peace*. "We took so much time, when I saw the bill for it all I thought, 'I could have made an entire studio for this!' "

Yet McCartney told White he was pleased with the results: "*Tug of War* worked as a commentary on my career thus far, an accurate summing up." The album also earned McCartney another pair of chart-toppers. On May 15, 1982, "Ebony and Ivory" hit the top of the Hot 100. Two weeks later, *Tug of War* joined it at Number One.

THE TOP FIVE
Week of May 29, 1982

1. **Tug of War**
   Paul McCartney

2. **Success Hasn't Spoiled Me Yet**
   Rick Springfield

3. **Asia**
   Asia

4. **Diver Down**
   Van Halen

5. **Stevie Wonder's Original Musiquarium 1**
   Stevie Wonder

WARNER BROS. 23607 **Mirage** **271**
FLEETWOOD MAC

Producers: Lindsey Buckingham, Richard Dashut, Ken Caillat, Fleetwood Mac

Track listing: Love in Store / Can't Go Back / That's Alright / Book of Love / Gypsy / Only Over You / Empire State / Straight Back / Hold Me / Oh Diane / Eyes of the World / Wish You Were Here

August 7, 1982
5 weeks

Following the success of *Rumours* [see 223], Fleetwood Mac earned the right to experiment and took advantage of it on the 1979 two-record set *Tusk*. The album's tribal, rhythm-driven title track was recorded live at Dodger Stadium with the USC Trojan Marching Band. Of course, *Tusk*, which reached number four, and the 1980 double-album *Fleetwood Mac Live*, which made number 14, were no match for *Rumours*, which eventually reached sales of more than 14 million.

Mirage was meant to be a return to the sound Fleetwood Mac had mastered on *Rumours*. "It was a reaction to *Tusk*," says Mick Fleetwood. "We all felt, 'Let's get back and not be so experimental and be less esoteric in our approach.' It's a little cruel to say it was a step back, but *Mirage* was certainly a reflec-tion of doing things the same sort of ways we had done on *Rumours*."

For *Mirage*, Fleetwood Mac once again recorded and wrote as a band. "Lindsey [Buckingham] was very much part of the band, whereas on *Tusk*, Lindsey did a lot of creative work at his house. There were even three or four things that he played drums on," says Fleetwood, the band's usual drummer. "*Mirage* was a departure [from that approach], because it was back to more of a band format."

All this talk of Fleetwood Mac working closer as a band on *Mirage* is somewhat ironic, since Stevie Nicks had completed her solo debut *Bella Donna* [see 262], which would go on to tremendous success almost right after the band wrapped up the *Mirage* sessions. "Stevie's solo career was not really problematic at the time," Fleetwood says. "Stevie is an honest enough person where she wouldn't arbitrarily hold back songs [for her solo albums]. She's very prolific." Indeed, "Gypsy," one of the biggest hits from *Mirage*, was written by Nicks.

Mirage was recorded primarily at the Le Chateau studio in France, which was made famous by Elton John's *Honky Chateau* [see 146]. The album was completed in seven months—fast compared to the time the band had spent recording its two previous studio efforts.

However, the sessions weren't completely smooth. "There were ghosts at the Chateau," Fleetwood says. "Weird things would end up on tape and we had a lot of trouble with some of the machines. My drum roadie was reduced to tears." In the long run, however, a few gremlins were nothing for Fleetwood Mac. Says Fleetwood, "After we got through the emotional boot camp of *Rumours*, we could get through anything." When *Mirage* reached Number One in a mere four weeks, becoming Fleetwood Mac's third Number One album, it was proof positive.

THE TOP FIVE
Week of August 7, 1982

1. **Mirage**
   Fleetwood Mac

2. **Asia**
   Asia

3. **Eye of the Tiger**
   Survivor

4. **American Fool**
   John Cougar

5. **Pictures at Eleven**
   Robert Plant

272 American Fool RIVA 7501
JOHN COUGAR

Producers: John Cougar Mellencamp,
Don Gehman

Track listing: Hurts So Good / Jack &
Diane / Hand to Hold on To / Danger
List / Can You Take It / Thundering
Hearts / China Girl / Close Enough /
Weakest Moments

September 11, 1982
9 weeks

To say that the success of John Cougar's *American Fool* was a surprise is to seriously understate the case. Distributing label PolyGram initially rejected the album, while the singer himself had to be talked into leaving "Jack & Diane"—an eventual Number One single—on the album.

Cougar, who would later reclaim his given surname, Mellencamp, had always dreamed of being a rock star. He was barely into his teens when he picked up the guitar and played with his first band, Crepe Soul. By 1975 he had gone through two years of college and another band, Trash. With demo tape in hand, he relocated to New York, where he hooked up with former David Bowie manager Tony DeFries, who renamed the would-be star "Johnny Cougar."

Cougar's debut album, *Chestnut Street Incident*, released in 1976 on MCA, failed to chart, and MCA balked at releasing the follow-up, *The Kid Inside*. A third album, *A Biography*, was not released in America, but became a hit in Australia.

After signing on with new manager Billy Gaff and his Riva label, Mellencamp's fortunes gradually began to change. *John Cougar*, released in 1979, included the top 30 hit "I Need

a Lover." The 1980 follow-up *Nothin' Matters and What If It Did* included "This Time" and "Ain't Even Done with the Night," two more top 30 entries, which paved the way for *American Fool*.

"We thought we were pretty heavy back in those days," Mellencamp says. "We were pretty young. We were actually the worst band in the world. We had no idea how to arrange or write a song or how to go onstage. We were, and still are, a bunch of hillbillies from Indiana."

Hillbillies or not, Mellencamp and his band jelled on *American Fool*. The bulk of the album was recorded at Cherokee-Criteria studios in Miami during late 1981 and early 1982, but the band and first-time producer Don Gehman also held sessions in L.A., London, and New York.

Former Bowie guitarist Mick Ronson was an uncredited guest on "Jack & Diane." Says Mellencamp, "A lot of credit should be given to Mick. He came in and said, 'You know Johnny,

you should get some baby rattles on this.' I said, 'Baby rattles? Ronson, what the fuck are you talking about?' " Even with the rattles and some tasty guitar licks from Ronson, Mellencamp still didn't like the song. "The guys in the band and Don had to talk me into leaving 'Jack & Diane' on the record," Mellencamp says.

PolyGram didn't like the rest of the album, including "Hurts So Good," which went on to become a number two hit. "When I delivered the record, they said, 'We don't want to put it out. We think it will ruin your career.' " The label suggested the Memphis Horns be added to the record, but Mellencamp hated the suggestion. "The Memphis Horns are fine players, but I always felt horns belonged in a marching band out in the street, not on a rock record," he says.

According to Mellencamp, Gaff had the last word. "He told PolyGram 'Your job isn't to like this record. It's to put it out and sell it or let him out of the deal.' So they put it out and I think they were as surprised as we were.' "

THE TOP FIVE
Week of September 11, 1982

1. **American Fool**
   John Cougar

2. **Mirage**
   Fleetwood Mac

3. **Eye of the Tiger**
   Survivor

4. **Abracadabra**
   Steve Miller

5. **Pictures at Eleven**
   Robert Plant

COLUMBIA 37978 # Business as Usual **273**
MEN AT WORK

Producer: Peter Mclan

Track listing: Who Can See It Be Now? / I Can See It in Your Eyes / Down Under / Underground / Helpless Automaton / People Just Love to Play with Words / Be Good Johnny / Touching the Untouchables / Catch a Star / Down by the Sea

November 13, 1982
15 weeks

It took 15 years to top the Monkees' record for the most weeks at Number One by a debut artist [see 91], and it took an Australian bar band called Men at Work to do it.

Singer-songwriter Colin Hay and bassist John Rees first joined forces in 1979, as an act that played regularly in Melbourne pubs. By the time the band, dubbed Men at Work, was rounded out by drummer Jerry Speiser, multi-instrumentalist Greg Ham, and guitarist Ron Strykert, the group had become the house band at a pub called Cricketer's Arms. The group held the gig for two years before being discovered by an executive at CBS Records in Australia. "He was a fan," says Hay. "He wasn't an A&R person. He was a guy who worked in accounting and he came to see us every Wednesday night."

Once signed to CBS, the band went into Richmond Recorders in Melbourne and cut *Business as Usual* in a mere two weeks. "We just got in there and kind of nipped and tucked at things," says Hay. "Playing live, we were usually in front of 500 drunkards and could do whatever we liked."

One track, "Down Under," which would become a theme song of sorts for the group, was altered significantly.

"We did this version before the album that was kind of like the hippie version. If you had about 25 bong hits it might sound okay. It was originally written by me and Ron on two acoustic guitars. When it ended up on the album, it became bigger and anthem-like, but we never really meant it to be like that. We never felt like we were waving any flag, but we enjoyed the fact that we were from Australia and we were coming to America."

Yet Men at Work almost didn't make it to the States. Although the group scored early success in Australia, topping the album chart for 10 weeks, Columbia Records wasn't quick to pick up the band for American release. "They rejected the album twice, because they didn't think there were any hits on it," Hay says. "It happened in different places, like Switzerland and Israel, before CBS in America decided to put it out."

A tour supporting Fleetwood Mac [see 271] and MTV's acceptance of the video clip for "Who Can It Be Now?" helped the group garner its first U.S. hit, as the single topped the Hot 100 on October 30, 1982. The song, a staple of the band's live set, was originally six minutes long but was cut in half for the album. "I wrote it when I was in the middle of the bush in Australia with my girlfriend," says Hay. "It was a great moment. She said, 'That's a great song. I think that might be Number One someday.' "

Men at Work topped the Hot 100 a second time on January 15, 1983, this time with "Down Under." Yet by then, Men at Work were already established stars, as *Business as Usual* rode out 1982 in the top position. It would take the star power of Michael Jackson's *Thriller* [see 274] to finally knock the band from the summit. Says Hay, "People genuinely found something about the record that they liked, whether it was because it was charming or a bit different—there was something there that they responded to."

THE TOP FIVE
Week of November 13, 1982

1. **Business as Usual**
   Men at Work

2. **Mirage**
   Fleetwood Mac

3. **Nebraska**
   Bruce Springsteen

4. **American Fool**
   John Cougar

5. **Lionel Richie**
   Lionel Richie

274 Thriller EPIC 38112
MICHAEL JACKSON

Producer: Quincy Jones

*Track listing: Wanna Be Startin'
Somethin' / Baby Be Mine / The Girl Is
Mine / Thriller / Beat It / Billie Jean /
Human Nature / P.Y.T. (Pretty Young
Thing) / The Lady in My Life*

*February 26, 1983
37 weeks (nonconsecutive)*

By the dawn of the '80s, Michael Jackson was already a superstar. He had grown up as the frontman of the Jackson 5 and recorded several successful solo albums, but Jackson wasn't truly launched into orbit until he began working with veteran producer Quincy Jones. *Off the Wall*, his first Jones-produced solo album, reached number three in October 1979 and spawned the Number One singles "Don't Stop Until You Get Enough" and "Rock with You," but it hardly prepared the world for what was to follow in its wake.

"We were very excited and happy with the results of *Off the Wall* and we were hoping that the next one would do as well," says Jones. For *Off the Wall*, Jackson wrote three songs. On *Thriller*, he composed four tracks: "Wanna Be Startin' Somethin'," "The Girl Is Mine," "Beat It," and "Billie Jean." Others contributing songs included ex-Heatwave member Rod Temperton (the writer of "Rock with You"), whose *Thriller* contributions included the title track.

Demos, or what Jones calls "Polaroids," for the album were cut in a studio located in the Jackson family's Encino, California, estate. "Rod brought his songs in and we'd try everything out." Jones recalls eating candy with a

young Janet Jackson at a makeshift candy store located next to the studio.

"The *Thriller* process was just fascinating," says Jones. "We were open to try anything our impulses told us to." For example, Jones contacted heavy metal maestro Eddie Van Halen to lay down a blazing guitar solo on "Beat It," while the title track features a spoken-word segment by actor Vincent Price.

Yet the album was recorded during a particularly frantic period. Jackson and Jones only had four months to complete *Thriller* and in the middle of the project, Jones's friend Steven Spielberg recruited the pair to record narration and a song for the *E.T.—The Extra-Terrestrial* storybook album. "In those four months we did *E.T.* and *Thriller*, and it almost put us in the hospital," says Jones. "But the one good thing about it is that we didn't have time to get into paralysis from analysis. We didn't have time to mess around."

Jones actually began working on *Thriller* in December 1981, before he wrapped up *State of Independence* with Donna Summer. "I had to take time off Donna's album to go to Tucson with Michael to record Paul McCartney and Michael on 'The Girl Is Mine.' That was the only time we could get with Paul, so we had to get it. We only had three

days," recalls Jones.

The bulk of the *Thriller* sessions, however, didn't take place until August 1982. In fact, Jones was still mixing the album when "The Girl Is Mine," released in advance of *Thriller*, was climbing the Hot 100. "That made us a little nervous," Jones says. The day before Jones was supposed to turn the album in, Jackson and Jones pulled an all-night session. "We worked until 9 A.M.," he says. "We were fixing 'Beat It' in one room and [engineer] Bruce [Swedien] was mixing something in another room." A few hours later, Jones and Jackson went to listen to the final master. "It sounded terrible," Jones says. "We had put too much music on each side. Since it was vinyl, you could only have about 20 minutes a side. Michael was crying at the time and we all felt terrible."

After a two-day break, Jones went back to work, editing the songs down. "The 'Billie Jean' intro was too long and we had to take one verse out of 'The Lady in My Life,' " Jones says. "From there on in, it was like magic."

The final version of *Thriller* was so magical that it spawned seven top 10 singles and went on to become the best-selling album of all time, with sales of over 24 million in the U.S. alone.

THE TOP FIVE
Week of February 26, 1983

1. **Thriller**
   Michael Jackson

2. **Built for Speed**
   Stray Cats

3. **H2O**
   Daryl Hall & John Oates

4. **Business as Usual**
   Men at Work

5. **The Distance**
   Bob Seger and the Silver
   Bullet Band

CASABLANCA 811492 **Flashdance**
SOUNDTRACK `275`

Score composer: Giorgio Moroder

Music supervisor: Phil Ramone

Track listing: Flashdance...What a Feeling [Irene Cara] / He's a Dream [Shandi] / Love Theme from Flashdance [Helen St. John] / Manhunt [Karen Kamon] / Lady, Lady, Lady [Joe Esposito] / Imagination [Laura Branigan] / Romeo [Donna Summer] / Seduce Me Tonight [Cycle V] / I'll Be Here Where the Heart Is [Kim Carnes] / Maniac [Michael Sembello]

June 25, 1983
2 weeks

Prior to *Flashdance*, Giorgio Moroder had shown the record and film industry that he was a proven hitmaker. Not only did Moroder discover and produce Donna Summer [see 275], he had scored such notable soundtracks as *Midnight Express*, *Cat People*, and *American Gigolo*.

Moroder became involved in *Flashdance* through a relationship he established with Jerry Bruckheimer, the film's co-producer, while working on *American Gigolo*. "In June 1982 he asked me if I would be interested in writing songs for a new film he was working on," says Moroder. The producer-composer also knew the film's director, Adrian Lyne. Summer's 1980 hit "On the Radio" [see 244] was written specifically for Lyne's *Foxes*.

At that time, Moroder was still one of the hottest dance-music producers in the business. Aside from all the hits he scored with Summer, he was also the man behind Blondie's "Call Me," from *American Gigolo*, which had become a Number One single.

But Moroder didn't sign on for Bruckheimer's new project until he saw a rough cut of the film months later. "The video that you get when the movie is half-done is mostly terrible," says Moroder. Yet even the rough cut made an impact on Moroder's girlfriend at the time. "I was watching it with her and I went to make a phone call," he says. "When I came back, she was crying. I thought, 'Wow, that's unusual. This is a rough cut without the music. This must be something special.'"

Inspired by his girlfriend's reaction to the film, Moroder sat down and composed "Flashdance...What a Feeling." Irene Cara, known for the theme from *Fame*, was chosen to sing the track and asked to co-write the lyrics with longtime Moroder associate Keith Forsey. "It was an easy one to record," Moroder says. "It only took two or three days and we had a very good response from Paramount [the film studio]."

Having successfully cut the title track, Moroder was tapped to compose the film's score and contribute several other tracks. Donna Summer's "Romeo" was a track from her ill-fated 1981 album *I'm a Rainbow*, which Geffen Records had declined to release. The Summer connection was also present in "Lady, Lady, Lady," performed by Joe Esposito, a member of Summer's Brooklyn Dreams vocal troupe and co-writer of "Bad Girls" [see 240].

Rounding out the soundtrack album was "Maniac," a song by Michael Sembello, a former Stevie Wonder sideman [see 219] who was recruited for the project by music supervisor Phil Ramone.

Flashdance...What a Feeling hit the summit on May 28, 1983, and was still holding fast in the top position when the soundtrack hit Number One on the album chart. Months later, "Maniac" also topped the Hot 100.

Jennifer Beals in *Flashdance*.

THE TOP FIVE
Week of June 25, 1983

1. **Flashdance**
   Soundtrack

2. **Thriller**
   Michael Jackson

3. **Pyromania**
   Def Leppard

4. **Let's Dance**
   David Bowie

5. **Cargo**
   Men at Work

276 Synchronicity A&M 3732
THE POLICE

Producers: Hugh Padgham and the Police

Track listing: Synchronicity I / Walking in Your Footsteps / O My God / Mother / Miss Gradenko / Synchronicity II / Every Breath You Take / King of Pain / Wrapped Around Your Finger / Tea in the Sahara / Murder By Numbers

July 23, 1983
17 weeks (nonconsecutive)

By the early '80s, the Police, which started out as a modest punk-influenced trio, had grown into a superstar attraction. Ghost in the Machine, the group's fourth album, spent six weeks at number two in late 1981. Meanwhile, the group's trademark blend of reggae, jazz influences, and pop had provided a blueprint for Men at Work [see 273] (whose detractors sometimes derisively referred to them as "Cops on the Beat"). But by the time the Police entered the studio to record their fifth album, the group's formula was getting tired.

"The trick was to try to keep the happening ingredients, add to them, and take them into new places," says drummer Stewart Copeland. "All the ingredients that were in the first album—a high-energy approach, the reggae thing, and

emotional lyrics—were still there on Synchronicity." Yet the band faced some new challenges, as Synchronicity became the most trying album, both emotionally and technically, of their career.

"The more we learned about how to use a studio and how to make records," Copeland says, "the more we wanted to push the parameters. We put ourselves into more challenging places creatively. Also, we were getting along less and less well."

By that time, the members of the band had found notoriety outside of the Police. Singer/bassist Sting had starred in the film Brimstone and Treacle and recorded a solo single for the soundtrack, while Copeland had scored Francis Ford Coppola's Rumblefish. Meanwhile, guitarist Andy Summers had cut an instrumental album with Robert Fripp.

Although Copeland says the Police's squabbles weren't "nearly as exotic as a lot of other groups'," he quips that "in those days, Sting thought he was the devil. It was my job in life to persuade him that he wasn't the devil, he was just an asshole."

One of the conflicts within the band was Sting's lofty lyrical themes. The album was inspired by psychologist Carl Jung's theory of synchronicity and Sting's painful divorce. "Lyrically, it was his personal odyssey through discovery

of these strange places of the mind, but I couldn't stop myself from popping the bubble occasionally, because I had studied all of this stuff in Psych 101," Copeland says. "It was exactly what they taught me in college."

Though Copeland would occasionally rib Sting about his lyrics, both he and Summers acknowledged that he was the best songwriter in the group. "Andy and I would show up with a third or a half of an album's worth of material and Sting would show up with two albums' worth," says Copeland. "By the end of the day, when we sat down to play, the stuff that sounded best usually ended up being Sting's."

For the Synchronicity sessions, held over a six-week period at Air Studios in Montserrat, Sting came armed with several gems, including "Every Breath You Take." The song, which Sting reportedly wrote in a mere five minutes, "was one of our simplest-sounding recordings, but the most complicated to record," says Copeland. "We knew we had a killer song and we didn't want to fuck it up. To present the simple elements of that song in a really important way, without just being trite or clichéd, took a lot of head-scratching." At one point, the band tried the song with a Hammond organ. "Finally, Andy came up with that guitar figure, then we had an idea about how to do the song," Copeland says.

"Every Breath You Take" was just one of several gems on Synchronicity, which turned out to be the Police's swan song. "We just scraped a whole bunch of new areas that would have been damned interesting to build on," Copeland says. "I'm very disappointed that we didn't go on to make three more albums."

THE TOP FIVE
Week of July 23, 1983

1. **Synchronicity**
   The Police

2. **Flashdance**
   Soundtrack

3. **Thriller**
   Michael Jackson

4. **Pyromania**
   Def Leppard

5. **The Wild Heart**
   Stevie Nicks

PASHA 38443 **Metal Health**
QUIET RIOT

Producer: Spencer Proffer

Track listing: Metal Health / Cum on Feel the Noize / Don't Wanna Let You Go / Slick Black Cadillac / Love's a Bitch / Breathless / Run for Cover / Battle Axe / Let's Get Crazy / Thunderbird

November 26, 1983
1 week

Quiet Riot singer Kevin DuBrow wasn't a particularly big fan of Slade or the British group's 1973 Number One British hit "Cum on Feel the Noize," yet Quiet Riot's cover of the song climbed to number five on the Hot 100 and helped propel Metal Health to Number One on the Billboard album chart. Says DuBrow, "The producer [Spencer Proffer] thought I sounded like Noddy Holder, the singer of Slade, and he suggested it. We were working up that song and the old Fontella Bass song 'Rescue Me.' I really wanted to do 'Rescue Me.' A heavy rock version of it. No one actually knew 'Cum on Feel the Noize.' We learned the basic chord pattern as we went along. It was done in sections. We really had to relearn it after the song was recorded."

Not only did the members of Quiet Riot—DuBrow, bass player Rudy Sarzo, guitarist Carlos Cavazo, and drummer Frankie Banali—fail to learn the song before entering the studio, they goofed off while recording it. "I remember being at one end of the studio and

Frankie at the other with the producer in the middle," DuBrow recalls. "I didn't want to record it, because I thought it was a silly song, so I made faces at Frankie so he would make mistakes. Eventually I was thrown out of the studio for screwing around too much." DuBrow also cut his vocals half-heartedly, but Proffer doubled up the vocal tracks and Pasha released it as a single.

Metal Health was Quiet Riot's American debut album, but the group members were certainly not newcomers. Quiet Riot formed in Los Angeles in 1975 with a lineup that included future Ozzy Osbourne guitarist Randy Rhodes. With Rhodes on guitar, the group recorded two albums that were released by CBS in Japan, Quiet Riot and Quiet Riot II, in 1977 and 1978. After Rhodes left, the group changed its name to DuBrow; they opted for their original moniker after Proffer was interested in signing the band to his Pasha label.

DuBrow says the majority of Metal Health was cut as demos recorded with Proffer before Pasha parent company CBS agreed to distribute the album. "Only two songs were cut after we had the actual signed deal," he says. "It had an immediacy about it, because with demos you can't overindulge yourself—you have to get in and get out of the studio. In that sense, it made it real raw."

"Bang Your Head," DuBrow's favorite track, almost was lost in the studio. "The tape was shedding oxide when we were mixing it and I remember thinking this was the best thing we

ever recorded and now it's being turned into magnetic dust." Luckily, the engineer was able to salvage the track.

Metal Health, and more specifically the track "Thunderbird," was dedicated to former member Rhodes, who died in a plane crash on March 19, 1982, at the age of 25. "He was actually going to come and play on that song, but unfortunately that didn't come to pass," DuBrow says.

Quiet Riot received the news about Metal Health topping the charts while the band was on tour supporting Black Sabbath in Rockford, Illinois. The chart-topping album proved to be a tough act to follow. "It was sort of like, 'What do we do for an encore?'," he says. "In a way, I knew it was the beginning of the end right then."

THE TOP FIVE
Week of November 26, 1983

1. **Metal Health**
   Quiet Riot

2. **Can't Slow Down**
   Lionel Richie

3. **Thriller**
   Michael Jackson

4. **Synchronicity**
   The Police

5. **An Innocent Man**
   Billy Joel

278 Can't Slow Down MOTOWN 6059
LIONEL RICHIE

Producers: Lionel Richie and James Anthony Carmichael

Track listing: Can't Slow Down / All Night Long (All Night) / Penny Lover / Stuck on You / Love Will Find a Way / The Only One / Running with the Night / Hello

December 3, 1983
3 weeks

As the lead vocalist of the Commodores and later as a solo artist, Lionel Richie had experienced his share of success. In the late '70s and early '80s, the R&B group racked up five top 10 albums and two Number One singles. Richie's 1982 self-titled debut album peaked at number three and included his first Number One solo single, "Truly." Yet in spite of the success, the top spot of the album chart remained elusive to Richie, at least until the release of his second solo effort, *Can't Slow Down.*

"It was a very creative period in my life," Richie says. "I had so many songs coming into my head that I didn't know which ones to put on the album." Initially, three songs—"Running with the Night," "Hello," and "All Night Long"—were dropped from the album. "It wasn't until the last two weeks of mixing that we came to our senses," Richie recalls. "Everyone started to say, 'Man, you just threw away the best three songs.' We almost threw the baby out with the bathwater, because we were burned out."

The ballad "Hello" was originally intended for Richie's first solo album. "I had a choice between 'Truly' and 'Hello,' and I chose to go with 'Truly,' " which turned out to be a wise choice.

THE TOP FIVE
Week of December 3, 1983

1. **Can't Slow Down**
   Lionel Richie

2. **Metal Health**
   Quiet Riot

3. **Synchronicity**
   The Police

4. **Thriller**
   Michael Jackson

5. **An Innocent Man**
   Billy Joel

For *Can't Slow Down,* Richie turned to Commodores producer James Anthony Carmichael, but also enlisted the help of David Foster [see 372] on the song "The Only One." Says Richie, "What made it work so well for me is the fact that he is also such a great writer. It only took about two and a half days to get the song done."

When Richie wrote several of the songs on the album, he didn't necessarily have himself in mind. "When I write, I always imagine writing for another artist," he says. "That way I don't freak myself out. If I was writing for myself, I never would have written 'All Night Long,' because it doesn't fit me."

Richie isn't sure what he had in mind when he came up with "All Night Long." Says Richie, "I was more interested in the rhythm than the actual song, and I was playing around with this Jamaican/Calypso kind of singing. I wasn't going to keep it, but when I tried to sing it straight, it didn't work."

Not only did Richie use Jamaican and calypso rhythms, he also used words in several different languages. "There is Jamaican in there, some African phrasing, and some Swahili." When searching for the right words, Richie turned to a friend, a doctor from Jamaica. "I asked him what Bob Marley meant with all those phrases, and he said it doesn't really mean anything. Once I found that out, I just went with a bunch of different phrases that worked well and some of them I made up myself, and they mean absolutely nothing," he says.

Even if some of the words were nothing but nonsense, they connected with Richie's fans. On November 12, 1983, "All Night Long (All Night)," became Richie's second Number One solo single. Three weeks later, with "All Night Long" still on top of the Hot 100, *Can't Slow Down* became Richie's first Number One album. The other two songs that almost didn't make the album also went on to become hits: "Running with the Night" reached number seven, while "Hello" became the album's second Number One single.

COLUMBIA 39242 **Footloose** **279**
SOUNDTRACK

Lori Singer and Kevin Bacon in *Footloose*.

Executive producers: Becky Shargo and Dean Pitchford

Track listing: Footloose [Kenny Loggins] / Let's Hear It for the Boy [Deniece Williams] / Almost Paradise (Love Theme from Footloose) [Mike Reno and Ann Wilson] / Holding Out for a Hero [Bonnie Tyler] / Dancing in the Sheets [Shalamar] / I'm Free (Heaven Helps the Man) [Kenny Loggins] / Somebody's Eyes [Karla Bonoff] / The Girl Gets Around [Sammy Hagar] / Never [Moving Pictures]

April 21, 1984
10 weeks

After working extensively on the *Fame* soundtrack, which reached number seven in 1980, songwriter Dean Pitchford relocated to Los Angeles in search of more work. "I began to do more songs in motion pictures, but every time I would get a call it would be for a song, or two songs," he says. "I was getting frustrated. I began to think it would be great if I could do a group of songs that would create the texture for a film."

In his quest for such a project, Pitchford came across a news clipping from Elmore City, Oklahoma. The town had outlawed dancing in 1889 but had finally repealed the law. "I took that and went with it and created a motion pic-

ture script," Pitchford says. "Then, when the motion picture went into production, I began working on all the songs for the soundtrack."

Pitchford co-wrote each song specifically for scenes in the movie. "I felt that all the songs were the alter egos of the actors on the screen, so I specifically set out to get those artists who would make sense," he says.

The first artist to commit to the project was Kenny Loggins. "He had always been a favorite of mine," Pitchford says. "When I contacted him about this movie idea I had, he asked me to write with him for the album he did right before *Footloose*." The result was a song called "Don't Fight It," a duet by Loggins and Journey frontman Steve Perry. "We knew we could work together," Pitchford adds. "I wanted him involved, because I felt there was a wonderful honesty to the way he sang and I heard him as the voice of the main character. He was really the only artist that I had in mind when I walked into Paramount [Pictures]."

The other artists on the soundtrack became involved through a variety of circumstances. "In some cases, it was because of their availability, or because they were on Columbia, or because they were absolutely the right voice for the moment in the movie," he says.

One of the most difficult recordings

to coordinate was "Almost Paradise," a duet by Mike Reno and Ann Wilson. "He was in Loverboy and she was touring with Heart," Pitchford says. "The only way we could get them together was on this one single night that they both had free in their schedule." Both artists flew into Chicago for the recording session, scheduled at a suburban studio. Reno flew in from Canada, arriving on the last plane before a storm shut down the airport. "He arrived, but Ann Wilson didn't show up," Pitchford says.

Finally, Pitchford received a phone call. Wilson had fallen in her hotel room and broken her wrist. "She went to the hospital, but refused pain killers, because she knew that they would mess up her voice," he says. Instead, Wilson requested only a beer. "It was enough to bring tears to your eyes. The woman was obviously in pain. She was wearing a sling and the plaster was hardly dry on the cast," he says. Nonetheless, the track was recorded that night.

Wilson's effort was rewarded, as the song went on to become a number seven hit, but that wasn't the biggest hit from *Footloose*. The title track, performed by Loggins, hit the top of the Hot 100 on March 31, 1984. Three weeks later, the album hit Number One on the album chart. With the album still at the top, Deniece Williams's "Let's Hear It for the Boy" also reached Number One on May 26, 1984. In the end, Shalamar's "Dancing in the Sheets," Bonnie Tyler's "Holding Out for a Hero," and Loggins's "I'm Free (Heaven Helps the Man)" also became hits, giving *Footloose* a grand total of five top 40 singles, a record for a soundtrack album matched only by *Saturday Night Fever* [see 226] and *Xanadu*.

THE TOP FIVE
Week of April 21, 1984

1. **Footloose**
   Soundtrack

2. **1984**
   Van Halen

3. **Thriller**
   Michael Jackson

4. **Can't Slow Down**
   Lionel Richie

5. **Sports**
   Huey Lewis and the News

280 Sports CHRYSALIS 41412
HUEY LEWIS AND THE NEWS

Producers: Huey Lewis and the News

Track listing: The Heart of Rock & Roll / Heart and Soul / Bad Is Bad / I Want a New Drug / Walking on a Thin Line / Finally Found a Home / If This Is It / You Crack Me Up / Honky Tonk Blues

June 30, 1984
1 week

The 1980 self-titled debut album by Huey Lewis and the News was a big disappointment, selling poorly and failing to chart. Rather than packing it in, Lewis and the News fought for more control and the right to produce their second album, 1982's Picture This. That album spawned the band's first hit single "Do You Believe In Love," written by producer Mutt Lange [see 319]. "We were allowed to produce the second album and we had a hit," says Lewis. "And that allowed us the chance to make a third record. If we hadn't had a hit on that second record, that would have been it. We would have had to look for a deal somewhere."

Instead, Lewis and the News cut Sports. "We were feeling really confident," Lewis says. "because I knew we were in the game." Having produced Picture This, the band had also learned its way around a recording studio. "We kept improving so much as a band and in the studio. We were just getting so much better. My view at the time was, 'Man, if you like this stuff, boy are you going to like the next one.' "

Even with that kind of confidence going into the project, Lewis admits that the sessions for Sports, at Fantasy Studios in Berkeley and the Plant Studios in Sausalito, California, were "fairly tedious." Says Lewis, "We were an R&B-based band, but since we were new, the idea was to use machines and embrace new technology and make blues and rhythm & blues cut to a drum machine."

Indeed several tracks, including "I Want a New Drug" and "Bad Is Bad," were recorded with a drum machine instead of live drums. The band also turned to other new technology. " 'I Want a New Drug' has a synthesized, sequenced bass," Lewis says. The latter track, however, wasn't complete until lead guitarist Chris Hayes added a human touch. "We knew we wanted it to be a sort of groove thing, but we couldn't come up with the right lick, until Chris said, 'I got it,' with a kind of sparkle in his eye. And sure enough, he did."

The album's final cut, a cover of Hank Williams's "Honky Tonk Blues," featured a reunion of sorts with John McFee, who played slide guitar on the track. Lewis, News keyboardist Sean Hopper, and McFee were members of the '70s San Francisco bar band Clover. That group, minus Lewis, backed Elvis Costello on his 1977 debut album, My Aim Is True, but disbanded shortly thereafter when McFee left the band to join the Doobie Brothers [see 238]. "That was fun," Lewis says.

Overall, Lewis was pleased with Sports but was surprised by its slow rise to the top. "I felt like the whole album was a good album, almost from begin-ning to end. It kind of went to pieces a little bit on the second side, but I felt like the first seven tracks were as good as they could be."

Included on the album's first side were three top 10 hits. "Heart and Soul," a track originally recorded by Exile, reached number eight in November 1983. In March, the News struck again with "I Want a New Drug," which peaked at number six. "The Heart of Rock & Roll" hit number six in June. The three hits were enough to push Sports to the top of the album chart in its 39th week, making it the slowest-climbing chart-topper since Fleetwood Mac's self-titled LP [see 218]. The News went on to score their fourth top 10 hit from Sports when "If This Is It" reached number six in September. Says Lewis, "We just felt like it was our time and we could do no wrong."

COLUMBIA 38653 ## Born in the U.S.A.
BRUCE SPRINGSTEEN

Producers: Bruce Springsteen, Jon Landau, Chuck Plotkin, and Steve Van Zandt

Track listing: Born in the U.S.A. / Cover Me / Darlington County / Working on the Highway / Downbound Train / I'm on Fire / No Surrender / Bobby Jean / I'm Goin' Down / Glory Days / Dancing in the Dark / My Hometown

July 7, 1984
7 weeks (nonconsecutive)

Following the success of *The River* [see 253] and its subsequent tour, Bruce Springsteen and the E Street Band reconvened to record a follow-up album. "We went in to record in the spring of 1982," recalls E Street drummer Max Weinberg. "We got some good renditions of the songs, but what we came up with was not what Bruce had in his head. When you put the full-blown E Street Band on it, the starkness of what he wanted disappeared." Springsteen opted to record that collection of songs solo on a four-track recorder at home. That album, *Nebraska*, peaked at number three.

While the E Street Band wasn't suited to the *Nebraska* material, it was the perfect accompaniment for Springsteen on another set of songs he was working on. "In April 1982, Bruce started writing more material, on the spot, because the whole band was there. Over a two-week period, we recorded a bunch of songs," says Weinberg. "It started with 'Born in the U.S.A.,' then we went on to 'Glory Days,' 'I'm Going Down,' 'Darlington County,' and 'I'm on Fire.' It was a tremendously prolific two or three weeks. We had eight of the 12 songs that ended up on that record recorded. The band was really playing the best we had played."

The title track, which set the tone for the album, was initially recorded with a different arrangement. "We did it with just Garry Tallent playing bass, myself, and Bruce playing guitar with sort of a rockabilly approach, but that wasn't working." The final version of the song came very late one night. "We were just hacking around," says Weinberg. "We didn't go out to revisit the arrangement, it just sort of materialized. We started playing and the tape was running." The second take from that session ended up as the album version. "We knew that song was very special when we record-ed it that night. We had never done anything like that before in the studio. It really did blow us away."

Weinberg says the track features his freest playing. "I was just responding to the lyrics and Bruce. There was tremendous power coming off him." The breakdown section of the song was spontaneous. "Bruce took his hand off his guitar and started playing air-drums," Weinberg recalls. "So I did a drum solo." In fact, the keyboard players didn't catch Springsteen's cue and can be heard continuing to play. "They stopped only after they realized the rhythm had stopped," Weinberg adds. "Then out of the corner of my eye, I saw Bruce count, one-two-three-four, and we went back into the ending of the song. It was an incredible emotional and musical experience."

After a break over the summer, Springsteen wrote more songs. "We probably recorded another 50, but of those tunes, 'Bobby Jean,' 'No Retreat,' and 'Dancing in the Dark' and one other ended up on the album."

"Dancing in the Dark" began in a different incarnation as well. "We recorded a real rock 'n' roll version of it," says Weinberg. "I remember sitting down at the drums after getting three or four takes of the rock version, and Jon Landau came over to me and whispered in my ear, 'Dance record.' He even referenced some current songs that were on the radio at the time."

With "Dancing in the Dark" peaking at number two on the Hot 100, *Born in the U.S.A.* became Springsteen's second Number One album in its third week on the chart. The album went on to generate six other top 10 hits: "Cover Me," "Born in the U.S.A.," "I'm on Fire," "Glory Days," "I'm Going Down," and "My Hometown." The Boss was bigger than ever.

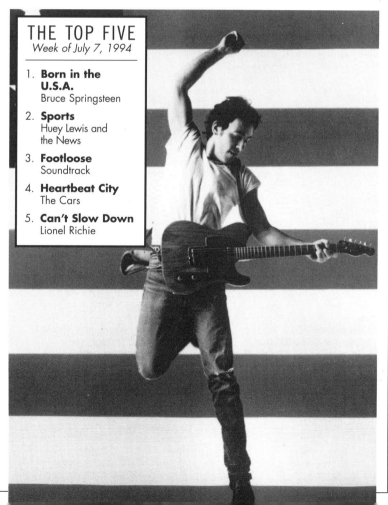

THE TOP FIVE
Week of July 7, 1994

1. **Born in the U.S.A.**
   Bruce Springsteen

2. **Sports**
   Huey Lewis and the News

3. **Footloose**
   Soundtrack

4. **Heartbeat City**
   The Cars

5. **Can't Slow Down**
   Lionel Richie

282 Purple Rain WARNER BROS. 25110
PRINCE AND THE REVOLUTION

Producers: Prince and the Revolution

Track listing: Let's Go Crazy / Take Me With U / The Beautiful Ones / Computer Blue / Darling Nikki / When Doves Cry / I Would Die 4 U / Baby I'm a Star / Purple Rain

August 4, 1984
24 weeks

As the '70s gave way to the '80s, a multi-instrumentalist/singer-songwriter named Prince Roger Nelson had emerged from Minneapolis to become one of the most exciting and innovative new acts in years. Initially, Prince, whose music often combined the rock-guitar instincts of Jimi Hendrix [see 108] with the funk flavor of Sly and the Family Stone [see 138], was a hit with rock critics and cutting-edge music fans, but with his fifth album, *1999*, Prince became a mainstream success. The two-record set, released in 1982, reached number nine and spawned the top 10 singles "Little Red Corvette" and "Delirious." Yet even the success of *1999* couldn't have prepared the world for Prince's next move, *Purple Rain*.

The album, which also served as the soundtrack to the film of the same name, began to take shape in the summer of 1983, at a concert held at 1st Avenue, a Minneapolis nightspot frequented by Prince. The concert was a benefit for the Minnesota Dance Theatre, but Prince had other things on his mind. Engineers David Rivkin and David Leonard recorded the show that night from the Record Plant mobile truck. Three of the songs recorded that night—"I Would Die 4 U," "Baby I'm a Star," and "Purple Rain"—would turn up on the album.

Thrilled by the experience of performing with his new band the Revolution and the spontaneity of a live setting, Prince opted to record additional tracks at a Minneapolis rehearsal space known as the Warehouse. "He said he wanted to record the whole band that night," recalls Leonard, "There were no remote trucks, so I just had to put a console up on road cases and plug it in so they could record." The result of that impromptu session was "Let's Go Crazy" and "Computer Blue." "Once we got set up, they just blew through it," Leonard says.

By then, the film was also in production. "He was planning out the film and the album simultaneously in his head," says Leonard. The film, a semi-biographical story of Prince's rise from an unhappy home life to become a star, had Prince cast as "the Kid." The film also featured several of Prince's protégés, including Morris Day of the Time as the Kid's arch rival, and Apollonia Kotero as Prince's love interest.

The album, particularly the confessional "When Doves Cry" and the gospel-flavored title track, also delved into Prince's life story. "It was a very personal album," says engineer Peggy McCready, who was married to Leonard at the time.

With the film in production, Prince traveled frequently between his home base of Minneapolis and Los Angeles, where he mixed the live tracks, recorded overdubs, and laid down the additional songs "Take Me With You," "The Beautiful Ones," and "When Doves Cry." The suggestive "Darling Nikki" was recorded in Prince's basement. "The live recordings were the band," says Leonard, "but Prince played most of the other stuff. He's a genius," Leonard adds. "He works really fast sometimes, but he would work all day and all night until a song was where he wanted it to be."

One of the last songs recorded was "When Doves Cry," a track for which Prince had big plans. "He wanted two boards together so he could have 48 tracks, which was something that he never did in the early days," says McCready. As Leonard recalls, initially, Prince layered guitar, keyboards, bass, drums, and strings on the track. But in the final mix, Prince stripped the song down. "He took the bass out," McCready says. "I remember him saying, 'It will be real different. No one else will have the guts to do that,' and he was right, because it became a hit."

"When Doves Cry" wasn't only a hit, it became Prince's first Number One single on July 7, 1984. Four weeks later, with the single still at Number One, *Purple Rain* bumped Bruce Springsteen's *Born in the U.S.A.* from the top spot on the album chart. And the Purple One's reign had just begun—"Let's Go Crazy" went on to top the Hot 100, while the title track reached number two, and "I Would Die 4 U" reached number eight.

THE TOP FIVE
Week of August 4, 1984

1. **Purple Rain**
   Prince and the Revolution

2. **Born in the U.S.A.**
   Bruce Springsteen

3. **Sports**
   Huey Lewis and the News

4. **Victory**
   The Jacksons

5. **Can't Slow Down**
   Lionel Richie

Like a Virgin
MADONNA

283

Producer: Nile Rodgers

Track listing: Material Girl / Angel / Like Virgin / Over and Over / Love Don't Live Here Anymore / Dress You Up / Shoo-Bee-Doo / Pretender / Stay

February 9, 1985
6 weeks

A former dancer and fixture on the New York club scene, Madonna Louise Ciccone became known to the world simply as Madonna with the release of her 1983 self-titled debut album. *Madonna*, fueled by such hit singles as "Holiday," "Borderline," and "Lucky Star," peaked at number eight. The singer's sexy image and her irresistible brand of dance-pop made her one of the most exciting new artists of the '80s. Following the surprise success of *Madonna*, a growing legion of fans was anxiously awaiting Madonna's next move.

For her sophomore effort, Madonna turned to former Chic member Nile Rodgers. "When I was making the record, I was just so thrilled and happy to be working with Nile Rodgers," Madonna says. "I had no idea it was going to do as well as it did or have the impact that it did." Rodgers can still remember the first time he saw the singer perform at a small club in New York in 1983. "I went to the club to see another woman sing," he says. "But when I got there Madonna was onstage. I loved her stage presence and then we met right after that. I kept thinking to myself, 'Damn, is she a star,' but she wasn't at the time." The admiration was mutual. "I idolized Nile because of the whole Chic thing," she says. "I couldn't believe the record company gave me the money so I could

work with him."

The album was recorded at the Power Station in New York at a relatively quick pace. Rodgers also played guitar, and his former Chic bandmates bassist Bernard Edwards and drummer Tony Thompson appeared on several tracks. The sessions usually didn't start until the afternoon. "I would go to the swim club on the Upper West Side and go swimming and walk from there to the recording studio," Madonna recalls. "We didn't start before 1 P.M., because Nile was a party animal and he stayed up all night, so there was no morning working for us."

As Rodgers recalls, Madonna was "a real hard worker and incredibly tenacious." At one point the producer threatened to quit the project, annoyed because he thought Madonna had treated a studio hand unfairly. "I was actually in the elevator and she walked up and smiled at me and said, 'Nile, I want to know one thing: Does this mean you don't love me anymore?' And then we both started laughing. Then we realized how ridiculous we were both being. That was it. We didn't have a serious fight after that."

Another emotional moment in the studio occurred when Madonna covered the 1978 Rose Royce hit "Love Don't Live Here Anymore." Says Rodgers, "Madonna had never performed with a live orchestra before. I was very much into doing everything live, so I just said, 'Madonna, you go out there and sing and we will follow you.'" At first Madonna was hesitant, but the live setting ended up producing memorable results. "She sang and she was overcome with emotion and started crying, but I left it on the record," Rodgers says.

Initially, neither Madonna nor Rodgers cared much for "Like a Virgin," written by the songwriting team of Billy Steinberg and Tom Kelly, and brought to Madonna's attention by Warner Bros. Records A&R executive Michael Ostin. "I remember hearing a demo and the guys who wrote it were singing," Madonna says. "It sounded really stupid and retarded. I was like, 'Oh my God,' but everyone was saying this was a great song and I was like, 'Gross me out.'" However, Madonna soon had second thoughts. "It's weird because I couldn't get it out of my head after I played it, even though I didn't really like it," she says. "It sounded really bubble-gummy to me, but it grew on me. I really started to like it, my little gears started clicking, and I thought, 'This could be really cool.' But, my first reaction to it was, 'This is really queer.'"

Rodgers credits Madonna with recognizing the song's potential. "Madonna had a vision. She knew that 'Like a Virgin' was the first single on that album. Since she was a woman and clued into what young girls like and feel, she was sold on the song," he says. "I liked her more sexy side that addressed men. I liked 'Material Girl' more."

Madonna's choice for a first single ended up right on the money, as "Like a Virgin" became her first Number One hit on December 22, 1984. A week after the single ended its six-week stay at the top of the Hot 100, *Like a Virgin* became Madonna's first Number One album, thanks in part to the second single, "Material Girl," which was climbing the Hot 100 and eventually peaked at number two. Subsequent singles from the album "Angel" and "Dress You Up" also went on to reach the top five.

THE TOP FIVE
Week of February 9, 1985

1. **Like a Virgin**
   Madonna

2. **Born in the U.S.A.**
   Bruce Springsteen

3. **Make It Big**
   Wham!

4. **Agent Provocateur**
   Foreigner

5. **Purple Rain**
   Prince and the Revolution

284 Make It Big COLUMBIA 39595
WHAM!

Producer: George Michael

Track listing: Wake Me Up Before You Go-Go / Everything She Wants / Heartbeat / Like a Baby / Freedom / If You Were There / Credit Card Baby / Careless Whisper

March 2, 1985
3 weeks

Engineer Chris Porter initially shared the widely held view that Wham!, a duo featuring British school pals George Michael and Andrew Ridgeley, was nothing more than a disposable pop group. Porter first worked with the pair on the single "Wham Rap" in 1981. "I didn't see a huge future for them," he says. "I thought they were just a teen band." Yet his impression changed a few years later when working on a B-side of the "Club Tropicana" single, "Blue." Says Porter, "I started to get the sense that there was more depth to George Michael than perhaps people had seen before."

With its early singles, Wham! became a hit in the U.K., but were hardly noticed in America, where their first album, *Fantastic*, stalled at number 83 in 1983. When Wham! and Porter regrouped to record "Wake Me Up Before You Go-Go," the first song cut for the group's second album, *Make It Big*, Porter once again noticed changes in Michael. "In that period between 1981 and 1984, he had definitely learned an awful lot about music and the music business," he says.

"Wake Me Up Before You Go-Go," which was inspired by a note Ridgeley left on his door for his mother, was cut quickly at Sarm West Studios in London, signaling the beginning of an album that would live up to its title. "It was based on a Linn drum track and we had live musicians playing along with it," recalls Porter. "We set up the drum pattern and had everyone rehearse it for an afternoon, and by about 7 P.M. that night we made a few fixes and basically that was it." The vocals were recorded in three days.

The single was released in the U.K. in the summer of 1984, where it went straight to Number One. "That was a good feeling, but to a certain extent it also put a lot of pressure on us to make a comparable album, and stylistically an album that was of that vein," says Porter. "There were a lot of '60s-sounding tracks on there."

In an attempt to get an authentic '60s feel, Michael originally cut the ballad "Careless Whisper" with legendary R&B producer Jerry Wexler at the Muscle Shoals studios in Alabama. "When I got a call saying we were going to do some work on 'Careless Whisper,' I couldn't believe it," says Porter, "because I knew that Jerry Wexler just worked on it. I thought, 'There really can't be much to do on it.' " Porter says. Surprisingly, Porter adds, Wexler's version sounded "European" and didn't have "quite as much of the soul I expected."

By the time "Careless Whisper" was recorded, it was clear that Wham! had essentially become George Michael. "He was taking a really big role in every part of the production," Porter says. "Andrew was still involved in being a pop star and thinking about other ways he wanted to enjoy himself, while George had his head down in the music."

Following the release of *Make It Big* in the fall of 1984, Wham! finally found success in America. "Wake Me Up Before You Go-Go," the first U.S. single from the album, reached Number One on November 17, 1984. Wham!'s reign continued in 1985, when "Careless Whisper," which was credited to "Wham! Featuring George Michael," hit Number One on Febraury 16. With "Careless Whisper" still in the top position, *Make It Big* reached Number One three weeks later in its 17th week on the chart.

"Everything She Wants" became the third Number One single from *Make It Big* on May 25, 1985, making Wham! the first group to score three chart-toppers from an album since the Bee Gees had done it with *Spirits Having Flown* [see 237].

Wham! would soon be no more. The group's last album, 1986's *Music from the Edge of Heaven*, peaked at number 10. However, George Michael's career was just beginning [see 316].

THE TOP FIVE
Week of March 2, 1985

1. **Make It Big**
   Wham!

2. **Like a Virgin**
   Madonna

3. **Born in the U.S.A.**
   Bruce Springsteen

4. **Centerfield**
   John Fogerty

5. **Agent Provacteur**
   Foreigner

WARNER BROS. 25203 **Centerfield** | **285**
JOHN FOGERTY

With Waronker's encouragement, Fogerty went back into the Plant Studios in Sausalito, California, to finish what would become the album's title track. "I was having trouble with the drumming on that song," says Fogerty, who played all the instruments on the album. "But after I came back from meeting Lenny, I finished that song in one day. I was ready."

One of the tracks that Fogerty played for Waronker was "The Old Man Down the Road," which went on to become Fogerty's first top 10 solo hit. "It was pivotal to the statement I was making about the music I was performing again," says Fogerty. "For a long time, I had lost the muse, the inspiration, and the ability to write a song, or at least I didn't know how to get it out of me."

Centerfield hit the summit in its ninth week on the Top Pop Albums chart, allowing Fogerty to join the ranks of John Lennon, Paul McCartney, the Rolling Stones, and Barbra Streisand, all of whom have had Number One albums in the '60s, '70s, and '80s. Yet Fogerty's triumphant return was dampened by Zaentz, who threatened legal action unless Fogerty changed the lyrics of "Zanz Kant Danz," a thinly veiled stab at the record executive that contains the lyrics, "Zanz can't dance/But he'll steal your money." On subsequent pressings, the song's title was changed to "Vanz Kant Danz." Zaentz went a step further by suing Fogerty, claiming that "The Old Man Down the Road" infringed on the copyright of the Creedence song "Run Through the Jungle"— a copyright that Zaentz held, even though Fogerty had written both songs. In the end, Fogerty prevailed.

Producer: John Fogerty

Track listing: The Old Man Down the Road / Rock and Roll Girls / Big Train (From Memphis) / I Saw It on TV / Mr. Greed / Searchlight / Centerfield / I Can't Help Myself / Zanz Kant Danz

March 23, 1985
1 week

After Creedence Clearwater Revival split in late 1972, John Fogerty first resurfaced in 1973 under the moniker the Blue Ridge Rangers. Despite the band-like name, the self-titled album was actually a solo effort with Fogerty playing all the instruments, although his name did not appear on the sleeve. It peaked at number 47. Fogerty made his official solo debut with a 1975 album on Asylum, which only made number 78. Fogerty had seemingly lost the magic touch that gave Creedence nine top 10 singles and two chart-topping albums.

"My first instincts were not jazz, bluegrass, or opera," says Fogerty. "I was raised right in the middle with pop music, and that's the hardest, coldest game in town, where people have one hit and that's it for the rest of their life. You learn very quickly that it's 'What

have you done for me lately?' with current product."

After *John Fogerty*, the singer/guitarist simply did not want to make records anymore. To make matters worse, he was engaged in a heated battle with Fantasy Records chief Saul Zaentz over the CCR catalog. "It did a lot of damage to my psyche and personality as far as confidence," says Fogerty. "There were times in those years when I was scared to go in and buy a pair of socks in a department store."

Slowly, Fogerty began to regain his confidence and started to write and record new material again. But it took a meeting with Warner Bros. Records president Lenny Waronker to put him back in the saddle. Fogerty played the executive six new songs he had recorded. "He was the first person who listened and he got all excited about it," Fogerty says. Waronker's positive feedback gave Fogerty a much-needed emotional boost. "The man who recorded those songs was not a guy who was full of confidence and filled with the knowledge that the world was waiting for him," Fogerty says. "I was the opposite way. I was a guy with his hat in his hand, wondering if the world still cared about this music or if I was some sort of a relic at the age of 38."

THE TOP FIVE
Week of March 23, 1985

1. **Centerfield**
   John Fogerty

2. **No Jacket Required**
   Phil Collins

3. **Born in the U.S.A.**
   Bruce Springsteen

4. **Make It Big**
   Wham!

5. **Beverly Hills Cop**
   Soundtrack

286 No Jacket Required ATLANTIC 81240
PHIL COLLINS

Producer: Phil Collins and Hugh Padgham

Track listing: Sussudio / Only You Know and I Know / Long Long Way to Go / I Don't Wanna Know / One More Night / Don't Lose My Number / Who Said I Would / Doesn't Anybody Stay Together Anymore / Inside Out / Take Me Home

March 30, 1985
7 weeks (nonconsecutive)

By 1985, Phil Collins had certainly enjoyed a lengthy and successful career. In 1970, he became the fourth drummer of the veteran British rock band Genesis. In 1975, when singer Peter Gabriel opted to leave the band, it was Collins who took the spotlight, surprising naysayers who had pronounced Genesis dead with Gabriel's departure. Not only did Collins flourish fronting Genesis, but in 1981 he launched a solo career with the album *Face Value.* That album and 1982's *Hello, I Must Be Going!* were top 10 hits that went on to sell more than four million and two million copies, respectively.

In 1984 Collins scored a pair of smash singles. "Against All Odds (Take a Look a Me Now)," from the film of the same name, became his first Number One in April, while "Easy Lover," a duet with Philip Bailey of Earth, Wind & Fire [see 198], climbed to number two, setting the stage for the most successful year of Collins's career.

"One More Night," the first single from *No Jacket Required,* wasn't a dramatic departure for Collins. The vocal track on the cut, and other ballads on the album, were recorded as demos at Collins's home, but that didn't stop the song from striking a nerve with the public. The single became Collins's second Number One, while *No Jacket Required* simultaneously topped the album chart—a career first for Collins.

Yet there was more to *No Jacket Required* than the ballads. "I was trying to do something a little differently than what I had done before," Collins says. "I was interested in trying to explore the R&B influence and taking it a step further." To achieve that goal, Collins enlisted the help of David Frank from the System, who played bass and keyboards on several tracks.

While the funky new direction won over fans—on July 6 "Sussudio" became Collins's second consecutive Number One—it made him an easy target of critics who charged that "Sussudio" was a virtual rehash of Prince's "1999." Says Collins, "Well, it ain't far wrong...There was something about '1999' that I liked, but Prince is a black American and I'm a white Englishman, so it's going to sound very different. They are basically the same kind of dance groove, but that's pretty much where the resemblance ends."

Nonetheless, the song helped Collins reach a new audience. "I suddenly found out I was really across the board. Black kids in the street were stopping me and saying 'Hey man, I love the new record,' as well as the usual spotty white kids."

The diverse selection of material also helped Collins win favor with the members of the National Academy of Recording Arts and Sciences, as *No Jacket Required* received a Grammy for Album of the Year. Says Collins, "Maybe that will be viewed as the peak of my career, at least commercially speaking. I may never go that way again."

THE TOP FIVE
Week of Marcy 30, 1985

1. **No Jacket Required**
   Phil Collins

2. **Centerfield**
   John Fogerty

3. **Born in the U.S.A.**
   Bruce Springsteen

4. **Beverly Hills Cop**
   Soundtrack

5. **Private Dancer**
   Tina Turner

Executive producer: Ken Kragen

Track listing: We Are the World [USA for Africa] / If Only for a Moment Girl [Steve Perry] / Just a Little Closer [The Pointer Sisters] / Trapped [Bruce Springsteen & the E Street Band / Tears Are Not Enough [Northern Lights (Canadian All Stars)] / 4 the Tears in Your Eyes [Prince and the Revolution] / Good for Nothing [Chicago] / Total Control [Tina Turner] / A Little More Love [Kenny Rogers] / Trouble in Paradise [Huey Lewis and the News]

April 27, 1985
3 weeks

On January 28, 1985, at approximately 10 P.M., some of the pop world's biggest stars began arriving at A&M Studios in Hollywood. The American Music Awards ceremony had just wrapped up at the Shrine Auditorium, but this was to be more than just another post-awards party. On this night, the assembled throng of 45 musicians, including Michael Jackson, Lionel Richie, Bruce Springsteen, Diana Ross, Stevie Wonder, and Bob Dylan, were gathered to record "We Are the World," a song written by Jackson and Richie to benefit African famine relief.

It was veteran performer Harry Belafonte [see 3] who initially came up with the idea for an American project to benefit famine relief. Belafonte had been impressed by the efforts of Bob Geldof, the former frontman of the Boomtown Rats, who had organized the union of British artists known as Band Aid. The

group's single "Do They Know It's Christmas?" sold more than a million copies in the U.K.

"I had spoken to Geldof," says Belafonte. "I said I thought we should do that in the U.S." Belafonte then telephoned personal manager Ken Kragen, who enlisted his client Richie. Richie asked Wonder to sign on, while Belafonte contacted Quincy Jones to produce the record. Jones in turn asked Jackson to participate. "Initially, when I called Ken Kragen and Quincy, I thought we would do it with the five or six of the top black acts—with Lionel, Stevie Wonder, and Ray Charles, I didn't even know if we could get Michael. For it to have blossomed into this multi-cultural, multi-racial response was very moving," says Belafonte.

Most of the talent assembled, which also included Billy Joel, Fleetwood Mac's Lindsey Buckingham, and Geldof, was top-notch. In fact, at least 18 artists on the project had previously been associated with Number One albums. "Recording that song with all of those people was one of the most incredible experiences in my life," says Kenny Rogers, who had his sheet music signed by the other participants at the all-night session.

But not all the superstars that wanted to participate could make the sessions. "A lot of other people felt they wanted to make a contribution," Belafonte says. "So we discussed it and agreed that we would accept material they would send us and we would put it on an album reflecting their support for the famine struggle."

Some artists, such as Springsteen,

Huey Lewis, Journey's Steve Perry, Rogers, and Tina Turner, did double duty, singing on "We Are the World" and also offering rare recordings. Other acts, such as Chicago and Prince & the Revolution, contributed songs but did not appear on the single. A group of Canadian performers known as Northern Lights, which included such stars as Bryan Adams, Gordon Lightfoot, and Neil Young, also recorded an anthem for the album.

On April 13, "We Are the World" went to Number One on the Hot 100. Two weeks later, the album joined it at the summit. By 1995, the *We Are the World* project had raised more than $100 million.

"It did the artists proud that participated in it," says Belafonte. "But most importantly, it raised global consciousness about an issue the people outside of Africa were ignoring."

THE TOP FIVE
Week of April 27, 1985

1. **We Are the World**
   USA for Africa

2. **No Jacket Required**
   Phil Collins

3. **Born in the U.S.A.**
   Bruce Springsteen

4. **Beverly Hills Cop**
   Soundtrack

5. **Centerfield**
   John Fogerty

288 Around the World in a Day PAISLEY PARK 25286
PRINCE AND THE REVOLUTION

Producer: Prince and the Revolution

Track listing: Around the World in a Day / Paisley Park / Condition of the Heart / Raspberry Beret / Tamborine / America / Pop Life / The Ladder / Temptation

June 1, 1985
3 weeks

Prince wasn't content merely to bask in the success of *Purple Rain* [see 282]—instead, he mounted the massive Purple Rain Tour. And when they weren't performing, Prince and the Revolution were busy writing and recording their next album, *Around the World in a Day*. It would have been easy to just duplicate the approach of the wildly successful *Purple Rain,* but instead Prince took a left turn, opting to explore neo-psychedelia with his own personal twist.

However, the elfin pop star did succumb to some of the usual trappings that often accompany superstar status. *Around the World in a Day* marked Prince's first album released on his own custom label, Paisley Park (also the name of the new state-of-the art studio where most of the album was recorded). Yet while Prince enjoyed the spoils of his success, he also mocked them in the track "Pop Life," which includes the lyric, "What u putting in your nose/Is that where all you money goes." Prince protégé Sheila E. performed drums on the track.

Engineer David Leonard recalls that Prince generally preferred to let his music do the talking. "He was always a moody guy who never really chatted about what he was feeling," Leonard recalls. Those feelings apparently were often about sexual desire and religion, as Leonard discovered when he recorded the track "Temptation" at Capitol Records studios in Hollywood. The religious theme was also prevalent in "The Ladder," a song Prince co-wrote with his father, John L. Nelson.

While Prince's band, the Revolution (featuring Lisa Coleman on keyboards and backing vocals, Wendy Melvoin on guitar and vocals, Bobby Z on percussion, Brown Mark on bass and backing vocals, and Matt Fink on keyboards and backing vocals), took a more active role, sharing writing and production credits on several songs, Prince still occasionally worked solo, as evidenced by the songs "Condition of the Heart" and "Tamborine," on which he played all the instruments.

Not all the tracks included on *Around the World in a Day* were new. " 'Raspberry Beret' was an old song. He wrote that before I met him," says engineer Peggy McCready, who began working with Prince in on 1981's *Controversy*.

On *Around the World in a Day*, Prince continued to explore the use of strings, and even opted for finger cymbals and darbuka on the title track. The use of the additional instrumentation gave the sessions "a Beatles flavor," McCready says.

While Prince was faced with the awesome task of following up *Purple Rain*, he seemed unfazed by the challenge during the making of *Around the World in a Day*. "I never sensed any pressure like that from Prince," says McCready. "He did what he felt in his heart, and that's where his genius lies."

Of course, *Around the World in a Day* couldn't match the blockbuster success of *Purple Rain*, but it did quite well in its own right, hitting Number One in its fourth week on the chart (just 20 weeks after the end of *Purple Rain*'s 24-week run) and spawning the hits "Raspberry Beret," which peaked at number two, and "Pop Life," which reached number seven.

THE TOP FIVE
Week of June 1, 1985

1. **Around the World in a Day**
   Prince and the Revolution

2. **No Jacket Required**
   Phil Collins

3. **Born in the U.S.A.**
   Bruce Springsteen

4. **Beverly Hills Cop**
   Soundtrack

5. **Diamond Life**
   Sade

MCA 5553 **Beverly Hills Cop**
SOUNDTRACK

289

Executive producers: Don Simpson, Jerry Bruckheimer, and Marty Brest

Track listing: New Attitude [Patti LaBelle] / Don't Get Stopped in Beverly Hills [Shalamar] / Do You Really (Want My Love?) [Junior] / Emergency [Rockie Robbins] / Neutron Dance [Pointer Sisters] / The Heat Is On [Glenn Frey] / Gratitude [Danny Elfman] / Stir It Up [Patti LaBelle] / Rock 'n Roll Again [The System] / Axel F [Harold Faltermeyer]

June 22, 1985
2 weeks

Following the success of *Flashdance*, the filmmaking team of Don Simpson and Jerry Bruckheimer would once again hit paydirt with a combination of cinema and music. This time the film didn't involved dancing, but that couldn't stop the duo from delivering a hit soundtrack with *Beverly Hills Cop*, the action/comedy film starring Eddie Murphy.

Like *Flashdance*, *Beverly Hills Cop* featured a mix of veterans and virtual unknowns. On *Flashdance*, it was newcomers Irene Cara and Michael Sembello who benefited the most from the soundtrack; *Beverly Hills Cop*, however, proved to be the launching pad that helped re-establish the careers of Patti LaBelle and Glenn Frey. "It was one of the first things that Patti did as a newly signed artist to MCA," says music consultant Kathy Nelson. "It sort of broke her back into the business." The appropriately titled "New Attitude" was a change for LaBelle. "It was a different kind of track for her, because it was very pop," adds Nelson. Released as a single, "New Attitude" reached number

17, becoming LaBelle's first top 20 single since the 1975 Number One hit "Lady Marmalade," which she recorded as a member of LaBelle. It also paved the way for *The Winner in You* [see 301], LaBelle's first album for MCA.

Once and future Eagle Frey [see 401] was in a similar situation. Since leaving the Eagles, his solo outings had been only mid-charters, until "The Heat Is On." The single reached number two, establishing Frey as a solo commercial force. "He hadn't done anything significant as solo artist before that," Nelson says. "Everyone just knew him from the Eagles."

The other veteran act to cop a hit from the Murphy film was the Pointer Sisters, whose "Neutron Dance" reached number six. Yet despite the star power of LaBelle, Frey, and the Pointer Sisters, *Beverly Hills Cop* didn't make that final surge to the summit until an instrumental called "Axel F" was

released as a single. The song was written and performed by Harold Faltermeyer, a German keyboardist who had worked on the film scores *Midnight Express* and *American Gigolo* but had no pop hits to his credit.

The song, named for Murphy's character Axel Foley, climbed all the way to number three, becoming the fourth top 20 hit from *Beverly Hills Cop*.

With its potent lineup of hits, *Beverly Hills Cop* rode up to the Number One position in its 24th week on the chart. It marked the first time MCA had scored a Number One album since Elton John's *Rock of the Westies* in 1975 [see 207]. It also had the distinction of being the first soundtrack to go to the pole position without the aid of a Number One single since *The Sting* in 1974 [see 175]. That album also contained a number three instrumental hit, "The Entertainer."

THE TOP FIVE
Week of June 22, 1985

1. **Beverly Hills Cop**
   Soundtrack

2. **Around the World in a Day**
   Prince and the Revolution

3. **No Jacket Required**
   Phil Collins

4. **Songs from the Big Chair**
   Tears for Fears

5. **Born in the U.S.A.**
   Bruce Springsteen

290 Songs from the Big Chair MERCURY 824300
TEARS FOR FEARS

Producer: Chris Hughes

Track listing: Shout / The Working Hour / Everybody Wants to Rule the World / Mother's Talk / I Believe / Broken / Head Over Heels / Listen

July 13, 1985
5 weeks (nonconsecutive)

The British duo Tears for Fears didn't initially take America by storm. *The Hurting*, the first album by school chums Roland Orzabal and Curt Smith, peaked at number 73 in the U.S., as did the group's first single, "Change." Yet in the U.K., the duo, named for a concept in Arthur Janov's book *The Primal Scream*, found success quickly. On the strength of three top five singles, *The Hurting* hit Number One in its second week on the U.K. charts.

The success, however, brought on high expectations for the young band. "It was a very high-pressured time," says Orzabal. "We were under so much pressure to keep putting out hit singles in England. That, in a sense, is how *Songs from the Big Chair* started. The record company would hear a song and say, 'Yeah, that'll do,' and we

would record it and put it out."

"Mother's Talk," which peaked at number 14 in the U.K., was the first of two new singles that would eventually turn up on Tears for Fears' second album. The other was "Shout," which climbed to number four in the U.K.

"When 'Shout' started off, it was just this chorus going around and around," says Orzabal. "I had this idea that it would be like 'Give Peace a Chance.' But we all got a bit tired of it and decided that it needed a verse."

To record the material, the group stuck with former Adam and the Ants drummer/producer Chris Hughes, who had co-produced *The Hurting*. The album's title, *Songs from the Big Chair*, was inspired by the film *Sybil*—the "big chair" was a place where the girl with 14 different personalities felt comfortable. However, recording the album wasn't necessarily a comfortable experience for TFF. "I aimed so high and I beat myself up when I didn't make records that were of the quality that I desired," says Orzabal.

For example, "Everybody Wants to Rule the World," the first American single from *Songs from the Big Chair*, almost didn't make it on the album. "It

was an afterthought," says Orzabal. "I had the song, but I really didn't care for it much. But Chris Hughes was very enthusiastic about it. So while we were recording the album, myself, Chris, and [keyboardist] Ian Stanley would just improvise the song." Eventually, Hughes talked Orzabal into including the song on the album. The final version, recorded in a week, was the last track recorded for *Songs from the Big Chair*.

In the U.S., "Everybody Wants to Rule the World" was released as the first single from *Songs from the Big Chair*. On June 8, it hit Number One. Just over a month later, TFF scored their first Number One album when *Songs from the Big Chair* hit the top in its 16th week on the chart. On August 3, less than a month later, the group scored their second U.S. Number One single with "Shout." Today, Orzabal still finds the group's success mind-blowing: "I'm one of these people that never feels like I've gotten anywhere. I'm still surprised when people know who I am and have heard of the band."

THE TOP FIVE
Week of July 13, 1985

1. **Songs from the Big Chair**
   Tears for Fears

2. **No Jacket Required**
   Phil Collins

3. **Around the World in a Day**
   Prince and the Revolution

4. **Reckless**
   Bryan Adams

5. **Beverly Hills Cop**
   Soundtrack

Producers: Bryan Adams and Bob Clearmountain

Track listing: One Night Love Affair / She's Only Happy When She's Dancin' / Run to You / Heaven / Somebody / Summer of '69 / Kids Wanna Rock / It's Only Love / Long Gone / Ain't Gonna Cry

August 10, 1985
2 weeks

In the mid-'80s, singer-songwriter Bryan Adams may have been the hardest-working Canadian in show business. In 1983 alone, he spent 283 days on the road. As a result of this relentless touring schedule and his catchy brand of hook-filled rock, *Cuts Like a Knife*, Adams's third album, reached number eight.

Before Adams and co-producer Bob Clearmountain regrouped to record a follow-up album, the pair met in the studio to cut "Heaven," a song for the soundtrack of *A Night in Heaven*, a box-office bomb about a male stripper. At the time, Clearmountain was obliged to complete another project. "We recorded it during off hours at the Power Station in New York," he says. "It was one of situations where I was mixing something else during the day and I'd usually work with Bryan at night until 6 A.M." The duo's unusual hours didn't hamper their work, however—when the soundtrack was released, radio programmers, hungry for new Adams material, jumped on the track and demanded that it be released as a single. But Adams had other plans. "Bryan didn't want it to be released as a single," says

Clearmountain. "He wanted to save it for *Reckless.*"

The album was initially recorded at Little Mountain Studios in Vancouver, Canada. Clearmountain, who had co-produced Adams's previous two albums, *You Want It, You Got It* and *Cuts Like a Knife*, says *Reckless* was a bit more difficult to make. "We were getting pickier," he says. "We wanted it to be better than the other two." Adams and Clearmountain even opted to re-record a few tracks. "When we finished 'One Night Love Affair' we decided that it was a little on the boring side, so we went back and re-recorded the drums and half of the guitars," Clearmountain says. "We thought that since it was going to be the opening song on the album, we should make it as good as it could be."

The re-recording of some of the tracks pushed the sessions past the scheduled deadline, putting Clearmountain in the position of working on two projects at once at Electric Ladyland Studios in New York. "We were supposed to have been finished with Bryan's album, so I was working on Hall & Oates's *Big Bam Boom* from 11 A.M. to 9 P.M. and then Bryan would come in and I would work with him until about 6 A.M."

It took approximately three months to complete the album, relatively long by Adams's previous standards. "We did *You Want It, You Got It* in two weeks," Clearmountain says. "*Cuts Like a Knife* took about six weeks."

When Adams first played Clearmountain the demos for the album, "Run to You" was at the end of the tape. "He said, 'Don't even bother with the last song, I'm probably going to give it

away.' But when I got to the song, I realized that it was one of the best songs on the tape. I had to talk him into doing it and I'm glad I did, because it came out really well."

If Clearmountain saved that track, he gives Adams all the credit for "It's Only Love," which almost didn't make the album. "It wasn't sounding that great," he recalls. "I thought maybe we needed another guitar or something, but then Bryan said, 'What if this was a duet with Tina Turner?' " All agreed it was a great idea, but that's all it was, until Adams's manager Bruce Allen put in a call to Turner's representative. "She was totally into it," recalls Clearmountain, "and it came out great. It was genius on Bryan's part to suggest it." Foreigner's Lou Gramm [see 261] also made a guest appearance, singing backing vocals on "She's Only Happy When She's Dancing."

In all, Clearmountain felt the extra effort on *Reckless* had paid off. "It was the most consistent songwriting he had done," he says. "*Cuts Like a Knife* was good. It had its high points, but this album seemed to have more to it songwise."

Clearmountain's hunch proved correct. In January 1985, "Run to You" became a top 10 hit. A second single, "Somebody," peaked at number 11, setting the stage for the long-awaited release of "Heaven." On June 22, 1985, the track became Adams's first Number One single and helped push *Reckless* to the top spot in its 38th week on the chart. It made Adams the first Canadian artist to top the album chart since Bachman-Turner Overdrive [see 184], an act also managed by Allen, had done it in 1974.

THE TOP FIVE
Week of August 10, 1985

1. **Reckless**
   Bryan Adams

2. **Songs from the Big Chair**
   Tears for Fears

3. **No Jacket Required**
   Phil Collins

4. **The Dream of the Blue Turtle**
   Sting

5. **Born in the U.S.A.**
   Bruce Springsteen

292 Brothers in Arms WARNER BROS. 25264
DIRE STRAITS

Producers: Mark Knopfler and Neil Dorfsman

Track listing: So Far Away / Money for Nothing / Walk of Life / Your Latest Trick / Why Worry / Ride Across the River / The Man's Too Strong / One World / Brothers in Arms

August 31, 1985
9 weeks

By 1985, Dire Straits had built a healthy following in the United States. Both the band and manager Ed Bicknell were confident the group's popularity would increase with the release of *Brothers in Arms*. Yet neither the Dire Straits nor Bicknell had any idea how popular the album would eventually be.

With their self-titled 1979 debut album, the London-based Dire Straits quickly made a name for themselves in America. The album, fueled by the top

10 single "Sultans of Swing," reached number two. While the group continued to be hugely successful in Europe, their subsequent five albums failed to crack the top 10 of the album chart in America, with 1983's *Twisting by the Pool* EP and 1984's *Dire Straits Live—Alchemy*, peaking at numbers 53 and 46, respectively.

To ensure the success of the band's next effort, singer-songwriter Mark Knopfler and the rest of the band (keyboardist Alan Clark, keyboardist/vocalist Guy Fletcher, bassist/vocalist John Illsley, and drummers Omar Hakim and Terry Williams) made demos of every song being considered for the album at Gallery Studio near London. "I remember going down to the rehearsals one day and hearing 'Money for Nothing,' " says Bicknell. "At the lunch break I said to John, 'I think that one might be a hit,' and he just smiled."

The chances of "Money for Nothing" becoming a hit increased considerably

when the band was recording the final version of the song at Air Studios in Montserrat, West Indies. Sting, the frontman of the Police [see 276], happened to be vacationing on the island. The members of Dire Straits were friendly with him, having shared several bills with the Police in the late '70s. "He came to the studio because one of the best places to eat was a restaurant at the studio," says Bicknell, "and Mark said to him, 'I've written this really stupid song about MTV, do you fancy singing on it?' " Sting agreed, singing the line "I want my MTV" to the melody of the Police hit "Don't Stand So Close to Me." It turned out to be a winning combination, as the song went on to become a hit, thanks in part to an innovative video clip that paired computer animation with live performance footage.

With "Money for Nothing" receiving heavy airplay on MTV and the single climbing the Hot 100, *Brothers in Arms* became Dire Straits' first Number One album in its 13th week on the chart. With the album still holding at the top, "Money for Nothing" joined it at the summit on September 21, 1985.

Knopfler initially didn't plan to include "Walk of Life" on the album. "When they were mixing the album at the Power Station in New York, it was playing when I went into the room," says Bicknell. "He said it was just a piece of nonsense and that it wasn't going on the album. It was a B-side." In the end, Bicknell persuaded Knopfler that the song had hit potential. Once again, he was right, as "Walk of Life" went on to become the second top 10 single from *Brothers in Arms* in January 1986.

THE TOP FIVE
Week of August 31, 1985

1. **Brothers in Arms**
   Dire Straits

2. **Songs from the Big Chair**
   Tears for Fears

3. **The Dream of the Big Turtles**
   Sting

4. **Reckless**
   Bryan Adams

5. **Born in the U.S.A.**
   Bruce Springsteen

"Miami Vice" made its network debut on September 16, 1984. Although it was embraced from the start by some TV critics, it took the public a while to catch on. By the summer of its first season, the show had worked its way into the top 10 of the Nielsen ratings.

Part of the show's success was due to its use of music incorporated along with visuals, an approach that clearly owed a stylistic debt to MTV. The series also featured songs by several hot artists, such as Phil Collins [see 286] and former Eagle Glenn Frey. As MCA soundtrack executive Kathy Nelson notes, Mann was particularly in tune with pop music. "When I gave him Glenn Frey's 'Smuggler's Blues,' he liked it so much he created a whole episode around it."

With Hammer's score and a rotating stable of pop stars featured prominently each week, a soundtrack album was a natural. MCA released *Miami Vice* in the fall of 1985 to coincide with the start of series's second season. The album debuted at number 28 on October 12, 1985. Four weeks later, it hit Number One, with Hammer's "Miami Vice Theme" reaching the top of the Hot 100 on November 9, 1985.

The album also spawned other hits, including Frey's "You Belong to the City" and "Smuggler's Blues," which reached numbers two and 12, respectively. Tina Turner's "Better Be Good to Me," a number five hit in 1984, was also included on the album.

Much like *The Music from Peter Gunn*, *Miami Vice* was successful enough to warrant a sequel. Yet *Miami Vice II*, released in late 1986, failed to recapture the magic of the original, peaking at number 82.

Executive producers: Danny Goldberg, Michael Mann

Track listing: Miami Vice Theme [Jan Hammer] / Smuggler's Blues [Glenn Frey] / Own the Night [Chaka Kahn] / You Belong to the City [Frey] / In the Air Tonight [Phil Collins] / Miami Vice Theme (Instrumental) / Vice [Grandmaster Mele Mell] / Better Be Good to Me [Tina Turner] / Flashback [Hammer] / Chase / Evan

November 2, 1985
11 weeks (nonconsecutive)

When Jan Hammer first met television producer Michael Mann, he knew nothing of Mann's new series in development called "Miami Vice." Hammer, a Czech native who was a former member of the Mahavishnu Orchestra, had worked with several noted musicians, including Carlos Santana [see 126], Al Di Meola, Stanley Clarke, and Jeff Beck. He had also scored the 1983 film *A Night in Heaven*. Upon meeting Mann in March 1984, Hammer played the TV producer a piece of music he was working on. Mann was impressed enough to hire Hammer to score the series. "I tried three or four other themes, but the first one I played him ended up being the 'Miami Vice Theme,' " says Hammer.

Henry Mancini had proven that TV show soundtracks could be big business with *The Music from Peter Gunn* [see 24], but that was more than 25 years earlier. Yet the timeless mix of drama and music would work again with *Miami Vice*. Hammer credits the success of the soundtrack to the fact that he was given full artistic control over the score: "I was left on my own and had my own very clear vision, as opposed to three different visions from the producer, the director, and the stars."

THE TOP FIVE
Week of November 2, 1985

1. **Miami Vice**
   Soundtrack

2. **Brothers in Arms**
   Dire Straits

3. **Whitney Houston**
   Whitney Houston

4. **Scarecrow**
   John Cougar Mellencamp

5. **Songs from the Big Chair**
   Tears for Fears

294 Heart CAPITOL 12410
HEART

Producer: Ron Nevison

Track listing: If Looks Could Kill / What About Love / Never / These Dreams / The Wolf / All Eyes / Nobody Home / Nothin' at All / What He Don't Know / Shell Shock

December 21, 1985
1 week

The success of *Heart* was a bittersweet triumph for sisters Ann and Nancy Wilson. The group, fronted by the two sisters, was formed in Seattle in 1974. Initially they experienced success with the top 10 albums *Dreamboat Annie, Little Queen,* and *Bebe Le Strange* and the hit singles "Magic Man" and "Barracuda," but by the early '80s, the group's popularity had waned. They even contemplated breaking up.

Instead, Heart regrouped, enlisted a new producer and manager, and signed to a new label, Capitol. "There was the feeling of a new beginning," says Ann Wilson. "The two previous albums, *Private Audition* and *Passionworks,* brought us to an end of our previous incarnation."

At the time, the group was also desperate for a big commercial breakthrough. Don Grierson, the A&R executive who brought the band to Capitol, suggested that Heart turn to outside writers for material. This didn't sit particularly well with the Wilson sisters, who were proud of their songwriting talents. "We both felt exposed," Ann says. "But even people in our own band weren't

excited about doing our songs."

To make matters worse, Ann Wilson didn't get along too well with producer Ron Nevison, who had worked as an engineer for Led Zeppelin and the Who, and was also producing Starship. "Some producers think they have to make the singer mad to get a good performance out of them, and he tried that on me," she says.

The album was recorded from January through April 1985 at the Record Plant in Sausalito, California. It was tough for Ann Wilson to get into the sessions. "I wasn't accustomed to singing other people's songs," she says. "They were kind of tough for me to identify with. But everyone was saying, 'This is brilliant.' I wasn't sure I agreed."

While Ann Wilson wasn't crazy about the bulk of the outside material, there was one song, written by Elton John's lyricist Bernie Taupin [see 146] and Martin Page, that she liked. " 'These Dreams' was the exception," she says. "It's a great song. Bernie was always kind of an idol to me. That was the best of whole bunch. When it came to us, I wanted to sing it really bad, but Nancy stood firm."

Nancy Wilson had a bad cold when she was laying down her guide vocal on the track, which gave her voice kind of a scratchy feel, Ann says. When Nancy was unable to duplicate the sound, Nevison decided to go with the demo vocal for the final mix.

Heart was released in July 1985. The album featured several high-gloss power ballads, a dramatic departure

THE TOP FIVE
Week of December 21, 1985

1. **Heart**
   Heart
2. **Miami Vice**
   Soundtrack
3. **Scarecrow**
   John Cougar Mellencamp
4. **Afterburner**
   ZZ Top
5. **The Broadway Album**
   Barbra Streisand

from the band's hard-rocking roots. "What About Love?," the first single from the album, reached number 10. The followup, "Never," did even better. When it peaked at number four, it became the group's highest charting single to date, and helped propel *Heart* to the top of the album chart. The roll continued with "These Dreams," which hit Number One on March 26, 1986, and "Nothin' at All," which hit number 10 in June.

Heart had found its long-sought commercial success with a Number One album featuring four top 10 singles, but for Ann Wilson it wasn't the band's finest moment. "It's not that I hate those songs," she says. "They just didn't ring a bell in me. We weren't forced to do those songs, but after a while I began to feel that we made a real devil's bargain creatively to get the hit."

COLUMBIA 40092 **The Broadway Album**
BARBRA STREISAND

295

Barbra Streisand with David Foster.

Producers: Barbra Streisand, Peter Matz, Richard Baskin, Bob Esty, Paul Jabara, and David Foster

Track listing: Putting It Together / If I Love You / Something's Coming / Not While I'm Around / Being Alive / I Have Dreamed/We Kiss in a Shadow/Something Wonderful / Send in the Clowns / Pretty Women/The Ladies Who Lunch / Can't Help Lovin' That Man / I Loves You Porgy/Porgy, I's You Woman Now (Bess, You Is My Woman) / Somewhere

January 25, 1986
3 weeks

Recording an album of songs made popular on the Broadway stage made perfect sense for Barbra Streisand. After all, the singer/actress's career began in the early '60s with roles in such musicals as *I Can Get It for You Wholesale* and *Funny Girl*. In fact, Streisand's first charting single, "People," was from the latter.

For *The Broadway Album*, Streisand drew selections from the some of the most acclaimed musicals of all time, including "Putting It Together" from Stephen Sondheim's *Sunday in the Park with George*, "If I Loved You" from Rodgers and Hammerstein's *Carousel*, "Something's Coming" and "Somewhere" from Leonard Bernstein and

Sondheim's *West Side Story*, and "I Loves You Porgy/Porgy, I's Your Woman Now" from George and Ira Gershwin's *Porgy and Bess*.

On several tracks, including "Putting It Together," Streisand and co-producer Peter Matz gave the songs the grand treatment with lush orchestral arrangements. That particular track also included cameos from filmmaker/actor Sydney Pollack and record mogul David Geffen, who are credited as "actors." They mimicked the lines Streisand heard from Columbia executives when she first approached them with the idea for *The Broadway Album*: "Why take chances?," "It's just not commercial," and "It won't sell."

Another special guest was Stevie Wonder, who played harmonica on Streisand's rendition of "Can't Help Lovin' That Man" from *Showboat*.

In the album's liner notes, Streisand thanked Sondheim "for his contribution to this project—and being so open to change, believing as I do, that art is a living, constantly evolving process."

Possibly the most dramatic interpretation was Streisand's version of "Somewhere," which was produced and arranged by David Foster, who also played keyboards and synthesizer on the track.

"I had been involved with her before," says Foster. "I had played piano on her records and arranged

some songs for her and had somewhat of a relationship established with her already. But when the call came to work on *The Broadway Album*, I was thrilled. When she explained to me that she wanted the song 'Somewhere' to sound like it wasn't created on this planet, that just piqued my interest even more."

"Somewhere" was the only single released from *The Broadway Album* and it made only number 43, yet that couldn't stop Streisand from scoring her sixth Number One album and first chart-topper in five years. *The Broadway Album* entered the chart on November 23, 1985, at number 59. Ten weeks later, it hit the top spot.

THE TOP FIVE
Week of January 25, 1986

1. **The Broadway Album**
   Barbra Streisand

2. **Miami Vice**
   Soundtrack

3. **Heart**
   Heart

4. **Scarecrow**
   John Cougar Mellencamp

5. **Promise**
   Sade

296 Promise PORTRAIT 40263
SADE

Producers: Robin Millar, Ben Rogan, Mike Pela, and Sade

Track listing: Is It a Crime / The Sweetest Taboo / War of the Hearts / You're Not the Man / Jezebel / Mr. Wrong / Punch Drunk / Never as Good as the First Time / Fear / Tar Baby / Maureen

February 15, 1986
2 weeks

Producer Robin Millar can still remember the first time he heard Sade's voice. Millar, who ran the Power Plant Willesden studio, had used keyboardist Andrew Hale and guitarist/saxophonist Stuart Matthewman, from the London-based group Pride, for a session. Pride's manager told Millar that the group had cut a demo tape with one of its backup singers, Helen Folsade Adu. A song called "Smooth Operator" was among the selections featured on the tape. "It was a really, really rough tentative demo," Millar says. "It was a girl's first steps at singing lead vocals, but I heard the turn of her voice and that was that. I took the tape home and I woke my wife up at 3 A.M. and told her, 'If I can produce this and get an album deal, it's going to be huge.'"

Millar's prediction proved to be correct. The group and its singer, both known as Sade (pronounced SHA-day), became a hit in the U.K. and in America. Their 1984 debut album, *The Diamond Life*, reached number five in the States and spawned the hit single "Smooth Operator." Sade's smooth blend of jazz and R&B had struck a nerve.

By the time Portrait/CBS Records released *The Diamond Life* in America, Sade was already a British superstar attempting to forge her own creative vision, without interference from record company executives, on her second album. The singer, band members, and Millar all felt that with the success of *The Diamond Life*, Sade had "earned the right to be wrong."

The group, which also included bassist Paul S. Denman and was augmented by several session players, began recording *Promise* at Millar's Power Plant Willesden studios. Tracks cut in London include "Is It a Crime," "Jezebel," "Fear," "The Sweetest Taboo," and "War of the Hearts." With a full tour in support of *The Diamond Life* under their collective belt, the group and Sade had grown tremendously since the sessions for the first album and thus wanted to push their newly honed chops to the limit. For example, "Is It a Crime" was cut completely live in the studio. "Nobody believes me to this day that the whole track was done live," says Millar. "It took two-and-a-half days to set up the instruments. When we cut it, we had everyone in the same room. It had to be one complete mood. It was Sade's moment to see if she could be a torch singer, and she really came of age on that record."

However, Sade's popularity also created problems. Journalists hung around the studio, trying to get the dirt on the new star. To escape all the attention, the group fled to Studio Miraval in France, but was unable to shake the spotlight. "She was still being pestered by the European press," Millar says. "I had never worked with a very famous group before. It was hard to get everyone to focus when they were doing interviews between the takes for vocals."

To make matters worse, record company executives from CBS in America were attempting to become involved in the creative process. "We were very much aware of the fact that people around us, who were making money off us, were attempting to push us around," Millar says.

Rather than succumb to the pressure of the outside forces, Sade and the group continued to follow their own muse. "There were great highs and deep lows, and that brought about intensity in the music," Millar says. "It was a painful record to make, in the best sense of the word."

When the album was completed some six months later, Millar and the group realized they didn't have a track suitable for release as a single. "We thought of recording a couple of other tracks, but then we decided to stick to our guns," Millar says.

The group's unwillingness to compromise paid off, even if their instincts regarding the album's commercial prospects were a bit off. *Promise* hit the top in its ninth week on the chart and "The Sweetest Taboo" became a top five hit.

THE TOP FIVE
Week of February 15, 1986

1. **Promise**
   Sade

2. **The Broadway Album**
   Barbra Streisand

3. **Welcome to the Real World**
   Mr. Mister

4. **Heart**
   Heart

5. **Whitney Houston**
   Whitney Houston

RCA 7180 # Welcome to the Real World 297
MR. MISTER

Producer: Mr. Mister and Paul DeVilliers

Track listing: Black/White / Uniform of Youth / Don't Slow Down / Run to Her / Into My Own Hands / Is It Love / Kyrie / Broken Wings / Tangent Tears / Welcome to the Real World

March 1, 1986
1 week

Mr. Mister's 1984 debut album, *I Wear the Face,* stalled at number 170. It wasn't singer/bassist Richard Page's first failed attempt at the big time. He and keyboardist Steve George had been members of a band called Pages, which recorded two albums for Epic and one for Capitol. All failed to chart.

After that experience, Page and George stuck together, working as session musicians for the likes of Michael Jackson, Patti LaBelle, Rick Springfield, the Pointer Sisters, and Donna Summer. In 1982, they formed Mr. Mister with drummer Pat Mastelotto and guitarist Steve Farris.

Following the disappointing sales of *I Wear the Face,* Mr. Mister weren't exactly aiming for the sky with their follow-up album. "We had absolutely no expectations, having had several commercially unsuccessful records before," says Page. "We figured it would be another one of those. It would be a record that we loved, but it wouldn't make any noise. It would catch a few people's ears and that would be the end of it."

Page's instincts, of course, were wrong. *Welcome to the Real World* would become a surprise hit, thanks largely to "Broken Wings," a song Page

initially didn't think was a particularly good choice for a single. "I've always been really bad at predicting things," he says. "When the executives at RCA and our manager all said that 'Broken Wings' should be the first single, I tried to talk them out of it. I thought it was a great song, I just didn't think it would be a big hit."

Although Page was initially unsure of the commercial potential of "Broken Wings," he knew he was on to something when he started composing the song at his Southern California home. "I just had the bass line and melody," he says. "But I called up my collaborator John Lang and said, 'Get in the car and get over here now. This is important.' He came over and jotted down some words and in an hour we were pretty much finished with it."

While "Broken Wings" came together quickly, it took the single more than a

dozen weeks just to chart. Eventually, however, it began to move up the Hot 100. On December 7, 1985, it hit Number One.

Yet it would take a second chart-topping single to push *Welcome to the Real World* to the top of the album chart. "Kyrie" was a song that Page initially didn't want to record. "John came up with the lyric," Page says. " 'Kyrie eleison' means 'Lord have mercy.' It's from the Greek Sanskrit. It's one of the oldest known sayings in history. I just thought that people would think it was a Christian thing and felt really uncomfortable about it." Yet Lang insisted, and the band recorded the track.

On March 1, "Kyrie" became Mr. Mister's second Number One single, as *Welcome to the Real World* hit the peak of the Top Pop Albums chart in its 27th week. "Don't anyone ask me for advice on hit records," quips Page.

THE TOP FIVE
Week of March 1, 1986

1. **Welcome to the Real World**
   Mr. Mister

2. **Promise**
   Sade

3. **Whitney Houston**
   Whitney Houston

4. **The Broadway Album**
   Barbra Streisand

5. **Scarecrow**
   John Cougar Mellencamp

298 Whitney Houston ARISTA 8212
WHITNEY HOUSTON

Producers: Jermaine Jackson, Kashif, Michael Masser, and Narada Michael Walden

Track listing: You Give Good Love / Thinking About You / Someone for Me / Saving All My Love for You / Nobody Loves Me Like You Do / How Will I Know / All At Once / Take Good Care of My Heart / Greatest Love of All / Hold Me

March 8, 1986
14 weeks (nonconsecutive)

When producer/songwriter Michael Masser first heard Whitney Houston's voice, she was singing "Greatest Love of All," a song Masser had written with Linda Creed for a film about Muhammad Ali called *The Greatest*. Masser had been invited by Arista president Clive Davis to attend a showcase featuring the young singer at Sweetwater's in New York. "I felt like I lost it," Masser says. "I was hearing this song that I loved and it was sung by this voice. Once I got past the shock, and I started listening, I knew that this was one of the greatest talents I have heard in my life."

Naturally, when Davis asked Masser if he was interested in producing the young singer, he jumped at the opportunity. The first track Masser recorded with Houston was "Hold Me," a song meant as a duet that he had promised to Teddy Pendergrass two days before the R&B singer was paralyzed in a car accident. When it was time for Masser to find a duet partner for Pendergrass, only one voice came to mind, the voice of Whitney Houston. "When she flew out to California, she was a young kid who was 18 years old with everything in front of her," says Masser. The duet with Pendergrass stalled at number 46 in June 1984, hardly hinting at what was to come.

Over the next six months, Masser recorded three more tracks with Houston, but he was only one of several producers involved in the project. Davis also turned to Kashif, Narada Michael Walden, and Jermaine Jackson, who sang with Houston on "Nobody Loves Me Like You Do" and "Take Good Care of My Heart."

Masser opted to dig up "Saving All My Love for You," a song he co-wrote with Gerry Goffin that was originally recorded by Marilyn McCoo and Billy Davis Jr. in 1978. "I rearranged the structure of the song and I thought it would be a great single for Whitney," he says. "When I did the track, the musicians and myself were stunned by the torchiness of the way she sang it."

While Masser was impressed with Houston's take of that song, his real goal was to have Houston record "Greatest Love of All," the first song he heard her sing. "That was why I took the project with Whitney. George Benson had originally recorded the track in 1977, but it wasn't a big hit, peaking at number 24. "Nobody knew the 'Greatest Love of All' would be that big," says Masser of Houston's version of the song. "At first it was released as a B-side to the first single, 'You Give Good Love.' But it became one of Whitney's greatest hits."

By the time *Whitney Houston* hit the top spot in its 50th week on the Top Pop Albums chart, Houston was no stranger to the Number One position. "Saving All My Love for You" had topped the Hot 100 on October 26, 1985 and "How Will I Know" turned the trick on February 15, 1986. With *Whitney Houston* still at Number One on the album chart, "Greatest Love of All" became the third chart-topping single from the album. The feat put Houston in the record books as the first female artist to score three Number One singles from one album, but it was only the beginning of the Whitney Houston story.

THE TOP FIVE
Week of March 8, 1986

1. **Whitney Houston**
   Whitney Houston

2. **Promise**
   Sade

3. **Welcome to the Real World**
   Mr. Mister

4. **The Broadway Album**
   Barbra Streisand

5. **Heart**
   Heart

WARNER BROS. 25394 5150 **299**
VAN HALEN

Producers: Van Halen, Mick Jones, and
Donn Landee

Track listing: Best of Both Worlds /
Dreams / Why Can't This Be Love /
Love Walks In / 5150 / Inside / Good
Enough / Summer Nights / Get Up

April 26, 1986
3 weeks

By late 1985, when singer David
Lee Roth announced he was leaving Van Halen, many assumed the
band had run its course. Named for
brothers—guitarist Eddie and drummer
Alex—Van Halen certainly had had its
share of success by that point. After the
group's 1978 self-titled debut made
number 19, each of their subsequent
five albums made the top 10, including
1984, which spent five weeks at number two. Yet the departure of the charismatic Roth put the band's future in jeop-
ardy, at least until the day Eddie Van
Halen went to pick up his Lamborghini
from the shop.

The guitar whiz noticed a Ferrari at
the shop and he asked his mechanic
whose car it was. The mechanic told
Van Halen it belonged to Sammy
Hagar, the one-time member of '70s
hard-rock band Montrose who had
gone on to a moderately successful solo
career. The mechanic urged Van Halen
to give Hagar a call. "I had only been
home about five days from my own tour
and Eddie asked me to join the band,"
Hagar says. "I said, 'Shit, I don't know.
I just came off tour, I don't think I want
to do anything.' " Yet Hagar did agree
to come down and meet the band at
Van Halen's newly constructed Los
Angeles home studio called 5150,

named after the police code for the
criminally insane. "I came down and
walked into the room and they played
two songs, 'Summer Nights' and 'Good
Enough,' and it was so bad-ass, I just
freaked."

Hagar left the jam session with a tape
in hand and wrote lyrics for the songs
that night. "I put the stuff on the next
morning and went nuts," Hagar says. "I
called up Eddie and said, 'Let's go.' "

For Hagar, the meeting with Eddie
Van Halen, considered among the premier guitarists of the '80s, was an artistic jolt. "5150 will always remain the
most exciting album I made since the
first Montrose album," says Hagar. "It
was a great, high-energy record."

The band, handling the production
duties along with longtime band associate Donn Landee and Foreigner's Mick
Jones, worked at a hectic pace. "We
were finishing songs in three days,"

says Hagar. "We'd write it, record it,
and go on to the next. We didn't even
turn around to look back. We were
done with everything in three months
max, and we were out on tour by the
time the album came out."

For Hagar, replacing Roth wasn't an
issue. "It was so magical, what we were
doing, I didn't feel like I was replacing
anybody," says Hagar. "It felt like we
were starting a new band. It was almost
like he didn't exist. His name was not
mentioned."

Van Halen fans apparently didn't
miss Roth either. 5150, named for the
band's studio, hit the top of the Top Pop
Albums chart in its third week. Roth was-
n't as fortunate. He reached his solo
career chart high later in 1986 with Eat
'Em and Smile, which reached number
four. But ever since, it has been downhill
for Roth, while Van Halen has continued
to thrive.

THE TOP FIVE
Week of April 26, 1986

1. **5150**
   Van Halen

2. **Whitney Houston**
   Whitney Houston

3. **Falco 3**
   Falco

4. **Heart**
   Heart

5. **Dirty Work**
   The Rolling Stones

300 Control A&M 5106
JANET JACKSON

Producers: Jimmy Jam and Terry Lewis

Track listing: Control / Nasty / What Have You Done for Me Lately / You Can Be Mine / The Pleasure Principle / When I Think of You / He Doesn't Know I'm Alive / Let's Wait Awhile / Funny How Time Flies (When You're Having Fun)

July 5, 1986
2 weeks

Janet Jackson had attempted to make a name for herself well before the release of *Control*. She starred on the TV shows "Good Times," "Diff'rent Strokes," and "Fame." She recorded two albums—her 1982 self-titled debut effort, which reached number 63, and 1984's *Dream Street,* which made only number 147. Yet Janet Jackson was still best known as the youngest sibling in the famous family that included her older brother Michael [see 274]. At least until she took control.

Jimmy Jam and Terry Lewis, meanwhile, were best known as members of the Time, a Minneapolis band affiliated with Prince and featured in the film *Purple Rain* [see 282]. After leaving the Time, the duo began a fledgling career as producers, working with such artists as the Force M.D.'s and Patti Austin. Initially they were set to produce former Atlantic Starr singer Sharon Bryant, but the deal fell apart. A&M Records A&R executive John McClain asked the duo if there was any other artist on the A&M roster that Jam and Lewis were interested in working with. Their response was Janet Jackson.

"She saw us play with the Time in Long Beach," Jam recalls. "We could see her in the front row." Since Jackson was a fan of the Time, she was anxious to meet with Jam and Lewis, but was a little surprised when they played her some of their productions. The Patti Austin material sounded "too adult" for Jackson. Janet's manager at the time, Jackson family patriarch Joe Jackson, also had a major concern. "He said, 'I know you guys are from Minneapolis, but don't make my daughter sound like Prince,' " says Jam. "We assured them that every artist we produce has their own sound and Janet wouldn't sound like Patti Austin or Prince."

To create an appropriate sound for Jackson, Jam and Lewis agreed that they had to get to know her, so when Jackson came to the duo's Flyte Tyme studios in Minneapolis, "we did everything but record," says Jam. "We sat down and talked, we went to the movies, we went to eat, and we just hung out."

Although she was just 19 at the time, Jackson had been through a lot. She was just 16 when she eloped with singer James DeBarge from another famed musical family. "We listened to her talk about going through her divorce, moving out of her parents' house, and the fact that she was really serious about her singing career," says Jam. "The album was definitely a product of how she was feeling at the time."

Control was recorded in a mere six weeks. When Jam and Lewis initially turned in the album to A&M, it was rejected. "John McClain said 'Control' and 'Nasty' are great songs and that it would be great to have another song like it," Jam says. "We said that we didn't want to do a clone, but we would do another uptempo song."

Back in Minneapolis, Jam and Lewis were already at work on another album. Lewis heard Jam play a bass line and was convinced it could serve as the basis of the new Jackson track. Jackson, sitting on a couch in the lobby of the studio, heard the riff. "When we opened the door she said, 'Oh, what's that?' We told her it was for her and she was really excited about it."

The track, titled "What Have You Done for Me Lately," became Jackson's first top five hit. The follow-up single, "Nasty" peaked at number three. In its 18th week on the chart, *Control* hit the pole position, making Janet Jackson the youngest artist since Little Stevie Wonder [see 61] to score a Number One album. The subsequent singles "When I Think of You," "Control," and "Let's Wait Awhile" also broke into the top five. Janet Jackson was no longer just Michael's little sister.

THE TOP FIVE
Week of July 5, 1986

1. **Control**
   Janet Jackson

2. **Winner in You**
   Patti LaBelle

3. **Whitney Houston**
   Whitney Houston

4. **Like a Rock**
   Bob Seger & the Silver Bullet Band

5. **So**
   Peter Gabriel

Executive Producer: Patti LaBelle

Track listing: Oh, People / On My Own / Something Special (Is Gonna Happen Tonight) / Kiss Away the Pain / Twisted / You're Mine Tonight / Finally We're Back Together / Beat My Heart Like a Drum / Sleep with Me Tonight / There's a Winner in You

July 19, 1986
1 week

By 1986, Patti LaBelle had been singing professionally for 25 years and had one of the most storied careers in pop music. Yet, the one thing that had eluded her was a Number One album.

LaBelle started her career in 1961, fronting the all-female quartet Patti LaBelle & the Blue Belles. When Cindy Birdsong left the group in 1967 to join the Supremes [see 97], the group, which also featured Nona Hendrix and Sarah Dash, abbreviated its name to LaBelle and continued as a trio. In 1975, the trio scored a Number One hit with the single "Lady Marmalade," which featured the unforgettable French chorus, "Voulez-vous couchez avec moi ce soir?"

Nightbirds, the 1974 album that featured that hit single, became the group's highest charting album when it reached number seven. However, the group was never able to match that success and by 1977 they disbanded, leaving LaBelle a solo artist.

Of LaBelle's first seven solo albums, only 1984's *I'm in Love Again* became even a moderate hit, reaching number 40. LaBelle's career had seemingly reached a commercial standstill, but things changed when the diva left the Philadelphia International label for MCA.

MCA cleverly put LaBelle back into the limelight by featuring the songs "New Attitude" and "Stir It Up" on the soundtrack to *Beverly Hills Cop* [see 289]. "New Attitude" reached number 17, priming the pump for LaBelle's MCA debut album, *Winner in You*.

To cut the album, LaBelle turned to several different producers, including Richard Perry, known for his work with Carly Simon [see 151] and Barbra Streisand [see 234]; longtime producer Budd Ellison; and Nickolas Ashford and Valerie Simpson, better known as the hit duo Ashford and Simpson.

Yet the most important collaborators on *Winner in You* turned out to be songwriter/producers Burt Bacharach and Carole Bayer Sager and former Doobie Brothers vocalist Michael McDonald [see 238]. Bachrach and Sager brought two songs to LaBelle, "On My Own" and "Sleep with Me Tonight," and it was Sager who asked McDonald if he would be interested in singing on one of the two tracks. He chose "On My Own."

McDonald and LaBelle didn't actually sing a duet in the studio. "I recorded my vocal track to her voice on tape," says McDonald. Yet it was still an honor for McDonald to cut a record with the queen of rock 'n' soul. "I admired Patti a lot and I was kind of thrilled that they had asked me to do it. They had actually asked me once before, but I wasn't able to do it because of contractual problems." When the second opportunity to duet with LaBelle arose, McDonald wouldn't let it slip away. "I pushed for it with [my] label and they were very accommodating. They cleared the way for me to do it and I'm glad they did, because it was a great song. Songs like that don't come around that often. I think everyone kind of saw that it had the potential to be a big record." LaBelle and McDonald both appeared in the video, but once again their parts were recorded separately, because they were in different cities. The two singers finally met at the NBC Studios in Burbank, just before they performed the song live for the first time on "The Tonight Show."

On June 14, 1986, "On My Own" became Patti LaBelle's first Number One solo hit. A month later, LaBelle knocked young Janet Jackson from the summit of the album chart, finally scoring that elusive Number One album.

THE TOP FIVE
Week of July 19, 1986

1. **Winner in You**
   Patti LaBelle

2. **Control**
   Janet Jackson

3. **So**
   Peter Gabriel

4. **Top Gun**
   Soundtrack

5. **Invisible Touch**
   Genesis

302 Top Gun COLUMBIA 40323
SOUNDTRACK

Executive Producers: Don Simpson and Jerry Bruckheimer

Track listing: Danger Zone [Kenny Loggins] / Heaven in Your Eyes [Loverboy] / Mighty Wings [Cheap Trick] / Take My Breath Away [Berlin] / Top Gun Anthem [Harold Faltermeyer & Steve Stevenes] / Hot Summer Nights [Miami Sound Machine] / Playing with the Boys [Kenny Loggins] / Lead Me On [Teena Marie] / Destination Unknown [Marietta] / Through the Fire [Larry Greene]

July 26, 1986
5 weeks (nonconsecutive)

After the success of *Flashdance* [see 275], Giorgio Moroder was the leading candidate to score Don Simpson and Jerry Buckheimer's next production—*Top Gun*. The only problem was that Moroder couldn't fit the job into his busy schedule. "I suggested to Jerry and Don to use Harold Faltermeyer," says Moroder, "because I couldn't do it." Faltermeyer worked on the score and a few tracks for the film at Mororder's Oasis Recording Studio in North Hollywood while Mororder was in Europe working on another project. "When I came back I stopped at the studio one afternoon," Moroder recalls. "Faltermeyer, Don Simpson, and Jerry Buckheimer were there with director Tony Scott. Jerry said, 'Why don't you compose a song?' " Moroder complied. The song, set to appear in the film's opening scene, was called "Danger Zone."

Moroder wrote the music for the track that afternoon after viewing a rough cut of the film. "They liked it immediately," says Moroder, who turned to collaborator Tom Whitlock for the song's lyrics.

Impressed with Moroder's first stab at music for the film, the producers asked the composer/producer to write a love theme for the movie as well. The action adventure starred Tom Cruise as a fighter pilot in love with a woman portrayed by Kelly McGillis. With Whitlock once again contributing lyrics, the duo wrote "Take My Breath Away."

A demo circulated around Los Angeles. "A lot of well-known singers wanted to sing that song," Moroder says. Yet Simpson, Bruckheimer, and Moroder had something else in mind. They decided to give the track to a Los Angeles–based new wave group known as Berlin. Moroder had co-produced a few tracks on the group's 1984 Geffen album *Love Life*.

Moroder recorded singer Terri Nunn's vocals in two days but couldn't get the largely synthesizer-based instrumental track to sound right. "We ended up using the demo track with Terri's vocal," Moroder says. "If you listen carefully, you can hear plenty of mis-takes, but the atmosphere on that demo was so good we couldn't recreate it."

"Danger Zone," the first track Moroder wrote for the movie, was initially recorded by another act. Although Moroder thought the demo recording was good, music consultant Michael Dilbeck had other ideas. Dilbeck was involved in *Footloose* [see 279] and thought that Kenny Loggins, who had scored a Number One single with the title track from *Footloose*, would be the perfect voice of the opening anthem.

Although Loggins didn't receive any songwriting credits, he did more than simply sing the track. "He had a lot of musical suggestions," says Mororder. "He called me at 11 at night from Santa Barbara with suggestions on which chords would fit the song better."

With help from Berlin, Loggins, and Whitlock, Moroder once again proved to have the Midas touch. "Danger Zone" made number two, and *Top Gun* flew to the peak in its eighth week on the chart. A few months later "Take My Breath Away" topped the Hot 100.

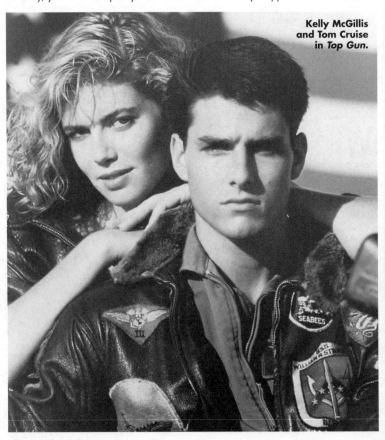

Kelly McGillis and Tom Cruise in *Top Gun.*

THE TOP FIVE
Week of July 26, 1986

1. **Top Gun**
   Soundtrack

2. **So**
   Peter Gabriel

3. **Control**
   Janet Jackson

4. **Invisible Touch**
   Genesis

5. **Winner in You**
   Patti LaBelle

Producers: Madonna, Patrick Leonard, and Stephen Bray

Track listing: Papa Don't Preach / Open Your Heart / White Heat / Live to Tell / Where's the Party / True Blue / La Isla Bonita / Jimmy Jimmy / Love Makes the World Go Round

August 16, 1986
5 weeks

When Patrick Leonard, a songwriter/producer whose credits included work on the Jacksons' Victory Tour, was asked if he was interested in a job as the musical director for Madonna's "Virgin Tour," he initially balked at the proposition. Leonard wasn't really a fan of the singer, but he agreed to meet with Madonna and discuss the job. "After meeting with her, I really couldn't say no," he says. "It seemed too intriguing."

It was during that 1985 tour, in support of Like a Virgin [see 283], that the singer's third album first began to take shape. "We wrote 'Love Makes the World Go Round' while we were on tour," Leonard recalls. "Then we wrote 'Live to Tell' and recorded it, and that sort of got the album going."

Madonna wrote the latter song for At Close Range, a film starring her then-husband, Sean Penn. "I wrote that song completely and totally out of mad crazy love for Sean and I wrote it in 10 minutes," Madonna says. "He showed me a rough cut of the movie and said, 'Write a song for this movie,' and we came up with that."

The song was also recorded quickly. "We recorded it on an eight-track at my house," Leonard says. "We transferred it and added to it, but the vocal was from the eight-track demo."

Much of True Blue was recorded in that fashion. Often demos cut at Leonard's Hollywood home would be turned into finished songs at Channel Recording, engineer Michael Verdick's home studio. "The studio was probably only about 10-by-12 [feet]," says Leonard. "It was a very small room."

The informal setting worked well for Madonna. "I didn't really come into my own skills as a writer until that point," she says. "Pat was a real collaborator in that respect. When I got together with him, I decided I liked writing better with people instead of in a vacuum."

Stephen Bray, who, like Madonna, had been a member of the early '80s-group the Breakfast Club, co-wrote three of the album's songs. " 'Where's the Party' was written after everything else was basically finished," Leonard says. "Steve and I and Madonna got together and we recorded it almost entirely in my family room." Although the home-recording atmosphere kept the sessions relaxed, it wasn't all fun and games. "Madonna's a taskmaster and always has been," says Leonard. "When we worked, we worked hard, but we also had some fun."

During the making of the album, Leonard became a father. "I remember we were working on 'Live to Tell' and I had to leave to go to the hospital, because my daughter was being born," he says. Coincidentally, the responsibilities of parenthood were discussed in the album's most controversial song, "Papa Don't Preach," in which Madonna takes on the persona of a pregnant, unwed teen who chooses to keep her baby. The song was embraced by such unlikely allies as Tipper Gore, head of the Parents Music Research Center (a lobbying group devoted to protesting the use of explicit rock lyrics), and right-wing pro-life groups.

"I knew that song was going to be controversial, because it can be read so many different ways," says Madonna. "The irony of that was that the Catholics were on my side, even though it was a teenage rebellion song. The subtext under all that was, 'Don't tell me what to do.' It was just a 'fuck you' to all authority figures."

While Madonna and Leonard may have been confident about their ability to record hits, executives at Warner Bros. Records, the parent company of Madonna's label, Sire, weren't so sure. "They were a little nervous, because I was basically an unknown," Leonard says. But once Warner Bros. A&R executive Michael Ostin and label president Lenny Waronker visited the studio to hear the playback, their fear subsided. "At one point they were laughing at each other, because it was apparently the right record," Leonard says.

On June 7, 1986, "Live to Tell" became Madonna's third Number One single; ten weeks later she scored her fourth with "Papa Don't Preach." That same week, True Blue became her second consecutive album chart-topper.

THE TOP FIVE
Week of August 16, 1986

1. **True Blue**
   Madonna

2. **Top Gun**
   Soundtrack

3. **So**
   Peter Gabriel

4. **Invisible Touch**
   Genesis

5. **Control**
   Janet Jackson

304 Dancing on the Ceiling MOTOWN 6158
LIONEL RICHIE

Producers: Lionel Richie and James Anthony Carmichael

Track listing: Dancing on the Ceiling / Sela / Ballerina Girl / Don't Stop / Deep River Woman / Love Will Conquer All / Tonight Will Be Alright / Say You, Say Me

September 27, 1986
2 weeks

One day when Lionel Richie was working on his third solo album at Ocean Way Recording in Los Angeles, an acquaintance stopped in to congratulate the singer on the success of his latest single. "This guy said, 'I just came back from Chicago and your record is doing great in Chicago. It's breaking out over the Midwest,' " Richie recalls. The news was a shock to Richie, because he didn't have a new single out. When the acquaintance told Richie that the new single was called "Say You, Say Me," the singer was floored. "I said, 'It can't be "Say You, Say Me," because I haven't mixed it yet.' "

As shocking as it seemed, an early version of "Say You, Say Me" had found its way into the hands of some program directors and onto the airwaves before Richie could finish the track. The song was slated to be included in the film White Nights, so the production company had asked Richie for a demo version of the song. Unbeknownst to Richie, a marketing executive for the film studio included a copy of the demo version of the song in a promotional package designed to drum up interest in the film, which was about a famed ballet dancer who defects from Russia to live in America.

"Four or five months later, I still hadn't finished the album," Richie says. Although "Say You, Say Me" appeared in the film, it wasn't included on the White Nights soundtrack because of contractual reasons. Motown, meanwhile, rush-released the song as a single. "I had to finish the song and let it go, because we couldn't have the demo out there on the radio," Richie says. On December 21, 1985, it topped the Hot 100; soon after, it received an Oscar nomination for Best Original Song. The publicity further delayed the release of the album, as frequent interview requests interrupted Richie's scheduled studio time.

On March 24, 1986, Richie picked up an Oscar for "Say You, Say Me" and performed the song on the awards show telecast. Prior to the telecast, director Stanley Donen visited Richie to brief him on his performance. Coincidentally, Donen had worked with Fred Astaire in the film Dancing on the Ceiling and Richie just happened to be working on a song of the same name at the time. Donen volunteered his services for the gravity-defying video clip of the song.

For the song "Deep River Woman," Richie turned to the popular country act Alabama. He flew into Nashville to work with the group. "They met me at the air-port and we had a quick dinner and then I said, 'What time do you guys want to record tomorrow?' " When the members of Alabama answered "Eight," Richie thought they meant 8 P.M., but they had morning in mind. "They gave me a wake up call at 6 A.M. and I didn't know where I was," Richie recalls. "At 8:30 they were ready to sing. My body was in the studio, but my mind didn't show up until about 2 P.M. But by that time, we had already recorded the song. I had no idea what we did."

Alabama wasn't the only special guest on the album. Eric Clapton [see 179] is featured on the song "Tonight Will Be Alright." To record Clapton's guitar solo, Richie had to fly up to Seattle, where he attended a Clapton concert and was invited to join the guitarist for an encore of "Knock on Wood" and "The Midnight Hour." After the show, Clapton laid down his guitar solo in one take. "It was magical," recalls Richie.

When Dancing on the Ceiling was finally released in August, it didn't disappoint. On September 13, the title track reached number two on the Hot 100, but was unable to unseat Berlin's "Take My Breath Away." Two weeks later, Dancing on the Ceiling hit Number One, becoming Richie's second consecutive album chart-topper.

THE TOP FIVE
Week of September 27, 1986

1. **Dancing on the Ceiling**
   Lionel Richie

2. **Top Gun**
   Soundtrack

3. **Raising Hell**
   Run-D.M.C.

4. **True Blue**
   Madonna

5. **Back in the Highlife**
   Steve Winwood

Producers: Huey Lewis and the News

Track listing: Jacob's Ladder / Stuck with You / Whole Lotta Lovin' / Doing It All for My Baby / Hip to Be Square / I Know What I Like / I Never Walk Alone / Forest for the Trees / Naturally / Simple as That

October 18, 1986
1 week

H uey Lewis and the News soon followed up the success of *Sports* [see 280] with their first Number One single. "The Power of Love," which Lewis wrote specifically for the film *Back to the Future*, hit the top of the Hot 100 on August 24, 1985. Lewis even had a cameo appearance in the film as a music teacher.

The single also became the band's first hit in England, so they toured Europe to take advantage of the momentum. Yet the newfound fame didn't make things easier for Lewis or the News, as they soon found themselves

pressed for material for their fourth album.

"You have all these impressions from 30 years of living when you're totally anonymous," says Lewis. "Then, for the next two years, you [do nothing but] stay in hotel rooms and go and play shows. So what are you going to write about?"

Since his own recent experiences had been limited to touring, Lewis contemplated tackling weightier subject matter. "I really wanted to write a record that said something, but I realized it wasn't honest," he says. "What we do is really simple stuff and our lives were fantastic, so it was really hard to complain about things. 'Doing It All for My Baby' was essentially what I was doing. I had two kids and I was groovin', so we made *Fore!*, which was a groovin' record."

As he'd done on *Sports*, with such tracks as "I Want a New Drug" and "Bad Is Bad," Lewis turned to a catchy phrase for a song title, this time with "Hip to Be Square." Meanwhile, "Stuck

with You," issued in advance of *Fore!*, turned out to be an ace in the hole. On September 20, the track hit Number One on the Hot 100 and stayed there for three weeks. That hit alone was enough to push *Fore!* to the top. It had been on the chart a mere six weeks—33 less than it had taken *Sports* to climb to the top spot.

"Hip to Be Square," one of two tracks on the album featuring guest vocals from San Francisco 49ers professional football players Joe Montana, Dwight Clark, Riki Ellison, and Ronnie Lott, was the next hit, climbing to number three on December 6. "We wanted to get a certain sound and the four of them sounded like a gang of 100 guys," says Lewis. "I liked them more for their voices than their names." Appropriately enough, Lewis and the News sang "The Star Spangled Banner" the following day at a 49ers game.

The News hit the summit on the Hot 100 again on March 14, 1987, with "Jacob's Ladder," a song written by Bruce and John Hornsby. Lewis first heard the tune while producing songs for *The Way It Is*, Bruce Hornsby's 1986 debut album. "It was one of my favorite songs and I wanted him to cut it, but he felt it didn't fit in with the other material," Lewis says. Instead, Lewis and the News gave the song a slightly different arrangement and recorded it themselves.

On *Fore!*, the News once again had success mixing the old with the new. Says Lewis, "We constantly tried to make records that would compete with the increasingly technological records in the marketplace, and I don't apologize for that. We were doing it ourselves in our own local studios in Northern California, and I'm proud of those hits."

THE TOP FIVE
Week of October 18, 1986

1. **Fore!**
   Huey Lewis and the News

2. **Slippery When Wet**
   Bon Jovi

3. **Top Gun**
   Soundtrack

4. **Dancing on the Ceiling**
   Lionel Richie

5. **Raising Hell**
   Run-D.M.C.

306 Slippery When Wet MERCURY 830264
BON JOVI

Producer: Bruce Fairbairn

Track listing: Let It Rock / You Give Love a Bad Name / Livin' on a Prayer / Social Disease / Wanted Dead or Alive / Raise Your Hands / Without Love / I'd Die for You / Never Say Goodbye / Wild in the Streets

October 25, 1986
8 weeks (nonconsecutive)

By 1986, the New Jersey–based rock band Bon Jovi was in danger of becoming "the ultimate opening act," says singer Jon Bon Jovi. The band had formed in March 1983. Its members—guitarist Richie Sambora, keyboardist David Bryan, bassist Alec John Such, and drummer Tico Torres—had played in a number of bands in the New Jersey area before joining forces. Their self-titled debut album reached number 43 in 1984. A year later, the follow-up album 7800 Fahrenheit climbed to number 37, as Bon Jovi built a decent following thanks to opening slots for such acts as ZZ Top. Yet Jon Bon Jovi wasn't particularly happy with the way things were going.

"I certainly thought it was time for a change," he says. "We had done two records prior, but I wasn't in love with either one. At that point we were being touted as the best-kept secret in rock 'n' roll, but we couldn't capture it on vinyl."

What impressed Jon Bon Jovi was an album by Los Angeles–based hard-rock band Black 'N Blue. "I liked the production on their album," he says. "It had great background vocal tricks." Bon Jovi's fortunes would change, thanks to John Kalodner, an A&R executive for Geffen Records. He hooked Bon Jovi up with producer Bruce Fairbairn, who had worked on the Black N' Blue album.

The band headed to Fairbairn's home base at Little Mountain Sound Studios in Vancouver, British Columbia, to record Slippery When Wet. "Bruce let us play," says Jon Bon Jovi. "He didn't tell us how to play. He just let us be ourselves."

Another important factor contributing to Bon Jovi's success was songwriter Desmond Child. Initially, Bon Jovi and Sambora thought they would try their hand at songwriting for other artists. Mercury A&R man Derek Shulman suggested they work with Child, who had scored a hit with Kiss called "I Was Made For Loving You."

"We got together to write a song for Loverboy," Jon Bon Jovi says. "We wrote 'You Give Love a Bad Name,' and I said, 'I think we'll keep that one for ourselves.' "

It turned out to be a good call, as the track was released as the first single from Slippery When Wet. It received heavy airplay on album rock stations before crossing over to top 40.

Slippery When Wet hit the top in its seventh week on the chart but was quickly displaced by such heavy hitters as Boston [see 307] and fellow New Jerseyite Bruce Springsteen [see 308]. "You Give Love a Bad Name" became the band's first Number One single on November 29, 1986.

The album returned to the Number One position for a second time in January for seven more weeks, as it spawned the group's second Number One single, "Livin' on a Prayer."

On that track, Sambora turned to a talk box to get the guitar effect he was after. "We tried a wah-wah, but that didn't work," Bon Jovi says. "So we tried a talk box. It worked on Frampton Comes Alive! [see 213], and Richie knew how to play it really well. And it worked. It was just different enough."

THE TOP FIVE
Week of October 25, 1986

1. **Slippery When Wet**
   Bon Jovi

2. **Fore!**
   Huey Lewis and the News

3. **Third Stage**
   Boston

4. **Top Gun**
   Soundtrack

5. **Dancing on the Ceiling**
   Lionel Richie

Producer: Tom Scholz

Track listing: Amanda / We're Ready / The Launch / Cool the Engines / My Destination / A New World / To Be a Man / I Think I Like It / Can'tcha Say / Still in Love / Hollyann

November 1, 1986
4 weeks

Boston hit paydirt with its 1976 self-titled debut, and the group's follow-up, *Don't Look Back* [see 230], came two years later. But anyone who was waiting for the third Boston album had a long wait in store for them—it took *eight years* to complete *Third Stage*.

"So many things were happening," says Boston leader and guitarist Tom Scholz. "There was a huge lawsuit with CBS and problems with managers. But mostly it just took a long time to get the music on tape the way I liked it."

Scholz's perfectionist work habits, and the resultant slow pace of his work on *Third Stage,* began to frustrate his record label. CBS-owned Epic Records, anxious to capitalize on the band's success and tired of waiting for the follow-up, filed a $20 million lawsuit, alleging breach of contract on the band's five-album, 10-year pact. The label also cut off the band's royalties from its first two albums. "They basically cut off the money," says Scholz, "which made it very difficult to continue working on the third album."

Frustrated by his lack of progress in the studio and the legal hassles, Scholz channeled his energies into a new pro-ject: developing a sandwich-sized guitar amplifier called the Rockman. "That became a serious venture as I got into it, because I realized that might be the only way that I might be able to make the money to finish the record."

The legal wrangling continued with Scholz filing a countersuit and preparing to move Boston to MCA Records. CBS then asked for an injunction to prevent Boston from signing with another label, but a U.S. District Court judge denied the request, clearing the way for Boston to sign with MCA. From that point, it would take the group "only" another two years to complete the album.

Although several other musicians were credited on the album, Scholz says, "*Third Stage* was done the same way all the Boston albums have been done, which was basically me overdub-bing the instruments and Brad Delp on the vocals. The reason why the sound is consistent is that I end up playing most of the parts."

Anyone concerned that the eight-year layoff might have significantly changed Boston's sound need not have worried. Although Scholz used new technology, including his Rockman amplifier, Boston continued to sound basically the same. Yet Scholz says the extra effort on *Third Stage* paid off. "I did feel much better about the sound quality on *Third Stage* compared to the first two albums," he says. "I felt that I finally learned how to make a record sound the way I wanted it to."

Recorded at Scholz's basement Hide-away Studio in a suburb of Boston, *Third Stage* was 12,000 hours of studio time in the making. Indeed, some tracks were recorded as early as 1980, while Scholz worked on the album-closer "Hollyann" during 1980, 1981, 1982, 1984, and 1985.

The power ballad "Amanda," which would go on to become Boston's first Number One single, was the first track recorded for the album. "That song fell together very quickly and very easily. There was one quick demo made of it and then we went straight to master tape. In fact, that song made me extremely optimistic in 1981, about the prospects of completing an album fairly quickly." While those hopes would soon be dashed, *Third Stage* nonetheless flew up the charts upon its eventual release. In its third week on the charts, *Third Stage* hit Number One, giving Boston its second consecutive Number One album—even if it took a bit longer than anyone had anticipated.

THE TOP FIVE
Week of November 1, 1986

1. **Third Stage**
   Boston

2. **Slippery When Wet**
   Bon Jovi

3. **Fore!**
   Huey Lewis and the News

4. **Top Gun**
   Soundtrack

5. **Break Every Rule**
   Tina Turner

308 Bruce Springsteen & the E Street Band Live/1975–85 COLUMBIA 40558
BRUCE SPRINGSTEEN & THE E STREET BAND

Producers: Bruce Springsteen, Jon Landau, and Chuck Plotkin

Track listing: Thunder Road / Adam Raised a Cain / Spirit in the Night / 4th of July, Asbury Park (Sandy) / Paradise by the "C" / Fire / Growin' Up / It's Hard to Be a Saint in the City / Backstreets / Rosalita (Come Out Tonight) / Raise Your Hand / Hungry Heart / Two Hearts / Cadillac Ranch / You Can Look (But You Better Not Touch) / Independence Day / Badlands / Because the Night / Candy's Room / Darkness on the Edge of Town / Racing in the Street / This Land Is Your Land / Nebraska / Johnny 99 / Reason to Believe / Born in the U.S.A. / Seeds / The River / War / Darlington County / Working on the Highway / The Promised Land / Cover Me / I'm on Fire / Bobby Jean / My Hometown / Born to Run / No Surrender / Tenth Avenue Freeze-Out / Jersey Girl

November 29, 1986
7 weeks

From the onset of his career, Bruce Springsteen was known for his marathon live performances. As his career progressed, the concerts would often stretch to four or five hours long. With Springsteen's popularity reaching new heights following the massive success of *Born in the U.S.A.*, a live album seemed like a natural. Yet for Springsteen and the E Street Band, a single- or double-disc set simply wouldn't do. To truly capture the essence of a Springsteen concert and provide an adequate sampling of his impressive body of work, it was decided that Springsteen's live album would be a sprawling five-LP set.

The album began to take shape in November 1985, when Springsteen received a four-song cassette along with a note from his manager/co-producer Jon Landau. The tape contained live versions of the Springsteen originals "Born in the U.S.A.," "Seeds," and "The River," and his interpretation of the Edwin Starr hit "War." Landau's note suggested the possibility of a live album.

After months of listening to tapes, 40 songs were chosen from concerts ranging from intimate club dates, such as 1975 and 1978 engagements at the Roxy in Hollywood, to stands at mammoth outdoor stadiums like Giants Stadium and the Los Angeles Coliseum in 1985.

Aside from such obvious choices and early favorites as "Born to Run," "Rosalita (Come Out Tonight)," and "Backstreets," *Live/1975–85* marked the first time that such Springsteen-penned hits as "Fire" (a number two hit for the Pointer Sisters in 1979) and "Because the Night" (a top 20 hit for co-writer Patti Smith in 1978) had appeared on a Springsteen album.

Springsteen also tipped his hat to some other artists, covering Eddie Floyd's "Raise Your Hand," Woody Guthrie's "This Land Is Your Land," Tom Waits's "Jersey Girl," and "War."

E Street Band drummer Max Weinberg recalls performing the latter track on September 30, 1985, at the L.A. Coliseum: "Right before the show Bruce called us into his dressing room and he said he wanted to do 'War.' We all knew the tune, so we went out and rehearsed it very briefly because we had never played it before in concert." Unbeknownst to the band, Springsteen had prepared a spoken prologue to the song. "He came back to me and said, 'Just watch my hand.' He went through this long, incredibly beautiful and touch-ing monologue and he started to raise his hand. When he brought his hand down, everybody in the E Street Band hit that downbeat perfectly. It was awesome."

The version of "Born to Run" on *Live/1975–85* was taken from a 1985 show at Giants Stadium, rather than from a '70s club date, a decision that was fine with Weinberg. "Most everything we played with equal passion, but much more precision," he says. "In the early days, we had a lot of energy and passion, but some of us didn't have as much precision as we would have liked."

Upon its release, *Bruce Springsteen & the E Street Band Live/1975–85* became Springsteen's first album to debut at the top, as well as the first album to do so since Stevie Wonder's *Songs in the Key of Life* in 1976 [see 219]. It also became the first five-record set ever to hit Number One—the last two-LP album to hit the summit had been Springsteen's *The River* [see 253].

THE TOP FIVE
Week of November 29, 1986

1. **Bruce Springsteen & the E Street Band Live/1975–85**
   Bruce Springsteen & the E Street Band

2. **Third Stage**
   Boston

3. **Slippery When Wet**
   Bon Jovi

4. **Fore!**
   Huey Lewis and the News

5. **Dancing on the Ceiling**
   Lionel Richie

COLUMNS 40238 **Licensed to III**
BEASTIE BOYS
309

Producers: Rick Rubin, Beastie Boys

Track listing: Rhymin & Stealin / The New Style / She's Crafty / Posse in Effect / Slow Ride / Girls / Fight for Your Right / No Sleep Till Brooklyn / Paul Revere / Hold It Now, Hit It / Brass Monkey / Slow and Low / Time to Get Ill

March 7, 1987
7 weeks

Who could have guessed that it would take three white punks to bring rap music to the top of the album chart? While it was certainly nothing new for white artists to achieve popular status with a form of music founded in the African-American community—Bill Haley's cover of Big Joe Turner's "Shake, Rattle and Roll," the 1955 song frequently cited as the first rock 'n' roll record, is a prime example—but the sudden rise of the Beastie Boys was particularly unusual.

The Beastie Boys formed in August 1981 to play a party for bass player Adam Yauch's 17th birthday. Yauch had heard the Los Angeles hardcore punk band Black Flag and found punk's do-it-yourself ethic appealing. After a few breakups, reunions, personnel changes, and the release of the hardcore *Polly Wog Stew* EP, the Beasties suddenly became enamored with the world of hip-hop. Their "Cookie Puss" 12-inch

single reflected this new passion, combining a prank phone call to a Carvel ice cream store with hip-hop beats. Eventually the band traded in their instruments for mics and a turntable, as Yauch, Mike Diamond, and Adam Horovitz became MCA, Mike D., and King Ad-Rock, respectively.

"If you're not gonna have as much equipment as AC/DC, you really shouldn't play instruments," Mike D. said at the time. "When we can be as rich as them and have that kind of stage show, we'll play instruments." Actually, rap and punk shared certain sensibilities. "Punk rockers have really funny hairdos," said Mike D. "And homeboys have really funny hats," added Ad-Rock.

With the Beastie Boys enjoying acceptance in the rap community, the band was soon signed to Rush Productions by manager Russell Simmons, whose brother Joseph was the "Run" in Run-D.M.C. By 1984, Simmons and Beastie DJ Rick Rubin had started Def Jam Records, with the Beasties and rapper LL Cool J among the first signings.

The Beasties recorded *Licensed to III* on and off during 1985 while completing tours as a support act for the likes of Madonna [see 203] and Run-D.M.C. Meanwhile, Columbia Records picked up Def Jam for distribution, but the major label didn't expect much from the Beastie Boys. "They looked at us as the curse of the whole deal," says Mike D.

On *Licensed to III*, the band sampled

everything from Led Zeppelin [see 118], the Clash, and War [see 152] to the theme from *Mr. Ed*. But there were also live instruments. "No Sleep Till Brooklyn" featured Slayer's Kerry King on guitar, while Rubin and Ad-Rock played guitar on the rap 'n' roll teen anthem "Fight for Your Right," which reached number seven on the Hot 100.

Although the Beasties' rapped their way into the hearts of millions of teens, their sometimes sexist, violent, and stupid lyrics outraged others. Even Mike D. finds some of *Licensed To III* a bit hard to swallow: "There are some things that I think are really fly and still stand up and there are songs that I am completely embarrassed to be involved with."

THE TOP FIVE
Week of March 7, 1987

1. **Licensed to III**
   Beastie Boys

2. **Slippery When Wet**
   Bon Jovi

3. **The Way It Is**
   Bruce Hornsby & the Range

4. **Invisible Touch**
   Genesis

5. **Control**
   Janet Jackson

310 The Joshua Tree ISLAND 90581
U2

Producers: Daniel Lanois and Brian Eno

Track listing: Where the Streets Have No Name / I Still Haven't Found What I'm Looking For / With or Without You / Bullet the Blue Sky / Running to Stand Still / Red Hill Mining Town / In God's Country / Trip Through Your Wires / One Tree Hill / Exit / Mothers of the Disappeared

April 25, 1987
9 weeks

Prior to 1987, Ireland's U2 was considered one of the most important rock acts of the '80s, despite the fact that they had yet to break into the top 10 of the Top Pop Albums chart. The band's highest-charting albums to that date had been 1983's *War* and 1984's *The Unforgettable Fire*, both of which had reached number 12.

It was a measure of U2's importance that the band was one of the star attractions of Amnesty International's Conspiracy of Hope tour, which included such star talent as Sting [see 276], Peter Gabriel, Lou Reed, Bryan Adams [see 291], Joan Baez, and Jackson Browne [see 250]. "We kind of got started on *The Joshua Tree*, but we had already committed to the Conspiracy of Hope tour, so we had to stop halfway through," says bassist Adam Clayton. Although the tour put more stress on the band, it turned out to be a blessing in disguise. "It was good for us, because we wanted to try this new material and we wanted [the album] to be performance-based," says Clayton.

The Conspiracy of Hope tour ran from June 4 to June 15, 1986. Once it was completed, the members of U2—singer Paul "Bono" Hewson, guitarist Dave "The Edge" Evans, drummer Larry Mullen Jr., and Clayton—resumed the recording of their fifth full-length album at a number of different locations, including Clayton's future home in Dublin. "Rather than use a commercial studio, we set up a studio in a room that we liked the sound of, and we made the room work for us," he says.

For the second consecutive studio album, Daniel Lanois and Brian Eno were enlisted as producers, and the sessions had a loose feel. "There was always someone playing an instrument, and everyone else just kind of joined in as they saw fit, including Danny and Brian," says Clayton. "It seemed that the division of control room and playing room didn't exist."

The album would capture U2 at a significant point in the band's career, as they were beginning to jell both instrumentally and lyrically. " 'Bullet the Blue Sky' was a song that definitely realized the potential of where Edge was going as a guitar player," says Clayton. "And lyrically, it was a real milestone for Bono. He really managed to write about some tough topics in a very clear way."

Some of Bono's finest lyrics were featured on the haunting ballad "With or Without You," the soul-searching "Still Haven't Found What I'm Looking For," and the heartfelt "One Tree Hill," dedicated to the late U2 roadie Greg Carroll, who had died in a motorcycle accident. Other standouts included the blis-

tering "Bullet the Blue Sky" and "Mothers of the Disappeared."

Says Clayton, "We all kind of felt like it was going to be a breakthrough record. We were quite clear about the album we wanted to make. We had this image of a spiritual desert, which was what we felt America had become in the mid-'80s. Greed and money was the big issue. We wanted to step back from that and look at the spirituality of the heart."

America heard U2's message, or at least its music, loud and clear. *The Joshua Tree* entered the chart at number seven on April 4, 1987. Three weeks later, the album hit the top. In the following months, U2 scored its highest-charting singles, as both "With or Without You" and "I Still Haven't Found What I'm Looking For" topped the Hot 100.

THE TOP FIVE
Week of April 25, 1987

1. **The Joshua Tree**
   U2

2. **Licensed to III**
   Beastie Boys

3. **Slippery When Wet**
   Bon Jovi

4. **Look What the Cat Dragged In**
   Poison

5. **Graceland**
   Paul Simon

ARISTA 8405 **Whitney**
WHITNEY HOUSTON

Ulvaeus of Abba and Tim Rice [see 129 and 395]. Houston recorded the song as a duet with her mother, Cissy. "That was a really touching moment, to see Whitney sing with her mother," Walden says. "They really, truly love each other."

Walden wasn't as impressed, initially, with "I Wanna Dance with Somebody (Who Loves Me)." He says the song, written by George Merrill and Shannon Rubicam, was "too pop and almost kind of country-sounding. The whole trick was to figure out how to make it black and more R&B, because I wanted her to keep her fans at black radio." Using a production technique that he describes as "like a black Phil Spector," Walden succeeded in making the cut groove.

On June 27, 1987, the song became Houston's fourth consecutive Number One single (as well as Walden's third Number One production in less than three months—he had also produced Starship's "Nothing's Gonna Stop Us Now" and Aretha Franklin and George Michael's "I Knew You Were Waiting [For Me]"). The success of "I Wanna Dance with Somebody (Who Loves Me)" also helped *Whitney* debut at Number One, making it the first album by a female artist ever to bow at the pole position.

While Houston's second album couldn't match the duration of her debut's reign at Number One, it did top the first album in another category. *Whitney* went on to yield three more Number One hits—"Didn't We Almost Have It All," "So Emotional," and "Where Do Broken Hearts Go"—giving Houston seven consecutive chart-topping singles. *Whitney Houston* had spawned the first three, but *Whitney* spun off four.

Producers: Narada Michael Walden, Jellybean, Michael Masser, and Kashif

Track listing: I Wanna Dance with Somebody (Who Loves Me) / Just the Lonely Talking Again / Love Will Save the Day / Didn't We Almost Have It All / So Emotional / Where You Are / Love Is a Contact Sport / You're Still My Man / For the Love of You / Where Do Broken Hearts Go / I Know Him So Well

June 27, 1987
11 weeks

Songwriter/producer Narada Michael Walden first worked with Whitney Houston on the track "How Will I Know," featured on her debut album, *Whitney Houston*. The song went on to become Houston's second Number One single, but after Walden cut the track, Houston wasn't as receptive as Walden had hoped. "When I finished putting the song together, I told I her I would like to be friends with her and asked if we could exchange phone numbers, but she said no," Walden recalls. "She didn't want to give me her phone number."

In spite of the rejection, Walden wasn't put off by Houston. "I took it in stride," he says. "She was a top model who had guys hit on her all the time, so she didn't want to give out her phone number." Walden, however, did receive a phone call from Arista president Clive Davis, who asked him to work with Houston on her second album.

"Clive gave me five songs to do, so I just did them really quick," says Walden. The producer had been impressed by Houston's professionalism when they'd worked together on "How Will I Know," and Houston was even more impressive on the second meeting. "I asked Whitney if she was nervous about doing the second album, because the first album was so successful. She said, 'No, if they liked me the first time, they'll like me again.' "

Walden recorded Houston's vocals fairly quickly. "Sometimes she didn't know the songs, so it may have taken her a day to sing it through a bunch of times to learn it, but then on the next day, she would knock things out in one or two takes."

A particular highlight for Walden was "I Know Him So Well," a song written by Benny Andersson and Bjorn

---

THE TOP FIVE
Week of June 27, 1987

1. **Whitney**
   Whitney Houston

2. **Girls, Girls, Girls**
   Motley Crue

3. **The Joshua Tree**
   U2

4. **Whitesnake**
   Whitesnake

5. **Slippery When Wet**
   Bon Jovi

312 La Bamba SLASH 25605
SOUNDTRACK

Lou Diamond Pillips (center) in *La Bamba.*

Executive Producers: Taylor Hackford and Joel Sill

Track listing: La Bamba [Los Lobos] / Come On, Let's Go / Ooh! My Head / We Belong Together / Framed / Donna / Lonely Teardrops [Howard Huntsberry] / Crying, Waiting, Hoping [Marshall Crenshaw] / Summertime Blues [Brian Setzer] / Who Do You Love [Bo Diddley] / Charlena [Los Lobos] / Goodnight My Love

September 12, 1987
2 weeks

Ritchie Valens never had a Number One album. In fact, his self-titled debut album wasn't even released until a few months after his life was cut tragically short in the February 3, 1959, plane crash that also claimed the lives of Buddy Holly and the Big Bopper. Yet Valens's influence lived well beyond his 17 years.

One of the bands that was affected by the Valens legacy was Los Lobos, an East Los Angeles quintet that had been together for nearly a decade before their traditional Mexican sounds became the toast of the L.A. club scene in 1981. Even before the members of Los Lobos knew of Valens, they were well aware of "La Bamba," a traditional song the band often heard and performed acoustically at weddings. "Later on," says Los Lobos singer/guitarist David Hidalgo, "We

looked into his life a little and found out how young he was and how short his career was. We found out he was from California, and he became a more important figure in our lives."

Yet Valens became even more important to Los Lobos when their friend, director Luis Valdez, wrote a screenplay based on Valens's life. "He knew we were doing some of Ritchie's material in our live set, so he asked us to do the music," Hidalgo says.

At the time, Los Lobos were adding the finishing touches to their latest album, *By the Light of the Moon,* "so we had to run back and forth between studios," says Hidalgo. While the rest of Los Lobos—Ceasar Rosas, Conrad Lozano, Louie Perez, and Steve Berlin—had little trouble knocking out the Valens covers, the sessions weren't as easy for Hidalgo. "For me, some of it was a bit of a challenge to sing because of the fact that it was going into a film. I had to almost act the songs out. I had to overdo it in a way," he says.

And, after Hidalgo's vocals were cut, they had to be sped up to make him sound like the 17-year-old Valens. When the band saw a final print of the film and heard Hidalgo's sped-up vocals coming out of the mouth of the film's star Lou Diamond Phillips, they couldn't help but laugh. "I think overall the film worked out well, but for me, knowing that I did the vocals and hearing my voice coming out of Lou Diamond

Phillips's face was funny," he says.

The success of the film and the soundtrack catapulted the critically acclaimed act into the mainstream. Los Lobos's version of "La Bamba" hit Number One on the Hot 100 on August 29, 1987, and held on for three weeks, making *La Bamba* the first film to have both its soundtrack album and its title song simultaneously hold the Number One slots since the *Flashdance* album and its title track had turned the trick in 1983 [see 275].

"The only regret about the success of *La Bamba* is that it kind of overshadowed our own material," Hidalgo says. "But at the same time, it got us out in front of a lot of people, so it was a positive thing."

THE TOP FIVE
Week of September 12, 1987

1. **La Bamba**
   Soundtrack

2. **Whitney**
   Whitney Houston

3. **Whitesnake**
   Whitesnake

4. **Hysteria**
   Def Leppard

5. **Bad Animals**
   Heart

EPIC 40600

Bad

MICHAEL JACKSON

313

Producer: Quincy Jones

Track listing: *Bad / The Way You Make Me Feel / Speed Demon / Liberian Girl / Just Good Friends / Another Part of Me / Man in the Mirror / I Just Can't Stop Loving You / Dirty Diana / Smooth Criminal*

September 26, 1987
6 weeks

Thriller [see 274] wasn't just a hard album to follow—it was nearly impossible. Nevertheless, when Michael Jackson went to work on his next album in the summer of 1986, he had his sights set on eclipsing *Thriller*, which had gone on to sell more than 40 million copies worldwide, making it the top-selling album of all time.

Initially, Jackson went to work on *Bad* without the assistance of producer Quincy Jones, who took time off from work after producing the film *The Color Purple*. "I went to Tahiti for a vacation and Michael started working on the new album with arranger John Barnes," says Jones. "That was the first time that I asked Michael to write the whole album." Jackson took the challenge seriously, coming up with 66 songs. "Eventually we boiled it down to 33, and then down to 10," says Jones.

Unlike *Thriller*, the recording of *Bad* was an extremely lengthy process, lasting 14 months. The album featured eight songs written by Jackson, including the title track, "The Way You Make Me Feel," "I Just Can't Stop Loving You," and "Dirty Diana." "Just Good Friends," which was recorded as a duet featuring Jackson and Stevie Wonder [see 219], was written by Terry Britten

and Graham Lyle, the team responsible for Tina Turner's "What's Love Got to Do with It." "Man in the Mirror" was a collaboration between Siedah Garrett and Glen Ballard, both of whom were signed to Jones's publishing company.

A few of the album's songs were written with superstar guests in mind. "'Bad' was originally written as a vehicle for Michael to do a duet with Prince [see 288]," says Jones. "It was a real confrontation song and it would have been very dramatic. But Prince didn't want to do it. He said, 'It would be just as good without me.'"

"I Just Can't Stop Loving You" was also initially set as a superstar duet. "We talked about having Barbra Streisand [see 295] or Whitney Houston [see 298], but I think it worked out just the way it was supposed to." It was the relatively unknown Garrett, whose voice strongly resembles Jackson's, who was eventually recruited as Jackson's singing partner. "They have the same register," says Jones. "It's

amazing, sometimes I couldn't tell the difference between their voices."

As was the case with *Thriller*, Jackson's elaborate music videos dominated the MTV airwaves and drove album sales. The video clip for the title track was directed by Jones's friend Martin Scorsese. "I called Marty, because he's one of my favorite directors," says Jones. "He was in the editing room doing *The Color of Money*. The timing was just right and he agreed to do it."

The combination of heavy airplay on radio and MTV once again made Jackson nearly unavoidable. *Bad* couldn't match the awesome sales of *Thriller*, but the album did manage to top its predecessor in one sense: Both "I Just Can't Stop Loving You" and "Bad" went on to top the Hot 100, as did "The Way You Make Me Feel," "Man in the Mirror," and "Dirty Diana." The feat made *Bad* the first album to spawn *five* Number One singles, an accomplishment not even *Thriller* could match.

THE TOP FIVE
Week of September 26, 1987

1. **Bad**
   Michael Jackson

2. **La Bamba**
   Soundtrack

3. **Whitney**
   Whitney Houston

4. **Whitesnake**
   Whitesnake

5. **Hysteria**
   Def Leppard

314 Tunnel of Love COLUMBIA 40999
BRUCE SPRINGSTEEN

Producers: Bruce Springsteen, Jon Landau, and Chuck Plotkin

Track listing: Ain't Got You / Tougher Than the Rest / All That Heaven Will Allow / Spare Parts / Cautious Man / Walk Like a Man / Tunnel of Love / Two Faces / Brilliant Disguise / One Step Up / When You're Alone / Valentine's Day

November 7, 1987
1 week

Following the success of *The River* [see 253], Bruce Springsteen retreated to his home studio to record the dark and introspective *Nebraska*. Approximately five years later, Springsteen made a similar retreat, moving from the bombastic anthems of *Born in the U.S.A.* [see 281] to the more personal and reflective songwriting style of *Tunnel of Love*. Even before its release, the album created a stir with longtime fans, as word spread that *Tunnel of Love* would not be a Springsteen album with the E Street Band, but rather a Springsteen solo album with various E Streeters providing occasional accompaniment on some of the tracks. Not one song featured the full band lineup.

Drummer Max Weinberg was the E Street Band member who appeared the most on *Tunnel of Love*, playing on eight of the album's 12 tracks. "I got a call from Bruce in February 1987. He was in his home in New Jersey," says Weinberg. "He said that he was making these tapes and asked me if I could come over and put some drums on." Springsteen had recorded demo versions of the tracks with a drum machine. "I really enjoyed being on that record, because I got to work with just Bruce, the engineer Toby Scott, and Chuck Plotkin for two or three months straight," says Weinberg. "Before, it had always been in a group situation with 12 people around."

For both Springsteen and Weinberg, the *Tunnel of Love* sessions marked a new way of recording an album. "I basically replaced all the pre-recorded [drum machine] tracks with real drums.

It was Bruce's first record that he had done that way and he was really having a great time and I was having a terrific time." The stark arrangements didn't call for a whole lot of drumming from Weinberg. "It was just little sound effects and percussion stuff here and there," he says. Most of the album was recorded in Springsteen's garage in New Jersey, except for "One Step Up," which was cut at A&M Studios in Hollywood.

Lyrically, *Tunnel of Love*, as its title suggests, delved into the sometimes dark recesses of human relationships. The album's songs would take on added meaning in the years to come, as Springsteen's four-year marriage to actress/model Julianne Phillips fell apart in 1989. Fittingly, his future wife and mother of his children, E Street Band member Patti Scialfa, is the lone voice backing Springsteen on the track "One Step Up."

In its third week on the chart, *Tunnel of Love* became the fourth chart-topper of Springsteen's career, making him the only artist to rack up a quartet of Number One albums in the '80s.

THE TOP FIVE
Week of November 7, 1987

1. **Tunnel of Love**
   Bruce Springsteen

2. **Bad**
   Michael Jackson

3. **Dirty Dancing**
   Soundtrack

4. **Whitesnake**
   Whitesnake

5. **A Momentary Lapse of Reason**
   Pink Floyd

RCA 6408 **Dirty Dancing**
SOUNDTRACK

315

Patrick Swayze and Jennifer Grey in *Dirty Dancing*.

Executive producer: Jimmy Ienner

Track listing: "(I've Had) the Time of My Life" [Bill Medley and Jennifer Warnes] / "Be My Baby" [The Ronettes] / "She's Like the Wind" [Patrick Swayze] / "Hungry Eyes" [Eric Carmen] / "Stay" [Maurice Williams and the Zodiacs] / "Yes" [Merry Clayton] / "You Don't Own Me" [The Blow Monkeys] / "Hey Baby" [Bruce Channel] / "Overload" [Zappacosta] / "Love Is Strange" [Mickey and Sylvia] / "Where Are You Tonight" [Tom Johnston] / "In the Still of the Night" [The Five Satins]

November 14, 1987
18 weeks (nonconsecutive)

"A lot of people wanted me committed. They were picking out rooms with little flowers." Those are the words of record executive Jimmy Ienner, recalling how some of his cohorts reacted to the concept that would make *Dirty Dancing* one of the biggest soundtrack hits of the '80s, second only to Prince's *Purple Rain*.

Ienner's concept was to find singers with voices that mirrored the film's lead characters portrayed by Patrick Swayze and Jennifer Grey. His choice of the Righteous Brothers' Bill Medley and singer-songwriter Jennifer Warnes was seen by some as less than righteous, but Ienner was certain it would work. "Bill had an emotional voice like the Johnny

character, and Jennifer had a voice that mirrored Baby," Ienner says. The pair would sing a duet on "(I've Had) The Time of My Life," the hit single that would help propel *Dirty Dancing* to the top of the album chart.

Yet it wasn't easy for Ienner to convince Medley to take part in the project. The singer had just come off a duet with Gladys Knight that had flopped. "Telling people they should get involved in something called *Dirty Dancing* was not easy," he admits.

The Medley–Warnes duet was only part of the *Dirty Dancing* phenomenon. The album also spawned hits by Eric Carmen and the film's male lead, Swayze. Ienner and Carmen had a relationship dating back to the early '70s, when Ienner had helped the Carmen-fronted Raspberries land a recording contract with Capitol Records. "Some of the film people wanted a larger name," Ienner admits. Yet Ienner stuck by his old friend and was rewarded for his loyalty, as "Hungry Eyes" climbed to number four, becoming Carmen's biggest hit since "All By Myself" made number two in 1975.

Swayze's musical contribution, which also featured singer Wendy Fraser, came as a bit of a surprise. "I got a call from the set," Ienner recalls. "Patrick just presented this demo, I heard it, and I loved it. We decided we should really try to fit it in."

Aside from the new material, *Dirty Dancing* also featured several classic sides from the late '50s and early '60s,

including the Ronettes' "Be My Baby," Bruce Channel's "Hey Baby," Mickey and Sylvia's "Love Is Strange," and the Five Satins' "In the Still of the Night."

Ienner says the album was so successful because of emotional impact tied into the film: "If you look at the hits, they all are from a specific place and time in the movie, so you relive those moments when you hear them."

Dirty Dancing was so successful that RCA released *More Dirty Dancing* less than a year later. The sequel peaked at number three. "People really had a thirst for it and wanted those other cuts," Ienner says. "This was an album that probably deserved to be a double album from the get-go."

THE TOP FIVE
Week of November 14, 1987

1. **Dirty Dancing**
   Soundtrack

2. **Tunnel of Love**
   Bruce Springsteen

3. **Bad**
   Michael Jackson

4. **Whitesnake**
   Whitesnake

5. **A Momentary Laspe of Reason**
   Pink Floyd

316 Faith COLUMBIA 40867
GEORGE MICHAEL

Producer: George Michael

Track listing: Faith / Father Figure / I Want Your Sex / One More Try / Hard Day / Hand to Mouth / Look at Your Hands / Monkey / Kissing a Fool

January 16, 1988
12 weeks (nonconsecutive)

After the break-up of Wham!, George Michael had already begun to establish himself as a solo star. In early 1987, he recorded "I Knew You Were Waiting (For Me)," a duet with legendary R&B diva Aretha Franklin. The single went to Number One on both sides of the Atlantic and would provide adequate momentum for the release of Michael's first solo album later that year.

The song "Faith," and much of the album, was recorded at Puk Studios in Denmark. "George wanted to do this acoustic guitar thing, but the only acoustic guitar that was around was this horrible aluminum-body guitar that [the British punk group] the Damned had left there," says engineer Chris Porter. A phone call was placed to have another acoustic guitar delivered to the studio, but by the time it arrived, the track had already been recorded. "So that's what you hear, and it became the signature sound of the record," says Porter. "He said he wanted a Bo Diddley kind of rhythm and he wanted everything stark and dry."

Also recorded during the sessions was "I Want Your Sex." The squelching sound heard throughout the track was the result of an accident, says Porter. "We were experimenting, trying to tie a bunch of machines together, and when we started the sequencer, this strange squelching sound came out." It was the song's lyrics, however, rather than its sound, that created a stir. "Since the AIDS issue was looming large, George felt it was important to say it was about monogamy," Porter says. To drive the point home, "Monogamy" was spelled out on the back of Michael's girlfriend in the video clip.

While working on Faith, Porter noticed once again that Michael's talent continued to grow. "I was completely knocked out by the vocal on 'One More Try,' " he says. "I really started to see what a good soul singer he was becoming. I think that track had a lot to do with the album's success on the R&B charts, rather than a lot of the poppier stuff."

"I Want Your Sex," which was released prior to the album and featured on the soundtrack of Beverly Hills Cop II, peaked at number two, yet there was no stopping "Faith." On December 12, 1987, the song became Michael's first Number One solo single. A little more than a month later, Michael also had his first Number One solo album.

Faith went on to yield three more chart-toppers— "Father Figure," "One More Try," and "Monkey"—and established Michael as a superstar. It also laid to rest Michael's teeny-bopper image from the Wham! days.

"We had no idea the album would sell as well as it did," says Porter, "but we did know that it would make people see him in a different light."

THE TOP FIVE
Week of January 16, 1988

1. **Faith**
   George Michael

2. **Dirty Dancing**
   Soundtrack

3. **Tiffany**
   Tiffany

4. **Bad**
   Michael Jackson

5. **Whitesnake**
   Whitesnake

sound and a Lone Justice kind of a sound with a little country influence, and I was just a happy camper," Tiffany says. "Then he found 'I Think We're Alone Now.' He did the track and he gave it to me and I said, 'This isn't really what I want to do.' I took it home and played it for my friends and they liked it."

At Tobin's urging, Tiffany also recorded a cover of the Beatles' "I Saw Her Standing There," retitled "I Saw Him Standing There." Says Tiffany, "George loved the Beatles, but at the time I was not a big Beatles fan. George brought me the track and I gave him a hard time, because I really didn't want to do it. It wasn't the sound that I wanted, but in the end I went ahead and did it anyway."

The one track that Tiffany did like was the ballad "Could've Been." Says Tiffany, "The lyrics are so meaningful and could mean so many different things to so many different people. I like the way I sang on that record. I can feel the emotion in that song."

Even if Tiffany didn't necessarily like the song, Tobin's choice of "I Think We're Alone Now," originally recorded by Tommy James, ended up being a winner. With help from Tiffany's novel tour of shopping malls, the single hit the top of the Hot 100 on November 7, 1987.

Tiffany hit the summit in its 18th week on the Top Pop Albums chart. Two weeks later, she scored her second Number One single with "Could've Been."

The gap between *Little Stevie Wonder/The 12 Year Old Genius* and *Tiffany* had been 25 years, but it would take only a bit over a year for the next Number One album from a teenager [see 327].

Producer: George E. Tobin

Track listing: Should've Been Me / Danny / Spanish Eyes / Feelings of Forever / Kid on a Corner / I Saw Him Standing There / Johnny's Got the Inside Moves / Promises Made / I Think We're Alone Now / Could've Been

January 23, 1988
2 weeks

On January 23, 1988, a high school girl from Norwalk, California, simply known as Tiffany, made history when she became the first teenage girl in history to score a Number One album. The last teenager to have a Number One album was Stevie Wonder, whose *Little Stevie Wonder/The 12 Year Old Genius* [see 61], hit the summit in 1963, when the singer was 13. The only other teen to score a Number One album prior to Tiffany was Ricky Nelson, who was 17 when his *Ricky* topped the chart in 1958 [see 12].

Tiffany was a mere 12 years old when she met producer George Tobin while recording a demo at a San Fernando Valley studio. "I was singing country at that time," she says. "He started a relationship with me over the phone." Tiffany's parents were divorced, and her father did not want her to enter the music business. But once she moved into her mother's home, she was able to sign on with Tobin, and began cutting her debut album when she was just 14.

"In the beginning we just recorded after school," Tiffany says. "I would get out of school at about 3 P.M. and there would be a car waiting for me to take me to the studio, and I would get back home at about 8 P.M." However, as the project progressed, Tiffany sometimes pulled all-nighters working in the studio. "I'd have to skip my first and second periods in school. It was hard to still be in school and get semi-good grades, because the music was all I wanted to do."

Tiffany's own musical tastes leaned toward classic rock, Janis Joplin [see 130], Stevie Nicks [see 262], and the country-rock of the Los Angeles band Lone Justice, but Tobin, a big fan of '60s pop, had other ideas. "When I first started recording with George, we did some songs with a Stevie Nicks kind of a

THE TOP FIVE
Week of January 23, 1988

1. **Tiffany**
   Tiffany

2. **Faith**
   George Michael

3. **Dirty Dancing**
   Soundtrack

4. **Bad**
   Michael Jackson

5. **Whitesnake**
   Whitesnake

318 OU812 WARNER BROS. 25732
VAN HALEN

Producer: Donn Landee

Track listing: Mine All Mine / When It's Love/ A.F.U. (Naturally Wired) / Cabo Wabo / Source of Infection / Feels So Good / Finish What Ya Started / Black and Blue / Sucker in a 3 Piece

June 25, 1988
4 weeks

Anyone who doubted Van Halen's ability to carry on without David Lee Roth needed only to look at the success of 5150 [see 299], the band's first album with new lead singer Sammy Hagar. Following a lengthy stretch of touring, the group re-entered guitarist Eddie Van Halen's 5150 home studio to prove that the previous album had been no fluke.

Van Halen was also attempting to prove that despite their mainstream commercial success, they were still first and foremost a hard-rock act. Even before the band finished their eighth album, they were booked to headline the Monsters of Rock tour, which also featured such metal bands as the Scorpions, Dokken, Metallica [see 353], and Kingdom Come.

With the tour scheduled to start in early summer, Van Halen had to rush to finish the album, which would eventually bear the title OU812. "We really didn't have time to screw around," says Hagar,

who notes the album was completely self-produced, although the band did not take a production credit on the album (the credits said the album was "recorded by" longtime Van Halen associate Donn Landee). "It's an unfinished album, in my opinion," Hagar adds. "It didn't get mixed properly. It doesn't have any bottom end." The album was recorded and mixed in a mere three months.

Despite the rush, OU812 contained "When It's Love," the second-biggest hit single of the band's post-Roth career. "I remember flying down from my house in the Bay Area the day we were ready to start recording," Hagar says. "Eddie and Al [Van Halen] picked me up at the airport and played me the music for 'When It's Love' and I got goosebumps all over me. I wrote the lyrics that night. It was done almost instantly."

The album's moniker didn't come as quickly. The working title for the album was Bone. "It wasn't a sexual thing," Hagar says. "It was like, down to the bone, real stark and not produced, but we thought people would take it the wrong way." One day in the studio Hagar came in and wrote out the license plate–like phrase "OU812." Says Hagar, "Everyone laughed real hard and thought it was funny, so we went with it."

At that point, it really didn't matter what Van Halen called their albums, as the band continued on a roll. Aside

from "When It's Love," the album contained "Black and Blue" and "Finish What Ya Started," two other tracks that received a substantial amount of airplay.

"Cabo Wabo" didn't turn out to be a legitimate hit, but it would serve as the name of a nightclub the band would open in 1989 in the Mexican resort town of Cabo San Lucas. Hagar had been inspired to write the lyrics after witnessing a drunk man bounce off a barbed-wire fence during one of his visits to the resort town.

OU812 hit the pole position in its second week on the chart, a week less than it took 5150 to hit the top. Van Halen had made it two straight.

THE TOP FIVE
Week of June 25, 1988

1. **OU812**
   Van Halen

2. **Faith**
   George Michael

3. **Hysteria**
   Def Leppard

4. **Open Up and Say...Ahh!**
   Poison

5. **Dirty Dancing**
   Soundtrack

MERCURY 830675 # Hysteria
DEF LEPPARD

319

Producer: John "Mutt" Lange

Track listing: Women / Rocket / Animal / Love Bites / Pour Some Sugar on Me / Armageddon It / Gods of War / Don't Shoot Shotgun / Run Riot / Hysteria / Excitable / Love and Affection

July 23, 1988
6 weeks (nonconsecutive)

By 1984, a young five-piece British hard rock band called Def Leppard had arrived. *Pyromania*, the group's third album peaked at number two—only Michael Jackson's *Thriller* could keep it from the top spot—and spent 92 weeks on the chart, securing the band a position as one of the most popular rock acts in the world. "With *Pyromania* we set out to make our version of *Sgt. Pepper's*," says vocalist Joe Elliot. "We didn't achieve that, but we made a damn good rock record. With the next record, we attempted to take that a step further."

In their quest for sonic perfection, Def Leppard went through a number of different studios, a few producers, and spent four years making *Hysteria*. At first, in August 1984, the band attempted to work with Meat Loaf producer/songwriter Jim Steinman, but nothing from those sessions ever saw the light of day. "It was a complete mismatch. It was like going from a Rolls Royce to a bicycle," says Elliot, comparing the production styles of *Pyromania* producer John "Mutt" Lange and Steinman.

Then, on New Year's Eve 1984, drummer Rick Allen had his left arm severed in an auto accident. "We all went to visit him in the hospital and it was

such a traumatic thing. We figured if we just sat around and waited for him to get well, we'd all just start cracking up," says Elliot. "We figured the best way to get around it was to go back to work."

Following the accident, the band attempted to produce itself, as Allen recuperated, using the drum tracks that had been recorded with Steinman. In April 1975, Allen rejoined the band, using a custom electronic drum kit equipped with foot pedals, allowing him to drum one-handed. "It gave us a good lift when Rick came back," says Elliot.

By the summer of 1985, Lange was ready to work with the band again and the sessions proceeded. The turning point came when the band recorded "Animal." Says Elliot, "We wanted the vocal to be really attention-grabbing. I thought it would take a long time to record it, but I nailed it in two days, which for me is damned quick. That was a very inspiring moment. It gave me the confidence to carry on with the rest of the record."

Hysteria also marked a dramatic change in the way the members of Def Leppard wrote their songs. "Everyone always commented when we first started

out about how great our songs were," says Elliot. "But there was always an element of the songwriter missing." For much of *Hysteria*, the band wrote around Elliot's vocal lines, rather than "writing a piece of music and letting me scream over the top in whatever fashion I could muster."

The new writing style led to the creation of "Love Bites." For the ballad, the group borrowed the lyrics from another of its songs. (The original track, retitled "I Wanna Be Your Hero," was subsequently released on *Retro Active*, a 1993 album of rarities.)

Yet Def Leppard's troubles weren't over. In November 1986, Elliot came down with the mumps and spent nine days in bed, while Lange was hospitalized for three weeks in December after a car accident. The album was mixed in the spring of 1987 and finally released in August. *Hysteria* debuted at number 36 and took 49 weeks to hit the top, but for Elliot and Def Leppard it was worth the wait. "It was a nightmare to make, but I still enjoy listening to it today," he says. "I'd rather have it that way than have an album that I had a great time making, but I can't listen to."

THE TOP FIVE
Week of July 23, 1988

1. **Hysteria**
   Def Leppard

2. **OU812**
   Van Halen

3. **Dirty Dancing**
   Soundtrack

4. **Appetite for Destruction**
   Guns N' Roses

5. **Faith**
   George Michael

320 Appetite for Destruction GEFFEN 24148
GUNS N' ROSES

Producer: Mike Clink

Track listing: Welcome to the Jungle /
It's So Easy / Nightrain / Out ta Get
Me / Mr. Brownstone / Paradise City /
My Michelle / Think About You / Sweet
Child o' Mine / You're Crazy /
Anything Goes / Rocket Queen

August 6, 1988
5 weeks (nonconsecutive)

The Guns N' Roses saga isn't exactly an overnight success story. The roots of the band date back to 1982, when friends Bill Bailey and Jeff Isbell arrived in Los Angeles from Lafayette, Indiana. After gigging with a number of other hard-rock bands, the duo formed Guns N' Roses in March 1985, recruiting bassist Duff McKagan, a refugee of the Seattle punk scene. Guitarist Saul Hudson and drummer Steven Adler rounded out the group. By then, Bailey was known as W. Axl Rose, Isbell was Izzy Stradlin, and Hudson was simply known as Slash.

By early 1986, the band had created enough of a buzz on the Sunset Strip in Hollywood to attract the attention of nearly every major label. In March, Geffen won the bidding war, but the battle was just beginning.

In August 1986, the band began recording their debut album at Rumbo Records in Canoga Park, California. "It only took 12 days for the basic tracks, but altogether it took several months," McKagan says. The sessions were reportedly interrupted while Slash and Stradlin attempted to kick their heroin habits.

Meanwhile, the band was attempting to survive on a shoestring budget. "We didn't have any money or nothing," says McKagan. "We had one van between all of us that Geffen made the mistake of renting us, and we tore it to shreds. And we didn't have anyplace to live."

To keep the buzz surrounding the group alive on the streets, the band issued the Live?!@Like a Suicide EP on its own Uzi Suicide label. The EP, released in the fall of 1986, was distributed by Geffen, but the major label's name was kept off the release to secure the band's then-underground reputation.

Appetite for Destruction was finally released on July 27, 1987. Robert Williams's cover art, depicting a woman who had apparently been raped by a robot, raised the ire of women's groups and retailers and led to the creation of an alternate cover design. Rose's raw lyrics about urban decay and his own personal struggles, in songs such as the aggressive album-opener "Welcome to the Jungle," were bound to offend some. The track "Mr. Brownstone" addressed heroin addiction, a recurring problem in the band's early days. Yet nobody else paid much attention to Appetite at first.

"We didn't think the thing would sell 10 copies," says McKagan. "We weren't expecting anything." Yet slowly, mostly due to the band's virtual non-stop touring, including dates opening for Iron Maiden, the Cult, and Aerosmith [see 370], the word on Appetite spread. "Sweet Child o' Mine," the most accessible track on the album, was rising up the Hot 100. The song was inspired by Rose's girlfriend at the time, Erin Everly, the daughter of Don Everly of the Everly Brothers.

"We were on tour and still staying in shitty hotels," says McKagan. "One day I was walking down the street in whatever city I was in, and I saw some preppy guy with a Walkman on singing 'Sweet Child o' Mine' and I said, 'What the fuck is this about?' "

The members of Guns N' Roses would soon find out, as Appetite For Destruction, in its 50th week on the Top Pop Albums chart, finally completed its slow climb to the top, knocking Def Leppard's Hysteria from the Number One spot. A month later, "Sweet Child o' Mine" topped the Hot 100, but the public's appetite for Guns N' Roses was only beginning to grow [see 355].

THE TOP
Week of August 6, 1988

1. **Appetite for Destruction**
   Guns N' Roses

2. **Hysteria**
   Def Leppard

3. **Roll With It**
   Steve Winwood

4. **Tracy Chapman**
   Tracy Chapman

5. **Dirty Dancing**
   Soundtrack

VIRGIN 90946 **Roll With It** **321**
STEVE WINWOOD

phis Horns' Wayne Jackson on trumpet and Andrew Love on saxophone, was reminiscent of the R&B sounds Winwood played as a teenager as a member of the Spencer Davis Group. "It was exciting working with those musicians," Winwood says. "I can't say I knew it was going to be a hit—I've made too many records to ever want to think that. But I did have a good feeling about *Roll With It*. I knew I liked it, but it didn't necessarily feel like a commercial success."

Winwood wrote seven of the album's eight tracks with Will Jennings, with whom he had collaborated previously. The duo had penned "While You See a Chance," a number seven hit from Winwood's 1981 *Arc of a Diver*. (Jennings would later share writing credits with Winwood's former Blind Faith mate Eric Clapton [see 368].) "Hearts on Fire," the eighth track, was a collaboration between Winwood and his one-time Traffic mate Jim Capaldi.

Yet it was the title track that would put *Roll With It* on top. The single hit Number One on the Hot 100 on July 30, 1988. Three weeks later, while "Roll With It" was still the top single, the album made Number One.

Winwood's triumph, however, wasn't without controversy. The follow-up single, "Don't You Know What the Night Can Do?," which reached number six, was featured in a Michelob commercial. "I certainly got my share of criticism for that, but most of it was unfounded," Winwood says. "Certain people tried to claim I had written a jingle for a beer commercial, but I had not. I wrote a seven-minute song, some of which was used in the commercial, but I don't regret that at all."

Producers: Steve Winwood and Tom Lord Alge

Track listing: Roll With It / Holding On / The Morning Side / Put on Your Dancing Shoes / Don't You Know What the Night Can Do? / Hearts on Fire / One More Morning / Shining Song

August 20, 1988
1 week

In his 27-year career, Steve Winwood had experienced success a number of times, from "Gimme Some Lovin'," recorded when he was a teenager with the Spencer Davis Group, to hit albums with Blind Faith [see 115] and Traffic. Yet Winwood experienced his greatest success at the age of 40 with *Roll With It*.

In the summer of 1988, Winwood was primed for a hit. As the title of his previous album, *Back in the High Life*, suggested, the veteran R&B vocalist/keyboardist had launched a comeback in 1986. That album climbed to number three, included the Number One single "Higher Love," and set the stage for *Roll With It*.

Says Winwood, "It was really the pinnacle of my solo career. I never expected at the age of 40 to be suddenly doing better than I had at any time before." There were a number of factors that helped Winwood reach new heights with *Roll With It*. For one, it was his first album for his new label, Virgin, which signed him to a deal reportedly worth $13 million. "It certainly was a new step up for me. Also, I had just got married and I had a family, which was very important to me. It was a new phase in my life."

In a few instances, *Roll With It* marked a return to Winwood's roots. The title track, which featured the Mem-

---

THE TOP FIVE
Week of August 20, 1988

1. **Roll With It**
   Steve Winwood

2. **Hysteria**
   Def Leppard

3. **Appetite for Destruction**
   Guns N' Roses

4. **Tracy Chapman**
   Tracy Chapman

5. **He's the D.J., I'm the Rapper**
   D.J. Jazzy Jeff & the Fresh Prince

322 Tracy Chapman ELEKTRA 60774
TRACY CHAPMAN

Producer: David Kershenbaum

Track listing: Talkin' Bout a Revolution / Fast Car / Across the Lines / Behind the Wall / Baby Can I Hold You / Mountains o' Things / She's Got Her Ticket / Why? / For My Lover / It Not Now... / For You

August 27, 1988
1 week

When Tracy Chapman's self-titled debut album hit the summit in its 18th week on the chart, it became the first album by a folk act to reach Number One since Peter, Paul & Mary's *In the Wind* [see 63] had turned the trick in 1963, a year before Chapman was born. Yet the album, which earned Chapman a Grammy for best new artist of 1988, might have been markedly different had the 24-year-old singer-songwriter not called a halt to the initial sessions.

"I started out with a different producer at Bearsville Studios in New York,"

Chapman says. "Steve Jordan was playing drums, and we had a couple of other guys on keyboard and guitar. I knew immediately that it wasn't working, even though everyone else felt pretty good about it." The initial sessions lasted about two weeks before Chapman pulled the plug. "I just said that it wasn't the way I heard things and the way I wanted to make a record."

In her search to find a producer more in sync with her vision, Chapman came across David Kershenbaum, whose credits included work with Joan Baez, Joe Jackson, and Graham Parker. "When I met David, I felt a rapport immediately," says Chapman.

To record the album at Powertrax Studio in Hollywood, the singer-songwriter left her home in Boston for Los Angeles. Just a year earlier, Chapman had graduated from Tufts University with a degree in anthropology. "There were so many unknowns for me," she says. "I had never been in a professional recording studio before. I had never worked with other musicians, I had just

played casually with friends."

The sessions began with Chapman and the rhythm section of bassist Larry Klein, known for his work with his wife Joni Mitchell, and drummer Denny Fongheiser. Chapman had been performing most of the material to be featured on the album in her performances in coffeehouses and the streets of Boston.

It was during those performances that Chapman had first gained attention. Brian Koppelman, the son of music executive Charles Koppelman, was also attending Tufts and frequented Chapman's shows. He told his father about the young talent and Charles Koppelman was impressed enough to sign Chapman to a production deal. It was SBK that landed Chapman on Elektra, a suitable home for her, given its history with acoustic music and folk artists.

One song that was new to Chapman's repertoire was "Fast Car." Says Chapman, "I actually had to play that song live for David Kershenbaum when I first met him, because it wasn't on my demo tape." While the album contained several striking cuts, from the folk anthem "Talkin' Bout a Revolution" to the harrowing tales of spousal abuse in "Behind the Wall" and racial violence in "Across the Line," it was "Fast Car" that drove *Tracy Chapman* to the summit.

Although Chapman's sound was distinctively different from anything else at the top of the charts, she credits another female folksinger with paving the way for her own breakthrough. "Right before my record came out, Suzanne Vega had already had some success with her records, which were very acoustic-based. I think that was very significant in terms of how my album was accepted."

THE TOP FIVE
Week of August 22, 1988

1. **Tracy Chapman**
   Tracy Chapman

2. **Hysteria**
   Def Leppard

3. **Roll With It**
   Steve Winwood

4. **Appetite For Destruction**
   Guns N' Roses

5. **He's The D.J., I'm The Rapper**
   D.J. Jazzy Jeff & The Fresh Prince

MERCURY 836345 **New Jersey** **323**
BON JOVI

Producer: Bruce Fairbairn

Track listing: Lay Your Hands on Me /
Bad Medicine / Born to Be My Baby /
Living in Sin / Blood on Blood /
Homebound Train / Wild Is the Wind /
Ride Cowboy Ride / Stick to Your Guns
/ I'll Be There for You / 99 in the
Shade / Love for Sale

October 15, 1988
4 weeks

"I don't think there was pressure," Jon
Bon Jovi says of following up *Slippery When Wet* [see 306], which
had sold more than 13.5 million copies
worldwide. "Because there wasn't anything calculated going into *Slippery*.
With *New Jersey*, it was like, 'This is an
amazing high, how do we continue it?'
After the constant thrills we had with the
Slippery project, we all said, 'Wow, let's
do it again.' Six weeks later we were
making demos of the songs for *New Jersey*."

Bon Jovi stayed with the same
team—producer Bruce Fairbairn, engineer Bob Rock, and contributing songwriter Desmond Child—and the group
once again returned to Little Mountain
Sound Studios in Vancouver, British
Columbia. "It was an extended family,
so going back to Bruce and Bob was
logical," says Bon Jovi. "Plus, selling 13
million records wasn't too fucking shabby."

The success of *Slippery When Wet*

gave Bon Jovi a jolt of confidence, as
the *New Jersey* sessions went fairly
smoothly. "It took about the same time
period to record and mix the whole
thing," he says. "We certainly came up
with the songs."

One track, "Living in Sin," was written by Jon Bon Jovi alone at his New
Jersey home. "I called [guitarist] Richie
[Sambora] up, because I had this idea,
but by the time he got there, it was finished. He was bummed he didn't have
a piece of it."

When Bon Jovi penned "I'll Be There
for You," Sambora did make it in time
to contribute. "When we finished that
one off, I remember going to bed with a
Walkman on so I wouldn't wake up my
girlfriend and listening to it with us on
two acoustic guitars and our voices. I
was very pleased with that. It reminded
me of sort of a Lennon-type of attitude,"
he says.

The track "Bad Medicine" was written with help from Child. "He didn't like
the 'B' section, so he said, 'Why don't
you put this other part in from another
song.' And I said, 'Because I don't want
to give you a piece of a Number One
song.' We made light of it, put it in, and
pushed all egos aside."

Bon Jovi's prediction was on the
mark, as "Bad Medicine" became the
band's third Number One single on
November 19, 1988. By that time,
New Jersey had already topped the
album chart, becoming Bon Jovi's second consecutive Number One album. It

also spawned four more top 10 singles:
"I'll Be There for You" (another Number
One), "Born to Be My Baby," "Lay Your
Hands on Me," and "Living in Sin."

New Jersey was important to Bon
Jovi for more than just its chart achievements. On August 11, 1989, it became
the first new recording by an American
act to be issued in the USSR by the gov-
ernment-run Melodiya label. The following day the group headlined the
Moscow Music Peace Festival at Lenin
Stadium.

"When you make a record and you
tour, it's not often that you can find
something that no one else has done,"
Bon Jovi says. "But when we released
that record on Melodiya, that was a
first. Elvis never did that."

THE TOP FIVE
Week of October 15, 1988

1. **New Jersey**
   Bon Jovi

2. **Appetite for Destruction**
   Guns N' Roses

3. **Hysteria**
   Def Leppard

4. **Cocktail**
   Soundtrack

5. **Tracy Chapman**
   Tracy Chapman

324 Rattle and Hum ISLAND 91003
U2

Producer: Jimmy Iovine

Track listing: Helter Skelter / Van Diemen's Land / Desire / Hawkwind / All Along the Watchtower / I Still Haven't Found What I'm Looking For / (Freedom for My People) / Silver and Gold / Pride (In the Name of Love) / Angel of Harlem / Love Rescue Me / When Love Comes to Town / Heartland / God Part II / (The Star Spangled Banner) / Bullet the Blue Sky / All I Want Is You

November 12, 1988
6 weeks

Following the success of The Joshua Tree [see 310], U2 embarked on its biggest tour to date. The band started in sports arenas in the spring of 1987 but graduated to huge outdoor stadiums by the summer months. "It was a new experience playing stadiums," says bassist Adam Clayton. To capture the moment, the band opted to commission a film documentary about their experiences. Yet U2 was interested in more than just playing stadiums, and the film, to be titled Rattle and Hum after a lyric in "Bullet the Blue Sky," would reflect that. "We wanted to go back to the basics," says Clayton.

Rather than signing on a big-name director, the band opted to go with a relatively unknown young talent named Phil Joanou. The USC film school graduate and hardcore U2 fan had directed two episodes of Steven Spielberg's "Amazing Stories" and was in the process of wrapping up his theatrical directorial debut, "Three O'Clock High," when he campaigned for the job. "It

really made a difference to them when they realized that I was such a fan that I really wanted to make the film with them, not for them," Joanou says.

In the film, Joanou not only captured the band on the concert trail but on a trek through America's musical heritage, which included a stop at the legendary Sun Studios in Memphis [see 1] and guest appearances by Bob Dylan [see 170] and B.B. King.

"A lot of people didn't really understand what the band was doing at Sun Studio," Clayton says. "We were re-examining the blues and traditional songwriting. We felt we needed to have an appreciation and an understanding of that genre of music. As products of the punk movement, we didn't really know what that stuff was about."

The band also paid tribute to its heroes. "Angel of Harlem," recorded at Sun Studio, was about jazz great Billie Holiday. The live selections included the band's cover of the Beatles' "Helter Skelter" [see 110] and Dylan's "All Along the Watchtower." The band also acknowledged "Watchtower" cover artist Jimi Hendrix by using his recording of "The Star Spangled Banner" as an introduction to the live version of its own "Bullet the Blue Sky."

Other influences and guests were evident: The album's first single, "Desire," rocked with a Bo Diddley beat. Elsewhere, Bono honored the late John Lennon [see 255] in "God Part II." The song, a sequel to Lennon's own "God," featured an attack on Lennon biographer Albert Goldman, who had written about the former Beatle in less-than-flattering terms. In addition, Dylan co-wrote and contributed backing vocals

to the studio cut "Love Rescue Me" and played Hammond organ on "Hawkmoon 269." B.B. King played guitar and dueted with U2 vocalist Bono on "When Love Comes to Town."

Although critics savaged U2 for attempting to align itself with rock's historical pantheon, Clayton says it was a necessary step for the band. "These were people that had tremendous track records, so it was very good for us. The kind of humbleness and humility and appreciation and love of music that they had was something that we needed to hold onto at the time, because we had been through a lot of razzmatazz."

Although Rattle and Hum was a disappointment at the box office, the album did not disappoint, vaulting to the pinnacle of the Top Pop Albums chart in its third week and becoming the first double album to top the chart since Bruce Springsteen's The River [see 253].

THE TOP FIVE
Week of November 12, 1988

1. **Rattle and Hum**
   U2

2. **Appetite for Destruction**
   Guns N' Roses

3. **New Jersey**
   Bon Jovi

4. **Cocktail**
   Soundtrack

5. **Hysteria**
   Def Leppard

ELEKTRA 60827 # Giving You the Best That I Got

ANITA BAKER

325

Producer: Michael J. Powell

Track listing: Priceless / Lead Me Into Love / Giving You The Best That I Got / Good Love / Rules / Good Enough / Just Because / You Belong to Me

December 24, 1988
4 weeks

With her 1986 album, *Rapture*, Anita Baker became a star. The album topped the R&B album chart, spawned the hit single "Sweet Love," and earned the R&B diva a Grammy Award for Best Female R&B Vocal Performance, while the single took the Grammy for Best R&B Song. Yet that success put pressure on the Detroit-born singer when she began planning her next album. "I was scared to death," says Baker. "It was the follow-up album

to my first hit record. *Rapture* stayed on the album chart for 157 weeks and I had picked up every accolade in the book. It was very, very scary, because I had to go in and do the follow-up."

With the success of *Rapture*, Baker soon found herself fielding offers from a number of big-name producers who wanted to work with her. "When you get a hit like that, you get all these big-shot producers who want to work on your project," she says. "But I decided I didn't want it to be a collaboration of big-shot producers. I decided I just wanted to stay the course." So Baker regrouped with producer Michael J. Powell, a former bandmate of the singer in Chapter 8, a Detroit-based band she recorded with in 1980. Other former Chapter 8 members, such as keyboardist Vernon Fails and background singer Valerie Pinkston, were also fea-

tured on the album.

"*Giving You the Best That I Got* wasn't a hard album to make in the studio," says Baker. "The hard work came before I went into the studio. I never go into the studio until I have all of my material, and I know exactly where I am going, and who is doing what. It was difficult for me to put the material together," adds Baker, who is credited as executive producer on the album.

Baker first heard a bare-bones demo of "Giving You the Best That I Got" while she was staying in a bungalow at the Sunset Marquis in West Hollywood. "The only thing that was on that tape was the chorus. I played it over and over again. There was no bridge. The melody and the verses I wrote myself, but that hook was inescapable."

Since the hook was already in place, Baker had no problem writing additional lyrics to the song in the bedroom of her home outside of Detroit. "The lyrics just rolled off my tongue," she says. "It was the most effortless thing. It was a lot like 'Sweet Love.' You know when a song like that is a hit."

Baker's intuition was right on target, as "Giving You the Best That I Got" topped the Hot R&B Singles chart on November 12, 1988, before crossing over to the Hot 100, where it climbed to number three. Meanwhile, the album hit Number One on the Top R&B Albums chart on November 19, 1988. Six weeks later, it knocked U2's *Rattle and Hum* from the peak of the Top Pop Albums chart at the height of the competitive holiday season. With *Giving You the Best That I Got*, Baker gave it her best, and it paid off.

THE TOP FIVE
Week of December 24, 1988

1. **Giving You the Best That I Got**
   Anita Baker

2. **Rattle and Hum**
   U2

3. **Cocktail**
   Soundtrack

4. **Appetite for Destruction**
   Guns N' Roses

5. **New Jersey**
   Bon Jovi

326 Don't Be Cruel MCA 42185
BOBBY BROWN

Producers: L.A. & Babyface, Gene Griffin, Larry White, Gordon Jones, and Bobby Brown

Track listing: Cruel Prelude / Don't Be Cruel / My Prerogative / Roni / Rock Wit'cha / Every Little Step / I'll Be Good to You / Take It Slow / All Day All Night / I Really Love You Girl / Cruel Reprise

January 21, 1989
6 weeks (nonconsecutive)

As a member of Boston-based R&B vocal group New Edition, Bobby Brown experienced his first taste of success before he was eligible to receive a driver's license. In 1985, the group's self-titled MCA album climbed all the way to number six, propelled by the hit singles "Cool It Now" and "Mr. Telephone Man." Yet the group was unable to match that accomplishment with its subsequent albums. In 1986, Brown, who had grown tired of the group's teeny-bopper image, left New Edition to go solo.

After his first solo effort, 1986's King of Stage, stalled at number 88, some may have wondered if Brown made a mistake leaving New Edition behind. Yet Brown was unfazed and MCA executive Louil Silas Jr. had other plans for the budding talent. By 1988, Silas had hooked up Brown with some of the hottest young R&B producers and songwriters in the music business, including the team of Antonio "L.A." Reid and Kenneth "Babyface" Edmonds. With help from Reid and Edmonds, Brown developed into a forerunner of a new musical movement dubbed "new jack swing," which combined traditional R&B with elements of hip-hop.

The duo, known collectively as LaFace, were only vaguely familiar with Brown before they began work on the project. "We were familiar with him mainly from New Edition," Edmonds says, "but we liked him, because he brought a lot of energy and fire to the table."

Expectations for the project were not high. "No one really cared what we did," admits Edmonds. "We really hadn't made a name yet for ourselves as producers and it was just Bobby's second record after his first one didn't do that well, so no one knew what to expect."

With Reid and Edmonds, Brown cut four full tracks that made the album, includ-ing the title track, "Roni," and "Every Little Step," as well as "Cruel Prelude" and "Cruel Reprise." The sessions were held at Silverlake Studios in Hollywood. The singer reacted immediately to "Don't Be Cruel"—not the Elvis Presley hit (a cover of which would be a top 10 hit for for the rock band Cheap Trick around the same time Brown's song was released), but a song written by Reid, Edmonds, and Daryl Simmons. "That was one of the first songs placed," says Edmonds, who adds he never had a second thought about the song sharing its title with the Elvis classic.

"Every Little Step" wasn't greeted as enthusiastically by Brown. He initially rejected the song. "When Bobby didn't want to do it, I took it back for myself," says Edmonds, "but then Louil Silas fought to get it back for Bobby."

It turned out to be a wise decision, as the single became Brown's fourth top 10 single from the album. "Don't Be Cruel," the album's first single, peaked at number eight on the Hot 100. "My Prerogative," written by Brown and producer Gene Griffin became Brown's first Number One single on January 14, 1989, while "Roni" went on to reach number three.

By the time Don't Be Cruel hit the summit in its 27th week on the chart, Brown had become a surprise solo star, competing with such heavyweights as Anita Baker [see 325] and Guns N' Roses [see 320]. At just 19, he was also the youngest male solo artist to top the chart since Stevie Wonder accomplished the feat with Little Stevie Wonder/The 12 Year Old Genius [see 61].

THE TOP FIVE
Week of January 21, 1989

1. **Don't Be Cruel**
   Bobby Brown

2. **Appetite for Destruction**
   Guns N' Roses

3. **Open Up and Say...Ahh!**
   Poison

4. **New Jersey**
   Bon Jovi

5. **Hysteria**
   Def Leppard

ATANTIC 81932 **Electric Youth**
DEBBIE GIBSON

327

Producers: Deborah Gibson and Fred Zarr

Track listing: Who Loves Ya Baby? / Lost in Your Eyes / Love in Disguise / Helplessly in Love / Silence Speaks (a Thousand Words) / Should've Been the One / Electric Youth / No More Rhyme / Over the Wall / We Could Be Together / Shades of the Past

March 11, 1989
5 weeks

In the fall of 1987, Tiffany and Debbie Gibson emerged from the suburbs of Norwalk, California, and Long Island, respectively, to become the two reigning teen queens of pop. Tiffany hit it big first, scoring Number One hits with a cover of "I Think We're Alone Now" and "Could've Been," which pushed her self-titled debut album to the top of the album chart [see 317]. Although Gibson's first Number One single came months later and *Out of the Blue*, her 1987 debut album, peaked at number seven, she proved to be the more substantial talent.

"A lot of people group us together, but we're very different artists," said Gibson at the time. For one thing, Gibson wrote her own material, while Tiffany relied on songs provided to her by producer/manager George Tobin. Gibson even produced "Foolish Beat," her first Number One single, which topped the Hot 100 on June 25, 1988. A week later, she graduated from high school.

Success gave Gibson added confidence. In the middle of making *Electric Youth*, Gibson vowed, "We did the first album in eight weeks. Wait until people see what I can really do."

Like portions of *Out of the Blue*, *Electric Youth* was recorded at Fred Zarr's Z Studio in Brooklyn. Yet this time Gibson took even more control, producing six of the album's 11 tracks herself.

Since the album was recorded in summer of 1988 on breaks from Gibson's extensive touring schedule, the singer frequently tested out new material in her live set. In May 1988, Gibson was invited to participate in an all-star concert celebrating the 40th anniversary of Atlantic Records. Others on the bill included a temporarily reunited Led Zeppelin, the Bee Gees, Genesis, Crosby, Stills & Nash, and Roberta Flack. Gibson's own performance was sandwiched between sets by veteran progressive rockers Yes and former Led Zeppelin vocalist Robert Plant. Rather than playing one of her bubbly dance hits, she opted for a ballad, "Lost in Your Eyes," which she performed solo at the piano.

"It was the most nerve-wracking and exciting thing I have ever done," Gibson said of the concert. "That show really helped me a great deal. People took me a lot more seriously after that. There was a rock audience there, and I kept them entertained. I consider that a compliment. I showed a lot of people I was for real."

"Lost in Your Eyes" was the first single released from *Electric Youth*. On March 4, 1989, it became Gibson's second Number One single. A week later, *Electric Youth* hit the top spot on the album chart, while "Lost in Your Eyes" held at the pole position of the Hot 100 for a second consecutive week, making Gibson the first teen artist to have a simultaneous Number One single and album since Little Stevie Wonder [see 61], and the first female teen ever to achieve the feat.

THE TOP FIVE
Week of March 11, 1989

1. **Electric Youth**
   Debbie Gibson

2. **Don't Be Cruel**
   Bobby Brown

3. **Appetite for Destruction**
   Guns N' Roses

4. **Traveling Wilburys**
   Traveling Wilburys

5. **Shooting Rubberbands at the Stars**
   Edie Brickell & New Bohemians

328 Loc-ed After Dark DELICIOUS VINYL 3000
TONE LOC

Producers: Matt Dike, Michael Ross, and the Dust Brothers

Track listing: On Fire (Remix) / Wild Thing / Loc'ed After Dark / I Got It Goin' On / Cutting Rhythms / Funky Cold Medina / Next Episode / Cheeba Cheeba / Don't Get Close / Loc'in on the Shaw / The Homies

April 15, 1989
1 week

By 1987, Mike Ross, who studied mass communications at UCLA, and Matt Dike, a former New Yorker, were the hottest club DJs in Los Angeles, spinning hip-hop records at the hippest nightspots. Yet the duo, both in their mid-20s, soon became bored with the routine. "We decided we would try our hand at making records, instead of playing other people's records all the time," Ross says. "We had some tracks we were fiddling around with, but we needed someone to come in and rap over them."

Ross and Dike, both heavily into the smooth, cool style of Eric B. & Rakim, put the word out that they were looking for a rapper. A friend suggested his cousin, a 22-year-old named Anthony Smith, who auditioned over the phone. "I called him up," Ross says. "And his voice was just so amazing, we knew we could do something cool with him."

After Ross borrowed some money from his father, he and Dike formed Delicious Vinyl. Smith, the first artist on the new label, started using his gang-banging tag Tone Loc, as in loco or crazy Tony. "I used to gang-bang for awhile," he admits. "But I was a different kind of gangster. I didn't do it

because I didn't have money or I didn't have love from my family, I did it because I just liked to fight."

It was Tone Loc's mother who can take credit for his distinctive baritone. When he was nine, his mother fixed him a mixture of hot tea and brandy to ease the pain of a strep throat, but young Tony drank it before allowing it to cool, scalding his throat and forever changing his voice.

After two initial singles created a buzz on the West Coast, Tone Loc struck gold with "Wild Thing." The cut (not a remake of the 1966 Troggs classic) was inspired by a line from the Spike Lee film *She's Gotta Have It*. For the track, Dike sampled a guitar and drum riff from Van Halen's "Jamie's Cryin'." After Tone Loc's initial rap was deemed too racy for radio play, Young MC, another rapper in the Delicious Vinyl posse, rewrote the lyrics.

"Wild Thing" found a home on the playlists of alternative rock stations. A

video parodying Robert Palmer's "Addicted to Love," produced for a mere $400, made its way onto MTV. It soon became the second-best-selling single of all time, next to USA for Africa's "We Are the World," but since radio programmers in middle America would not program the track, it never topped the Hot 100 chart, where rankings are determined by a mix of sales and air-play.

When *Loc-ed After Dark* was released, Tone Loc finally made it to the top, hitting the Number One spot in just eight weeks and becoming the first African-American rap act to top the album chart. A second similarly party-themed single, "Funky Cold Medina," was also a huge hit, leading many to overlook the fact that Tone Loc's roots were firmly planted in the streets. "*Loc-ed After Dark* is full of gang-banging rhetoric," Ross says. "It's an autobiographical record that is as tough as Tone is."

THE TOP FIVE
Week of April 15, 1989

1. **Loc-ed After Dark**
   Tone Loc

2. **Electric Youth**
   Debbie Gibson

3. **Like a Prayer**
   Madonna

4. **Don't Be Cruel**
   Bobby Brown

5. **Mystery Girl**
   Roy Orbison

SIRE 25844 ## Like a Prayer
MADONNA

329

Producers: Madonna, Patrick Leonard, Stephen Bray, and Prince

Track listing: Like a Prayer / Express Yourself / Love Song / Till Death Do Us Part / Promise to Try / Cherish / Dear Jessie / Oh Father / Keep It Together / Spanish Eyes / Act of Contrition

April 22, 1989
6 weeks

Things were decidedly different for Madonna when the singer went to work on her fourth full-length album in early 1988. For one, her marriage to actor Sean Penn had begun to sour. Also, having already dabbled in such films as *Desperately Seeking Susan, Shanghai Surprise,* and *Who's That Girl,* Madonna decided it was time to take a stab at Broadway with a role in *Speed the Plow.* Meanwhile, on the recording front, Madonna and producer Patrick Leonard agreed it was time to abandon the small home studios used for *True Blue* [see 303] in favor of Leonard's Johnny Yuma Recording in Burbank, California.

"It was a real coming-of-age record for me emotionally," says Madonna. "I was at the end of my marriage and I was working with Pat, who was also in a very dark state of mind, and we worked in a very isolated place in the Valley. I was very lonely when I was working on the record. I had to do a lot of soul-searching and I think it is a reflection of that."

Perhaps the most telling song on the album is "Till Death Do Us Part," a track originally titled

"State of Matrimony," which can be taken as an autobiographical account of Madonna's ill-fated marriage to Penn.

Despite the troubles that were brewing in Madonna's personal life, several of the songs on the album came together very quickly. "I would start working on the music and then Madonna would come in the afternoon and work on some lyrics, then we would do a vocal and that was usually the vocal we kept," says Leonard. "In the first week, we wrote 'Cherish,' 'Like a Prayer,' and 'Spanish Eyes.' " The track "O Father" was written in New York, while Madonna was working on *Speed the Plow,* Leonard says.

Madonna also had her mother on her mind when she was working on *Like a Prayer.* "This album is dedicated to my mother, who taught me how to pray," Madonna wrote in the liner notes. The singer's mother, also named Madonna, died of cancer. Madonna was six at the time.

" 'Like a Prayer' is a very important

song to me," she says. "I felt the impact that it was going to make. That song means a lot more to me than 'Like a Virgin.' I wrote it and it's from my heart. It's a very spiritual song. I think I was much more spiritually in touch with the power of words and music by the time I was recording that album."

Another emotionally charged cut on the album is "Oh Father." Says Madonna, "It was like the second half of 'Live to Tell,' in a way. It was a combo package—it was about my father and my husband. I was dealing with male authority figures once again. That is a great source of inspiration to my writing."

To give various songs the appropriate atmosphere, Madonna turned to a number of outside sources. On "Like a Prayer," for example, the singing of the Andre Crouch Choir added an authentic hymn-like feel to the song, while "Love Song" is a collaboration between Madonna and Prince [see 331], recorded at the latter's Paisley Park Studios.

"We were friends and talked about working together, so I went to Minneapolis to write some stuff with him, but the only thing I really dug was 'Love Song,' " Madonna says. "We ended up writing it long-distance, because I had to be in L.A. and he couldn't leave Minneapolis, and quite frankly I couldn't stand Minneapolis. When I went there, it was like 20 degrees below zero, and it was really desolate. I was miserable and I couldn't write or work under those circumstances."

In all, Leonard says *Like a Prayer* is a better record than *True Blue.* "It is much more musician-oriented and much more live," he says. The musicianship, however, took a back seat to controversy. The video clip for "Like a Prayer," which crossed an interracial love story with religious imagery, raised the ire of fundamentalist groups and led Pepsi-Cola to yank a TV commercial featuring the song from the air. But Madonna had the last laugh, pocketing the money from the commercial and benefitting from the publicity, as the single went on to top the Hot 100. The same week *Like a Prayer* hit the summit in its third week on the chart, making it Madonna's fastest-climbing album to date.

THE TOP FIVE
Week of April 22, 1989

1. **Like a Prayer**
   Madonna

2. **Loc-ed After Dark**
   Tone Loc

3. **Electric Youth**
   Debbie Gibson

4. **Don't Be Cruel**
   Bobby Brown

5. **The Raw & the Cooked**
   Fine Young Cannibals

330 The Raw & the Cooked I.R.S. 6273
FINE YOUNG CANNIBALS

Producers: David Z, Fine Young Cannibals, and Jerry Harrison

Track listing: She Drives Me Crazy / Good Thing / I'm Not the Man I Used to Be / I'm Not Satisfied / Tell Me What / Don't Look Back / It's OK (It's Alright) / Don't Let It Get You Down / As Hard As It Is / Ever Fallen in Love

June 3, 1989
7 weeks

In the early '80s, British ska group the Beat scored several top 10 singles in England, but didn't have much luck in America, where a conflict with a similarly named band forced them to identify themselves as the English Beat. The English Beat achieved their album chart high in 1982, when their final studio album, *Special Beat Service*, reached number 39. The sum of that group's parts may have been better, at least commercially, than its whole. While English Beat frontmen Dave Wakeling and Ranking Roger went on to marginal success as General Public, former Beat guitarist Andy Cox and bassist David Steele recruited actor/musician Roland Gift to front their new group, named after the 1960 Natalie Wood–Robert Wagner film *All the Fine Young Cannibals*.

The group's 1985 self-titled debut album reached number 49, while its only single, "Johnny Come Home," stalled at number 76. In spite of the group's mediocre chart performance, some took notice of the Cannibals, including director Barry Levinson, who used songs from the group's first album as temporary tracks in an early version of the film *Tin Men*, which starred Richard Dreyfuss and Danny DeVito.

THE TOP FIVE
Week of June 3, 1989

1. **The Raw & the Cooked**
   Fine Young Cannibals

2. **Like a Prayer**
   Madonna

3. **Beaches**
   Soundtrack

4. **G N' R Lies**
   Guns N' Roses

5. **Don't Be Cruel**
   Bobby Brown

Levinson was such a fan that he eventually contacted the Cannibals and asked the group to write new music for the film. The result was "Good Thing, "Tell Me What," and "As Hard as It Is." Levinson also cast the group in the film as a soul band. Meanwhile, the Cannibals also covered "Ever Fallen in Love," written and originally recorded by British pop-punk aces the Buzzcocks, for the 1986 soundtrack to Jonathan Demme's *Something Wild*.

While the songs for the films would serve as the heart of the Cannibals' follow-up album, they were having trouble coming up with more material. In an effort to end their writer's block, the Cannibals asked a record company executive to hook them up with Prince. The elfin superstar wasn't available, but David Z, a Prince cohort whose brother Bobby was a member of the Revolution, was up for the job. The plan was to bring the Cannibals to Minneapolis, which to them was "nowheresville," David Z says. Since they would have nothing else to do, they would have little choice but to complete the album. "When they got off the plane, Roland Gift had a big bag of brown rice, because he probably thought that he couldn't get any in Minneapolis," David Z recalls.

The producer booked the band at Prince's Paisley Park Studio. "The rest of the album was basically done in the studio," he says. "They had some songs, but they were all disjointed."

One of those songs was a track called "She's Me Baby." As the song began to take shape, Steele changed the title to "She Drives Me Crazy," and it was suggested that Gift sing in a falsetto. "Roland was still very shy about singing in the studio," says David Z, "especially on that falsetto part on 'She Drives Me Crazy.' He was very uncertain about singing that, but it came out pretty cool."

Gift's hesitancy could be attributed to the fact that he mostly played saxophone in his pre-Cannibals bands, Blue Kitchen and Akrylyx. "He didn't consider himself a singer at all," says David Z. "He was a saxophone player."

Gift also proved to be somewhat of an enigma during the sessions at Paisley Park. "He led us to believe he was a vegetarian the whole time, eating brown rice," says David Z. "On the last day of recording we decided to get some steaks and throw them on the grill. Roland sat down and started eating a steak and someone said, 'The head Cannibal is eating meat.' Everyone was surprised."

Many were likely surprised by the Cannibals' success, too. "She Drives Me Crazy" became the group's first hit and climbed all the way to Number One on April 15, 1989. Less than two months later, *The Raw & the Cooked* reached the pole position. With the album still lodged in the Number One position, "Good Thing" became the trio's second chart-topping single on July 8, 1989.

WARNER BROS. 25936 # Batman

PRINCE/SOUNDTRACK

Producer: Prince

Track listing: The Future / Electric Chair / The Arms of Orion / Partyman / Vicki Waiting / Trust / Lemon Crush / Scandalous / Batdance

July 22, 1989
6 weeks

Prior to 1989, the careers of both Prince and Batman were on the decline. In the mid-'80s, Prince had scored back-to-back Number One albums with *Purple Rain* [see 282] and *Around the World in a Day* [see 288], but his popularity took a dip with his subsequent releases. *Parade*, his 1986 album, featuring music from the flop film *Under the Cherry Moon*, peaked at number three. *Sign "O" the Times*, a 1987 double album, reached number six; and *Lovesexy*, his 1988 album, stalled at number 11, becoming his first album not to reach the top 10 since 1981. Batman, meanwhile, had been the subject of a hugely successful TV program in the '60s, but after the series was canceled, the superhero was relegated to reruns and comic book stores, at least until 1989. That's when director Tim Burton's theatrical version of *Batman* would help put the Purple One and the Caped Crusader back on top.

When executives at Warner Bros. films and records began thinking of a pop star to contribute to the soundtrack of the film, most everyone agreed that Prince was the man for the job. "He was the perfect artist for that picture," says Gary LeMel, president of music for Warner Bros. Inc. "It may have been kind of subliminal. The Joker wore purple, so that kind of leads you to the Purple One. We didn't think of any other artist. We knew he was the one."

The prospect of writing music for *Batman* appealed to Prince, who in January 1989 took the Concorde to London to meet Burton on the set and see some footage from the film-in-progress. "We all wanted Prince real badly, but he wasn't going to commit until he met with Tim," says LeMel. Burton showed the visitors a 20-minute reel. "It was very exciting, because it was the first *Batman* movie and Prince loved what he saw," LeMel adds. After a discussion over lunch, the deal was sealed.

Enthused by the prospects, Prince canceled a scheduled vacation and headed home to Minneapolis to write and record material at his Paisley Park Studios. "Not only did Prince write songs, he also wrote a score for the movie, even though he knew we were going with a score by Danny Elfman." Prince composed the songs specifically

for the characters in the film, as the liner notes of the album suggest. Batman is listed as lead vocalist on "The Future," the Joker on "Electric Chair," and "The Arms of Orion" is credited as a duet by Vicki Vale and Bruce Wayne (it's actually Sheena Easton and Prince).

The crowning achievement was "Batdance," which features the dialogue of Jack Nicholson's Joker, Michael Keaton's Batman, and Kim Basinger's Vicki Vale in the mix. "That was a total surprise," says LeMel. "He knew that it wouldn't be in the movie, but he wanted it to be the lead single and it ended up leading off the entire campaign for the movie. It was like a thumbnail sketch of the movie. It was almost like a piece of advertising for the movie."

Although only approximately six minutes of Prince's 42-minute *Batman* soundtrack made it into the film, the album and the movie were both smashes in their respected mediums. The film went on to gross more than $251 million in the U.S. alone, while the album made Number One in its third week on the chart, giving Prince his second Number One soundtrack and third career chart-topping album. Two weeks after *Batman* first hit the peak, "Batdance" joined it at the top, hitting Number One on the Hot 100. Prince and the Caped Crusader were back.

THE TOP FIVE
Week of July 22, 1989

1. **Batman**
   Prince/Soundtrack

2. **The Raw & the Cooked**
   Fine Young Cannibals

3. **Don't Be Cruel**
   Bobby Brown

4. **Hangin' Tough**
   New Kids on the Block

5. **Full Moon Fever**
   Tom Petty

332 Repeat Offender EMI 90380
RICHARD MARX

Producer: Richard Marx and David Cole

Track listing: Nothin' You Can Do About It / Satisfied / Angelia / Too Late to Say Goodbye / Right Here Waiting / Heart on the Line / Real World / If You Don't Want My Love / That Was Lulu / Wait for the Sunrise / Children of the Night

September 2, 1989
1 week

Even before Richard Marx became an established artist, he was no stranger to the top of the charts. He sang backing vocals on Lionel Richie's *Can't Slow Down* and *Dancing on the Ceiling* [see 278, 304], and a song he wrote for Chicago was included on *We Are the World* [see 287]. Yet the Chicago-born singer-songwriter wouldn't stand alone at the summit of the album chart until the release of his second album, *Repeat Offender.*

In his formative years, Marx literally lived music. His father, a jazz pianist, recorded jingles, and Marx was only five when he was lured into the business; his mother was also a singer. Moving to Los Angeles at 18, Marx found work as a back-up singer for Richie and later worked as an assistant for producer David Foster. After years of working for Foster, the producer broke the news to the aspiring singer-songwriter. "One day he said, 'You might be a big producer and win a Grammy over me, but you're never going to make it as a singer,' " Marx says. "It was like having your father tell you you're ugly. It totally devastated me."

Yet Marx would soon prove Foster

wrong. At a songwriters' seminar in Canada, Marx met former Blood, Sweat & Tears drummer Bobby Colomby, who was working as an A&R consultant to Manhattan Records. He set up an audition, which led to Marx's signing. Marx's self-titled debut album climbed to number eight on the strength of four top three singles, including his first Number One, "Hold on to the Nights."

High on his newfound success, Marx wrote 25 songs for *Repeat Offender* while on tour in support of his first album. He recorded 15 tracks for the album at various studios in Los Angeles. "Satisfied," the last song written for the album, became the first single.

Marx, a big fan of the veteran rock band the Tubes, collaborated with Tubes frontman Fee Waybill on two songs on *Repeat Offender*, but not on "Satisfied," the most Tubes-like of the bunch. "I think I stole the riff from the Tubes' "She's a Beauty,' " Marx says. "It's slightly different, but when I wrote 'Satisfied,' I definitely was trying to write my version of 'She's a Beauty.' " On June 24, "Satisfied" became Marx's second consecu-

tive Number One single, yet it would take the ballad "Right Here Waiting" to push *Repeat Offender* to the top spot.

Initially, Marx didn't consider releasing the track he wrote as a musical love letter to his soon-to-be wife, actress Cynthia Rhodes. "It was based upon a separation that we had no control over," Marx says. "She was working in another country and I was touring. For various circumstances, three and a half months went by. When you are in a relationship and you love somebody, that is a hell of a long time. The only thing that got me through that was that song, but I had no intention of putting it on the record. It is a very personal song. It would be like writing a love letter and letting *Entertainment Weekly* publish it."

Yet Colomby changed Marx's mind, telling him that it was the best song he had ever written. Apparently the public agreed, as "Right Here Waiting" became Marx's third consecutive Number One single. Three weeks later *Repeat Offender* ended Prince's six-week reign at Number One.

COLUMBIA 40985 **Hangin' Tough**
NEW KIDS ON THE BLOCK

333

Producer: Maurice Starr

Track listing: You Got It (The Right Stuff) / Please Don't Go Girl / I'll Be Loving You (Forever) / Cover Girl / I Need You / Hangin' Tough / I Remember When / What'cha Gonna Do (About It) / My Favorite Girl / Hold On

September, 9 1989
2 weeks

Maurice Starr had it all and then lost it. In 1981, Starr put together a group of five black youths called New Edition. But after their first album, the group was lured away by MCA Records.

Even before the split, Starr had other ambitions. He wanted to start a white version of New Edition that would appeal to an even broader audience. Starr's first attempt, in which he left his phone number with a teenager at a flower shop, led to a phone call from the F.B.I., who were wondering why a grown man was leaving his number with children.

After that mishap, Starr's first recruit was Mark Wahlberg, who later scored hits as Marky Mark. Although Mark left the group because he was more interested in rapping than singing, his older brother Donnie stayed on and suggested other possible members. Danny Wood and brothers Jordan and Jon Knight, who Wahlberg knew from elementary school, were enlisted, and Joe McIntyre rounded out the quintet.

The group was originally called Nynuk, but Columbia Records, which was courting the group, suggested the name be replaced by one of the group's song titles. The rechristened New Kids

were signed to Columbia Records black music division in January 1986.

Later that year, the group recorded its self-titled debut album, but it only sold 5,000 copies upon its release in 1987, as the single "Be My Girl" failed to crack the Hot 100 and stalled at number 90 on the Hot Black Singles chart. "We had high hopes and big dreams when we were doing the first album," says Jordan Knight. "We thought it was going to be real big, but it didn't do anything."

"But we didn't give up," Jordan adds. "We had the same hopes and dreams for *Hangin' Tough*," much of which was recorded at Starr's home. "It didn't have regular studio walls," says Wahlberg. "So if a truck drove by, we had to stop recording." In spite of such nuisances, Walhberg says that *Hangin' Tough* was the group's best collaboration with Starr. "It was just a total vibe session with Danny, myself, Jordan, and Maurice," Wahlberg says. "We would sit down with Maurice for days and talk about what kind of music we wanted to do and we would go through Maurice's

whole song library and find the songs we liked."

Among the songs the Kids chose was "Please Don't Go Girl," a song originally recorded by another Starr discovery, Irving & the Twins. The New Kids' version caught the ear of WRBQ Tampa program director Randy Kabrich. Eventually, it became a hit, climbing to number 10. The follow-up, "You Got It (The Right Stuff)," hit number three. Then, "I'll Be Loving You (Forever)," a song Starr penned with Smokey Robinson in mind, topped the Hot 100.

Buoyed by the hits, *Hangin' Tough* was on a slow climb to the top, but it would need another hit for the final push. "Hangin' Tough" entered the Hot 100 on July 15, 1989. Eight weeks later, it hit the pole position as the album also hit Number One in its 55th week on the Top Pop Albums chart, making the New Kids the first teen group to have a simultaneous Number One album and single. "That was probably the truest reward that we ever had," says Wahlberg. "There's been nothing like it ever since."

THE TOP FIVE
Week of September 9, 1989

1. **Hangin' Tough**
   New Kids on the Block

2. **Repeat Offender**
   Richard Marx

3. **Forever Your Girl**
   Paula Abdul

4. **Girl You Know it's True**
   Milli Vanilli

5. **Batman**
   Prince/Soundtrack

334 Girl You Know It's True ARISTA 8592
MILLI VANILLI

Producer: Frank Farian

Track listing: Girl You Know It's True / Baby Don't Forget My Number / More Than You'll Ever Know / Blame It on the Rain / Take It as It Comes / It's Your Thing / Dreams to Remember / All or Nothing / I'm Gonna Miss You / Girl You Know It's True (N.Y. Subway Extended Mix)

September 23, 1989
8 weeks (nonconsecutive)

German record producer Frank Farian began working on a project known as Milli Vanilli in April 1988. The name was borrowed from a Berlin disco that was popular in the '60s. By 1988, Farian was already an established hit-maker, having scored nine top 10 singles in England with the West Indies group Boney M.

To front Milli Vanilli, Farian recruited Rob Pilatus and Fabrice Morvan, a pair of dreadlocked video models and dancers. The album was recorded in three months at Far Studios in Frankfurt, Germany. The resulting album, All or Nothing, was issued on a small label in Europe and soon garnered the attention of Clive Davis, the president of Arista Records.

"Clive Davis suggested three new songs for the album for the American release," recalls Farian. One of those tracks, "Blame It on the Rain," was penned by the hot songwriter Diane Warren, who had written such chart-toppers as Starship's "Nothing's Gonna Stop Us Now," Chicago's "Look Away," and Bad English's "When I See You Smile."

With the release of the American version of the album, retitled Girl You Know It's True, Milli Vanilla began to experience success with the title track. The song, which was already a number three hit in the U.K., was released as the group's first American single and went on to reach number two on the Hot 100. The follow-up single, "Baby Don't Forget My Number," penned by Farian, Brad Howell, and Bernd Berwanger, was even more successful. On July 1, 1989, it became Milli Vanilli's first Number One hit.

In spite of the group's success, rumors began to circulate that Pilatus and Morvan, credited with "vocals" in the album's liner notes, did not really sing on the album. Despite the rumors, Milli Vanilli's success continued. A third single, "Girl I'm Gonna Miss You," also became a hit, reaching the top spot on September 23, 1989. The third hit single was enough to drive Girl You Know It's True to Number One in its 27th week on the album chart.

Milli Vanilli's hot streak continued when "Blame It on the Rain" became the group's third consecutive Number One single on November 25, 1989. On February 21, 1990, Milli Vanilli was named best new artist at the 32nd Annual Grammy Awards by members of the National Academy of Recording Arts and Sciences. With all the success, however, the rumors that Pilatus and Morvan didn't sing just became louder.

Finally, on November 14, 1990,

almost a year after Milli Vanilli had topped the album chart, Farian held a press conference to announce that it was true: Pilatus and Morvan did not sing on the album. "Rob and Fab were supposed to do a dance video and it developed from there," says Farian. However, the duo wanted to sing and actually thought that their vocals, which were in fact recorded in the course of the studio sessions, appeared on the album. "During the album recordings there was a funny situation in the studio. We were listening to the record and Rob started to claim that he expected his voice to be louder. As we all know by now, he never sang one tune."

Farian says he opted not to use Pilatus and Morvan's vocals because they simply were "not good enough." Instead he turned to his friend, Howell, who co-wrote "Baby Don't Forget My Number," to handle the lead vocals.

In retrospect, Farian has mixed feelings about the Milli Vanilli experience. "Even though what happened is common procedure in the music business, I felt really bad," he says. However, he is proud of his work on the album. "Girl You Know It's True was an excellent production and deserved all the positive attention it received."

The duo were later forced to return their Grammy, but chart history cannot be undone — Girl You Know It's True remained one of the best-selling albums of 1989.

THE TOP FIVE
Week of September 23, 1989

1. **Girl You Know It's True**
   Milli Vanilli

2. **Hangin' Tough**
   New Kids on the Block

3. **Forever Your Girl**
   Paula Abdul

4. **Repeat Offender**
   Richard Marx

5. **Full Moon Fever**
   Tom Petty

VIRGIN 90943 **Forever Your Girl** **335**
PAULA ABDUL

Executive producer: Gemma Corfield

Track listing: The Way That You Love Me / Knocked Out / Opposites Attract / State of Attraction / I Need You / Forever Your Girl / Straight Up / Next to You / Cold Hearted / One or the Other

October 7, 1989
10 weeks (nonconsecutive)

The recording, release, and subsequent success of *Forever Your Girl* "was the most exciting time of my life," says Paula Abdul. "It was an incredible three years." In that time, Abdul would go from a virtually unknown dancer to one of the most popular female performers in pop music.

Born June 19, 1962, and raised in the San Fernando Valley, Abdul knew from a young age that she wanted to be a performer. While her peers favored the hits of the day, Paula was intrigued by such all-around entertainers as Gene Kelly.

Abdul's big break came when she was in college working as the head choreographer of the Laker Girls, the cheerleading squad for basketball's Los Angeles Lakers, a high-profile job that led to other gigs. Soon she was serving as choreographer on Fox-TV's *Tracey Ullman Show* and for music videos by Janet Jackson, Dolly Parton, and others. But merely dancing wasn't enough—Abdul dreamed of being a star. She shared her desire with Warner Bros. executive Jeff Ayeroff while working on ZZ Top's "Velcro Fly" video. When Virgin Records launched its American wing in 1988, Ayeroff was named co-chairman. He remembered Abdul and made

her one of the label's first signings. "It was me, Roy Orbison, Steve Winwood [see 314], and Warren Zevon," she says.

But Paula still had her day job. "I was winning awards for my choreography, but after we recorded the first song, I had to make the decision to put choreography on hold," she recalls. "To put everything aside was a risky thing. There was no guarantee that they would even release the album, but I figured even if it didn't work out, at the very least it was something I could tell my grandchildren about."

Once the decision was made, Paula devoted her life to making *Forever Your Girl*, jetting from L.A. to Minneapolis and back again for recording sessions with a variety of songwriters and producers, including L.A. Reid and Babyface, Oliver Leiber (the son of Jerry Leiber of Leiber & Stoller fame), former Time member Jesse Johnson, Darryl Simmons, and others. "Sometimes I would spend the night and I'd sleep on the couch in the studio, because I didn't want to leave," Paula recalls.

Once the album was released, Paula's star did not rise overnight. The first two singles, "Knocked Out" and "The Way That You Love Me," failed to crack the top 40, but then a track called "Straight Up" started receiving airplay. Virgin followed the lead of the radio programmers and released it as a single. It took a few months, but "Straight Up" went straight to the top of the Hot 100, with "Forever Your Girl," and "Cold Hearted" also reaching the summit. With three Number One singles to its credit, *Forever Your Girl* hit the top in its 64th week on the album chart. On February 10, 1990, "Opposites Attract" hit Number One, making *Forever Your Girl* the first debut album to hit Number One and generate four Number One singles.

THE TOP FIVE
Week of October 7, 1989

1. **Forever Your Girl**
   Paula Abdul

2. **Girl You Know It's True**
   Milli Vanilli

3. **Steel Wheels**
   Rolling Stones

4. **Hangin' Tough**
   New Kids on the Block

5. **Dr. Feelgood**
   Mötley Crüe

336 Dr. Feelgood ELEKTRA 60829
MÖTLEY CRÜE

Producer: Bob Rock

Track listing: T.n.T. (Terror 'n Tinseltown) / Dr. Feelgood / Slice of Your Pie / Rattlesnake Shake / Kickstart My Heart / Without You / Same Ol' Situation / Sticky Sweet / She Goes Down / Don't Go Away Mad (Just Go Away) / Time for Change

October 14, 1989
2 weeks

By 1989, Los Angeles hard-rock group Mötley Crüe had certainly had a taste of success and excess. After becoming a sensation on the L.A. club scene in the early '80s, the band released Too Fast for Love on its own independent Leathür label. That album, coupled with the band's live performances, generated such a buzz that Elektra signed the band. Shout at the Devil, the band's first album for the label, reached number 17, with the follow-ups, 1985's Theatre of Pain and 1987's Girls, Girls, Girls, hitting numbers six and two, respectively. Yet the success took its toll. In June 1987, the band was forced to scrap a tour when bassist/songwriter Nikki Sixx was sidelined after an overdose. That scare led the band to clean up its act.

Dr. Feelgood was inspired, in part, by the band's days at a detox clinic. The title track tells the story of a drug pusher and the album art features the band in straitjackets. Dr. Feelgood was recorded at Little Mountain Sound Studios in Vancouver, while fellow hard-rockers Aerosmith laid down tracks for their Pump album. With Aerosmith also sobering up, the members of the two bands shared common ground. The Crue invited Aerosmith frontman Steven Tyler to sing backing vocals on "Sticky Sweet." Says Sixx, "Knowing where he came from, he's got a lot of power and self-will." Tyler even fronted the Crue on a take of "Slice of Your Pie," which was never released but remains in Sixx's possession. "It's a bad-ass version," he says. "I put it on every now and then."

In a sense, it was appropriate that Mötley Crüe was recording in such close proximity to Aerosmith, for many would later compare the riff of "Dr. Feelgood," which became the band's first top 10 single, to classic Aerosmith. "That's a compliment to me," says Sixx. "They're one of my favorite bands. I really like those down-and-dirty riffs that Aerosmith does."

To produce the album, the band called on Bob Rock, who would soon become one of the most sought-after hard-rock producers. "It was a very high compliment that Metallica chose Bob Rock to do their next album after hearing what he did on Dr. Feelgood," says Sixx.

During the sessions, the band cut 12 tracks. "Rock 'n' Roll Junkie" didn't make the final cut, but later turned up on the soundtrack to The Adventures of Ford Fairlane.

Perhaps the most telling song on Dr. Feelgood was the final cut, "Time for Change." Says Sixx, "We almost left that off the record. When I wrote it, it was almost church-like. It was organ-based with a lot of weird background vocals. The demo version is actually better than the one that's on the album." Nonetheless, the song proved prophetic, as vocalist Vince Neil would leave the band in February 1992, making Dr. Feelgood the final full album by the original lineup of Mötley Crüe and the band's first Number One.

THE TOP FIVE
Week of October 14, 1989

1. **Mötley Crüe**
   Dr. Feelgood

2. **Forever Your Girl**
   Paula Abdul

3. **Steel Wheels**
   Rolling Stones

4. **Girl You Know It's True**
   Milli Vanilli

5. **Hangin' Tough**
   New Kids on the Block

A&M 3920 # Janet Jackson's Rhythm Nation 1814

JANET JACKSON

Producers: Jimmy Jam & Terry Lewis

Track listing: Interlude: Pledge / Rhythm Nation / Interlude: T.V. / State of the World / Interlude: Race / The Knowledge / Interlude: Let's Dance / Miss You Much / Interlude: Come Back / Love Will Never Do (Without You) / Livin' in a World (They Didn't Make) / Alright / Interlude: Hey Baby / Escapade / Interlude: No Acid / Black Cat / Lonely / Come Back to Me / Someday Is Tonight / Interlude: Livin'...in Complete Darkness

October 28, 1989
4 weeks

With the success of *Control* [see 300], Janet Jackson was a superstar and Jimmy Jam and Terry Lewis became one of the hottest production teams in the music business. Yet success didn't necessarily make working together easier for Jackson and Jam and Lewis. "When we made the *Control* album, basically everyone left us alone," says Jam. "After it was successful, it seemed like everyone had their two cents they wanted to put in about the next album." Lawyers and managers for both parties and A&M Records tried

unsuccessfully to hammer out a deal for six months. Then Jackson put a call into Jam. "She said, 'Do you guys want to do this album?' And I said, 'Yeah.' And I asked her, 'Do you want us to do this album?' and she said, 'Yeah'," Jam says. "Once we figured that out, we were ready to record that week."

In the initial stages, *Rhythm Nation* was not a concept album. "The thing we set out to do was not make *Control Part II*," says Jam. "We purposely didn't do any songs that were like 'Nasty' or 'What Have You Done for Me Lately' updated." It was only after Jackson spent some time in the studio lounge watching television that the album began to take on its political bent. "The actual *Rhythm Nation* idea wasn't formed until about six or seven songs into the project," Jam says. "We realized there was a theme taking shape. We were watching a lot of CNN and there were a lot of world events that were happening that were screwed up. That was on Janet's mind while we were making the album."

Not all the subject matter, however, was heavy. "Miss You Much" was inspired by a card Jam received from his girlfriend. "At the bottom of it she signed it, 'Miss you much,' and I just thought

that was a cool term.' " The rhythm track was actually cut before Jackson arrived at Flyte Tyme Studios in Minneapolis. "She walked into the studio while I was getting ready to lay down a keyboard part," Jam recalls. "I pointed at the key I was going to play and that was how we started the album."

Former Time member Jellybean Johnson, who had also contributed to *Control*, was tapped to co-produce the hard-rocking track "Black Cat." Says Jam, " 'Bean is very much a closet rock 'n' roller. That song came from a riff Janet had in her head. We laid down the beat and then 'Bean came in and put down a guitar part."

While *Control* was recorded in a relatively quick six weeks, *Rhythm Nation* took six months. "We didn't play it for the record company until it was totally done with all the little snippets in between the songs," says Jam. "It was almost like we treated it as a painting. We didn't want to let anyone hear it until it was finished."

When *Rhythm Nation* hit Number One in its fourth week on the Top Pop Albums chart, "Miss You Much" had already held the top position of the Hot 100 for three weeks. The album went on to spawn six more top five hits, including the Number One singles "Escapade," "Black Cat," and "Love Will Never Do (Without You)." The feat earned Jackson and *Rhythm Nation* a place in the history book, as the album was the first to generate seven top five hits. "We felt like we had some hits on there," says Jam. "But we also felt it didn't have as much [youth] appeal as *Control* and it wasn't a given that it would work. It could have gone the other way."

THE TOP FIVE
Week of October 28, 1989

1. **Janet Jackson's Rhythm Nation 1814**
   Janet Jackson

2. **Girl You Know It's True**
   Milli Vanilli

3. **Dr. Feelgood**
   Mötley Crüe

4. **Steel Wheels**
   Rolling Stones

5. **Forever Your Girl**
   Paula Abdul

338 Storm Front COLUMBIA 44366
BILLY JOEL

Producers: Mick Jones and Billy Joel

Track listing: That's Not Her Style / We Didn't Start the Fire / The Down-easter "Alexa" / I Go to Extremes / Shameless / Storm Front / Leningrad / State of Grace / When in Rome / And So It Goes

December 16, 1989
1 week

Storm Front marked a major change for Billy Joel: It was the singer/pianist's first album in 12 years that wasn't produced by Phil Ramone. "The album that came out in 1986, The Bridge, was not a happy experience," says Joel. "It felt like a marriage that had gotten old. The band wasn't really motivated and there was a lot of complaining about stuff other than the music. Also, I didn't feel like Phil and I were sparking any more."

While recording The Bridge was an ordeal, the album reached number seven, continuing Joel's run of top 10 studio albums, which had begun in 1977 with The Stranger. Yet prior to the recording of Storm Front, Joel decided to take a step back and re-evaluate his career. "I decided that I had to find out why I do what I do," Joel says. "Every artist has to reinvent themselves constantly, which I try to do on every album, but aside from that you have to find your motivation. At that point I had forgotten. On Storm Front, I rediscovered the joy of rock 'n' roll."

In his quest to rediscover his inspiration, Joel enlisted Mick Jones of Foreigner [see 261] as his co-producer. Jones also had a co-producer credit on Van Halen's 5150 [see 299], that group's

first Number One album. "Mick brought an English rock sensibility, which is somewhat perverse and deviant," Joel says. "He was also someone who was very material-oriented, because he was a songwriter in his own right."

As with his previous efforts, Joel went for a whole album of quality recordings, rather than a few choice hit singles and some filler. The title track, which features the Memphis Horns, was a particular favorite, although "it didn't get a lot of airplay, because it wasn't released as a single," he says. Another album track, "Shameless," which Joel calls his tribute to Jimi Hendrix [see 108], would go on to become a hit for country superstar Garth Brooks [see 354].

Yet Storm Front wasn't without its share of hits. "We Didn't Start the Fire" became Joel's third Number One single. "Originally, that was a completely different song, a country song that I had in the spare-parts bin called 'Jolene,'" says Joel. The song was inspired by a visit to the studio by Sean Lennon, the son of late Beatle John Lennon, and a group of his friends. "One of his friends had just turned 21," Joel says. "And he was saying that it was really a tough time in the world to be that age. 'We've

got AIDS, homeless people, and crack.' I said, 'Hey, it was a tough time when I was that age, too. We had Vietnam, there were drug problems, there was a lot of violence, and presidents were getting assassinated.'" The youngster turned to Joel and said, "Well, at least you grew up as a kid in the '50s. Everyone knows nothing happened in the '50s." As Joel recalls, "I said, 'What? Didn't you ever hear of the Korean War, the Suez Canal, and Castro?' So I started writing these things down and I realized that there was this whole generation that really didn't know anything about history, except what went on in their lives. Also, I had just hit 40 years old, and as most people know that's a good time to take inventory. The combination of me turning 40 and the conversation with that kid inspired me to kind of sum up where I was. I started with Harry Truman, because in the year I was born, 1949, Harry Truman was president. From there it kind of wrote itself."

On December 9, 1989, "We Didn't Start the Fire" hit the top of the Hot 100, becoming Joel's third Number One single. A week later Storm Front joined the single at the top, giving Joel his third chart-topping album.

THE TOP FIVE
Week of December 16, 1989

1. **Storm Front**
   Billy Joel

2. **Girl You Know It's True**
   Milli Vanilli

3. **Janet Jackson's Rhythm Nation 1814**
   Janet Jackson

4. **Forever Your Girl**
   Paula Abdul

5. **Hangin' Tough**
   New Kids on the Block

ATLANTIC 82050 **...But Seriously**
PHIL COLLINS | **339**

Producers: Phil Collins and Hugh
Padghm

Track listing: Hang in Long Enough /
That's Just the Way It Is / Find a Way
to My Heart / Colours / Father to Son
/ Another Day in Paradise / All of My
Life / Something Happened on the
Way to Heaven / Do You Remember?
/ I Wish It Would Rain Down

January 6, 1990
3 weeks (nonconsecutive)

When Phil Collins looks back at
...But Seriously, he thinks of
"Another Day in Paradise," his
seventh solo single to top the Hot 100
and third consecutive Number One in
a little more than a year. Yet Collins
remembers "Another Day in Paradise"
not for its impact on the chart, but for
how it raised consciousness about the
plight of the homeless.

"That song ended up, albeit not by
design, but by action, as a sort of mini-
anthem for the shelters. It kind of typifies
the feel of the album," Collins says. "It
was called ...But Seriously because I
was trying to draw people to some of
the serious issues I was singing about,
as opposed to some of the more frivolous songs."

The big hits from Collins's previous
album, No Jacket Required, [see 286],
were the intimate ballad "One More
Night" and the funky "Sussudio." In
between albums, Collins scored Number
One singles with "Separate Lives," a
duet with Marilyn Martin from the film
White Nights, and "Groovy Kind of
Love" and "Two Hearts." The latter two
songs were covers of '60s hits featured
on the soundtrack from Buster, a 1988

THE TOP FIVE
Week of January 6, 1990

1. **...But Seriously**
   Phil Collins

2. **Girl You Know It's True**
   Milli Vanilli

3. **Storm Front**
   Billy Joel

4. **Janet Jackson's
   Rhythm Nation 1814**
   Janet Jackson

5. **Forever Your Girl**
   Paula Abdul

film that starred Collins in the title role
as the Great Train Robber–turned–flower
salesman, Buster Edwards.

With ...But Seriously, Collins made a
conscious decision to challenge his audience. "I wanted to call the album something that would at least imply that there
was something going on that the audience wasn't expecting," Collins says.

As he had done with No Jacket
Required, which included guest shots by
Sting, onetime Culture Club backing
vocalist Helen Terry, ex-Genesis mate
Peter Gabriel, and the System's David
Frank, Collins once again called upon
his famous friends to lend a hand. Eric
Clapton [see 179, 361] plays guitar on
"I Wish It Would Rain Down." Steve
Winwood [see 314] plays organ on
"All of My Life." Stephen Bishop lends
some backing vocals to "Do You
Remember?," and David Crosby [see

120, 131, 186] sings back-up on
"That's Just the Way It Is" and "Another
Day in Paradise."

Collins, a longtime Byrds and
Crosby, Stills & Nash fan, had asked
Crosby if he would sing on his album
when the two met at the Atlantic
Records 40th Anniversary Concert at
Madison Square Gardens in 1988.
"Getting him to sing was a major buzz
on the album for me," Collins says.
"He just came down, picked those
notes out of the air and laid down
some great harmonies."

"Another Day in Paradise" went to
Number One on December 23, 1989,
and held that position when ...But Seriously reached the top of the album chart
two weeks later, giving Collins his second consecutive Number One album
and another simultaneous Number One
album and single.

340 Nick of Time CAPITOL 91268
BONNIE RAITT

Producer: Don Was

Track listing: Nick of Time / Thing Called Love / Love Letter / Cry on My Shoulder / Real Man / Nobody's Girl / Have a Heart / Too Soon to Tell / I Will Not Be Denied / I Ain't Gonna Let You Break My Heart Again / The Road's My Middle Name

April 7, 1990
3 weeks

Nick of Time didn't come a moment too soon for Bonnie Raitt, whose career seemed as good as dead following her 1986 album *Nine Lives*. The daughter of Broadway actor/singer John Raitt had recorded several critically acclaimed albums for Warner Bros. in the '70s, but had enjoyed little commercial success. After *Nine Lives*, Raitt's ninth album for Warner Bros., stalled at number 115, the label decided to drop her, a decision that would later haunt the Warner Bros. top brass for years to come.

After the split with Warner Bros., Raitt hooked up with Capitol and producer Don Was, then known primarily as a member of the Detroit R&B band Was (Not Was). Many credited Was with revitalizing Raitt's career, but he downplays his role. "I feel uncomfortable with that," he says. "I wasn't asleep during those sessions, but there were a lot of factors that came into play. You don't just revitalize someone. The best that you can do is help them realize what their strengths are and aim for them."

Was's game plan was to have Raitt make a record that they would both be proud of, rather than cater to the marketplace. "Radio wasn't playing anything that sounded remotely like the kind of record Bonnie Raitt should have been making," Was says. "So, we made the record that we wanted to make, not the record that we thought people wanted to buy."

In keeping with that spirit, the bulk of *Nick of Time* was recorded in approximately five days with very few overdubs. "As a result, it was unself-conscious. It was stripped-down, and everybody had a good time making it. And I believe you can hear that joy of music-making on the tracks."

Was found himself moved by Raitt's performance during the sessions. "I remember cutting 'Nick of Time,'" he says. "It struck me that it really had a universal ring of truth. You don't have to be a woman wanting to have a baby to appreciate it." Working with Raitt also helped Was gain some insight on the art of producing. "There's something larger than technique," he says. "It wasn't about hitting the right notes, it was about telling the truth."

For material, Raitt opted for a mix of originals and covers, such as John Hiatt's "Thing Called Love" and Bonnie Hayes's "Love Letter." Several notable players guested on the album, including David Crosby and Graham Nash, who supplied backing vocals on "Cry on My Shoulder," and Herbie Hancock, who accompanied Raitt on "I Ain't Gonna Let You Break My Heart Again." While recording the latter track, Raitt began to cry. "That was one of the few things we had to do over," Was says. "She got so caught up in the song, she couldn't get through it."

Despite the big-name guests, sales expectations for *Nick of Time* were relatively low. "Everybody expected to sell about 150,000 records and we would break even," says Was. "But then it shipped 300,000." *Nick of Time* originally peaked at number 22 in June 1989 and had fallen to number 119 toward the end of that year. But after it received a Grammy nomination for album of the year in January 1990, it began to rebound up the chart.

On February 21 at the Shrine Auditorium in Los Angeles, Raitt surprised many by taking the awards for album of the year, female pop and rock vocals, and best traditional blues recording. The following week, *Nick of Time* matched its previous peak at number 22. Four weeks later, in its 52nd week on the Top Pop Albums chart, *Nick of Time* hit Number One, giving Raitt history's longest chart span from an artist's chart debut (1972, in her case) to the top. For Raitt, it was worth the wait.

THE TOP FIVE
Week of April 7, 1990

1. **Nick of Time**
   Bonnie Raitt

2. **Forever Your Girl**
   Paula Abdul

3. **Janet Jackson's Rhythm Nation 1814**
   Janet Jackson

4. **Soul Provider**
   Michael Bolton

5. **Alannah Myles**
   Alannah Myles

ENSIGN 21759 # I Do Not Want What I Haven't Got

SINEAD O'CONNOR

341

Producer: Sinead O'Connor and Nellee Hooper

Track listing: Feel So Different / I Am Stretched on Your Grave / Three Babies / The Emperor's New Clothes / Black Boys on Mopeds / Nothing Compares 2 U / Jump in the River / You Cause as Much Sorrow / The Last Day of Our Acquaintance / I Do Not Want What I Haven't Got

April 28, 1990
6 weeks

With her stunning 1988 debut album, *The Lion and the Cobra*, and her striking, clean-shaven head, Irish-born Sinead O'Connor became one of the most promising and refreshing new talents in rock. With her 1990 follow-up, O'Connor became a superstar, albeit one of the most controversial in the pop world.

The one-time lead vocalist of the Dublin-based Ton Ton Macoute, O'Connor made her recording debut on the *Captive* soundtrack, which also featured a score co-written by U2 guitarist the Edge. After signing to Ensign records in 1985, O'Connor recorded her debut album with a cast of musicians that included former Adam & the Ants members Marco Pirroni on guitar and Kevin Mooney on bass, Irish chanteuse Enya, and O'Connor's then-husband John Reynolds on drums. Yet it was O'Connor herself, whose unusual voice suggested a more aggressive version of Kate Bush, who garnered all the attention. The album reached number 36, even though it failed to generate a hit single. O'Connor wouldn't face the same problem

with *I Do Not Want What I Haven't Got*.

Although only a rising talent in America, in the U.K. O'Connor was already a full-fledged star, and the new-found pressures of stardom served as a central theme in songs such as "Feel So Different" and "The Emperor's New Clothes." The former song opens with the Serenity Prayer ("Grant me the serenity to accept the things I cannot change..."). The prayer, taught to O'Connor as a youth by her mother, is familiar to those in 12-step programs.

"A lot of very dramatic changes have taken place in my life," O'Connor explained to Edna Gundersen in *USA Today*. "I've had to make a lot of big decisions when I wasn't too sure of what I was doing. And [the prayer] seemed the most appropriate way of asking for assistance. I only recently discovered there was no reason for me to worry, that everything was fine. I got to know myself a bit better."

Possibly the biggest change in O'Connor's life was a split with her manager and close friend Fachtan O'Ceallaigh. Before the break-up, it was O'Ceallaigh who suggested that O'Connor cover "Nothing Compares 2 U," an obscure Prince tune originally recorded by the Family in 1985. The video for the track, taped only days after her split

with O'Ceallaigh, featured a close-up of a teary-eyed O'Connor. Ironically, O'Connor found a new manager in Steve Fargnoli, whose former client was Prince.

Buoyed by heavy MTV play, "Nothing Compares 2 U" hit the top of the Hot 100 on April 21. A week later, with the single still holding on to the Number One position, *I Do Not Want What I Haven't Got* hit the top of the album chart.

But life didn't get any easier for O'Connor, as she found herself in the center of several media furors in the ensuing months. At a concert in New Jersey, she refused to have "The Star Spangled Banner" played before she took the stage, leading several radio stations to ban her music. She also canceled an appearance on NBC-TV's "Saturday Night Live" when she learned that shock-comedian Andrew Dice Clay was the scheduled host. When she finally did appear on the show, she tore up a photo of Pope John Paul II, leading to another wave of anti-O'Connor fervor. Even her meeting with Prince ended up a disaster when she told the Irish music publication *Hot Press* that Prince had "threatened her with physical violence," an allegation that Prince dismissed. In any case, the encounter gave "Nothing Compares 2 U" new resonance.

THE TOP FIVE
Week of April 28, 1990

1. **I Do Not Want What I Haven't Got**
   Sinead O'Connor

2. **Janet Jackson's Rhythm Nation 1814**
   Janet Jackson

3. **Soul Provider**
   Michael Bolton

4. **Nick of Time**
   Bonnie Raitt

5. **Forever Your Girl**
   Paula Abdul

342 Please Hammer Don't Hurt 'Em CAPITOL 92857
M.C. HAMMER

Producer: M.C. Hammer

Track listing: Here Comes the Hammer / U Can't Touch This / Have You Seen Her / On Your Face / Help the Children / Dancin' Machine / Pray / Crime Story / She's Sort and Wet / Lets Go Deeper

June 9, 1990
21 weeks (nonconsecutive)

By 1989, M.C. Hammer's pop-oriented brand of rap music had already proven successful. His Capitol Records debut, Let's Get It Started, topped the Top Black Albums chart and peaked at number 30 on the Top Pop Albums list, spawning two top five Hot Rap Singles, "Pump It Up" and "Turn This Mutha Out." Yet few could have predicted the enormous success of his follow-up album, Please Hammer Don't Hurt 'Em.

As a youth, Stanley Kirk Burrell had two loves: baseball and music. He idolized James Brown, but it was his passion for baseball that led him to the Oakland Coliseum to watch the A's. One day, A's owner Charlie Finley caught a glimpse of the 11-year-old Burrell performing a James Brown–styled dance routine in the stadium parking lot. Finley was impressed enough to invite him to work as a batboy. Burrell was soon dubbed Little Hammer because of his resemblance to home run king "Hammerin' " Hank Aaron.

Although Hammer's pro baseball dreams didn't pan out, his ties to the A's did help him launch his recording career. Two A's players invested

$20,000, allowing him to launch his Bustin' Records. He sold his first single, "Ring 'Em," out of the trunk of his car and eventually recorded an album called Feel My Power. The album and Hammer's dance-floor antics were enough to secure a contract with Capitol, which advanced Hammer $750,000 to record additional songs. The album, with the new songs, was retitled Let's Get It Started.

Please Hammer Don't Hurt 'Em was recorded on the Bust It Mobile Studio Bus while Hammer was on tour in support of Let's Get It Started. "We did it when we could," Hammer says, "during the day when we were traveling down the road and at night after the shows. It was a work in progress made in America—from city-to-city, from state-to-state."

For the musical backbone of several songs on the album, Hammer turned to his heroes. He recorded rap remakes of the Chi-Lites' "Have You Seen Her," Earth, Wind & Fire's "On Your Face," and the

Jacksons' "Dancing Machine." Elsewhere, he sampled Prince and Marvin Gaye significantly enough to give them co-writing credits. "They're all people that I think are great musicians," Hammer says.

Yet it was Hammer's take of Rick James's 1981 hit "Super Freak," titled "U Can't Touch This," which drove Please Hammer Don't Hurt 'Em up the album chart. Hammer cleared his sample of the track with James's lawyers. Yet James, who was opposed to having his music sampled, didn't know about Hammer's use of his music until he heard the song on the radio. By that time, it was too late. "U Can't Touch This" peaked at number eight a week after Please Hammer Don't Hurt 'Em hit the top of the album chart, as Capitol deleted the single to spur on album sales.

With "Have You Seen Her" and "Pray" later becoming top five hits, Please Hammer Don't Hurt 'Em became the rapper's grand slam, racking up the most weeks at Number One since Prince's Purple Rain [see 282].

THE TOP FIVE
Week of June 9, 1990

1. **Please Hammer Don't Hurt 'Em**
   M.C. Hammer

2. **I Do Not Want What I Haven't Got**
   Sinead O'Connor

3. **Brigade**
   Heart

4. **Pretty Woman**
   Soundtrack

5. **Poison**
   Bell Biv Devoe

Producer: Maurice Starr

Track listing: Step by Step / Tonight /
Baby, I Believe in You / Call It What
You Want / Let's Try It Again / Happy
Birthday / Games / Time Is on Our
Side / Where Do I Go From Here? /
Stay with Me Baby / Funny Feeling /
Never Gonna Fall in Love Again

June 30, 1990
1 week

In March 1990, the readers of *Rolling
Stone* voted the New Kids on the
Block worst band, worst tour, and
Hangin' Tough [see 333] and its title
track worst album and single, respectively. But that didn't matter much to the
New Kids on the Block or their fans. The
New Kids had become such a phenomenon that Hasbro announced it would
launch a line of dolls modeled after the
group in time for Christmas. And when
Step by Step was released in June, it hit
the peak of the Top Pop Albums chart in
a mere two weeks.

But success was taking its toll on the
New Kids. Constant touring left little
time for the band to work in the recording studio, so much of *Step by Step* was
recorded on the road with Maurice
Starr once again at the helm. "It was a
totally different situation," says Donnie
Wahlberg. "We recorded in hotel
rooms. We would come off the stage,

go right to the hotel, and sing all night."

Jordan Knight says he laid down the
vocals for "Baby, I Believe in You" the
same day he heard the demo of the
track. "I didn't even have a lyric sheet,"
he says. "Maurice sang it to me into
headphones and I would repeat it and
put in on tape."

Other times, the band would record
before shows. "I remember recording
'Step by Step,' " says Jordan Knight. "I
had a bad cold, but we still had to
record it. It took a long time to get it
done and then we had to do a show."

Like some of the New Kids' previous
hits, "Step by Step" was a song Starr
had penned for another act. The song,
originally recorded for Motown by the
Boston-based group the Superiors, had
flopped. "We liked the song, so Maurice decided to give it to us," Wahlberg
says. The public also loved the New
Kids' version, as the track, released as
the first single from *Step by Step*,
debuted at number 27. Four weeks
later, as *Step by Step* hit Number One
on the Top Pop Albums chart, "Step by
Step" hit the top of the Hot 100, giving
the New Kids another simultaneous
Number One album and single.

The New Kids scored their ninth consecutive top 10 hit with "Tonight," which
recalled the Beatles. That single climbed
to number seven, but the third single
from the album, "Let's Try Again," didn't
fare as well, stalling at number 53.

If that wasn't bad enough, Gregory
McPherson, credited as an "associate
producer" and "string arranger" on *Step
by Step*, filed a breach-of-contract lawsuit against the group. McPherson
claimed that Starr recorded many of the
group's vocals and that the New Kids
lip-synched on stage. The group had the
last word, however, canceling an Australian tour to appear live on "The Arse-
nio Hall Show" to set the record
straight. It also filed a countersuit
against McPherson, who later dropped
his suit. "I don't think it hurt us," says
Wahlberg. "It's one of those things you
try to use to your advantage."

THE TOP FIVE
Week of June 30, 1990

1. **Step by Step**
   New Kids on the Block

2. **Please Hammer
   Don't Hurt 'Em**
   M.C. Hammer

3. **I'm Breathless**
   Madonna

4. **I Do Not Want What
   I Haven't Got**
   Sinead O'Connor

5. **Poison**
   Bell Biv Devoe

344 To the Extreme SBK 95325
VANILLA ICE

Producers: *Vanilla Ice, Earthquake, Khayree, Paul Loomis, George Anderson, David Deberry, Kim Sharp, Wayne Stallings, and Darryl Williams*

Track listing: *Ice Ice Baby / Yo Vanilla / Stop That Train / Hooked / Ice Is Workin' It / Life Is a Fantasy / Play That Funky Music / Dancin' / Go Ill / It's a Party / Juice to Get Loose Boy / Ice Cold / Rosta Man / I Love You / Havin' a Roni*

November 10, 1990
16 weeks

With M.C. Hammer's *Please Hammer Don't Hurt 'Em* [see 342] showing the incredible commercial potential of rap music, the timing was perfect for Robert Van Winkle to become a star. Under the name Vanilla Ice, the young rapper had a pop sensibility like Hammer and teen-idol good looks like Elvis, which made his brand of rap music safe enough for white preteens in the suburbs. Yet Vanilla Ice wasn't an overnight sensation.

The Miami-born Van Winkle fell in love with rap when he heard the Sugarhill Gang's "Rapper's Delight" in 1980, when he was 12. Van Winkle's love of rap stayed with him as his family relocated to Dallas and he was bumped from school to school. In 1987 he entered a talent contest at the City Lights nightclub in Dallas. The club's owner, Tommy Quon, was impressed enough to sign on as his manager on the spot. At Quon's club, Ice opened for such future chart-toppers as Tone Loc and Paula Abdul. He later laid down demo tracks with City Lights' DJ Earthquake.

THE TOP FIVE
Week of November, 1990

1. **To the Extreme**
   Vanilla Ice

2. **Please Hammer Don't Hurt 'Em**
   M.C. Hammer

3. **The Razors Edge**
   AC/DC

4. **Mariah Carey**
   Mariah Carey

5. **Wilson Phillips**
   Wilson Phillips

"We were shopping for a record deal, but no one was interested," Ice recalls. Undaunted, Quon decided to form his own record label, Ultrax, and release Ice's music himself. The single he issued featured a cover of Wild Cherry's 1976 Number One hit "Play That Funky Music" on the A-side and a cut called "Ice Ice Baby" on the flip. The latter track borrowed a sample from the Queen–David Bowie collaboration "Under Pressure."

The single was serviced to urban radio stations in March 1990 but failed to make a dent until several months later, when a DJ named Darrell J at WAGH Columbus, Georgia, flipped it over and started playing "Ice Ice Baby." The single, and Ice's album *Hooked*, released in July on Ultrax, started to sell. Meanwhile, a low-budget video became the Number One request on the newly established Video Jukebox Network.

The buzz on Ice was sufficient to elicit interest from some of the major labels that had initially turned Ice away. By August, SBK Records had inked Ice to a deal. The label decided to release *Hooked* under a new title, *To the Extreme*, with new artwork. One song, a cover of the Rolling Stones classic "(I Can't Get No) Satisfaction," was deleted for legal reasons, although Ice's version of the song would later turn up on his follow-up album *Extremely Live*.

With the muscle of SBK behind it, "Ice Ice Baby" became the first rap song ever to top the Hot 100 on November 3, 1990. The week "Ice Ice Baby" hit the summit, SBK deleted the single to spur album sales. The strategy paid off as *To the Extreme* knocked M.C. Hammer's *Please Hammer Don't Hurt 'Em* from the Number One spot for good a week later. At the time, Ice was Hammer's opening act.

COLUMBIA 45202 **Mariah Carey**
MARIAH CAREY

Executive producer: Tommy Mottola

Track listing: Vision of Love / There's Got to Be a Way / I Don't Wanna Cry / Someday / Vanishing / All in Your Mind / Alone in Love / You Need Me / Sent From Up Above / Prisoner / Love Takes Time

March 2, 1991
11 weeks

"I've been writing songs my whole life," says Mariah Carey. It was that preparation, a little luck, and an unforgettable voice that help Carey secure a record deal at the age of 18.

Carey grew up with music. Her mother, Patricia, was a vocal coach who sang with the New York City Opera. At the age of 16, Carey was already making demo tapes and writing songs with partner Ben Margulies. "'Someday' and 'Alone in Love' I wrote while I was in high school," Carey says of the two tracks, which turned up on her debut album.

Carey's first professional gig, however, didn't come until after she graduated high school. Through a friend, Carey learned that Brenda K. Starr was looking for a back-up singer. Carey auditioned and got the job.

During a break in touring, Starr encouraged Carey to accompany her to a CBS Records party. Starr passed Carey's demo tape to CBS Records Group president Tommy Mottola, who listened to the tape in his limousine on the way home from the party. Mottola was so impressed after hearing a mere two songs that he ordered his driver to return to the party, but Carey had

already left. (Mottola's fondness for Carey would eventually go beyond her music—the two were married in 1993.)

Eventually, Mottola tracked down Carey and offered her a recording contract. He subsequently became so involved in the project that he served as executive producer.

"I had a lot of the songs before I got my record deal," says Carey, "so the songs remind me of different things in my life while I was growing up. Right after I got the record deal, I wrote 'Vision of Love' and 'Vanishing.' It was an ongoing process."

Instead of going for a single, big-name producer, Mottola hooked Carey up with a number of different people to work with in the studio, including Rhett Lawrence, Ric Wake, Narada Michael Walden, and Walter Afanasieff. Margulies also received production credits, as did Carey herself on "Vanishing."

Once the album was completed, Carey's success came quickly. "Vision of Love," her debut single, hit the top on August 4, 1990, a mere nine weeks after debuting on the Hot 100. The follow-up single, "Love Takes Time," a last-minute addition to the album that was not even listed on the initial pressing, proved Carey was no fluke. That track hit the top on November 10, eight weeks after its chart debut.

With "Someday," her third single, in the number two position on the Hot 100, *Mariah Carey* hit the top spot in its 36th week on the Top Pop Albums chart.

Yet Carey's Number One single streak was far from over. On March 9, "Someday" knocked Whitney Houston's "All the Man That I Need" from the top spot, to become her third consecutive chart-topper. When "I Don't Wanna Cry" became Carey's fourth Number One, she became the first artist since the Jackson Five to have their first four chart singles go to Number One. Says Carey, "It was the culmination of a lot of hard work and a lot of dreams."

THE TOP FIVE
Week of March 2, 1991

1. **Mariah Carey**
   Mariah Carey

2. **To the Extreme**
   Vanilla Ice

3. **The Soul Cages**
   Sting

4. **Please Hammer Don't Hurt 'Em**
   M.C. Hammer

5. **I'm Your Baby Tonight**
   Whitney Houston

346 Out of Time WARNER BROS. 26496
R.E.M.

Producers: R.E.M. and Scott Litt

Track listing: Radio Song / Losing My Religion / Low / Near Wild Heaven / Endgame / Shiny Happy People / Belong / Half a World Away / Texarkana / Country Feedback / Me in Honey

May 18, 1991
2 weeks (nonconsecutive)

In 1981, R.E.M. emerged out of the small college town of Athens, Georgia, and into the hearts of rock critics across America with "Radio Free Europe." The single, released on the tiny Hib-Tone label, was voted the top independent single of 1981 in the *Village Voice*'s annual critics' poll. It took the American public a decade to catch up with critical opinion, as R.E.M. finally hit Number One on the Top Pop Albums chart with *Out of Time.*

With the release of its first four albums on I.R.S. Records—1983's *Murmur,* 1984's *Reckoning,* 1985's *Fables of the Reconstruction,* and 1986's *Lifes Rich Pageant*—the quartet remained critics' darlings, but failed to crack the top 20 of the album chart. R.E.M.'s big commercial breakthrough came in 1987 with its fifth album, *Document,* and the blistering folk-rock single "The One I Love." The album reached number 10, while the single peaked at nine. With *Green,* its debut for Warner Bros., R.E.M.'s success continued. The album reached number 12, while the single "Stand" climbed to number six.

When R.E.M. returned to recording after a year-long hiatus, the band decided it was time for a change. Guitarist Peter Buck had grown tired of playing

---

THE TOP FIVE
Week of May 18, 1991

1. **Out of Time**
   R.E.M.

2. **Mariah Carey**
   Mariah Carey

3. **Gonna Make You Sweat**
   C + C Music Factory

4. **Wilson Phillips**
   Wilson Phillips

5. **Shake Your Money Maker**
   The Black Crowes

---

electric guitar. "He just wanted to explore more acoustic things and get away from loud guitar," says singer Michael Stipe. As a result, Buck picked up the mandolin, while bassist Mike Mills opted for keyboards on several tracks, and drummer Bill Berry picked up the bass duties on a few songs. In addition, the band recruited a string section, tour sideman and former dB's member Peter Holsapple, and saxophonist Kidd Jordan for the recording sessions.

The band also called in guest vocalists: rapper KRS-1 of Boogie Down Productions and fellow Athens music scenester Kate Pierson of the B-52's. KRS-1 was featured on the album opener "Radio Song." Says Stipe, "It was really exciting to involve him in the project. He was really into it, and it made sense, since we both had similar gripes about radio and formatting." Pierson's guest shots came on "Shiny Happy People" (a pure-pop delight punctuated by a string section playing a different time signature), "Country Feedback," and "Me in Honey." Says Mills, "It was fun working with Kate. That was a highlight."

Yet the most memorable song on *Out of Time* was "Losing My Religion," which

was accompanied by a video clip as striking as the track itself. The single climbed to number four, becoming the biggest hit of R.E.M.'s career, while the video, directed by a visual artist simply known as Tarsem, picked up six awards at the 1991 MTV Video Music Awards.

"I really hit the nail on the head with that one," says Stipe. "My idea with that song was to try to rewrite 'Every Breath You Take' [see the Police's *Synchronicity*—276]. I guess I did a pretty good job of it." Still, the success of the single took the members of R.E.M. by surprise. "Nobody expected that at all," says Mills. "It was nice to see that a mandolin-based quasi-folk song could be a big hit in America."

Thanks in part to the success of "Losing My Religion," *Out of Time* hit Number One in its eighth week on the Top Pop Albums chart. The following week, *Billboard* began utilizing SoundScan data in compiling the album chart and Michael Bolton's *Time, Love & Tenderness* temporarily dethroned R.E.M. On June 1, 1991, however, *Out of Time* returned to Number One, becoming the only album to top the chart in both the pre- and post-SoundScan eras.

COLUMBIA 46771 **Time, Love & Tenderness** 347
MICHAEL BOLTON

Producer: Walter Afanasieff and
Michael Bolton

Track listing: Love Is a Wonderful Thing
/ Time, Love and Tenderness / Missing
You Now / Forever Isn't Long Enough /
Now That I Found You / When a Man
Loves a Woman / We're Not Makin'
Love Anymore / New Love / Save Me
/ Steel Bars

May 25, 1991
1 week

Success certainly didn't happen
overnight for Michael Bolotin, but
when it did happen there was no
stopping him. The one-time hard-rocker
fronted the group Black Jack in the late
'70s, but he changed his named to
Bolton in 1983 for his self-titled Columbia Records debut, and altered his
sound to a more pop-oriented approach
with the 1987 album The Hunger. But it
was the 1989 effort, Soul Provider, that
really landed Bolton on the musical
map.

That album peaked at number three,
spawned five top 10 singles, including
Bolton's first Number One, "How Am I
Supposed to Live Without You," and led
an incredible chart life. In fact, when
Time, Love & Tenderness debuted on
May 11, 1991, Soul Provider was still
in the top half of the Top Pop Albums
chart after 95 weeks.

Upon the release of Time, Love &
Tenderness, Bolton vowed that the
album would yield at least four hit singles. His prediction was right on target.
Although "Missing You Now" stalled at
number 12, "Love Is a Wonderful
Thing" and "Time, Love and Tenderness"
were top 10 hits, while Bolton's version

of Percy Sledge's "When a Man Loves
a Woman" became his second Number
One single.

Bolton's recording of "When a Man
Loves a Woman" continued the tradition
of covering R&B classics he began on
The Hunger with his take of Otis Redding's "(Sittin' on) The Dock of the Bay."
On Soul Provider he covered "Georgia
on My Mind," a hit for Ray Charles [see
53] in 1960.

The cover of "When a Man Loves a
Woman" may have also helped Bolton
win over a few males to his predomi-
nantly female fan base. "There are a lot
of male fans of that remake," Bolton
says. "When I perform the song live I
see couples squeezing and hugging
each other."

Time, Love & Tenderness includes collaborations with sax master Kenny G,
who's featured on "Missing You Now,"
and R&B belter Patti LaBelle [see 294],

who duets with Bolton on "We're Not
Makin' Love Anymore." Yet one of the
most surprising and rewarding collaborations on the album is "Steel Bars," a
song Bolton co-wrote with Bob Dylan
[see 170, 194, and 211].

"Someone who works for Bob Dylan
came to me. When they extended the
invitation, I took it immediately. I had
other things booked, but I didn't even
have to think about it. I moved my
schedule to meet with him. The first session went well, so we met again,"
Bolton says. "He's a unique individual.
He was very receptive to finishing this
song and it turned out to be a hit. It
wasn't released as a single, but the airplay on it was phenomenal. It was one
of those rare experiences that's up there
with doing a duet with Ray Charles on
'Georgia' or singing 'When a Man
Loves a Woman' with Percy Sledge, or
having lunch with Joe DiMaggio."

THE TOP FIVE
Week of May 25, 1991

1. **Time, Love & Tenderness**
   Michael Bolton

2. **New Jack City**
   Soundtrack

3. **Mariah Carey**
   Mariah Carey

4. **No Fences**
   Garth Brooks

5. **Out of Time**
   R.E.M.

348 Spellbound
PAULA ABDUL

CAPTIVE 91611

Rush' and I carried it everywhere I went. I couldn't wait to record it," she recalls. Working primarily with V. Jeffrey Smith and Peter Lord of the group the Family Stand allowed Abdul to be more focused. "With *Forever Your Girl*, I was traveling back and forth from Los Angeles and Minneapolis and working with a bunch of different producers," she says. "With *Spellbound*, I was more experienced. I was much more involved, co-writing some of the songs. I was there during the whole process."

The bulk of the material of *Spellbound* was written and produced with the Family Stand, but other producers and songwriters contributed: The song "U" was credited to "Paisley Park," better known as Prince, while "Alright Tonight" was written by John Hiatt and produced by Don Was.

Yet it was the material written collaboratively by Abdul and the Family Stand that proved the most popular. "Rush Rush" hit Number One on the Hot 100 on June 15 and stayed there for five weeks. For Abdul, it was important that the ballad was the first single released from *Spellbound*, rather than another dance track. "It showed versatility and a different side of me and won me some new fans," she says. Abdul scored another Number One single with "The Promise of a New Day."

"Will You Marry Me?" was also released as a single, only weeks after Abdul and actor Emilio Estevez announced their engagement in March 1992. "It was recorded two years before I met him," she says. "I didn't want it to be released, but radio stations started playing it. People didn't understand. I had to explain that I didn't have to ask him to marry me."

Executive producer: Gemma Corfield

Track listing: The Promise of a New Day / Rock House / Rush Rush / Spellbound / Vibeology / U / My Foolish Heart / Blowing Kisses in the Wind / To You / Alright Tonight / Will You Marry Me?

June 8, 1991
2 weeks

For Paula Abdul, the making of *Spellbound* was "a growing experience." Coming off the unprecedented success of her debut album *Forever Your Girl* [see 328], Abdul was able to stretch out on *Spellbound*.

Yet Abdul's triumph was dampened weeks before the release of "Rush Rush," the single that preceded *Spellbound*. In a *Globe* tabloid article, singer Yvette

Marine claimed that she had sung lead vocals on several tracks on *Forever Your Girl*. Weeks later, Marine filed a multi-million-dollar "false and deceptive packaging" lawsuit against Virgin Records, Abdul's label. Although Virgin went on to win the suit in August 1993, the legal action hurt Abdul. "It robbed me of some of the excitement and joy from *Spellbound*," she says. Yet even with the allegations questioning Abdul's singing abilities, her fans showed their support. *Spellbound*, the first release on Captive, Abdul's own Virgin-distributed label, debuted at number five on June 1, 1991, before hitting to top of the album chart the following week.

Abdul began searching for material for a follow-up album while *Forever Your Girl* was still riding high on the charts. "I remember when 'Opposites Attract' was a hit, I received a cassette of 'Rush

---

THE TOP FIVE
Week of June 8, 1991

1. **Spellbound**
   Paula Abdul

2. **Time, Love, & Tenderness**
   Michael Bolton

3. **Out of Time**
   R.E.M.

4. **Mariah Carey**
   Mariah Carey

5. **Gonna Make You Sweat**
   C + C Music Factory

Producers: Dr. Dre and Yella

Track listing: Prelude / Real Niggaz
Don't Die / Niggaz 4 Life / Protest /
Appetite for Destruction / Don't Drink
That Wine / Alwayz Into Somethin' /
Message to B.A. / Real Niggaz / To
Kill a Hooker / One Less Bitch /
Findum, Fuckum & Flee / Automobile /
She Swallowed It / I'd Rather Fuck You
/ Approach to Danger / 1-900-2-
COMPTON / The Dayz of Wayback

June 22, 1991
1 week

Other rap albums, like the Beastie
Boys' bratty Licensed to Ill [see
302], Tone Loc's funky Loc-ed After
Dark [321], and M.C. Hammer's pop-
flavored Please Hammer Don't Hurt 'Em
[335], had hit the top of the album
chart, but there had never been a Number One album like N.W.A's EFIL4ZAG-
GIN.

N.W.A—short for Niggaz with Attitude—formed in the late '80s in Compton, California. The group was first featured on the 1987 album N.W.A and
the Posse, which included its earliest

raps and presaged a new sub-genre
known as gangsta rap. However, it was
the group's 1988 album Straight Outta
Compton that brought N.W.A out of its
home turf and into instant infamy. That
album featured a track called "Fuck tha
Police," which raised the ire of law-
enforcement organizations around the
country, even prompting a letter from
the FBI to the group's label.

With the resulting controversy and
plenty of street credibility, N.W.A
proved to be a surprisingly potent commercial force, even though the group's
profanity-laced raps and hard beats
were far too extreme for radio and
video outlets. The album, which offered
a dose of urban reality in graphic and
often shocking terms, climbed to number
37, and went on to sell more than two
million copies.

Yet all was not well in the N.W.A
posse. Ice Cube, one of the group's
most notable voices, left the group over
a dispute with management, but there
was no stopping N.W.A. A follow-up EP
featuring the four remaining members—
Eazy-E, Dr. Dre, D.J. Yella, and M.C.
Ren—titled 100 Miles and Runnin'
peaked at number 27 in 1990, setting

the stage for EFIL4ZAGGIN.

According to N.W.A leader Eazy-E,
there were those who doubted the crew
would be able to carry on without Ice
Cube. "At first they thought we couldn't
do it without him, so we had to prove
we could," he said. Some critics complained that when N.W.A lost Ice Cube,
it also lost its conscience, as the material
on EFIL4ZAGGIN was even more
graphic and shocking than the previous
effort, as evidenced by song titles like
"I'd Rather Fuck You" and "Findum,
Fuckum & Flee."

"We just did whatever we felt like
doing," explained Eazy-E. "A lot of people were afraid to put it on wax, but we
didn't give a fuck." And the group also
didn't mind the negative reviews. "Publicity is publicity," Eazy-E said. "It does-
n't matter if it is good or bad. It's all
good to me."

However, the group did make one
small concession: The album was originally slated to be Niggaz4life. "Everyone complained, so we put it backward
and it looked kind of cool," Eazy-E
recalled.

EFIL4ZAGGIN was so controversial
that many retailers balked at carrying
the album. Like its predecessor,
EFIL4ZAGGIN didn't benefit from radio
or video airplay, but it didn't matter. The
album rose to the top of The Billboard
200 in two short weeks. Even Eazy-E
was surprised.

EFIL4ZAGGIN proved to be
N.W.A.'s finale, as the group's mem-
bers opted to go solo at the album's
release. Years later, plans for a full
N.W.A reunion were scrapped after
Eazy-E announced he had contracted
AIDS. He died of AIDS-related complica-
tions on March 26, 1995.

THE TOP FIVE
Week of June 22, 1991

1. **EFIL4ZAGGIN**
   N.W.A

2. **Spellbound**
   Paula Abdul

3. **Out of Time**
   R.E.M.

4. **Gonna Make You Sweat**
   C + C Music Factory

5. **Time, Love & Tenderness**
   Michael Bolton

350 Slave to the Grind ATLANTIC 82242
SKID ROW

Producer: Michael Wagener

Track listing: Monkey Business / Slave to the Grind / The Threat / Quicksand Jesus / Psycho Love / Beggars Day / Livin' on a Chain Gang / Creepshow / In a Darkened Room / Riot Act / Mudkicker / Wasted Time

June 29, 1991
1 week

Skid Row was the first hard-rock band to benefit from the use of SoundScan data in compiling *Billboard*'s album chart. The New York band's self-titled 1989 debut certainly showed there was a market for the band's mix of hard-rocking tunes and power ballads when it climbed to number six and generated two top 10 singles—"18 and Life" and "I Remember You." Yet *Slave to the Grind*'s entry at Number One likely turned a lot of heads.

Skid Row was founded in 1986 by bassist/songwriter Rachel Bolan and guitarist Dave "The Snake" Sabo. Guitarist Scotti Hill and drummer Rob Affuso rounded out the band. After a nearly year-long search for a frontman, the band hooked up with Sebastian Bach, who caught the eye of the band's friend David Feld at a jam session following a wedding. Soon the band signed on with McGhee Entertainment, which also managed Bon Jovi [see 306], and Atlantic Records. The band's debut album and a support spot on the Bon Jovi tour made Skid Row stars.

Yet it wasn't necessarily easy to follow up the debut album. "We had our whole life to write the first one," says Bolan. "For the second album, we really had to put our noses to the grindstone." Only two of the songs on the album, "Psycho Love" and "Monkey Business" were written on the road, despite the fact that the band also toured with Aerosmith [see 370] and Mötley Crüe [see 336].

Success gave Skid Row some time to relax while recording its second album. The band recorded the album in two and a half months at New River Studios in Fort Lauderdale, Florida, and Scream Studios in Studio City, California. "At times it was a little more relaxed, but then it got to be crunch time," says Bolan. The band was hoping to complete the album so it could be released prior to starting a summer tour supporting Guns N' Roses [see 320]. "We wanted to have something on the radio before the tour," says Bolan.

Wagener, who had also produced the band's debut album, was the only candidate considered for *Slave to the Grind*. "Michael understands the band as well as any of guys in the band," says Bolan. "He was partially responsible for the Skid Row sound."

While many regarded the harder, less commercial sound of *Slave to the Grind* as a big departure from *Skid Row*, Bolan saw the second album as a "gradual and natural step."

The lyrical themes of the songs on *Slave to the Grind* may also have surprised some. "Psycho Love" was inspired by a news story Bolan caught on CNN. "It was about hookers putting sleeping pills in their Johns' drinks," he says. "I thought let's take it one step further and put some necrophilia in there.

It's kind of like a horror movie, but I can't make a movie, so I wrote a song." Another song, "Creepshow" also reflected the band's love of horror movies, as does the album cover art, painted by Bach's father David Beirk. It appears to depict a man about to be buried alive while spectators watch.

Unlike *Skid Row*, *Slave to the Grind* failed to spawn a top 40 hit. "Wasted Time," the only single released from the album, stalled at number 88 on the Hot 100. Still, the album itself entered the chart at Number One. "That's when I started to pay attention," says Bolan, who hadn't taken much interest in following the charts prior to that. "I asked who was coming out with a record that week." When he learned that a new Van Halen album had just hit the stores, Bolan knew Skid Row's stay at Number One would be short. "I said, 'Oh well, let's love it while it lasts.'"

THE TOP FIVE
Week of June 29, 1991

1. **Slave to the Grind**
   Skid Row

2. **Spellbound**
   Paula Abdul

3. **EFIL4ZAGGIN**
   N.W.A

4. **No Fences**
   Garth Brooks

5. **Gonna Make You Sweat**
   C + C Music Factory

WARNER BROS. 26594 # For Unlawful Carnal Knowledge

VAN HALEN

351

Producers: Andy Johns, Ted Templeman, and Van Halen

Track listing: Poundcake / Judgement Day / Spanked / Runaround / Pleasure Dome / In 'n' Out / Man on a Mission / The Dream Is Over / Right Now / 316 / Top of the World

July 6, 1991
3 weeks

Van Halen intended its ninth album to be its "masterpiece," says singer Sammy Hagar. "We decided we were going to go into the studio and overwrite. We were going to spend as much time as it takes to make the greatest record we could ever make. For once, we were going to get together as a band and work hard."

Yet the band's best intentions went slightly awry. "We were going to produce ourselves, basically, but we got so damned lost we had songs that were 20 minutes long," Hagar says. "So we called in Ted Templeman. Andy Johns had been there working with us, but he wasn't so much producing—he was there for the sound."

With two consecutive Number One albums [see 299, 318], Van Halen were feeling confident that a "masterpiece" was within their reach. "That was our intent," says Hagar. "And it was close. I think that's a great record. Song by song, each song was pretty good, but no one was there to beat me up on the lyrics, so I just sang the first thing I wrote."

Although *For Unlawful Carnal Knowledge* was a year in the making, Hagar doubts it would have ever been completed if the band hadn't turned to Templeman. "If we would have brought Ted in from the beginning, it would have been done a lot sooner." Templeman, a veteran staff producer at Warner Bros., had worked with Hagar in the early '70s when he was a member of Montrose, and also produced the early Van Halen records, but *For Unlawful Carnal Knowledge* marked the first time that Templeman had worked with Van Halen since Hagar had replaced original vocalist David Lee Roth in 1985.

Unlike Van Halen's prior two albums, *For Unlawful Carnal Knowledge* didn't spawn any top 10 hits. "Right Now," the second single released from the album, stalled at number 55 but became one of the group's best-known songs, thanks to extensive album rock play, a striking video that won the band an MTV award, and its subsequent use in a Pepsi commercial. "It's been used in every football game, every baseball game, every basketball game, and by Pepsi," says Hagar. "It wasn't because we sold out, it was just because all these people wanted to use our song, which is very flattering."

The album's title wasn't just a joke like *OU812*. Says Hagar, "That's when censorship was a big issue. I wanted to name the album just *Fuck*. I thought, 'How are they going to stop us? We're one of the biggest bands in the world. We are worth all this money to all these people. If the big chains are going to

carry it, the mom-and-pop stores will.' I wanted to be rebellious. I guess I was a couple years younger then, but I wanted to push the censorship issue, because I thought it was bullshit. People were blaming rock bands for all the violence in the world."

Yet Hagar's original plan was a little too radical. As a compromise, he turned to his friend, boxer Ray "Boom Boom" Mancini, who told him "fuck" was actually an acronym for "For unlawful carnal knowledge." Says Hagar, "I thought that was great, we will enlighten our fans. We thought it was pretty intellectual for Van Halen."

For Unlawful Carnal Knowledge entered The Billboard 200 at the top, giving the band its third consecutive Number One album.

THE TOP FIVE
Week of July 6, 1991

1. **For Unlawful Carnal Knowledge**
   Van Halen

2. **Slave to the Grind**
   Skid Row

3. **Spellbound**
   Paula Abdul

4. **No Fences**
   Garth Brooks

5. **Gonna Make You Sweat**
   C + C Music Factory

352 Unforgettable with Love ELEKTRA 61049
NATALIE COLE

Executive producers: Tommy LiPuma and Natalie Cole

Track listing: The Very Thought of You / Paper Moon / Route 66 / Mona Lisa / L-O-V-E / This Can't Be Love / Smile / That Sunday That Summer / Orange Colored Sky / A Medley of: For Sentimental Reasons, Tenderly, Autumn Leaves / Straighten Up and Fly Right / Avalon / Don't Get Around Much Anymore / Too Young / Nature Boy / Darling, Je Vous Aime Beaucoup / Almost Like Being in Love / Thou Swell / Non Dimenticar / Our Love Is Here to Stay / Unforgettable

July 27, 1991
5 weeks

"I'm sure that there have been other artists and producers who wanted to do a record like this, but everyone was so afraid, because it wouldn't sell," says Natalie Cole. "That's what I was told. I just had to get to the point of saying, 'Okay, so it won't sell, I'm going to do it anyway.'"

Natalie Cole eventually reached that point when she decided to record an album of songs made famous by her father Nat King Cole [see 7], but it didn't happen overnight.

Born in Los Angeles on February 6, 1950, Cole first performed professionally at the age of 11. By her college years, she was regularly performing in clubs and soon secured a contract with Capitol Records, which yielded a string of gold and platinum albums beginning in 1975, when she won a Grammy for best new artist.

By the late '70s, Cole's album sales were beginning to slide. Yet, after signing with EMI in the late '80s, she racked up several top 20 singles, including her version of Bruce Springsteen's "Pink Cadillac," which climbed to number five in 1988.

"I was still establishing who I was," she says. "That meant not doing any of my dad's music for however long it took, until people were convinced I could sing my own stuff. I had to wait until I could pull it off and I feel good about it."

When Cole finally felt the time was right, EMI did not, leading her to leave that label. Upon signing with Elektra, Cole proposed to do a pop album first, then an album of her father's classics. Cole recalls, "Then I went back to L.A. and [Elektra CEO] Bob Krasnow called me up and said, 'I think you should do it now.' And I said, 'What are you talking about?' He said, 'The album of your father's music, do it now.'"

Finally going to work on the project was frightening at first, Cole admits, but the recording sessions, which were conducted in several different studios, "went like clockwork."

"Unforgettable," the title track, featured Cole exchanging verses with her father's original recording. Initially, the single was serviced only to adult contemporary radio stations, but it soon crossed over to top 40, peaking at number 14 in the summer of 1991.

Unforgettable with Love featured several musicians who had played on Nat King Cole's recordings. In addition, portions of the album were recorded on the 26th anniversary of the late crooner's death at the same studio at Capitol Records that he frequently used. "The one thing that saved that session from being a total disaster was that we were doing big band stuff," Cole says, "so it was real up."

The album and "Unforgettable" went on to garner seven Grammy Awards, including record, album, and song of the year, as well as best traditional pop performance, and producer of the year for David Foster, who worked on the project with Tommy LiPuma, Cole, and her husband, Andre Fischer.

The success of the project was a surprise to Cole. "You could say that," she says. "I was stupefied."

THE TOP FIVE
Week of July 27, 1991

1. **Unforgettable with Love**
   Natalie Cole

2. **For Unlawful Carnal Knowledge**
   Van Halen

3. **Spellbound**
   Paula Abdul

4. **Gonna Make You Sweat**
   C + C Music Factory

5. **Slave to the Grind**
   Skid Row

ELEKTRA 61113 **Metallica** **353**
METALLICA

Producers: Bob Rock with James
Hetfield & Lars Ulrich

Track listing: Enter Sandman / Sad But
True / Holier Than Thou / The Unfor-
given / Wherever I May Roam / Don't
Tread on Me / Through the Never /
Nothing Else Matters / Of Wolf and
Man / The God That Failed / My
Friend of Misery / The Struggle Within

August 31, 1991
4 weeks

By the late '80s, the Bay Area–based quartet known as Metallica had proven itself as one of the best and most influential new heavy metal bands. Metallica was much more than a fashion statement—it was a musical force to be reckoned with, as each of the band's members showed uncanny musical chops that allowed the group to twist and turn its way through its complex song structures at breakneck speed. The group's innovations and instrumental virtuosity didn't go unnoticed. By 1988, Metallica's loyal cult following had grown large enough to push the band's fourth album, ...And Justice for All, to number six on the album chart.

Yet despite their success, Metallica felt a need to change. "We had come off the ...And Justice for All album and tour. For me, it was pretty obvious that we had taken the progressive, compli-cated side of Metallica as far as we could take it," says drummer Lars Ulrich, who writes the bulk of the band's songs with singer/guitarist James Hetfield. "The songs kept getting longer and more and more sideways. When we

took those songs out on the road, we realized that was it. We really needed to make a major change—not so much for commercial reasons, but creatively we had exhausted that route."

At the same time, Ulrich had begun to rediscover his hard-rock roots by lis-tening to classic sides by the Rolling Stones [see 145] and AC/DC [see 265]. "The one thing in Metallica that we had not done was to really sit down and try to write a bunch of short and more to-the-point songs," he says. "We decided to take what we do in Metalli-ca and make it a little more straightfor-ward and not be so concerned about trying to show our musicianship."

In June 1990, Ulrich and Hetfield sat down to write songs for Metallica's fifth album. The first song the duo churned out was "Enter Sandman." Says Ulrich, "That was the most straightforward, sim-plest song we had ever written. We did that in two days. That kind of set the tone for the whole record."

Over the course of the next three months, the band composed the other 11 songs that would round out the album. After initially planning to record the album with longtime producer Flem-ming Rasmussen, the group opted for a change in the control room as well. Metallica had been impressed with the sound on Mötley Crüe's Dr. Feelgood [see 336] and decided to ask producer Bob Rock to mix their new album. But Rock wasn't interested in merely mixing the record—he was familiar with Metal-lica and wanted to produce the band.

At first, Metallica balked at Rock's proposition. "But then it became increas-ingly apparent that we should let some-

one else in," says Ulrich. "All those other bands he worked with don't have much in common with us, but with Bob, they all made their best records. We felt that we still had our best record in us and Bob could help us make it."

At first, Rock's professionalism caught the band off-guard. "But once we realized that this guy wasn't here to fuck up our music, he was here to enhance it, it was full speed ahead," says Ulrich. Rock brought hundreds of ideas into the studio. He even suggested the use of strings on "Nothing Else Mat-ters." Quips Ulrich, "When Bob suggest-ed that, after we threw him across the room, we actually discussed it with an open mind."

With its back-to-basics approach and Rock's ace production, Metallica proved to be a winner. "Everyone has one album when everything comes together," says Ulrich. "This was ours."

354 Ropin' the Wind CAPITOL NASHVILLE 96330
GARTH BROOKS

Producer: Allen Reynolds

Track listing: Against the Grain / Rodeo / What She's Doing Now / Burning Bridges / Papa Loved Mama / Shameless / Cold Shoulder / We Bury the Hatchet / In Lonesome Dove / The River

September 28, 1991
18 weeks (nonconsecutive)

With *Ropin' the Wind* Garth Brooks knocked the pop music world on its ear, as the young Oklahoman's third album became the first by a country performer to debut at Number One on the *Billboard* album chart.

While *Ropin' the Wind*'s debut at the top likely shocked many, keen chart-watchers saw it coming. *Ropin' the Wind* also debuted at Number One of the Top Country Albums chart, ending the 41-week reign of Brooks's previous album, *No Fences*. That album reached number three on the pop album chart and had sold more than four million copies by the time *Ropin' the Wind* was released.

Brooks's previous success put him on the brink of superstardom, which was something he was well aware of. "With the success of *No Fences* there was a lot of pressure, but it was put on by myself," he says. "I wanted to try and repeat the success."

Ropin' the Wind, like Brooks's first two albums, was produced by Allen Reynolds, known for his work with country stars Kathy Mattea and Emmylou Harris. It was recorded in roughly six months at Jack's Tracks Recording Studio in Nashville at a cost of approximately $100,000.

While Brooks stuck with the same

producer and recorded *Ropin' the Wind* in approximately the same time period and at the same cost as his two prior releases, the album did mark a departure. "It was a very big stretch for us, because of songs like 'Shameless,' 'Papa Loved Mama,' and 'The River,'" says Brooks. "Those songs were big stretches for me as a country performer at the time."

"Shameless" is a Billy Joel song featured on Joel's *Storm Front* [see 338]. Since Joel never released the song as a single, Brooks decided to record it for *Ropin'*. While Brooks had yet to make an impact on the Hot 100, his decision to record the Joel track showed that his musical influences reached beyond Nashville's Music Row.

"Papa Loved Mama" and "The River" were co-written by Brooks. The former is an up-tempo track chronicling the story of adultery and murder, while

the later is a philosophical ballad.

"Coming off *No Fences*, we could have just tried to make another album just like it, but we tried to do something different, and to be rewarded with a Number One album was really quite an honor," says Brooks.

Country musicians had long maintained that *Billboard*'s previous methods of chart tabulation had short-changed their sales and commercial achievements, and the advent of SoundScan appeared to prove them right, a fact not lost on Brooks. "[*No Fences*] was my biggest-selling album," he says, "but it didn't go to Number One because it was before SoundScan. SoundScan put country music on a level playing field with every other form of music. The [recent] success that country music has had, along with the success that I have had, truly is due to SoundScan, along with God and the people themselves."

THE TOP FIVE
Week of September 28, 1991

1. **Ropin' the Wind**
   Garth Brooks

2. **Metallica**
   Metallica

3. **Unforgettable**
   Natalie Cole

4. **C.M.B.**
   Color Me Badd

5. **Luck of the Draw**
   Bonnie Raitt

Producers: Mike Clink and Guns N' Roses

Track listing: Civil War / 14 Years / Knockin' on Heaven's Door / Get in the Ring / Shotgun Blues / Breakdown / Pretty Tied Up / Locomotive / So Fine / Estranged / You Could Be Mine / Don't Cry (Alt. Lyrics) / My World

October 5, 1991
2 weeks

Following the success of *Appetite for Destruction* [see 320], Guns N' Roses had not only became a success, but also a phenomenon, albeit a controversial one. First, singer Axl Rose was taken to task for some seemingly racist and homophobic lyrics in the song "One in a Million," included on the 1988 EP *G N' R Lies*, which climbed all the way to number two. Then Rose was charged with inciting a disturbance after jumping off the stage during a performance in St. Louis. Once again, drugs clouded the picture, as the band sacked drummer Steven Adler, who allegedly wasn't able to kick his habit. And, finally there was the music—so much music, in fact, that it couldn't be contained on one CD. So Guns N' Roses went against logic and tradition: The band's official follow-up to *Appetite for Destruction* would not be one album, but two released simultaneously.

Use Your Illusion I and *Use Your Illusion II* were released on September 17, 1991. When the albums entered at number two and Number One, respectively, the Guns became the first act to hold down the top two positions on the album chart since Jim Croce had achieved the feat with *You Don't Mess*

Around with Jim [see 169] and *I Got a Name* in 1974. While that triumph was certainly significant, the future had appeared anything but rosy for the Gunners in the months prior to the albums' release.

"We had just gone through the whole fiasco of trying to get Steven off drugs," recalls bassist Duff McKagan. "We did everything we could, but it didn't work out. We were really frustrated because we didn't have a drummer." The band auditioned several, but nothing clicked. "It was kind of depressing," he says. Finally, one night McKagan and guitarist Slash went to see the Cult. Both were impressed by the performance of the band's drummer Matt Sorum, who informed them that the group was going on hiatus. "It was like bing, bang, boom. A month later we were in recording. We were elated. We were a band again." The Guns' sixth member, keyboardist Dizzy Reed, a friend of the band from their club days, was added in 1990.

"There was no pressure," McKagan says. "There was no pressure of trying to follow up anything." At first, the band had no plans to issue two separate

albums. "We knew we had tons of shit, but we didn't know how much we were going to record. But we just kept recording more and more. We didn't think we would put them all out."

A few of the tracks were familiar to the group's fans. "You Could Be Mine," featured in the blockbuster film *Terminator 2: Judgment Day*, was released as a single on June 25. Early versions of the Guns' original "Civil War" and a cover of Bob Dylan's "Knockin' on Heaven's Door" appeared in 1990 on *Nobody's Child* (a Warner Bros. benefit album for Romanian orphans) and the Geffen soundtrack to *Days of Thunder*, respectively.

Illusion II was the higher-charting album, likely due to the inclusion of the familiar material, but there was no master plan in sequencing the albums. "We just made our own tapes and wrote down our own sequences without talking to each other, and kind of mashed them altogether," says McKagan.

At first Geffen was caught a bit off-guard by the band's ambitious plans. "It was pretty much inevitable that we were going to have to have two albums, so we told Geffen," says McKagan. "And they got over the shock."

356 Achtung Baby ISLAND 10347
U2

Producer: Daniel Lanois with Brian Eno

Track listing: Zoo Station / Even Better Than the Real Thing / One / Until the End of the World / Who's Gonna Ride Wild Horses / So Cruel / The Fly / Mysterious Ways / Tryin' to Throw Your Arms Around the World / Ultra Violet (Light My Way) / Acrobat / Love Is Blindless

December 7, 1991
1 week

Following the incredible commercial success of *The Joshua Tree* [see 310] and the critical lashing they received for *Rattle and Hum* [see 324], U2 decided to return to their alternative-rock roots for their first album of the '90s.

While U2 had devoted much of their previous two albums to exploring Americana, *Achtung Baby*, which took its name from a line in the Mel Brooks's film *The Producers*, would be decidedly different. "We wanted a more European kind of location and sound," says bassist Adam Clayton. "It wasn't so much a record about America. We were aware that people maybe wouldn't get off on that as much, but that was where we were coming from."

U2 opted to record most of *Achtung Baby* in Berlin, where David Bowie had collaborated with Brian Eno in the mid-'70s. And just as Bowie had emerged from Berlin with a more electronic-oriented sound, so did U2. In the album's opening track, for instance, Bono's vocals were distorted to the point that they were barely recognizable. "I always liked it when we got back to the loud, noisy rock 'n' roll," says Clayton.

"And, that was the kind of record we needed to make."

Although U2's direction on *Achtung Baby* may have seemed to some like a radical departure, Clayton says that there were clues to the new direction on *Rattle and Hum*. "We wanted to strengthen the traditional songwriting base of the band, but at the other end of the scale, we started getting into remixing and using more electronics as a foundation with songs like 'God Part II.'"

Also affecting the album was an air of uncertainty in the lives of the members of U2, as guitarist the Edge was going through a painful divorce while the album was being written. "I don't think it was a good time for anyone necessarily," says Clayton. "Part of the reason for going to Berlin was to try to separate ourselves from that domestic environment. We needed to focus on redefining what the band was doing away from all the distractions."

Yet Berlin, during the German reunification, was not a comfortable place. "Berlin had always had this great underground art scene and it had always been an open city, but when the wall came down, it was a very confusing time there," says Clayton. "There weren't massive celebrations, it was just a time of real uncertainty."

Adding to confusion, the band's early demos for the album, recorded in Dublin, were stolen and released on a bootleg before the real album was completed. "At the time it made us feel very paranoid, but now it's real flattering for an artist's unfinished work to be released."

While much of *Achtung Baby* featured electronic effects, there were still hints of the old U2 in material such as the heartfelt ballad "One." Says Clayton, "We did want to do something that in some way was relevant to a world that was living with AIDS," says Clayton. "We didn't want to tap into a highly emotional subject in an emotional way, we just wanted to connect with people."

Bono, meanwhile, who had been criticized for taking himself too seriously, began to reveal new personae, such as "The Fly." Says Clayton, "With a career like we've had, it is very hard to sustain people's involvement if they become too familiar with just one character."

Achtung Baby debuted at Number One, becoming the first U2 album to enter at the top, but it stayed at the summit for only a week, the shortest span of any of U2's chart-toppers. Nonetheless, its success proved that U2 had successfully redefined themselves for a new decade.

EPIC 45400 **Dangerous**
MICHAEL JACKSON

Executive producer: Michael Jackson

Track listing: Jam / Why You Wanna Trip On Me / In the Closet / She Drives Me Wild / Remember the Time / Can't Let Her Get Away / Heal the World / Black or White / Who Is It / Give in to Me / Will You Be There / Keep the Faith / Gone Too Soon / Dangerous / Planet Earth

December 14, 1991
4 weeks

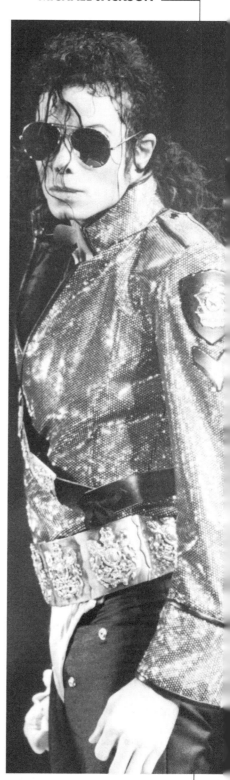

Although it was never spoken, Michael Jackson had his mind set on exceeding the 38-million-selling *Thriller* [see 274] and the 25-million-selling *Bad* [see 313] when he went to work on *Dangerous*. "You always will see that with Michael," says producer and mixer Bruce Swedien. "He wants to exceed what the last effort was. He doesn't express that while he is doing it, but the thought was always there."

Yet *Dangerous* would be decidedly different from Jackson's previous two efforts, as well as their predecessor, *Off the Wall*. Famed producer Quincy Jones, who had worked with Jackson on all three of those albums, had signed a joint venture with Time Warner for his own label, making it impossible to work with Jackson, who himself had just inked a new contract with Sony, said to be worth approximately $50 million. "It definitely had an impact that Quincy's musical approach was absent," says Swedien, who had worked with Jackson and Jones since the breakthrough *Off the Wall* album. "What Michael wanted to do on *Dangerous* was to have a much more street-oriented sound on the album and less of a studio approach."

Initially, Jackson turned to L.A. Reid and Babyface [see 326] before settling on Teddy Riley, Bill Bottrell, and Swedien. The decision to bring Riley in was "a masterstroke," says Swedien. "Teddy did an absolutely incredible job on 'Why You Wanna Trip On Me,' 'She Drives Me Wild,' and 'In the Closet.'"

Bottrell, who would later work with Sheryl Crow, co-wrote and co-produced the first single, "Black or White," which featured Slash from Guns N' Roses [see 355] on guitar. Slash also lent his guitar to "Give in to Me." For "Jam," Swedien worked with his partner Rene Moore, and Riley. "The idea was to combine old sounds with new, so we got a couple of tape loops and put the newer sounds over it," Swedien says. "We played it for Michael and he just freaked, he started dancing and he loved it."

Another track, "Keep the Faith," written by Glen Ballard, Siedah Garrett, and Jackson, was somewhat troublesome. "We recorded the track, overdubbed all the instruments and the Andre Crouch Singers and then started the session where we were going to do Michael's vocal. When we got to the key change, it was in the wrong key. It was a little too high," says Swedien. "I looked into the studio and Michael had disappeared. I went back into the office to find him and I heard this sobbing and crying. He was absolutely heartbroken. I told him, 'Michael, it's no big deal, we will take care of it.' He was so geared up for that piece of music that it was really a trauma for him when it was in the wrong key." Swedien ended up re-recording the entire track and takes full credit for the mistake. "It was our own fault," he says. "We should have been more careful, but it seemed fine at the time."

Elsewhere on the album, Jackson hearkened back to earlier hits. "Remember the Time" is like "Rock with You" with "a '90s approach," says Sweiden. "Michael sings all those incredible harmonies in the background like no one else can."

On December 7, 1991, "Black or White" became Jackson's 12th Number One single. A week later, *Dangerous* became his third consecutive album to top the album chart and second to debut at the summit. While *Dangerous* went on to sell more than 17 million copies worldwide, Jackson was undoubtedly disappointed that his album sales had begun to decline, and that he was unable to meet his goal of bettering the sales of his two previous efforts.

THE TOP FIVE
Week of December 14, 1991

1. **Dangerous**
   Michael Jackson

2. **Ropin' the Wind**
   Garth Brooks

3. **Achtung Baby**
   U2

4. **Too Legit to Quit**
   Hammer

5. **Time, Love & Tenderness**
   Michael Bolton

358 Nevermind DGC 24425
NIRVANA

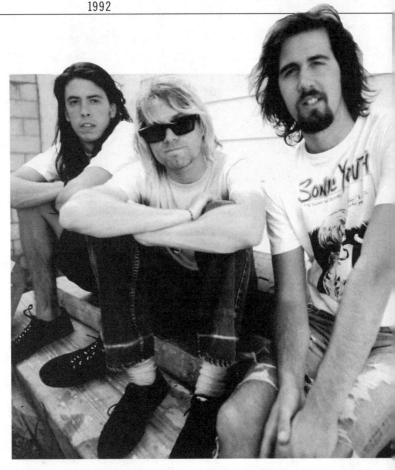

Producers: Butch Vig and Nirvana

Track listing: Smells Like Teen Spirit / In Bloom / Come as You Are / Breed / Lithium / Polly / Territorial Pissings / Drain You / Lounge Act / Stay Away / On a Plain / Something in the Way

January 11, 1992
2 weeks (nonconsecutive)

Punk rock, a genre that emerged from the streets of New York and London in the late '70s, returning rock 'n' roll to its raw, rebellious roots, had a tremendous influence on music and fashion. Yet it failed to make a significant dent on the album chart, at least until Nirvana's Nevermind.

Nirvana was born in December 1987 in Aberdeen, Washington, with the core of singer/guitarist Kurt Cobain and bassist Chris Novoselic. After a series of lineup changes and gigs in the Seattle area, the band was signed to the up-and-coming independent label Sub Pop, which in 1989 released the group's debut single, "Love Buzz," and album, Bleach. After their first U.S. tour, Nirvana finally settled on a permanent lineup when Dave Grohl, formerly of the Washington, D.C., punk band Scream, signed on as drummer.

With their Sub Pop releases and live shows garnering a tremendous buzz, Nirvana became the subject of a fierce bidding war, which was won by Geffen in early 1991. In May, the band temporarily relocated to Los Angeles to record their major label debut with producer Butch Vig. The bulk of Nevermind was recorded at Sound City in Van Nuys, the same studio used to mix part of Fleetwood Mac's Rumors [see 223].

THE TOP FIVE
Week of January 11, 1992

1. **Nevermind**
   Nirvana
2. **Ropin' the Wind**
   Garth Brooks
3. **Too Legit to Quit**
   Hammer
4. **Achtung Baby**
   U2
5. **Dangerous**
   Michael Jackson

"We had no idea what was going to happen," says Vig. "We thought we were just making another punk record." Yet Vig did notice that Cobain had an uncanny knack with melody that separated him from other underground songwriters. "There was this song 'About a Girl' on Bleach, which was my favorite track, because it was the poppiest one. It has this really cool almost Beatle-esque kind of hook line right at the end of the chorus. When I heard some of the demos for Nevermind, I was blown away, because they were so poppy, even though the band was totally onslaught rockin' when they played—it had a very hooky pop sense to it."

The sessions were extremely loose. "We screwed around," says Novoselic. "We would sleep in every day and then lay on the couch and play pinball all day and then we would stroll in and occasionally lay down a few tracks."

It wasn't the first time Nirvana had recorded with Vig. In 1990, the band recorded many of the songs that would be released on Nevermind at Vig's Smart studio in Madison, Wisconsin. "We didn't know what the future was with Sub Pop, and then we lost a drum-

mer," says Novoselic. "It was never the right time. But we saved all the good songs for Nevermind, like 'Lithium,' 'In Bloom,' and 'Stay Away,' which was called 'Pay to Play' back then." One track from the Smart sessions, an acoustic ballad called "Polly," which describes a rape from the rapist's point of view, did make the album.

Yet the song that put Nevermind on top was "Smells Like Teen Spirit," an anti-anthem that simultaneously mocks and celebrates the slacker generation's apathy. Some said its monster riff resembled a punked-up version of Boston's 1976 hit "More Than a Feeling." A video clip of the track, which featured the band performing at a high school gym from hell, complete with moshing students and cheerleaders with uniforms bearing the symbol for anarchy, slammed into MTV's Buzz Bin with radio also airing the rallying cry.

In one of the most significant and telling pop music happenings in the young decade, Nevermind hit Number One on Billboard's album chart in its 14th week, knocking off the self-proclaimed King of Pop's Dangerous. Rock 'n' roll would never be the same.

Executive producers: Michael Ostin and Ted Templeman

Track listing: Bohemian Rhapsody [Queen] / Hot and Bothered [Cinderella] / Rock Candy [Bullet Boys] / Dream Weaver [Gary Wright] / Sikamikanico [Red Hot Chili Peppers] / Time Machine [Black Sabbath] / Wayne's World Theme (Extended Version) [Mike Myers and Dana Carvey] / Ballroom Blitz [Tia Carrere] / Foxy Lady [Jimi Hendrix] / Feed My Frankenstein [Alice Cooper] / Ride with Yourself [Rhino Bucket] / Loving Your Lovin' [Eric Clapton] / Why You Wanna Break My Heart [Tia Carrere]

April 4, 1992
2 weeks

"It's an ironic twist that the main factor in Queen's reemergence in the States was *Wayne's World*," says Queen drummer Roger Taylor. "Especially after losing Freddie."

After the success of *The Game* in 1980 [see 251], Queen's following in the United States began to dwindle, despite the fact that the band remained tremendously popular internationally. On November 23, 1991, frontman Freddie Mercury announced that he had AIDS. The following day, at age 45, he died.

To honor Mercury and raise money for AIDS research, Queen's British label re-released "Bohemian Rhapsody" in late 1991. The single entered the U.K. chart at Number One, topping the list for the second time in 16 years.

In the summer of 1991, months before Mercury's death, "Bohemian Rhapsody" was slated to be included in a key scene in *Wayne's World*, a film adaptation of a popular recurring sketch on NBC-TV's "Saturday Night Live." It featured comedians Mike Myers and Dana Carvey as two suburban dudes hosting their own public-access cable show.

In January 1992, Hollywood Records released the double A-side single of "The Show Must Go On" / "Bohemian Rhapsody" in the U.S. Even before the single's official release, the classic mini-pop-opera began picking up play at album rock and top 40 stations, while Queen's original video clip started turning up on MTV and VH1. Yet Reprise Records chose to promote a clip of film star Tia Carrare's version of Sweet's "Ballroom Blitz" on MTV, rather than the Queen classic.

Another hard-rocking clip, Cinderella's "Hot and Bothered," was also serviced to MTV. Finally, a new video of "Bohemian Rhapsody," combining the efforts of Hollywood Records, Paramount Pictures, and Reprise, was released to MTV as an exclusive on March 4, 1992. The clip, which mixed classic Queen footage with film clips of the *Wayne's World* crew banging their heads to the song, was the knockout punch.

Wayne's World also included Jimi Hendrix's 1967 classic "Foxy Lady," a re-recording of Gary Wright's 1975 hit "Dream Weaver," as well as cuts by the Red Hot Chili Peppers, the reunited Black Sabbath, and Alice Cooper, but it was "Bohemian Rhapsody" that made it a success.

The album debuted on The Billboard 200 at number 14 on March 7. "We thought all along that 'Bohemian Rhapsody' would be the big, big hit off the soundtrack," said co-executive producer Michael Ostin. Hollywood Records executive Wes Hein noted that *Wayne's World* was responsible for "introducing the 17-year-old 'Bohemian Rhapsody' to a new audience.' "

Less than a month after it debuted, *Wayne's World* knocked Garth Brooks' *Ropin' the Wind*, which had been king of the hill for 18 of the previous 27 weeks, from the top of The Billboard 200. It also became the second album inspired by a *Saturday Night Live* spin-off to reach Number One [see the Blues Brothers' *Briefcase Full of Blues*—235].

The use of "Bohemian Rhapsody" in *Wayne's World* was just fine by Queen's Taylor. "It was hilarious," he says. "It was a very funny film. But a lot of my contemporaries didn't like it very much. I guess either I'm regressing or they're losing their sense of humor."

THE TOP FIVE
Week of April 4, 1992

1. **Wayne's World**
   Soundtrack

2. **Ropin' The Wind**
   Garth Brooks

3. **Nevermind**
   Nirvana

4. **No Fences**
   Garth Brooks

5. **Metallica**
   Metallica

Mike Meyers (left) and Dana Carvey in *Wayne's World*.

360 Adrenalize MERCURY 512185
DEF LEPPARD

Producers: Mike Shipley and Def Leppard

Track listing: Let's Get Rocked / Heaven Is / Make Love Like a Man / Tonight / White Lightning / Stand Up (Kick Love into Motion) / Personal Property / Have You Ever Needed Someone So Bad / I Wanna Touch U / Tear It Down

April 18, 1992
5 weeks

Following the trauma Def Leppard endured in making *Hysteria*, the members of the band expected the follow-up album to be a little easier to make. Unfortunately, they were wrong.

"We finished a tour in October 1988 and then we went straight into the studio in December, which was the stupidest thing we have ever done, because we didn't have that much material," says vocalist Joe Elliot. After six weeks, the sessions were aborted and the band took a five-month rest.

When the band regrouped, it became apparent that guitarist Steve Clark had a serious drinking problem. "It became obvious that the record wasn't going to be very important to us without contributions from Steve, but Steve was much more interested in picking up a bottle than his guitar," says Elliot.

The band put recording on hold while Clark checked himself into rehab. Elliot built a studio at his home in Dublin so the band wouldn't end up with the tremendous studio bills it had racked up during the recording of *Hysteria*. But even in the more relaxed atmosphere, Clark was having a hard time working.

"Steve went in and out of rehab about five times during the making of the album," Elliot says. "After the fourth time, he came out and walked into a bar and got annihilated and ended up in a coma. We decided that the best thing to do, for his own sake, was to give him six months' leave of absence to let him sort himself out and decide what he wanted to do. We didn't fire him."

Clark did contribute to six songs in the early stages of the album, but he never completed his six-month leave from the band. "He was due back in February or March, but unfortunately, he never made it," says Elliot. On January 8, 1991, Clark was found dead of a lethal mix of alcohol and drugs at his home in the Chelsea section of London.

"After Steve died, we went through six weeks of hell," says Elliot. "But we went back to work the same way we did after Rick [Allen, the group's drummer] lost his arm. But after about six weeks, we sat around a coffee table and looked at each other and said, 'This is bullshit. There's no soul in what we're doing. He's not coming back, he's dead, he's gone, and we got to get on with it.' After that, there was a big relief."

The band once again started fresh in late March, and by December the album was complete. Clark was remembered in the song "White Lightning." Says Elliot, "It isn't some sappy thing, it is looking steely-faced at the crowd and singing about what happened to him. We wanted the lyrics to hit home and maybe someone that wants to listen will learn and think, 'I better quit.' It was therapeutic to do that kind of song."

But *Adrenalize* wasn't only about heavy subject matter. "After we did that song, the last thing we had was this funky, mid-tempo, rock thing," says Elliot. "Because we just went through this really heavy thing, we decided to go the opposite way and write the most stupid thing we could think about. That's how 'Let's Get Rocked' came about. It was a big chunk of fun going back to our youth and bands like Slade, T. Rex, and even Gary Glitter." The upbeat rocker ended up being the ideal opening track. Says Elliot, "We didn't want the album to end up to be like some Leonard Cohen–type thing."

There was certainly little chance of that. *Adrenalize* became the first album of 1992 to debut at the top spot. It had plenty of competition that week, as new entries by Bruce Springsteen and Wynonna rounded out the top four. But Def Leppard had prevailed through turmoil once again.

THE TOP FIVE
Week of April 18, 1992

1. **Adrenalize**
   Def Leppard

2. **Human Touch**
   Bruce Springsteen

3. **Lucky Town**
   Bruce Springsteen

4. **Wynonna**
   Wynonna

5. **Wayne's World**
   Soundtrack

Totally Krossed Out **361**

KRIS KROSS

while Smith opted for "Daddy Mack."

Apparently Dupri's hip-hop training camp worked. It wasn't long before a demo tape landed the duo a contract with Ruffhouse Records, distributed by the major label Columbia. Kris Kross recorded the majority of *Totally Krossed Out* in a week at Studio 4 in Philadelphia. Although the duo thought the album was complete, Dupri had other plans. "We needed one more song," Dupri recalls. "I went home and came up with it real quick." That song was a hip-hop jam titled "Jump," which would launch Kris Kross's career.

The song took the singles chart by storm, bounding from number 61 to the top in three short weeks, thanks in part to the duo's national television debut on Fox-TV's *In Living Color*.

Yet Kris Kross wasn't just about a sound. The pint-sized rappers also grabbed headlines with their unusual fashion sense. The duo favored their clothes baggy and worn backwards. According to Dupri, the duo tested the fashion fad in a mall. "People in the mall were flipping out," he recalls. "Like, 'They got their clothes backwards.' We were like, 'Yeah, that's it right there. We've got something to catch people's eyes.'"

Despite their pop success and built-in teen appeal, Kris Kross didn't want to be known as just another kiddie act. The duo attempted to emulate their favorite hardcore rappers, including Run-D.M.C. and N.W.A, on tracks such as "Lil' Boys in da Hood." Says Kelly, "Our first album was nowhere near pop. It just crossed over, and everybody said it was pop. But we didn't go into the studio and say we wanted to make a pop record."

Producer: Jermaine Dupri

Track listing: *Intro Interview / Jump / Lil' Boys in da Hood / Warm It Up / The Way of Rhyme / Party / We're in da House / A Real Bad Dream / It's a Shame / Can't Stop the Bum Rush / You Can't Get with This / I Missed the Bus / Outro / Party (Krossed Mix) / Jump (Extended Mix)*

May 23, 1992
2 weeks (nonconsecutive)

The story of Kris Kross reads like a '90s hip-hop version of actress Lana Turner, who, as legend has it, was discovered at the soda fountain at Schwab's Drugstore in Hollywood. Chris Smith, 13, and Chris Kelly, 12, were hanging out at a shopping mall in their native Atlanta when they crossed paths with an 18-year-old producer named Jermaine Dupri, who was shopping with the female rap group Silk Tymes Leather. "Me and Chris were just hanging out at the mall and Jermaine asked us if we rapped and danced," recalls Chris Smith.

From that day on, Dupri took the two young would-be rappers under his wing. According to Dupri, they had some natural talent. "They could keep up," he says. "I was writing the lyrics. I put the lyrics on tape, and then they would go home and study them. They just had to get into the mode of becoming total hip-hoppers every day, so I just started taking them out with me clubbing." Kelly adopted the nickname "Mack Daddy,"

THE TOP FIVE
Week of May 23, 1992

1. **Totally Krossed Out**
   Kris Kross

2. **Adrenalize**
   Def Leppard

3. **Blood Sugar Sex Magik**
   Red Hot Chili Peppers

4. **Ropin' The Wind**
   Garth Brooks

5. **Classic Queen**
   Queen

362 The Southern Harmony and Musical Companion DEF AMERICAN 26976
THE BLACK CROWES

Producers: The Black Crowes and George Drakoulias

Track listing: Sting Me / Remedy / Thorn in My Pride / Bad Luck Blue Eyes Goodbye / Sometimes Salvation / Hotel Illness / Black Moon Creeping / No Speak No Slave / My Morning Song / Time Will Tell

May 30, 1992
1 week

In 1990, the Black Crowes came from nowhere to deliver *Shake Your Money Maker*, the first hit album for the Def American label, which was helmed by Rick Rubin, who'd been known as a hot rap producer [see 309] before becoming a record mogul. With a sound reminiscent of the Rolling Stones and the Faces, *Shake Your Money Maker* became a sleeper hit. After 54 weeks on the chart and hundreds of live dates, the album reached number four.

When the madness of non-stop touring and so-called overnight success subsided, the Crowes flew home to Atlanta to record their follow-up album. Original guitarist Jeff Cease bowed out, to be replaced by Marc Ford from Burning Tree, a band that had opened for the Crowes on the road.

"We spent so much time on the road after *Shake Your Money Maker*, we just wanted to go right back into the studio," says singer Chris Robinson. The band's success allowed the group more musical freedom. "The first album was more sort of George's production, whereas the second record was more what we wanted to do. We added some gospel singing elements and more percussion without anybody saying no."

THE TOP FIVE
Week of May 30, 1992

1. **The Southern Harmony and Musical Companion**
   The Black Crowes
2. **Totally Krossed Out**
   Kris Kross
3. **Adrenalize**
   Def Leppard
4. **Blood Sugar Sex Magik**
   Red Hot Chili Peppers
5. **Ropin' the Wind**
   Garth Brooks

The album was recorded in a mere eight days at Southern Tracks studio in Atlanta, as Ford's addition to the band raised its confidence. "All of a sudden we had these new tools," says Robinson. "We were confident and competent enough to say, 'This is a take, let's move on.'"

There was no plan to record so quickly—it just happened. "Everyone showed up on a Monday and by Wednesday, Steve [Gorman] was finished with his drum tracks, because we did all the live tracks and then we started overdubbing. Steve came back on Saturday, we cut three songs over, and then it was done," says Chris Robinson. "It was one huge emotional—but hilarious—drunken blur."

When the Crowes first blasted onto the scene, the band attempted to distance itself from the South. Yet with their second album's title, taken from an old book of

religious songs, they played up the connection. "For a long time, it was a weird concept for us to be considered Southern, because we never left. But once we went around the world and came back home, we knew we couldn't escape it. It was sort of owning up to our roots."

The inclusion of a cover of Bob Marley's "Time Will Tell" as the album's finale may have caught some by surprise. "Actually, the recording is us just learning the song," says Chris Robinson. "All the lyrics are wrong, but it came out pretty good. The choruses are right."

With "Remedy" riding high on top of the Album Rock Tracks chart for five consecutive weeks, *The Southern Harmony and Musical Companion* debuted at Number One on the album chart. "Being the sort of cynic I am, I said, 'Oh great, what's next, number two?'" says Robinson. "But I dug it and my parents have the chart on their wall."

MERCURY 510635 **Some Gave All** | 363

BILLY RAY CYRUS

Producers: Joe Scaife and Jim Cotton

Track listing: Could've Been Me / Achy Breaky Heart / She's Not Cryin' Anymore / Wher'm I Gonna Live? / These Boots are Made for Walkin' / Someday, Somewhere, Somehow / Never Thought I'd Fall in Love with You / Ain't No Good Goodbye / I'm So Miserable / Some Gave All

June 13, 1992
17 weeks

Billy Ray Cyrus always knew that if he was given the chance to make an album, it would be a hit. "For over a decade we would play in the tri-state area of Kentucky, Ohio, and West Virginia," he recalls. "Our clientele always ranged from very young people to a lot of older people and everything in between. I always felt if someone would just give me and the music a chance, its appeal would be equally wide."

Cyrus found that person in 1989 when he hooked up with manager Jack McFadden, who had helped guide the career of a number of artists, including Buck Owens and Keith Whitley. The following year, with McFadden's help, Cyrus signed with Mercury Records, but the struggle wasn't over. On February 23, 1991 Cyrus, his band Sly Dog, and producers Scaife and Cotton, cut the song "Some Gave All" as an audition for Mercury. The label wanted Cyrus to play with session players, but he insisted that he work with his own band. "Everyone loved it, but they didn't schedule us in studio to do the rest of the album until the first two weeks of June 1991," Cyrus says.

When June rolled around, Cyrus and company cut two songs a day, completing the entire album in the allotted two weeks. But Mercury was in no rush to release Some Gave All. "The album was done and in the can for almost a year," Cyrus recalls. "That was a very dark period for me. They always say it's darkest just before the dawn. I didn't know if I would live to see the album come out." Cyrus's wife also lost faith, divorcing the would-be star who was waiting for his big break.

That break came in March 1992 when Mercury issued the music video of "Achy Breaky Heart," which featured Cyrus's country-hunk good looks and a dance step that would go on to sweep the nation as the song crossed over from country to top 40 radio stations.

Finally, on May 19, 1992, Mercury issued Some Gave All. Within a month, it topped the album chart, becoming, at the time, the fastest-selling debut album in history. "I was on an airplane traveling that morning," Cyrus recalls. "I picked up USA Today and it said, 'Fastest-rising debut ever to hit Number One, Billy Ray Cyrus, Some Gave All.' You better believe that Billy Ray Cyrus prayed a very humble prayer that second."

With "Achy Breaky Heart" topping the Hot Country Singles & Tracks chart and reaching number four on the Hot 100, and with two other top 10 country hits—"She's Not Cryin' Anymore" and "Could've Been Me"—Some Gave All went on to become the best-selling album of 1992.

However, the tremendous success also led to a backlash, particularly from critics who found "Achy Breaky Heart" insipid and compared Cyrus's music unfavorably with that of Garth Brooks, country music's other new pop sensation. "Every sword definitely has two edges," Cyrus says. "A lot of people have judged Billy Ray Cyrus like a book by the cover, by the first impression, but nine million people around the world took time to listen to Some Gave All, to listen to the pages between the chapters."

THE TOP FIVE
Week of June 13, 1992

1. **Some Gave All**
   Billy Ray Cyrus

2. **Totally Krossed Out**
   Kris Kross

3. **Blood Sugar Sex Magik**
   Red Hot Chili Peppers

4. **The Southern Harmony and Musical Companion**
   The Black Crowes

5. **Adrenalize**
   Def Leppard

364 The Chase LIBERTY 98743
GARTH BROOKS

Producer: Allen Reynolds

Track listing: We Shall Be Free /
Somewhere Other Than the Night / Mr.
Right / Every Now and Then /
Walking After Midnight / Dixie
Chicken / Learning to Live Again / That
Summer / Night Rider's Lament / Face
to Face

October 10, 1992
7 weeks (nonconsecutive)

With *The Chase*, lightning struck twice. For the second time in less than a year, a new Garth Brooks album had entered The Billboard 200 and the Top Country Albums chart at Number One. Meanwhile, *Beyond the Season*, Brooks's Christmas album, released a full four months before the holiday, was at number five after peaking at number two.

Yet in spite of all the success Brooks was experiencing, the time making and leading up to the release of *The Chase* wasn't particularly happy. "*The Chase* was tough because of the personal thing I was going through at the time," Brooks says. "I was expecting a child, I wasn't real happy with my record deal, and I was wondering what my future was."

In fact, just before the album's release, Brooks publicly contemplated retiring, saying that he wanted to spend time with his family. His wife Sandy had gone through a difficult pregnancy. Finally, on July 8, 1992, his first child, Taylor Mayne Pearl, was born. She was healthy, and Brooks was happy with his new life as a family man, yet he wasn't quite sure he wanted to continue to live life as a superstar, touring for months on end. Meanwhile, his contract with Liberty, signed long before he became one of the most popular performers in the world, suddenly seemed onerous.

"I was just feeling really dark and while all that was going on, I was still trying to do what I enjoyed most—making albums," he says.

"We Shall Be Free," one of five tracks co-written by Brooks on the album, suggested the country star still had not found what he was seeking. The song was inspired by the riots that erupted in Los Angeles after the Rodney King verdicts (Brooks was in Los Angeles the night portions of the city burned, picking up Entertainer of the Year honors at the Academy of Country Music Awards), but neither King nor Los Angeles are mentioned by name in the lyrics. "We Shall Be Free" also speaks out for sexual as well as racial tolerance.

Another song on the album, "Face to Face" addresses date rape. The heaviness of the topics addressed on *The Chase* perhaps hinted at Brooks's mood while making the album. "My eyebrows were real low," he says.

Yet there was some relief. The album also features several lyrical snapshots of days gone by, and Brooks was also working on *Beyond the Season* while making *The Chase*. The Christmas album, he says, "was my favorite album to make. *The Chase* was very intense and *Beyond the Season* was very light and well felt, so it was a good marriage. It was exactly what I needed at the time, or I probably would have gone off the deep end."

THE TOP FIVE
Week of October 10, 1992

1. **The Chase**
   Garth Brooks

2. **Unplugged**
   Eric Clapton

3. **Some Gave All**
   Billy Ray Cyrus

4. **Ten**
   Pearl Jam

5. **Beyond the Season**
   Garth Brooks

COLUMBIA 52783 # Timeless (The Classics)
MICHAEL BOLTON

Producers: David Foster, Michael Bolton, and Walter Afanasieff

Track listing: Since I Fell for You / To Love Somebody / Reach Out I'll Be There / You Send Me / Yesterday / Hold On, I'm Coming / Bring It On Home to Me / Knock on Wood / Drift Way / White Christmas

November 21, 1992
1 week

With his 1987 album *The Hunger*, which featured a cover of Otis Redding's "(Sitting on) The Dock of the Bay," Michael Bolton became as well known for his interpretations of classic songs as he was for his own material. When his cover of Percy Sledge's "When a Man Loves a Woman" became his second Number One single and the biggest hit from *Time, Love & Tenderness* [see 340], an album full of cover versions seemed like the next logical step.

"It was really meant as an enjoyable departure," Bolton says of *Timeless*. "In the industry we call it a 'bridge album.' It was not meant to be my next major project."

Timeless (The Classics) was inspired by Bolton's participation in the 1991 all-star Walt Disney tribute album *Simply Mad About the Mouse*. Bolton performed the song "A Dream Is a Wish Your Heart Makes," from the animated classic *Cinderella*, backed by an orchestra. "I loved singing to an orchestra so much, I was just kind of intoxicated with the vision of doing a record like that, but I didn't want to write 10 songs that were orchestrations. *The Classics* was the way to do that," he says.

While Bolton says *Timeless* was "a labor of love," it was harder to make than he expected. "It got to the point where I was getting fanatical about quality control," he says. "It turned out to be a huge amount of labor." Originally the sessions were set to last six to eight weeks, but that soon turned into three months. "The deeper I got into it, the more I realized I couldn't just put out a record and just toss it out there."

Six of the 10 tracks on the album were co-produced by David Foster, who also had a production credit on Natalie Cole's Number One album of standards *Unforgettable with Love* [see 345]. Bolton says that he had become spoiled by the modern technology used in recording his previous albums. "When I got into performing with an orchestra, after spending thousands of hours trying to make a perfect record, I heard things that weren't perfect. Some of them I let go, others I tried to correct. There are things that the average person would not notice or hear, but every time they come up on the record, I hear it and I almost cringe, but I look around and nobody else hears them."

While *Timeless* wasn't an easy album to make, one thing made the recording a bit more pleasurable: Some of the sessions were held at Passion Studios at Bolton's home in Connecticut. "I finally built a studio in my home so I could spend some time there and have dinner with my kids at 6:30 P.M. After many years of not doing that, it's great."

THE TOP FIVE
Week of November 21, 1992

1. **Timeless (The Classics)**
   Michael Bolton

2. **The Chase**
   Garth Brooks

3. **Love Deluxe**
   Sade

4. **Unplugged**
   Eric Clapton

5. **Keep the Faith**
   Bon Jovi

366 The Predator PRIORITY 57285
ICE CUBE

Executive producer: Ice Cube

Track listing: The First Day of School (Intro) / When Will They Shoot? / I'm Scared (Insert) / Wicked / Now I Gotta Wet 'Cha / The Predator / It Was a Good Day / We Had to Tear This _____ Up / _____ 'Em (Insert) / Dirty Mack / Don't Trust 'Em / Gangsta's Fairytale 2 / Check Yo Self (Featuring Das EFX) / Who Got the Camera? / Integration (Insert) / Say Hi to the Bad Guy

December 5, 1992
1 week

Ice Cube made history when *The Predator* knocked off Garth Brooks's *The Chase* to become the first rap album to debut at Number One on The Billboard 200. It also debuted at Number One on the Top R&B Albums chart, making it the first album to debut at the top of both charts since Stevie Wonder's *Songs in the Key of Life* [see 219]. Cube achieved the feat with a combination of hardcore rap and controversy.

"He's in the eye of the storm," said Priority Records president Bryan Turner at the time of album's success, "and it's gratifying to see him achieve this and remain true to his form of expression."

In 1991, Ice Cube raised the ire of Korean and Jewish groups with tracks on his *Death Certificate* album that some deemed anti-Korean and anti-Semitic. *Billboard* published an editorial denouncing two songs on the album, "Black Korea" (in which Ice Cube's protagonist vowed to burn down a Korean market if its owners continued to disrespect blacks) and "No Vaseline." Controversy or no, *Death Certificate* debuted and peaked at number two on November 16, 1991, one position above Hammer's *Too Legit to Quit*. Six months later, after four Los Angeles police officers were acquitted in the beating of black motorist Rodney King, dozens of buildings were burned and looted by rioters, including some operated by Koreans.

On *The Predator*'s title track, Ice Cube addressed the riots and his beef with *Billboard* and his other rivals. For

backing support, Cube once again turned to Lench Mob crew members Pooh and Jinx, but on three other tracks he was joined in the studio by Mixmaster Muggs of Cypress Hill [see 374]. Live horns and acoustic bass were featured on "We Had to Tear This _____ Up."

Priority's Turner attributed Cube's record-setting debut to a number of factors: his active core audience, the single "Wicked," which created an advance buzz on the album, and Cube's appearance on the Lollapalooza '92 tour. In addition, Turner cited the home-video release of the film *Boyz N The Hood* and the publicity preceding the release of another film, *Trespass*, which was set for theatrical release a few weeks after *The Predator* hit the street. Both films featured Cube in acting roles and on their soundtrack.

For Cube, who left N.W.A prior to their chart-topping *EFIL4ZAGGIN* [see 349], *The Predator* was a true triumph. However, its stay on top was short-lived, as it would soon prove to be no match for *The Bodyguard* [see 367].

THE TOP FIVE
Week of December 5, 1992

1. **The Predator**
   Ice Cube

2. **The Bodyguard**
   Soundtrack

3. **The Chase**
   Garth Brooks

4. **Timeless (The Classics)**
   Michael Bolton

5. **Unplugged**
   Eric Clapton

ARISTA 18699 **The Bodyguard**
SOUNDTRACK **367**

Executive producers: Clive Davis and Whitney Houston

Track listing: I Will Always Love You / I Have Nothing / I'm Every Woman / Run to You / Queen of the Night / Jesus Loves Me [Whitney Houston] / Even If My Heart Would Break [Kenny G and Aaron Neville] / Someday (I'm Coming Back) [Lisa Stansfield] / It's Gonna Be a Lovely Day [the S.O.U.L. S.Y.S.T.E.M.] / (What's So Funny 'Bout) Peace, Love and Understanding [Curtis Stigers] / Theme from the Bodyguard / Trust in Me [Joe Cocker featuring Sass Jordan]

December 12, 1992
20 weeks (nonconsecutive)

"I kind of knew that it would have some potency to it, being Whitney Houston's first acting role in a film starring Kevin Costner," producer/songwriter David Foster says of *The Bodyguard*. "It seemed like a winning combination. We knew it would be hot, but I don't think we knew that it would sell 25 million copies."

Of course, the prospects for *The Bodyguard* soundtrack looked pretty good right from the start. Houston's first two albums had topped the chart [see 298 and 311], while 1990's *I'm Your Baby Tonight* had climbed to number three.

Foster and his wife, Linda Thompson, became involved in the project at the script stage. They wrote the song "I Have Nothing," and Foster produced Houston's recordings of "I Will Always Love You" and "Run to You" and co-produced Kenny G and Aaron Neville's contribution.

Says Foster, "Whitney was such a treat to work with and we had a lot of positive influence from Kevin, director Mick Jackson, [Arista president] Clive Davis, and scriptwriter Lawrence Kasdan. They all had ideas of how they wanted the music, but they all pretty much agreed, so it wasn't that confusing."

The standout track from *The Bodyguard* was Houston's cover of "I Will Always Love You," a two-time Number One country hit for the song's writer, Dolly Parton. Houston's version was decidedly different. It began with the diva singing the opening lines a cappella. "I would love to take credit for it, but it was Kevin Costner's idea," says Foster. "I said, 'Kevin, I don't like that idea. Maybe for the movie we'll do it, but for the record, I don't think that is such a good idea.' " Yet when Foster recorded Houston's vocal in Miami, he changed his mind. "She started singing with no music and I just went, 'Wow, this is incredible.' "

Although Arista was initially a little concerned that pop radio might not take to an a cappella intro, the label held their ground, and issued the single in its original form. On November 28, 1992, the single began its run atop the Hot 100. Two weeks later, *The Bodyguard* joined the single at the summit. (During its 20-week run, *The Bodyguard* would return to the top spot after being knocked out from Number One three different times.)

"I Will Always Love You" held the top position on the Hot 100 for a total of 14 weeks, topping Boyz II Men's "End of the Road" for the record for most weeks at Number One on Hot 100 [see 396]. (That record, however, was later bested by the Mariah Carey–Boyz II Men collaboration "One Sweet Day" [see 418].)

The album featured other hits as well. The song Foster and Thompson opted to write for the film needed to fit some specific requirements. "In the script it called for a big, Shirley Bassey/ 'Goldfinger'–type [see 75] Oscar-winning hit. That was quite a challenge, to think of something Shirley Bassey would sing, but could be a hit in 1992."

Foster and Thompson lived up to the challenge, but "I Have Nothing" didn't become a hit until 1993. On April 3, it peaked at number four on the Hot 100. It also spent two weeks on top of the Hot Adult Contemporary chart. On February 20, 1993, Houston's version of Ashford & Simpson's "I'm Every Woman" also reached number four.

One of the albums *The Bodyguard* kept from the pole position was Kenny G's *Breathless*, which spent 10 weeks at number two. Said Kenny G, "When you're at number two...it's nice to know that the album at Number One is something that you're rooting for."

THE TOP FIVE
Week of December 12, 1992

1. **The Bodyguard**
   Soundtrack

2. **Unplugged**
   Eric Clapton

3. **The Predator**
   Ice Cube

4. **Timeless (The Classics)**
   Michael Bolton

5. **The Chase**
   Garth Brooks

368 Unplugged DUCK/REPRISE 45024
ERIC CLAPTON

Producer: Russ Titelman

Track listing: Signe / Before You Accuse Me / Hey Hey / Tears in Heaven / Lonely Stranger / Nobody Knows You When—You're Down & Out / Layla / Running on Faith / Walkin' Blues / Alberta / San Francisco Bay Blues / Malted Milk / Old Love / Rollin' & Tumblin'

March 13, 1993
3 weeks

Before Eric Clapton agreed to perform on MTV's "Unplugged" acoustic showcase, such heavyweights as Don Henley, Elton John, and R.E.M. had been featured on the program. Paul McCartney even allowed Capitol Records to release an album of his performance. Yet Clapton wasn't so sure the acoustic setting was right for him. After all, as a solo artist [see 179] and a former member of the Yardbirds, Cream [see 104], Blind Faith [see 115], and Derek & the Dominos, Clapton was known for his virtuosity on electric guitar.

"It had been talked about for some time," recalls producer Russ Titelman, "but Eric was kind of reluctant. He didn't want to do it at first." After some coaxing from record company and MTV executives, Clapton agreed to do the show. On January 16, 1992, Clapton, backed by bassist Nathan East, guitarist Andy Fairweather-Low, percussionist Ray Cooper, drummer Steve Ferrone, keyboardist Chuck Leavell, and vocalists Katie Kissoon and Tessa Niles, gathered at Bray Studios in Windsor, England, to tape "Unplugged." The one-hour program premiered on MTV on March 11.

"It was never thought of as an album," says Titelman, who mixed the audio portion of the show for broadcast in a weekend. "Eric really didn't want to put the record out, because if he had intended it to be a record, he would have done things differently."

Yet once again, Clapton's label and associates attempted to persuade him. "There was a huge response to it and everyone put their two cents in," says Titelman. "I called him and said, 'Look, I understand how you feel, but it was a great show with some beautiful performances.' "

Clapton's show was so popular that it garnered MTV's highest "Unplugged" ratings since the acoustic series' January 1990 debut. An estimated 1.3 million viewing households tuned in. For the program, Clapton culled various songs from his 25-year career, including the first live recording of the Derek & the Dominos classic "Layla," which was given a dramatic reworking, and a cover of Bo Diddley's "Before You Accuse Me," one of the first records Clapton had ever heard. Yet the emotional high point of the set was "Tears in Heaven," written following the death of Clapton's son Conor, who accidentally fell to his death from a 53rd-floor Manhattan apartment in 1991. A studio version of the track, featured on the *Rush* soundtrack, had become a number two hit for Clapton in March 1992, setting the stage for *Unplugged*.

Yet it took a Grammy triumph to help *Unplugged* temporarily knock *The Bodyguard* from the top of The Billboard 200, much in the same way that Bonnie Raitt's 1990 Grammy sweep helped push *Nick of Time* [see 340] to the top.

On February 24, 1993, at the Grammy Awards ceremony in Los Angeles, the version of "Tears of Heaven" from *Rush* was named record of the year and earned Clapton the male pop vocal award, while *Unplugged* took the honors for album of the year and male rock vocal performance. In addition, "Layla," from *Unplugged*, took the award for rock song of the year, even though it was originally recorded by Derek & the Dominos in 1970.

In the evening's most emotional moment, Clapton made his final trip to the podium to accept his sixth award of the night. "I want to thank a lot of people, but the one person I want to thank is my son, for the love he gave me and the song he gave me," Clapton said.

The following week, *Unplugged* jumped from number five to the pole position, giving Clapton his first Number One album in nearly two decades.

SIRE/REPRISE 45243 # Songs of Faith and Devotion
DEPECHE MODE
369

Producers: Depeche Mode & Flood

Track listing: I Feel You / Walking in My Shoes / Condemnation / Mercy in You / Judas / In Your Room / Get Right with Me / Rush / One Caress / Higher Love

April 10, 1993
1 week

"When you haven't released a record in three years, you don't know if fans are still there," says Depeche Mode's Andrew Fletcher. If the British band had any doubts, those misgivings disappeared the week after their tenth album was released, when *Songs of Faith and Devotion* entered The Billboard 200 at Number One.

The chart-topping entry might have come as a surprise to the band and some music industry observers, but over the years Depeche Mode had become a textbook example of how an alternative act can grow from cult status to mass success. The band had steadily built a larger audience with each album release and subsequent tour, culminating with 1990's *Violator*. That album, which included the band's first top 10 single, "Enjoy the Silence," climbed to number seven on the album chart, sold more than two million units, and primed the pump for *Songs*.

Recording in a series of six-week stints in Madrid and Hamburg in early 1992, Depeche Mode—which also includes lead vocalist David Gahan, and multi-instrumentalists Martin Gore and Alan Wilder—were quite aware that the expectations for *Songs* would be high. "We were very conscious of the fact that the last album had done so well," Fletcher says. "So there was a bit of pressure on us initially. But we wanted to make an album that sounded different. We really didn't want to make *Violator 2*, and I think we achieved that."

The band's intentions were made quite clear on the album's opening track and first single, "I Feel You," which featured a blistering metallic guitar sound rather than the bouncy techno-pop that had become Depeche Mode's trademark. "Since we had been away for so long we wanted to come back with a track that sort of created an impression," Fletcher says. "People react to that track. They may not like it or they may love it. It makes a statement...If we'd released a more commercial track first, there is a danger that people might say, 'Oh, here they are again with the same old stuff.' "

Although top 40 radio programmers didn't react positively to the track, the single, which peaked at number 37, served its purpose: It showed that Depeche Mode was continuing to evolve. "That's what makes the fans go

out and buy the record in the first week," Fletcher says. "Because they are so curious as to what we might come up with next."

Songs also offered other surprises. Gahan was listening to a lot of gospel music prior to recording the album, and that influence can be heard on various tracks, including "Get Right with Me," which features a choir. Another track, "One Caress," includes a string section. "That was probably the most exciting part of the whole album," Fletcher says. "Martin sang along live to the string section. It was all done in three hours. It was all very emotional."

THE TOP FIVE
Week of April 10, 1993

1. **Songs of Faith and Devotion**
   Depeche Mode

2. **The Bodyguard**
   Soundtrack

3. **Breathless**
   Kenny G

4. **Eric Clapton**
   Unplugged

5. **Sting**
   Ten Summoner's Tales

370 Get a Grip GEFFEN 24455
AEROSMITH

Producer: Bruce Fairbairn

Track listing: Intro / Eat the Rich / Get a Grip / Fever / Livin' on the Edge / Flesh / Walk on Down / Shut Up and Dance / Cryin' / Gotta Love It / Crazy / Line Up / Amazing / Boogie Man

May 8, 1993
1 week

In their 23 years, Aerosmith had literally been there and back—from a Boston garage to the top of the rock heap to a rock-bottom, drug-induced haze. Yet one place the band had never been was atop the *Billboard* album chart—until the release of *Get a Grip*.

Aerosmith was born in 1970, playing a mix of hard rock, R&B, and the blues. The band's first two albums were regional hits but hardly noticed outside of Boston, as singer Steven Tyler and guitarist Joe Perry were written off as Mick Jagger–Keith Richards clones. That all changed with the 1975 release of *Toys in the Attic,* their third album. "Dream On," a ballad from the band's 1973 debut album was re-released and climbed to number six. Then came "Walk This Way," with its irresistible guitar riff and lyrics full of sexual innuendo—it became Aerosmith's second top 10 hit. With 1976's *Rocks,* the band reached new heights, both artistically and commercially. The album climbed to number three and Aerosmith was America's premiere hard-rock band. Then the bottom fell out.

The excesses of success took their toll as internal squabbles and drug abuse led to Perry's departure in 1979, with rhythm guitarist Brad Whitford following in 1981. Tyler, bassist Tom Hamilton, and drummer Joey Kramer continued, but it wasn't the same.

The original line-up regrouped in 1984, but it was a series of drug-rehab stints and Tyler and Perry's participation in a 1986 cover of "Walk This Way" by rap crew Run-D.M.C. that relit the band's creative fuse. *Permanent Vacation* introduced the band to a new generation of fans and climbed to number 11 in the fall of 1987. In 1989, *Pump* hit number five and sold more than five million copies, prompting Columbia Records to woo the band back to the label with a deal reportedly worth $30 million, even though Aerosmith still owed Geffen two more albums.

Get a Grip, Aerosmith's penultimate album for Geffen, was initially recorded at A&M Studios in Los Angeles. But the band wasn't completely satisfied with the results and ventured to Little Mountain Sound Studio in Vancouver, British Columbia, to complete the project. "Usually you're up against the ceiling," says Tyler. "You have a due date, you know it's going to be six pounds, five ounces, everybody's ready, and the clothes are out. This time, we said, 'Wait a minute,' and we got a second wind."

In cuts like "Eat the Rich," the band returned to the harder, driving guitar sound that marked their earlier work. Says Tyler, "In the beginning it was

'Back in the Saddle' and "Train Kept a Rollin',' and that was the side that always got me off."

The album also marked some new collaborations. Lenny Kravitz guested and co-wrote "Line Up," ex-Eagle Don Henley sang back-up on "Amazing," and Mark Hudson, from the '70s TV group the Hudson Brothers, co-wrote "Livin' on the Edge." The latter track has been interpreted as a commentary on the 1992 L.A. riots, but Tyler says it's much more personal: "It was inspired by finding out that I'm addicted to adrenalin and the way I am is the way I am, so let's just celebrate it and sing about it."

The band had more to celebrate when *Get a Grip* temporarily dethroned *The Bodyguard* by debuting at Number One.

THE TOP FIVE
Week of May 8, 1993

1. **Get a Grip**
   Aerosmith

2. **The Bodyguard**
   Soundtrack

3. **Breathless**
   Kenny G

4. **Pocket Full of Kryptonite**
   Spin Doctors

5. **Unplugged**
   Eric Clapton

VIRGIN 87825 **janet.** **371**
JANET JACKSON

Producers: Jimmy Jam and Terry Lewis

Track listing: Morning / That's the Way Love Goes / You Know... / You Want This / Be a Good Boy... / If / Back / This Time / Go On Miss Janet / Throb / What'll I Do / The Lounge / Funky Big Band / Racism / New Agenda / Love Pt. 2 / Because of Love / Wind / Again / Another Lover / Where Are You Now / Hold on Baby / The Body That Loves You / Rain / Any Time, Any Place / Are You Still Up / Sweet Dreams

June 5, 1993
6 weeks

Following the landmark success of *Janet Jackson's Rhythm Nation 1814* [see 337], the singer was wooed away from A&M Records by Virgin. On March 11, 1991, the label announced that Jackson had been signed to a $32 million, three-album contract. The megadeal could have put pressure on Jackson and producers Jimmy Jam and Terry Lewis, but Jam says it was pretty much business as usual when the trio went to work on *janet.*

Although Jam and Lewis refused to let A&M executives hear *Rhythm Nation* prior to its completion, Virgin Records co-presidents Jeff Ayeroff and Jordan Harris were invited to get an early taste of *janet.* "Normally we wouldn't do something like that, but we had a lot of respect for them," Jam says. Jam had worked with Harris before on a Human League project, "so it wasn't so much like record company people coming out—they were creative people. We were about two or three weeks into the project." Three tracks were completed at the time of the visit: "Because of Love," "If," and "Again." Says Jam, "We played them those three songs and we never saw them again, so I think they were happy. They thought we were doing okay."

Although *Rhythm Nation* was mixed at Jam and Lewis's new Flyte Tyme studios, it was recorded at the duo's first studio, which went by the same name. *janet.* was the first full album project completed at the new complex, which included a rehearsal space with a dance room. "As we were recording the album, Janet's choreographer Tina Landon was in town. As we were getting the songs done, we would make her a cassette and she started working out routines for the songs. Literally when Janet wasn't singing, she would go to the back room and work out routines," Jam says. "It was very interesting to watch the videos and the stage show come alive as the record was being made."

On *janet.*, Jackson once again showed significant artistic growth. "She was older, more mature, and much more confident as a songwriter and a producer," says Jam. "Our collaboration was at the point where there were no punches being pulled at all."

Jackson wrote her thoughts about what the album should be about in her Powerbook, while Jam and Lewis jotted down notes on paper. "When we compared notes we were about 95 percent on," Jam says. The artist and the producers had some lofty ambitions. "History will tell us whether we deserve to even be mentioned in the same breath, but we felt like *Rhythm Nation* was like *What's Going On* and *janet.* was *Let's Get It On*," Jam says. "We felt we wanted to do the same thing that Marvin Gaye did by going from a social consciousness–type album to a love album."

The love theme made perfect sense. "Terry had been recently married, I was engaged, and Janet had been with her boyfriend Rene for about five years," Jam adds. "It was a very lovey-dovey period in all of our lives."

Jackson was also influenced by her role in the John Singleton film *Poetic Justice*. "She felt very confident and very womanly," Jam says. "Our job was just to make that happen musically. So *janet.* has a very seductive feel to it."

And *janet.* seduced the public, becoming Jackson's first album to debut in the pole position and eventually spawning seven top 10 singles, including the back-to-back Number Ones "That's the Way Love Goes" and "Again."

THE TOP FIVE
Week of June 5, 1993

1. **janet.**
   Janet Jackson

2. **The Bodyguard**
   Soundtrack

3. **Get a Grip**
   Aerosmith

4. **Pocket Full of Kryptonite**
   Spin Doctors

5. **Breathless**
   Kenny G

372 Back to Broadway COLUMBIA 44189
BARBRA STREISAND

Producers: David Foster, Barbra Streisand, Andrew Lloyd Webber, and Nigel Wright

Track listing: Some Enchanted Evening / Everybody Says Don't / The Music of the Night / Speak Low / As If We Never Said Goodbye / Children Will Listen / I Have a Love/One Hand, One Heart / I've Never Been in Love Before / Luck Be a Lady / With One Look / The Man I Love / Move On

July 17, 1993
1 week

In 1986, Barbra Streisand scored her sixth Number One album with The Broadway Album [see 295]. It took seven years for Streisand to return to the Broadway theme and the summit of the album chart, but for her fans, it was well worth the wait.

Streisand first revealed plans for Back to Broadway in the booklet to her 1991 Just for the record... box set. The four-CD retrospective contained Streisand's version of Frank Loesser's "Warm All Over" from his show The Most Happy Fella. Streisand vowed it would be included on the Back to Broadway album, but when the album was released, the track was absent.

Much like The Broadway Album, Streisand produced much of Back to Broadway herself. However, she did on occasion turn to David Foster, who produced "Somewhere" on The Broadway Album.

"On this album she was involved every step of the way, from early rehearsals at her house to the final mix," says Foster. "Every day with Barbra is intense, invigorating, and thrilling. I pushed hard to be involved in it, because this is the material she does best and I knew it would be a milestone, since it was her 50th album."

Foster wasn't Streisand's only collaborator. Andrew Lloyd Webber [see 129] and Nigel Wright co-produced "The Music of the Night," "With One Look," and "As If We Never Said Goodbye" from the Webber musicals The Phantom of the Opera and Sunset Boulevard. The latter two tracks made their debut on Back to Broadway, as Sunset Boulevard did not open in London until weeks after the album's release.

A few male vocalists were also called upon to share the spotlight. Phantom star Michael Crawford was featured on Streisand's version of "The Music of the Night," while Johnny Mathis [see 28] joined Streisand on "I Have a Love/One Hand, One Heart" from West Side Story [see 52].

Even with the big-name guests, there was no doubt Streisand remained the star attraction. "She and Sinatra [see 86] are the greatest voices of our time," says Foster. "I always joke about the fact that people literally pay thousands and thousands of dollars to hear her sing, and she paid me to hear her sing every night for eight months."

Although the eight months of recording the album were broken up into weeks of work followed by week-long breaks, the making of Back to Broadway was quite intense. "She's the kind of person that watches over every movement," says Foster. "She's intensely interested in the final product. Probably more than any artist I have met before, Barbra realizes that once it goes onto disc, it is there forever. She is acutely aware of it and she strives for perfection."

For example, Streisand occasionally even caught mistakes in the sheet music. "I wouldn't notice that it had the wrong word, but she would pick up on it right away," Foster says. "It was very important for her to have the lyrics be exactly the way they were supposed to be."

Although A&R executive Jay Landers and Streisand's manager Martin Erlichman made suggestions, "what appeared on the album is exactly what Barbra wanted to appear," says Foster.

No one could argue with Streisand's choices, which included tunes from both classic and contemporary productions. Back to Broadway debuted at Number One, becoming Streisand's seventh career chart-topper and first entry at the peak.

THE TOP FIVE
Week of July 17, 1993

1. **Back to Broadway**
   Barbra Streisand

2. **janet.**
   Janet Jackson

3. **It Won't Be the Last**
   Billy Ray Cyrus

4. **Core**
   Stone Temple Pilots

5. **Unplugged...and Seated**
   Rod Stewart

Producers: Flood, Brian Eno, and the Edge

Track listing: Zooropa / Babyface / Numb / Lemon / Stay (Faraway, So Close!) / Daddy's Gonna Pay for Your Crashed Car / Some Days Are Better Than Others / The First Time / Dirty Day / The Wanderer

July 24, 1993
2 weeks

With the success of *Achtung Baby,* U2 again launched a massive tour, this one dubbed "Zoo TV." The trek began with multiple-night stands at indoor arenas, but like the *The Joshua Tree* tour, it soon moved to huge outdoor arenas, carrying a new title, "Zoo TV: Outside Broadcast." Yet "Zoo TV" was different from the band's previous tours—the stage was covered with video monitors, displaying TV broadcasts and other messages via satellite from around the globe. Bono came onstage wearing a gold lame Elvis-type suit and "Fly" glasses. Just as *Achtung Baby* had redefined U2's sound, "Zoo TV" had effectively recast the band's live shows.

Still brimming with creative energy from *Achtung Baby* and "Zoo TV," U2 opted to enter the recording studio in Dublin during a break between the U.S. and European legs of the tour. "We had to wait until summer to tour Europe," says bassist Adam Clayton. "We had three months, so we thought we would go back and dig up some of the tracks from *Achtung Baby* that we hadn't finished. We thought we would put together some sort of an EP just to keep ourselves busy, but then it turned into an album."

The band continued on the path it had forged with *Achtung Baby,* as several of the tracks, including "Lemon" and "Numb," rocked with an electronic dance beat. Longtime co-producer Daniel Lanois had only limited involvement with the sessions. With Brian Eno still on board, Flood, who had been credited with recording *The Joshua Tree,* was tapped as a co-producer, along with guitarist the Edge. "Eno and Edge contributed to the record the most," says Clayton. "In a sense, [producer] was a role that Edge always had played. On *Zooropa,* since we were under time pressure, there was a lot more handed over to him. He would work on some of the chord structures on his own and have the work prepared for us, so when we came in the next day there was less messing around and we knew what we had to do."

The Edge also took on the role as lead vocalist on "Numb," the first track from the album released to radio. Although the Edge had contributed lead vocals in the past, this was the first time one of his vocal contributions had received such a high profile.

Other voices appeared on *Zooropa* as well. "The Wanderer," the album's final track, features Johnny Cash [see 114] on lead vocals. "That was just magical," says Clayton. "Bono and myself spent some time with Johnny after we finished the *Rattle and Hum* sessions and we talked about the possibility of doing a track together. It just so happened that when we started *Zooropa,* Johnny was touring with the Carter Family and Kris Kristofferson [see 222] in Dublin. We played Johnny the track. Bono said he would finish up some words for him and asked Johnny if he would come in the next day and sing it."

For Cash, the collaboration was also a special moment. "I felt really honored that they wanted me to be on their album," he says. "That was a bold step in my career and it opened up a lot of doors for me."

Like *Achtung Baby, Zooropa* debuted at the summit, giving U2 its fourth consecutive Number One album. Clayton says the deadline pressure contributed to the quality of the album. "Since we only had three months, it meant we really got the best of each other," he says. "And that was a good way to work."

THE TOP FIVE
Week of July 24, 1993

1. **Zooropa**
   U2

2. **Back to Broadway**
   Barbra Streisand

3. **janet.**
   Janet Jackson

4. **Sleepless in Seattle**
   Soundtrack

5. **It Won't Be the Last**
   Billy Ray Cyrus

374 Black Sunday RUFFHOUSE 53931
CYPRESS HILL

Executive producers: D.J. Muggs, Joe "the Butcher" Nicolo, and Chris Schwartz

Track listing: I Wanna Get High / I Ain't Goin' Out Like That / Insane in the Brain / When the Sh— Goes Down / Lick a Shot / Cock the Hammer / Interlude / Lil' Putos / Legalize It / Hits from the Bong / What Go Around Come Around, Kid / A to the K / Hand on the Glock / Break 'Em Off Some

August 7, 1993
2 weeks

In 1991, in a cloud of marijuana smoke, the trio known as Cypress Hill exploded onto the rap scene straight out of South Gate, a section of Los Angeles located about five minutes from the mean streets of South Central.

Initially, fans thought the group, which brought a Latin flavor to hip-hop, was from New York. "The East Coast crowd was the ones that made us," says Sen Dog, a Cuban-born rapper/lyricist whose real named is Senen Reyes. "It got us that first bit of notoriety."

Before Sen Dog hooked up with Cypress Hill lead rapper B-Real (Louis Freese), he was a member of DVX, a group that included his brother, Mellow Man Ace. Producer DJ Muggs (Larry Muggerud), who rounds out the trio, was once a member of the rap act 7A3. Cypress Hill's self-titled debut album, released in 1991, became a sleeper hit. It peaked at number 31, but spent more than a year on the chart, during which

time Muggs became one of the hottest producers on the rap scene, working with the likes of the Beastie Boys, Ice Cube, and House of Pain.

The trio spent about three years working on their debut album before being signed to Ruffhouse/Columbia. However, their second album was an entirely different story—constant touring put the group in a bind and the album had to be completed in a mere two months. "We were kind of hurried on the whole thing," says Sen Dog. "We all knew there was stuff missing and everything, but we were trying to beat the deadline."

Lyrically, Cypress Hill returned one of their favorite themes—the joys of smoking pot—in such tracks "I Wanna Get High," "Legalize It," and "Hits from the Bong." But the group didn't just rap about cannabis—they put their money where their mouths were, becoming official spokesmen for the National Organization for the Reform of Marijuana Laws. Elsewhere on the album, Cypress Hill offered tales of street violence in such songs as "Cock the Hammer" and "Hand on the Glock." The album title Black Sunday adequately summed up the group's dark vision.

"Insane in the Brain," the album's first single, covered some new ground. "That song's a freestyle party type of tune," says Sen Dog. "It's about describing the crowd at concerts and how crazy they go when they mosh and dive on each other."

Some fans thought that "Cock the Hammer" was meant as a put down of

M.C. Hammer [see 342], a highly commercial rapper who lacked street credibility, but Sen Dog insists that's not the case. "I'm not gonna drop no names, cause I'm not a name-dropper," he says. "If I can't stand you or don't like you, I'll tell you to your face."

Although Cypress Hill was nearly two years old when Black Sunday was released, the group retained a high profile with tracks appearing on the soundtrack albums of Juice, White Men Can't Jump, and Last Action Hero. With interest in Cypress Hill running high, Black Sunday entered the album chart at Number One, smoking past such stiff competitors as U2 and Barbra Streisand. "I never dreamed it would be Number One," says B-Real. "That's something you fantasize about and when you see it, it's like, 'What did I do to deserve this?' "

THE TOP FIVE
Week of August 7, 1993

1. **Black Sunday**
   Cypress Hill

2. **Zooropa**
   U2

3. **Sleepless in Seattle**
   Soundtrack

4. **janet.**
   Janet Jackson

5. **Back to Broadway**
   Barbra Streisand

EPIC SOUNDTRAX 53764 **Sleepless in Seattle**
SOUNDTRACK

Executive producer: Nora Ephron

Track listing: As Time Goes By [Jimmy Durante] / A Kiss to Build a Dream On [Louis Armstrong] / Stardust [Nat King Cole] / Makin' Whoopee [Dr. John featuring Rickie Lee Jones] / In the Wee Small Hours of the Morning [Carly Simon] / Back in the Saddle Again [Gene Autry] / Bye Bye Blackbird [Joe Cocker] / A Wink and a Smile [Harry Connick Jr.] / Stand By Your Man [Tammy Wynette] / An Affair to Remember / Make Someone Happy [Jimmy Durante] / When I Fall in Love [Celine Dion and Clive Griffin]

August 21, 1993
1 week

When pop music fans woke up to find *Sleepless in Seattle* on top of The Billboard 200, they might have wondered what year they were in. The album included such golden oldies as Jimmy Durante's version of "As Time Goes By," Louis Armstrong's "A Kiss to Build a Dream On," and Nat King Cole's "Stardust."

Sleepless in Seattle was a romantic comedy starring Tom Hanks and Meg Ryan. For filmmaker Nora Ephron, the musical selections on the soundtrack made perfect sense. "The word we started with was 'timeless,' " Ephron wrote

in the album's liner notes. "We were making a movie we hoped would be the kind of love story people would go back to for years and years, and I didn't want anything in *Sleepless in Seattle*, from the clothes to the hairstyles to the couches to (most of all) the music—to date it in any way. So we went with the classic."

Ephron didn't just stick with classic recordings, such as Gene Autry's "Back in the Saddle Again." Instead, she turned to several contemporary artists, such as Harry Connick Jr. and Joe Cocker, to record their own versions of the classics. She also included previously recorded covers of classy tunes by such contemporary artists as Dr. John and Carly Simon.

While the album was loaded with talent, Epic chose to release Celine Dion and Clive Griffin's version of "When I Fall in Love," originally a hit for Cole, as a single. Super-producer David Foster, known for his work with Barbra Streisand [see 372] and Whitney Hous-

ton [see 367], was called in to produce the session.

"I worked really hard on that with Jeremy Lubbock, who is a great arranger-composer," says Foster. "We did three different demos before we arrived at the right format. It was not an easy song to make into a duet. I wanted to maintain the integrity of the direction Nora wanted to go musically."

Long before Foster began working on the track, he had interest in *Sleepless in Seattle*. At one point, Ephron considered hiring him to score the film. Although Foster didn't end up landing that gig (Mark Shaiman did, but his work was showcased on a separate score album), he was impressed by working with Ephron. "If people want to learn about music in a movie, they should take a lesson from what Nora did with that album and the way she used the old music in the movie," he says. "It was just flawlessly done."

After seven weeks on the chart, *Sleepless in Seattle* hit Number One, even without a big hit single (Dion & Griffin's version of "When I Fall in Love" reached number six on the Hot Adult Contemporary chart on September 18, 1993). The soundtrack's success even inspired a sequel album, *More Songs for Sleepless Nights*, which wasn't nearly as successful—it stalled at number 124 on January 8, 1994.

THE TOP FIVE
Week of August 21, 1993

1. **Sleepless in Seattle**
   Soundtrack

2. **Black Sunday**
   Cypress Hill

3. **janet.**
   Janet Jackson

4. **Zooropa**
   U2

5. **Core**
   Stone Temple Pilots

From left: Meg Ryan, Ross Malinger, and Tom Hanks in *Sleepless in Seattle*.

376 River of Dreams COLUMBIA 53003
BILLY JOEL

Producer: Dan Kortchmar

Track listing: No Man's Land / The Great Wall of China / Blonde Over Blue / A Minor Variation / Shades of Grey / All About Soul / Lullabye (Goodnight, My Angel) / The River of Dreams / Two Thousand Years / Famous Last Words

August 28, 1993
3 weeks

Billy Joel initially began to work on his first album since 1989's *Storm Front* in the summer of 1992. "But I had been through some pretty hairy legal mine fields at that point," he says. "So my take on how life was going was not the greatest, so I put off writing."

Joel's legal battles actually dated back to 1989, when he sued his former manager Frank Weber for fraud. In 1992, he filed a lawsuit against his former attorneys, Allen Grubman and Arthur Indursky, for fraud, malpractice, and breach of contract. To help himself get through the legal hassles, Joel turned to the music of some of his favorite composers—Beethoven, Chopin, and John Lennon [see 255]. "I realized that a lot of these guys maybe weren't in such a great mood when they were writing, but that was okay, because they expressed what they were feeling very eloquently.

"When I finally sat down and did the bulk of the writing on the album, it came very naturally," Joel says. So naturally, in fact, that much of the music came to Joel in his sleep, including the album's title track. "I keep trying to shake that song off," he says. "I woke up one morning and I had this thing in my head. I heard it as this old doo-wop song done by guys on a street corner, but I felt like it wasn't the type of thing that I wanted to write at the time, because it was too lighthearted, but it wouldn't go away."

Joel decided to sequence the album in the order that the songs were written. After composing "All About Soul," Joel came down with a case of writer's block. For inspiration, he turned to his seven-year-old daughter, Alexa Ray, and wrote "Lullabye (Goodnight, My Angel)." Says Joel, "That song enabled me to rush out 'River of Dreams,' which had been going around in my head about sleepwalking and dreams. It all made sense. How do you get into a dream state? You go to sleep. How do you get to sleep? Someone sings you a lullabye."

It was while working on *River of Dreams*—his first album to debut at Number One and his second consecutive chart-topper—that Joel stumbled on a personal revelation. "The writing process for me is difficult, because I dream the music and I forget it. When I'm able somehow to get the dream to recur in my conscious mind, there is a moment of insecurity, some people call it inspiration. Sometimes there is a feeling, 'Wait a minute, haven't I heard this before?' And the answer is, 'Yes, you've heard it before, stupid, you dreamt it and then you forgot it.'"

The piano man's wife at the time, supermodel Christie Brinkley, also played a role in *River of Dreams*, contributing the cover portrait of Joel surrounded by the dreamlike imagery of several of the album's songs.

THE TOP FIVE
Week of August 28, 1993

1. **River of Dreams**
   Billy Joel

2. **Sleepless in Seattle**
   Soundtrack

3. **Black Sunday**
   Cypress Hill

4. **janet.**
   Janet Jackson

5. **Core**
   Stone Temple Pilots

LIBERTY 80857

In Pieces
GARTH BROOKS

377

Producer: Allen Reynolds

Track listing: Standing Outside the Fire / The Night I Call the Old Man Out / American Honky-Tonk Bar Association / One Night a Day / Kickin' and Screamin' / Ain't Going Down (Til the Sun Comes Up) / The Red Strokes / Callin' Baton Rouge / The Night Will Only Know / The Cowboy Song

September 18, 1993
5 weeks (nonconsecutive)

In the summer of 1993, Garth Brooks began to take an increasingly visible stand in the debate over used CDs. The industry had long opposed the sale of used records, claiming it cheapened the value of CDs and cut into profits on new releases. Brooks felt the sale of used CDs robbed songwriters, artists, and producers of royalties, since none are collected for the sale of used discs.

Brooks was so firm in his beliefs that he initially requested that Liberty Records not sell his new album, In Pieces, to retailers dealing in used CDs. Although the label later backed away from that plan for fear of a lawsuit, Brooks continued to speak out on the matter. Angered by his comments, many smaller retailers refused to stock his albums, leading to fears that sales of In Pieces would be jeopardized.

Not to worry—a full-fledged Brooks backlash never materialized. In fact, with first-week sales of more than 405,000, In Pieces got off to the fastest start of any album of Brooks's career, fast enough to become his third album to debut simultaneously at the top of The Billboard 200 and the Top Country Albums Chart.

While Brooks and the record companies' efforts to curb the sale of used CDs eventually proved futile, the country superstar proved that he could speak out and not be hurt by the conse-

quences. And Brooks had plenty to talk about. With In Pieces, the dark cloud haunting him while recording The Chase [see 364] had finally lifted. He had learned to balance his family and career lives and, after protracted negotiations, signed a multimillion-dollar, 20-year pact with Liberty Records. "The new deal was in, and part of the new deal was no deadlines," says Brooks. "So In Pieces was probably one of the most relaxed albums we ever made."

With no deadline to meet, Brooks actually finished the album in record time—less than six months. "In Pieces reflects the live show more than any album we have done," Brooks adds. "The first two cuts, 'Ain't Going Down,' and 'American Honky-Tonk Bar Association,' pretty much reflect the fun of it all." While The Chase showed the dark and brooding side of Garth, In Pieces reminded people that he could have fun and rock out.

Brooks's favorite song on the album is "The Cowboy Song," which features many key session players, including bassist Roy Huskey Jr., fiddle player Rob Hajacos, and mandolin picker Sam Bush. "That's the first time I've ever dispersed the studio band and brought in some different pickers," says Brooks. "We even got rid of the drum kit." Brooks had attempted to record the song for Ropin' the Wind [see 354] and The Chase, "but we just couldn't seem to get it right."

With the lineup of guest players, Brooks finally captured the song on tape. "It sure flowed well for me," he says. "Whether it is done well or not is a matter of opinion, but it sure felt good to me."

THE TOP FIVE
Week of September 18, 1993

1. **In Pieces**
   Garth Brooks

2. **Music Box**
   Mariah Carey

3. **River of Dreams**
   Billy Joel

378 In Utero DGC 24607
NIRVANA

Recorded by Steve Albini

Track listing: Serve the Servants / Scentless Apprentice / Heart-Shaped Box / Rape Me / Frances Farmer Will Have Her Revenge on Seattle / Dumb / Very Ape / Milk It / Pennyroyal Tea / Radio Friendly Unit Shifter / Tourette's / All Apologies

October 9, 1993
1 week

Following the incredible rise of *Nevermind*, the members of Nirvana found themselves under the microscope of celebrity. They never wanted to be rock stars, or so they said. Yet singer Kurt Cobain had fallen for some rock star trappings: He became addicted to heroin, although he would say that he used the drug to treat a chronic and painful stomach ailment. There were even reports that his wife, Hole singer Courtney Love, had taken heroin while pregnant with the couple's first child, a charge she vehemently denied. In the midst of the media circus, *In Utero* was conceived.

The media frenzy surrounding Nirvana wasn't limited to Cobain's personal life. Months before the release of *In Utero*, *Newsweek* reported that Geffen/DGC felt that the album, recorded by noted underground producer Steve Albini, was too harsh. Scott Litt, known for his work with R.E.M. [see 346], was called in to remix "Heart-Shaped Box" and "All Apologies." DGC/Geffen took out a full-page ad in *Billboard* slamming the *Newsweek* piece.

In hindsight, Nirvana bassist Krist Novoselic (who changed the spelling of his first name from Chris to reflect his

Croatian heritage) and Albini say the whole thing was blown out of proportion. Novoselic says he, Cobain, and drummer Dave Grohl frequently jammed before settling on material for *In Utero*. With the majority of songs in a more aggressive vein, Cobain suggested bringing Albini (who frequently eschews the "Producer" credit, preferring "Recorded by") onto the project. "After I heard the way the songs turned out, it was like, 'Yeah, Albini would be cool. He would be the man for the job,' " says Novoselic. "We didn't trust anyone else."

In Utero was recorded and mixed in about 12 days in a studio in the woods 40 miles from Minneapolis. "The band and I both were trying to make a record that was very straightforward, very accurate, a powerful hi-fi recording without doing the contemporary studio tricks," Albini says. "The band recorded essentially live in the studio."

After the sessions, Nirvana weren't completely satisfied with the album. "I was really happy with the record, but

'Heart-Shaped Box' irked me. It just wasn't right. There was a horrible effect on the guitar," Novoselic says. "Then Kurt wanted to add some background vocals." Albini and another candidate, Andy Wallace, were booked up, says Novoselic. "We wanted to do it right away, so I called up Scott Litt," he says. "I really like the way that [R.E.M.'s] 'Automatic for the People' and 'Document' sound." Litt then handled the additional recording sessions.

Controversy erupted again following the release of *In Utero*, as Wal-Mart and Kmart declined to carry the album, citing its back-cover artwork (by Cobain) depicting human fetuses scattered in a bed of flowers. A song titled "Rape Me" obviously didn't help matters. (Subsequent pressings of the album featured toned-down artwork and the newly retitled "Waif Me.") Perhaps proving the notion that there's no such thing as bad publicity, *In Utero* entered the album chart at Number One, temporarily displacing country superstar Garth Brooks.

MCA 10699 # Bat Out of Hell II: Back into Hell

MEAT LOAF

Producer: Jim Steinman

Track listing: I'd Do Anything for Love (But I Won't Do That) / Life Is a Lemon and I Want My Money Back / Rock and Roll Dreams Come Through / It Just Won't Quit / Out of the Frying Pan (and into the Fire) / Objects in the Rear View Mirror May Appear Closer Than They Are / Wasted Youth / Everything Louder Than Everything Else / Good Girls Go to Heaven (Bad Girls Go Everywhere) / Back into Hell / Lost Boys and Golden Girls

October 30, 1993
1 week

In the late '60s and early '70s, before Meat Loaf became more than just a ground beef casserole, the singer who adopted the moniker had a fairly impressive resume: One of his early bands had opened for the likes of the Who and Iggy Pop; he had appeared in several Broadway productions, including *Hair,* and also in *The Rocky Horror Picture Show;* and he had contributed vocals on Ted Nugent's *Free For All* album. However, Meat Loaf didn't truly make his mark until 1977 with *Bat Out of Hell.*

That album, released on the Cleveland International label in conjunction with CBS Records, teamed the hefty singer with fellow Broadway alumnus and songwriter Jim Steinman. With the overheated rock of such songs as "Paradise By the Dashboard Light," "Two Out of Three Ain't Bad," and "You Took the Words Right Out of My Mouth," *Bat Out of Hell* peaked at number 14 and went on to sell more than 25 million copies worldwide.

Yet, Meat Loaf (whose real name is Marvin Lee Aday) had a hard time digesting his newfound fame. "When we had the success with *Bat Out of Hell,* I didn't know how to deal with it," he says. "I went into self-inflicted exile. I said, 'I don't want to do this, because I don't like this.' "

As a result, Steinman recorded *Bad for Good* as a solo effort. The album was originally intended as the follow-up to *Bat Out of Hell,* but Meat Loaf lost his voice and will to record. *Bad for Good,* as well as Meat Loaf's subsequent albums, were major commercial disappointments. Although he continued to draw healthy crowds on tour, Meat Loaf could no longer be counted on to sell records. He was dropped from Cleveland International and later from Arista as well.

But Meat Loaf's fortunes began to change in the late '80s, when he and Steinman agreed to work together again. The reunion sparked the interest of record executive Al Teller, who had relocated from CBS Records to MCA. In 1989, Teller signed Meat Loaf to MCA and the singer and Steinman went to work on a sequel to *Bat Out of Hell.*

The pair worked in secrecy at Ocean Way Studios in Los Angeles and the Power Station in New York, but the results didn't come quickly. "Jim and I work great together, but physically we are very different, not only in size but in appearance. He works at night, while I sleep and I work in the day, while he sleeps. We meet to work at the end of my day, which is the beginning of his."

The scheduling conflict was exacerbated by Steinman's perfectionism and need to take breaks away from the project. "He spends more time out of the studio than in it, for long periods of time," Meat Loaf explains. "It tends to drive people really loony."

Yet the album, which was filled with songs with titles that read like bumper sticker slogans, was worth the wait. Todd Rundgren, who produced the original *Bat,* sang backing vocals on several tracks, while E Street pianist Roy Bittan and John Mellencamp drummer Kenny Aronoff lent instrumental support.

The album's first single, "I'd Do Anything for Love (But I Won't Do That)" became Loaf's first hit in 12 years. In its fifth week on the chart, *Bat Out of Hell II* flew to Number One, as the single topped the Hot 100.

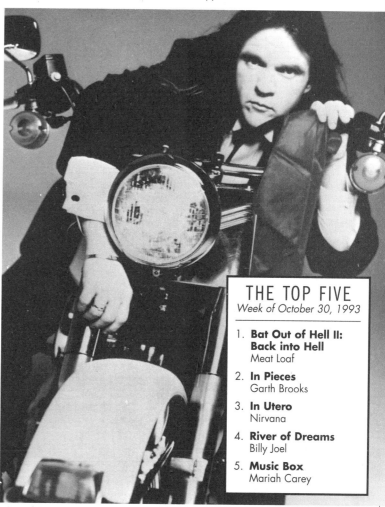

THE TOP FIVE
Week of October 30, 1993

1. **Bat Out of Hell II: Back into Hell**
   Meat Loaf

2. **In Pieces**
   Garth Brooks

3. **In Utero**
   Nirvana

4. **River of Dreams**
   Billy Joel

5. **Music Box**
   Mariah Carey

380

Vs. EPIC 53136
PEARL JAM

Producers: Brendan O'Brien and
Pearl Jam

Track listing: Go / Animal / Daughter
/ Glorified G / Dissident / W.M.A. /
Blood / Rearviewmirror / Rats / Elderly
Woman Behind the Counter in a Small
Town / Leash / Indifference

November 6, 1993
5 weeks

Pearl Jam rose from the ashes of Seattle glam-rock band Mother Love Bone, which self-destructed in March 1990 on the eve of the release of their first album when singer Andrew Wood died of a heroin overdose. Mother Love Bone guitarist Stone Gossard and bassist Jeff Ament stuck together, recruiting additional guitarist Mike McCready and drummer Dave Krusen. All the band needed was a lead singer, until a young San Diego vocalist named Eddie Vedder heard the group's demo tape.

First dubbed Mookie Blaylock after the basketball star, the group was eventually rechristened Pearl Jam. Their 1991 debut album, Ten, named for the number on Blaylock's jersey, wasn't an immediate hit, debuting at number 155 on January 4, 1992. By August, however, the album had climbed to number two, where it spent four weeks. Ten eventually went on to sell more than five million copies. Within a year, Pearl Jam had become one of the most popular rock bands in the world.

The pressure of the band's newfound stardom inspired much of Vs. "We tried really hard to not have the making of that record be a pressure situation," says Ament. "But if you think of that record and that time, it was a really stressful situation. There was an incredible pressure on us. We had the eyes of the music world on us to see if we would fall on our face."

That pressure was reflected in Vedder's lyrics to such tunes as "Go," "Animal," and "Indifference." Says Ament, "He was just being honest with himself about what he was going through." Musically, Vs. ranged from the punk rock–styled "Blood" to the folk rock of "The Elderly Woman Behind the Counter in a Small Town." The album's cover, which featured a photo by Ament of a goat sticking his nose through a fence, also summed up the band's plight. "It captured the way we felt," says Ament. "We all felt like that goat."

Vs. was recorded at Potatohead studios in Seattle and the Site in Nicasio, California, in approximately five weeks in the spring of 1993. Brendan O'Brien, who had remixed tracks culled from Ten and worked on albums by the Red Hot Chili Peppers and the Black Crowes, handled the production duties with the band.

The recording of Vs. wasn't a complete downer. The band found some relief from its own intense material while recording "Crazy Mary" with the multiple sclerosis–stricken songwriter Victoria Williams. The track turned up on the 1993 album Sweet Relief, an all-star benefit album of artists performing Williams's songs, with proceeds targeted at alleviating Williams's medical costs.

Vs., originally titled Five Against One after a lyric in "Animal," was initially issued as a vinyl LP on October 12 (the CD followed a week later). Since the title of the album was changed at the last minute, early copies do not carry the Vs. title. As had been the case with Ten, Pearl Jam once again insisted that no singles be commercially released from Vs. In addition, the band refused to make promotional video clips, which had been instrumental in the success of Ten.

It became clear that it didn't really matter if Pearl Jam didn't play the promotional game by the rules. Even without a video clip to drum up interest in the album, Vs. debuted at Number One, setting a record for most first week sales—more than 950,000—since Billboard began using SoundScan sales data in May 1991.

THE TOP FIVE
Week of November 6, 1993

1. **Vs.**
   Pearl Jam

2. **Counterparts**
   Rush

3. **Bat Out of Hell II:
   Back into Hell**
   Meat Loaf

4. **In Utero**
   Nirvana

5. **It's on (Dr. Dre)
   187um Killa**
   Eazy-E

"It took a lot of time and we went through a lot of trouble, but we made it," says Dr. Dre, who notes the album took 10 months of actual recording time at various studios in the Los Angeles area. It was time well spent, adds Dre, who prefers *Doggystyle* to his own *The Chronic*.

Dr. Dre wasn't the only big name connected to *Doggystyle*. The D.O.C., whose self-titled 1989 album reached number 20, was featured on "Serial Killa." Warren G & Nate Dogg, who had a hit in 1994 with the single "Regulate," lent their talents to "Aint No Fun," while veteran R&B vocal group the Dramatics backed up Snoop on "Doggy Dogg World."

Although *Doggystyle* is filled with misogynist and violent lyrics, Snoop says the album's success shows that hardcore rap can be positive. "I was on the total wrong side of the world, as far as gang violence, drugs, and gang-banging," he says. "Now I'm in a position now where people love and respect me. That shows no matter where you are at, if you keep your head up and keep your mind on what you want to do, it's going to happen."

By December 1994, *Doggystyle* had eclipsed sales of four million copies. At the Billboard Music Awards on December 7, 1994, Snoop was named top male artist of the year over such stiff competition as Garth Brooks [see 404], Michael Bolton [see 365], Meat Loaf [see 379], and R. Kelly. Snoop marveled that he'd gone up against such heavy hitters and come out on top. "It was wild I was even in a category with them," he says. "I was happy to even be able to be compared to someone like that."

Producer: Dr. Dre

Track listing: Bathtub / G Funk Intro / Gin and Juice / W Balls / Tha Shiznit / Lodi Dodi / Murder Was the Case / Serial Killa / Who Am I (What's My Name)? / For All My Niggaz & Bitches / Aint No Fun (If the Homies Cant Have None) / Doggy Dogg World / Gz and Hustlas / Pump Pump / Gz Up, Hoes Down / The Next Episode

December 11, 1993
3 weeks (nonconsecutive)

In April 1992, Dr. Dre's first post-N.W.A recording was featured as the title track to the *Deep Cover* soundtrack. The album topped out at number 166 on May 9, 1992, but is important for its historical significance. Lending Dre a hand at the mic was his protégé, a young Long Beach–based rapper named Snoop Doggy Dogg.

Snoop, whose real name is Calvin Broadus, was also on hand when Dre made his full-length solo debut with *The Chronic* in late 1992. By February 13, 1993, *The Chronic* had peaked at number three on The Billboard 200. Although Dre failed to top the chart, he did succeed in establishing himself as a solo star and Snoop Doggy Dogg as a fast-rising talent. Snoop also gained infamy without the aid of a microphone. On August 25, 1993, he was arrested in connection with a fatal drive-by shooting. (A jury acquitted him of second-degree murder on February 20, 1996, but deadlocked on the charges of voluntary manslaughter, resulting in a mistrial.)

By the time Snoop's debut, *Doggystyle*, was ready for release in late 1993, after several delays, there was talk of it becoming the first debut album to enter The Billboard 200 at Number One. *Doggystyle* didn't disappoint. On December 11, 1993, it knocked Pearl Jam's *Vs.* from the summit with sales of more than 800,000 copies in its first week, becoming the fastest-selling debut album in history.

THE TOP FIVE
Week of December 11, 1993

1. **Doggystyle**
   Snoop Doggy Dogg

2. **Vs.**
   Pearl Jam

3. **Music Box**
   Mariah Carey

4. **The Spaghetti Incident?**
   Guns N' Roses

5. **The Beavis & Butt-Head Experience**
   Various artists

382 Music Box COLUMBIA 53205
MARIAH CAREY

Producers: Mariah Carey, Walter Afanasieff, Dave Hall, Babyface, and Daryl Simmons

Track listing: Dreamlover / Hero / Anytime You Need a Friend / Music Box / Now That I Know / Never Forget You / Without You / Just to Hold You Once Again / I've Been Thinking About You / All I've Ever Wanted

December 25, 1993
8 weeks (nonconsecutive)

With 1991's "Emotions," Mariah Carey made chart history by becoming the first artist to have her first five singles go to Number One on the Hot 100. On the Top Pop Albums chart, however, Carey was falling just short of the mark. *Emotions*, her second album, peaked at number four, while *The MTV Unplugged EP*, released in June of 1992, climbed to number three on the album chart, and yielded another Number One single—a cover of the Jackson Five's "I'll Be There." Yet it took *Music Box* to put Carey back on top of the album chart.

For *Music Box*, Carey turned to several big-name producers, including Robert Clivilles and David Cole of C + C Music Factory fame. When working with the different producers, "each situation had its own vibe," Carey says. "So we went from one mood to an entirely different mood on *Music Box*."

Since *Music Box* was Carey's third studio album, she was becoming more seasoned as a vocalist. "In a lot of ways, *Music Box* let me let loosen up a lot more and be myself vocally. I really

THE TOP FIVE
Week of December 25, 1993

1. **Music Box**
   Mariah Carey

2. **Doggy Style**
   Snoop Doggy Dogg

3. **Vs.**
   Pearl Jam

4. **Bat Out of Hell II: Back into Hell**
   Meat Loaf

5. **Lethal Injection**
   Ice Cube

let go on a lot of performances and didn't scrutinize everything as much as I used to do. I didn't do things over and over again. Instead, we went with some of my first performances of things and really tried to get the authenticity there."

Music Box, like Carey's previous efforts, was a virtual hit-fest. The album's first single, "Dreamlover," which contains a sample of the Emotions song "Blind Alley," hit the top on September 11, 1993, and "Hero," the second single released from the album, hit the top of the Hot 100 on Christmas Day, the same day that *Music Box* went to Number One. A Thanksgiving-night NBC Television special helped push *Music*

Box to the top in its 15th week on the chart.

The third single released from *Music Box* was "Without You," a cover of the song Nilsson took to Number One in 1972. "I was in a restaurant in Florida and I heard it being played," Carey says. "I hadn't heard it for a really long time, since I was a little girl. I thought it would really add to the album. So we did it, but I really tried to keep it as close to the original as I could." Carey's version made number three, good enough to push *Music Box*, which had fallen from Number One twice by that point, back to the top for a third time on March 5, 1994.

COLUMBIA 57628 **Jar of Flies**
ALICE IN CHAINS

383

Producer: Alice in Chains

Track listing: Rotten Apple / Nutshell / I Stay Away / No Excuses / Whale & Wasp / Don't Follow / Swing on This

February 12, 1994
1 week

Alice In Chains made history when *Jar of Flies* became the first EP to top The Billboard 200 (for good measure, it also debuted at Number One). The accomplishment also made Alice in Chains the third act from the much-heralded "Seattle scene" to top the album chart—Pearl Jam accomplished the feat with *Vs.* [see 380], while Nirvana hit Number One with *Nevermind* [see 358] and *In Utero* [see 378].

Nirvana and Pearl Jam were the two bands that gained the most attention when the Seattle music scene began to garner headlines in the early '90s, but Alice in Chains was also making plenty of noise. The foursome of singer Layne Staley, guitarist Jerry Cantrell, bassist Mike Starr, and drummer Sean Kinney, formed in early 1987. Two years later, the band was signed to Columbia. They made their recording debut on *We Die Young*, an EP released in June 1990, followed by the full album *Facelift* in August, which would eventually climb to number 42.

A second EP, *SAP*, was released in November 1991, as Alice's following grew. The band was featured performing the song "Would?" in Cameron Crowe's 1992 film *Singles*, which chronicled the love lives of a group of twentysomethings and used the Seattle music scene as a backdrop. The film's soundtrack album also included the song, as well as tracks by other noted Seattle-ites like Pearl Jam and Soundgarden.

Dirt, the band's second full-length album, climbed to number six in 1992. Added exposure on the *Last Action Hero* soundtrack, a hit despite the film's disappointing showing, paved the way for *Jar of Flies*.

With new bassist Mike Inez now on board, the band decided to re-enter the studio on a whim following the completion of Lollapalooza '93, the annual alternative-rock fest. "Right after Lollapalooza we just booked a week in the studio and we went in and fucked around," says Cantrell. "We talked about doing an EP like *SAP*. At the end of two or three days we had four or five good song ideas." In a mere seven days at Seattle's London Bridge Studio, the seven-track *Jar of Flies* was written and recorded. Its primarily acoustic-based approach was a departure from the band's usual hard-rocking sound.

"It was meant as something fun, and more for the fans," Cantrell says. In keeping with that spirit, Columbia didn't issue a single, but shipped radio stations the entire EP. The track "No Excuses" began picking up airplay on modern rock and album rock stations the week prior to the album's January 25 release. Columbia also issued a special double-10-inch vinyl version of the EP, coupled with the previously released *SAP*.

Although *Jar of Flies* was a hit, temporarily knocking Mariah Carey's *Music Box* from the top spot, initial reaction to Alice's acoustic approach wasn't positive. The band performed some of the songs at a benefit concert at the Hollywood Palladium, where the rest of the bands on the bill played electric sets. Says Cantrell, "We did four or five songs and we were pelted with ice."

THE TOP FIVE
Week of February 12, 1994

1. **Jar of Flies**
   Alice in Chains

2. **Music Box**
   Mariah Carey

3. **Kickin' It Up**
   John Michael Montgomery

4. **Doggystyle**
   Snoop Doggy Dogg

5. **Greatest Hits**
   Tom Petty & the Heartbreakers

384 Kickin' It Up ATLANTIC 82559
JOHN MICHAEL MONTGOMERY

Producer: Scott Hendricks

Track listing: Be My Baby Tonight / Full-Time Love / I Swear / She Don't Need a Band to Dance / All in My Heart / Friday at Five / Rope the Moon / If You've Got Love / Oh How She Shines / Kick It Up

February 19, 1994
1 week

For the second time in as many weeks, there was a surprise at the top of The Billboard 200, as country newcomer John Michael Montgomery's *Kickin' It Up* knocked Alice in Chains' *Jar of Flies* [see 383] from the Number One position. Montgomery's rise to the top showed the continuing strength of country music, as Montgomery joined Garth Brooks [see 354] and Billy Ray Cyrus [see 363] as members of the new breed of chart-topping country hitmakers.

Montgomery grew up with music in Lexington, Kentucky, performing with his family onstage. When his parents retired, the young Montgomery took center stage as a solo act and soon landed a contract with Atlantic Records.

Life's a Dance, Montgomery's January 1992 debut album, peaked at number 27 on The Billboard 200 and number six on the Top Country Albums chart, thanks to the title track and "I Love the Way You Love Me," both of which were country radio hits.

On *Life's a Dance,* Montgomery proved to be the master of the country power ballad. *Kickin' It Up,* meanwhile, as its title suggests, showed off his rowdy side. While *Kickin' It Up* does have its share of uptempo songs, it was the ballad "I Swear" that set the album up for success. That track and "Kick It Up" were the first two songs Montgomery recorded for the album at Woodland Recording Studios in Nashville. "When we got through 'I Swear' and 'Kick It Up,'" he recalls, "we had two songs that went from one extreme to the other. All we had to do was fill in the void and I felt I would have an album I would be very proud of."

Atlantic serviced "I Swear" to radio on November 19, 1993, a full nine weeks in advance of the album's release. Eight weeks later, "I Swear" topped the Hot Country Singles and Tracks chart, setting the stage for *Kickin' It Up.* The album debuted at Number One on the Top Country Albums chart and number three on The Billboard 200. A week later, it rode high in the saddle atop both album charts, while "I Swear" also held its Number One position.

"I think this is a sign to everyone that country music is big because of the new influences," says Montgomery. "This isn't the 'Urban Cowboy' thing. This is something that is for real." Montgomery says those new influences are the artists he listened to as a teenager, including Bob Seger, Lynyrd Skynyrd, Eric Clapton [see 179], the Eagles [see 201], and Lionel Richie [see 278]. He also points to his country influences at home. "I couldn't help but be influenced by country," he says. "My mom and dad were singing all the time. They both were weekend performers."

Montgomery learned of *Kickin It Up*'s ascent to Number One the night after he picked up an American Music Award for favorite new country artist. "I'm still trying to gather my thoughts," he said at the time. "It's been one heck of a ride. It's almost too much to handle."

THE TOP FIVE
Week of February 19, 1994

1. **Kickin' It Up**
   John Michael Montgomery

2. **Music Box**
   Mariah Carey

3. **Doggy Style**
   Snoop Doggy Dogg

4. **Jar of Flies**
   Alice in Chains

5. **12 Play**
   R. Kelly

LAFACE 26007 **Toni Braxton**
TONI BRAXTON

385

weren't the only producers involved in the project. She also worked with a number of up-and-coming producers and songwriters, including Vincent Herbert, with whom Braxton co-wrote "How Many Ways," and Tim Thomas and Ted Bishop, who wrote "Love Affair." Other producers involved in the album included Three Boys from Newark ("How Many Ways"), former Midnight Starr members Melvin & Moe ("Spending My Time"), and Ernesto Phillips, who co-wrote and co-produced "Best Friends" with Braxton.

One of the standout tracks is "Breathe Again," which was among the last tunes written and recorded for the album. Says Edmonds, "While I was writing it she came in and said, 'That's the one for me.'" Braxton's hunch was right. On January 22, 1994, "Breathe Again" reached number three, becoming Braxton's second consecutive top 10 single. ("Another Sad Love Song" had peaked at number seven in November 1993.)

The hit singles were only the beginning of Braxton's roll. On February 7, 1994, she picked up awards for favorite new artist in the soul/R&B and adult contemporary categories at the American Music Awards; she was also featured performing "Another Sad Love Song" on the show. The awards and the added exposure from the TV performance were enough to boost *Toni Braxton* from number seven all the way to the top in its 31st week on the chart. After a one-week stay at the top, the album fell and then returned to the summit a month later in the wake of Braxton's Grammy wins for best new artist and best R&B vocal performance for "Another Sad Song."

Executive producers: Antonio "L.A." Reid and Kenny "Babyface" Edmonds

Track listing: Another Sad Love Song / Breathe Again / Seven Whole Days / Love Affair / Candlelight / Spending My Time with You / Love Shoulda Brought You Home / I Belong to You / How Many Ways / You Mean the World to Me / Best Friend / Breathe Again (Reprise)

February 26, 1994
2 weeks (nonconsecutive)

Initially Toni Braxton was just one of the Braxtons, a group she formed with her four sisters. The group's 1990 album was a commercial failure, but Toni garnered the attention of the red-hot production team of Antonio "L.A." Reid and Kenny "Babyface" Edmonds, known for their work with Bobby Brown [see 326]. The LaFace duo first put Braxton in the spotlight on the 1992 *Boomerang* soundtrack. She was featured on two tracks, "Love Shoulda

Brought You Home" and "Give U My Heart," a duet with Babyface. The singles reached numbers four and two, respectively, on the Hot R&B Singles chart, serving as the perfect setup for Braxton's self-titled solo album.

"It was kind of all coming together at the same time," says Edmonds of Braxton's debut album and contributions on *Boomerang*. "'Love Shoulda Brought You Home' was from *Boomerang* and during the same time that we did that song, 'You Mean the World to Me' was written and recorded." The latter track, written by Edmonds, Daryl Simmons, and Bo Watson, was originally penned with Anita Baker [see 325] in mind, says Edmonds.

While the producers were putting together *Boomerang*, Braxton never wandered far from the scene. "She was kind of like a little sister hanging around," Edmonds says. "We finished that project and then went on to do more things with her."

Although Edmonds and Reid supervised Braxton's entire album, they

THE TOP FIVE
Week of February 26, 1994

1. **Toni Braxton**
   Toni Braxton

2. **Music Box**
   Mariah Carey

3. **Doggystyle**
   Snoop Doggy Dogg

4. **Kickin' It Up**
   John Michael Montgomery

5. **12 Play**
   R. Kelly

386 Superunknown A&M 0198
SOUNDGARDEN

Producers: Michael Beinhorn and Soundgarden

Track listing: Let Me Drown / My Wave / Fell on Black Days / Mailman / Superunknown / Head Down / Black Hole / Spoonman / Limo Wreck / The Day I Tried to Live / Kickstand / Fresh Tendrils / 4th of July / Half / Like Suicide

March 26, 1994
1 week

It's only appropriate that Soundgarden reached the top of The Billboard 200. After all, the foursome can be credited with paving the way for a number of chart-topping Seattle acts, from Nirvana [see 358] and Pearl Jam [see 380] to Alice in Chains [see 383].

While Pearl Jam and Mudhoney precursor Green River is often cited as the early pioneer of the Seattle scene, Soundgarden was one of the first grunge bands to make the leap from an independent label to the majors with their integrity intact. The band's earlier efforts, which combined the power of heavy metal with the energy and attitude of punk rock, were also noteworthy. Nirvana's Kurt Cobain cited the band's 1987 Screaming Life and 1988

FOPP EPs on Sup Pop as the reason his band opted to sign with that label before moving on to Geffen.

Ultramega OK, released in 1988 on independent SST, managed to stoke the buzz, but it wasn't until the band's 1989 A&M debut, Louder Than Love, which reached number 108, that Soundgarden managed to crack the album chart.

Soundgarden continued to pick up steam in 1991 and 1992. The band's Badmotorfinger, released in late 1992, climbed to number 39. The self-titled album by Temple of the Dog, a side project/tribute to the late Mother Love Bone singer Andrew Wood, featuring Soundgarden vocalist Chris Cornell and drummer Matt Cameron with members of Pearl Jam, reached number five in the fall of 1992. Hater, an eponymous spin-off featuring bassist Ben Shepherd and Cameron, failed to chart. But that album and a Cornell solo track, included on the hit 1992 Singles soundtrack, showed off the diverse talents of Soundgarden's members.

The group's proven track record and the success of its fellow Seattle bands set the stage for Soundgarden's commercial and artistic triumph, Superunknown.

"I think Hater and Temple of the Dog helped out a lot," says guitarist Kim

Thayil. "Everyone in the band learned a little bit about the other dimensions the band has creatively and learned that other members of the band have more to offer." As a result, Soundgarden's sound evolved. The band, whose hard, bluesy sound was initially compared to Black Sabbath and Led Zeppelin, found itself called "the Beatles of grunge," with songs like "Head Down" and "Half." Says Thayil, "The aggression in the performances has been toned down, so it might be a little more palatable to the people who may have been intimidated by us in the past."

Soundgarden spent five months at Heart's [see 294] Bad Animals studio in Seattle working on the album. "That's the longest we've ever spent on an album, but it's also the longest album we've ever produced. It's 72 minutes," says Thayil.

During the sessions, the band turned to some unusual instrumentation. "Spoonman," the first single from the album, and its video, featured the Seattle artist Spoonman, playing his namesake utensil. "The title actually came from Jeff Ament of Pearl Jam. He coined the title for a fictitious album for Singles. Chris thought it would be fun to write songs with the titles Jeff came up with. But after we heard it, we said, ' "Spoonman" is definitely a Soundgarden song.' "

When Superunknown entered The Billboard 200 at Number One (A&M's first chart-topping album since the Police had achieved the feat in 1983 [see 276]), Soundgarden were no longer unknowns, but they were a bit surprised. Says Thayil, "We expected this album to do better, based on the way we were growing, but this is a little beyond what we had suspected."

THE TOP FIVE
Week of March 26, 1994

1. **Superunknown**
   Soundgarden

2. **The Downward Spiral**
   Nine Inch Nails

3. **The Sign**
   Ace of Base

4. **12 Play**
   R. Kelly

5. **Toni Braxton**
   Toni Braxton

ARISTA 18740

The Sign   387
ACE OF BASE

Producers: Joker, Buddha, PoP, Ekman, Adebrratt, Carr, and T.O.E.C.

Track listing: All That She Wants / Don't Turn Around / Young and Proud / The Sign / Living in Danger / Dancer in a Daydream / Wheel of Fortune / Waiting for Magic (Total Remix 7") / Happy Nation / Voulez-Vous Danser / My Mind (Mindless Mix) / All That She Wants (Banghra Version)

April 4, 1994
2 weeks (nonconsecutive)

When the Swedish quartet Ace of Base first washed up on U.S. shores, the group was compared with ABBA, another Swedish foursome with two male and two female members. The comparison irked Ace of Base, who claimed it was cooked up by the group's European record label. Although Ace of Base's coed lineup and pop sensibilities certainly could be compared to ABBA, Ace of Base accomplished something that neither ABBA nor any other Swedish group has ever done: score a Number One album in America.

Ace of Base, which includes Jonas "Joker" Berggren, his sisters Jenny and Linn, and Ulf "Buddha" Ekberg, officially formed in 1991. At first Jonas and Ulf wrote their own music and produced reggae acts at a studio in Gothenburg.

Eventually, after most of the songs that would turn up on The Sign were written, Jonas's sisters were recruited to round out the group. "We had around 40 songs and then we picked the best ones to record," recalls Ekberg. One of those tracks, the mid-tempo "Wheel of Fortune" was released by a Danish

independent label called Mega Records, a label name that became most appropriate when the single became a smash in Denmark, garnering the attention of the German label Metronome, which signed the band to a European licensing agreement. On Metronome, Ace of Base scored a European hit with "All That She Wants," which in turn caught the ear of Arista Records in the U.S.

"Before our album was released in the U.S., we had time to refresh the album, because it was two years," says Ekberg. "We did some remixes and we added a few new songs." Added for the U.S. release were "Living in Danger," "Don't Turn Around," and "The Sign." Says Ekberg of the latter track, " 'The Sign' is about teenage memories. It was probably the fourth reggae tune we wrote. We wrote it at the same time we wrote 'All That She Wants,' 'Wheel of Fortune,' and 'Happy Nation,' but it was the last song we produced. We did 'All That She Wants' two years before that, and you can tell that the sound has developed."

The public may have been able to tell the difference. "All That She Wants," Ace of Base's debut U.S. single, peaked at number two in December 1993, but "The Sign" did the trick. On March 12, the single topped the Hot 100. Four weeks later, the album joined the single at Number One.

Then, something truly remarkable happened: The single and the album both returned to the Number One position after being displaced. When "The Sign" returned to Number One on May 7, 1994, it marked the first time a single had reclaimed the top spot in 11 years. The album's return to the top on June 11 wasn't as dramatic or unexpected. "Don't Turn Around," the group's third single, had entered the top 10, spurring album sales.

Ekberg could scarcely believe that the group had gone to Number One even once. "I had a dream that we would be Number One in maybe Germany or France," he says, "but to reach over to the U.S., I never ever even dreamed of that."

THE TOP FIVE
Week of April 4, 1994

1. **The Sign**
   Ace of Base

2. **Superunknown**
   Soundgarden

3. **12 Play**
   R. Kelly

4. **August & Everything After**
   Counting Crows

5. **Music Box**
   Mariah Carey

388 Far Beyond Driven EASTWEST 92302
PANTERA

Producers: Terry Date & Vinnie Paul

Track listing: Strength Beyond Strength / Becoming / 5 Minutes Alone / I'm Broken / Good Friends and a Bottle of Pills / Hard Lives, Sunken Cheeks / Slaughtered / 25 Years / Shedding Skin / Use My Third Arm / Throes of Rejection / Planet Caravan

April 9, 1994
1 week

When Pantera's *Far Beyond Driven* entered The Billboard 200 at Number One, *USA Today* ran a story about the group's "overnight success," but nothing could have been further from the truth.

Pantera, which is Spanish for Panther, was formed in 1983 in Dallas by drummer Vinnie Paul, his brother "Dimebag" Darrell on guitar, and bassist Rex. The group released three albums on their own Metal Magic label before replacing their original lead singer with Philip Anselmo. After one more release on Metal Magic, they were signed to Atco.

Pantera's 1990 major label debut, *Cowboys from Hell*, didn't crack The Billboard 200, but appeared on the Heatseekers new artist chart and went on to sell more than 500,000 copies—an extraordinary total for an album that failed to chart. *Vulgar Display of Power*, released in 1992, debuted and peaked at number 44, showing that the band had an active and growing fan base.

With four and a half years of virtually constant touring, Pantera were primed for success when *Far Beyond Driven* was released on March 22, 1994. "Touring has been the total key to our

---

THE TOP FIVE
Week of April 9, 1994

1. **Far Beyond Driven**
   Pantera

2. **Longing in Their Hearts**
   Bonnie Raitt

3. **The Sign**
   Ace of Base

4. **Above the Rim**
   Soundtrack

5. **Live at the Acropolis**
   Yanni

---

success," says Paul. "We're not on regular AOR radio. We're not on MTV, except for 'Headbanger's Ball.' People find out about us from our playing live. They see us and they tell their friends, and their friends tell their friends."

For *Far Beyond Driven*, Pantera took a different approach. "Usually we do demos and then we fly Terry in and re-record everything," Paul says. "This time around, we wrote as we recorded. Whatever felt right ended up on the record. It was more spontaneous and more fun." During the sessions the band would focus on three songs at a time and then take a break. "Good Friends and a Bottle of Pills" was recorded at the end of a very long day. "It was about 4 A.M. and everyone was pretty wasted," he says. "And we thought, 'Let's do something different.' So we ended up with this two-and-a-half-minute song. It was recorded on the first take and it ended up being one of a lot of people's favorite song on the record."

Pantera also paid tribute to one of their influences by recording Black Sabbath's "Planet Caravan," an obscure track featured on Sabbath's 1970 *Paranoid* LP. Pantera's version of the cut was originally recorded for inclusion on a Sabbath tribute album but was left off for contractual reasons. "Everyone else was doing the obvious songs like 'Iron Man,' " Paul says. "We wanted to do something that would set us apart and it turned out killer. When we found out we couldn't put it on the tribute album, we said, 'Fuck it, let's put it on our album.' "

Far Beyond Driven's huge success may have caught some observers by surprise, in part because it was Pantera's hardest-rocking record to date, as the band continued to push the limits rather making their sound more accessible. "Other bands have tried to commercialize their sound and they lose their fan base," Paul says. "We didn't want to do that, so we went the other direction."

Far Beyond Driven also became the hardest rock record to top The Billboard 200. "Metallica's [see 353] last record was amazing," says Paul, "but it's not nearly as hard as this album."

CAPITOL 81427 ## Longing in Their Hearts
BONNIE RAITT

389

Producers: Don Was and Bonnie Raitt

Track listing: Love Sneakin' Up on You / Longing in Their Hearts / You / Cool, Clear Water / Circle Dance / I Sho Do / Dimming of the Day / Feeling of Falling / Steal Your Heart Away / Storm Warning / Hell to Pay / Shadow of Doubt

April 16, 1994
1 week

Ironically it was another comeback record by a veteran artist, Natalie Cole's *Unforgettable* [see 352], that kept Bonnie Raitt from scoring two consecutive Number One albums. *Luck of the Draw*, Raitt's follow-up to the Grammy-winning *Nick of Time* [see 340], stayed at number two for two weeks in August 1991, but wasn't able to unseat *Unforgettable*. Cole's tribute to her father Nat "King" Cole also took the album of the year Grammy over *Luck of the Draw*, but Raitt didn't go home empty-handed. She won three Grammys that year, including the award for best rock vocal performance and best female pop vocal performance. Simply put, Raitt's hot steak was far from over.

From August through October 1993, Raitt teamed with Don Was a third time for *Longing in Their Hearts*, the 12th studio album of her 23-year career. Once again, Raitt drew on a mix of originals and songs penned by her favorite songwriters. The title track was written by Raitt and her husband, actor Michael O'Keefe, who also contributed lyrics to "One Part Be My Lover" from *Luck of the Draw*. Several guests also made appearances on *Longing in Their Hearts*, including Richard Thompson, who played guitar on Raitt's cover of his "Dimming of the Day." Others lending their musical support on the album included keyboardist Benmont Tench from Tom Petty & the Heartbreakers, the Band's Levon Helm, and David Crosby. Once again, however, the real star was Raitt.

"She was blowing everyone's mind by singing better than she ever had in her life," says Was. "Guys like [drummer] Ricky Fataar and [bassist James] 'Hutch' [Huchinson], who have been in her band for 15 years, were amazed that she continued to improve."

Part of Raitt's enhanced vocal prowess could likely be attributed to confidence. "When we did *Nick of Time* we weren't quite sure where we fit in the commercial spectrum," says Was. "But after that success of that album and *Luck of the Draw*, we knew that there were five million people or so who were willing to buy an album when we did a good job. That gave us the confidence to stay true to what we wanted to do

and take some risks in terms of under-production."

On *Longing in Their Hearts*, Raitt and Was took the sparse production of *Nick of Time* and *Luck of the Draw* a step further. "I was trying to get a little closer to what she does live," Was says. "So 99 percent of Bonnie's vocals were cut live with the band and there are very few fixes."

With the success of *Nick of Time* and *Luck of the Draw*, Raitt had a healthy following awaiting the release of *Longing in Their Hearts*. On April 9, 1994, the album was one of three new albums to debut in the top five. However, Raitt's following was not as rabid as Pantera's. The Texas-based heavy metal act took the top spot with *Far Beyond Driven* [see 388], leaving Raitt at number two with the highest debut of her career. Yet the following week, *Longing in Their Hearts* was able to push its way to Number One, giving Raitt the second chart-topper of her career.

THE TOP FIVE
Week of April 16, 1994

1. **Longing in Their Hearts**
   Bonnie Raitt

2. **The Sign**
   Ace of Base

3. **Above the Rim**
   Soundtrack

4. **August & Everything After**
   Counting Crows

5. **12 Play**
   R. Kelly

390 The Division Bell COLUMBIA 64200
PINK FLOYD

Producers: Bob Ezrin and David Gilmour

Track listing: Cluster One / What Do You Want From Me / Poles Apart / Marooned / A Great Day for Freedom / Wearing the Inside Out / Take It Back / Coming Back to Life / Keep Talking / Lost for Words / High Hopes

April 23, 1994
4 weeks

To record their first studio album since 1987, Pink Floyd regrouped at Astoria, David Gilmour's floating studio on the River Thames. A lot had transpired since the chart-topping triumph of The Wall [see 246] in 1979. In 1983, Pink Floyd recorded one more album with Roger Waters before the bassist/vocalist left the band. That album, appropriately dubbed The Final Cut, reached number six. Four years later, the Floyd fared better when A Momentary Lapse of Reason, their first album recorded as a trio, reached number three.

The Division Bell was spawned from two weeks of jamming and then close to a year of work, on and off, in the studio. "We started off with the band going into a rehearsal studio for a few weeks, where they basically reconnected with each other and jammed and played together as a band," says co-producer Bob Ezrin. "We recorded the whole thing and in that there were a lot of Pink

Floyd musical moments, so we extracted those from the tape of the jam session and began there with those germs to construct the material for the album."

With Floyd's Gilmour, Nick Mason, and Rick Wright seasoned professionals, the sessions were workmanlike. "The band hadn't changed that much over the years," Ezrin says. "Sometimes they were a little frivolous, but mostly they were quite serious. They have maintained their sense of humor and sense of humanity, and everyone has stayed relatively unpretentious."

Ezrin, who worked on The Wall and A Momentary Lapse of Reason, wasn't the only person to reunite with Pink Floyd for The Division Bell. Michael Kamen, who arranged the strings on The Wall, also returned, as did saxophonist Dick Parry, who had last worked with the band on "Money" from The Dark Side of the Moon [see 157]. "It was a really sweet and wonderful type of reunion," says Ezrin. "Dick was a little nervous and self-deprecating. He was saying that he wasn't sure that he would be able to cut it, but as soon as he started to blow his horn, we realized he was the right guy, because he had the sort of vibe we were looking for."

While most of the songs were an outgrowth of the initial jam sessions, the album's closing track, "High Hopes," came later. "Dave literally went in one week on his own and had inspiration and came back and presented it in

almost finished form to the band," says Ezrin. "The demo sounds very much like what is on the record. We just added a few things to it in terms of the arrangement."

With the release of The Division Bell on the horizon, Pink Floyd announced that they would again launch a massive North American tour. Even before the album's release, the band had sold more than a million tickets to the first 22 dates on the tour, which included a stop at Yankee Stadium in New York.

With the excitement of the tour in full swing, The Division Bell became the first Pink Floyd album to debut in the pole position, and the band's fourth career chart-topper.

THE TOP FIVE
Week of April 23, 1994

1. **The Division Bell**
   Pink Floyd

2. **Above the Rim**
   Soundtrack

3. **The Sign**
   Ace of Base

4. **Longing in Their Hearts**
   Bonnie Raitt

5. **August & Everything After**
   Counting Crows

CURB 77659 **Not a Moment Too Soon 391**

TIM MCGRAW

Producers: James Stroud and Byron Gallimore

Track listing: It Doesn't Get Any Countrier Than This / Give It to Me Strait / Wouldn't Want It Any Other Way / Down on the Farm / Not a Moment Too Soon / Indian Outlaw / Refried Dreams / Don't Take the Girl / 40 Days and 40 Nights / Ain't That Just Like a Dream

May 21, 1994
2 weeks

Tim McGraw's second album couldn't have been more aptly titled. "I was just trying to cut a good enough record to keep my record deal," says McGraw of *Not a Moment Too Soon*. "We thought we cut a good one before and it didn't do much. We kind of felt like we were at our last rope. This record had to do something in order for me to keep a deal."

McGraw's self-titled 1993 album failed to crack both The Billboard 200 and the Top Country Albums charts. The country crooner grew up in the tiny town of Start, Louisiana, where he originally planned to follow in the footsteps of his biological father, former major league baseball pitching ace Tug McGraw. "I didn't get to know my father until I was 18, after I got out of

high school," says McGraw, who was raised by his mother and step-father. At age 11, McGraw learned that his real father was the baseball star.

The young McGraw eventually gave up baseball for music. "I thought I wanted to become a ballplayer until I got into college and discovered keg floatin' and things like that," he says. "That kind of cramps your athletic style." Shortly thereafter, McGraw established his own musical style, "turbo-tonk," which mixes rock influences with honky-tonk, and played clubs in Louisiana and Jacksonville.

Not a Moment Too Soon was recorded and mixed in approximately five weeks at Loud Studio in Nashville. The song that gave McGraw the most trouble was the title track. "Every morning I would come in and warm up with that song, but I could never get it to sound like I wanted it to, until the last day we were in the studio, I decided I was going to lay it down on track and we got it in 30 minutes."

The album's best-known track is "Indian Outlaw," written by Tommy Barnes, Gene Simmons, and John D. Loudermilk. McGraw first heard the song in March 1989 during his first visit to Nashville. "Tommy Barnes was in this little bar called the Hall of Fame Lounge playing guitar and that was one of the songs he played," says McGraw. "So I

heard my first hit song on my first trip to Nashville and didn't even know it."

Although McGraw considered "Indian Outlaw" for his first album, he opted not to record the song at the time. "Timing is everything. I don't think we would have got the airplay two years before that we got in 1994," he says. "Because of how different the song is and how much country music changed. It's probably a good thing we didn't cut it on the first album."

When "Indian Outlaw" became a hit on country radio, its rise up the chart was greeted with controversy, as some Native American Activists attacked the song as racist. "I didn't expect the controversy," he says. "All we were trying to do was cut a good record and a fun record. We weren't trying to make any social statements. We weren't trying to make any great piece of artwork out of it. Some people read some things into that just weren't there in my opinion."

Yet at the end of the day, the controversy surrounding "Indian Outlaw" helped make McGraw a star and push *Not a Moment Too Soon* to the top of the album chart. "You know the old saying, 'Just spell the name right.' Any time there is publicity, it is going to create interest. But I also hope that just by gaining some attention it will help [Native Americans] get some attention for problems that they need looked at."

THE TOP FIVE
Week of May 21, 1994

1. **Not a Moment Too Soon**
   Tim McGraw

2. **Read My Mind**
   Reba McEntire

3. **The Sign**
   Ace of Base

4. **The Division Bell**
   Pink Floyd

5. **Chant**
   Benedictine Monks of Santo Domingo de Silos

392 The Crow ATLANTIC/INTERSCOPE 82519
SOUNDTRACK

Executive producers: Jeff Most, Jolene Cherry, and Tom Carolan

Track listing: Burn [The Cure] / Golgotha Tenement Blues [Machines of Loving Grace] / Big Empty [Stone Temple Pilots] / Dead Souls [Nine Inch Nails] / Darkness [Rage Against the Machine] / Color Me Once [Violent Femmes] / Ghostrider [Rollins Band] / Milktoast [Helmet] / The Badge [Pantera] / Slip Slide Melting [For Love Not Lisa] / After the Flesh [My Life with the Thrill Kill Kult] / Snakedriver [The Jesus and Mary Chain] / Time Baby III [Medicine] / It Can't Rain All the Time [Jane Siberry]

June 4, 1994
1 week

Much like the film it accompanied, *The Crow* soundtrack overcame various obstacles and flew to the top. The future of the film, based James O'Barr's cult comic book, was left in limbo when its star, Brandon Lee, 28, died on March 31, 1993, after being hit by a blast from an improperly loaded prop gun during filming. After mourning Lee's death, the cast and crew decided to finish the remaining scenes as a tribute to the young actor, the son of late martial-arts legend Bruce Lee. Although the movie's initial distributor, Paramount, decided to pass on the film, it was picked up by Miramax. *The Crow* opened on Friday the 13th of May and surprisingly topped that weekend's box-office chart. A few weeks later, *The Crow* soundtrack hit Number One on The Billboard 200.

The soundtrack had begun to take shape more than two years earlier,

before a studio had signed on to produce the film. Jolene Cherry, who executive-produced the soundtrack with film producer Jeff Most and Tom Carolan, became involved in the project through the film's other producer, Ed Pressman. Cherry and Pressman are partners in a music publishing company.

The film script and the comic book naturally lent themselves to an alternative rock–leaning set. "In the comic book, it refers to the Cure and Joy Division," says Cherry. In fact, comic book creator O'Barr is also a member of the industrial act Trust/Obey, signed to Nine Inch Nails leader Trent Reznor's Nothing imprint.

The first artist Cherry approached for the album, appropriately enough, was Reznor. "He was familiar with the comic book," says Cherry. Reznor met with Cherry while he was writing material for Nine Inch Nails' *The Downward Spiral*.

"He was living at Sharon Tate's old house and working on his record at the time," says Cherry, who also supervised, compiled, and sequenced the soundtrack with Leslie Reed. "Fortunately for us, he agreed to be a part of it. That was the cornerstone of the record." NIN recorded a cover of the Joy Division song "Dead Souls" for the album. With Nine Inch Nails signed on, Interscope Records also became involved in the

project, as two of the label's other acts, Helmet and My Life with the Thrill Kill Kult, contributed tracks.

A number of acts featured on the set contributed material recorded specifically for the film, including the Cure, Machines of Loving Grace, and Stone Temple Pilots. Others, such as Rollins Band, Rage Against the Machine, and Violent Femmes, contributed previously unreleased material.

"I was looking for a tone and feel evocative of [director] Alex Proyas's past work, the tone of the comic, and the feeling I got from reading the script," says Cherry. "One of the most interesting things about this album is that there's 14 bands, yet there is a cohesiveness in the sound."

The soundtrack, like the film, is dedicated to the memory of Lee. "Brandon's death affected everyone who worked on the film and the record," says Cherry. "It was a very tragic, sad experience for all of us, and it's to everyone's credit that we decided to carry on....All the bands involved in this project were very brave to stay aboard. There were so many bumps along the way. There was a lot of bad press, accidents on the set, and Brandon's death. They could have panicked and dropped out, but they stuck with it, and now they are being rewarded for it."

THE TOP FIVE
Week of June 4, 1994

1. **The Crow**
   Soundtrack

2. **Not a Moment Too Soon**
   Tim McGraw

3. **The Sign**
   Ace of Base

4. **Chant**
   Benedictine Monks of
   Santo Domingo de Silos

5. **Above the Rim**
   Soundtrack

Brendan Lee in *The Crow.*

CAPITOL 28599 | ||| Communication

BEASTIE BOYS

393

Producers: Beastie Boys and Mario
Caldator Jr.

Track listing: Sure Shot / Tough Guys /
B-Boys Makin' with the Freak Freak /
Bobo on the Corner / Root Down /
Sabotage / Get It Together / Sabrosa
/ The Update / Futterman's Rule /
Allright Hear This / Eugene's Lament /
Flute Loop / Do It / Ricky's Theme /
Heart Attack Man / The Scoop /
Shambala / Bodhisattva Vow /
Transitions

June 18, 1994
1 week

In 1986, the Beastie Boys became the
first rap act to top the album chart with
Licensed to Ill [see 309]. Paul's Bou-
tique, the group's 1989 followup, was
hailed by critics but failed to match the
commercial knockout of the debut album,
as it stalled at number 14. Check Your
Head, released in 1992, struck a balance between critical and commercial
appeal, debuting and peaking at number
10 and selling more than a million
copies. Still, many wrote off the trio as
one-hit wonders who would never match
the commercial success of Licensed to Ill.

That all changed with the release of
Ill Communication. The album features
the Beasties dabbling in everything from
hardcore punk and hip-hop to funk
jams. The Beasties' Mike D notes that
the musical climate had changed to the

group's advantage. "Increasingly, there
are a number of bands that incorporate
different styles into what they do," he
says. "There's an audience for everything from hip-hop to the rare groove
funky shit to hardcore. There are actually kids now that have grown up on all
those kinds of music, like we have."

The Beastie Boys, whose ranks also
include bassist MCA (Adam Yauch) and
guitarist Adrock (Adam Horovitz), recorded Ill Communication in record time.
"Seven months is a world's record for us,"
says Mike D. "We worked on Check Your
Head for a long time and we learned
how to make records, and touring taught
us a lot about playing together."

As had been the case with Check
Your Head, Ill Communication features a
mix of samples and live instrumentation.
Material sampled on the set includes
"everything from Richard Pryor to the
Keychains," says Mike D.

On the live instrument side, the Middle Eastern–flavored "Eugene's Lament"
features the Beasties' pal Eugene Gore
on violin. Other tracks include keyboardist Money Mark and percussionist
Eric Bobo, for whom the track "Bobo on
the Corner" is named. The latter two
instrumentalists played with the band on
the tour in support of Check Your Head.

"When we started playing instruments for Check Your Head, a lot of that
was based on the music that inspired
it—whether it was the Meters or the
J.B.'s, it was the stuff that we had been

sampling. As soon as we started to do
that, we realized we could still play
hardcore, too," says Mike D. "With this
album it was just a matter of getting
even more out there"

Capitol issued a white-label 12-inch
of "Get It Together," which features a
guest appearance by Q-Tip of Tribe
Called Quest, to clubs in early April. A
second track, "Sabotage," went to college and modern rock radio in mid-
May. The combination of working the
two tracks at different formats was
enough to push Ill Communication to
the top in its first week, making the Beastie
Boys, who were already the first rap act
to have topped the album chart, the first
rap act to do it twice.

THE TOP FIVE
Week of June 18, 1994

1. **Ill Communication**
   Beastie Boys

2. **The Sign**
   Ace of Base

3. **The Crow**
   Soundtrack

4. **Not a Moment Too Soon**
   Tim McGraw

5. **Above the Rim**
   Soundtrack

394 Purple ATLANTIC 82607
STONE TEMPLE PILOTS

THE TOP FIVE
Week of June 25, 1994

1. **Purple**
   Stone Temple Pilots

2. **Regulate...
   G Funk Era**
   Warren G

3. **The Sign**
   Ace of Base

4. **Ill Communication**
   Beastie Boys

5. **Not a Moment
   Too Soon**
   Tim McGraw

Producer: Brendan O'Brien

Track listing: Meatplow / Vasoline / Lounge Fly / Interstate Love Song / Still Remains / Pretty Penny / Silvergun Superman / Big Empty / Unglued / Army Ants / Kitchen Ware & Candy Bars

June 25, 1994
3 weeks

The Stone Temple Pilots' debut album, *Core*, peaked at number three and spawned three hits on the Modern Rock and Album Rock Tracks charts. When the new STP track "Big Empty" was included on *The Crow* soundtrack [see 392], radio programmers were quick to gravitate toward the introspective rocker, although it wasn't officially released as a single.

Since the track was also included on STP's sophomore set, *Purple*, singer Scott Weiland had mixed feelings about radio going on the track weeks before the band's second album. "When we were writing and recording the second record, we decided we wanted ["Big Empty"] on there," he says. "It fit the vibe." By the time STP

decided that they wanted the song for their album, "Big Empty" was already slated for inclusion on *The Crow*. Says Weiland, "We didn't want to give away too much before the album was finished, but radio started playing the song when we were still in the process of recording the album."

Yet, he adds, "If people want to hear it, they want to hear it. It would be pretty pompous of me to make a stink about it and say, 'Don't play this song. You're tainting the feeling of the album.'"

Most of *Purple* was recorded at Atlanta's Southern Tracks studio with Brendan O'Brien, who had also produced *Core*, once again manning the board. Says Weiland, "It's far away and removed from the industry, so we didn't have to worry about distractions." The band completed the album in approximately two weeks.

A few additional tracks were recorded while the band was on the road. "Lounge Fly" was cut at Paisley Park Studios in Minneapolis and features Paul Leary of the Butthole Surfers on guitar. "Big Empty" was recorded in L.A., during a break from touring. An unlisted 12th track, performed by a Washington-based lounge singer, showed off the

band's warped sense of humor.

Weiland says *Purple* is much more personal than *Core*. "I wasn't writing to explain or put any point across or any opinion to a mass audience," he says. "The more successful we became, the less responsible I felt about instilling any type of ideas. I don't know if that works anyway. It doesn't work for me. I'm just expressing myself."

Musically, the band had grown as well, escaping the comparisons to Pearl Jam [see 380] that dogged them around the release of *Core*. In fact, the subtle acoustic number "Pretty Penny" is more reminiscent of Led Zeppelin [see 118] than any of STP's contemporaries. "I would be very bored making an album the sounds completely like the last record with nothing more than copycat songs, just for the sake of making money," says Weiland.

Yet squabbles between band members over the album's title and artwork almost delayed the release of *Purple*. The title of the album only appears on the package in Chinese. Says Weiland, "As long as we can still dig each other and communicate with each other while arguing about album titles, we will make other albums."

WALT DISNEY RECORDS 60858 **The Lion King** **395**
SOUNDTRACK

Producers: *Hans Zimmer, Mark Mancina, Jay Rifkin, and Chris Thomas*

Track listing: Circle of Life / I Just Can't Wait to Be King / Be Prepared / Hakuna Matata / Can You Feel the Love Tonight / This Land / ...To Die For / Under the Stars / King of Pride Rock / Circle of Life / I Just Can't Wait to Be King / Can You Feel the Love Tonight

July 16, 1994
10 weeks (nonconsecutive)

When *The Lion King* rose to the throne of The Billboard 200 in its fifth week on the chart, it became Disney's first Number One album since *Mary Poppins* [see 74], on the Buena Vista label, had reached the top nearly 30 years earlier.

Although the Number One position remained elusive, Disney had continued to have its share of hits. With the 1989 release of *The Little Mermaid*, the label began a new streak of hit soundtracks that was nearly as impressive as its animated films' box office and home-video successes. *The Little Mermaid* climbed to number 32 and went on to sell more than two million copies. *Beauty and the Beast*, released in 1991, reached number 19 and 1992's *Aladdin* peaked at number six. Both sold more than three million copies.

The latter two albums also spawned hit singles. From *Aladdin*, "A Whole New World" by Peabo Bryson & Regina

Belle reached number three on the Hot 100 and topped the Hot Adult Contemporary chart, while Bryson & Celine Dion's "Beauty & The Beast" reached number nine on the Hot 100 and number three on the Hot Adult Contemporary list.

The Lion King was actually in the works before *Aladdin*, says lyricist Tim Rice, whose first major success was the rock opera *Jesus Christ Superstar* [see 129], but it was put on the back burner until *Aladdin* was completed. Once Disney was ready to get back on the project, Rice was asked which composer he would like to work with. "I said, 'Well, Elton John would be terrific,'" he says. "I didn't know at the time that he would have any interest in doing it, and even if he did he probably wouldn't have the time. And, even if he had the time, I didn't think Disney would be able to persuade him to do it."

To Rice's surprise, John came aboard. It wasn't the first time the two had collaborated together—John had written the music for Rice's "Legal Boys" and included it on his 1982 *Jump Up!* album.

For *The Lion King*, Rice and John rarely actually worked together. "Elton was always on the road and he likes to be sent the lyrics," says Rice. "For me,

Tim Rice

it's unusual to write lyrics without a tune, but it worked very well. I would send him the lyrics, then he would send me a demo tape back."

The Lion King features five songs composed by John and Rice, plus score music by Hans Zimmer. The production numbers include vocals by stars Matthew Broderick, Jeremy Irons, Whoopi Goldberg, and Cheech Marin, who provided the voices to the film's animated characters. The album also includes John's own versions of three key songs.

When John and Rice did get together to collaborate, Rice was amazed by the singer's songcrafting abilities. Rice had asked John for a few more days to complete the lyric to "Circle of Life," but John insisted he bring it to him as is. "He said, 'No, don't worry.' I turned up at Air Studios in London and he sat down at the piano with the lyrics. He made one suggestion. He wanted one more phrase. Then he sat down and played over and over again while singing the lyrics and gradually a tune emerged. It really sounded sensational. That version by Elton already sounded like a hit."

Rice's first impression wasn't off the mark. John's version of "Can You Feel the Love Tonight," which ran during the film's closing titles, topped the Hot Adult Contemporary chart for eight weeks and peaked at number four on the Hot 100 Singles chart. "Circle of Life" fared almost as well, reaching Number two on the Hot Adult Contempoary chart and number 18 on the Hot 100.

Elton John

THE TOP FIVE
Week of July 16, 1994

1. **The Lion King**
   Soundtrack

2. **Purple**
   Stone Temple Pilots

3. **The Sign**
   Ace of Base

4. **Regulate...G Funk Era**
   Warren G

5. **Not a Moment Too Soon**
   Tim McGraw

396

II MOTOWN 530323

BOYZ II MEN

Executive producers: Jheryl Busby & Boyz II Men

Track listing: Thank You / All Around the World / U Know / Vibin' / I Sit Away / Jezzebel / Khalil (Interlude) / Trying Times / I'll Make Love to You / On Bended Knee / 50 Candles / Water Runs Dry / Yesterday

September 17, 1994
4 weeks (nonconsecutive)

The "End of the Road" was just the beginning for Boyz II Men, as the vocal group's *II* debuted at Number One on The Billboard 200, while the album's first single held the top position on the Hot 100.

"End of the Road," culled from the *Boomerang* soundtrack, topped the Hot 100 for 13 weeks, breaking a record previously held by Elvis Presley's "Don't Be Cruel"/"Hound Dog," although it was subsequently topped by Whitney Houston's "I Will Always Love You" from *The Bodyguard* [see 367], the Boyz' own "I'll Make Love to You," and, later, by the Boyz' collaboration with Mariah Carey, "One Sweet Day" [see 418].

Cooleyhighharmony, the quartet's 1991 debut album, climbed to number three, while *Christmas Interpretations*, their 1993 seasonal album, made number 19. The success of "End of the Road" put Boyz II Men on top, and also somewhat intimidated the group's members, Shawn Stockman, Michael S. McCary, and brothers Wanya and Nate Morris. "It took us a long time to get the

album done," says Stockman. "It took six to nine months, not only because of the intimidation factor. People were coming up to us and saying, 'The last album was good, this one better be even better.' And we were being pressured by the record company. They said it wasn't only an important album for us, but for the record company, too. They had their hands in a lot of the creative processes. There were a lot of chefs in the kitchen."

Boyz II Men initially began writing the songs for *II* even before their Christmas album was recorded. At first, the group planned on recording the album in their home base of Philadelphia, but they subsequently ditched the plan. "It was hard to concentrate on the music with all of our families and friends around," says Stockman.

So the group went to Reno, Nevada, to work and live in a studio called Granny's House. "We could concentrate better there, and get away from the distractions," says Stockman.

At the studio, the group cut their cover of the Beatles' "Yesterday" [see 87] and "50 Candles." The former dates back to the high school days of group members McCary and Morris, who used to perform the song in the choir.

After Boyz II Men reignited their creative spark at Granny's House, they opted to contact a number of different producers, including such past collaborators as Babyface, who had worked on "End of the Road," and Dallas Austin, who had produced the group's first hit, "Motownphilly."

Says Stockman, "After 'End of the Road' it made sense to go back and work with Babyface, and he came up with some really nice songs." Babyface's contributions were "I'll Make Love to You," which picks up where "End of the Road" left off, and "Water Runs Dry."

The success of *II* wasn't only a triumph for Boyz II Men, it was a victory for Motown, which scored its first album to debut at Number One since Stevie Wonder's *Songs in the Key of Life* [see 219]. The Motown tradition is something that Boyz II Men are proud to be a part of. "We think about it every day," says Stockman. "It's a dream come true to be part of that legacy, and we are responsible for carrying that tradition on."

THE TOP FIVE
Week of September 17, 1994

1. **II**
   Boyz II Men

2. **The Lion King**
   Soundtrack

3. **Forrest Gump**
   Soundtrack

4. **The 3 Tenors in Concert 1994**
   Carreras, Domingo, Pavarotti (Mehta)

5. **Dookie**
   Green Day

DUCK 45735 # From the Cradle

ERIC CLAPTON

Producers: Eric Clapton and
Russ Titelman

Track listing: Blues Before Sunrise /
Third Degree / Reconsider Baby /
Hoochie Coochie Man / Five Long
Years / I'm Tore Down / How Long
Blues / Goin' Away Baby / Blues Leave
Me Alone / Sinner's Prayer / Mother-
less Child / It Hurts Me Too / Someday
After a While / Standin' Round Crying
/ Driftin' / Groanin' the Blues

October 1, 1994
1 week

Eric Clapton's desire to cut a blues
album dates back to at least 1989,
when the acclaimed guitarist
began working with producer Russ Titelman. "We wanted to make a blues
album at first," says Titelman, "but then
we decided we would make a studio
album to set up the blues album."
While 1989's *Journeyman* has some
bluesy material, Clapton's full-scale
blues album didn't materialize until the
singer-guitarist hit paydirt with the multiple Grammy-winner *Unplugged* [see
368]. "The success of *Unplugged*
allowed him to feel comfortable about
doing it at last," says Titelman.

Atlhough *From the Cradle* was basically recorded live, it took approximately three months for Clapton and his cast
of eight musicians to complete the
album full of blues standards. "There
was a certain level of excellence set,"
says Titelman. "There would be these
amazing performances of things, but
they were just not quite acceptable."
Only two tracks had overdubs—"Motherless Child," had additional drums,
while "How Long Blues" had a dobro
overdub. "But other than that they were
all live, so it was like a show," says Titel-

man. "That's why the energy is at such
a high level."

For material, Clapton chose songs
from some of his heroes, including such
blues greats as Leroy Carr, Eddie Boyd,
Lowell Fulson, Willie Dixon, Freddie
King, Elmore James, and Muddy
Waters. One track, "Motherless Child"
had special meaning to Clapton, since
he was born out of wedlock and raised
by his grandmother.

To capture the original spirit of the
songs, guitarist Andy Fairweather-Low
brought in his collection of blues CDs.
"We'd play the original records then
they would go out in the studio and
play it, so the spirit of the original was
always there, even if they changed
things entirely," says Titelman.

For example, on "Goin' Away
Baby," Clapton and band incorporated
a Bo Diddley flavor, making the track
significantly different than the original.
"It came off great," says Titelman.
"[Drummer] Jim Keltner really shines on
that album. He swings like nobody's
business."

While the band's instrumental prowess
made *From the Cradle* swing, Clapton's
vocals give it heart. "His singing technique is amazing. Now people are real-
izing what a great singer he is," says
Titelman. "He has so much control, so
much passion, and so much inventive-
ness in the way he does things."

Without the aid of a hit single or
heavy video play, *From the Cradle*
debuted atop The Billboard 200,
becoming Clapton's second consecutive
Number One. It was also a triumph for
the musical genre Clapton chose to
salute, as *From the Cradle* was the first
traditional blues album ever to top the
album chart.

THE TOP FIVE
Week of October 1, 1994

1. **From the Cradle**
   Eric Clapton

2. **II**
   Boyz II Men

3. **Rhythm of Love**
   Anita Baker

4. **The Lion King**
   Soundtrack

5. **Dookie**
   Green Day

398 Monster
WARNER BROS. 45740
R.E.M.

Producers: Scott Litt and R.E.M.

Track listing: What's the Frequency, Kenneth? / Crush with Eyeliner / King of Comedy / I Don't Sleep, I Dream / Star 69 / Strange Currencies / Tongue / Bang and Blame / I Took Your Name / Let Me In / Circus Envy / You

October 15, 1994
2 weeks

For *Monster*, R.E.M. packed the acoustic instruments away and plugged in to record the hardest-rocking album of their career. As a result, the band, which managed to increase in popularity despite a hiatus from touring, hit the road for the first time in five years.

"To go on the road with three albums of slow, quiet material would be kind of a snore," says vocalist Michael Stipe, "so we made a loud record."

Automatic for the People, R.E.M.'s largely acoustic follow-up to the chart-topping *Out of Time* [see 346], debuted and peaked at number two on October 24, 1992. R.E.M. started writing material for *Monster* about a year later, in September 1993. The album was recorded between March and July 1994 at studios in New Orleans, Miami, Atlanta, and Los Angeles "and a couple of parking lots," Stipe says.

Both Stipe and bassist/keyboardist Mike Mills say the album was difficult to record. "It took about one-eighth of my life," quips Stipe. "There were a lot of life things happening around us. It was a very intense record."

During the recording process, guitarist Peter Buck became the father of twins, and Nirvana frontman Kurt Cobain, who

THE TOP FIVE
Week of October 15, 1994

1. **Monster**
   R.E.M.

2. **II**
   Boyz II Men

3. **From the Cradle**
   Eric Clapton

4. **Rhythm of Love**
   Anita Baker

5. **Songs**
   Luther Vandross

Stipe had befriended, committed suicide. Following Cobain's death, Stipe released a statement saying the two had planned to collaborate on a project. "I knew basically what was going on, so I was trying to offer a diversion to where he was at," Stipe says.

Monster includes "Let Me In," a haunting track that pits Stipe's vocals against a wall of guitar reverb, organ, and tambourine, but no drums. "I wrote that to Kurt, for Kurt, and about him," Stipe says. "I had just written an entire album [*Automatic for the People*] about death, mortality, and passage and really didn't want to repeat myself on this record, but his death profoundly affected me. I couldn't really ignore it much longer."

Yet taken in its entirety, *Monster* isn't a downer, but generally rather upbeat, loud, and raucous. "We set out to do that with *Automatic for the People*," Stipe says. "It was going to be kind of a loud punk rock record, but then it went the other way."

Musically, *Monster* runs the gamut. Fuzzed-out, guitar-heavy rockers "Crush with Eyeliner," "Star 69," and "Circus Envy" recall the obscure R.E.M. oldie "Wind Out," T. Rex, and Iggy Pop. In fact, in "I Took Your Name," Stipe wryly

states, "I wanna be Iggy Pop."

"If it would have been left to my devices, the record would sound like Fugazi on 45," says Stipe, referring to the Washington, D.C., punk band. "I'm kind of like the punk rocker of the four of us. I would make the loudest, fastest, most fucked-up record in the world."

Sonic Youth's Thurston Moore contributes backing vocals on "Crush with Eyeliner," while Stipe's sister, Lynda, is one of the backing vocalists on "Bang and Blame."

Lyrically, Stipe takes on the media in "What's the Frequency, Kenneth?" The track was inspired by an incident involving Dan Rather, in which the CBS-TV news anchor was accosted by a man on the streets of New York. Yet Stipe says the song isn't aimed just at Rather. "It's so far beyond him," he says.

Monster, R.E.M.'s ninth full studio album, came as the band's 15th anniversary approached. Throughout the years, R.E.M. found success, while retaining its artistic integrity and original lineup. Says Stipe, "We have a great deal of respect and love for each other and we like working together. There has yet to be a real turd in the punch bowl in terms of records, so it seems whatever we are doing, we're doing it right."

DEATH ROW/INTERSCOPE 92484 # Murder Was the Case
SOUNDTRACK **399**

Executive producer: Suge Knight

Track listing: Murder Was the Case (remix) [Snoop Doggy Dogg] / Natural Born Killaz [Dr. Dre & Ice Cube] / What Would U Do? [Tha Dogg Pound] / 21 Jumpstreet [Snoop Doggy Dogg & Tray Dee] / One More Day [Nate Dogg] / Harvest for the World [Jewell] / Who Got Some Gangsta Shit? [Snoop Doggy Dogg featuring tha Dogg Pound, Lil' Style, Young Swoop] / Come When I Call [Danny Boy] / U Better Recognize [Sam Sneed featuring Dr. Dre] / Come Up to My Room [Jodeci featuring Tha Dogg Pound] / Woman to Woman [Jewell] / The Eulogy [Slip Capone & CPO] / Horny [B-Rezell] / Eastside-Westside [Young Soldierz]

November 5, 1994
2 weeks

Clocking in at just over 73 minutes, *Murder Was the Case* isn't just another Number One soundtrack album. It's likely the only soundtrack album in history that runs more than four times longer than the film that inspired it. Based on a song from Snoop Doggy Dogg's *Doggystyle* [see 381], the 18-minute film directed and co-written by Dr. Dre, starred Snoop as a gang member. In the film, a drive-by shooting leaves Snoop near death until he has a close encounter with the devil.

For Snoop and Dre, the film *Murder Was the Case* was an important vehicle. "We wanted to put this out so people would look at it and say, 'These men are real talented,' instead of, 'They're criminals,' and this and that," says Snoop. The rapper, whose real name is Calvin Broadus, was anxious to prove to the public he wasn't just a thug following his arrest on August 25, 1993, in connection with a real drive-by shooting. "I gave a lot as far as acting goes, because I wanted to show people that I'm more than just a basic rapper," he adds. "We wanted to dig deep and show what we can't show because the media won't let us."

Murder Was the Case, which was released on home video, was certainly more graphic than the average music video. Yet the visuals weren't the only part of the project that raised eyebrows—the track "Natural Born

Killaz," which marked the reunion of former N.W.A [see 349] members Dr. Dre and Ice Cube [see 366], featured references to the Simpson, Menendez, and Manson murder cases.

Aside from a remixed version of "Murder Was the Case," Snoop was represented on the soundtrack with two new songs, "21 Jump Street" and "Who Got Some Gangsta Shit?" Yet the majority of the *Murder Was the Case* soundtrack featured developing artists.

"Now it's my turn to expose people like the way I was exposed," says Snoop. The rapper made his debut in 1992 joining Dr. Dre on the title track of the *Deep Cover* soundtrack. Dr. Dre and Snoop weren't the only artists from *Deep Cover* who made appearances on *Murder Was the Case*—R&B diva Jewell did likewise.

With Snoop's popularity still riding high, *Murder Was the Case* entered The Billboard 200 at Number One, knocking off Boyz II Men's *II* and fending off stiff competition from Scarface's *The Diary*, another hot hardcore rap title that debuted the same week. While it's debatable whether the film actually achieved Snoop's goal of showcasing him as more than just a rapper, *Murder* proved his recording career was alive and well.

THE TOP FIVE
Week of November 5, 1994

1. **Murder Was the Case**
   Soundtrack

2. **The Diary**
   Scarface

3. **Promised Land**
   Queensryche

4. **II**
   Boyz II Men

5. **Smash**
   Offspring

Snoop Doggy Dogg

400 MTV Unplugged in New York DGC 24727
NIRVANA

Producers: Nirvana and Scott Litt

Track listing: About a Girl / Come as You Are / Jesus Doesn't Want Me for a Sunbeam / The Man Who Sold the World / Pennyroyal Tea / Dumb / Polly / On a Plain / Something in the Way / Plateau / Oh Me / Lake of Fire / All Apologies / Where Did You Sleep Last Night

November 19, 1994
1 week

Almost a year to the day after Nirvana recorded an *MTV Unplugged* special, the audio souvenir from the show topped The Billboard 200, becoming Nirvana's third chart-topper, and a fitting tribute to a band whose end came too soon.

On April 8, 1994, Nirvana frontman Kurt Cobain was found dead from a self-inflicted shotgun blast to the head. Cobain, like Janis Joplin, Jimi Hendrix, and Jim Morrison, died at the age of 27. MTV paid its respects by airing *Nirvana Unplugged* repeatedly in the days following Cobain's death. Several of the songs featured in the performance, taped November 18, 1993 at Sony Studios in New York City, took on a haunting new meaning. In "Come As You Are," originally featured on *Nevermind* [see 358], Cobain sings, "And I swear I don't have a gun." *In Utero*'s "Pennyroyal Tea," given a stark solo reading by Cobain on the *Unplugged* disc, includes the lyric "Give me a Leonard Cohen afterworld/ So I can sigh eternally." Even Nirvana's choice of covers was eerie. In "Jesus Doesn't Want Me for a Sunbeam," originally by the Scottish group the Vaselines, Cobain sings, "Don't expect me to die for you."

Yet the death references and Cobain's unhappiness were nothing new. *In Utero* [see 378] was originally to be titled *I Hate Myself and Want to Die*, but the title was scrapped, because the title track, which later ended up on the 1993 Geffen compilation *The Beavis and Butt-head Experience*, didn't fit the mood of the album.

For *Unplugged*, Nirvana was joined by second guitarist Pat Smear, best known as a member of the Los Angeles punk band the Germs (whose frontman, Darby Crash, was another rock 'n' roll tragedy, dying of a heroin overdose in December 1979). Also on hand during the taping was cellist Lori Goldston. Nirvana drummer Dave Grohl played his kit with brushes to fit the soft mood of the set.

Instead of performing only his own songs, Cobain opted to showcase some of his favorites. Along with "Jesus Doesn't Want Me for a Sunbeam," Nirvana performed David Bowie's "The Man Who Sold the World," Leadbelly's "Where Did You Sleep Last Night," and the Meat Puppets' "Plateau," "Lake of Fire," and "Oh Me." On the latter three tracks, originally on 1984's *Meat Puppets II*, Nirvana was joined by Pups Curt and Cris Kirkwood, a guest spot that boosted the Arizona band's career.

MTV Unplugged in New York kicks off with "About a Girl," a Beatle-esque track from Nirvana's 1989 Sub Pop debut album, *Bleach*. The band's acoustic approach may have helped them connect with those initially put off by the sheer power of their electric approach. Either way, by the time *Unplugged* was released, it was clear that Nirvana had changed the face of rock 'n' roll. For proof, one need only to look at The Billboard 200 the week *MTV Unplugged* debuted at Number One. At number five was *Smash* by the punk band Offspring, on the independent Epitaph label, a record that likely would never have charted if not for the path blazed by Nirvana.

THE TOP FIVE
Week of November 19, 1994

1. **MTV Unplugged in New York**
   Nirvana

2. **II**
   Boyz II Men

3. **Murder Was the Case**
   Soundtrack

4. **Youhanasia**
   Megadeth

5. **Smash**
   Offspring

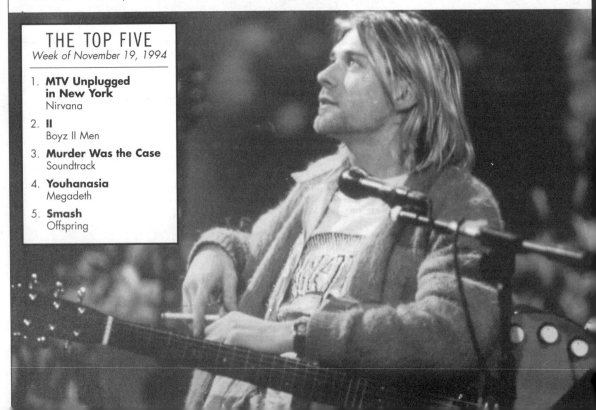

GEFFEN 24725

Hell Freezes Over
EAGLES

401

Producers: Eagles with Elliot Scheiner and Rob Jacobs

Track listing: Get Over It / Love Will Keep Us Alive / The Girl From Yesterday / Learn to Be Still / Tequila Sunrise / Hotel California / Wasted Time / Pretty Maids All in a Row / I Can't Tell You Why / New York Minute/ The Last Resort / Take It Easy / In the City / Life in the Fast Lane / Desperado

November 26, 1994
2 weeks

Following the release of *Eagles Live* in 1980, a two-record set that peaked at number six, the Eagles broke up and flew solo with Glenn Frey and Don Henley enjoying the most success. Frey scored a number of hit singles on soundtracks, including "You Belong to the City" on *Miami Vice* [see 293] and "The Heat Is On" from *Beverly Hills Cop* [see 289], but his own albums failed to break into the top 20. Henley's 1984 effort, *Building the Perfect Beast*, reached number 13, while his third solo effort, 1989's *The End of the Innocence*, peaked at number eight.

After a particularly bitter split, an Eagles reunion seemed unlikely. "We tried it in 1990, but the timing was all wrong," says Don Henley. "I'd just come off the *End of the Innocence* tour. I wasn't physically or emotionally prepared to start the Eagles process again and Glenn was having health problems."

Yet things changed in 1994. Irving Azoff, the Eagles' longtime manager,

put together a tribute album with some top country stars preforming Eagles songs. Dubbed *Common Thread: The Songs of the Eagles*, the album benefited Henley's preservation campaign to save Walden Woods in Massachusetts, and launched the Nashville division of Azoff's Giant Records. The album peaked at number three on The Billboard 200. "That was part of the catalyst," Henley says, "when we saw what kind of demand there still was for our music."

When Henley, Frey, Don Felder, Timothy B. Schmit, and Joe Walsh reunited in April to rehearse for an MTV special, the band's first show in 14 years, Henley says "it felt like maybe three years had gone by since we had broken up."

The band had managed to get past the bitter feelings that tore them apart in 1980. "We'd all grown up a lot. A lot of the guys were married and had children," says Henley. "We talked about it before we got back together. We brought up everything in the past and agreed to go forward based on mutual respect and understanding."

Yet the Eagles reunion wouldn't just be an exercise in nostalgia. The band also wrote and recorded four new songs. "It was imperative," Henley says. "We didn't want to reunite unless we could [do new material]."

Hell Freezes Over, an appropriate title for the band's unlikely reunion album and tour, featured 11 Eagles classics recorded at an MTV special in April 1994 and the new studio tracks. Henley calls "Get Over It," one of the

new songs, "probably the best rock 'n' roll track we've ever cut, and I think Glenn would concur with that."

During the live performance, some of the Eagles classics were given new arrangements, including "Hotel California," which was recast to showcase the Latin-flavored guitar work.

While Eagles fans flocked to *Hell Freezes Over*—it was the first Eagles album to debut at the top—Henley wasn't completely satisfied with the band's performance. "In retrospect, we should have toured for a month or two before we did the TV show, instead of making that our first performance in 14 years. That put a lot of undue pressure on us and we were stiffer than we might have been if we'd toured first," he says, "but we always did like to do things the hard way."

THE TOP FIVE
Week of November 26, 1994

1. **Hell Freezes Over**
   Eagles

2. **MTV Unplugged in New York**
   Nirvana

3. **II**
   Boyz II Men

4. **No Quarter**
   Jimmy Page & Robert Plant

5. **Murder Was the Case**
   Soundtrack

402 Miracles: The Holiday Album ARISTA 18767
KENNY G

Producer: Kenny G

Track listing: Winter Wonderland / White Christmas / Have Yourself a Merry Little Christmas / Silent Night / Greensleeves / Miracles / Little Drummer Boy / The Chanukah Song / Silver Bells / Away in a Manger / Brahms Lullaby

December 10, 1994
3 weeks (nonconsecutive)

When saxophonist Kenny G's *Miracles: The Holiday Album* moved from number six to the summit in its fourth week on The Billboard 200, it became the first Christmas album to reach Number One since Mitch Miller's *Holiday Sing Along with Mitch* [see 50] reached the top in January 1962. *Miracles* also had the distinction of being the first instrumental album to top the album chart since Vangelis's *Chariots of Fire* soundtrack in April 1982 [see 268], and the first Christmas instrumental album ever to top the album chart.

The commercial success of the record was no surprise. Kenny G's previous album, *Breathless*, spent 10 weeks at number two in late 1992. The only thing keeping that album from Number One was *The Bodyguard* soundtrack [see 367], which featured a duet between the saxophonist and Aaron Neville. What was surprising is how quickly the holiday set took off.

The rise of *Miracles* marked the earliest date in a given year that a Christmas album had hit the top spot. Elvis Presley's *Elvis' Christmas Album* [see 10], the previous record-holder, had gone to Number One on December 16, 1956.

THE TOP FIVE
Week of December 10, 1994

1. **Miracles: The Holiday Album**
   Kenny G

2. **II**
   Boyz II Men

3. **Hell Freezes Over**
   Eagles

4. **Merry Christmas**
   Mariah Carey

5. **MTV Unplugged in New York**
   Nirvana

When Arista president/CEO Clive Davis called Kenny G to tell him that *Miracles* had gone to Number One, the artist was in his back yard playing with his year-old son Max, whose photo is featured on the album. "I'm in shock," Kenny G said when he heard the news. "It's a dream to be Number One."

Yet when Davis originally suggested the holiday album, the saxophonist was lukewarm to the idea. "It was not something that I immediately jumped on," he says. "I really like to do my own originals, and I wasn't sure my sax and holiday music fit together."

After Kenny G recorded "Silent Night," he changed his mind. "When I listened to it again, it sounded really good, like a beautiful lullaby. These are melodies I grew up listening to."

There was another dilemma as well:

Kenny G, whose full surname is Gorelick, is Jewish. "That was another thing about doing a Christmas album that I was concerned about," he says. The musician was able to come to terms with the concept by calling it a "holiday" album, and since the album is all-instrumental, it does not include any religious lyrics.

To pay respect to his own religion, Kenny G composed the original "The Chanukah Song" with collaborator Walter Afanasieff, who also co-arranged the album. The duo also co-wrote the title track, the only other original composition on the album.

Says Kenny G, "The biggest challenge was to write original songs that could fit in with the other songs, which are some of the most beautiful melodies ever written."

EPIC 66900 **Vitalogy** **403**
PEARL JAM

Producers: Brendan O'Brien and Pearl Jam

Track listing: Last Exit / Spin the Black Circle / Not for You / Tremor Christ / Nothingman / Whipping / Pry, to / Corduroy / Bugs / Satan's Bed / Better Man / Aye Davanita / Immortality / Hey Foxymophandlemama, That's Me

December 24, 1994
1 week

"Spin the Black Circle," Pearl Jam's punk rock–style ode to vinyl records, took on new meaning on December 10, 1994, when *Vitalogy*, the album featuring the track, entered The Billboard 200 at number 55 based on sales of the vinyl LP alone. It was the first time an album available only on vinyl had charted since LPs began disappearing from record store shelves in the late '80s. The band chose to release its third album on vinyl two weeks before the CD and cassette version as a tribute to the LP and as a treat for its hardcore fans. The following week, the vinyl version of *Vitalogy* dropped to number 173, allowing the band to make history a second time a week later, when the cassette and CD were released and *Vitalogy* rocketed up 172 places to Number One, marking the biggest jump in the history of the album chart.

The impressive sales of the vinyl version of *Vitalogy* represented a victory of sorts for the band. Says bassist Jeff Ament, "[Pearl Jam vocalist] Eddie [Vedder] wrote 'Spin the Black Circle' because he loves vinyl. He loves the way it looks, sounds, and feels." The vinyl version of *Vitalogy* has the look and feel of a '70s rock album. The cover of the gatefold sleeve looks like an old photo album. One sleeve of the two-pocket jacket houses an eight-page booklet filled with photos, handwritten and typed lyrics, and passages and graphics culled from the 1927 book by Dr. E.H. Ruddick after which the album is named.

"Besides the sound quality and the warmth it presents, a lot of it has to do with the package," says Ament. "A jewel box, and even worse a cassette case, seems really cold and impersonal, and it's really bad to put a piece of art on.

"It was fun putting the package together," he adds. "There's lots of little surprises. There was something cool about buying a favorite band's record when you were a kid. It was fun to see what was inside."

The CD version is also housed in a special package containing no plastic. The booklet, reduced to CD size, is 36 pages, and the disc is stored in a black sleeve, reminiscent of an old 78 jacket. "Essentially what we tried to do with the CD package is make it more like an album package. It feels really organic," Ament says.

Vedder found the book *Vitalogy* in a thrift store, Ament says. "He had it in the studio about six or seven months ago, and we thought it would be great for the album. The word itself, 'vitalogy,' is really amazing. It really brings to mind what music means to us—this science of being vital."

After the pressure-cooker making of *Vs.* [see 380], Pearl Jam opted to take a different approach, although on cuts such as "Not for You" Vedder sounds just as angry and disillusioned as he had on the hardest *Vs.* tracks. "We'd get together and record a song here and there and tried to take the whole scheduling thing out of it," says Ament. "There was no pressure. We just got together and jammed and three or four songs would come out of it."

Vitalogy was recorded at dates in New Orleans, Atlanta, and Seattle. "Last Exit," "Tremor Christ," and "Nothingman" were recorded in New Orleans, while Atlanta sessions generated "Immortality," "Not for You," and "Corduroy."

Says Ament, "We just make music that is important to us and feels good to us. If people like it, it's a bonus." With *Vitalogy*, Pearl Jam once again got their bonus.

THE TOP FIVE
Week of December 24, 1994

1. **Vitalogy**
   Pearl Jam

2. **Miracles: The Holiday Album**
   Kenny G

3. **Live at the BBC**
   The Beatles

4. **Merry Christmas**
   Mariah Carey

5. **II**
   Boyz II Men

404 The Hits LIBERTY 29689
GARTH BROOKS

Producer: Allen Reynolds

Track listing: Ain't Goin' Down (Til the Sun Comes Up) / Friends in Low Places / Callin' Baton Rouge / The River / Much Too You (to Feel This Damn Old) / The Thunder Rolls / American Honky-Tonk Bar Association / If Tomorrow Never Comes / Unanswered Prayers / Standing Outside the Fire / Rodeo / What She's Doing Now / We Shall Be Free / Papa Loved Mama / Shameless / Two of a Kind, Workin' on a Full House / That Summer / The Dance

January 7, 1995
5 weeks (nonconsecutive)

The Hits, Garth Brooks's first greatest-hits album, was the country super-star's first Number One album not to debut at the top. Facing such stiff competition as Pearl Jam's *Vitalogy* [see 403] and Kenny G's *Miracles: The Holiday Album* [see 402], *The Hits* debuted at number three on December 31, 1994. Yet it only took a week for the album to push its way to the top.

When superstar artists reach a certain point in their careers, a compilation of their hits is a natural. Yet Brooks, an artist with a keen business sense, was initially a little leery of releasing such a collection, fearing it might cut into sales of his previous releases. While Brooks' six previous albums, including the chart-toppers *Ropin' the Wind* [see 354], *The Chase* [see 364], and *In Pieces* [see 377], are all multi-platinum sellers, their sales potential had yet to be completely tapped.

Brooks finally agreed to allow Liberty to release a hits album, but only if the label played by his rules. He wanted to

THE TOP FIVE
Week of January 7, 1995

1. **The Hits**
   Garth Brooks

2. **Miracles: The Holiday Album**
   Kenny G

3. **Vitalogy**
   Pearl Jam

4. **II**
   Boyz II Men

5. **Hell Freezes Over**
   Eagles

keep the CD's list price low, at $15.98, instead of the usual superstar price of $17.98 or $18.98. The pricing was particularly unusual for a country album featuring 18 songs, as most country artists, including Brooks, limit their albums to 10 tracks. Brooks also wanted the album to be available only for a limited time period, so that *The Hits* would promote his previous albums instead of cannibalizing his catalog sales. An added bonus was a free "CD Zooming" sampler, which featured snippets of the 60 songs featured on his six albums, giving consumers a taste of a potential purchase.

Although not assembled chronologically and lacking any cuts from Brooks's 1992 *Beyond the Season* Christmas album, *The Hits* offers an ample overview of Brooks's career, with three

tracks from his 1990 self-titled debut; four tracks from 1990's breakthrough *No Fences* album; five tracks from Brooks's most successful album, 1991's *Ropin' the Wind*; only two from 1992's *The Chase*, an album recorded during a particularly difficult period for Brooks; and four from 1993's *In Pieces*.

On the eve of the album's release, Brooks told *Billboard*'s Melinda Newman that *The Hits* effectively capped a phase in his career. "That's another reason why we decided to do it now," he said. "It's the end of the beginning for us."

Liberty stopped shipping *The Hits* to retailers on September 22, 1995. Even though the album was mothballed after less than a year, SoundScan figures show that it still managed to sell over 5.9 million copies.

WARNER BROS. 45760 **Balance**
VAN HALEN 405

Producer: Bruce Fairbairn

Track listing: The Seventh Seal / Can't Stop Lovin' You / Don't Tell Me (What Love Can Do) / Amsterdam / Big Fat Money / Strung Out / Not Enough / Aftershock / Doin' Time / Baluchitherium / Take Me Back (Déjà Vu) / Feelin'

February 11, 1995
1 week

Van Halen had been on a major roll since Sammy Hagar joined them in 1985. Their first three post–David Lee Roth albums—1986's *5150* [see 299], 1988's *OU812* [see 318], and 1991's *For Unlawful Carnal Knowledge* [see 351]—all topped the album chart. *Live: Right Here, Right Now,* the band's 1993 two-disc live set, peaked at number five and went on to sell more than a million copies. However, Van Halen's good luck streak came to an end on October 16, 1993, when their longtime manager Ed Leffler died of thyroid cancer. Says vocalist Sammy Hagar, "With Ed dying, it was the first time that we had a reality check in the time I've been with the band."

Following, Leffler's death, Van Halen had a quick meeting. "At least 50,000 managers had called offering their condolences and putting in their bid," says Hagar, "but we just told our offices, Warner Bros., and our agent, 'We're not speaking to anyone about management. We are going to let the dust settle. We need some time.' "

Hagar headed to Maui for a three-month vacation. Upon his return in early 1994, the band started to work on new material. Without Leffler around as its

"fearless leader and protector," guitarist Eddie Van Halen's 5150 studio became "a sanctuary" for the band, says Hagar. "Just the four of us would get together, turn the phones off and jam."

As a result, *Balance* is the most serious record the band has ever recorded. Says Hagar, "Not only did we take it seriously, but it's a serious record with no filler."

While the band was in the middle of recording *Balance,* they opted to sign longtime Rush manager Ray Daniels—drummer Alex Van Halen's brother-in-law—as their new manager.

"What Ed Leffler was to me, Ray has been to Alex," says Hagar. "If Alex wasn't sure about some deal that came down, he would always call Ray for his sounding board...Ray was already there for Al, but after Ed died, Alex started turning to Ray more and more.

"He was the obvious guy," adds Hagar. "Also, he had the track record

of staying with a band for so long with Rush, for the 23 years they have been together. It was important that we found someone who showed commitment, rather than someone after the flavor of the month."

The band turned to producer Bruce Fairbairn because they were impressed with his work with Aerosmith [see 370]. "We wrote 17 songs for this album," says Hagar. "It was the first time in our history that we actually overwrote." For Hagar, the extra effort paid off, as *Balance* represented his personal best. "This is the best thing I've ever done in my life," he says. "I'm at a whole other place vocally and lyrically. And this album has songs that I can sing with dignity for the rest of my life."

The public responded to Van Halen's serious approach, making *Balance* the first Number One debut of 1995 and Van Halen's fourth chart-topper.

THE TOP FIVE
Week of February 11, 1995

1. **Balance**
   Van Halen

2. **The Hits**
   Garth Brooks

3. **Dookie**
   Green Day

4. **Hell Freezes Over**
   Eagles

5. **II**
   Boyz II Men

406 Greatest Hits COLUMBIA 67060
BRUCE SPRINGSTEEN

Producers: Bruce Springsteen, Mike Appel, John Landau, Steve Van Zandt, Chuck Plotkin, and Roy Bittan

Track listing: Born to Run / Thunder Road / Badlands / The River / Hungry Heart / Atlantic City / Dancing in the Dark / Born in the U.S.A. / My Hometown / Glory Days / Brilliant Disguise / Human Touch / Better Days / Streets of Philadelphia / Secret Garden / Murder Incorporated / Blood Brothers / This Hard Land

March 18, 1995
2 weeks

Nearly a decade after the release of *Bruce Springsteen & the E Street Band Live/1975–85*, a single-CD set of Springsteen studio hits may have seemed like too little, too late. Yet *Greatest Hits* did pack a little something extra for diehard fans: three new songs and one previously unreleased cut from the vaults. These four tracks featured Springsteen backed by the E Street Band, marking the first release of E Street Band studio recordings since *Born in the U.S.A.* [see 281].

Despite its title, *Greatest Hits* is not restricted to "hits" and isn't made up of all the obvious choices. In fact, the top 10 singles "Cover Me," "I'm on Fire," and "I'm Goin' Down," all from *Born in the U.S.A.*, and "War," from *Live/1975–85*, were left off the album in favor of such earlier album rock staples as "Thunder Road," "The River" and "Atlantic City," none of which charted on the Hot 100. The earlier tracks that did chart, "Born to Run" and "Badlands," failed to crack the top 20. It wasn't until 1980 that Springsteen scored his first top 10 single with "Hungry Heart," which reached number five.

Greatest Hits also includes one track each from Springsteen's simultaneously released 1992 albums, *Human Touch* and *Lucky Town*. On April 18, 1992, the albums entered and peaked at numbers two and three, respectively, behind Def Leppard's *Adrenalize* [see 360]. It marked the first time since 1982, when *Nebraska* rose to number three, that a Springsteen album failed to go to Number One. The double-A side single of "Human Touch"/"Better Days" peaked at number 16.

"Streets of Philadelphia," Springsteen's next new recording, would win the artist an Oscar and four Grammys, including song of the year. Springsteen

wrote the song for the 1993 Jonathan Demme film *Philadelphia*, a harrowing tale of a man coming to grips with AIDS. Longtime producer Chuck Plotkin says that the singer didn't commit to the project until he had a conversation with Demme. "Jonathan told him not simply about the story, but about the atmosphere and the main character in such sufficient depth that it began to work on Bruce," he says. Springsteen recorded a demo of the track at his home in Los Angeles with a drum machine, synthesizer, his guitar, and vocals before actually seeing the film. In the track, Springsteen managed to capture the despair of the film's lead character, portrayed by Tom Hanks.

"Bruce's gift is to locate the heart in some character's dilemma," says Plotkin. "I don't think he has ever set out to write something about a character that didn't come from his own experience or imagination, but he certainly managed to do it this time." On April 23, 1994, the single became Springsteen's 12th top 10 single, when it reached number nine on the Hot 100.

While Springsteen recorded "Streets of Philadelphia" solo, he reunited the E Street Band for the songs that round out *Greatest Hits*. "We did one track in the summer of '87 for a Woody Guthrie tribute album, but we hadn't recorded together as a full band since the *Born in the U.S.A.* sessions in 1984," says E Street drummer Max Weinberg, "and we came back better and stronger than ever." While the recording of "Murder Incorporated" dates back to 1982 during the *Nebraska* and *Born in the U.S.A.* writing and recording sessions, "Secret Garden," "Blood Brothers," and "This Hard Land" were recorded in 1995. "It was amazing," says Weinberg of the sessions, which lasted approximately four days. "It felt like we never stopped. It felt like we were at home."

Hot on the heels of Springsteen's Grammy triumph for "Streets of Philadelphia," *Greatest Hits* entered at Number One, becoming Springsteen's second Number One album to debut at the top, his fifth career chart-topper, and his first Number One of the '90s.

THE TOP FIVE
Week of March 18, 1995

1. **Greatest Hits**
   Bruce Springsteen

2. **II**
   Boyz II Men

3. **The Hits**
   Garth Brooks

4. **Tuesday Night Music Club**
   Sheryl Crow

5. **Dookie**
   Green Day

INTERSCOPE 92399 **Me Against the World** **407**
2PAC

THE TOP FIVE
Week of April 1, 1995

1. **Me Against the World**
   2Pac

2. **Greatest Hits**
   Bruce Springsteen

3. **Hell Freezes Over**
   The Eagles

4. **Cracked Rear View**
   Hootie & the Blowfish

5. **The Lion King**
   Soundtrack

Producers: Tony Pizarro, Easy Mo B., SoulShock & Karlin, D-Flizno Production Squad, Moe Z.M.D. and Le-morrious "Funky Drummer" Tyler, Mike Mosley & Sam Bostic, and Brian G

Track listing: Intro / If I Die 2Nite / Me Against the World / So Many Tears / Temptations / Young Niggaz / Heavy in the Game / Lord Knows / Dear Mama / It Ain't Easy / Can U Get Away / Old School / F*** the World / Death Around the Corner / Outlaw

April 1, 1995
4 weeks

Elvis sang "Jailhouse Rock," and *Johnny Cash at San Quentin* [see 114] topped the album chart, yet 2Pac's combination of pop music and prison was truly unique. When *Me Againt the World* hit Number One, the album title likely mirrored 2Pac's feelings all too well. The rap artist, whose real name is Tupac Shakur, celebrated his first Number One album while in prison at the Clinton Correctional Facility in Dannemora, New York, serving up to four and a half years for sexual

abuse. It earned 2Pac a dubious place in the history books—he is the first artist to have an album go to Number One on The Billboard 200 while serving time behind bars.

The New York–born, Oakland, California=bred rapper first gained notice as a member of the funky and funny hip-hop troupe Digital Underground. By 1991, 2Pac had set out on his own with his solo debut, *2Pacalypse Now*, which reached number 64. In 1993, 2Pac captured an even larger audience with *Strictly 4 My N.I.G.G.A.Z...*, which included the rap, R&B, and Hot 100 hits "I Get Around" and "Keep Ya Head Up." That album peaked at number 24.

Meanwhile, 2Pac was also making himself known on the big screen, appearing in the 1992 film *Juice* and starring opposite Janet Jackson [see 371] in 1993's *Poetic Justice*.

The rapper was also gaining noteriety for his non-artistic endeavors. In 1993, he spent 10 days in jail for swinging a baseball bat at a rival rapper. Later that same year, a 19-year-old woman alleged that 2Pac and three friends sodomized and sexually abused her. In 1994, he returned to jail for 15

days for assaulting film director Allen Hughes.

His legal troubles, however, didn't stop 2Pac from recording. In 1994 he released Thug Life's *Volume I* in his own Out Da Gutta label. The album, by the group consisting of 2Pac, his brother MoPreme, Syke, Macadoshis, and The Rate R, reached number 42.

2Pac also found time to record the aptly titled *Me Against the World*. "When 2Pac writes songs, he writes very quickly," says Tom Whalley, the Interscope Records artist and repertoire executive who signed 2Pac in 1990 and is credited for A&R direction on *Me Against the World*. "Sometimes he can cut five songs in an evening."

Me Against the World took shape before and during 2Pac's highly publicized sexual abuse trial in late 1994. The first single from the album, "Dear Mama," was originally scheduled to come out on Mother's Day 1994. Yet 2Pac wanted to ensure that *Me Against the World* was up to snuff. "We had 30 songs to choose from," says Whalley. "We just wanted to take the best and then we had some sound and mix issues to deal with." All told, it took two years to complete the album.

"Dear Mama," an ode to his own mother, a former Black Panther named Afeni Shakur, became 2Pac's first top 10 pop hit as *Me Against the World* entered the chart at the summit. "The first time he played ['Dear Mama'] for me, I thought it was a hit record," says Whalley. "But that was one of the songs that I had to convince 2Pac to put on the record."

To the casual listener, it may appear that 2Pac is obsessed with death in such songs as "If I Die 2Nite" and "Death Around the Corner." On November 30, 1994, he had his own brush with death, as he was shot four times and robbed at a New York recording studio. Two bullets actually hit 2Pac in the head, but failed to pierce his skull.

Never one to shy away from controversy, 2Pac opted to open *Me Against the World* with "Intro," a series of simulated audio news clips about his various legal troubles and his shooting. "The original idea was to use actual news pieces and headlines from his trial," says Whalley. Including the actual news footage, however, would have required Interscope to obtain permission from the news organizations involved. Instead, the label opted to recreate their own soundbites.

408 Throwing Copper RADIOACTIVE 10997
LIVE

Producers: Jerry Harrison and Live

Track listing: The Dam at Otter Creek / Selling the Drama / I Alone / Iris / Lightning Crashes / Top / All Over You / Shit Towne / T.B.D. / Stage / Waitress / Pillar of Davidson / White, Discussion

May 6, 1995
1 week

Even before the release of *Throwing Copper*, the second album from Live, singer Ed Kowalczyk had a premonition: The band that he formed with three middle school chums—guitarist Chad Taylor, drummer Chad Cracey, and bassist Patrick Dahlheimer—would be huge. He wrote the song "Selling the Drama" to sum up how it would feel to go from a small town garage band to national stardom.

"I pretty much knew that from the beginning that this would be a big record for us," he says. "It was just a gut feeling that we had made a bunch of great songs that sounded really good. We figured we would be in front of a lot of people doing interviews. We probably won't write another song like it again, but being that it was going to be the first time that the mass media was going to pay attention to our band, we figured why not do a song about how fucked-up we feel and also about how good we feel onstage, because it is a weird mixture of emotions."

Live formed in 1987 under the moniker Public Affection. Two years later, the band had produced its own 10-track cassette and was landing shows at famed New York nightspot CBGB's. It

was there that that the band caught the ear of Gary Kurfirst, an artist manager who was launching a new label, Radioactive Records. Live's first Radioactive release, a 1991 EP titled *Four Songs*, failed to chart. In early 1992, the band made its first appearance on The Billboard 200 when *Mental Jewelry*, their first full-length album, reached number 73. However, that hardly prepared anyone for *Throwing Copper*.

Recorded in August and September of 1993, *Throwing Copper* was co-produced by former Talking Heads guitarist Jerry Harrison, who had worked with the band since *Four Songs*. "Jerry's pretty much a father figure in the studio," says Kowalczyk. "He just keeps everyone organized and psyched." The album was recorded at Pachyderm Studio in Cannon Falls, Minnesota, the same studio where Nirvana cut its final studio album [see 378]. "It was really easy," says Kowalczyk. "We did everything in pretty much one or two takes with very few overdubs. I went back and sang most of the vocals over, but other than that, we tried to keep everything as live-to-tape as possible."

To mix the album, the band called on Tom Lord-Alge, known for his work with Steve Winwood [see 321]. "He brought a punchiness, crunch, and sheen that I hadn't heard before with our music," says Kowalczyk. "The first one he did was 'Selling the Drama.' It just blew me away, how well it came across and how immediate it was, so we had him mix the whole record. That's probably why it did so well at radio."

The tracks "Selling the Drama," "I Alone," and "Lightning Crashes" all

became hits at modern rock and album rock radio, as well as at MTV, as Live's fan base multiplied. The group's earnest, no-nonsense approach earned it comparisons to R.E.M. [see 398] and U2 [see 373], which suits Kowalczyk just fine. "We don't make any apologies for that," he says. "U2 and R.E.M. made me look at music as more than just pop stuff. I never saw them as message bands. I saw them as normal guys who wanted to bring more to music and they do it in a real soulful and gritty way."

Throwing Copper debuted at number 38 on The Billboard 200 on May 14, 1994. In stark contrast to the SoundScan era's trend of albums debuting at Number One, the album reached the top spot in its 52nd week on the chart, tying Bonnie Raitt's *Nick of Time* as the album with the longest chart run prior to reaching Number One. Says Kowalczyk, "It was the perfect year anniversary."

Producer: Ice Cube

Track listing: Friday [Ice Cube] / Keep Their Heads Ringin' [Dr. Dre] / Friday Night [Scarface] / Lettin' Niggas Know [Threat] / Roll It Up, Light It Up, Smoke It Up [Cypress Hill] / Take a Hit [Mack 10] / Tryin' to See Another Day [The Isley Brothers] / You Got Me Wide Open [Bootsy Collins and Bernie Worrell] / Mary Jane [Rick James] / I Wanna Get Next to You [Rose Royce] / Superhoes [Funkdoobiest] / Coast II Coast [Tha Alkaholiks] / Blast If I Have To [E-A-Ski] / Hoochie Mama [2 Live Crew] / I Heard It Through the Grapevine [Roger]

May 13, 1995
2 weeks

In John Singleton's 1991 film *Boyz N The Hood*, rap star Ice Cube became a film star. But his ambitions didn't stop there. He also had his sights on writing a movie. With *Friday*, Cube's dream became a reality.

"It was born out of Ice Cube and [his manager] Pat Charbonnet's frustration with major film studios," says Priority Records president Bryan Turner. After Cube's success as an actor, he began to write treatments. One script was accepted by a major film studio, only to sit on the shelf for months. Cube was frustrated by the experience, but not defeated. One day he paid a visit to the Hollywood offices of Priority. "He brought up this idea for a day-in-the-life–type buddy-movie thing," Turner recalls. "As it started to come together, it sounded really great to me." Cube was reluctant to go back to a major studio, and asked Turner if Priority Records would fund the pro-

ject. Turner agreed.

"Being record people first and film-makers second, the first thing we thought about was the soundtrack," Turner says. In its 10 year-history, Priority had done business with just about every heavy hitter in the rap business, while Cube often appeared on other artists' albums and in their videos. "We thought if we called in all of our favors, if nothing else we would get a slammin' soundtrack," says Turner, "and we would be able to pay for the movie with the soundtrack."

Together, Turner, Cube, Charbonnet, and co-executive producer Andrew M. Shack lined up such hip-hop heavy-weights as Cube's former N.W.A [see 349] partner Dr. Dre, Cypress Hill [see 374], and Scarface. "Dre read the script and he loved it," Turner says. "He thought it was hilarious, so he wanted to do it. Most of the others are Cube's friends or my friends, so they all came to the party willing and able."

Yet the soundtrack wasn't limited to rappers. New material by the Isley Brothers [see 203] and funk veterans Bootsy Collins and Bernie Worrell also appears on the album, as well as old-

school favorites by Rick James and Rose Royce. "Part of the appeal was that it wasn't just a youth thing," Turner says. "The movie was for older folks too, so we put some of the '70s stuff in there too."

The diversity of the music reflects the various scenes in the movie. "We wanted to make sure the movie was full of music, from the first frame to the last frame," says Turner. The label also kept the artists involved in the project. "We made sure they were part of the film-making process by showing them the dailies," Turner says. "A lot of the tracks were written for specific scenes that were in the movie." The marriage of music and the film went so far as to include the video clip of Dr. Dre's "Keep Their Heads Ringin' " at the opening of the film during its theatrical release.

Friday debuted at number two on April 22, 1995. Three weeks later, it blew to the top. For Turner, it wasn't a big surprise. "We knew we were going to have a certain degree of success because of the name value of the artists involved," he says. "When the tracks started coming in, we really knew we had something tremendous."

Ice Cube

THE TOP FIVE
Week of May 13, 1995

1. **Friday**
   Soundtrack

2. **Throwing Copper**
   Live

3. **Cracked Rear View**
   Hootie & the Blowfish

4. **Me Against the World**
   2Pac

5. **The Lion King**
   Soundtrack

410 Cracked Rear View ATLANTIC 82613
HOOTIE & THE BLOWFISH

Producer: Don Gehman

Track listing: Hannah Jane / Hold My Hand / Let Her Cry / Only Wanna Be With You / Running from an Angel / I'm Goin' Home / Drowning / Time / Look Away / Not Even the Trees / Goodbye

May 27, 1995
8 weeks (nonconsecutive)

Before any major label would take notice, Hootie & the Blowfish had already proven themselves quite successful on their home turf of Columbus, South Carolina. The quartet, fronted by lead singer/guitarist Darius Rucker, formed in the late '80s. It found a moniker by taking the nicknames of two of Rucker's friends—Hootie and Blowfish—and combining them. The band, which also includes drummer Jim Sonefeld, guitarist Mark Bryan, and bassist Dean Felber, released three independent EPs: 1990's *Hootie & the Blowfish*, 1992's *Time*, and 1993's *Kootchypop*. The last title, which sold more than 50,000 copies—an impressive sum for an indie release—caught the attention of Atlantic Records A&R executive Tim Sommer, who signed the band in 1994. "We sold so many copies of *Kootchypop*, people couldn't believe it," says Rucker.

Although Hootie & the Blowfish now had the backing of a major label, there wasn't a lot of pressure on the band to do things differently in the studio. "We didn't expect this record to do anything," says Rucker. "We just went in and made a Hootie & the Blowfish record. We just went in and had a lot of fun, played and sang, and came out

real happy."

Producer Don Gehman was enlisted to work on the project by Sommer. "The second you meet him, you fall in love with him," says Rucker, who was a fan of Gehman's work with John Cougar [see 272] and R.E.M. The album, recorded at N.R.G. Recording Services in North Hollywood, California, took four weeks to record and another three weeks to mix. While that was still relatively quick compared to most major label releases, it was a big change for the Blowfish. "All the other records we did before were like five songs in five days," says Rucker. "On this album we were able to try everything we wanted to do."

Five of the songs featured on *Cracked Rear View*—"Hold My Hand," "Only Wanna Be With You," "Let Her Cry," "Running from an Angel," and "Time"—first appeared on the band's indie EPs. Yet Rucker notes the new versions are "significantly better" than the originals. "We had the time to record the songs the way we actually wanted to hear them." They had some help, too—labelmate David Crosby [see 186]

was recruited to lend background vocals to "Hold My Hand."

Initially, the adult-leaning video network VH1, and rock, adult alternative, and top 40 radio all played "Hold My Hand." But Hootie's biggest break came from David Letterman. The talk show host heard "Hold My Hand" on his car radio and invited his "favorite new band" to perform on *The Late Show* three times. "Letterman was a turning point," says Rucker. "That's when you could see the record sales start to happen. Letterman adopting us like he did helped our career immensely."

Cracked Rear View, named after a lyric in a John Hiatt song, cracked the top 10 in late February. By April, it had crept into the top five. Finally, in its 44th week on The Billboard 200, the album hit Number One. After its initial four-week stay at the top, *Cracked Rear View* would not go away. It returned to Number One for four additional nonconsecutive weeks. Yet the Blowfish weren't going to let success go to their heads. "Nothing has changed," says Rucker. "I'm still doing the same things that I did two years ago."

THE TOP FIVE
Week of May 27, 1995

1. **Cracked Rear View**
   Hootie & the Blowfish

2. **Throwing Copper**
   Live

3. **Friday**
   Soundtrack

4. **Forrest Gump**
   Soundtrack

5. **Hell Freezes Over**
   Eagles

Producers: James Guthrie and David Gilmour

Track listing: Shine on You Crazy Diamond / Astronomy Domine / What Do You Want from Me / Learning to Fly / Keep Talking / Coming Back to Life / He You / Great Day for Freedom / Sorrow / High Hopes / Another Brick in the Wall (Part Two) / Speak to Me / Breathe / On the Run / Time / The Great Gig in the Sky / Money / Us and Them / Any Colour You Like / Brain Damage / Eclipse / Wish You Were Here / Comfortably Numb / Run Like Hell

June 24, 1995
1 week

Although *The Dark Side of the Moon* [see 157] only held the pole position for one week, it stayed on the album chart for 741 consecutive weeks and, perhaps more importantly, it was the album that launched Pink Floyd into the orbit of rock superstardom.

On the album's 20th anniversary, in March 1993, Capitol Records released a limited-edition commemorative version of *The Dark Side of the Moon*. However, the ultimate tribute to the album didn't take place until a year later, when Pink Floyd began performing *The Dark Side of the Moon* in its entirety, for the first time in more than a decade, during dates on the *Division Bell* tour.

It was during the tour that James Guthrie, who had previously worked with Floyd as a co-producer and engineer on *The Wall* [see 246], received a phone call from Floyd manager Steve O'Rourke. "He said, 'We want to record a live version of *The Dark Side of the Moon* and he asked me to come over and do it with them.'"

The prospect of re-recording one of the most popular albums in the history of rock in a concert setting was initially intimidating to Guthrie. A series of meetings was held with Guthrie, O'Rourke, and Floyd members David Gilmour, Nick Mason, and Rick Wright. "We had two concerns," says Guthrie. "The first was to try to capture as much of the feel and excitement of a Pink Floyd concert as possible, which is a difficult thing to do because it's hard to compete with the excitement of being at a gig and the sheer level of their quadraphonic P.A. system. The other concern was to try to capture as much of the feel and atmosphere of the original recording. It's such an atmospheric record and everyone is so attached to it." In fact, in order to conjure up the spirit of the original album, the band and Guthrie listened to *The Dark Side of the Moon* repeatedly before attempting to record the live version. "We listened very carefully, not to try to copy it, but to remind ourselves of the feel of the record, and that was crucial," says Guthrie.

In all, 20 shows on the *Division Bell* tour were recorded for the album, including some huge European dates. "All the European gigs were outdoor stadium gigs with 80,000 to 100,000 people a night, but when they got to England they did a residency at Earl's Court [in October 1994] for 14 nights and we recorded 10 of those shows," says Guthrie.

Between the mammoth stadium dates and the Earl's Court shows, it was quite clear that the project was evolving into more than just a live recording of *The Dark Side of the Moon*. "In typical Pink Floyd fashion, it grew at an alarming rate," Guthrie says. "Since *The Dark Side of the Moon* didn't really fill out a full CD, we decided we should add the encores, and before we knew it, we had a double CD."

In the end, almost all of Pink Floyd's live set was included on the album, which was called *Pulse*. Among the exceptions was "One of These Days," which later resurfaced on the limited-edition four-LP vinyl set released in November 1995.

As an added attraction, the initial run of the CD edition of *Pulse* featured a slipcase with a built-in blinking red light. The combination of *The Dark Side of the Moon* live and the nifty packaging drove *Pulse* to Number One in its first week on the chart, far outdistancing the chart performance of Floyd's previous live set, 1988's *The Delicate Sound of Thunder*, which made number 11.

THE TOP FIVE
Week of June 24, 1995

1. **Pulse**
   Pink Floyd

2. **Cracked Rear View**
   Hootie & the Blowfish

3. **Pocahontas**
   Soundtrack

4. **Throwing Copper**
   Live

5. **Crazysexycool**
   TLC

412 HIStory: Past, Present and Future—Book 1 EPIC 59000
MICHAEL JACKSON

Executive producer: Michael Jackson

Track listing: Billie Jean / The Way You Make Me Feel / Black or White / Rock with You / She's Out of My Life / Bad / I Just Can't Stop Loving You / Man in the Mirror / Thriller / Beat It / The Girl Is Mine / Remember the Time / Don't Stop 'Til You Get Enough / Wanna Be Startin' Somethin' / Heal the World / Scream / They Don't Care About Us / Stranger in Moscow / This Time Around / Earth Song / D.S. / Money / Come Together / You Are Not Alone / Childhood (Theme from "Free Willy 2") / Tabloid Junkie / 2 Bad / History / Little Susie / Smile

July 8, 1995
2 weeks

The initial plan was to release a Michael Jackson hits album called *Decade*, featuring four new songs, prior to the release of *Dangerous* [see 357], but when a whole new album began to take shape, the project was shelved. After *Dangerous*, the Jackson camp began to again think about a possibility of releasing a single-disc hits set with some new tracks. "We had gone through 36 or 37 different sequences for the album," says producer/mixer Bruce Swedien. "But then, as we began to experiment with the new songs, it became evident that we had an awful lot of good new material to deal with, so Michael decided that we should make it a double and have the old stuff on a separate disc from the new material." And that's exactly what happened.

The first disc, dubbed *HIStory Begins*, features 15 of the best tracks from *Off the Wall*, *Thriller* [see 274], *Bad* [see 313], and *Dangerous*, including eight Number One singles.

While Jackson was hard at work on the new material in the summer of 1993, his world came crashing down around him after a 13-year-old boy claimed that the self-proclaimed King of Pop had sexually molested him. Police searched Jackson's Neverland Ranch near Santa Barbara, California, for evidence, and even photographed the singer's genitals, but no charges were filed. Still, the allegations stunned Jackson's fans around the globe and sent the singer into seclusion. Jackson reportedly reached a multi-million-dollar settlement with the boy's family.

Yet the accusations provided Jackson with fuel for much of his new material.

"Stranger in Moscow" was one of the first songs to be inspired by the ordeal. "Michael was in Russia when he was having all the trouble," says Swedien. "He was literally alone in Moscow, sitting in his hotel room with the rain pounding down outside, and he wrote this incredible song. I think it is one of the best things he has ever done. That's really what started the ball rolling on the album."

While "Stranger in Moscow" had Jackson in a more subdued and reflective mood, other cuts on the album's second disc, *HIStory Continues*, found him downright angry. "Scream," the album's first single, which paired Jackson with his sister Janet [see 371] and producers Jimmy Jam and Terry Lewis, took on the media, as did "Tabloid Junkie."

On another track, "They Don't Care About Us," perhaps Jackson's anger went a bit too far. The song never identifies the titular "they," but the lyrics include the lines, "Jew me, sue me / everybody do me / kick me, Kike me / Don't you black or white me." On a nationally televised interview with Diane Sawyer on ABC-TV's *Prime Time Live*, Jackson denied that he was anti-Semitic, noting that his close friends include David Geffen, Jeffrey Katzenberg, and Steven Spielberg, all of whom are Jewish.

Initially, Jackson apologized, explaining that his message was to say "no" to racism. When the outcry continued, Jackson decided to re-record the offending lyrics, but the millions of copies of the album already issued remained either on retailers' shelves or in the hands of fans.

Perhaps the damage was already done. The double-A-side single of "Scream" and "Childhood (Theme from 'Free Willy 2')" became the highest debut single in the history of the Hot 100 when it entered the Hot 100 at number five June 17, but that lofty debut was also its peak.

HIStory debuted at Number One, no small feat for a pricey two-CD set, but it only held the top spot for two weeks, giving it the dubious distinction of having the shortest reign of Jackson's four chart-toppers. In spite of this, Jackson managed to make history again when "You Are Not Alone" became the first single to enter the Hot 100 at Number One on September 2, 1995.

THE TOP FIVE
Week of July 8, 1995

1. **HIStory: Past, Present and Future–Book 1**
   Michael Jackson

2. **Pocahontas**
   Soundtrack

3. **Cracked Rear View**
   Hootie & the Blowfish

4. **CrazySexyCool**
   TLC

5. **Batman Forever**
   Soundtrack

Executive producer: Chris Montan

Track listing: The Virginia Company [chorus] / Ship at Sea / The Virginia Company (Reprise) [Chorus and Mel Gibson] / Steady as the Beating Drum (Main Title) [chorus] / Steady as the Beating Drum (Reprise) [Jim Cummings] / Just Around the Riverbend [Judy Kuhn] / Grandmother Willow / Listen with Your Heart I [Linda Hunt and Bobbi Page] / Mine, Mine, Mine [David Ogden Stiers, Mel Gibson, and chorus] / Listen with Your Heart II [Linda Hunt and Bobbi Page] / Color in the Wind [Judy Kuhn] / Savages (Part 1) [David Ogden Stiers, Jim Cummings, and chorus] Savages (Part 2) [Judy Kuhn, David Ogden Stiers, Jim Cummings, and chorus] / I'll Never See Him Again / Pocahontas / Council Meeting / Percy's Bath / River's Edge / Skirmish / Getting Acquainted / Ratcliffe's Plan / Picking Corn / The Warriors Arrive / John Smith Sneaks Out / Execution / Farewell / Colors of the Wind (End Title) [Vanessa Williams] / If I Never Knew You (End Title) [Jon Secada and Shanice]

July 22, 1995
1 week

Alan Menken, along with his late partner, lyricist Howard Ashman, was responsible for making Walt Disney a significant chart force in the '90s. The company scored its first Number One album in 1965 with the *Mary Poppins* soundtrack [see 74], released on the Buena Vista subsidiary. But over the next 24 years, Disney failed to score a hit album, at least until the release of *The Little Mermaid.* That album reached

number 32 and went on to sell more than two million copies. *Beauty and the Beast,* released in 1991, reached number 19 and 1992's *Aladdin* peaked at number six, both selling three million copies along the way. All three releases featured the music of Menken and words of Ashman, who died of complications from AIDS in 1991.

It was in 1992 when Menken first began to work on the music for *Pocahontas.* Lyricist Stephen Schwartz was enlisted to collaborate with Menken. The two songwriters, coincidentally, were already friends, having been introduced years earlier by *Footloose* songwriter Dean Pitchford [see 279].

Two years later, after Menken and Schwartz first began work on *Pocahontas,* Walt Disney Records enjoyed its biggest success to date with *The Lion King* [see 395], which featured music by Elton John, lyrics by Tim Rice, and a score by Hans Zimmer. "I didn't feel any pressure from the success of *Lion King* during the writing process, because what I do is so different from what Elton John and Hans Zimmer do, and what Stephen does is very different from what Tim Rice does. This is a very different kind of score," says Menken.

Indeed, *Pocahontas* marked a departure for Disney. "All the other Disney projects I've worked on prior to *Pocahontas* take place in a mythical land, long ago, and far away," says Menken. "*Pocahon-*

tas takes place in a real place, not so long ago, and not so far away, so the score is more literal and more adult. It's more from the Rodgers and Hammerstein school of musicals as opposed to the Ashman–Menken school."

Like Disney's previous soundtracks, superstar talent was recruited to sing the film's main themes. Whitney Houston was among the artists approached to be featured on the album, but she declined. Instead, Disney recruited former Miss America Vanessa Williams to sing the track "Colors of the Wind" and Jon Secada and Shanice to duet on "If I Never Knew You."

Appropriately, "Colors of the Wind," the first song composed by Menken and Schwartz for the project, was the first single released from the album. "That was the song that started it all," says Menken. "When we finished it, I got a call from [Disney executive] Jeffrey Katzenberg, who said it was the best song ever written for a Disney animated feature."

Pocahontas hit Number One in its sixth week on The Billboard 200, dethroning Michael Jackson's *HIStory* [see 412]. Menken had met Jackson a few years earlier. Originally, Jackson was one of the artists in consideration to record "A Whole New World" from *Aladdin.* "You can judge the quality of what you do by the quality of your competition," says Menken.

414 Dreaming of You EMI LATIN 34123
SELENA

Producers: Keith Thomas, Guy Roche, Rhett Lawrence, Arto Lindsay, Susan Rogers, David Byrne, A.B. Quintanilla III, K.C. Porter, and Jose Hernandez

Track listing: I Could Fall in Love / Captive Heart / I'm Getting Used to You / God's Child (Baila Conmigo) / Dreaming of You / Missing My Baby / Amor Prohibido / Wherever You Are (Dondequiera Que Estes) / Techno Cumbia / El Toro Relajo / Como La Flor / Tu Solo Tu / Bidi Bidi Bom Bom

August 5, 1995
1 week

When 17-year-old Selena Quintanilla became the first artist signed to the newly established EMI Latin label in 1989, Jose Behar, president of the imprint, didn't have his eyes specifically set on the Hispanic market. "I was more secure about signing her with a vision of having crossover into the Anglo market," he says, "as opposed to her becoming huge with the Hispanic market. Because when I signed her, females were not known to be great sellers [among Hispanics]. It was a male-dominated genre."

However, that would soon change. Initially, Selena fronted a group called Selena y Los Dinos, which featured her older siblings Abraham III on bass and Suzette on drums. The group's 1991 album, Ven Conmigo, topped Billboard's regional Mexican chart. A year later, Selena was billed as a solo act with the release of Entre a Mi Mundo.

Although Selena wasn't fluent in Spanish ("She understood it perfectly, but she could only speak about 50 per-

cent Spanish at first," says Behar), she became a superstar of Tejano music. Entre a Mi Mundo and Live! also topped Billboard's Mexican chart, while in 1993 Selena picked up her first Grammy and was signed to EMI Records in a deal that Behar hoped would realize Selena's crossover dreams.

As part of that plan, 1994's Amor Prohibido included a diverse selection of music, from Tejano to R&B and hip-hop. The mix proved successful, as the album topped The Billboard Latin 50.

With crossover stardom on the horizon, Selena appeared as a mariachi singer in the film Don Juan de Marco and began working on her English-language debut album. Then, on March 31, 1995, Selena arranged a business meeting with Yolanda Saldivar, the former president of her fan club and manager of the singer's two clothing boutiques. Selena had hoped to clear up reports that Salvidvar was embezzling money from the singer's stores, but Saldivar had other things on her mind. She shot the singer in the back with a .38-caliber revolver. Despite a blood transfusion, Selena died later that afternoon. She would have been 24 on April 16.

With the music world mourning the singer's loss, EMI announced only days after her death that it would release an album to pay tribute to the artist. That

album evolved into Dreaming of You. It includes five songs in English, some of which Selena had recorded for her English-language debut, and two English/Spanish duets, including "God's Child (Baila Conmigo)," a duet with former Talking Heads frontman David Byrne. It also features four unreleased Spanish songs, originally recorded for Don Juan de Marco, as well as her three biggest hits: "Amor Prohibido," "Bidi Bidi Bom Bom," and "Como La Flor."

"We felt after the tragedy that it would be important to include the hits that brought her to this point in her career, as well as the Spanish- and English-language music that would take her into the future," says Behar. "That would enable her new fans to really understand what she was about musically."

The concept proved to be a winner, as Dreaming of You entered The Billboard 200 at Number One. It made Selena only the fourth act of primarily Hispanic descent to top the album chart, following Santana [see 137], Los Lobos [see 374], and Cypress Hill [see 374].

While cynics attributed the success of the album to the publicity surrounding Selena's death, Behar strongly disagrees. "I'm not convinced that the 11 o'clock news drives hundreds of thousands of people to a record store to spend $14 on a CD," he says. "I'm convinced it's about the music."

THE TOP FIVE
Week of August 5, 1995

1. **Dreaming of You**
   Selena

2. **The Show, the After Party, the Hotel**
   Jodeci

3. **Cracked Rear View**
   Hootie & the Blowfish

4. **CrazySexyCool**
   TLC

5. **Pocahontas**
   Soundtrack

RUTHLESS 5539 ## E. 1999 Eternal
BONE THUGS-N-HARMONY
415

Executive producer: Eric (Eazy-E) Wright

Track listing: Da Introduction / Easy 1999 / Eternal / Crept and We Came / Down '71 (The Getaway) / Mr. Bill Collector / Budsmokers Only / Crossroad / Me Killa / Land of Tha Heartless / No Shorts, No Losses / 1st of tha Month / Buddah Lovaz / Die Die Die / Mr. Ouija 2 / Mo' Murda / Shotz to Tha Double Glock

August 12, 1995
2 weeks

On March 26, 1995, Eric "Eazy-E" Wright, the founder of N.W.A [see 349] and one of the forefathers of hardcore rap, died of AIDS at the age of 31. His death shocked the rap world, particularly a young group from Cleveland known as Bone Thugs-N-Harmony. One of Wright's final artistic endeavors was to serve as executive producer of the group's album, which was recorded in early 1995.

Wright had signed the group to his Ruthless Records label after the group traveled from Cleveland to Los Angeles and back in hopes of landing a recording contract. "We knew that all it would take was for one person with some power to hear us," says Krayzie Bone, who, like the group's other members, adopted the surname Bone in 1992. The group consists of brothers Layzie Bone and Flesh-N-Bone, stepbrother Bizzy Bone, cousin Wish Bone, and longtime friend Krayzie. While in L.A., the group found out where rapper Tone Loc [see 328] lived and walked to his house. "We rapped for him, but he

acted like he wasn't interested."

The group left a phone message for Eazy-E and were surprised when he returned the call. He was interested in the group but was about to hit the road and didn't have time for an audition. When the Bones found out that the N.W.A tour included a Cleveland date, they hustled some bus tickets to return home, where they secured the opening spot at the N.W.A concert. After the show, the group rapped for Eazy in his dressing room. "He signed us right there and the rest is history," says Krayzie.

In 1994, the group's debut EP, *Creepin' On Ah Come Up*, reached number 12, spending seven weeks in the top 20 and a total of 55 weeks on The Billboard 200, giving the group ample confidence for its full-length debut.

Although Bone Thugs-N-Harmony songs like "Me Killa" and "Die Die Die" deal with harsh urban realities, Krayzie says the group isn't a gangsta rap crew. "A gangsta is out to get a reputation," he says. "A thug is someone incognito who is trying to keep it on the low." The group's sound, which includes some singing mixed in with rapping, also sets it apart from the rap crowd. "That's how we got the name 'Thugs-N-Harmony,'

because we're throwing harmony in with it on the way," he says.

Lyrically, the group explores real-life circumstances in its old Cleveland neighborhood. "1st of Tha Month," for example, is about the day when everyone receives their welfare checks. "That's when everyone pays the bills, buys clothes, and has parties, because that's the only time when they got any money."

Another track, "Crossroad," was written in the memory of a friend from the neighborhood. "He got shot in his chest trying to break up a fight," Krayzie says. While the track was recorded months before Eazy-E's death, the song can also serve as a tribute to their mentor.

"He had a copy of the album before he died," says Krayzie. "He knew it was going to end up on top." While Wright may have predicted big things for his protégés, the Bones were somewhat surprised when the album debuted at Number One. "The EP went triple-platinum, and I knew that this product was better than the last one," Krayzie says. "I was surprised how quick it went to Number One, but I knew it would get there sooner or later."

THE TOP FIVE
Week of August 12, 1995

1. **E. 1999 Eternal**
   Bone Thugs-N-Harmony

2. **Cracked Rear View**
   Hootie & the Blowfish

3. **Dreaming of You**
   Selena

4. **CrazySexyCool**
   TLC

5. **The Show, the After Party, the Hotel**
   Jodeci

416 Dangerous Minds MCA 11228
SOUNDTRACK

Michelle Pfeiffer and Coolio.

Executive producers: Don Simpson & Jerry Bruckheimer, and DeVante

Track listing: Gangsta's Paradise [Coolio] / Curiosity [Aaron Hall] / Havin Thangs [Big Mike] / Problems [Rappin' 4-Tay] / True O.G. [Dalvin & Static] / Put Ya Back into It [Tre Black] / Don't Go There [24-K] / Feel the Funk [Immature] / It's Alright [Sista featuring Craig Mack] / A Message for You Mind [Rappin' 4-Tay] / Gin & Juice [DeVante] / This Is the Life [Wendy & Lisa]

September 2, 1995
3 weeks

Movie producers Don Simpson and Jerry Bruckheimer may have been the most successful music executives not in the record business. When a soundtrack album to one of their films was released, chances were that it would become a big hit or at least spawn a hit single. In the '80s alone, Simpson and Bruckheimer racked up three Number One albums with the soundtracks to *Flashdance* [see 275], *Beverly Hills Cop* [see 289], and *Top Gun* [see 302].

While Simpson and Bruckheimer seemingly couldn't go wrong in the '80s, the first half of the '90s didn't prove as fruitful, at least until they brought a project called *Dangerous Minds* to Kathy Nelson of MCA Soundtracks, the label that had success with *Beverly Hills Cop* and *Beverly Hills Cop II.*

In early 1994, three months before the duo began production on the film, they took the script about an ex-Marine

who teaches at an inner-city high school to Nelson, who helped enlist the artists. "We would try to keep the music true to the genre of the picture and what the story was about," says Bruckheimer. "It's a classroom drama and it's about kids, so we wanted the music to be realistic to what the kids would be listening to."

To accomplish that, Nelson first turned to Coolio, a rapper known for the 1994 number three hit "Fantastic Voyage." Says Nelson, "I wanted Coolio, because I'm a huge fan of his. He was one of my first calls."

Nelson had showed the rapper about six scenes from the film, starring Michelle Pfeiffer, which was still in production at the time. "It was written for the movie. He had the movie in his head, a couple of guys were fooling around with this track and that was it," says Bruckheimer of Coolio's "Gangsta's Paradise," which contains a sample of Stevie Wonder's "Pastime Paradise" [see 219]. Bruckheimer and Simpson were impressed by the results. "Kathy played it for me over the phone and then she sent it over, and I said, 'Oh God, this is a Number One record.' Everyone thought we were both nuts."

DeVante, a member of the hit R&B group Jodeci, was also intrigued by the project, and contributed his first solo single "Gin & Juice" (not to be confused with the Snoop Doggy Dogg single of the same name). "He ended up being so interested in the project, he came on as an executive producer to the album," says Nelson. DeVante's involvement led to the inclusion of "True O.G.," by Mr. Dalvin & Static. Mr. Dalvin is DeVante's brother and a fellow Jodeci member,

and also produced "Curiosity" by Aaron Hall. "DeVante loves Michelle as an actress and he loved the movie," says Bruckheimer. "He added credibility to the project, and that's how we got all of these acts."

On the other end of the spectrum, former Prince and the Revolution [see 282] members Wendy & Lisa contributed "This Is the Life." When the first musician hired to compose the score for the film didn't work out, Bruckheimer turned to Wendy & Lisa. "We kept using the rhythm and the melody of that song in the film and it worked," he says. "They were up for scoring the film and did a sensational job."

Dangerous Minds wasn't a blockbuster initially, entering The Billboard 200 at number 130 on August 11, 1995. But then an unusual cross-promotional effort launched by Hollywood Pictures and MCA Soundtracks began to kick in. Since the film's star Pfeiffer agreed to appear alongside Coolio in the video clip for "Gangsta's Paradise," the companies opted to use the video clip for its television spots for the film. As a result, the song rocketed up the charts.

On September 2, "Gangsta's Paradise" seemed a shoo-in for Number One on the Hot 100, but was surprisingly held out of the top spot by the Number One debut of Michael Jackson's "You Are Not Alone" [see 412]. Jackson, however, couldn't keep *Dangerous Minds* from the peak, as it hit the top of The Billboard 200 in its fourth week on the chart. For Simpson and Bruckheimer, it was their fourth chart-topper.

A week later, with *Dangerous Minds* holding at Number One, "Gangsta's Paradise" was able to slip by Jackson's single.

THE TOP FIVE
Week of September 2, 1995

1. **Dangerous Minds**
   Soundtrack

2. **Cracked Rear View**
   Hootie & the Blowfish

3. **Jagged Litte Pill**
   Alanis Morissette

4. **The Show**
   Soundtrack

5. **E. 1999 Eternal**
   Bone Thugs-N-Harmony

MAVERICK 45901 **Jagged Little Pill** **417**
ALANIS MORISSETTE

Producer: Glen Ballard

Track listing: All I Really Want / You Oughta Know / Perfect / Hand in My Pocket / Right Through You / Forgiven / You Learn / Head Over Feet / Mary Jane / Ironic / Not the Doctor / Wake Up

October 7, 1995
2 weeks

When Madonna was interviewed for this book in the summer of 1995, she predicted that a young Canadian woman named Alanis Morissette, who was signed to her Maverick Recording Co., would soon be joining her as a chart-topper. A few months later, Madonna's prediction became a reality, as Morissette's *Jagged Little Pill* hit Number One in its 15th week on The Billboard 200. It earned Morissette the distinction of being the first Canadian woman ever to top the album chart.

To Americans, the 21-year-old singer-songwriter may have seemed like a newcomer, but in fact Morissette was already a seasoned professional. In the mid-'80s, she was a regular on the Nickelodeon show "You Can't Do That on Television." By the early '90s, she had recorded two dance-oriented albums for MCA/Canada, which earned her comparisons with American teen pop queens Debbie Gibson [see 327] and Tiffany [see 317]. "There are little pieces of me in them," Morissette says of her early recordings. "You can hear me forming my identity as far as the way I sing, but it was my 15-year-old self. I'm not sure if I was secure enough to make a record as unadulterated and forthright as the music I make now."

After Morissette's initial taste of the music business left her cold, she left her native Ottawa for Toronto and eventually Los Angeles. "I had to sort of clear my head and get a perspective on not only music, and the whole industry side of it, and also myself as a person," she says.

After several failed attempts to collaborate with other artists, an executive at MCA Music Publishing introduced Morissette to songwriter/producer Glen Ballard, known for his work with such pop stars as Michael Jackson and Paula Abdul.

"We just hit it off on every different level," Morissette says. "It was compatibility at first sight. Stylistically we had the same history, so it was wonderful for he and I to start off with a clean slate."

On their first meeting, the duo composed a song called "The Bottom Line" in 25 minutes. Although that song didn't make *Jagged Little Pill*, it set the tone for the collaborative effort.

Nearly the entire album was recorded at Ballard's Encino, California, home over a two-month period. "It was just a very stream-of-consciousness, spiritual way of writing, and we recorded it that way too," Morissette says. "We would write and record at the same time and the vocals are all one- or two-take vocals, and the guitars are the same. Essentially, 80 percent of the record is the original demos."

The spontaneous method of writing led to Morissette's brutally frank lyrics about relationships. For example, in the hit single "You Oughta Know," Morissette questions an ex-boyfriend who left her for an older woman. "I in no way wrote these songs for the sake of revenge. I wrote them for the sake of release on my part," she says. "I never mention anyone's name. I don't feel I have the right to drag someone else through the emotional mud with me."

While Morissette's angst-ridden tales of tainted love are extremely personal, they still found a mainstream audience. "During the writing of this album, I felt I was being very self-indulgent with the lyrics and the music," she admits. "I was writing what I wanted and it was from a very personal place. The fact that it was received so well on the outside I found sort of ironic."

THE TOP FIVE
Week of October 7, 1995

1. **Jagged Little Pill**
   Alanis Morissette

2. **Dangerous Minds**
   Soundtrack

3. **Cracked Rear View**
   Hootie & the Blowfish

4. **All I Want**
   Tim McGraw

5. **Greatest Hits 1985–1995**
   Michael Bolton

418 Daydream COLUMBIA 66700
MARIAH CAREY

Producers: Walter Afanasieff, Mariah Carey, Dave Hall, Jermaine Dupri, Manuel Seal, and David Morales

Track listing: Fantasy / Underneath the Stars / One Sweet Day / Open Arms / Always Be My Baby / I Am Free / When I Saw You / Long Ago / Melt Away / Forever / Daydream Interlude (Fantasy Sweet Dub Mix) / Looking In

October 21, 1995
4 weeks (nonconsecutive)

With *Daydream*, her fifth full-length studio album, Mariah Carey made history. "Fantasy," the album's first single, entered the Hot 100 at Number One on September 30, 1995, making Carey the only female artist ever to debut at the top of that chart. Three weeks later, with "Fantasy" still holding the pole position on the Hot 100, *Daydream* bowed at Number One on The Billboard 200, earning Carey the additional distinction of the first artist to debut at the top with an album and its initial single. If that wasn't enough, Carey kept the streak alive when "One Sweet Day," the second single from *Daydream*, entered the Hot 100 at Number One on December 2, 1995, making Carey the only artist—male or female—to debut at Number One on the singles chart twice in a row. Carey's record-breaking streak continued on March 9, 1996, when "One Sweet Day" became the longest-running Number One single of the rock era, logging its 15th week at the top.

"The overall feeling surrounding the sessions on *Daydream* was much more calm than on the sessions for *Music Box*," Carey says. "I took a little more time on this one." Once again Carey

collaborated with several noted producers, including Walter Afanasieff and David Morales, but initially she found some of the most rewarding moments on her own. "There were times when I was in the studio alone doing vocals on 'Underneath the Stars' and 'I Am Free,'" she says. "It was a really creative time." On several tracks, Carey also recorded her own background vocals.

For "Fantasy," Carey opted to sample "Genius of Love," a 1982 hit for the Tom Tom Club. "I grew up loving that song," she says. "I think that is one of the best tracks ever produced. I just thought that the melody I had would go really well with that track...It really complimented what I was doing."

For the single release, several different remixes were recorded, including one version featuring Wu Tang Clan rapper Ol' Dirty Bastard. One of Morales's remixes ended up on the album. "It's an interlude, but it's actually one of my favorite things on the album," she says. "It sort of inspired the title *Daydream*." The song, recorded at 5 A.M., was one of the first cuts recorded at Carey's home studio. Morales surprised Carey by having her sing over a remix she had never heard before. "It

was at the very end of the session," Carey says. "When I got to that part of the song it was very jazzy, so it inspired me to start scatting on the top of it. It had this dreamy, ethereal feeling."

Also included on *Daydream* is "One Sweet Day," Carey's collaboration with Boyz II Men. "I had the idea for the song and finished the first verse and chorus, but then I stopped writing, because the style of background vocals I wanted to do would be perfect for Boyz II Men," she says. Carey presented the idea to her manager. "Months later, after getting through all the drama that it takes to bring our schedules together, they came in and I played it for them, and as it turned out Nate Morris was writing something similar dedicated to his road manager, who was shot to death. Lyrically and melodically, it was almost identical to mine, so we combined it all. It was just a crazy coincidence. The melodies could literally be woven together."

Since Carey and the Boyz both have busy schedules, the recording session was taped for the music video clip. "We just felt it was very important to document the session and that's what the video is," says Carey, "a documentary about making the record."

THE TOP FIVE
Week of October 21, 1995

1. **Daydream**
   Mariah Carey

2. **Jagged Little Pill**
   Alanis Morissette

3. **Dangerous Minds**
   Soundtrack

4. **Cracked Rear View**
   Hootie & the Blowfish

5. **Starting Over**
   Reba McEntire

VIRGIN 40861 # Mellon Collie and the Infinite Sadness
THE SMASHING PUMPKINS

419

Producers: Flood, Alan Moulder, and Billy Corgan

Track listing: Mellon Collie and the Infinite Sadness / Tonight, Tonight / Jellybelly / Zero / Here Is No Why / Bullet with Butterfly Wings / To Forgive / An Ode to No One / Love / Cupid de Locke / Galapogogs / Muzzle / Porcelina of the Vast Oceans / Tame Me Down / Where Boys Fear to Tread / Bodies/ Thirty-three / In the Arms of Sleep / 1979 / Tales of a Scorched Earth / Thru the Eyes of Ruby / Stumbleine / X.Y.U. / We Only Come Out at Night / Beautiful / Lily (My One and Only) / By Starlight / Farewell and Goodnight

November 11, 1995
1 week

Virgin Records' decision to release the Smashing Pumpkins' *Mellon Collie and the Infinite Sadness* as a two-CD set was a risky move for the label and the band. Certainly, the sprawling, double-disc opus would separate the Chicago-based band from its alternative rock peers. But in the CD era, double-disc packages are usually reserved for greatest-hits sets or live albums, not 28 new songs. In fact, few rock artists have dared to release so much new material at once since the CD became the dominant configuration for recorded music. Indeed, in 1991, when Columbia and Geffen released, respectively, Bruce Springsteen's *Human Touch* and *Lucky Town* and Guns N' Roses' *Use Your Illusion I* and *II* [see 355], in both cases the labels opted to spread the artist's material out over two simulta-

neously but separately released CDs.

At the time of the release of *Mellon Collie and the Infinite Sadness*, the Pumpkins had secured their position as one of modern rock's brightest commercial forces. The band's previous album, 1994's *Pisces Iscariot*, was a collection of B-sides and rarities, but it still managed to reach number four, while 1993's *Siamese Dream* made number 10.

Despite the success, the question remained: Was the Pumpkins' fan base loyal enough to shell out for a double CD?

That's just the kind of challenge Pumpkins frontman Billy Corgan wanted to make with the album. "It's not what anyone would expect from a band that is supposedly going to be big," he says. "These days, selling records has become so formulized. This is the record that we should be going after top 40 radio with, [but] I wanted to do the best artistic thing I could do, and if it sells, it sells because of its artistic success, not because we are conforming to some kind of preconceived idea about how to make a band big."

Corgan began working on the album immediately after the Pumpkins completed their headlining stint on the 1994 Lollapalooza tour. From the initial stages, he had a double CD in mind. Each disc has a subtitle—*Dawn to Dusk* and *Twilight to Starlight*—but Corgan says that was just a device to separate the music.

Mellon Collie and the Infinite Sadness is not a concept album, he says.

The album, produced by Flood, Alan Moulder, and Corgan, was written and recorded in 10 months at several studios in Chicago and Los Angeles. Impressed by Flood's work with Depeche Mode [see 369] and U2 [see 373], Corgan invited the producer to a Lollapalooza date, where he agreed to work with the band, which includes bassist/vocalist D'Arcy, drummer Jimmy Chamberlin, and guitarist James Iha. Co-producer Moulder mixed *Siamese Dream*.

Opening with the piano-based instrumental title track, *Mellon Collie and the Infinite Sadness* runs the gamut from rockers to ballads, and incorporates a variety of instrumentation, including pedal and lap steel guitar, strings, and mellotron. As a whole, the album "is not self-indulgent," says Corgan. "It doesn't have long-winded guitar solos or space jams—it's a song-based album."

The Pumpkins' bold move paid off when *Mellon Collie* entered The Billboard 200 at Number One, becoming the first two-disc set of all new material to bow at the top in the CD era. (Among previous double-CD chart-toppers, Pink Floyd's *Pulse* [see 411] featured live versions of old material, while Michael Jackson's *HIStory* [see 412] included a disc of hits and a disc of new material.) The Pumpkins' experiment had paid off.

THE TOP FIVE
Week of November 11, 1995

1. **Mellon Collie and the Infinite Sadness**
   The Smashing Pumpkins

2. **Daydream**
   Mariah Carey

3. **Jagged Little Pill**
   Alanis Morissette

4. **Ozzmosis**
   Ozzy Osbourne

5. **The Greatest Hits Collection**
   Alan Jackson

420 Dogg Food DEATH ROW 50546
THA DOGG POUND

Producer: Dat Nigga Daz

Track listing: Intro / Dogg Pound Gangstaz / Respect / New York, New York (Tha Night I Served 2,000 M.C.s) / Smooth / Cyco-Lic-No (Bitch Azz Niggaz) / Ridin', Slipin' and Slidin' / U Can't Cee Me / Big Pimpin 2 / Let's Play House / I Don't Like to Dream About Gettin Paid / Do What I Feel / If We All Fuc* / Some Bomb Azz Pussy / A Dogg'z Day Afternoon / Reality / One By One (Subtracting Sucka Azz Niggaz from the Face of the Earth) / Sooo Much Style

November 18, 1995
1 week

Months before the release of Dogg Food, Tha Dogg Pound was no stranger to controversy and the top of the charts. The duo, consisting of Delmar "Dat Nigga Daz" Arnaud and Ricardo "Kurupt the Kingpin" Brown, appeared on such hit albums as Dr. Dre's The Chronic, Snoop Doggy Dogg's Doggystyle [see 381], and the Murder Was the Case soundtrack [see 399].

With such an impressive list of credits and connections—Daz is Snoop Doggy Dogg's cousin—anticipation for Tha Dogg Pound's album was already high when a political firestorm in May 1995 brought things to the boiling point. Senate majority leader and presidential candidate Bob Dole publicly attacked Time Warner for selling what he called "violent and sexually degrading" rap music. Other influential leaders, including former Secretary of Education and federal drug czar William J.

THE TOP FIVE
Week of November 18, 1995

1. **Dogg Food**
   Tha Dogg Pound

2. **Daydream**
   Mariah Carey

3. **Cypress Hill III (Temple of Boom)**
   Cypress Hill

4. **Jagged Little Pill**
   Alanis Morissette

5. **Mellon Collie and the Infinite Sadness**
   The Smashing Pumpkins

Bennett and C. DeLores Tucker, chair of the National Political Congress of Black Women, also applied pressure on Time Warner to divest itself of Interscope Records, the label that distributed Death Row Records, home to Dr. Dre, Snoop Doggy Dogg, and Tha Dogg Pound.

The pressure was so great that Warner Music Group chairman Michael Fuchs opted to sever ties with Interscope, leaving Death Row free to pact with the independent Priority label for distribution of Dogg Food.

While the anti–gangsta rap political forces were celebrating a victory, Tha Dogg Pound wasn't going to go away. In fact, in the midst of the hoopla, the duo continued working tirelessly on the album, almost oblivious to the controversy. "It was just a campaign thing," says Daz. "We didn't give a fuck about that shit. We were just trying to get our album done."

While Tha Dogg Pound was bound to have similarities to Dr. Dre's The Chronic and Snoop Doggy Dogg's Dog-

gystyle, Daz says each album is unique. "It's all different coming from different areas," Daz says. "We're all different individuals, so we all have our own perspective." Dr. Dre, who produced Doggystyle, served as co–executive producer of Dogg Food, along with Death Row CEO Suge Knight.

Although the album was originally scheduled to bow in July 1995, it wasn't released until Halloween day, as the duo made sure to enjoy the sessions held at Can Am studios and Dr. Dre's studio, known as Dre's Crib. "There was all kinds of shit going on," Daz says. "Late nights, phone calls, bitches, all kinds of shit. It was like a goddamn party in there. I like a lot of people around when I'm working. It all inspired us to do better."

Hardcore rap fans didn't need to be convinced. Like Doggystyle and Murder Was the Case, Dogg Food entered The Billboard 200 at Number One. Bob Dole, William Bennett, and C. DeLores Tucker had to be disappointed.

COLUMBIA 67243 **Alice in Chains**
ALICE IN CHAINS `421`

Producers: Tony "Flobee" Wright and Alice in Chains

Track listing: Grind / Brush Away / Sludge Factory / Heaven Beside You / Head Creeps / Again / Shame in You / Go Am / So Close Nothin' Song / Frogs / Over Now

November 25, 1995
1 week

Alice in Chains recorded their first chart-topper, the *Jar of Flies* EP [see 383], on a whim following their appearance on Lollapalooza '93. *Alice in Chains* wasn't as easy. In fact, following the release of *Jar of Flies*, the Seattle-based hard-rock quartet nearly broke up. "We were pretty worn out," says guitarist Jerry Cantrell. "We really needed to sit down and leave the gig and chill out. If we didn't stop, we definitely would have broken up."

Alice in Chains' ride to the top was relatively quick. Prior to *Jar of Flies*, the band had only two albums and two EPs to its credit. The quick rise to stardom wasn't without its price. Singer Layne Staley battled a drug habit, but apparently beat his demons by immersing himself in a side project with Pearl Jam's Mike McCready, Barrett Martin, and Mysterious Baker. The group, initially known as Gacy's Gang, changed their name to Mad Season for the March 1995 release of their self-titled album.

While Staley was working on *Mad Season*, Cantrell began working on his own material, much of which ended up on *Alice in Chains*. The demo sessions, which began in March 1995, were held at London Bridge, the studio where the band recorded *Jar of Flies*. During this period, Cantrell wrote "Grind" and "Over Now." In fact, the demo of Sean Kinney's drum track ended up on the album version of "Over Now," even if the drummer was initially less than pleased with his performance. "He was playing this take with me and it's a long song, so we really had to be locked in together," Cantrell says. "I thought the take was fucking great, but apparently he thought it was shitty, so he picked up his drums and threw them across the room."

Once the band regrouped with Staley in April 1995 at Bad Animals Studio, the sessions proved to be difficult, but ultimately worth the effort. "Layne had pretty much creatively cleared himself with Mad Season, but that was ultimately good for this record," Cantrell says. "When you put yourself in the situation where you don't know what the fuck you are going to do, you come up with some of your best work off the top of your head and off the cuff. Other than 'Grind' and 'Over Now,' the rest of the stuff was all just music and riffs that we pieced together in the studio."

Also on board was co-producer Toby Wright, who first worked with the band as an engineer on its contributions to the *Last Action Hero* soundtrack. "We have kind of moved more into a producer's role ourselves," says Cantrell. "So we were really looking for an engineer with a producer's ear to take the heat off of us a little bit."

The sessions ended up running five months, but it was time well spent. *Alice in Chains* became the band's second title to enter The Billboard 200 at the top. "We're happy we stuck it out and made the record," says Cantrell. "During the time we took off, we just cut ourselves off from the press, because we really didn't have anything to say at that point. Now, we've said it all on this record."

THE TOP FIVE
Week of November 25, 1995

1. **Alice in Chains**
   Alice in Chains

2. **Daydream**
   Mariah Carey

3. **Jagged Little Pill**
   Alanis Morissette

4. **Dogg Food**
   Tha Dogg Pound

5. **Mellon Collie and the Infinite Sadness**
   The Smashing Pumpkins

422

R. Kelly JIVE 41579
R. KELLY

Producer: R. Kelly

Track listing: Intro—The Sermon /
Hump Bounce / Not Gonna Hold On /
You Remind Me of Something / Step in
My Room / Baby, Baby, Baby, Baby,
Baby... / (You to Be) Be Happy / Down
Low (Nobody Has to Know) / I Can't
Sleep Baby (If I) / Thank God It's
Friday / Love Is on the Way / Heaven
If You Hear Me / Religious Love /
Tempo Slow / As I Look into My Life /
Trade in My Life

December 2, 1995
1 week

Some pop music fans may have
been surprised that R. Kelly, known
primarily for the racy 1994 Number One R&B hit "Bump and Grind,"
was the same R. Kelly who wrote and
produced Michael Jackson's "You Are
Not Alone," which became the first single to debut atop the Hot 100 [see
412]. With his 1995 self-titled album,
Kelly attempted to show that he could
score with his suggestive and sensitive
sides.

It was on 1991's aptly titled Born
into the '90s that Robert Kelly proved to
be a hot new talent on the R&B scene.
The album reached number three on the
Top R&B Albums chart and spawned
two Number One R&B hits: "Honey
Love" and "Slow Dance (Hey Mr. DJ)."

Kelly turned up the heat on his 1993
follow-up, 12 Play, which included
"Bump and Grind," among other hot
and spicy numbers. That album topped
the R&B chart for nine weeks and
climbed all the way to number two on
The Billboard 200. Adding to Kelly's
bad-boy image was talk that he'd mar-

THE TOP FIVE
Week of December 2, 1995

1. **R. Kelly**
   R. Kelly

2. **Daydream**
   Mariah Carey

3. **Waiting to Exhale**
   Soundtrack

4. **Jagged Little Pill**
   Alanis Morissette

5. **The Greatest Hits Collection**
   Alan Jackson

ried teenage R&B star Aaliyah.

Yet Kelly's success came at a price.
"I'm not Robert anymore," he told Cheo
H. Coker in the Los Angeles Times. "I
love to be Robert, but everybody is trying to make me R. Kelly. When you
become successful, you're suddenly
under the magnifying glass. If I'm on a
court and I shoot a ball, it's not like it
used to be. I'm R. Kelly now, I can't miss
a single shot."

The singer/producer had also grown
tired of his music being labeled sexist or
just plain nasty. Whether by coincidence
or design, R. Kelly revealed the star's
more sensitive side. To show off his
diverse talents, Kelly called on a number
of guests to appear on the album. Ernie
and Ronald Isley appear on "Down Low
(Nobody Has to Know)," while rapper
the Notorious B.I.G. turns up on "(You
to Be) Be Happy." To show his gospel
influence, Kelly called on gospel star
Kirk Franklin to direct the choir on
"Trade in My Life." However, R. Kelly
still includes an occasional racy couplet.

For example, the single "You Remind
Me of Something," includes the lyric,
"You remind me of my Jeep / I wanna
ride it."

Some have said that Kelly's music is
somewhat derivative, something he
doesn't try to hide. "Some people will
hear the 'Wooo!' that I used from Total's
'Can't You See' in 'Hump Bounce,' " he
admitted to Coker. "But Marvin Gaye
used 'Wooo!' too. Never think you
came up with something first. I can't
really say, 'This is my sound,' 'cause I
was inspired by Quincy Jones, Stevie
Wonder, and Teddy Riley. You should
never be too proud to admit someone
inspired you."

Even before R. Kelly debuted at
Number One, R. Kelly was humble
enough to admit his rapid rise was a bit
of a surprise. "It's amazing to know that
five years ago I was writing songs in a
basement in the ghetto and now I'm
writing for Michael Jackson," he told
Newsweek's Allison Samuels. "I'd be a
fool not to say it's a dream come true."

Producer: George Martin

Track listing: Free as a Bird / Speech: John Lennon / That'll Be the Day / In Spite of All the Danger / Speech: Paul McCartney / Hallelujah, I Love Her So / You'll Be Mine / Cayenne / Speech: Paul / My Bonnie / Ain't She Sweet / Cry for a Shadow / Speech: John / Speech: Brian Epstein / Searchin' / Three Cool Cats / The Sheik of Araby / Like Dreamers Do / Hello Little Girl / Speech: Brian Epstein / Beasame Mucho / Love Me Do / How Do You Do It / Please Please Me / One After 909 (False Starts) / One After 909 / Lend Me Your Comb / I'll Get You / Speech: John / I Saw Her Standing There / From Me to You / Money (That's What I Want) / You Really Got a Hold of Me / Roll Over Beethoven / She Loves You / Till There Was You / Twist and Shout / This Boy / I Want to Hold Your Hand / Speech: Eric Morecambe and Ernie Wise / Moonlight Boy / Can't Buy Me Love / All My Loving / You Can't Do That / And I Love Her / A Hard Day's Night / I Wanna Be Your Man / Long Tall Sally / Boys / Shout / I'll Be Back (Complete) / You Know What to Do / No Reply (Demo) / Eight Days a Week (False Starts) / Eight Days a Week / Kansas City / Hey-Hey-Hey-Hey!

December 9, 1995
3 weeks

Long before the Beatles' *Anthology 1* sailed to the top of The Billboard 200, a series of meetings between top executives at Capitol, EMI, and Apple Corps. were held to pave the long and winding road to new Beatles releases.

Prior to 1994's two-CD *Live at the BBC* set, which reached number three on The Billboard 200, there hadn't been a new Beatles compilation released in America since 1988's *Past Masters* CDs, which featured singles and B-sides not included on the British versions of the Beatles' albums, which were issued on CD in the U.S. When Gary Gersh took over as president/CEO of Capitol Records in July 1993, he took stock of the situation.

"When I arrived at Capitol, the relationship between the Beatles and EMI had gotten to the point where it was

continually being stalled in terms of getting new product out, making a new deal, or trying to move forward with what the potential was for releasing new Beatles product," Gersh says.

Gersh took his concerns to Charles Koppelman, chairman/CEO of the EMI-Capitol Music Group, and suggested that the executives and their counterparts in the U.K. examine the Beatles' future.

"I said, 'We should take a real serious look at reassessing the Beatles situation with EMI worldwide. We should open our eyes to what the future could be,' " Gersh says.

Rather than be content with the catalog sales of the Beatles albums already on the market, Gersh suggested changing the structure of EMI-Capitol's arrangement with the Beatles and Apple Corps. in hopes of generating new product.

Although Gersh stops short of revealing specifics of the new deal, he says it "is extremely beneficial for both the Beatles and EMI, and, from the Beatles' perspective, I would think they would say it has never been fairer than it is today."

It was those secret negotiations that paved the way for *Anthology 1*, the first of three double-CDs featuring Beatles rarities, tied into a three-part, six-hour television documentary that aired on ABC-TV in November 1995.

Fueling the anticipation for *Anthology 1* and the TV documentary was the release of "Free as a Bird," the first new Beatles song in 25 years. The song was constructed from a 1977 John Lennon home demo recorded in mono. In March 1994, Paul McCartney, George Harrison, and Ringo Starr completed the

track with producer Jeff Lynne at McCartney's home studio in Sussex, England.

"It was strange because I warned Ringo that he'd better have a handkerchief ready when he listened to the tape for the first time, because he's a very emotional guy, and I know I had a bit of a cry," McCartney told Robert Hilburn of the *Los Angeles Times*. "It's a powerful thing hearing your friend on a very beautiful song. When we got in the studio, however, it felt like John was there. It was like he had done his vocal and maybe gone off to the toilet or something while the rest of us worked on the track."

The excitement of "Free as a Bird" and *Anthology 1* earned the Beatles a few more historic achievements. The first two hours of the documentary were watched by an estimated 27.3 million viewers, tops in its time slot. Meanwhile, the album entered The Billboard 200 at Number One, with sales of more than 855,000 units, making it the fastest-selling double-CD and the highest-grossing album debut (raking in over $22 million, according to Capitol) in history.

Anthology 1 gave the Beatles their 16th Number One album and set the mark for the longest time span for a run of Number One albums in the rock era—it was 31 years and 10 months between *Anthology 1* and *Meet the Beatles!* [see 65]. The Fab Four's previous chart-topping album, *The Beatles/1967–1970* [see 160], had hit the pole position 12 years and seven months prior to *Anthology 1*'s move to the top—another record.

THE TOP FIVE
Week of December 9, 1995

1. **Anthology 1**
   The Beatles

2. **Fresh Horses**
   Garth Brooks

3. **Daydream**
   Mariah Carey

4. **Christmas in the Aire**
   Mannheim Steamroller

5. **Waiting to Exhale**
   Soundtrack

APPENDIX: FACTS AND FIGURES

The Most Number Ones

BY ARTIST		BY PRODUCER		BY LABEL*	
The Beatles	16	George Martin	16	Columbia	68
Elvis Presley	9	Gus Dudgeon	7	Capitol	37
The Rolling Stones	9	James William Guercio	6	Warner Bros.	25
Elton John	7	Paul McCartney	6	RCA	24
Paul McCartney/Wings	7	Jimmy Page	6	Atlantic	20
Barbra Streisand	7	Phil Ramone	6*	MCA	17
Led Zeppelin	6	Herb Alpert and Jerry Moss	5	A&M	15
Herb Alpert & the Tijuana Brass	5	Glimmer Twins	5	Apple	13
Chicago	5	Bruce Springsteen and Jon Landau	5*	Epic	10
Eagles	5	Bill Szymczyk	5	Mercury	9
The Kingston Trio	5	Walter Afanasieff	4*	Asylum	8
Pink Floyd	5	Bruce Fairbarin	4	Rolling Stones	8
Bruce Springsteen	5	Jimmy Miller	4	Elektra	8
Garth Brooks	4	Giorgio Mororder	4*	Arista	7
Michael Jackson	4	Chuck Plotkin	4*	Reprise	7
Billy Joel	4	Allen Reynolds	4	Motown	7
The Monkees	4	Barbra Streisand	4*	Geffen	6
Frank Sinatra	4	Neil Young	4*	Liberty	5
U2	4			Decca	5
Van Halen	4				

*Includes co-production credits.

*Tallied by a count of the actual label on the record, not distributing labels.

The Most Weeks at Number One

BY ARTIST

The Beatles	122
Elvis Presley	64
Michael Jackson	49
The Kingston Trio	46
Whitney Houston	45*
Elton John	39
Garth Brooks	38
The Rolling Stones	38
Fleetwood Mac	37
The Monkees	37
Harry Belafonte	31
Prince	33
Bee Gees	31*
Eagles	29
Led Zeppelin	28
Herb Alpert & the Tijuana Brass	26
Simon & Garfunkel	26*
Mariah Carey	23
Pink Floyd	23
Barbra Streisand	23
Henry Mancini	22
Paul McCartney/Wings	22
Chicago	22
Bruce Springsteen	21

*Includes soundtrack albums prominently featuring the artist.

BY ALBUM

ALBUM	ARTIST	WEEKS	YEAR(S)
West Side Story	Soundtrack	54	1962–1963
Thriller	Michael Jackson	37	1983
Calypso	Harry Belafonte	31	1956–1957
South Pacific	Soundtrack	31	1958–1959
Rumours	Fleetwood Mac	31	1977–1978
Saturday Night Fever	Soundtrack	24	1978
Purple Rain	Prince and the Revolution	24	1984–1985
Please Hammer Don't Hurt 'Em	M.C. Hammer	21	1990
Blue Hawaii	Elvis Presley/Soundtrack	20	1961–1962
The Bodyguard	Soundtrack	20	1992–1993
More of the Monkees	The Monkees	18	1967
Dirty Dancing	Soundtrack	18	1987–1988
Ropin' the Wind	Garth Brooks	18	1991–1992
Synchronicity	The Police	17	1983
Some Gave All	Billy Ray Cyrus	17	1992
The Days of Wine and Roses	Andy Williams	16	1963
The Sound of Music	Original Cast	16	1960
To the Extreme	Vanilla Ice	16	1990–1991
My Fair Lady	Original Cast	15	1956–1959
Sgt. Pepper's Lonely Hearts Club Band	The Beatles	15	1967
Tapestry	Carole King	15	1971
Hi Infidelity	REO Speedwagon	15	1981
Business as Usual	Men At Work	15	1982
The Button-Down Mind of Bob Newhart	Bob Newhart	14	1960
Exodus	Soundtrack	14	1961
Modern Sounds in Country and Western Music	Ray Charles	14	1962
Songs in the Key of Life	Stevie Wonder	14	1976–1977
Whitney Houston	Whitney Houston	14	1986
Persuasive Percussion	Enoch Light/Terry Snyder and The All-Stars	13	1960
The Monkees	The Monkees	13	1966–1967
Hair	Original Cast	13	1969
The Music Man	Original Cast	12	1958
Sold Out	The Kingston Trio	12	1960
Breakfast at Tiffany's	Henry Mancini/Soundtrack	12	1961
The First Family	Vaughn Meader	12	1962–1963
Grease	Soundtrack	12	1978
Faith	George Michael	12	1988
Calcutta!	Lawrence Welk	11	1961
Meet the Beatles	The Beatles	11	1964
Miami Vice	TV Soundtrack	11	1985
Whitney	Whitney Houston	11	1987
Mariah Carey	Mariah Carey	11	1991
Elvis Presley	Elvis Presley	10	1956
Around the World in 80 Days	Soundtrack	10	1957
Gigi	Soundtrack	10	1958
The Music From Peter Gunn	Henry Mancini	10	1959
G.I. Blues	Elvis Presley	10	1960
String Along	The Kingston Trio	10	1960
The Singing Nun	The Singing Nun	10	1963–1964
Bridge Over Troubled Water	Simon and Garfunkel	10	1970
Elton John—Greatest Hits	Elton John	10	1974–1975
Frampton Comes Alive!	Peter Frampton	10	1976
4	Foreigner	10	1981
Footloose	Soundtrack	10	1984
Forever Your Girl	Paula Abdul	10	1989
The Lion King	Soundtrack	10	1994–1995

Albums Debuting at Number One

1975

Captain Fantastic and the Brown Dirty Cowboy	Elton John
Rock of the Westies	Elton John

1976

Songs in the Key of Life	Stevie Wonder

1986

Bruce Springsteen & the E Street Band Live/1975–85	Bruce Springsteen & the E Street Band

1987

Whitney	Whitney Houston
Bad	Michael Jackson

1991*

Slave to the Grind	Skid Row
For Unlawful Carnal Knowledge	Van Halen
Metallica	Metallica
Ropin' the Wind	Garth Brooks
Use Your Illusion II	Guns N' Roses
Achtung Baby	U2
Dangerous	Michael Jackson

1992

Adrenalize	Def Leppard
The Southern Harmony and Musical Companion	The Black Crowes
The Chase	Garth Brooks
The Predator	Ice Cube

*In 1991, *Billboard* began basing the chart on SoundScan data, resulting in a marked increase in albums debuting at Number One.

1993

Songs of Faith and Devotion	Depeche Mode
Get a Grip	Aerosmith
janet.	Janet Jackson
Back to Broadway	Barbra Streisand
Zooropa	U2
Black Sunday	Cypress Hill
River of Dreams	Billy Joel
In Pieces	Garth Brooks
In Utero	Nirvana
Vs.	Pearl Jam
Doggystyle	Snoop Doggy Dogg

1994

Jar of Flies	Alice in Chains
Superunknown	Soundgarden
Far Beyond Driven	Pantera
The Division Bell	Pink Floyd
Ill Communication	Beastie Boys
Purple	Stone Temple Pilots
II	Boyz II Men
From the Cradle	Eric Clapton
Monster	R.E.M.
Murder Was the Case	Soundtrack
MTV Unplugged in New York	Nirvana
Hell Freezes Over	Eagles

1995

Balance	Van Halen
Me Against the World	2Pac
Pulse	Pink Floyd
HIStory: Past, Present and Future–Book 1	Michael Jackson
Dreaming of You	Selena
E. 1999 Eternal	Bone Thugs-N-Harmony
Daydream	Mariah Carey
Mellon Collie and the Infinite Sadness	The Smashing Pumpkins
Dogg Food	Tha Dogg Pound
Alice In Chains	Alice In Chains
R. Kelly	R. Kelly
Anthology 1	The Beatles

The Biggest Jumps to Number One

From 173 to 1*	Vitalogy	Pearl Jam	1994
From 122 to 1	More of the Monkees	The Monkees	1967
From 98 to 1	The Beatles '65	The Beatles	1965
From 61 to 1	Help!	The Beatles	1965
From 60 to 1	Rubber Soul	The Beatles	1966
From 53 to 1	Ballads of the Green Berets	SSgt. Barry Sadler	1966
From 48 to 1	The Beatles VI	The Beatles	1965
From 47 to 1	Greatest Hits	Elton John	1974
From 45 to 1	Revolver	The Beatles	1966
From 29 to 1	Pisces, Aquarius, Capricorn & Jones, Ltd.	The Monkees	1967
From 19 to 1	Planet Waves	Bob Dylan	1974
From 18 to 1	Chicago VI	Chicago	1973
From 16 to 1	The Beatles' Second Album	The Beatles	1964
From 14 to 1	Gigi	Soundtrack	1958
From 14 to 1	Step By Step	New Kids on the Block	1991
From 13 to 1	Red Rose Speedway	Paul McCartney & Wings	1973
From 12 to 1	In the Wind	Peter, Paul & Mary	1963
From 12 to 1	A Hard Day's Night	The Beatles	1964
From 12 to 1	Harvest	Neil Young	1972
From 12 to 1	Wish You Were Here	Pink Floyd	1975
From 11 to 1	Loving You	Elvis Presley	1957
From 11 to 1	First Family	Vaughn Meader	1962
From 11 to 1	Living in the Material World	George Harrison	1973
From 11 to 1	Double Fantasy	John Lennon/Yoko Ono	1980

*The vinyl version of Vitalogy, which was released two weeks prior to the CD and cassette edition, debuted at number 55 and then fell to number 173 the next week; sales of the CD and cassette versions puhed it to Number One the following week.

The Biggest Falls from Number One

From 1 to off the 25-position chart	Elvis' Christmas Album	Elvis Presley	1958
From 1 to 13	Endless Summer	The Beach Boys	1974
From 1 to 12	Alice In Chains	Alice In Chains	1995
From 1 to 9	Far Beyond Driven	Pantera	1994
From 1 to 7	Frank Sinatra Sings for Only the Lonely	Frank Sinatra	1958
From 1 to 7	Wrap Around Joy	Carole King	1974
From 1 to 7	Fire	Ohio Players	1975
From 1 to 7	Red Octopus	Jefferson Starship	1975
From 1 to 7	Greatest Hits	Kenny Rogers	1980
From 1 to 7	R. Kelly	R. Kelly	1995
From 1 to 6	Something for Everybody	Elvis Presley	1961
From 1 to 6	There's a Riot Goin' On	Sly & the Family Stone	1972
From 1 to 6	Not Fragile	Bachman-Turner Overdrive	1974
From 1 to 6	So Far	Crosby, Stills, Nash & Young	1974
From 1 to 6	Walls and Bridges	John Lennon	1974
From 1 to 6	Still Crazy After All These Years	Paul Simon	1975
From 1 to 6	Giving You the Best That I Got	Anita Baker	1989

Most Return Visits to Number One in Nonconsecutive Weeks

4	My Fair Lady	Original Cast	1957–1959
4	The Music Man	Original Cast	1958
4	Cracked Rear View	Hootie & the Blowfish	1995
3	Around the World in 80 Days	Soundtrack	1957
3	South Pacific	Soundtrack	1958–1959
3	Persuasive Percussion	Enoch Light/Terry Snyder and the All Stars	1960
3	Frampton Comes Alive!	Peter Frampton	1976
3	Rumours	Fleetwood Mac	1977–1978
3	Grease	Soundtrack	1978
3	Thriller	Michael Jackson	1983
3	Girl You Know It's True	Milli Vanilli	1989–1990
3	Ropin' the Wind	Garth Brooks	1992
3	The Bodyguard	Soundtrack	1993
3	II	Boyz II Men	1994–1995

The Most Weeks on the Chart Before Hitting Number One

64	Forever Your Girl	Paula Abdul	1989
58	Fleetwood Mac	Fleetwood Mac	1976
55	Hangin' Tough	New Kids on the Block	1989
52	Nick of Time	Bonnie Raitt	1990
52	Throwing Copper	Live	1995
50	Appetite for Destruction	Guns N' Roses	1988
50	Whitney Houston	Whitney Houston	1986
49	Hysteria	Def Leppard	1988
47	You Don't Mess Around with Jim	Jim Croce	1974
44	Cracked Rear View	Hootie & the Blowfish	1995
39	Hair	Original Cast	1969
39	Sports	Huey Lewis & the News	1984
38	Reckless	Bryan Adams	1985
36	Mariah Carey	Mariah Carey	1991
35	The Sound of Music	Soundtrack	1965
34	Dr. Zhivago	Soundtrack	1966
32	Beauty and the Beat	The Go-Go's	1982
32	Metal Health	Quiet Riot	1983
31	Toni Braxton	Toni Braxton	1994
29	Whipped Cream and Other Delights	Herb Alpert's Tijuana Brass	1965
28	West Side Story	Soundtrack	1962
27	Between the Lines	Janis Ian	1975
27	Chariots of Fire	Vangelis	1982
27	Welcome to the Real World	Mr. Mister	1986
27	Don't Be Cruel	Bobby Brown	1989
27	Girl You Know It's True	Milli Vanilli	1989
27	Unplugged	Eric Clapton	1993
26	Peter, Paul & Mary	Peter, Paul & Mary	1962
24	Mary Poppins	Soundtrack	1965
24	Beverly Hills Cop	Soundtrack	1985
24	Heart	Heart	1985
23	Jazz Samba	Stan Getz & Charlie Byrd	1963
23	AWB	Average White Band	1975

PHOTO CREDITS

The author and publisher gratefully acknowledge the following parties, which provided photos for the entries listed:

A&M Records: 80, 82, 85, 93, 103, 149, 213, 239, 257, 276, 291, 300, 337, 371, 386
ABC/Dunhill Records: 53, 169
ABC-TV: 168
American Recordings: 362
Apple Records: 65, 110, 117, 121, 128, 135, 162, 188, 423
Apple/20th Century-Fox: 170
Arista Records: 224, 298, 311, 334, 367, 387, 402
Atlantic Records: 118, 120, 127, 131, 143, 166, 186, .216, 242, 261, 262, 265, 286, 327, 339, 350, 384, 394, 410
The *Billboard* Archives: 19, 28, 60, 87, 91, 92, 109, 117, 127, 144, 145, 149, 153, 158, 164, 166, 181, 183, 184, 189, 195, 206, 241, 247, 268, 275, 280
Capitol Records: 4, 13, 20, 21, 27, 29, 34, 36, 37, 71, 157, 160, 187, 205, 294, 340, 342, 389, 393
Capricorn Records: 165
Casablanca: 232, 240, 244
CBS-Fox: 1
CBS-TV: 187
Carol Channing: 67
Chrysalis: 144, 260, 341
The Church of Jesus Christ of Latter-Day Saints Archives: 30
Columbia Pictures: 5, 171, 197, 198, 312, 314, 365, 372
Columbia Records: 102, 112, 114, 124, 126, 130, 147, 163, 174, 194, 197, 204, 208, 209, 210, 211, 233, 234, 246, 248, 252, 253, 263, 270, 273, 274, 281, 284, 287, 295, 308, 309, 316, 333, 338, 343, 345, 347, 361, 374, 376, 382, 383, 390, 406, 418, 421
Curb Records: 391
Death Row Records: 381, 399, 420,
Delicious Vinyl: 328
Martin Denny: 25
The Disney Channel: 9, 12, 77
EastWest America: 388
Elektra/Asylum Records: 151, 192, 201, 212, 220, 225, 231, 243, 250, 251, 322, 325, 336, 352, 353
Embassy/Lawrence Turman, Inc.: 101
EMI/SBK Records: 258, 332, 344, 414
Epic Records: 203, 230, 256, 277, 296, 313, 380, 403, 412
Fantasy Records: 116, 125
Ken Fritz Management: 63
Gabbe - Lutz - Heller & Loeb: 42
Geffen/DGC Records: 255, 269, 320, 355, 358, 370, 378, 400, 401
Greengage Productions: 43
HBO/Cinemax: 357
Interscope Records: 407
I.R.S. Records: 267, 330
Island: 310, 356, 373
ITC Entertainment: 161
Jive Records: 422
LaFace: 385
Lisa Law: 107

Liberty Records: 354, 364, 377, 404
Legacy Recordings: 22, 133, 136, 138, 139
Mantovani Production Associates: 26
Paul Mauriat: 100
Maverick Recordings: 417
Mercury Records: 290, 306, 319, 323, 360, 363,
MCA Records: 146, 152, 167, 177, 190, 207, 301, 307, 317, 326, 379, 416
MCA Universal Home Video: 105
Onnie McIntyre: 193
MGM: 18, 64, 90
Mitch Miller: 50,
Motown/Tamla Records: 61, 97, 111, 180, 219, 278, 304, 396
MPL Communications: 173, 200, 221, 214
NBC-TV: 39, 96
Paramount Pictures: 155, 279, 289, 302, 324, 359
Parlophone: 88, 95
PBS: 2
Photofest: 14, 32, 48, 56, 58 (Charlie Byrd), 113
Picture Music: 66
PolyGram/Polydor/Chronicles: 104, 115, 191, 229, 259, 272
Radioactive: 408
RCA Records: 3, 10, 24, 72, 83, 172, 178, 202, 297
Rhino Records: 16, 94, 98, 106, 266
The Rodgers & Hammerstein Organization: 23, 31
Rolling Stones Records: 228, 249, 264
RSO Records: 226, 237, 245
Ruthless Records/Relativity: 415
Priority Records: 349, 366, 409
The Samuel Goldwyn Company: 15
Sire Records: 283, 303, 329, 369
Showtime: 305
The Showtime Music Archives (Toronto): 57, 58 (Stan Getz), 62, 115, 199
Space Agency Concerts & Theatricals: 18
Swan Song Records: 159, 196, 215, 242
TNN: 38
TriStar Pictures: 375
20th Century-Fox: 46, 79
United Artists Records: 140, 227, 254
United Artists: 41, 52, 75, 78, 81
Universal Studios, Inc.: 175, 235
USA Network: 293
Virgin Records: 348, 419
Vestron Films: 315
Walt Disney Records/Walt Disney Company: 74, 395, 413
Hal B. Wallis and Joseph H. Hazen: 49
Walter Shenson Films: 69
Warner Bros./Reprise Records: 35, 51, 54, 55, 86, 134, 141, 156, 176, 179, 217, 218, 236, 285, 292, 299, 318, 331, 346, 351, 368, 397, 398, 405
Warner Bros. Inc.: 8, 108, 123, 142, 148, 154, 182, 222, 238, 271, 282
Eric Weissberg: 154
Barry White: 185